LIVING
RELIGIONS

LIVING
RELIGIONS

EIGHTH EDITION — MARY PAT FISHER

CONSULTANTS

JOSEPH A. ADLER *Kenyon College*

AFE ADOGAME *University of Edinburgh*

ROBIN RINEHART *Lafayette College*

KARMA LEKSHE TSOMO *University of San Diego*

MINQIN WANG (王敏琴) *Hunan University, China and Cornell University*

VANESSA OCHS *University of Virginia*

AMY DEROGATIS *Michigan State University*

ALI IHSAN YITIK *Dokuz Eylul University, Izmir, Turkey*

DR. MOHINDER SINGH *Bhai Vir Singh Sahitya Sadan, New Delhi*

CHRISTINE GUDORF *Florida International University*

ARVIND SHARMA *McGill University, Montreal*

Prentice Hall

Boston Columbus Indianapolis New York San Francisco Upper Saddle River
Amsterdam Cape Town Dubai London Madrid Milan Munich Paris Montréal Toronto
Delhi Mexico City São Paulo Sydney Hong Kong Seoul Singapore Taipei Tokyo

Editorial Director: Craig Campanella
Editor in Chief: Dickson Musslewhite
Publisher: Nancy Roberts
Project Manager: Nicole Conforti
Editorial Assistant: Nart Varoqua
Managing Editor: Maureen Richardson
Operations Specialist: Amanda Smith

Credits and acknowledgments borrowed from other sources and reproduced,
with permission, in this textbook appear on page 558.

This book was designed
and produced by
Laurence King
Publishing Ltd, London
www.laurenceking.com

Every effort has been made to contact
the copyright holders, but should
there be any errors or omissions,
Laurence King Publishing Ltd would
be pleased to insert the appropriate
acknowledgment in any subsequent
printing of this publication.

Senior Editor: Clare Double
Picture Researcher: Amanda Russell
Designer: Daniel Sturges
Production: Simon Walsh

Printed in Hong Kong

Front Cover: Shutterstock/
© Orhan Cam

Library of Congress Cataloging-in-Publication Data

Fisher, Mary Pat, 1943-
    Living religions / Mary Pat Fisher ; consultants, Joseph Adler ... [et al]. -- 8th ed.
        p. cm.
    Includes bibliographical references and index.
    ISBN-13: 978-0-205-83585-0 (pbk. : alk. paper)
    ISBN-10: 0-205-83585-6 (pbk. : alk. paper)
    1. Religions. I. Adler, Joseph Alan. II. Title.
    BL80.3.F57 2011
    200--dc22

                        2010019790

Student edition: ISBN-13: 978-0-205-83585-0
ISBN-10: 0-205-83585-6
Examination copy: ISBN-13: 978-0-205-83587-4
ISBN-10: 0-205-83587-2

Prentice Hall
is an imprint of

CONTENTS

Preface ix
Teaching and learning resources xiii
MAP *Religions of the World Today* xiv
TIMELINE xvi

CHAPTER 1

RELIGIOUS RESPONSES 1
Why are there religions? 3
— Materialistic perspective: humans invented religion 3
— Functional perspective: religion is useful 4
— Belief perspective: Ultimate Reality exists 7
Understandings of Sacred Reality 10
EXCLUSIVISM VS. UNIVERSALISM *A letter from
    I. H. Azad Faruqi* 12
Ritual, symbol, and myth 14
TEACHING STORY *Descendants of the Eagle* 17
Absolutist and liberal interpretations 18
BOX *Angels Weep* 19
The encounter between science and religion 20
RELIGION IN PRACTICE *When Science Approaches Religion* 25
Women in religions 26
Negative aspects of organized religions 28
Suggested reading 29
Key terms 31
Review questions 32
Discussion questions 32
Additional Internet resources 32

CHAPTER 2

INDIGENOUS SACRED WAYS 33
Understanding indigenous sacred ways 34
MAP *Distribution of Indigenous Groups* 34
Cultural diversity 38
The circle of right relationships 39
— Relationships with spirit 40
YORUBA TEACHING STORY *Osun and the Power of Woman* 43
— Kinship with all creation 43
— Relationships with power 48
Spiritual specialists 50
— Storytellers and other sacred roles 50
— Mystical intermediaries 53
LIVING INDIGENOUS SACRED WAYS *An Interview with
    Nadezhda Ananyevna Stepanova* 55
Group observances 56
RELIGION IN PRACTICE *The Sun Dance Way
    of Self-Sacrifice* 58
— Individual observances 61

Contemporary issues 62
RELIGION IN PRACTICE *The Orang Asli of Malaysia:
    Traditions being Lost* 64
RELIGION IN PUBLIC LIFE *Winona LaDuke* 68
Suggested reading 70
Key terms 71
Review questions 72
Discussion questions 72
Additional Internet resources 72

CHAPTER 3

HINDUISM 73
Philosophical and metaphysical origins 74
— The Indus Valley Civilization 74
MAP *The Indian Subcontinent* 75
TIMELINE *Hinduism* 76
— The Vedas 77
Major philosophical systems 80
— Samkhya 80
— Advaita Vedanta 81
— Yoga 81
Religious foundations and theistic paths 85
— Shaktas 86
— Shaivites 88
— Vaishnavites 90
— The epics and Puranas 91
TEACHING STORY *Hanuman, the Monkey Chief* 94
The Hindu way of life 97
— Rituals 97
— Castes, duties, and life goals 99
— Life stages 100
RELIGION IN PRACTICE *Sacred Thread Ceremony* 101
— The guru 102
— Women's duties 103
— Fasts, prayers, and auspicious designs 103
— Reverence of trees and rivers 104
LIVING HINDUISM *An Interview with Somjit Dasgupta* 105
— Pilgrimages 106
— Festivals 107
RELIGION IN PRACTICE *Holi* 108
Hinduism in the modern world 111
— Modern movements 111
— Global Hinduism 112
RELIGION IN PRACTICE *Dharmic Principles:
    The Swadhyaya Movement* 113
RELIGION IN PUBLIC LIFE *Dr. Karan Singh* 116
— Hindu identity 117
Suggested reading 118
Key terms 119

Review questions 120
Discussion questions 120
Additional Internet resources 120

CHAPTER 4

JAINISM 121

The Tirthankaras and ascetic orders 121
Freeing the soul: the ethical pillars 123
— Karma 123
TEACHING STORY *The Story of Bahubali* 124
— Ahimsa 125
RELIGION IN PRACTICE *Jain Purification* 127
— Aparigraha 127
— Anekantwad 128
Spiritual practices 128
Festivals and pilgrimages 130
LIVING JAINISM *An Interview with M. P. Jain* 131
World Jainism 132
Suggested reading 133
Key terms 134
Review questions 134
Discussion questions 134
Additional Internet resources 134

CHAPTER 5

BUDDHISM 135

The life and legend of the Buddha 135
TIMELINE *Buddhism* 137
The Dharma 141
— The Four Noble Truths 142
— The Noble Eightfold Path to liberation 143
— The wheel of birth and death 144
TEACHING STORY *The Great Ape Jataka Tale* 146
— Nirvana 147
Branches of Buddhism 148
MAP *The Spread of Buddhism* 149
— Theravada: the path of mindfulness 149
— Mahayana: the path of compassion and wisdom 156
MAP *Distribution of Theravada and Mahayana Buddhism* 157
— Chan and Zen: the great way of enlightenment 160
CHART Major Branches of Buddhism 160
RELIGION IN PRACTICE *Zen Oxherding Pictures* 162
— Pure Land: devotion to Amitabha Buddha 164
— Nichiren: salvation through the *Lotus Sutra* 164
— Vajrayana: the indestructible path 166
RELIGION IN PUBLIC LIFE *His Holiness the Dalai Lama* 169
— Festivals 170
Buddhism in the West 171
RELIGION IN PRACTICE *Life in a Western Zen Monastery* 172
LIVING BUDDHISM *An Interview with Karma Lekshe Tsomo* 176
Socially engaged Buddhism 177
Suggested reading 181
Key terms 182
Review questions 183
Discussion questions 183

Additional Internet resources 183

CHAPTER 6

DAOISM AND CONFUCIANISM 184

Ancient traditions 184
— Worship and divination 185
MAP *Historic Sites of Daoism and Confucianism* 185
— Cosmic balance 187
TIMELINE *Daoism and Confucianism* 188
Daoism—the way of nature and immortality 189
— Teaching of Daoist sages 190
TEACHING STORY *Three in the Morning* 192
— Popular religion and organized Daoism 194
— Inner alchemy 195
— Daoist sects 196
RELIGION IN PRACTICE *The Lantern Festival* 198
— Daoism today 199
Confucianism—the practice of virtue 203
— Master Kong's life 204
— The Confucian virtues 205
— Divergent followers of Confucius 206
— The state cult 207
— Neo-Confucianism 208
— Confucianism under communism 209
LIVING CONFUCIANISM *An Interview with Ann-ping Chin* 212
— Confucianism in East Asia 213
Suggested reading 214
Key terms 216
Review questions 216
Discussion questions 216
Additional Internet resources 216

CHAPTER 7

SHINTO 217

The roots of "Shinto" 217
— Kinship with nature 218
— Honoring the kami 219
— Shrines 220
MAP *Major Shinto Shrines* 221
TEACHING STORY *Amaterasu comes out of the cave* 222
— Ceremonies and festivals 223
— Purification 225
RELIGION IN PRACTICE *Purification by Waterfall* 226
Buddhist and Confucian influences 227
State Shinto 228
"Sect Shinto" 229
Shinto today 230
LIVING SHINTO *An Interview with Hitoshi Iwasaki* 232
Suggested reading 233
Key terms 234
Review questions 234
Discussion questions 234
Additional Internet resources 234

ZOROASTRIANISM 235

CHAPTER 8

JUDAISM   239
A history of the Jewish people   239
TIMELINE *Judaism*   240
— Biblical stories   241
MAP *The Early Israelites*   243
TEACHING STORY *Abraham's Willingness to Sacrifice Isaac*   245
BOX *The Ten Commandments*   248
— Return to Jerusalem   251
— Rabbinic Judaism   255
— Judaism in the Middle Ages   259
— Kabbalah and Hasidism   262
— Judaism and modernity   264
— The Holocaust   266
MAP *Jewish Populations and the Holocaust*   269
— Zionism and contemporary Israel   269
Torah   273
— The one God   273
— Love for God   274
— The sacredness of human life   275
— Law   275
LIVING JUDAISM *An Interview with Eli Epstein*   276
— Suffering and faith   277
Sacred practices   278
Holy days   282
RELIGION IN PRACTICE *Passover Innovations*   285
Contemporary Judaism   286
— Major branches today   286
CHART *Major Branches of Judaism Today*   287
RELIGION IN PUBLIC LIFE *Rabbi David Saperstein*   288
— Jewish feminism   291
— Jewish renewal   293
Suggested reading   294
Key terms   296
Review questions   297
Discussion questions   297
Additional Internet resources   297

CHAPTER 9

CHRISTIANITY   298
Historical evidence   298
Evidence of the Bible   299
The life and teachings of Jesus   301
— Birth   301
— Preparation   302
— Ministry   304
MAP *Jesus' Ministry*   304
LIVING CHRISTIANITY *An Interview with David Vandiver*   307
TEACHING STORY *The Good Samaritan*   308
— Challenges to the authorities   310
TIMELINE *Christianity*   311
— Crucifixion   313
— Resurrection and Ascension   316
BOX *Books of the New Testament*   317
The early Church   318
— From persecution to empire   318

MAP *St. Paul's Missionary Journeys*   320
— Evolving organization and theology   322
— Early monasticism   325
Church administration   326
MAP *Distribution of Christians Today*   326
— East–West division   327
— Social chaos and the papacy   329
Intellectual revival and monasticism   330
Medieval mysticism   331
RELIGION IN PRACTICE *Russian Orthodox Kenoticism*   333
The Protestant Reformation   334
CHART *Major Divisions of Christianity Today*   335
The Roman Catholic Reformation   339
Liberal trends   340
The Second Vatican Council   341
The Orthodox world today   342
BOX *Eastern Orthodox Church*   343
— The Russian Orthodox Church   344
— Distinctive features of Orthodox spirituality   345
Central beliefs in contemporary Christianity   347
Sacred practices   349
— Worship services and sacraments   349
— The liturgical year   352
— Contemplative prayer   355
— Devotion to Mary   357
— Veneration of saints and angels   359
Contemporary trends   360
— Evangelicalism   363
— Spirit-oriented movements   365
— The great reversal   368
— Liberation theology   370
RELIGION IN PUBLIC LIFE *Archbishop Desmond M. Tutu*   371
— Feminist theology   373
— Creation-centered Christianity   375
— Ecumenical movement   375
Suggested reading   377
Key terms   378
Review questions   379
Discussion questions   379
Additional Internet resources   380

CHAPTER 10

ISLAM   381
Pre-Islamic Arabia   381
TIMELINE *Islam*   382
The Prophet Muhammad   383
The Qur'an   388
The central teachings   391
— The Oneness of God and of humanity   391
— Prophethood and the compass of Islam   392
— Human relationship to the divine   393
— The unseen life   394
— The Last Judgment   394
The Five Pillars   396
— Belief and witness   396
— Daily prayers   397
RELIGION IN PRACTICE *Salaat*   398

— Zakat   399
— Fasting   399
— Hajj   400
LIVING ISLAM *An Interview with Dr. Syed M. Hussain*   401
Sunni and Shi'a   404
— Sunnis   404
— Shi'a   406
Sufism   407
The spread of Islam   411
MAP *The spread of Islam*   411
TEACHING STORY *Transformation by Islam*   412
— Islamic culture   413
— Eastward expansion   415
Relationships with the West   418
— Islam in the West   420
Muslim resurgence   421
— Tradition and modern life   423
— Outreach and education   424
RELIGION IN PUBLIC LIFE *Shirin Ebadi*   425
— Islam in politics   427
— Islam for the future   435
Suggested reading   436
Key terms   438
Review questions   438
Discussion questions   439
Additional Internet resources   439

CHAPTER 11

SIKHISM   440
The *sant* tradition   440
Guru Nanak   441
TIMELINE *Sikhism*   443
The succession of Gurus   444
TEACHING STORY *Guru Arjun Dev's Devotion*   445
Central beliefs   450
LIVING SIKHISM *An Interview with Inderpreet Kaur*   451
Sacred practices   453
RELIGION IN PUBLIC LIFE *His Holiness Baba Virsa Singh*   456
Sikhism today   457
RELIGION IN PRACTICE *Amrit Ceremony on Baisakhi*   458
MAP *The Punjab*   459
Suggested reading   463
Key terms   463
Review questions   464
Discussion questions   464
Additional Internet resources   464

CHAPTER 12

NEW RELIGIOUS MOVEMENTS   465
Social context of new religious movements   465
Charismatic leadership   468
— Unification Movement   468
— Sathya Sai Baba   470

Offshoots of older religions   471
— Mormon Church   471
— Jehovah's Witnesses   473
— Radhasoami   475
LIVING TRANSCENDENTAL MEDITATION
    An Interview with Wolfgang Hecker   476
Combinations of older religions   477
— Caodaism   477
— African-inspired syncretic religions   478
— Theosophical Society   480
— Baha'i   482
RELIGION IN PRACTICE *The Baha'i Model for
    Governance of the World*   483
Social trends   484
— Ethnic identity: Rastafari   484
— Nature spirituality   486
— New Age spirituality   491
Opposition to new religious movements   494
Will new religious movements last?   497
Suggested reading   497
Key terms   499
Review questions   499
Discussion questions   499
Additional Internet resources   499

CHAPTER 13

RELIGION IN THE
TWENTY-FIRST CENTURY   500
Globalization   500
Secularism   501
Religious pluralism   502
— Hardening of religious boundaries   503
— Religion after 11 September   505
Religion in politics   507
RELIGION IN PRACTICE *Excerpts from
    Obama's Historic Cairo Speech*   509
Interfaith movement   510
— Responses to other faiths   511
— Interfaith initiatives   513
Religion and social issues   517
RELIGION IN PUBLIC LIFE *Jimmy Carter*   518
Religion and materialism   522
Religion and the future of humanity   523
Suggested reading   524
Key terms   525
Review questions   525
Discussion questions   525
Additional Internet resources   525

Notes   526
Glossary   539
Index   548
Credits   558

PREFACE

Religion is not a museum piece. Religion is a vibrant force in the lives of many people around the world, and many religions are presently experiencing a renaissance. *Living Religions* is a sympathetic approach to what is living and significant in the world's major religious traditions and in various new movements that are arising. This book provides a clear and straightforward account of the development, doctrines, and practices of the major faiths followed today. The emphasis throughout is on the personal consciousness of believers and their own accounts of their religion and its relevance in contemporary life.

WHAT'S NEW IN THIS EDITION?

This eighth edition of *Living Religions* has been thoroughly revised and updated. In preparing the text I worked with a team of specialist consultants who provided detailed suggestions and resources for improving the text in the light of recent scholarship.

Old approaches to understanding and explaining religions are being increasingly challenged, so in this edition I have given special attention to sensitive issues raised by current scholarship and by voices from within the religions. Since the first edition of *Living Religions*, which was published in 1991, and this eighth edition, there have been sea changes in understandings of Daoism and of Shinto, for instance, and the presumed history of an Aryan invasion of India and its links to the Vedas is being very carefully re-examined. Much more emphasis is being placed on cultural customs, popular spiritual practices, mixtures of religions, and varieties of religious ways, as opposed to distinct monolithic institutionalized religions, and this emphasis is reflected in new material woven throughout this edition. It is now more difficult to make sweeping generalizations about any religion, for they do not fit the facts that are coming to light.

Violence perpetrated in the name of religion is still distressingly prevalent in the news, so the eighth edition continues to follow this disturbing trend throughout the discussion of each major religion and also within some new religious movements. Distinctions are made between the basic teachings of religions, none of which condones

wanton violence, and the ways in which religions have been politicized. Every religion is struggling with its responses to modernity, including fundamentalist and exclusivist reactions to increasing pluralism within our societies, and these struggles are discussed in each chapter.

People of many faiths are looking at ways in which their religious practices and beliefs are interwoven with and affect the natural environment. This edition, therefore, includes material on religious approaches to contemporary ecological concerns, such as pollution resulting from rapid industrialization in China, and destruction of the environment and ancestral graves in Nigeria as a result of oil extraction by multinational companies. Included are contemporary responses of religious leaders to ominous signs of climate change. Many other social issues are being taken up by religious leaders. Examples in this edition include AIDS, illiteracy, poverty, and female infanticide.

Women's voices and women's contributions are woven into the discussion of each religion. Feminist theologies now span decades of work and have reached the point of self-criticism, rather than focusing largely on criticism of traditional patriarchal attitudes that barred women from roles of spiritual power. Obstacles to women's expression of their spirituality still exist, however, and are discussed within the context of the various religious traditions.

This new edition also preserves and improves upon the features that make *Living Religions* special.

Personal interviews with followers of each faith provide interesting and informative first-person accounts of each religion as perceived from within the tradition. I have presented these first-person quotations from many people, from a Siberian shamaness to a practitioner of Transcendental Meditation, in "Living..." feature boxes and also in excerpts woven throughout the text, such as a new quotation by Christian earth-advocate Father Thomas Berry about the connection between our misuse of the earth's resources and our own spiritual losses. There are new interview boxes—which focus on how the practitioner of each faith experiences the beliefs and rituals of his or her tradition—in the Judaism and New Religious Movements chapters.

Eighteen Religion in Practice feature boxes portray the spiritual activities and beliefs of religious groups or individuals, such as the indigenous American sun dance and the Hindu sacred thread ceremony. Five new boxes in the Religious Responses, Hinduism, Judaism, Islam, and Religion in the Twenty-First Century chapters provide fascinating insights into significant practices and festivals.

Eight Religion in Public Life feature boxes portray the spiritual roots of people who are making significant contributions to modern society, such as Jimmy Carter, the Dalai Lama, and Desmond Tutu. A new feature box has been added in the Islam chapter on Nobel Peace Prize winner Shirin Ebadi, exploring how her work toward establishing democracy in her native Iran is informed by her faith.

Eleven Teaching Story feature boxes contain tales which serve as take-off points for discussions about core values embedded in each faith. New to this edition are boxes on Abraham's Sacrifice and Transformation by Islam.

An enhanced image program provides forty new images which, along with over 200 existing images, help to bring religions to life. Narrative captions accompanying illustrations offer additional insights into the characteristics and orientation of each tradition and the people who practice it.

Quotations from primary sources are incorporated throughout the book to give a direct perception of the thinking and flavor of each tradition. New memorable quotes have been included, such as a piece from Laozi on Daoist ethics that illustrates their still-fresh relevance to everyday life. MyReligionLab icons in the margins provide specific references to entries in the second edition of *An Anthology of Living Religions*, a companion volume of significant primary source material that follows the same organization as *Living Religions*.

Pedagogical aids are included throughout the text. A list of Key Topics to help readers organize their thinking about the material as it is presented appears at the beginning of each chapter. Key Terms, defined and highlighted in boldface when they first appear, are included in an extensive glossary and many of these are also listed and defined at the end of each chapter for immediate understanding and review. Because students are often unfamiliar with terms from other cultures, useful guides to the pronunciation of many words are included in the glossary.

All the Review Questions and Discussion Questions at the end of each chapter have been reviewed for this edition, as have the Suggested Reading lists and Additional Internet Resources, which provide suggestions for generally accurate and useful websites.

CHAPTER-BY-CHAPTER REVISIONS

Chapter 1: Religious Responses has been reorganized for greater clarity, as readers step into the maze of interacting influences and scholarly perspectives on the study of religion. A new Religion in Practice box is included on "When Science Approaches Religion," from the point of view of a theoretical physicist who discusses the borderline between science and philosophy or theology. Revisions have been made to the section on "The Encounter between Science and Religion," incorporating the latest research on evolutionary biology and Creationist responses. New images include those discussing atheism and Baha'i.

Chapter 2: Indigenous Sacred Ways includes expanded coverage of African indigenous religions and of the contemporary issues faced by modern and indigenous societies needing to share the same space. There is a new image of the International Council of Indigenous Grandmothers to support this discussion.

Chapter 3: Hinduism begins with a new discussion about the labeling of Indian religious traditions, including that called Hinduism. The material on the Aryan invasion has been revised in the light of recent scholarship and there is a completely new section on "Women's Duties." A new Religion in Practice box with original photos explores the sacred thread ceremony in which a Hindu boy is initiated into Vedic rites. Other new images include the renowned teacher Vivekananda.

Chapter 4: Jainism has been updated throughout, with particular reference to the religion's emphasis on sustainability and respect for the environment, and quotations to reinforce these points.

Chapter 5: Buddhism contains some reorganization for clarity, with a renamed section "Chan and Zen: The Great Way of Enlightenment" covering Chinese Chan Buddhism for the first time. Several sections have been revised, including the material on Jodo Shinshu and the Perfection of Wisdom scriptures. "Buddhism in the West" has a new introduction with more discussion of Buddhism's spread to the U.S. New images include monks seeking alms in Laos and the British Tibetan Buddhist nun Tenzin Palmo at a Buddhist women's conference in Mongolia.

Chapter 6: Daoism and Confucianism now includes a map of China, North and South Korea, Japan, Taiwan, and Hong Kong, showing important religious sites. The timeline and "Worship and Divination" section have been revised. In the Daoism material, translations of the *Dao de jing* have been standardized. "Daoism Today" has been revised and discussion of Neo-Confucianism expanded. The image related to Mao Zedong is now a contemporary one of a stallholder selling Mao statues.

Chapter 7: Shinto contains new text on Shinto myths. A new Teaching Story box, "Amaterasu Comes out of the Cave," reinforces this content. The map of Shinto shrines is now placed next to the relevant section. There is also more text on Buddhist and Confucian influences, and the practice of Shinto outside Japan today.

Chapter 8: Judaism includes much new material and many new images. There is a new Teaching Story box on "Abraham's Willingness to Sacrifice Isaac" and a new Living Judaism box in which an Orthodox businessman discusses the long tradition of Jewish philanthropy. New material discusses how customs are evolving, and becoming more inclusive, with a new Religion in Practice box on "Passover Innovations." The material on Jewish feminism is revised, with an image of the first black female rabbi.

Chapter 9: Christianity begins with a new section on "Historical Evidence" of Jesus and a revised section on "Evidence of the Bible." The material on the history of Jesus' life and teachings has been reorganized to improve chronology, and text on the Orthodox churches has been refined into a single section. There is a greater concentration on modern movements in Christianity, including a revised section on evangelicalism with new quotes, new material on "megachurches," including photographs of such churches in Korea and the U.S., and discussion of how today's Christians are responding to environmental challenges such as global warming.

Chapter 10: Islam begins with new background material on Pre-Islamic Arabia and also contains a new sidebar on the Twelver Shi'a imams, plus a new Teaching Story box on "Transformation by Islam" and a new Religion in Practice box on the custom of *salaat* (prayers). There is much new material on contemporary Islam and Muslims today, with a new quote from a Turkish *hajji* (pilgrim to Mecca), an updated section on "Islam in the West," and a new Religion in Public Life box on Iranian lawyer Shirin Ebadi, the first Muslim woman to win the Nobel Peace Prize.

Chapter 11: Sikhism has been revised throughout and has an updated timeline, plus improvements to the "Sikhism Today" section.

Chapter 12: New Religious Movements has been extensively updated to reflect current practice, including extra material on Scientology (including a picture of Tom Cruise opening a new center in Spain), the Unification Movement, Jehovah's Witnesses, and Falun Gong. A new Living Transcendental Meditation box features practitioner Wolfgang Hecker, who describes his experience of the benefits of the technique.

Chapter 13: Religion in the Twenty-First Century has been updated throughout and has a new introduction covering globalization and the growth of secularism. There is new text on religious tolerance and new material covering religion's bearing on modern sexual and reproductive issues, plus a revised section on "Religion and Materialism." A new Religion in Practice box features the historic speech made by President Obama in Cairo, July 2009.

ACKNOWLEDGMENTS

In order to try to understand each religion from the inside, I have traveled for many years to study and worship with devotees and teachers of all faiths, and to interview them about their experience of their tradition. People of all religions also come to the Gobind Sadan Institute for Advanced Studies in Comparative Religions, in New Delhi, where it is my good fortune to meet and speak with them about their spiritual experiences and beliefs.

In preparing this book, I have worked directly with consultants who are authorities in specific traditions and who have offered detailed suggestions and resources. For breadth of scholarship, I have engaged the help of a new group of consultants for each edition. For this eighth edition, a number of very helpful and dedicated scholars have carefully reviewed the various chapters and made excellent suggestions for their improvement in the light of current scholarship. Two of them also hosted me in their own countries and thus helped me to understand the current ways of religion there. They are Dr. Ali Ihsan Yitik of Dokuz Eylul University in Izmir, Turkey, and Dr. Minqing Wang of Hunan University in Changsha, China. They very graciously arranged my visits to people and places and helped me to understand what I was seeing. Their families are now my own beloved family members.

The other consultants who have served as excellent advisers on particular chapters are the Tibetan Buddhist nun and scholar, Karma Lekshe Tsomo of the University of San Diego, Joseph Adler of Kenyon College, Afe Adogame of University of Edinburgh, Robin Rinehart of Lafayette College, Vanessa Ochs of the University of Virginia, Amy DeRogatis of Michigan State University, Dr. Mohinder Singh of Bhai Vir Singh Sahitya Sadan in New Delhi, Christine Gudorf of Florida International University, and Arvind Sharma of McGill University. Robin Rinehart has also thoroughly revised and updated the Review Questions, Discussion Questions, and Internet resources at the end of each chapter. All the consultants understood what makes *Living Religions* special and gave generously of their time and knowledge to help improve this edition.

I am extremely grateful for their sensitive, knowledgeable, and enthusiastic help, and also for the assistance of the many scholars who have served as consultants to the previous editions and are acknowledged therein.

Many other people have helped with insights and resources. Among them are Elisabeth Ingles, Melissa Damelio, Kristi Paasuke, Bert Gunn, Noordin Kassam, Galina Ermolina, Somjit Dasgupta, Devdatta Mhaiskar, David and Marianne Vandiver, Michelle Brand, Justin Fisher, Shannon Hunt, I. H. Azad Faruqi, Ashin Nyana Dipa, Sonam Wangmo, Bob Maat, Sister Santacitta, Maria Lewis, Lee Bailey, Liu, Robert Carter, Eli Epstein, Vazhayil Babu, John Farina, Rabbi Tzipi Radonsky, Amy Reiss, Dahlia Sabry, Ibrahim Keskin Hafiz, Riffat Hassan, Kuek Chee Ying, Mohammad Habib, Daya Baweja, Bhai Kirpal Singh, Wolfgang Hecker, Santokh Singh, Vijaydeep Singh, Manbir Singh, Jathedar Iqbal Singh, Ronki Ram, Irene Hasapes, Hillel Levine, Priya Stolyarova, Katya Egorova, and Alan Nykamp.

As always, Laurence King Publishing has provided me with excellent editorial help. Melanie White, Clare Double, and Lee Ripley have guided this edition through its development and production with brilliance, patience, and extraordinary helpfulness. Amanda Russell has

worked hard to find the new illustrations that so enhance this edition. The designer Dan Sturges has put everything together beautifully. And at Prentice Hall, Nancy Roberts and Nicole Conforti have been discerning and supportive.

Finally, I cannot adequately express my gratitude to my own revered teacher, Baba Virsa Singh of Gobind Sadan. People of all faiths from all over the world came to him for his spiritual blessings and guidance. In the midst of sectarian conflicts, his place is an oasis of peace and harmony. Now that he has left his physical body, he is still teaching us to regard each other as members of one human family. May God bless us all to move in this direction.

Mary Pat Fisher

Gobind Sadan Institute for Advanced Studies

For this eighth edition the reviewers were Linda Villareal, University of West Florida; Mark Graham, College of Wooster; Margaret Huff, Northeastern University; Beth Benedix, Depauw University; Alexandria Egler, St. Francis College; Walter Kaelber, Wagner College; Fritz Wenisch, University of Rhode Island; Fotini Katsanos, University of NC at Charlotte; Cheryl Rhodes, Coastal Carolina University, University of South Carolina; Pasquale Simonelli, Monmouth University; William Darrow, Williams College; Emily Tai, Queensborough Community College, CUNY; Jane Crosthwaite, Mount Holyoke College; Hong Qu, Iowa State University; David Nikkel, University of North Carolina at Pembroke; Youru Wang, Rowan University; Christine Gudorf, Florida International University; Eric Rovie, Georgia State University; Jeffrey Robbins, Lebanon Valley College; Sarah McCombs, University of West Florida; Diana Cates, University of Iowa; Johnny Flynn, Indiana University Purdue University, Indianapolis; Christopher Martinez, St. Petersburg College; Randi McLeod, Western Michigan University; Jay G. Williams, Hamilton College; Wayne Husted, Indiana University Purdue University, Indianapolis; Robert Kenney, Northern Kentucky University; Donald Berry, Gardner-Webb University; Jon Brammer, Three Rivers Community College; Jayne Klein, Florida International University; Ivory Lyons, Mount Union College; Antoinette Denapoli, Dillard University; Jonathan Tan, Xavier University; Julie Ingersoll, University of North Florida; Dianne Oliver, University of Evansville; Larry Poston, Nyack College; David O'Leary, Tufts University; Joseph Kelly, John Carroll University; Steven Godby, Broward College, South Campus; Barbara Darling-Smith, Wheaton College; Robert Chamberlain, Brevard Community College; Shin-Yi Chao, Rutgers University; Charlene Burns, University of Wisconsin-Eau Claire; Mary Beth O'Halloran, Century College; Felecia McDuffie, Young Harris College; Stephen Sapp, University of Miami; Jamsheed Choksy, Indiana University; Carolyn Medine, University of Georgia; Wendy Turner, Augusta State University; Suzanne Morrison, Ohio Northern University; Terris Neuman, Southeastern University; Jonathan Lawrence, Canisius College; Andreas Reif, Southern New Hampshire University; Kelly Hayes, Indiana University-Purdue University, Indianapolis; Robert Steed, Hawkeye Community College; Kenneth Atkinson, University of Northern Iowa; Sang Kim, Hillsborough Community College; Charles Johnson, Washtenaw Community College; Nathan Rousseau, Jacksonville University; Clifford Cain, Franklin College; Wesley Mills, York County Community College; Sedgwick Heskett, Florida Community College at Jacksonville; Celia Sinclair, University of North Carolina at Charlotte; Leena Taneja, Stetson University; Nicholas Marziani, Flagler College; David Fenrick, Northwestern College; Alexander Miller, Northern Kentucky University; Todd Lavin, Clarion University of Pennsylvania; Bernard Roy, Ramapo College of New Jersey; Joseph Thomas, Ohio Northern University and Heidelberg College; P. Head, John Carroll University; Daniel Leister, Alverno College; Gregory Spinner, Central Michigan University; Vernon Naffier, Grand View College; Franklin Proano, The Ohio State University at Marion; Rick Rogers, Eastern Michigan University; Marvin Elliott, Catawba Valley Community College; Andrew Bolton, Graceland University; Steve Spina, University of Wisconsin, Eau Claire; Cyril Orji, University of Dayton, Ohio; James Goulding, Edgewood College; Nathaniel Murrell, UNC Wilmington; Chris Newcomb, Bethune-Cookman University; Matt Jackson-McCabe, Cleveland State University; James Moore, Georgia Perimeter College; Henry Parker, University of Tennessee, Martin;

TEACHING AND LEARNING RESOURCES FOR LIVING RELIGIONS

Whether you want to enhance your lectures, create tests, or assign outside material to reinforce content from the text, you and your students will find the most comprehensive set of instructional materials available with Living Religions to reinforce and enliven the study of world religions.

Instructor's Manual with Tests

This manual includes chapter outlines, key terms, and summaries. As in previous editions, there are class activities and discussion questions. New to this edition will be a list of relevant movies pertaining to each chapter. Test questions have been moved to the end of the manual in their own section. ISBN: 0-20-583590-2

My Test

This computerized test bank includes the test item file and allows flexibility in creating tests, editing questions, and adding instructor generated items. ISBN: 0-20-583589-9

Power Point Slides

New to this edition, these slides are illustrated with many of the photos from the text and also contain chapter outlines, provocative quotes, key terms, and timelines from each religion. ISBN: 0-20-583588-0

MyReligionLab   myreligionlab

MyReligionLab provides an outstanding array of student and faculty resources for learning and teaching with Fisher's Living Religions. Students are given robust self-assessment opportunities, including quizzes with feedback, access to dynamic video clips of the world's religions with assessment questions, and a unique collection of primary and secondary sources reflecting the world's major scriptural traditions.

The Prentice Hall Atlas of World Religions

Through the use of over 50 visually arresting maps, this atlas shows the origins, historical development, and present state of all the world's religions. ISBN: 0-13-193885-1

Joel Chernikoff, The College of New Jersey; Greg Loving, University of Cincinnati Clermont College; Harriet Luckman, College of Mount Saint Joseph; Jenny Caplan, Sinclair Community College; Doug Webb, Lakeland Community College; Cristobal Serran-Pagan, Valdosta State University; Jennifer Harvey, Drake University; Ida Baltikauskas, Century College; Alexander Conroy, Florida International University; Wayne Brouwer, Hope College; Carlos Cardoza, Columbia Theological Seminary; Lisa Knight, Furman University; Jamillah Karim, Spelman College; Donald Turner, Nashville State Community College; John Sheveland, Gonzaga University; Garry Morgan, Northwestern College, Minnesota; Alan Smith, Florida Southern College; Mark Berkson, Hamline University; Edwin Tait, Huntington University; Renee Levant, Florida Community College at Jacksonville; Derek Penwell, University of Louisville; Joseph Snow, Lemoyne College; Rob Gwaltney, Madisonville Community College/Muhlenberg Campus; Bradley Malkovsky, University of Notre Dame; Margaret Kamitsuka, Oberlin College; Daniel Rieger, Broward College; C.W. Huntington, Hartwick College; Stephen Murray, Skidmore College; June Watkins,

University of West Florida; John Easterling, Northwestern College; Don Peavy Sr., Victor Valley College; Annick Safken, Pima Community College; Billie R. Swanson, Coconino Community College; John Pahucki, SUNY Rockland; Ashley Cleere, Piedmont College; Chris McAllister, Lenoir Community College; Ronald Pachence, University of San Diego; Kenneth Zanca, Marymount College, Palos Verdes; Diana Pasulka, University of North Carolina Wilmington; Fr. Brad Karelius, Saddleback College; Chris Jackson, Mt. Hood Community College; Patrick Nnoromele, Eastern Kentucky University; Diana Dimitrova, Michigan State University; Sam Hughes, Mt. San Jacinto College; Michael O'Malley, Bakersfield College and College of the Canyons; Derry Seaton, Fullerton College; David Suter, Saint Martin's University; Mary Thurlkill, University of Mississippi; Steven Jacobs, University of Alabama; Barry Sang, Catawba College; Winston Thompson, Broward Community College; Santos Roman, Riverside Community College; Wayne Wooten, Catawba Valley Community College; Hun Lye, Warren Wilson College; Samuel Thomas, California Lutheran University; Joseph Price, Whittier College; Philip Tite, Willamette University.

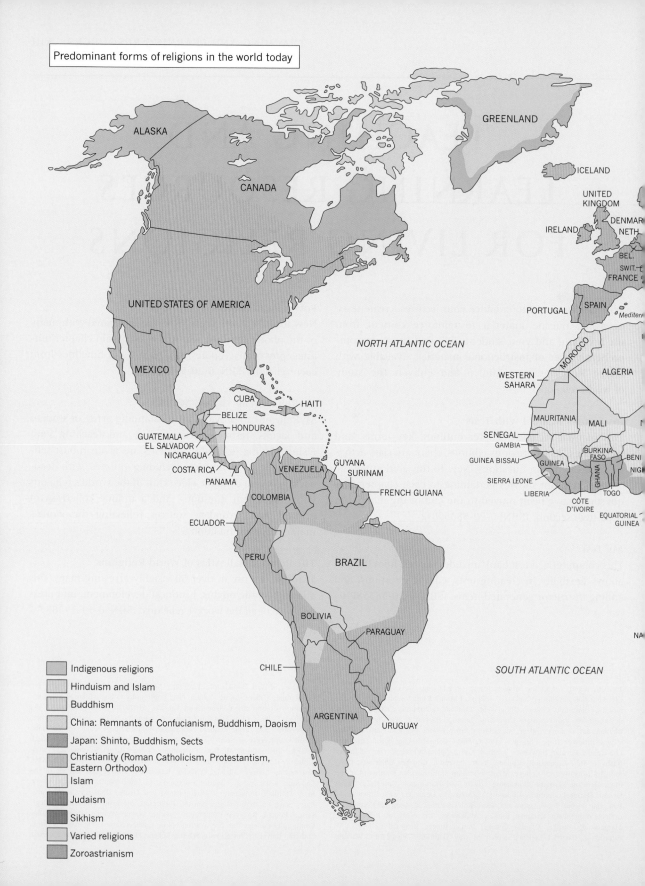

Predominant forms of religions in the world today

GREENLAND

ICELAND

ALASKA

UNITED KINGDOM

CANADA

IRELAND

DENMAR
NETH
BEL.
SWIT.-E
FRANCE

UNITED STATES OF AMERICA

NORTH ATLANTIC OCEAN

PORTUGAL

SPAIN

Mediter

MOROCCO

MEXICO

WESTERN SAHARA

ALGERIA

CUBA

HAITI

MAURITANIA

MALI

BELIZE
HONDURAS

SENEGAL

GUATEMALA
EL SALVADOR
NICARAGUA

GAMBIA
GUINEA BISSAU

BURKINA FASO

BENI

COSTA RICA
PANAMA

GUYANA
SURINAM

SIERRA LEONE

GUINEA

GHANA

TOGO

NIG

VENEZUELA

LIBERIA

CÔTE D'IVOIRE

COLOMBIA

FRENCH GUIANA

EQUATORIAL GUINEA

ECUADOR

PERU

BRAZIL

BOLIVIA

CHILE

PARAGUAY

SOUTH ATLANTIC OCEAN

NA

ARGENTINA

URUGUAY

Indigenous religions

Hinduism and Islam

Buddhism

China: Remnants of Confucianism, Buddhism, Daoism

Japan: Shinto, Buddhism, Sects

Christianity (Roman Catholicism, Protestantism, Eastern Orthodox)

Islam

Judaism

Sikhism

Varied religions

Zoroastrianism

TIMELINE	2000 BCE	1500	1000	500	0 CE
INDIGENOUS	←				
HINDUISM	← Vedas heard	Vedas first written down c.1500 BCE		*Ramayana* and *Mahabharata* in present form after 400 BCE	Code of Manu compiled 100–300 CE Patanjali systematizes Yoga Sutras by 200 BCE
JAINISM		Series of 23 Tirthankaras before c.777 BCE ⟶		Life of Mahavira 599–527 BCE Digambaras and Svetambaras diverge from 3rd century BCE	
BUDDHISM				Life of Gautama Buddha c.5th century BCE	Theravada Buddhism develops 200 BCE–200 CE King Asoka spreads Buddhism c.258 BCE	Mahayana Buddhism develops 1s century CE
DAOISM AND CONFUCIANISM				Life of Laozi c.600–300 Life of Confucius c.551–479	Educational system based on Confucian Classics from 205 BCE Life of Zhuangzi c.365–290
SHINTO	Shinto begins in pre-history as local nature- and ancestor-based traditions				
JUDAISM	Life of Abraham c.1900–1700 BCE	Moses leads Israelites out of Egypt c.13th or 12th century BCE	David, King of Judah and Israel c.1010–970 BCE First Temple destroyed; Jews exiled 586 BCE	Jerusalem falls to Romans 70 CE	
CHRISTIANITY					Life of Jesus c.4 BCE–30 CE Paul organizes early Christians c.50–60 CE Gospels written down c.70–95 c
ISLAM					
SIKHISM					
INTERFAITH					

| | 2000 BCE | 1500 | 1000 | 500 | 0 CE |

...t ways passed down and adapted over millennia ⟶

...s written Bhakti movement 600–1800 ⟶ Life of Ramakrishna
c.300 1836–1886

Jain monks establish
Jain centers outside
India 1970s–1980s

Life of Songstan Persecution of Ch'an Buddhism Buddhism spreads in
(c.609–650) who Buddhism begins to Japan as Zen the West 20th century
declares Buddhism in China 845 13th century
national religion Full ordination of nuns
of Tibet from 23 countries 1998

Japan imports Sung dynasty Cultural Revolution attacks
Confucianism revives ritualistic religions 1966–1976
to unite tribes Confucianism Confucian revival in China;
into empire ("neo-Confucianism") International Association of
Confucianism established; Daoist
sects and temples re-established
1990–2000

Shinto name adopted State Shinto
6th century CE established 1868

...binical Life of Expulsion of Jews The Holocaust 1940–1945
...ition Maimonides from Spain 1492 Independent state of Israel 1948
...elops 1135–1204
...to 4th The Baal Shem Israeli wall for
...turies Tov 1700–1760 separation from
Palestinians 2003

Centralization Split between Monastic orders Protestantism Second Vatican
of papal power Western and proliferate 1300s established 1521 Council 1962–1965
after 800 Eastern Orthodox
Churches 1054 Spanish Inquisition Churches reopened
established 1478 in USSR 1989

Life of Muhammad c.570–632 Akbar becomes European Terrorism and
Mogul emperor dominance counterterrorism
Spread of Islam begins 633 in India 1556 1800s–1900s increase 2001
Sunni–Shi'a split c.682

Islam's cultural peak 750–1258 Muslim resurgence and OPEC 1970s

Life of Guru At death of Guru 300th anniversary
Nanak Gobind Singh (1708), of Khalsa 2003
1469–1504 living presence of the
guru is embodied in
Guru Granth Sahib
(scriptures)

Mogul emperor Akbar First International Human
initiates interfaith Unity Conference 1974
dialogues 1556–1605 Parliament of the World's
Religions centenary
celebrations 1993

CHAPTER 1

RELIGIOUS RESPONSES

KEY TOPICS

• WHY ARE THERE
RELIGIONS? 3

• UNDERSTANDINGS
OF SACRED
REALITY 10

• RITUAL, SYMBOL,
AND MYTH 14

• ABSOLUTIST
AND LIBERAL
INTERPRETATIONS
18

• THE ENCOUNTER
BETWEEN SCIENCE
AND RELIGION 20

• WOMEN IN
RELIGIONS 26

• NEGATIVE ASPECTS
OF ORGANIZED
RELIGIONS 28

Before sunrise, members of a Muslim family rise in Malaysia, perform their purifying ablutions, spread their prayer rugs facing Mecca, and begin their prostrations and prayers to Allah. In a French cathedral, worshipers line up for their turn to have a priest place a wafer on their tongue, murmuring, "This is the body of Christ." In a South Indian village, a group of women reverently anoint a cylindrical stone with milk and fragrant sandalwood paste and place around it offerings of flowers. The monks of a Japanese Zen Buddhist monastery sit cross-legged and upright in utter silence, which is broken occasionally by the noise of the *kyosaku* bat falling on their shoulders. On a mountain in Mexico, men, women, and children who have been dancing without food or water for days greet an eagle flying overhead with a burst of whistling from the small wooden flutes they wear around their necks.

These and countless other moments in the lives of people around the world are threads of the tapestry we call "religion." The word is probably derived from the Latin, meaning "to tie back," "to tie again." All of religion shares the goal of tying people back to something behind the surface of life—a greater reality, which lies beyond, or invisibly infuses, the world that we can perceive with our five senses.

Attempts to connect with this greater reality have taken many forms. Many of them are organized institutions, such as Buddhism or Christianity. These institutions are complexes of such elements as leaders, beliefs, rituals, symbols, myths, scriptures, ethics, spiritual practices, cultural components, historical traditions, and management structures. Moreover, they are not fixed and distinct categories, as simple labels such as "Buddhism" and "Christianity" suggest. Each of these labels is an abstraction that is used in the attempt to bring some kind of order to the study of religious patterns that are in fact complex, diverse, ever-changing, and overlapping. In addition, not all religious behavior occurs within institutional confines. The inner dimensions of religion—such as experiences, beliefs, and values—can be referred to as **spirituality**. This is part of what is called religion, but it may occur in personal, noninstitutional ways, without the ritual and social dimensions of organized religions.

Religion is multifaceted. The influential scholar of world religions, Ninian Smart, distinguished seven dimensions of religion:

1 Ritual (public or private ceremonies).
2 Narrative and mythic (stories, including overall accounts of the universe and its creatures).
3 Experiential and emotional (feelings of guilt, dread, awe, devotion, ecstasy, peace, etc.)
4 Social and institutional (group dimensions involving shared beliefs, identity, membership).
5 Ethical and legal (rules concerning human behavior).
6 Doctrinal and philosophical (systematic belief structure and intellectual framework).
7 Material (things and places representing or manifesting the sacred).

Any of these dimensions may be thought to be divinely revealed and manifested, but in a religion all of them will in some way refer to the sacred.

Religion is such a complex and elusive topic that some contemporary scholars of religion are seriously questioning whether "religion" or "religions" can be studied at all. They have determined that no matter where and at what point they try to define the concept, other parts will get away. Nonetheless, this difficult-to-grasp subject is central to many people's lives and has assumed great political significance in today's world so it is important to try sincerely to understand it. In this introductory chapter, we will try to develop some understanding of religion in a generic sense—why it exists, its various patterns and modes of interpretation, its encounters with modern science, its inclusion or exclusion of women, and its potentially negative aspects—before trying in the subsequent chapters to understand the major traditions known as "religions" practiced around the world today.

From candles and oil lamps to sacred fires, light is universally used to remind worshipers of an invisible reality. At Gobind Sadan, outside New Delhi, worship at a sacred fire continues twenty-four hours a day.

Why are there religions?

In many cultures and times, religion has been the basic foundation of life, permeating all aspects of human existence. But from the time of the European Enlightenment, religion has become in the West an object to be studied, rather than an unquestioned basic fact of life. Cultural anthropologists, sociologists, philosophers, psychologists, and even biologists have peered at religion through their own particular lenses, trying to explain what religion is and why it exists to those who no longer take it for granted. In the following pages we will briefly examine some of the major theories that have evolved. They are not mutually exclusive.

MATERIALIST PERSPECTIVE: HUMANS INVENTED RELIGION

During the nineteenth and twentieth centuries, **scientific materialism** gained considerable prominence as a theory to explain the fact that religion can be found in some form in every culture around the world. The materialistic point of view is that the supernatural is imagined by humans; only the material world exists.

An influential example of this perspective can be found in the work of the nineteenth-century philosopher Ludwig Feuerbach (1804–1872). He reasoned that deities are simply projections, objectifications of human qualities such as power, wisdom, and love onto an imagined cosmic deity outside ourselves. Then we worship it as Supreme and do not recognize that those same qualities lie within ourselves; instead, we see ourselves as weak and sinful. Feuerbach developed this theory with particular reference to Christianity as he had seen it.

Other scientific materialists believe that religions have been created or at least used to manipulate people. Historically, religions have often supported and served secular power. The nineteenth-century socialist philosopher Karl Marx (1818–1883), author of *The Communist Manifesto*, argued that a culture's religion—as well as all other aspects of its social structure—springs from its economic framework. In Marx's view, religion's origins lie in the longings of the oppressed. It may have developed from the desire to revolutionize society and combat exploitation, but in failing to do so it became otherworldly, an expression of unfulfilled desires for a better, more satisfying life:

> *Man makes religion: religion does not make man. ... The religious world is but the reflex of the real world. ... Religion is the sigh of the oppressed creature, the sentiment of a heartless world, and the soul of soulless conditions. It is the opium of the people.*[1]

According to Marx, not only do religions pacify people falsely; they may themselves become tools of oppression. For instance, he charged Christian authorities of his times with supporting "vile acts of the oppressors" by explaining them as due punishment of sinners by God. Other critics have made similar complaints against Eastern religions that blame the sufferings of the poor on their own misdeeds in previous lives. Such interpretations and uses of religious teachings lessen the perceived need for society to help those who are oppressed and suffering. Marx's ideas thus led toward twentieth-century atheistic communism, for he had asserted, "The abolition of religion as the illusory happiness of the people is required for their real happiness."[2]

myreligionlab
The Study of
World Religions
LEE W. BAILEY

myreligionlab
Religion as the
Opium of the People
KARL MARX

FUNCTIONAL PERSPECTIVE: RELIGION IS USEFUL

Another line of reasoning has emerged in the search for a theory explaining the universal existence of religions: They are found everywhere because they are useful, both for society and for individuals. Religions "do things" for us, such as helping us to define ourselves and making the world and life comprehensible to us. Functional explanations have come from many disciplines.

One version of the functional explanation is based on sociology. Pioneering work in this area was done by French sociologist Emile Durkheim (1858–1917). He proposed that humans cannot live without organized social structures, and that religion is a glue that holds a society together. Surely religions have the potential for creating harmony in society, for they all teach social virtues such as love, compassion, altruism, justice, and discipline over our desires and emotions. The role of religion in the social process of identity formation at individual, family, community, and national levels is now being carefully examined, for people's identification with a particular religion can be manipulated to influence social change—either to thwart, moderate, or encourage it.

Biology also offers some functional reasons for the existence of religion. For instance, John Bowker, author of *Is God a Virus?*, asserts that religions are organized systems that serve the essential biological purpose of bringing people together for their common survival. To Bowker, religion is found universally because it protects gene replication and the nurturing of children. He proposes that because of its survival value, the potential for religiosity may even be genetically inherent in human brains.

Medical professionals have found yet another way of explaining the usefulness of religions: Religious faith is good for our health. Research conducted by the Center for the Study of Religion/Spirituality and Health at Duke University found that those who attend religious services or read scriptures frequently are significantly longer lived, less likely to be depressed, less likely to have high blood pressure, and nearly ninety percent less likely to smoke. Many other studies have indicated that patients with strong faith recover faster from illness and operations.

Many medical studies have also been done on the potential of prayer to heal illness, but results have been mixed. However, meditation has been proved to reduce mental stress and also to help develop positive emotions, even in the face of great difficulties. Citing laboratory tests of the mental calmness of Buddhists who practice "mindfulness" meditation, the Fourteenth Dalai Lama points out that:

> *Over the millenniums, many practitioners have carried out what we might call "experiments" in how to overcome our tendencies toward destructive emotions. The world today needs citizens and leaders who can work toward ensuring stability and engage in dialogue with the "enemy"—no matter what kind of aggression or assault they may have endured. If humanity is to survive, happiness and inner balance are crucial. We would do well to remember that the war against hatred and terror can be waged on this, the internal front, too.*[3]

From the point of view of individual psychology, there are many explanations of the usefulness of religion. Psychoanalyst Sigmund Freud (1856–1938) suggested that religion fulfills neurotic needs. He described religion as a collective fantasy, a "universal obsessional neurosis"—a replaying of our loving and fearful relationships with our parents. Religious belief gives us a God powerful enough to protect us from the terrors of life, and will reward or punish us for obedience or nonobedience to social norms. From Freud's extremely sceptical point of view, religious belief is an illusion springing from people's infantile insecurity and neurotic guilt; as such it closely resembles mental illness.

On a more positive note, the twentieth-century psychoanalyst Erich Fromm (1900–1980) concluded that humans have a need for a stable frame of reference, and that religion fulfills this need. As Mata Amritanandamayi, a contemporary Indian spiritual teacher, explains:

> Faith in God gives one the mental strength needed to confront the problems of life. Faith in the existence of God makes one feel safe and protected from all the evil influences of the world. To have faith in the existence of a Supreme Power and to live accordingly is a religion. When we become religious, morality arises, which, in turn, will help to keep us away from malevolent influences. We won't drink, we won't smoke, and we will stop wasting our energy through unnecessary gossip and talk. … We will also develop qualities like love, compassion, patience, mental equipoise, and other positive traits. These will help us to love and serve everyone equally. … Where there is faith, there is harmony, unity and love. A nonbeliever always doubts. … He cannot be at peace; he's restless. … The foundation of his entire life is unstable and scattered due to his lack of faith in a higher principle.[4]

For many, the desire for material achievement offers a temporary sense of purposefulness. But once achieved, material goals may seem hollow. A longing for something more lasting and deeply meaningful may then arise. The Buddha said:

> Look!
> The world is a royal chariot, glittering with paint.
> No better.
> Fools are deceived, but the wise know better.[5]

Religions propose ideals that can radically transform people. In fact, Frederick Streng (1933–1993), an influential scholar of comparative religion, proposed that the central definition of religion is that it is a "means to ultimate transformation." Mahatma Gandhi (1869–1948) was an extremely shy, fearful child. His transformation into one of the great political figures of the twentieth century occurred as he meditated single-mindedly on the great Hindu scripture, the *Bhagavad-Gita*, particularly the second chapter, which he says was "inscribed on the tablet of my heart."[6] It reads, in part:

> He is forever free who has broken
> Out of the ego-cage of I and mine
> To be united with the Lord of Love.
> This is the supreme state. Attain thou this
> And pass from death to immortality.[7]

People need inner strength for dealing with personal problems. Those who are suffering severe physical illness, privation, terror, or grief often turn to the divine for help. Agnes Collard, a Christian woman, reported that her impending death after four painful years of cancer was bringing her closer to God:

myreligionlab
The Future
of an Illusion
SIGMUND FREUD

I don't know what or who He is, but I am almost sure He is there. I feel His presence, feel that He is close to me during the awful moments. And I feel love. I sometimes feel wrapped, cocooned in love.[8]

Rather than seeking help from without, an alternative approach encourages the idea of changing our ways of thinking. According to some Asian religions, the concept that we are distinct, autonomous individuals is an illusion; what we think of as "our" consciousnesses and "our" bodies are in perpetual flux. Thus, freedom from problems lies in accepting temporal change and devaluing the "small self" in favor of the eternal self. The ancient sages of India called it "This eternal being that can never be proved, ... spotless, beyond the ether, the unborn Self, great and eternal, ... the creator, the maker of everything."[9]

The existential loneliness some feel is hauntingly depicted by the sculptures of Alberto Giacometti, such as his Walking Man, *c.1947–1948.*

We may look to religions for understanding, for answers to our many questions about life. Is life just a series of random and chaotic incidents, or is there some meaning and order behind what is happening? Who are we? Why are we here? What happens after we die? Why is there suffering? Why is there evil? Is anybody up there listening? We have difficulty accepting the commonsense notion that this life is all there is. We are born, we struggle to support ourselves, we age, and we die. If we believe that there is nothing more, fear of death may inhibit enjoyment of life and make all human actions seem pointless. Confronting mortality is so basic to the spiritual life that, as the Christian monk Brother David Steindl-Rast observes, whenever monks from any spiritual tradition meet, within five minutes they are talking about death.

> *It appears that throughout the world man* [sic] *has always been seeking something beyond his own death, beyond his own problems, something that will be enduring, true and timeless. He has called it God, he has given it many names; and most of us believe in something of that kind, without ever actually experiencing it.*
>
> *Jiddu Krishnamurti*[10]

For those who find security in specific answers, some religions offer **dogma**—systems of doctrines proclaimed as absolutely true and accepted as such, even if they lie beyond the domain of one's personal experiences. Absolute faith provides some people with a secure feeling of rootedness, meaning, and orderliness in the midst of rapid social change. Religions may also provide rules for living, governing everything from diet to personal relationships. Such prescriptions may be seen as earthly reflections of the order that prevails in the cosmos. Some religions, however, encourage people to explore the perennial questions by themselves, and to live in the uncertainties of not knowing intellectually, breaking through old concepts until nothing remains but truth itself.

A final need that draws some people to religion is the discomforting sense of being alone in the universe. This isolation can be painful, even terrifying. The divine may be sought as a loving father or mother, or as a friend. Alternatively, some paths offer the way of self-transcendence. Through them, the sense of isolation is lost in mystical merger with the One Being, with the Ultimate Reality.

BELIEF PERSPECTIVE: ULTIMATE REALITY EXISTS

From the point of view of religious belief, there truly is an underlying reality that cannot readily be perceived. Human responses to this Supreme Reality have been expressed and institutionalized as the structures of religions.

How have people of all times and places come to the conclusion that there is some Unseen Reality, even though they may be unable to perceive it with their ordinary senses? Some simply accept what has been told to them or what is written in their holy books. Others have come to their own conclusions. In general, we have two basic ways of apprehending reality: rational thought and nonrational modes of knowing. Both modes have been highly developed in Indian religious traditions. The eminent twentieth-century philosopher and erstwhile president of India, S. Radhakrishnan (1888–1975) observed:

> Every attempt at solving the problem of the ultimate basis of existence from a religious point of view has come to admit an Absolute or God. Rationalistic logic and mystic contemplation favour as a rule the former conception, while ethical theism is disposed to the latter. Hindu thought believes in the evolution of our knowledge of God. We have to vary continually our notions of God until we pass beyond all notions into the heart of the reality itself, which our ideas endeavour to report.[11]

Another path to belief is through deep questioning. Martin Luther (1483–1546), father of the Protestant branches of Christianity, recounted how he searched for faith in God through storms of doubt, "raged with a fierce and agitated conscience."[12]

The human mind does not function in the rational mode alone; there are other modes of consciousness. In his classic study *The Varieties of Religious Experience*, the philosopher William James (1842–1910) concluded:

> Our normal waking consciousness, rational consciousness as we call it, is but one special type of consciousness, whilst all about it, parted from it by the flimsiest of screens, there lie potential forms of consciousness entirely different. …
> No account of the universe in its totality can be final which leaves these other forms of consciousness quite disregarded.[13]

To perceive truth directly, beyond the senses, beyond the limits of human reason, beyond blind belief, is often called **mysticism**. George William Russell (1867–1935), an Irish writer who described his mystical experiences under the pen name "AE," was lying on a hillside:

> not then thinking of anything but the sunlight, and how sweet it was to drowse there, when, suddenly, I felt a fiery heart throb, and knew it was personal and intimate, and started with every sense dilated and intent, and turned inwards, and I heard first a music as of bells going away … and then the heart of the hills was opened to me, and I knew there was no hill for those who were there, and they were unconscious of the ponderous mountain piled above the palaces of light, and the winds were sparkling and diamond clear, yet full of colour as an opal, as they glittered through the valley, and I knew the Golden Age was all about me, and it was we who had been blind to it but that it had never passed away from the world.[14]

Sufi dervishes in Sudan chant names of God's qualities as a way to God-realization.

myreligi⊛nlab
Ground of Being
TARTHANG TULKU

Encounters with Unseen Reality are given various names in spiritual traditions: **enlightenment**, **realization**, illumination, *satori*, **awakening**, self-knowledge, **gnosis**, ecstatic communion, "coming home." Such a state may arise spontaneously, as in near-death experiences in which people seem to find themselves in a world of unearthly radiance, or may be induced by meditation, fasting, prayer, chanting, drugs, or dancing.

Many religions have developed meditation techniques that encourage intuitive wisdom to come forth. Whether this wisdom is perceived as a natural faculty within or an external voice, the process is similar. The consciousness is initially turned away from the world and even from one's own feelings and thoughts, letting them all go. Often a concentration practice, such as watching the breath or staring at a candle flame, is used to collect the awareness into a single, unfragmented focus. Once the mind is quiet, distinctions between inside and outside drop away. The seer becomes one with the seen, in a fusion of subject and object through which the inner nature of things often seems to reveal itself.

Kabir, a fifteenth-century Indian weaver who was inspired alike by Islam and Hinduism and whose words are included in Sikh scripture, described this state of spiritual bliss:

> *The blue sky opens out farther and farther,*
> *the daily sense of failure goes away,*
> *the damage I have done to myself fades,*
> *a million suns come forward with light,*
> *when I sit firmly in that world.*[15]

> [The "flash of illumination" brings] a state of glorious inspiration, exaltation, intense joy, a piercingly sweet realization that the whole of life is fundamentally right and that it knows what it's doing.
>
> Nona Coxhead[16]

Our ordinary experience of the world is that our self is separate from the world of objects that we perceive. But this **dualistic** understanding may be transcended in a moment of enlightenment in which the Real and our awareness of it become one. The *Mundaka Upanishad* says, "Lose thyself in the Eternal, even as the arrow is lost in the target." For the Hindu, this is the prized attainment of liberation, in which one enters into awareness of the eternal reality. This reality is then known with the same direct apprehension with which one knows oneself. The Sufi Muslim **mystic** Abu Yazid in the ninth century CE said, "I sloughed off my self as a snake sloughs off its skin, and I looked into my essence and saw that 'I am He.'"[17]

An alternative kind of spiritual experience brings one into contact with what the German professor of theology Rudolf Otto (1869–1937) called the "Wholly Other." Otto referred to this as numinous—a nonrational, nonsensory experience of that which is totally outside the self and cannot be described. In his landmark book *The Idea of the Holy*, Otto wrote of this mysterious experience as the heart of religion. It brings forth two general responses in a person: a feeling of great awe or even dread and, at the same time, a feeling of great attraction. These responses, in turn, have given rise to the whole gamut of religious beliefs and behaviors.

A sense of the presence of the Great Unnamable may burst through the seeming ordinariness of life. (Samuel Palmer, The Waterfalls, Pistyll Mawddach, North Wales, 1835–1836.)

Though ineffable, the nature of genuine religious experience is not unpredictable, according to the research of Joachim Wach (1898–1955), a German scholar of comparative religion. In every religion, it seems to follow a certain pattern: (1) It is an experience of what is considered Unseen Reality; (2) It involves the person's whole being; (3) It is the most shattering and intense of all human experiences; and (4) It motivates the person to action, through worship, ethical behavior, service, and sharing with others in a religious grouping.

Understandings of Sacred Reality

The concept of God as an old man with a beard who rules the world from the sky has been supported by the art of patriarchal monotheistic traditions, such as William Blake's frontispiece to "Europe," The Act of Creation, *1794.*

In the struggle to understand what the mind cannot readily grasp, individuals and cultures have come to rather different conclusions. Mircea Eliade (1907–1986) was a very influential scholar who helped to develop the field of **comparative religion**. This discipline attempts to understand and compare religious patterns found around the world. He used the terms "sacred" and "profane": the **profane** is the everyday world of seemingly random, ordinary, and unimportant occurrences. The **sacred** is the realm of extraordinary, apparently purposeful, but generally imperceptible forces. In the realm of the sacred lie the source of the universe and its values. However relevant this dichotomy may be in describing some religions, there are some cultures that do not make a clear distinction between the sacred and the profane. Many indigenous peoples who have an intimate connection with their local landscape feel that spiritual power is everywhere; there is nothing that is not sacred. Trees, mountains, animals—everything is perceived as being alive with sacred presence.

Another distinction made in the study of comparative religion is that between "immanent" and "transcendent" views of sacred reality. To understand that reality as **immanent** is to experience it as present in the world. To understand it as **transcendent** is to believe that it exists outside of the material universe (e.g. "God is out there").

The concept of sacred Being is another area in which we find great differences among religious traditions. Many people perceive the sacred as a personal being, as Father, Mother, Teacher, Friend, Beloved, or as a specific deity. Religions based on one's relationship to a Divine Being are called **theistic**. If the being is worshiped as a singular form, the religion is called **monotheistic**. If many attributes and forms of the divine are emphasized, the religion may be labeled **polytheistic**. Religions that hold that beneath the multiplicity of apparent forms there is one underlying substance are called **monistic**. Unseen Reality may also be conceived in **nontheistic** terms, as a "changeless Unity," as "Suchness," or simply as "the Way." There may be no sense of a personal Creator God in such understandings; in nontheistic traditions, Ultimate Reality may instead be perceived as impersonal.

Some people believe that the sacred reality is usually invisible but occasionally appears visibly in human **incarnations**, such as Christ or Krishna, or in special manifestations, such as the flame Moses reportedly saw coming from the center of a bush but not consuming it. Or the deity that cannot be seen may be described in human terms. Christian theologian Sallie McFague thus writes of God as "lover" by imputing human feelings to God:

> God as lover is the one who loves the world not with the fingertips but totally and passionately, taking pleasure in its variety and richness, finding it attractive and valuable, delighting in its fulfilment. God as lover is the moving power of love in the universe, the desire for unity with all the beloved.[18]

Throughout history, there have been **exclusivist** religious authorities—in other words, those who claim that they worship the only true deity and label all others as "pagans" or "nonbelievers." For their part, the others apply similar negative epithets to them. When these rigid positions are taken, often to the point of violent conflicts or forced conversions, there is no room to consider the possibility that all may be talking about the same indescribable thing in different languages or referring to different aspects of the same unknowable Whole—which may be defined as **universalism**.

Atheism is the belief that there is no deity. Atheists may reject theistic beliefs because they seem to be incompatible with the existence of evil in the world, or

Buddhism is sometimes referred to as a nontheistic religion, for its beliefs do not refer to a personal deity. Practitioners try to perceive the impermanence and interdependence of all things.

myreligionlab
Oneness of the Divine
ABRAHAM HESCHEL

myreligionlab
New Polytheism
DAVID MILLER

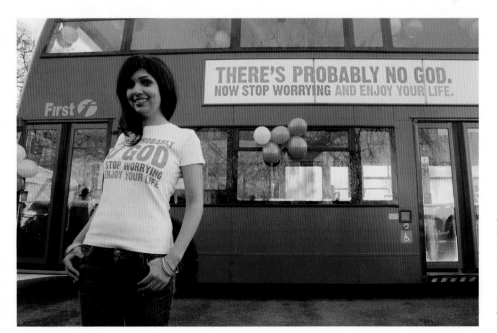

Atheists in England ran a large-scale campaign to advertise their point of view, posting large "There's probably no God. Now stop worrying and enjoy your life." signs on buses and in public places.

A Letter from I. H. Azad Faruqi

In this letter, the highly respected Muslim scholar Dr I. H. Azad Faruqi, Professor of Islamic Studies and Honorary Director of the Centre for the Study of Comparative Religions and Civilizations, Jamia Milia Islamia, New Delhi, gives his views on exclusivist and universalist standpoints.

"Despite the attitude of the majority of the followers of world religions justifying the claims of exclusive nature found in almost all world religions, there are sufficient grounds in the scriptures of these traditions which allow a universalistic interpretation of the phenomenon of the multiplicity of religions. That is, the scriptures of the various world religions within themselves contain the elements which can be interpreted to claim a viewpoint looking at various religious traditions as so many paths leading to the same Goal.

"Secondly, almost all world religions contain a vision of a Supreme Reality, which ultimately is considered beyond the categories of the rational thought, Incomprehensible and Unlimited. Thus, by their own admission these traditions appear to claim their vision of, and approach to, the Supreme Reality as short of exhausting It, and limited to a particular view of It.

"Otherwise also, although almost all the basic truths and aspects of religious life are represented in each of the religious traditions, each of these traditions tends to emphasize certain dimensions of the religious experience more than others. And these particular accentuations, at the core of the spiritual experience of these traditions, are the factors which appear to determine the special hue or distinctiveness of these traditions. Thus, each of the different religious traditions can be claimed to express some particular aspects of the Ultimate Reality which, in spite of Its myriad manifestations, remains unfathomable and far beyond the sum of all Its expressions. Seen from this perspective, the uniqueness of each religious tradition, and Its particular experience of the Supreme Reality, should no more remain as a hindrance in the cordial relations amongst them, as the usual case has been hitherto. Rather, these very particularities and distinctions would turn into the grounds for mutual attraction between them.

"Thirdly, the individualistic claims of various religions can be taken as true only in a relative sense. Each of the religious traditions being a close and complete world in itself, these are bound to claim their particular standpoints as absolute. Perhaps these could not develop into self-sufficient traditions in their own right without their exclusivist claims of being the only truly guided ones. But today, in the pluralistic societies of modern times, the claims of these traditions having the monopoly of the Supreme Truth can be considered as relatively absolute only, if the term of a relative absolute can be permitted. That is, we can attempt to approach and study these traditions on their own grounds, with a more humble attitude, and let them speak from within their own world, while being aware that this is only one world out of many such worlds. And ultimately, they all revolve around the same Sun."[19]

because there is little or no concrete proof that God exists, or because theistic beliefs seem unscientific, or because they inhibit human independence. In 2009, atheists in England mounted a major campaign to put up billboards and signs on buses proclaiming, "There's probably no God. Now stop worrying and enjoy your life." A movement called "New Atheism" is attacking religious faith as being not only wrong, but actually evil because it can be used to support violence. As we will see throughout this book, extremist religious views have indeed been used throughout history to justify political violence and oppression. The leading figure in the New Atheism movement is Richard Dawkins, Oxford Professor of the Public Understanding of Science and author of *The Selfish Gene* and *The God*

Delusion. Around him a debate is raging about whether science itself is fully "scientific," in the sense of being totally objective, or whether it is a culturally shaped enterprise based on unproven assumptions—the same criticism that its atheistic proponents make about religious faith.

Agnosticism is not the denial of the divine but the feeling, "I don't know whether it exists or not," or the belief that if it exists it is impossible for humans to know it. Religious scepticism has been a current in Western thought since classical times; it was given the name "agnosticism" in the nineteenth century by T. H. Huxley, who stated its basic principles as a denial of metaphysical beliefs and of most (in his case) Christian beliefs since they are unproven or unprovable, and their replacement with scientific method for examining facts and experiences.

These categories are not mutually exclusive, so attempts to apply the labels can sometimes confuse us rather than help us understand religions. In some polytheistic traditions there is a hierarchy of gods and goddesses with one highest being at the top. In Hinduism, each individual deity is understood as an embodiment of all aspects of the divine. In the paradoxes that occur when we try to apply human logic and language to that which transcends rational thought, a person may believe that God is both a highly personal being and also present in all things. An agnostic may be deeply committed to moral principles. Or mystics may have personal encounters with the divine and yet find it so unspeakable that they say it is beyond human knowing. The Jewish scholar Maimonides (1135–1204) asserted that:

> *the human mind cannot comprehend God. Only God can know Himself. The only form of comprehension of God we can have is to realize how futile it is to try to comprehend Him.*[20]

Jaap Sahib, the great hymn of praises of God by the Tenth Sikh Guru, Guru Gobind Singh, consists largely of the negative attributes of God, such as these:

> *Salutations to the One without colour or hue,*
> *Salutations to the One who hath no beginning.*
> *Salutations to the Impenetrable,*
> *Salutations to the Unfathomable …*
> *O Lord, Thou art Formless and Peerless*
> *Beyond birth and physical elements. …*
> *Salutations to the One beyond confines of religion. …*
> *Beyond description and Garbless*
> *Thou art Nameless and Desireless.*
> *Thou art beyond thought and ever Mysterious.*[21]

Some people believe that the aspect of the divine that they perceive is the only one. Others feel that there is one being with many faces, that all religions come from one source. Bede Griffiths (1906–1993), a Catholic monk who lived in a community in India attempting to unite Eastern and Western traditions, was one who felt that if we engage in a deep study of all religions we will find their common ground:

> *In each tradition the one divine Reality, the one eternal Truth, is present, but it is hidden under symbols. … Always the divine Mystery is hidden under a veil, but each revelation (or "unveiling") unveils some aspect of the one Truth, or, if you*

like, the veil becomes thinner at a certain point. The Semitic religions, Judaism and Islam, reveal the transcendent aspect of the divine Mystery with incomparable power. The oriental religions reveal the divine Immanence with immeasurable depth. Yet in each the opposite aspect is contained, though in a more hidden way.[22]

Ritual, symbol, and myth

Many of the phenomena of religion are ways of worship, symbols, and myths. Worship consists in large part of attempts to express reverence and perhaps to enter into communion with that which is worshiped or to request help with problems such as ill health, disharmony, or poverty. Around the world, rituals, sacraments, prayers, and spiritual practices are used to create a sacred atmosphere or state of consciousness necessary to convey the requests for help, to bring some human control over things that are not ordinarily controllable (such as rainfall), to sanctify and explain the meaning of major life stages such as birth, puberty, marriage, and death, or to provide spiritual instruction.

When such actions are predictable and repeated rather than spontaneous, they are known as **rituals**. Group rituals may be conducted by priests or other ritual specialists or by the people themselves. There may be actions such as recitation of prayers, chants, scriptures or stories, singing, dancing, sharing of food, spiritual purification by water, lighting of candles or oil lamps, and offerings of flowers, fragrances, and food to the divine. Professor Antony Fernando of Sri Lanka explains that when food offerings are made to the deities:

Places of worship are often designed as visual symbols of religious ideals. The Baha'i Temple in New Delhi was crafted in the shape of a lotus, symbol of beauty and purity rising divinely above stagnant water, and its nine-sided structure symbolizes the unity of all world religions.

Even the most illiterate person knows that in actual fact no god really picks up those offerings or is actually in need of them. What people offer is what they own. Whatever is owned becomes so close to the heart of the owner as to become an almost integral part of his or her life. Therefore, when people offer something, it is, as it were, themselves they offer. … Sacrifices and offerings are a dramatic way of proclaiming that they are not the ultimate possessors of their life and also of articulating their determination to live duty-oriented lives and not desire-oriented lives.[23]

What religions attempt to approach may be considered beyond human utterance. Believers build statues and buildings through which to worship the divine, but these forms are not the divine itself. Because people are addressing the invisible, it can be suggested only through metaphor. Deepest consciousness cannot speak the language of everyday life; what it knows can be suggested only in **symbols**—images borrowed from the material world that are similar to ineffable spiritual experiences. For example, attempts to allude to spiritual merging with Unseen Reality may borrow the language of human love. The great thirteenth-century Hindu saint Akka Mahadevi sang of her longing for union with the Beloved by using powerful symbolic language of self-surrender:

Like a silkworm weaving her house with love
From her marrow and dying in her body's threads
Winding tight, round and round, I burn
Desiring what the heart desires.[24]

> *Our religious ceremonies are but the shadows of that great universal worship celebrated in the heavens by the legions of heavenly beings on all planes, and our prayers drill a channel across this mist separating our earthbound plane from the celestial ones through which a communication may be established with the powers that be.*
>
> *Pir Vilayat Inayat Khan*[25]

Tracing symbols throughout the world, researchers find many similarities in their use in different cultures. Unseen Reality is often symbolized as a Father or Mother, because it is thought to be the source of life, sustenance, and protection. It is frequently associated with heights, with its invisible power perceived as coming from a "place" that is spiritually "higher" than the material world. The sky thus becomes heaven, the abode of the god or gods and perhaps also the pleasant realm to which good people go when they die. A vertical symbol—such as a tree, a pillar, or a mountain—is understood as the center of the world in many cultures, for it gives physical imagery to a connection between earth and the unseen "heavenly" plane. The area beneath the surface of the earth is often perceived as an "underworld," a rather dangerous place where life goes on in a different way than on the surface.

Some theorists assert that in some cases these common symbols are not just logical associations with the natural world. Most notably, the psychologist Carl Jung (1875–1961) proposed that humanity as a whole has a collective unconscious, a global psychic inheritance of archetypal symbols from which

myreligionlab
Mandalas
CARL JUNG

This symbolic representation of a World Tree comes from 18th-century Iran. It is conceived as a tree in Paradise, about which the Prophet Muhammad reportedly said, "God planted it with His own hand and breathed His spirit into it."

geographically separate cultures have drawn. These archetypes include such symbolic characters as the wise old man, the great mother, the original man and woman, the hero, the shadow, and the trickster.

Extended metaphors may be understood as **allegories**—narratives that use concrete symbols to convey abstract ideas. The biblical book attributed to the Hebrew prophet Ezekiel, for instance, is full of such allegorical passages. In one he says that God's spirit led him to a valley full of dry bones. As he watched and spoke as God told him, the bones developed flesh and muscles, became joined together into bodies, and rose to their feet. The voice of God in the scripture explains the allegorical meaning: the bones represent the people of Israel, who have been abandoned by their self-serving leaders and become scattered and preyed upon by wild beasts, like the sheep of uncaring shepherds. God promises to dismiss the shepherds, raise the fallen people and restore them to the land of Israel, where they will live peacefully under God's protection (Ezekiel 34–37).

Descendants of the Eagle

A long time ago, a really long time when the world was still freshly made, Unktehi the water monster fought the people and caused a great flood. Perhaps the Great Spirit was angry with us for some reason. Maybe he let Unktehi win out because he wanted to make a better kind of human being.

The waters got higher and higher. Finally everything was flooded except the hill next to the place where the sacred red pipestone quarry lies today. The people climbed up there to save themselves, but it was no use. The water swept over that hill. Waves tumbled the rocks and pinnacles, smashing them down on the people. Everyone was killed, and all the blood jelled, making one big pool. The blood turned to pipestone and created the pipestone quarry, the grave of those ancient ones. That's why the pipe, made of that red rock, is so sacred to us. Its red bowl is the flesh and blood of our ancestors, its stem is the backbone of those people long dead, the smoke rising from it is their breath. I tell you, that pipe comes alive when used in a ceremony; you can feel the power flowing from it.

Unktehi, the big water monster, was also turned to stone. Maybe Tunkashila, the Grandfather Spirit, punished her for making the flood. Her bones are in the Badlands now. Her back forms a long, high ridge, and you can see her vertebrae sticking out in a great row of red and yellow rocks. I have seen them. It scared me when I was on that ridge, for I felt Unktehi. She was moving beneath me, wanting to topple me.

When all the people were killed so many generations ago, one girl survived, a beautiful girl. It happened this way: When the water swept over the hill where they tried to seek refuge, a big spotted eagle, Wanblee Galeshka, swept down and let her grab hold of his feet. With her hanging on, he flew to the top of a tall tree which stood on the highest stone pinnacles in the Black Hills. That was the eagle's home. It became the only spot not covered with water. If the people had gotten up there, they would have survived, but it was a needle-like rock.

Wanblee kept that beautiful girl with him and made her his wife. There was a closer connection then between people and animals, so he could do it. The eagle's wife became pregnant and bore him twins, a boy and a girl. She was happy, and said, "Now we will have people again. *Washtay*, it is good." The children were born right there, on top of that cliff. When the waters finally subsided, Wanblee helped the children and their mother down from his rock and put them on the earth, telling them: "Be a nation, become a great Nation—the Lakota Oyate." The boy and girl grew up. He was the only man on earth, she was the only woman of child-bearing age. They married; they had children. A nation was born.

So we are descended from the eagle. We are an eagle nation. That is good, something to be proud of, because the eagle is the wisest of birds. He is the Great Spirit's messenger; he is a great warrior. That is why we always wore the eagle plume and still wear it.

As told by Lame Deer to Richard Erdoes[26]

Such allegories may assume great significance in a people's self-understanding, as in the Lakota myth of the eagle (see Box).

Symbols are also woven together into **myths**—the symbolic stories that communities use to explain the universe and their place within it. Like many cultures, Polynesians tell a myth of the world's creation in which the world was initially covered with water and shrouded in darkness. When the Supreme Being, Io, wanted to rise from rest, he uttered words that immediately brought light into the darkness. Then at his word the waters and the heavens were separated, the land was shaped, and all beings were created. Myths may purport to explain how

myreligionlab

Hero with a
Thousand Faces
JOSEPH CAMPBELL

things came to be as they are, perhaps incorporating elements of historical truth, and in any case are treated as sacred history.

Joseph Campbell (1904–1987), who carried out extensive analysis of myths around the world, found that myths have four primary functions: mystical (evoking our awe, love, wonder, gratitude); cosmological (presenting explanations of the universe based on the existence and actions of spiritual powers or beings); sociological (adapting people to orderly social life, teaching ethical codes); and psychological (opening doors to inner exploration, development of one's full potential, and adjustment to life cycle changes). Understood in these senses, myths are not falsehoods or the works of primitive imaginations; they can be deeply meaningful and transformational, forming a sacred belief structure that supports the laws and institutions of the religion and the ways of the community, as well as explaining the people's place within the cosmos. Campbell paid particular attention to myths of the hero's journey, in which the main character is separated from the group, undergoes hardships and initiation, and returns bearing truth to the people. Such stories, he felt, prepare and inspire the listener for the difficult inward journey that leads to spiritual transformation:

myreligionlab

Perseus Myth
APOLLODORUS

> *It is the business of mythology to reveal the specific dangers and techniques of the dark interior way from tragedy to comedy. Hence the incidents are fantastic and "unreal": they represent psychological, not physical, triumphs. The passage of the mythological hero may be overground, [but] fundamentally it is inward—into depths where obscure resistances are overcome, and long lost, forgotten powers are revivified, to be made available for the transfiguration of the world.*[27]

Absolutist and liberal interpretations

Within each faith people often have different ways of interpreting their traditions. The **orthodox** stand by an historical form of their religion, strictly following its established practices, laws, and creeds. Those who resist contemporary influences and affirm what they perceive as the historical core of their religion could be called **absolutists**. In our times, many people feel that their identity as individuals or as members of an established group is threatened by the sweeping changes brought by modern industrial culture. The breakup of family relationships, loss of geographic rootedness, decay of clear behavioral codes, and loss of local control may be very unsettling. To find stable footing, to attempt to preserve their distinctive identity as a people in the face of modernity and secularization, some people may try to stand on selected religious doctrines or practices from the past. Religious leaders may encourage this trend toward rigidity by declaring themselves absolute authorities or by telling the people that their scriptures are literally and exclusively true. They may encourage antipathy or even violence against people of other religious traditions.

The term **fundamentalism** is often applied to this selective insistence on parts of a religious tradition and to violence against people of other religions. This use of the term is misleading, for no religion is based on hatred of other people and because those who are labeled "fundamentalists" may not be engaged in a return to the true basics of their religion. A Muslim "fundamentalist" who insists on the veiling of women, for instance, does not draw this doctrine from the foundation of Islam, the Holy Qur'an, but rather from historical cultural practice in some Muslim countries. A Sikh "fundamentalist" who concentrates on externals, such as wearing a turban, sword, and steel bracelet, overlooks the central insistence of the Sikh Gurus on the inner rather than outer practice of religion.

A further problem with the use of the term "fundamentalism" is that it has a specifically Protestant Christian connotation. The Christian fundamentalist movement originated in the late nineteenth century as a reaction to liberal trends, such as historical-critical study of the Bible, which will be explained below. Other labels may, therefore, be more cross-culturally appropriate, such as "absolutist," "extremist," or "reactionary," depending on the particular situation.

Those who are called religious **liberals** take a more flexible approach to religious tradition. They may see scriptures as products of a specific culture and time rather than the eternal voice of truth, and may interpret passages metaphorically rather than literally. If activists, they may advocate reforms in the ways their religion is officially understood and practiced.

While conservatives tend to take their scriptures and received religious traditions as literally and absolutely true, liberals have for several centuries been engaged in a different approach to understanding their own religions and those of others: historical-critical studies. These are academic attempts to reconstruct the historical life stories of prophets and their cultures as opposed to legends about them, and to subject their scriptures to objective analysis. Such academic study of religion neither accepts nor rejects the particular truth-claims of any religion.

Non-faith-based research methods reveal that "sacred" scriptures may include polemics against opponents of the religion, myths, cultural influences, ethical instruction, later interpolations, mistakes by copyists, literary devices, factual history, and genuine spiritual inspiration. This process began with historical-critical

Angels Weep

Wherever there is slaughter of innocent men, women, and children for the mere reason that they belong to another race, color, or nationality, or were born into a faith which the majority of them could never quite comprehend and hardly ever practice in its true spirit; wherever the fair name of religion is used as a veneer to hide overweening political ambition and bottomless greed, wherever the glory of Allah is sought to be proclaimed through the barrel of a gun; wherever piety becomes synonymous with rapacity, and morality cowers under the blight of expediency and compromise, wherever it be—in Yugoslavia or Algeria, in Liberia, Chad, or the beautiful land of the Sudan, in Los Angeles or Abuija, in Kashmir or Conakry, in Colombo or Cotabato—there God is banished and Satan is triumphant, there the angels weep and the soul of man cringes; there in the name of God humans are dehumanized; and there the grace and beauty of life lie ravished and undone.

Dr. Syed Z. Abedin, Director of the Institute for Muslim Minority Affairs[28]

study of the Bible at the end of the eighteenth century and has expanded to include scriptures of other traditions, such as the Holy Qur'an of Islam, the *Dao de jing* of Daoism, and Buddhist and Hindu texts.

One area of research is to try to determine the original or most reliable form of a particular text. Another focus is ferreting out the historical aspects of the text, with help from external sources such as archaeological findings, to determine the historical setting in which it was probably composed, its actual author or authors, and possible sources of its material, such as oral or written traditions. Such research may conclude that material about a certain period may have been written later and include perspectives from that later period, or that a text with one person's name as author may actually be a collection of writings by different people. A third area of research asks, "What was the intended audience?" A fourth examines the language and meanings of the words. A fifth looks at whether a scripture or passage follows a particular literary form, such as poetry, legal code, miracle story, allegory, parable, hymn, narrative, or sayings. A sixth focuses on the **redaction**, or editing and organizing, of the scripture and the development of an authorized canon designed to speak not only to the local community but also to a wider audience. Yet another approach is to look at the scripture in terms of its universal and contemporary relevance, rather than its historicity.

Although such research attempts to be objective, it is not necessarily undertaken with sceptical intentions. To the contrary, these forms of research are taught in many seminaries as ways of reconciling faith with reason. Nevertheless, such analyses may be seen as offensive and/or false by orthodox believers. In any case, they are not perfect, for there are gaps in the available data and they can be interpreted in various ways. Scriptures also serve different purposes in different traditions, and these differences must be understood.

The encounter between science and religion

Divisions among absolutist, liberal, and sceptical interpretations of religion are related to the development of modern science. Like religion, science is also engaged in searching for universal principles that explain the facts of nature. The two approaches have influenced each other since ancient times, when they were not seen as separate endeavors. In both East and West, there were continual attempts to understand reality as a whole.

In ancient Greece, source of many "Western" ideas, a group of thinkers who are sometimes called "nature philosophers" tried to understand the world through their own perceptions of it. By contrast, Plato (c.427–347 BCE) distrusted the testimony of the human senses. He thus made a series of distinctions: between what is perceived by the senses and what is accessible through reason, between body and soul, appearance and reality, objects and ideas. In Plato's thought, the soul was superior to the body, and the activity of reason preferable to the distraction of the senses. This value judgment dominated Western thought through the Middle Ages, with its underlying belief that all of nature had been created by God for the sake of humanity.

In the seventeenth century, knowledge of nature became more **secularized** (that is, divorced from the sacred) as scientists developed models of the universe as a giant machine. Its ways could be discovered by human reason, by studying its component parts and mathematically quantifying its characteristics. However, even in discovering such features, many scientists regarded them as the work of a divine Creator or Ruler. Isaac Newton (1642–1727), whose gravitational theory shaped modern physics, speculated that space is eternal because it is the emanation of "eternal and immutable being." Drawing on biblical quotations, Newton argued that God exists everywhere, containing, discerning, and ruling all things.

During the eighteenth-century Enlightenment, rational ways of knowing were increasingly respected, with a concurrent growing scepticism toward claims of knowledge derived from such sources as divine revelation or illuminated inner wisdom. The sciences were viewed as progressive; some thinkers attacked institutionalized religions and dogma as superstitions. As we saw earlier, according to scientific materialism, which developed during the nineteenth and twentieth centuries, the supernatural is imaginary; only the material world is real.

The old unitary concepts of science and religion received another serious challenge in 1859, when the naturalist Charles Darwin (1809–1882) published *On the Origin of Species*, a work that propounded the theory of evolution by natural selection. Darwin demonstrated that certain genetic mutations give an organism a competitive advantage over others of its species. As evolutionary biology has continued to develop since Darwin through genetic research, it shows that those carrying advantageous genes statistically produce more offspring than others, so the percentage of the new gene gradually increases in the gene pool. Evolutionary studies are revealing more and more evidence of what appear to be gradual changes in organisms, as recorded in fossil records, footprints, and genetic records encoded in DNA. According to evolutionary biology theory, over great lengths of time such gradual changes have brought the development of all forms of life. The theory of natural selection directly contradicted a literal understanding of the biblical Book of Genesis, in which God is said to have created all life in only six days.

myreligionlab
Darwinian Account
of Religion
MIKAEL STENMARK

Mapping of human DNA reveals that its six-and-a-half foot (two-meter)-long chain, carrying trillions of times more data than a computer chip, is super-dense, folding without tangles into the nucleus of a cell which is only one-fifth the width of a human hair.

By the end of the nineteenth century, all such beliefs of the Judeo-Christian tradition were being questioned.

However, as science has progressed during the twentieth and twenty-first centuries, it has in some senses moved back toward a more nuanced understanding of religious belief. Science has always questioned its own assumptions and theories, and scientists have given up trying to find absolute certainties. From contemporary scientific research, it is clear that the cosmos is mind-boggling in its complexity and that what we perceive with our five senses is not ultimately real. For instance, the inertness and solidity of matter are only illusions. Each atom consists mostly of empty space with tiny particles whirling around in it. These subatomic particles—such as neutrons, protons, and electrons—cannot even be described as "things." Theories of quantum mechanics, in trying to account for the tiniest particles of matter, uncovered the Uncertainty Principle: that the position and velocity of a subatomic particle cannot be simultaneously determined. These particles behave like energy as well as like matter, like waves as well as like particles. Their behaviors can best be described in terms of a dynamic, interde-

The Hubble space telescope reveals an unimaginably vast cosmos, with billions of galaxies in continual flux. The Eagle nebula shown here is giving birth to new stars in "pillars of creation" which are six trillion miles high.

pendent system which includes the observer. As physicist David Bohm (1917–1994) put it, "Everything interpenetrates everything."[29]

Our own bodies appear relatively solid, but they are in a constant state of flux and interchange with the environment. Our eyes, ears, noses, tongues, and skin do not reveal absolute truths. Rather, our sensory organs may operate as filters, selecting from a multidimensional universe only those characteristics that we need to perceive in order to survive. Imagine how difficult it would be simply to walk across a street if we could see all the electromagnetic energy in the atmosphere, such as X-rays, radio waves, gamma rays, and infrared and ultraviolet light, rather than only the small band of colors we see as the visible spectrum. Though the sky of a starry night appears vast to the naked eye, the giant Hubble telescope placed in space has revealed an incomprehensibly immense cosmos whose limits have not been found. It contains matter-gobbling black holes, vast starmaking clusters, intergalactic collisions, and cosmic events that happened billions of years ago, so far away that their light is only now being captured by the most powerful instruments we have for examining what lies far beyond our small place in this galaxy. We know that more lies beyond what we have yet been able to measure. And even our ability to conceive of what we cannot sense may perhaps be limited by the way the human brain is organized.

As science continues to question its own assumptions, various new hypotheses are being suggested about the nature of the universe. "Superstring theory" proposes that the universe may not be made of particles at all, but rather of tiny vibrating strings and loops of strings. According to Superstring theory, whereas we think we are living in four dimensions of space and time, there may be at least ten dimensions, with the unperceived dimensions "curled up" or "compactified" within the four dimensions that we can perceive. According to another current theory, the cosmos is like a soccer ball, a finite closed system with many facets.

New branches of science are finding that the universe is not always predictable, nor does it always operate according to human notions of cause and effect. Physicist Murray Gell-Mann says that we are "a small speck of creation believing it is capable of comprehending the whole."[30] And whereas scientific models of the universe were until recently based on the assumption of stability and equilibrium, physicist Ilya Prigogine observes that "today we see instability, fluctuations, irreversibility at every level."[31]

The most beautiful and profound emotion that we can experience is the sensation of the mystical. It is the sower of all true science. He to whom this emotion is a stranger, who can no longer wonder and stand rapt in awe, is as good as dead. To know that what is impenetrable to us really exists, manifesting itself as the highest wisdom and the most radiant beauty which our dull faculties can comprehend only in their most primitive forms—this knowledge, this feeling is at the center of true religiousness. … A human being is part of the whole. … He experiences himself, his thoughts and feelings as something separated from the rest—a kind of optical delusion of his consciousness. … Our task must be to free ourselves from this prison by widening our circle of compassion to embrace all living creatures, and the whole [of] nature in its beauty.

Albert Einstein[33]

In the work of physicists such as David Bohm, physics approaches **metaphysics**—philosophy based on theories of subtle realities that transcend the physical world. Bohm described the dimensions we see and think of as "real" as the *explicate* order. Behind it lies the *implicate* order, in which separateness resolves into unbroken wholeness. Beyond may lie other subtle dimensions, all merging into an infinite ground that unfolds itself as light. This scientific theory is very similar to descriptions by mystics from all cultures about their intuitive experiences of the cosmos. They speak of realities beyond normal human perceptions of space and time. The Hindu term *"Brahma,"* for instance, means "vast"—a vastness perceived by sages as infinite dimensions of a Supreme Consciousness that started without any material and then Itself became the Creation. In the realization of Guru Nanak, first of the Sikh Gurus, God is *"Akal Murat"*—Reality that transcends time.

Science is moving beyond its earlier mechanical models toward more dynamic biological models. For instance, James Lovelock has proposed the Gaia Theory of the earth as a complex, self-regulating organism of sorts, but he does not see it as the work of any Grand Planner. He explains:

> Gaia theory sees the earth as a complete system made up of all the living things—all of them, from bacteria all the way up to whales, from tiny algae living in the ocean all the way up to giant redwood trees, and all of the great ecosystems of the forests and so on. All of that life part is not alone but tightly integrated with the atmosphere, the ocean, and the surface rocks. The whole of that constitutes a single system that regulates itself, keeps the climate constant and comfortable for life, keeps the chemical composition of the atmosphere so that it's always breathable. [The earth] is not alive like an animal. What I am implying is alive in the sense of being able to regulate itself. It's a system that evolved automatically, without any purpose, foresight, or anything. It just happened and has been in existence now for about three and a half to four billion years. A very tough system... .[32]

myreligionlab
Not-So-Random Universe
PATRICK GLYNN

In the United States, the conservative Christian community has objected to mechanistic scientific theories of biological evolution, preferring **Creationism**, the concept of intentional divine creation of all life forms. **Intelligent design** theory has been cited to support the religious concept of Creationism. According to intelligent design theorists, scientific discoveries of the complexities and perfections of life can be said to prove the existence of an Intelligent Designer. For instance, if the weak force in the nucleus of an atom were a small fraction weaker, there would be no hydrogen in the universe—and thus no water. Biologists find that the natural world is an intricate harmony of beautifully elaborated, interrelated parts. Even to produce the miniature propeller that allows a tiny bacterium to swim, some forty different proteins are required.

The question then arises: Can the complex maps that produce life be the consequences of chance arrangements of atoms, or are they the result of deliberate design by some First Cause? The intelligent design movement concludes that there must be a Creator. However, science is a method of proposing testable hypotheses and testing them, whereas the intelligent design hypothesis is not testable. In 2005, the judge in a landmark case in Dover, Pennsylvania, ruled that intelligent design could not be recommended to ninth-grade biology students because intelligent design does not qualify as science—unless the definition of

When Science Approaches Religion

Theoretical physicist Paul Davies (b. 1946) has won the Templeton Prize, a prestigious international award for contribution to thinking about religion. He suggests that science approaches religion when it asks fundamental questions:

"If you are a biologist and you get stuck, you might go to a chemist to help you out. If a chemist gets stuck, you might get a physicist. If you're a physicist and you get stuck, there's nowhere to go except theology, because physics is the most basic science. It's at the base of the explanatory pyramid upon which everything else is built. It deals with the fundamental laws of nature. And that inevitably prompts us to ask questions like, 'Why those laws? Where have they come from? Why are they mathematical? What does it mean? Could they be different?' Clearly these are questions on the borderline between science and philosophy, or science and theology.

"The early scientists perceived this natural order and its hidden mathematical content, and they thought it derived from a creator-being. What happened in the centuries that followed was that science accepted the existence of a real order in nature. You can't be a scientist if you don't believe that there is some sort of order that is at least in part comprehensible to us. So you have to make two enormous assumptions—which don't have to be right. But to be a scientist, you've got to believe they're true. First, that there is a rational order in nature. Second, that we can come to understand nature, at least in part. What an extraordinary thing this is to believe in! There is a rational, comprehensible order in nature. Science asserts that the world isn't arbitrary or absurd.

"If I use the word 'God,' it is not in the sense of a super-being who has existed for all eternity and, like a cosmic magician, brings the universe into being at some moment in time on a whimsical basis. When I refer to 'God,' it is in the sense of the rational ground in which the whole scientific enterprise is rooted. The God I'm referring to is not really a person or a being in the usual sense. In particular, it is something that is outside of time. That is a very significant issue, and one on which there can be a very fruitful exchange, in my opinion, between physics and philosophy.

"Almost all of my physics colleagues, and scientists from other disciplines, even if they would cast themselves as militant atheists, are deeply inspired by the wonder, the beauty, the ingenuity of nature, and the underlying, law-like mathematical order.

"It could be that there are some things that are simply going to be forever beyond scientific enquiry— not because we're lacking the money or the expertise or something of that sort, but because there are inherent limits to how far rational enquiry can take us. If science leaves us with mystery, is there a way that we can come to know about the world, about existence, not through scientific enquiry but through some other method? I'm open-minded as to whether that is the case. I'm talking here about revelatory or mystical experiences, where somehow the answer is grasped—not through rational enquiry, nor through experimentation, but by 'knowing' in some internal sense.

"Nothing I have said deals with the sort of issues we struggle with in daily life, which are ethical and moral issues. The weakness of restricting to a God who's just some sort of abstract, mathematical, rational ground for the world is that it doesn't provide us with any sort of moral guidance. Most people turn to religion not because they want to understand how the universe is put together, but because they want to understand how their own lives are put together, and what they should do next. You don't go to a physicist to ask about right and wrong."[34]

science is changed to include supernatural explanations—and because the First Amendment of the Constitution prevents government officials from imposing any particular religion or religious belief.

In the current dialogue between science and religion, four general positions have emerged. One is a conflict model, which is most apparent in issues such as creation, with some scientists holding onto faith in scientific method and some religionists holding onto faith in a Creator God whose existence cannot be proved by scientific method. A second position is that science and religion deal with separate realms. That is, religions deal with matters such as morality, hope, answers to philosophical questions ("Why are we here?"), and ideas about life after death, whereas science deals with quantifiable physical reality. In this position, a person can live with "two truths," and neither side is required to venture into the other's domain. A third position is that of dialogue, in which scientists and religious believers can find common ground in interpreting religious propositions as metaphors and bases for the moral use of scientific research. Claims to absolute truth are softened on each side. A fourth position is that of integration, in which science and religion overlap. One example is illustrated by the boxed excerpt from physicist Paul Davies; another is what is sometimes called "creation theology," referring to scientific enquiries by people who believe in a creative deity or deities. Environmentalist Ellen Bernstein explains this exploration from a Jewish perspective:

> Creation theology refers to any kind of reflection on God and the world as a whole, or the elements of the world. It is interested in the nature of nature, and the nature of humanity, and the interplay of the two. It understands God as the continual, creative Presence in the world. … Jews who accept the logic of evolution theory should be relieved to learn that embracing a theology of creation in no way requires a suspension of rational thought or scientific integrity. The ancients paid attention to nature and their environment—they were astute observers in their own right; so much of the sense we can detect in the [biblical story of creation] results from their own grasp of natural history.[35]

At the cutting edge of research, scientists themselves find they have no ultimate answers that can be expressed in scientific terms. The renowned theoretical physicist Stephen Hawking asks, "What is it that breathes fire into the equations and makes a universe for them to describe?"[36]

Women in religions

myreligionlab

Image of God as Dominating Other
JUDITH PLASKOW

Another long-standing issue in the sphere of religion is the exclusion of women in male-dominated systems. Most institutionalized religions are **patriarchal**, meaning that men lead like father figures. Women are often relegated to the fringes of religious organizations, given only supporting roles, thus reflecting existing social distinctions between men and women. In some cases, women are even considered incapable of spiritual realization or dangerous to men's spiritual lives. Founders of religion have in many cases attempted to temper cultural restraints on women. Jesus, for example, apparently included women among his close disciples, and the Prophet Muhammad gave much more respect to women

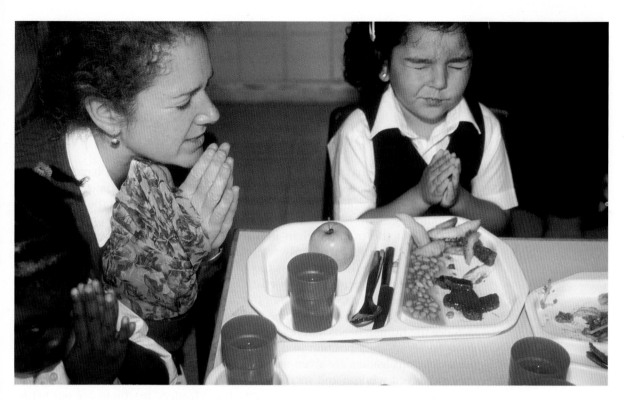

than had been customary in the surrounding culture. However, the institutions that developed after the prophets often reverted to exclusion and oppression of women, sometimes giving a religious stamp of approval to gender imbalances.

Although women are still barred from equal spiritual footing with men in many religions, this situation is now being widely challenged. The contemporary feminist movement includes strong efforts to make women's voices heard in the sphere of religion. Women are trying to discover their own identity, rather than having their identities defined by others, and to develop full, purposeful lives for themselves and their families. Scholars are bringing to light the histories of many women who have been religious leaders. Feminists are challenging patriarchal religious institutions that have excluded women from active participation. They are also challenging gender-exclusive language in holy texts and authoritarian masculine images of the divine. Their protests also go beyond gender issues to question the narrow and confining ways in which religious inspiration has been institutionalized. Many Buddhist centers in the West and some in Asia are run by women, and female scholars are having a major impact on the ways that Buddhist teachings are being understood. At prestigious Christian seminaries in the United States, women preparing for the ministry now outnumber men and are radically transforming views of religion and religious practice. Many women are deeply concerned about social ills of our times—violence, poverty, ecological disaster—and are insisting that religions be actively engaged in insuring human survival, and that they be life-affirming rather than punitive in approach.

Even in traditional roles, women are redefining themselves as important spiritual actors. Buddhist practitioner Jacqueline Kramer observes:

Even when denied access to public leadership roles in religions, women have been spiritually influential as mothers, nurses, Sunday school teachers, and the like.

The life occupation of mothering and homemaking has been both glorified and demeaned, but seldom has it been seen as the valid spiritual path it can be. Yet, the practices the mothers engage in, day in and day out—selfless service, generosity, letting go, developing a deep love for all beings, patience, faith, and mindfulness— are the way of practice for monks and nuns of all the world's wisdom traditions.[37]

Negative aspects of organized religions

Tragically, religions have often split rather than unified humanity, have oppressed rather than freed, have terrified rather than inspired. Institutionalization of religion is part of the problem. As institutionalized religions spread the teachings of their founders, there is the danger that more energy will go into preserving the outer form of the tradition than into maintaining its inner spirit. Max Weber (1864–1920), an influential early twentieth-century scholar of the sociology of religion, referred to this process as the "routinization of charisma." **Charisma** is the rare quality of personal magnetism often ascribed to founders of religion. When the founder dies, the center of the movement may shift to those who turn the original inspirations into routine rituals and dogma.

Since the human needs that religions answer are so strong, those who hold religious power are in a position to dominate and control their followers. In fact, in many religions leaders are given this authority to guide people's spiritual lives, for their perceived wisdom and special access to the sacred are valued. Because religions involve the unseen, the mysterious, these leaders' teachings are not verifiable by everyday physical experience. They must more often be accepted on faith and it is possible to surrender to leaders who are misguided or unethical. Religious leaders, like secular leaders, may not be honest with themselves and others about their inner motives. They may mistake their own thoughts and desires for divine guidance. Some people believe, however, that the most important thing for the disciple is to surrender the ego; even an unworthy leader can help in this goal simply by playing the role of one to whom one must surrender personal control.

Another potential problem is exaggeration of guilt. Religions try to help us make ethical choices in our lives, to develop a moral conscience. But in people who already have perfectionist or paranoid tendencies, the fear of sinning and being punished can be exaggerated to the point of neurosis or even psychosis by blaming, punishment-oriented religious teachings. If people try to leave their religion for the sake of their mental health, they may be haunted with guilt that they have done a terribly wrong thing. Religions thus have the potential for wreaking psychological havoc on their followers.

Another potentially negative use of religion is escapism. Because some religions, particularly those that developed in Asia, offer a state of blissful contemplation as the reward for spiritual practice, the faithful may use religion to escape from their everyday problems. Psychologist John Welwood observes that Westerners sometimes embrace Eastern religions with the unconscious motive of avoiding their unsatisfactory lives. He calls this attempt "spiritual bypassing."

Because religions may have such a strong hold on their followers—by their fears, their desires, their deep beliefs—they are potential centers for political power. When church and state are one, the belief that the dominant national religion is the only true religion may be used to oppress those of other beliefs within the country. Religion may also be used as a rallying point for wars against other nations, casting the desire for control as a holy motive. Throughout history, huge numbers of people have been killed in the name of eradicating "false" religions and replacing them with the "true" religion. Rather than uniting us all in bonds of love, harmony, and mutual respect, this has often divided us with barriers of hatred and intolerance.

In our times, dangerous politicized polarizations between religions are increasing in some areas, albeit cooling off in others. Some of the most worrisome conflicts are pitting Christians and Jews against Muslims to such an extent that some have predicted a catastrophic "clash of civilizations." No religion has ever sanctioned violence against innocent people, but such political clashes have given a holy aura to doing just that, posing a grave threat to life and peace. Sadism, terrorism, wars over land and resources, political oppression, and environmental destruction can all be given a thin veneer of religious sanctification, thus obscuring their evil aspects.

His Highness the Aga Khan, spiritual leader of Isma'ili Shia Muslims, maintains that the real problem today is a "clash of ignorance."[38] This is not the time to think of the world in terms of superficial, rigid distinctions between "us" and "them." It is the time when we must try to understand each other's beliefs and feelings clearly, carefully, and compassionately, and bring truly religious responses into play. To take such a journey does not mean forsaking our own religious beliefs or our scepticism. But the journey is likely to broaden our perspective and thus bring us closer to understanding other members of our human family.

Scholars of different disciplines have their own lens through which they attempt to describe and explain religions. In this book we will look through various lenses, including history, sociology, psychology, anthropology, theology, politics, economics, feminist studies, and **phenomenology**—a special field devoted specifically to the study of religions. Phenomenology involves an appreciative investigation of religious phenomena from the perspective of the practitioners and believers—an "insider's" rather than an "outsider's" point of view. This includes "thick description," a term used by the cultural anthropologist Clifford Geertz (1926–2006)—not only reporting outward behaviors but also attempting to explain their meaning for members of particular cultural systems. This approach follows real people into the depths of their search for meaning, order, and inner peace in a world that may otherwise seem chaotic and sometimes violent. Therefore, in addition to exploring various scholarly perspectives, we will try to listen carefully to individuals of all faiths as they tell their own stories.

myreligionlab
Lost Dimension in Religion
PAUL TILLICH

Suggested reading

Campbell, Joseph, *The Hero with a Thousand Faces,* second edition, Princeton, New Jersey: Princeton University Press, 1968. Brilliant leaps across time and space to trace the hero's journey—seen as a spiritual quest—in all the world's mythologies and religions.

Campbell, Joseph with Bill Moyers, *The Power of Myth*, New York: Doubleday, 1988. More brilliant comparisons of the world's mythologies, with deep insights into their common psychological and spiritual truths.

Capra, Fritjof, *The Tao of Physics*, third edition, Boston: Shambhala, 1991. A fascinating comparison of the insights of Eastern religions and contemporary physics.

Carter, Robert E., ed., *God, The Self, and Nothingness—Reflections: Eastern and Western*, New York: Paragon House, 1990. Essays from major Eastern and Western scholars of religion on variant ways of experiencing and describing Ultimate Reality.

Dawkins, Richard, *The God Delusion*, Boston: Houghton Mifflin; London: Transworld (Bantam Press), 2006. Controversial arguments against belief in a personal God by a leading atheistic evolutionary biologist.

Eliade, Mircea, *Patterns in Comparative Religion*, trans. Rosemary Sheed, Lincoln, Nebraska: University of Nebraska Press, 1958, 1996. A classic study of beliefs, rituals, symbols, and myths from around the world.

Eliade, Mircea, *The Sacred and the Profane: The Nature of Religion*, New York: Harcourt, 1959. A good basic introduction to Eliade's theories of sacred space and sacred time.

Ferguson, Kitty, *The Fire in the Equations: Science, Religion and the Search for God*, New York/London: Bantam Books, 1994. A wide-ranging, perceptive analysis of the implications of scientific research for religious beliefs.

Fisher, Mary Pat, *Women in Religion*, New York: Pearson Longman, 2007. Many women's stories and analysis of how each major religion has included or excluded them.

Hick, John, *An Interpretation of Religion*, New Haven: Yale University Press, 1992. A leading philosopher of religion offers a rational justification for seeing the major world religions as culturally conditioned forms of response to the great mystery of Being.

King, Ursula, *Women and Spirituality: Voices of Protest and Promise*, second edition, University Park, Pennsylvania: Pennsylvania State University Press, 1993. Excellent cross-cultural survey of feminist theology and spiritual activism.

Lincoln, Bruce, *Holy Terrors: Thinking about Religion after September 11*, Chicago and London; University of Chicago Press, 2003. Thought-provoking examination of the rhetoric of religious extremists and the interactions of politics, culture, and religion.

Marty, Martin E. and R. Scott Appleby, *The Fundamentalism Project*, five volumes, Chicago: University of Chicago Press, 1991–2000. Scholarly analyses of fundamentalist phenomena in all religions and around the globe.

McCutcheon, Russell T., *Manufacturing Religion: The Discourse on Sui Generis Religion and the Politics of Nostalgia*, New York and Oxford: Oxford University Press, 1997. Critique of the comparative study of religions as isolated phenomena without social and historical contexts.

McGrath, Alister E., *Dawkins' God: Genes, Memes, and the Meaning of Life*, Oxford: Blackwell, 2005. A biochemist and Christian theologian refutes Richard Dawkins' criticism of religion.

Otto, Rudolf, *The Idea of the Holy*, second edition, London: Oxford University Press, 1950. An important exploration of "nonrational" experiences of the divine.

Paden, William E., *Interpreting the Sacred: Ways of Viewing Religion*, Boston: Beacon Press, 1992. A gentle, readable introduction to the complexities of theoretical perspectives on religion.

Sharma, Arvind, ed., *Women in World Religions*, Albany, New York: State University of New York Press, 1987. Analyses of the historical and contemporary place of women in each of the major religions.

Shinn, Larry D., ed., *In Search of the Divine: Some Unexpected Consequences of Interfaith Dialogue*, New York: Paragon House Publishers, 1987. Scholars from various religions present a tapestry of understandings of the Sacred Reality.

Smart, Ninian, *Worldviews: Crosscultural Explorations of Human Beliefs*. Upper Saddle River, New Jersey: Prentice Hall, 2000. In-depth exploration of many dimensions of religious ideologies that influence beliefs around the world.

Stone, Merlin, *When God was a Woman*, San Diego, California: Harcourt Brace

Jovanovich, 1976. Pioneering survey of archaeological evidence of the early religion of the Goddess.

Ward, Keith, *God, Chance and Necessity*, Oxford: Oneworld Publications, 1997. A leading Christian theologian critiques scientific theories that deny the existence of God.

Ward, Keith, *The Case for Religion*, Oxford: Oneworld Publications, 2004. An attempt to justify and define religion in historical contexts and also contemporary understandings.

Key terms

absolutist Believing in one's received traditions as completely and exclusively true.

agnosticism Belief that if there is anything beyond this life it is impossible for humans to know it.

allegory Narrative using symbols to convey abstract ideas.

atheism Belief that there is no deity.

awakening Full awareness of invisible Reality.

charisma Magnetic attraction, a quality often ascribed to spiritual leaders.

comparative religion A discipline that attempts to compare and understand patterns found in different religious traditions.

Creationism Belief that all life was created by God.

dogma Doctrines proclaimed as absolutely true by religious institutions.

enlightenment Wisdom that is thought to come from direct experience of Ultimate Reality.

exclusivism Belief that one's own tradition is the only true religion and that others are invalid.

fundamentalism Insistence on what is perceived as the historical form of one's religion.

gnosis Intuitive knowledge of spiritual realities.

heretic One whose assertions about religion are considered false by his or her religious institution.

immanent Present in the visible world.

incarnation Physical embodiment of the divine.

intelligent design Theory that scientific discoveries prove the existence of an all-encompassing Designer, since they reveal complexities that seem to be beyond chance or evolutionary process.

liberal Taking a flexible, nondogmatic approach.

metaphysics Philosophy based on theories of subtle realities that transcend the physical world.

monotheism Belief that there is only one deity.

mysticism The intuitive perception of spiritual truths beyond the limits of reason.

myth A symbolic story expressing ideas about reality or spiritual history.

orthodox Strictly standing by received traditions.

phenomenology Study of religious practices to comprehend their meaning for their practitioners.

polytheism Belief that there are many deities.

profane Worldly, secular, as opposed to sacred.

realization Personal awareness of the existence of Unseen Reality.

redaction Editing and organization of a religion's scriptures.

religion A particular response to dimensions of life considered sacred, as shaped by institutionalized traditions.

ritual Repeated, patterned religious act.

sacred The realm of the extraordinary, beyond everyday perceptions, the supernatural, holy.

scientific materialism Belief that only the material world exists and that the supernatural is only imagined by humans.

spirituality Any personal response to dimensions of life that are considered sacred.

symbol Visible representation of an invisible reality or concept.

theism Belief in a deity or deities.

transcendent Spiritual reality that exists apart from the material universe.

universalism Acceptance that truth may be found in all religions.

Review questions

1. What are some of the different perspectives available for understanding religion?
2. Describe absolutist and liberal interpretations of religious traditions, and how each might react to historical-critical studies of religious texts.
3. What are the major positions that have emerged in the dialogue between science and religion?

Discussion questions

1. To what extent do you find materialistic arguments rejecting the reality posited by religion and spirituality useful in understanding religion?
2. In what ways is the patriarchal nature of institutionalized religions changing?
3. What factors do you believe contribute to the negative aspects of organized religions?

myreligionlab

For further activities and resources, including access to MyReligionLibrary, please visit MyReligionLab at www.myreligionlab.com

Additional Internet resources

American Religious Identification Survey 2008 http://livinginliminality.files.wordpress.com/2009/03/aris_report_2008.pdf

Beliefnet http://www.beliefnet.com/

Encyclopedia Mythica http://www.pantheon.org

Films for the Humanities and Sciences http://www.films.com

Internet Sacred Text Archive http://www.sacred-texts.com/index.htm

Introduction to Religion and Ecology http://environment.harvard.edu/religioninformation/index.html

National and World Religions Statistics http://www.adherents.com

The Pew Forum on Religion and Public Life http://pewforum.org/

The Pluralism Project at Harvard University http://pluralism.org

Religion Facts http://religionfacts.com

Religion and Science: Stanford Encyclopedia of Philosophy http://plato.stanford.edu/entries/religion–science

Religious Tolerance http://www.religioustolerance.org/chrmovie.htm

Virtual Religion Index http://virtualreligion.net/vri/

Wabash Center Guide to Internet Resources http://www.wabashcenter.wabash.edu/resources/guide_headings.aspx

CHAPTER 2

INDIGENOUS SACRED WAYS

"Everything is alive"

Here and there around the globe, pockets of people still follow local sacred ways handed down from their remote ancestors and adapted to contemporary circumstances. These are the traditional **indigenous** peoples—descendants of the original inhabitants of lands now controlled by larger political systems in which they may have little influence. Their distribution around the world, suggested in the map overleaf, reveals a fascinating picture with many indigenous groups surviving in the midst of industrialized societies.

Indigenous peoples comprise at least four percent of the world's population. Some who follow the ancient spiritual traditions still live close to the earth in nonindustrial, small-scale cultures; many do not. But despite the disruption of their traditional lifestyles, many indigenous peoples maintain a sacred way of life that is distinctively different from all other religions. These enduring ways, which indigenous peoples may refer to as their "original instructions" on how to live, were almost lost under the onslaught of genocidal colonization, conversion pressures from global religions, mechanistic materialism, and the destruction of their natural environments by the global economy of limitless consumption.

KEY TOPICS

- **UNDERSTANDING INDIGENOUS SACRED WAYS** 34
- **CULTURAL DIVERSITY** 38
- **THE CIRCLE OF RIGHT RELATIONSHIPS** 39
- **SPIRITUAL SPECIALISTS** 50
- **GROUP OBSERVANCES** 56
- **CONTEMPORARY ISSUES** 62

> *To what extent can [indigenous groups] reinstitute traditional religious values in a world gone mad with development, electronics, almost instantaneous transportation facilities, and intellectually grounded in a rejection of spiritual and mysterious events?*
>
> *Vine Deloria, Jr.*[1]

Much of the ancient visionary wisdom has disappeared. To seek paying jobs and modern comforts such as electricity, many people have shifted from their natural environments into urban settings. There are few traditionally trained elders left and few young people willing to undergo the lengthy and rigorous training necessary for spiritual leadership in these sacred ways. Nevertheless, in our time there is a renewal of interest in these traditions, fanning hope that what they offer will not be lost.

While globalization has on the one hand tended to absorb and dilute indigenous sacred ways, it has also helped to spread them internationally. In African indigenous societies, communal rituals and ceremonies commemorating specific local divinities are becoming internationalized. For instance, the annual Yoruba festival dedicated to Osun now attracts devotees and tourists from across the world. At the same time, indigenous African religions are being spread to the African diaspora, leading to the development of African-derived religions such as Santeria, Candomble, Vodun, and Yoruba-Orisa traditions across the Americas, and including the "export" of indigenous spiritual specialists (see Chapter 12).

Understanding indigenous sacred ways

Outsiders have known or understood little of the indigenous sacred ways, many of which have long been practiced only in secret. In Mesoamerica, the ancient teachings have remained hidden for 500 years since the coming of the conquistadores, passed down within families as a secret oral tradition. The Buryats living near Lake Baikal in Russia were thought to have been converted to Buddhism and Christianity centuries ago; however, almost the entire population of the area gathered for indigenous ceremonies on Olkhon Island in 1992 and 1993.

In parts of aboriginal Australia, the indigenous teachings have been underground for 200 years since white colonialists and Christian missionaries appeared. As aborigine Lorraine Mafi Williams explains:

The approximate distribution of indigenous groups mentioned in this chapter.

> *We have stacked away our religious, spiritual, cultural beliefs. When the missionaries came, we were told by our old people to be respectful, listen and be obedient, go to church, go to Sunday school, but do not adopt the Christian*

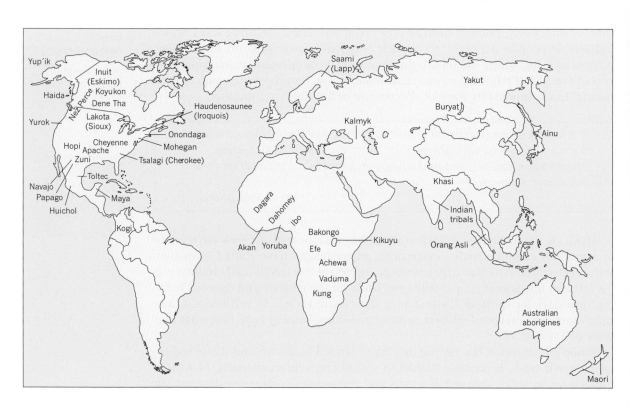

*doctrine because it takes away our cultural, spiritual beliefs. So we've always
stayed within God's laws in what we know.*[2]

Not uncommonly, the newer global traditions have been blended with the
older ways. For instance, Buddhism as it spread often adopted existing customs,
such as the recognition of local deities. Now many indigenous people practice one
of the global religions while still retaining many of their traditional ways.

Until recently, those who attempted to ferret out the native sacred ways had
little basis for understanding them. Many were anthropologists who approached
spiritual behaviors from the nonspiritual perspective of Western science or else
the Christian understanding of religion as a means of salvation from sinful earthly existence—a belief not found among most indigenous peoples. Knowing that
researchers from other cultures did not grasp the truth of their beliefs, native peoples have at times given them information that was incorrect in order to protect
the sanctity of their practices from the uninitiated.

Academic study of traditional ways is now becoming more sympathetic and
self-critical, however, as is apparent in this statement by Gerhardus Cornelius
Oosthuizen, a European researching African traditional religions:

> *[The] Western worldview is closed, essentially complete and unchangeable, basically
> substantive and fundamentally non-mysterious; i.e. it is like a rigid programmed
> machine. ... This closed worldview is foreign to Africa, which is still deeply
> religious. ... This world is not closed, and not merely basically substantive, but it
> has great depth, it is unlimited in its qualitative varieties and is truly mysterious;
> this world is restless, a living and growing organism.*[3]

*Uluru (Ayers Rock),
a unique mass rising
from the plains of
central Australia, has
long been considered
sacred by the aboriginal
groups of the area, and
in its caves are many
ancient paintings.*

Indigenous spirituality is a **lifeway**, a particular approach to all of life. It is not a separate experience, like meditating in the morning or going to church on Sunday. Rather, spirituality ideally pervades all moments. There is no sharp dichotomy between sacred and secular domains. As an elder of the Huichol in Mexico puts it:

> *Everything we do in life is for the glory of God. We praise him in the well-swept floor, the well-weeded field, the polished machete, the brilliant colors of the picture and embroidery. In these ways we prepare for a long life and pray for a good one.*[4]

In most native cultures, spiritual lifeways are shared orally. There are no scriptures of the sort that other religions are built around (although some written texts, such as the Mayan codices, were destroyed by conquering groups). Instead, the people create and pass on songs, proverbs, myths, riddles, short sayings, legends, art, music, and the like. This helps to keep the indigenous sacred ways dynamic and flexible rather than fossilized. It also keeps the sacred experience fresh in the present. Oral narratives may also contain clues to the historical experiences of individuals or groups, but these are often carried from generation to generation in symbolic language. The symbols, metaphors, and humor are not easily understood by outsiders but are central to a people's under-standing of how life works. To the Maori of New Zealand, life is a continual dynamic process of becoming in which all things arise from a burst of cosmic energy. According to their creation story, all beings emerged from a spatially confined liminal state of darkness in which the Sky Father and Earth Mother were locked in eternal embrace, continually conceiving but crowding their offspring until their children broke that embrace. Their separation created a great burst of light, like wind sweeping through the cosmos. That tremendously freeing, rejuvenating power is still present and can be called upon through rituals in which all beings—plants, trees, fish, birds, animals, people—are intimately and primordially related.

The lifeways of many small-scale cultures are tied to the land on which they live and their entire way of life; they are meaningful only within this context. However, traditional worldviews are not inevitably linked to materially simple ways of life. The Dene Tha of northwestern Alberta, Canada, now live in houses built by the government and ride snowmobiles instead of their traditional dog sleds, but they still seek spiritual help from "animal helpers" and find important meaning and guidance in their visionary experiences. Indigenous sacred ways are not static traditions. Even though they draw on ancient spiritual sensitivities, they encounter change, and they change with time.

Despite the hindrances to understanding of indigenous forms of spirituality, the doors to understanding are opening somewhat in our times. Firstly, the traditional elders are very concerned about the growing potential for planetary disaster. Some are beginning to share their basic values, if not their esoteric practices, in hopes of preventing industrial societies from destroying the earth. Secondly, those of other faiths are beginning to recognize the value of indigenous ways, which were in the past suppressed by global religions. Thirdly, many people who have not grown up in native cultures are attempting to embrace indigenous spiritual ways, finding their own traditions lacking in certain qualities for which they long, such as love for the earth. However, even outsiders who

myreligionlab
Theft of Light
TSIMSHIAN NATION

The indigenous community of Acoma Pueblo—built on a high plateau in New Mexico—may live in the oldest continuously occupied city in the United States.

value the sacred teachings may disrupt or alter the indigenous practices. Osage theologian George Tinker describes what often happens in North America:

The first Indian casualty today in any such New Age spiritual-cultural encounter is most often the strong deep-structure cultural value of community and group cohesion that is important to virtually every indigenous people. ... Well-meaning New Agers drive in from New York and Chicago or fly in from Austria and Denmark to participate in annual ceremonies originally intended to secure the well-being of the local, spatially configured community. These visitors see little or nothing at all of the reservation community, pay little attention to the poverty and suffering of the people there and finally leave having achieved only a personal, individual spiritual high.[5]

Indigenous traveling teachers are swamped with eager students. But many native peoples are wary of this trend. They feel that their sacred ways are all they have left and worry that even these may be sold, stolen, and ruined. Elders of the Lakota tribes have urged all indigenous nations to use every means possible to prevent the exploitation of their spiritual traditions by "'the New Age Movement,' 'the men's movement,' 'neo-paganism' cults, 'shamanism' workshops—a scandalous assortment of pseudo-Indian charlatans, 'wannabes,' commercial profiteers, cultists and 'New Age shamans.'"[6]

Nevertheless, although initially linked to their local environments, indigenous beliefs and practices can be exported from their local contexts through migration and use of media. African-derived religions, for instance, are increasingly appropriating new communication technologies such as the Internet to transmit their religious ideologies, via websites such as "orishanet."

Cultural diversity

In this chapter we are considering the faithways of indigenous peoples as a whole. However, behind these generalizations lie many differences in social contexts, as well as in religious beliefs and practices. Some contemporary scholars even question whether "indigenous" is a legitimate category in the study of religions, for they see it as a catchall "other" category consisting of varied sacred ways that do not fit within any of the other major global categories of organized religions.

To be sure, there are hundreds of different indigenous traditions in North America alone, and at least fifty-three different ethnolinguistic groups in the Andean rainforests. And Australian aboriginal lifeways, which are some of the world's oldest surviving cultures, traditionally included over 500 different clan groups, with differing beliefs, living patterns, and languages.

Indigenous traditions have evolved within materially as well as religiously diverse cultures. Some are descendants of civilizations with advanced urban technologies that supported concentrated populations. When the Spanish conqueror Cortés took over Tenochtitlán (which now lies beneath Mexico City) in 1519, he found it a beautiful clean city with elaborate architecture, indoor plumbing, an accurate calendar, and advanced systems of mathematics and astronomy. Former African kingdoms were highly culturally advanced with elaborate arts, such as intricate bronze and copper casting, ivory carving, goldworking, and ceramics. In recent times, some Native American tribes have become quite materially successful via economic enterprises, such as gambling complexes.

Among Africa's innumerable ethnic and social groupings, there are some indigenous groups comprising millions of people, such as the Yoruba. At the other extreme are those few small-scale cultures that still maintain a survival strategy of hunting and gathering. For example, some Australian aborigines continue to live as mobile foragers, though restricted to government-owned stations. A nomadic survival strategy necessitates simplicity in material goods; whatever can be gathered or built rather easily at the next camp need not be dragged along. But material simplicity is not a sign of spiritual poverty. The Australian aborigines have complex **cosmogonies**, or models of the origins of the universe and their purpose within it, as well as a working knowledge of their own bioregion.

Some traditional peoples live in their ancestral enclaves, somewhat sheltered from the pressures of modern industrial life, though not untouched by the outer world. Tribal peoples have lived deep in the forests and hills of India for thousands of years, utilizing trees and plants for their food and medicines, although since the twentieth century their ancestral lands have been taken over for "development" projects and encroached upon by more politically and economically powerful groups, rendering many of the seventy-five million Indian tribespeople landless laborers. The Hopi people have continuously occupied a high plateau area of the southwestern United States for between 800 and 1,000 years; their sacred ritual calendar is tied to the yearly farming cycle.

Other indigenous peoples visit their sacred sites and ancestral shrines but live in more urban settings because of job opportunities. The people who participate in ceremonies in the Mexican countryside include subway personnel, journalists, and artists of native blood who live in Mexico City.

In addition to variations in lifestyles, indigenous traditions vary in their adaptations to dominant religions. Often native practices have become interwoven with those of global religions, such as Buddhism, Islam, and Christianity. In Southeast Asia, household Buddhist shrines are almost identical to the spirit houses in which the people still make offerings to honor the local spirits. In Africa, the spread of Islam and Christianity saw the introduction of new religious ideas and practices into indigenous sacred ways. The encounter transformed indigenous religious thought and practice but did not supplant it; indigenous religions preserved some of their beliefs and ritual practices but also adjusted to the new sociocultural milieu. The Dahomey tradition from West Africa was carried to Haiti by African slaves and called **Vodou**, from *vodu*, one of the names for the chief nonhuman spirits. Forced by European colonialists to adopt Christianity, worshippers of Vodou secretly fused their old gods with their images of Catholic saints. In Cuba, Yoruba slaves did the same, resulting in the practices known as **Santeria** (see Chapter 12).

Despite their different histories and economic patterns, and their geographical separation, indigenous sacred ways have some characteristics in common. Perhaps from ancient contact across land-bridges that no longer exist, there are similarities between the languages of the Tsalagi in the Americas, Tibetans, and the aboriginal Ainu of Japan. Similarities found among the myths of geographically separate peoples can be accounted for by global diffusion through trade, travel, and other kinds of contact, and by parallel origin because of basic similarities in human experience, such as birth and death, pleasure and pain, and wonderment about the cosmos and our place in it.

Certain symbols and metaphors are repeated in the inspirational art and stories of many traditional cultures around the world, but the people's relationships to, and the concepts surrounding, these symbols are not inevitably the same. Nevertheless, the following sections look at some recurring themes in the spiritual ways of diverse small-scale cultures.

The circle of right relationships

For many indigenous peoples, everything in the cosmos is intimately interrelated. A symbol of unity among the parts of this sacred reality is a circle. This is not used by all indigenous people; the Navajo, for instance, regard a completed circle as stifling and restrictive. However, many other indigenous peoples hold the circle sacred because it is infinite—it has no beginning, no end. Time is circular rather than linear, for it keeps coming back to the same place. Life revolves around the generational cycles of birth, youth, maturity, and physical death, the return of the seasons, the cyclical movements of the moon, sun, stars, and planets. Rituals such as rites of passage may be performed to help keep these cycles in balance.

This understanding of life as a complex of circles is thought to be the perfect framework for harmony. As Lame Deer, a Lakota Sioux holy man, explained:

Nature wants things to be round. The bodies of human beings and animals have no corners. With us the circle stands for the togetherness of people who sit with one

Among the gentle Efe pygmies of the Ituri Forest in the Democratic Republic of Congo (formerly Zaire), children learn to value the circle by playing the "circle game." With feet making a circle, each child names a circular object and then an expression of roundness (the family circle, togetherness, "a complete rainbow").

another around the campfire, relatives and friends united in peace while the pipe passes from hand to hand. The camp in which every tipi had its place was also a ring. The tipi was a ring in which people sat in a circle and all the families in the village were in turn circles within a larger circle, part of the larger hoop which was the seven campfires of the Sioux, representing one nation. The nation was only a part of the universe, in itself circular and made of the earth, which is round, of the sun, which is round, of the stars, which are round. The moon, the horizon, the rainbow—circles within circles within circles, with no beginning and no end.[7]

To maintain the natural balance of the circles of existence, most indigenous peoples have traditionally been taught that they must develop right relationships with everything that is. Their relatives include the unseen world of spirits, the land and weather, the people and creatures, and the power within.

RELATIONSHIPS WITH SPIRIT

The cosmos is thought to contain and be affected by numerous divinities, spirits, and also ancestors. Many indigenous traditions worship a Supreme Being who they believe created the cosmos. This being is known by the Lakota as "Great Mysterious" or "Great Spirit." African names for the being are attributes, such as "All-powerful," "Creator," "the one who is met everywhere," "the one who exists by himself," or "the one who began the forest." The Supreme Being is often referred to by male pronouns, but in some groups the Supreme Being is a female. Some tribes of the southwestern United States call her "Changing Woman"—sometimes young, sometimes old, the mother of the earth, associated with women's reproductive cycles and the mystery of birth, the creatrix. Many traditional languages make no distinction between male and female pronouns, and some see the divine as androgynous, a force arising from the interaction of male and female aspects of the universe.

Awareness of one's relationship to the Great Power is thought to be essential, but the power itself remains unseen and mysterious. An Inuit spiritual adept described his people's experience of:

> *a power that we call Sila, which is not to be explained in simple words. A great spirit, supporting the world and the weather and all life on earth, a spirit so mighty that [what it says] to mankind is not through common words, but by storm and snow and rain and the fury of the sea; all the forces of nature that men fear. But Sila has also another way of [communicating]; by sunlight and calm of the sea, and little children innocently at play, themselves understanding nothing. … When all is well, Sila sends no message to mankind, but withdraws into endless nothingness, apart.[8]*

To traditional Buryats of Russia, the chief power in the world is the eternally blue sky, Tengry. African myths suggest that the High God was originally so close to humans that they became disrespectful. The All-powerful was like the sky, they say, which was once so close that children wiped their dirty hands on it, and women (blamed by men for the withdrawal) broke off pieces for soup and bumped it with their sticks when pounding grain. Although southern and central Africans believe in a high being who presides over the universe, including less powerful spirits, they consider this being either too distant, too powerful, or too dangerous to worship or call on for help.

It cannot therefore be said that indigenous concepts of, and attitudes toward, a Supreme Being are necessarily the same as that which Western monotheistic religions refer to as God or Allah. In African traditional religions, much more emphasis tends to be placed on the transcendent dimensions of everyday life and doing what is spiritually necessary to keep life going normally. Many unseen powers are perceived to be at work in the material world. In various traditions, some of these are perceived without form, as mysterious presences, who may be benevolent or malevolent. Others are perceived as having more definite, albeit invisible, forms and personalities. These may include deities with human-like personalities, the nature spirits of special local places, such as venerable trees and mountains, animal spirit helpers, personified elemental forces, ancestors who

Deity may be conceived as either male or female in indigenous religions. In Navajo belief, divinity is personified as both Father Sky and Mother Earth. In this traditional sand-painting, Father Sky is on the left, with constellations and the Milky Way forming his "body." Mother Earth is on the right, with her body bearing the four sacred plants: squash, beans, tobacco, and corn.

still take an interest in their living relatives, or the *nagas*, known to the traditional peoples of Nepal as invisible serpentine spirits who control the circulation of water in the world and also within our bodies.

Ancestors may be extremely important. Traditional Africans understand that the person is not an individual, but a composite of many souls—the spirits of one's parents and ancestors—resonating to their feelings. Rev. William Kingsley Opoku, International Coordinator of the African Council for Spiritual Churches, says:

> *Our ancestors are our saints. Christian missionaries who came here wanted us to pray to their saints, their dead people. But what about our saints? ... If you are grateful to your ancestors, then you have blessings from your grandmother, your grandfather, who brought you forth. ... Non-Africans came in and said we should not obey our ancestors, should not call upon them at all, because they are evil people. This has been a mental bondage, a terrible thing.[9]*

Continued communication with the "living dead" (ancestors who have died within living memory) is extremely important to some traditional Africans. In libation rituals, food and drink are offered to the ancestors, acknowledging that they are still in a sense living and engaged with the people's lives. Failure to keep in touch with the ancestors is a dangerous oversight, which may bring misfortunes to the family.

The Dagara of Burkina Faso in West Africa are familiar with the *kontombili*, who look like humans but are only about one foot (thirty centimeters) tall, because of the humble way they express their spiritual power. Other West African groups, descendants of ancient hierarchical civilizations, recognize a great pantheon of deities, the *orisa* or *vodu*, each the object of special cult worship. The *orisa* are embodiments of the dynamic forces in life, such as Oya, powerful goddess of change, experienced in winds; Osun, *orisa* of fresh waters, associated with sweetness, healing, love, fertility, and prosperity; Olokun, ruler of the mysterious depths of consciousness; Shango, a former king who is now honored as the stormy god of electricity and genius; Ifa, god of wisdom; and Obatala, the source of creativity, warmth, and enlightenment. At the beginning of time, in Yoruba cosmology, there was only one godhead, described by psychologist Clyde Ford as "a beingless being, a dimensionless point, an infinite container of everything, including itself."[10] According to the mythology, this being was smashed by a boulder pushed down by a rebellious slave, and broke into hundreds of fragments, each of which became an *orisa*. According to some analysts, *orisa* can also be seen as archetypes of traits existing within the human psyche. Their ultimate purpose—and that of those who pay attention to them as inner forces—is to return to that presumed original state of wholeness.

The spirits are thought to be available to those who seek them as helpers, as intermediaries between the people and the power, and as teachers. A right relationship with these spirit beings can be a sacred partnership. Seekers respect and learn from them; they also purify themselves in order to engage their services for the good of the people. As we will later see, those who are considered most able to call on the spirits for help are the shamans who have dedicated their lives to this service.

myreligionlab
Feminine Leadership
JUDITH GLEASON

Osun and the Power of Woman

Olodumare, the Supreme Creator, who is both female and male, wanted to prepare the earth for human habitation. To organize things, Olodumare sent the seventeen major deities. Osun was the only woman; all the rest were men. Each of the deities was given specific abilities and specific assignments. But when the male deities held their planning meetings, they did not invite Osun. "She is a woman," they said.

However, Olodumare had given great powers to Osun. Her womb is the matrix of all life in the universe. In her lie tremendous power, unlimited potential, infinities of existence. She wears a perfectly carved, beaded crown, and with her beaded comb she parts the pathway of both human and divine life. She is the leader of the *aje*, the powerful beings and forces in the world.

When the male deities ignored Osun, she made their plans fail. The male deities returned to Olodumare for help. After listening, Olodumare asked, "What about Osun?" "She is only a woman," they replied, "so we left her out." Olodumare spoke in strong words, "You must go back to her, beg her for forgiveness, make a sacrifice to her, and give her whatever she asks."

The male deities did as they were told, and Osun forgave them. What did she ask for in return? The secret initiation that the men used to keep women in the background. She wanted it for herself and for all women who are as powerful as she is. The men agreed and initiated her into the secret knowledge. From that time onward, their plans were successful.[11]

Teachings about the spirits also help the people to understand how they should live together in society. Professor Deidre Badejo observes that in Yoruba tradition there is an ideal of balance between the creativity of women who give and sustain life, and the power of men who protect life. Under various internal and external pressures, this balance has swung toward male dominance, but the stories of feminine power (see Box) and the necessity for men to recognize it remain in the culture, teaching an ideal symmetry between female and male roles. In many indigenous cultures, women appear as powerful beings in myths and they are thought to have great ritual power.

KINSHIP WITH ALL CREATION

In addition to the unseen powers, all aspects of the tangible world are believed to be imbued with spirit. Josiah Young III explains that in African traditional religion, both the visible and invisible realms are filled with spiritual forces:

The visible is the natural and cultural environment, of which humans, always in the process of transformation, are at the center. The invisible connotes the numinous field of ancestors, spirits, divinities, and the Supreme Being, all of whom, in varying degrees, permeate the visible. Visible things, however, are not always what they seem. Pools, rocks, flora, and fauna may dissimulate invisible forces of which only the initiated are conscious.[12]

Within the spiritually charged visible world, all things may be understood as spiritually interconnected. Everything is therefore experienced as family. In

myreligionlab
Of Water and Spirit
MALIDOMA
PATRICE SOMÉ

African traditional lifeways, "we" may be more important than "I," and this "we" often refers to a large extended family and ancestral village, even for people who have moved to the cities. In indigenous cultures, the community is paramount, and it may extend beyond the living humans in the area. Many traditional peoples know the earth as their mother. The land one lives on is part of her body, loved, respected, and well known. Oren Lyons, an elder of the Onondaga Nation Wolf Clan, speaks of this intimate relationship:

> [The indigenous people's] knowledge is profound and comes from living in one place for untold generations. It comes from watching the sun rise in the east and set in the west from the same place over great sections of time. We are as familiar with the lands, rivers and great seas that surround us as we are with the faces of our mothers. Indeed we call the earth Etenoha, our mother, from whence all life springs. … We do not perceive our habitat as wild but as a place of great security and peace, full of life.[13]

Some striking feature of the natural environment of an area—such as a great mountain or canyon—may be perceived as the center from which the whole world was created. Such myths heighten the perceived sacredness of the land. Western Tibet's Mount Kailas, high in the Himalayas, is seen by the indigenous people of that area as the center of the earth, a sacred space where the earthly and the supernatural meet. Spiritual specialists therefore climb the mountain seeking visions.

myreligienlab

That Mountain has Spirit
SOUTHWEST INDIGENOUS PEOPLES

An indigenous earthwork in Ohio represents a snake and an egg, symbols of fertility and transformation. The spiral in the snake's tail may be an appreciative symbol of the life force and wisdom inherent in the earth.

The Western Apache remember vivid symbolic narratives about the exploits of people in specific places in their environment and contemplate them as aids to the spiritual goal of making their minds smooth, steady, and resilient. Dudley Patterson's grandmother taught him:

Wisdom sits in places. It's like water that never dries up. You need to drink water to stay alive, don't you? Well, you also need to drink from places. You must remember everything about them. You must learn their names. You must remember what happened at them long ago. You must think about it and keep on thinking about it. Then your mind will become smoother and smoother. Then you will see danger before it happens. You will walk a long way and live a long time. You will be wise. People will respect you.[14]

Because of the intimate relationship indigenous peoples have with their particular environments, forced removal from that environment can be devastating. Pushed onto the most marginal lands by colonizers, nation-states, or multinational companies who regard land as a valuable commercial resource rather than a sacred place, indigenous peoples may feel they have lost their own identity. New Zealand traditional elders, who were systematically forced off their ancestral homeland from the nineteenth century onward, explain:

It is important to know where we come from, to know where we belong. To identify who I am I identify my mountain, my river, my lands, our tribal and subtribal community. Knowing these things helps to bring about and to keep together the healing, the wellbeing of our people. We have suffered the loss of our lands, our connection to the land. We belong to the mountains, to the sea, to the forest. With the loss of the land, there has been a tremendous alienation from who we are. As a people we are currently in a renaissance, in a reclamation of our cultural identity, our land works, our traditional practices, our healing methods, because without these things we become a lost people, we become invisible, we become submerged into the dominant culture. The connection we had to the land was a spiritual connection. The loss of the land is a loss to us as guardians and protectors of the land. We are not owners of the land.[15]

In contrast to the industrial world's attempts to dominate the earth, native peoples consider themselves caretakers of their mother, the earth. They are now raising their voices against the destruction of the environment, warning of the potential for global disaster. Nepali shamans who have recently undertaken the difficult pilgrimage to Lake Mansarovar at the base of revered Mount Kailas report that the lake level is low and the spirits are unhappy. Their prophecies indicate difficult times ahead unless we humans take better care of our planetary home. Some indigenous visionaries say they hear the earth crying. Contemporary Australian aboriginal elder Bill Neidjie speaks of feeling the earth's pain:

I feel it with my body,
with my blood.
Feeling all these trees,
all this country ...
If you feel sore ...
headache, sore body

that mean somebody killing tree or grass.
You feel because your body in that tree or earth. ...
You might feel it for two or three years.
You get weak ...
little bit, little bit ...
because tree going bit by bit ...
dying.[16]

The earth abounds with living presences, in traditional worldviews. Rocks, bodies of water, and mountains—considered inanimate by other peoples—are personified as living beings. Before one can successfully climb a mountain, one must ask its permission. Visionaries can see the spirits of a body of water, and many traditional cultures have recognized certain groves of trees as places where spirits live, and where spiritual specialists can communicate with them. As a Pit River Indian explained, "Everything is alive. That's what we Indians believe."[17] Australian aboriginal people see their local landscape in terms of the "every-when" of the **Dreaming**, the primordial time when the ancestors appeared from

Australian aborigines understand their environment as concentric fields of subtle energies. Snakes and Emus by Nym Bunduk (1907–74).

beneath the surface of the earth, investing the environment with their own presence and establishing the law.

All creatures may be perceived as kin, endowed with consciousness and the power of the Great Spirit. Many native peoples have been raised with an "ecological" perspective: they know that all things depend on each other. They are taught that they have a reciprocal, rather than dominating, relationship with all beings. Hawaiian *kahuna* (shaman–priest) Kahu Kawai'i explains:

> *How you might feel toward a human being that you love is how you might feel toward a dry leaf on the ground and how you might feel toward the rain in the forest and the wind. There is such intimacy that goes on that everything speaks to you and everything responds to how you are in being— almost like a mirror reflecting your feelings.*[18]

Trees, animals, insects, and plants are all to be approached with caution and consideration. If one must cut down a tree or kill an animal, one must first explain one's intentions and ask forgiveness. Those who harm nature may themselves be harmed in return. Tribal peoples of Madhya Pradesh in central India will avoid killing a snake, for they feel that its partner would come after them to seek revenge. When a Buryat cuts a tree to build a house, he must first offer milk, butter, rice, and alcohol to the spirits of the forest and ask their forgiveness. In 1994, a half-French, half-Buryat businessman returned to Buryatia and started to build a guesthouse in a picturesque place that had long been considered sacred to the god Huushanbaabay. When the businessman began cutting trees, he was warned by the traditional people that he would not be successful. Nonetheless, he proceeded and finished the guesthouse. Three months later, it burned down.

Many traditional peoples learn a sense of reverence for, and kinship with, the natural world, as suggested in this image from Botswana created by Elisabeth Sunday.

Respect is always due to all creatures, in the indigenous worldview. The Yup'ik of southwestern Alaska know animals as thinking, feeling fellow beings. In fact, they may be even more sensitive and aware than humans. No one should handle the geese's eggs or goslings, lest the human smell should frighten the adults and they abandon the babies, to be eaten by predators. In Yup'ik belief, if humans treat animal populations carefully as guests, they will come back in plentiful numbers the following year to intentionally offer themselves to the Yup'ik hunters.

In the challenging environment of the Koyukon people of northern Canada, all interactions between humans and animals are conducted carefully according to a respectful moral code so that the animals will allow themselves to be caught. The animal spirits are very easily offended, not by animals being killed but by disrespect shown to the animals or their remains. Killing must be done prayerfully and in a way that does not cause suffering to the animal; wounded animals must be found and put out of their misery. If displeased, the spirits can bring bad luck in the hunt for that species or perhaps illness or even death for the hunters. But if humans maintain good relationships with the animals, they will give themselves freely to the hunters and keep coming back year after year. It is the natural world that is dominant, not humans.

There are many stories of indigenous peoples' relationships with nonhuman creatures. Certain trees tell the healing specialists which herbs to use in curing the people. Australian aboriginal women are adept at forming hunting partnerships with dogs. Birds are thought to bring messages from the spirit world. A crow, a wild yak, and a pack of silver wolves revealed the sacred path to Mount Kailas in Tibet, revered as the center of the outer world and also of our inner world, the doorway through which other realms can most easily be reached. A Hopi elder said he spent three days and nights praying with a rattlesnake. "Of course he was nervous at first, but when I sang to him he recognized the warmth of my body and calmed down. We made good prayer together."[19]

RELATIONSHIPS WITH POWER

Another common theme in indigenous lifeways is developing an appropriate relationship with spiritual energy.

> *All animals have power, because the Great Spirit dwells in all of them, even a tiny ant, a butterfly, a tree, a flower, a rock. The modern, white man's way keeps that power from us, dilutes it. To come to nature, feel its power, let it help you, one needs time and patience for that. … You have so little time for contemplation. … It lessens a person's life, all that grind, that hurrying and scurrying about.*
>
> *Lame Deer, Lakota nation[20]*

myreligionlab
Essence of
Cosmic Man
TLAKAELEL

In certain places and beings, the power of spirit is believed to be highly concentrated. It is referred to as *mana* by the people of the Pacific islands. This is the vital force that makes it possible to act with unusual strength, insight, and effectiveness.

Tlakaelel, a contemporary spiritual leader of the descendants of the Toltecs of Mexico, describes how a person might experience this power when looking into an obsidian mirror traditionally made to concentrate power:

> *When you reach the point that you can concentrate with all your will, inside there, you reach a point where you feel ecstasy. It's a very beautiful thing, and everything is light. Everything is vibrating with very small signals, like waves of music, very smooth. Everything shines with a blue light. And you feel a sweetness. Everything is covered with the sweetness, and there is peace. It's a sensation like an orgasm, but it can last a long time.[21]*

Sacred sites may be recognized by the power that believers feel there. Some sacred sites have been used again and again by successive religions, either to capitalize on the energy or to co-opt the preceding religion. Chartres Cathedral in France, for instance, was built on an ancient ritual site. In New Zealand, the traditional Maori people know of the revivifying power of running water, such as waterfalls (now understood by scientists as places of negative ionization, which do indeed have an energizing effect). The Maori elders have told the public of the healing power of a certain waterfall on North Island; the area is now dedicated to anyone who needs healing.

Because power can be built up through sacred practices, the ritual objects of spiritually developed persons may have concentrated power. Special stones and animal artifacts may also carry power. A person might be strengthened by the spiritual energy of the bear or the wolf by wearing sacred clothing made from its fur. Power can also come to one through visions, or by being given a sacred pipe or the privilege of collecting objects into a personal sacred bundle.

In some cultures women are thought to have a certain natural power; men have to work harder for it. Women's power is considered mysterious, dangerous, uncontrolled. It is said to be strongest during menstruation. Women are secluded during their menstrual periods in many cultures, not necessarily because they are considered polluting. Among the Yurok of northern California, houses have a separate back room for women who are menstruating so that they can concentrate on their inner selves, becoming inwardly stronger and purified by the flow of blood. In certain rituals in which both men and women participate, women's menstrual blood is often thought to diminish or weaken the ritual or the men's spiritual power. In most Native American nations that have sweat lodge ceremonies for ritual purification, menstruating women are not allowed to enter the

At a remote shrine used by indigenous people in New Mexico, a ring of stones protects the sacred area where sun-bleached antlers and offerings have been placed around two stones naturally shaped like mountain lions.

lodge. A few cultures, such as the Ainu of Japan, have prized menstrual blood as a potent offering returned to the earth.

Gaining power is both desirable and dangerous. If misused for personal ends, it becomes destructive and may turn against the person. To channel spiritual power properly, native peoples are taught that they must live within certain strict limits. Those who seek power or receive it unbidden are supposed to continually purify themselves of any selfish motives and dedicate their actions to the good of the whole.

Spiritual specialists

In a few remaining hunting and gathering tribes, religion is a relatively private matter. Each individual has direct access to the unseen. Although spirit is invisible, it is considered a part of the natural world. Anyone can interact with it spontaneously, without complex ceremony and without anyone else's aid.

More commonly, however, the world of spirit is thought to be dangerous. Although everyone is expected to observe certain personal ways of worship, such as offering prayers before taking plant or animal life, many ways of interacting with spirit are thought to be best left to those who are specially trained for the roles. These specialists are gradually initiated into the secret knowledge that allows them to act as intermediaries between the seen and the unseen. They sacrifice themselves through ritual purification, struggle, hardship, and protocol in order to remain in proper relationship with the spirits.

STORYTELLERS AND OTHER SACRED ROLES

Specialists' roles vary from one group to another, and the same person may play several of these roles. One common role is that of storyteller. Because the traditions are oral rather than written, these people must memorize long and complex stories and songs so that the group's sacred traditions can be remembered and taught, generation after generation. The orally transmitted epics of the indigenous Ainu of Japan are up to 10,000 "lines" long. Chants of the Yoruba *orisa* comprise 256 "volumes" of 800 long verses each.

These Yoruban chants about the *orisa* include an explanation of the genesis of the earth, with its center in what is now the Nigerian city of Ife. When time began, where the earth now exists there was only a vast watery area, with a dim and misty atmosphere, the domain of Olokun. The other *orisa* lived in an upper world of light until Obatala decided to go down to see if some solid land could be created so that the *orisa* could inhabit the earth. He had a sacred chain of gold made for his descent, and carried a shell of sand, a white hen, a palm nut, and a black cat. He climbed down to the watery world by means of the chain, but it was too short. Thus he poured the sand downward and then released the hen, who by scratching in the sand created the contours of the earth. Obatala settled on the land and planted his palm nut, which flourished and sent its seed far and wide, developing the plant life of the earth. At first he was alone, with only the black cat as his companion, but as the story continues, many things happen, accounting for the features of the earth and its inhabitants as we know them today. The golden chain is a common mythological symbol of a World Axis connecting heaven and earth; the palm tree also commonly appears in myths of the World Tree, giver and protector of the first forms of life on earth.

Such stories are important clues to understanding the universe and one's place in it. What is held only in memory cannot be physically destroyed, but if a tribe is small and all its storytellers die the knowledge is lost. This happened on a large scale during contacts with colonial powers, as indigenous people were killed by war and imported diseases. Professor Wande Abimbola, who is trying to preserve the oral tradition of the Yoruba, has made thousands of tapes of the chants, but there are few people who can understand and interpret their meaning.

There are also bards who carry the energy of ancient traditions into new forms. In Africa, poets are considered "technicians of the sacred," conversing with a dangerous world of spirits. Players of the "talking drums" are highly valued as communicators with the spirits, ancestors, and Supreme Being. As the Akan of Ghana say:

The thumb, finger with mouth, wake up and speak!
The thumb armed with sticks for drumming
Is more loquacious and more eloquent
Than a human being sleeping;
Wake up and come![22]

Drumming creates a rhythmic environment in which the people can draw close to the unseen powers. By counterposing basic and complex cross-rhythmic patterns with a "return beat," Yoruba drummers create a tension that draws listeners into the unfilled spaces between the beats.

"Tricksters" such as foxes often appear in the stories of indigenous traditions. They are paradoxical, transformative beings. Similarly, sacred clowns may endure the shame of behaving as fools during public rituals in order to teach the people through humor. Often they poke fun at the most sacred of rituals, keeping the people from taking themselves too seriously. A sacred fool, called *heyoka* by the Lakota, must be both innocent and very wise about human nature, and must have a visionary relationship with spirit as well.

> *Life is holiness and everyday humdrum, sadness and laughter, the mind and the belly all mixed together. The Great Spirit doesn't want us to sort them out neatly.*
> Leonard Crow Dog, Lakota medicine man[23]

Another coveted role is that of being a member of a secret society in which one can participate by initiation or invitation only, whether to enhance one's prestige or to draw closer to the spirit world. When serving in ceremonial capacities, members often wear special costumes to hide their human identities and help them take on the personas of spirits they are representing. In African religions, members of secret societies periodically appear as impersonators of animal spirits or of dead ancestors, demonstrating that the dead are still watching the living and protecting the village. The all-male Oro secret society in some Yoruba tribes uses this authority to enforce male domination; when Oro appears, "roaring" by swinging a piece of wood on a cord, women stay inside their huts.

Women also have their secret societies, whose activities are yet little known by outsiders. Among aboriginal peoples of Australia, the men's and women's groups initiate members into separate but interrelated roles for males and females. For instance, when boys are separated from the tribe for circumcision by the men's secret society, the women's secret society has its own separation rituals and may stage mock ritual fights with the men's society. But men's and women's rituals ultimately refer to the eternal Dreaming, in which there is no male/female differentiation.

Sacred dancers likewise make the unseen powers visible. Body movements are a language in themselves expressing the nature of the cosmos, a language that is understood through the stories and experiences of the community. Such actions keep the world of the ancestors alive for succeeding generations.

In some socially stratified societies there are also priests and priestesses. These are specially trained and dedicated people who carry out the rituals that ensure proper functioning of the natural world, and perhaps also communicate with particular spirits or deities. Though West African priests or priestesses may have part-time earthly occupations, they are expected to stay in a state of ritual purity and spend much of their time in communication with the spirit being, paying homage and asking for guidance. In West Africa, there are also mediums associated with the temples; they enter a state of trance or allow themselves to be possessed by gods or spirits in order to bring messages to the people.

MYSTICAL INTERMEDIARIES

There is another distinctive type of spiritual specialist found among many indigenous peoples. They are called by many names, but the Siberian and Saami word **"shaman"** is used by scholars as a generic term for those who offer themselves as mystical intermediaries between the physical and the nonphysical world for specific purposes, such as healing. Archaeological research has confirmed that shamanic methods are extremely ancient—at least 20,000 to 30,000 years old. Shamanic ways are remarkably similar around the globe.

These mystical intermediaries may be helpers to society, using their skills to benefit others. They are not to be confused with sorcerers, who practice black magic to harm others or promote their own selfish ends, interfering with the cosmic order. Spiritual power is neutral; its use depends on the practitioner. What Native Americans call **"medicine** power" does not originate in the **medicine person**. Black Elk explained:

A traditional shaman at work in Trinidad, making offerings and receiving guidance.

> *Of course it was not I who cured. It was the power from the outer world,*
> *and the visions and ceremonies had only made me like a hole through which*
> *the power could come to the two-leggeds. If I thought that I was doing it myself,*
> *the hole would close up and no power could come through.*[24]

There are many kinds of medicine. One is the ability to heal physical, psychological, and spiritual problems. Techniques used include physical approaches to illness, such as therapeutic herbs, sweat-bathing, massage, cauterization, and sucking out toxins. But the treatments are given to the whole person—body, mind, and spirit, with emphasis on healing relationships within the group—so there may also be divination, prayer, chanting, and ceremonies in which group power is built up and spirit helpers are called in. If an intrusion of harmful power, such as the angry energy of another person, seems to be causing the problem, the medicine person may attempt to suck it out with the aid of spirit helpers and then dry-vomit the invisible intrusion into a receptacle.

myreligionlab

The Great Vision
BLACK ELK

These healing methods are now beginning to earn respect from the scientific medical establishment. Medicine people are permitted to attend indigenous patients in some hospitals, and in the United States the National Institute of Mental Health has paid Navajo medicine men to teach young Indians the ceremonies that have often been more effective than Western psychiatry in curing the mental health problems of Navajos.

In addition to healing, certain mystical intermediaries are thought to have gifts such as being able to talk with plants and animals, control the weather, see and communicate with the spirit world, and prophesy. A gift highly developed in Africa is that of divination, using techniques such as reading patterns supposed to be revealed by a casting of cowrie shells. According to Mado Somé of the Dagara:

> *Divination is a way of accessing information that is happening now, but not right*
> *where you live. ... The cowrie shells work like an intermediary between us and the*
> *other world. Divination is actually the inscription of information on those physical*
> *things, allowing the shaman—whose eyes have been modified through the course*
> *of her various medicine journeys—to be able to read and interpret them.*[25]

Traditional diviners in Mali rake sand and leave it overnight. The tracks of animals that run over it are interpreted the next day for information the client seeks.

The role of shaman may be hereditary or it may be recognized as a special gift. Either way, training is rigorous. In order to work in a mystical state of ecstasy, moving between ordinary and nonordinary realities, shamans must experience physical death and rebirth. Some have spontaneous near-death experiences. Uvavnuk, an Inuit shaman, was spiritually initiated when she was struck by a lightning ball. After she revived, she had great power, which she dedicated to serving her people.

Other potential mystical intermediaries undergo rituals of purification, isolation, and bodily torment until they make contact with the spirit world. Igjugarjuk from northern Hudson Bay chose to suffer from cold, starvation, and thirst for a month in a tiny snow hut in order to draw the attention of Pinga, a helping female spirit:

My novitiate took place in the middle of the coldest winter, and I, who never got anything to warm me, and must not move, was very cold, and it was so tiring having to sit without daring to lie down, that sometimes it was as if I died a little. Only towards the end of the thirty days did a helping spirit come to me, a lovely and beautiful helping spirit, whom I had never thought of; it was a white woman; she came to me whilst I had collapsed, exhausted, and was sleeping. But still I saw her lifelike, hovering over me, and from that day I could not close my eyes or dream without seeing her. … She came to me from Pinga and was a sign that Pinga had now noticed me and would give me powers that would make me a shaman.[26]

For many mystical intermediaries, initiation into the role is not a matter of their own choice. The spirit enters whom it will. Tsering, an aged Nepali *dhami* (shaman), relates:

We never wanted to become dhamis. *In fact, we tried hard to get the gods to leave us. We pleaded, performed worship ceremonies, even carried manure around with us to offend them, but nothing seemed to work. When calamities began to hit my family—when my brother died falling off the roof and our best horse drowned in the river—I realized I had no choice and had to make the initiatory journey to Kailas.[27]*

Once there, the new *dhamis* had to plunge naked with unbound hair into the freezing Lake Mansarovar in order to commune with the spirits. Then, when they returned to their village, the deities who had possessed them insisted that they prove their spiritual connection by terrible feats, such as drinking boiling oil. Thereafter, those *dhamis* were respected as authorities.

In addition to becoming familiar with death, a potential mystical intermediary must undergo lengthy training in spiritual techniques, the names and roles of the spirits, and secrets and myths of the tribe. Novices are taught both by older shamans and reportedly by the spirits themselves. If the spirits do not accept and teach the shaman, he or she is unable to carry the role.

The helping spirits that contact would-be mystical intermediaries during the death-and-rebirth crisis become essential partners in their sacred work. Often it

An Interview with Nadezhda Ananyevna Stepanova

 One of the remaining traditional shamans of Buryatia, Nadezhda Ananyevna Stepanova comes from a family of very powerful shamans. Her mother tried to prevent her from becoming a shaman. Buddhist lamas had spread the impression that shamans were to be avoided, saying that they were ignorant, primitive servants of dark, lower spirits. The reputation of shamans has also been recently damaged by pseudo-shamans—some of whom have certain extrasensory powers and others of whom are simply cheats. But when a shaman receives a true spiritual call, to deny that pull is dangerous. Nadezhda explains:

"As a child I knew when I would fall ill, and I could repeat by heart anything the teacher said or anything I read in a book, but I thought that was normal. When I was twenty-six, I was told I would be a shaman, a great shaman. When I told Mother, she said, 'No, you won't.' She took a bottle, went to her native town, and then came back. 'Everything will be taken away; you won't become a shaman,' she said. I didn't understand. The year I was said to become a shaman, I became seriously ill, and Mother was paralyzed. Usually paralyzed people have high blood pressure, but hers was normal. The doctors were surprised, but I understood then: We were both badly ill because she went against the gods.

"Nobody could heal me. Then one seer said, 'You must cure.' I replied, 'I don't know anything about curing.' But a voice inside me said, 'If you don't become a shaman, you will die. You will be overrun by a lorry with a blue number.' I began to collect materials about medicine, about old rites. Then I could do a lot, for all we need is seeing and feeling. I was initiated by the men shamans of all the families, each praying to his god in a definite direction, for every god has his direction. I sat in the middle. Every shaman asked his gods to help me, to protect me, to give me power. The ritual was in early March. It was very frosty and windy, and I was only lightly dressed, but I wasn't cold at all. The wind didn't touch me. I sat motionless for about four hours, but I was not cold.

"I began to cure. It is very difficult. You go through pain, through the tears of children and adults. I am able to see whether I will be able to cure a specific person. The main thing to me is to help a person if I can. I pray to my gods, ask them for mercy, I ask them to pay attention, to help. I feel the pain of those who come to me, and I want to relieve it. I have *yodo*—bark from a fir tree scratched by a bear; its smoke purifies. I perform rituals of bringing back the soul; often they work. My ancestors are very close to me; I see them as well as I see you.

"Last year in the island Olkhon in Lake Baikal, there was a great gathering of shamans from Tchita, Irkutsk, Ulan-Ude, Yakutiya, and Buryatia to pray to the great spirits of Baikal about the well-being and prosperity of the Buryat land. For a long time these spirits were not turned to. They were forgotten by the people, and they fell asleep. They could not take an active part in the life of people; they could not help them any more. *Teylagan*, the prayer of the shamans for the whole Buryatia, was to awaken the great spirits.

"It was a clear, clear sunny day, without a cloud. When the prayer began, it started to rain. It was a very good sign. There had been a long drought before. The Olkhon shamans had tried to call rain, but they couldn't. But when everyone gathered and three sheep were sacrificed, then they could, and the shamans of that district were grateful.

"We had always prayed to thirteen northern *nainkhats*, the great spirits of this area. But when the Buddhists came, persecution began, and people prayed secretly, only for their families. They could not pray for the whole Buryat nation, and they did not. They forgot. Shamans were killed. Then the atheistic Soviet regime tried to make us forget the faith, and we forgot. The most terrible thing about them was that they wanted to make people forget everything, to live by the moment and forget their roots. And what is man without roots? Nothing. It is a loss of everything. That is why now nobody has compassion for anybody. Now we are reaping the fruit: robbery, drinking, drugs. This is our disaster. That is why we must pray to our own gods.

"When we had the *teylagan*, on the first day three blue pillars rose from earth to the sky—it was a prayer to Ehon-Bahve, the head spirit of Baikal, and to all three gods. The second day we prayed to the bird-god, and there were very many birds flying and a rainbow in the sky."[28]

A shaman in Senegal invokes the power of a spirit and then, as its vehicle, sprays energized water onto a girl who needs healing.

is a spirit animal who becomes the shaman's guardian spirit, giving him or her special powers. The shaman may even take on the persona of the animal while working. Many tribes feel that healing specialists need the powers of the bear; Lapp shamans metamorphosed into wolves, reindeer, bears, or fish.

Mystical intermediaries may have the ability to enter parallel, spiritual realities at will in order to bring back knowledge, power, or help for those who need it. An altered state of consciousness is needed. Techniques for entering this state are the same around the world: drumming, rattling, singing, dancing, and in some cases hallucinogenic drugs. The effect of these influences is to open what the Huichol shamans of Mexico call the *narieka*— the doorway of the heart, the channel for divine power, the point where human and spirit worlds meet. It is often experienced and represented artistically as a pattern of concentric circles.

The "journey" then experienced by mystical intermediaries is typically into the Upperworld or the Lowerworld. To enter the latter, they descend mentally through an actual hole in the ground, such as a spring, hollow tree, cave, animal burrow, or special ceremonial hole regarded as a navel of the earth. These entrances typically lead into tunnels that, if followed, open into bright landscapes. Reports of such experiences include not only what the journeyer saw but also realistic physical sensations, such as how the walls of the tunnel felt during the descent.

The shaman enters into the Lowerworld landscape, encounters beings there, and may bring something back if it is needed by the client. This may be a lost guardian spirit or a lost soul, brought back to revive a person in a coma. The mystical intermediary may be temporarily possessed by the spirit of departed relatives so that an afflicted patient may finally clear up unresolved tensions with them that are seen as causing illness. Often a river must be crossed as the boundary between the world of the living and the world of the dead. A kindly old man or woman may appear to assist this passage through the Lowerworld. In cultures that have subdued the indigenous ways, this mystical process is retained only in myths, such as the Orpheus story.

Group observances

Indigenous ways are community-centered. Through group rituals, traditional people not only honor the sacred but also affirm their bonds with each other and all of creation. Humans can help to maintain the harmony of the universe by their ritual observances.

In order to maintain the natural balance and to ensure success in the hunt or harvest, ceremonies must be performed with exactitude. For instance, there is a specific time for the telling of specific stories. Chona, a Tohono O'odham (Papago) medicine woman, told anthropologist Ruth Underhill:

I should not have told you this [the origin of Coyote, who helped to put the world in order, with a few mistakes]. These things about the Beginning are holy. They should not be told in the hot time when the snakes are out. The snakes guard our secrets. If we tell what is forbidden, they bite.[29]

Rituals often take people out of everyday consciousness and into awareness of the presence of the sacred. In such altered states, participants may experience a heightened group consciousness that powerfully binds individuals together as a community.

Each group has its own ways of ritual dedication to the spirits of life, but they tend to follow certain patterns everywhere. Some honor major points in the human life cycle, such as birth, naming, puberty, marriage, and death. These rites of passage assist people in the transition from one state to another and help them become aware of their meaningful contribution to life. When a Hopi baby is twenty days old, it is presented at dawn to the rays of Father Sun for the first time and officially given a name. Its face is ritually cleansed with sacred cornmeal, a ceremony that will be repeated at death for the journey to the Lowerworld.

Girls commonly go through a special ceremony marking their first menstruation, which signals the end of childhood and preparation for becoming wives and mothers. For both boys and girls, the rituals of reaching puberty typically involve separation from the community, then a transition phase in which they are secluded with no clear identity and prepared for adulthood, and finally a third phase in which they are reincorporated into the community with a new adult identity. Girls in traditional Lakota households spend the transition time practicing such useful skills as stitching and cooking. Madonna Swan reports that she was secluded in part of her grandmother's cabin for her first moon ceremony, and that each day her grandmother would coach her in domestic skills and ethical principles. Her grandmother and mother daily bathed her in water with purifying sage and green cedar, and prayed for her in this fashion:

Grandfathers above and in the four directions, make Madonna a good woman. Help her to treat guests with hospitality. Grandfathers, help her to be a good worker. Grandfathers, and Maka Ina (Mother Earth), help Madonna to be a good mother. I pray that the food she cooks in her life will be good for those that eat it. Grandfathers, help her to be a good wife and live with the same man all her life. Grandfathers, bless her with healthy children.[30]

There are also collective rituals to support the group's survival strategies. In farming communities these include ways of asking for rain, of insuring the growth of crops, and of giving thanks for the harvest. In the Great Drought of 1988, Sioux holy man Leonard Crow Dog was asked by three nonindigenous Midwestern communities to perform rainmaking ceremonies for them, thus honoring the power of the traditional medicine ways.

Ritual dramas about the beginnings and sacred history of the people engage performers and spectators on an emotional level through the use of special costumes, body paint, music, masks, and perhaps sacred locations. These dramas provide a sense of orderly interface among humans, the land, and the spiritual

myreligionlab
Women's
Health Rituals
DIANE BELL

The Sun Dance Way of Self-Sacrifice

Sacrificing oneself for the sake of the whole is highly valued in most indigenous traditions. Through purification ceremonies, the people attempt to break through their small selves in order to serve as clear vehicles for the energy of the Great Spirit. In the Americas a powerful ceremony for these purposes is the sun dance. Among the Oglala Lakota, participants may dance for four days without food or water, looking at the sun and praying for blessings for the people. They say the ceremony as they practice it was first given to them through a vision received by a man named Kablaya.

In diverse forms, sun dances are now performed at many sites each spring and summer, most of them on the midwestern and northern plains of North America. In theory, only those who have had visions that they should perform the dance should do so. Some come in penance, for purification; others offer themselves as vehicles to request blessings for all people or for specific people who need help. It is not considered proper to dance for one's own needs.

Dancers make a commitment to do the dance for a certain number of times. Some sun dances include women dancers; some who dance are children. Non-indigenous people are generally barred from dancing.

The power of the sun dance requires that everything be handled in a sacred way. Dancers must do vision quests and purify themselves in sweat lodges before the ceremony begins. In spite of thirst and exhaustion, those in some sun dances continue to participate in sweat lodges each day of the dance. A tree is chosen to be placed at the center of the circle (among the Lakota, it is always a cottonwood, which when cut crosswise reveals a multipointed star pattern representing the sun). The tree's sacrifice is attended with ritual prayers. Participants may string prayer flags onto its branches before it is hoisted in the center of the dancing circle.

Sacred tree at the center of an area prepared for a Mexican version of the sun dance: Tonal Mitotianilitzli. Cloth strips tied to the tree carry prayers for the people.

*Names of individual dancers interviewed are not given here, to preserve their privacy and the sacredness of the dance.

During the dance itself, the participants are guided through patterns with symbolic meanings. The choreography varies from one group to another. The Sioux sun dancers do not move around the circle except to shift slightly during the day so that they are always facing the sun. In Mexico the patterns continually honor the powers of the four directions by facing each one in turn.

As they dance, the dancers blow whistles traditionally made from the wing bones of the spotted eagle, but now often whittled from hollow sticks. When giving instructions for the dance, Kablaya reportedly explained, "When you blow the whistle always remember that it is the voice of the Spotted Eagle; our Grandfather, Wakan Tanka, always hears this, for you see it is really His own voice."[31]

At a recent sun dance held in Mexico, one participant* reports:

When the energy of the Dancers was probably at their lowest and most exhausted, nearing the end of a very long and hot and sunny day, an eagle flew overhead and kept circling the Dance for maybe five minutes, flying back and forth, and again and again to the sound of the Dancers' whistles and the Huehuetl drum. It brought tears to the eyes of many. The Dancers just kept whistling and saluting and greeting the huge and graceful bird. I have often seen an eagle fly over our circle during the Dance for a minute, but never have we seen one just keep circling and returning so long. It was truly breathtaking, like a message from the Creator that all was well, and our prayers were heard.

A group of people support the dancers by singing special sacred songs and beating a large drum. If their energy flags, so does that of the dancers. A woman sun dancer says that after a while, "The drum is no longer outside of you. It is as if in you and you don't even know that you're dancing." The dancers also support each other in ways such as using the feathers they carry to fan those whose energy seems low. There may also be communal vision ceremonies.

Each dancer is the carrier of a sacred pipe. Between rounds, the pipes may be shared with group onlookers who are led into the circle and who pass them around among the dancers to strengthen them with the power of the smoke.

Nondancers may also be led into the circle for a special healing round on the third or fourth day. By that time, the dancers have been so purified and empowered that they can all act as healers, using their eagle feathers as instruments to convey the divine power.

The suffering that each dancer willingly undergoes is heightened during piercing. For those whose visions suggest it—and whose tribes use piercing, for some do not—at some point during the dance incisions are made in the skin of their chest, back, or arms and sharpened sticks are inserted. There are then various ways of tearing through the skin. One reserved for chiefs is to drag buffalo skulls from ropes attached to the piercing sticks, symbolizing their carrying of the burdens of the people. More often, ropes are thrown over the trees and attached to the piercing sticks. Each person who pierces is then pulled upward, "flying" by flapping eagle wings, until the sticks break through the skin. It is thought that the more a person asks to do when making the sacrifice the more difficult it will be to break free. One Lakota dancer was instructed in a vision that he should be hung from the tree for a whole night. They had to pierce him in many places in order to distribute his weight, and then pull him down in the morning.

Why must the dance involve so much suffering? A Lakota sun dancer explains, "Nobody knows why, but suffering makes our prayers more sincere. The sun dance tests your sincerity, pushes your spirit beyond its limits." And as the dance goes on, many of the dancers transcend their physical agony and experience an increasing sense of euphoria. A Mexican dancer explains:

It's not pain. It's ecstasy. We get the energy from the sun and from the contact with Mother Earth. You also feel the energy of the eagles [who often fly overhead], all the animals, all the plants that surround you, all the vegetation. That energy comes to sustain you for the lack of food and water. Also when you smoke the pipe it serves as food or energy; the smoke feeds you energy so that you can continue. And every so often we put our palms to the sun to receive the energy from the sun. You can feel it in your whole body, a complete bath of energy.

world. They also dramatize mysticism, drawing the people toward direct contact with the spirit world. Those who have sacred visions and dreams are supposed to share them with others, and often this is done through dramatization.

According to legend, the Plains Indians were given the sacred pipe by White Buffalo Calf Woman as a tool for communicating with the mysteries and understanding the ways of life. The bowl of the pipe represents the female aspect of the Great Spirit, the stem the male aspect. When they are ritually joined, the power of the spirit is thought to be present as the pipe is passed around the circle for collective communion with each other and with the divine.

Groups also gather for ritual purification and spiritual renewal of individuals. Indigenous peoples of the Americas "smudge" sites and possessions, cleansing them with smoke from special herbs, such as sage and sweetgrass. Many groups make an igloo-shaped "sweat lodge" into which hot stones are carried. People huddle together in the dark around the stone pit. When water is poured on the stones, intensely hot steam sears bodies and lungs. Everyone prays earnestly. Leonard Crow Dog says of the *inipi* (sweat lodge):

The inipi *is probably our oldest ceremony because it is built around the simplest, basic, life-giving things: the fire that comes from the sun, warmth without which there can be no life;* inyan wakan, *or* tunka, *the rock that was there when the earth began, that will still be there at the end of time; the earth, the mother womb; the water that all creatures need; our green brother, the sage; and encircled by all these, man, basic man, naked as he was born, feeling the weight, the spirit of endless generations before him, feeling himself part of the earth, nature's child, not her master.*[32]

To the Efe pygmies of the Ituri Forest in the Democratic Republic of Congo, the Great Spirit is embodied in the forest itself, a benevolent presence that is Mother and Father. Men perform a dance of gratitude to the forest for the animal food it provides.

Pilgrimages to sacred sites are often communal. Buryats gather on top of Erde, the mountain where the spirit of the earth lives, and all join hands to encircle it; a great energy is said to appear in the huge circle. The Huichol Indians of the mountains of western Mexico make a yearly journey to a desert they call Wirikuta, the Sacred Land of the Sun. They feel that creation began in this place. And like their ancestors, they gather their yearly supply of peyote cactus at this sacred site. Peyote has the power to alter consciousness: it is their "little deer," a spirit who helps them to communicate with the spirit world.

When indigenous groups are broken up by external forces, they lose the cohesive power of these group rituals. Africans taken to the New World as slaves lost not only their own individual identity but also their membership in tight-knit groups. In an attempt to re-establish a communal sense of shared spiritual traditions among African Americans, Professor Maulana Ron Karenga created a contemporary celebration, Kwanzaa, based on indigenous African "first fruits" harvest festivals. Using symbolic objects to help create a special atmosphere (such as candles, corn, fruits and vegetables, and a "unity cup," all called by their Swahili names), families and groups of families meet from December 26 to January 1 to explore their growth over the past year. They look at their own experiences of the "seven principles"—unity, self-determination, collective work, family centeredness, purpose, creativity with limited resources, and confidence—and reward each other for progress by giving gifts.

INDIVIDUAL OBSERVANCES

In indigenous sacred ways, it is considered important for each person to experience a personal connection with the spirits. The people acknowledge and work with the spirits in many everyday ways. For instance, when searching for herbs, a person is not to take the first plant found; an offering is made to it, with the prayer that its relatives will understand one's needs. Guardian spirits and visions may be sought by all the people, not just mystical specialists. The shaman may have more spirit helpers and more power, but visionary experiences and opportunities for worship are available to all. Indigenous traditions have therefore been called "democratized shamanism."

Temples to the spirits may exist, but one can also worship them anywhere. Wande Abimbola observes:

In West Africa, the gods and the spirits of the dead appear to the living in masquerades. The mysteries of spirit are made semivisible by costumed initiates.

> *Big temples aren't necessary to worship the* orisa, *even though there are temples for most* orisa *in Africa. If you are a devotee of Ifa, you can carry the objects of Ifa in your pocket. If you want to make an offering to Ogun, put any piece of iron on the floor and make an offering to it. It's just like a Christian would carry a Bible or maybe a cross.*[33]

To open themselves for contact with the spirit world, individuals in many indigenous cultures undergo a **vision quest**. After ritual purification, they are sent alone to a sacred spot to cry to the spirits to help them in their journey.

Prepuberty or the onset of puberty is commonly thought to be the best time for vision quests, for children are closest to the spirit world. Among the Dene Tha, children are informally encouraged to go out to the bush before the age of puberty and spend time alone, seeking a spirit helper. Intimate knowledge of the animal spirit is considered essential for a Dene Tha who helps others:

> *When you are young, you go alone in the bush and you stay there and an animal comes to you. He talks to you just like we do now [sitting next to each other], and he tells you about him and with his power he gives you his power to heal other people. With it you heal people. If it tells you all how he is from beginning to end, you help someone, you cure him. If he does not tell everything, and you do not know all about him, then, when you help someone, you cure him, but you get the sickness.*[34]

Adults may also make vision quests before undertaking a sacred mission, such as the sun dance. Indigenous Mexican leader Tlakaelel describes the vision quest as he observes it:

This altar in the home of a Mexican healer illustrates the blending of indigenous ways with those of later religions. The serpent, masks, vegetables, eggs, and "bird's nest" derive from indigenous sacred ways, but are juxtaposed with Christian symbols.

You stay on a mountain, desert, or in a cave, isolated, naked, with only your sacred things, the things that you have gained, in the years of preparation—your eagle feathers, your pipe, your copal *[tree bark used as incense]. You are left alone four days and four nights without food and water. During this time when you are looking for your vision, many things happen. You see things move. You see animals that come close to you. Sometimes you might see someone that you care about a lot, and they're bringing water. You feel like you're dying of thirst, but there are limits around you, protection with hundreds of tobacco ties. You do not leave this circle, and this vision will disappear when they come to offer the water or sometimes they will just drop it on the ground. Or someone comes and helps you with their strength and gives you messages.*[35]

One is not supposed to ask for a vision for selfish personal reasons. The point of this individual ordeal, which is designed to be physically and emotionally stressful, is to ask how one can help the people and the planet.

Contemporary issues

Sadly, traditional spiritual wisdom has been largely obliterated in many parts of the world by those who wanted to take the people's lands or save their souls with some other path to the divine. Under the slogan "Kill the Indian and save the man," the American founder of the boarding-school system for native children took them away from their families at a young age and transformed their cultural identity, presenting the native ways as inferior and distancing the children from normal participation in the traditional sacred life. They were exposed to the "modern" worldview, which does not believe in miracles, supernatural healings, or divine intervention—thus contradicting thousands of years of received wisdom in their own tradition.

Native Americans who converted to Christianity have sometimes been missionaries themselves, helping to spread Christian devotion among indigenous peoples. Sometimes Natives converted to try to appease the dominant non-Natives, but sometimes it was the personal example of these missionaries that caused Native Americans to embrace the "White Man's Faith," even though it was the religion of those who were oppressing them. For example, a young nineteenth-century Choctaw Christian named Kanchi drowned while trying to save teenagers whose raft swamped as the Choctaw tribe crossed the swollen and turbulent Mississippi River under forcible removal from their ancestral lands. So touched were tribe members by his sacrifice that they began reading his Bible in his memory and eventually formed a new Christian community in what is now Oklahoma. Indigenous spirituality has become so mixed with Christianity that many Native American Christians are now trying to re-examine their religious lives and identities honestly. Marie Therese Archambault asserts:

> When we read the Gospel, we must read it as Native people, for this is who
> we are. We can no longer try to be what we think the dominant society wants
> us to be. ... We just learn to subtract the chauvinism and cultural superiority
> with which this Gospel was often presented to our people. We have to go beyond
> the white gospel in order to perceive its truth.[36]

A similar policy of attempted acculturation was conducted between the 1880s and 1960s with Australian aboriginal children. Taken away from their parents by force, the "stolen generation" were often abused or used as slaves. Five children of Eliza Saunders were taken away by social workers while she and her husband were looking for employment. She recalls, "You walk miles and miles and find they're not there. It's like your child has been killed." One of her children, the Green Party politician Charmaine Clarke, managed to run away from foster care after eleven years and rejoin her mother, but she says of her missing family history, "When myself and my brothers and sisters go home, we five have to sit there quite mute and just listen, observe. Because we were never there."[37] In 1998, Australian citizens tried to apologize for this "attempted genocide," with some 300,000 signatures in Sorry Books and hundreds of emotional multiracial ceremonies in churches, schools, and cities across Australia.

In Mexico, decades of rebellion of indigenous people against central rule and cultural suppression seemed to be turning a corner in 2001, when a caravan of rebel leaders from the south was welcomed by tens of thousands as they entered Mexico City to request political autonomy for the ten million indigenous people of Mexico. Chiapas rebel leader Subcommander Marcos declared, "It is the hour of the Indian people, of the people of the color of the earth. What they fear is that there is no more 'you' and 'us,' because we are all the color of the earth."[38] However, a proposed indigenous rights bill which would have brought considerable autonomy for indigenous people in Mexico was altered to the extent that they may now have even fewer legal rights than before.

The Orang Asli of Malaysia: Traditions being Lost

In peninsular Malaysia, about 147,412 indigenous people known as the Orang Asli ("original peoples") still maintain some of their traditional ways. Among them are a subgroup known as the Jakun, inhabitants of what was once an extensive peat swamp forest. Traditionally the Jakun lived by hunting and gathering, as well as cultivating small plots temporarily before moving on after harvesting the crops. They lived simply, with great respect for the forest, the forest animals, and the invisible spirits around them. Now, however, much of the peat swamp forest has been logged, drained, and converted into oil palm or rubber plantations. Destruction of the sponge-like peat swamp forest has brought increased flooding to the Jakuns' traditional home along the Bebar River, so severe that the Department of Orang Asli Affairs shifted them to a permanent settlement on higher ground in Kampung Simpai. Their children have been sent to distant boarding schools along with Malay children; there they are exposed to popular culture, and have become very fond of televisions, cell phones, and Western clothing. The Orang Asli remain one of the poorest sectors within Muslim-majority Malaysia.

In the past, the lives of the Jakun were governed by a series of taboos. For example, they were not to chop down unfamiliar trees or joke or shout in the forest, lest the spirit of a tree might possess or curse them. No animals thought to have the quality of *badi* (sacred spirits or spirits of the dead) should be killed or harmed, lest those spirits might retaliate in a manner resembling the way in which the animal was harmed.

Through these and other such taboos, the people were traditionally taught to live carefully, always mindful of the spirits around them. Thus they behaved respectfully everywhere, whether in the forest, in the river, or at home. Abu Bin Le, a fifty-three-year-old man who is now helping in the Heritage Garden Project sponsored by the European Commission and the United Nations Development Program to document and conserve indigenous medicinal plants and promote sustainable use of the forest, decries the loss of reverence among the younger generations:

Kids these days do not believe because [the dire results of breaking taboos] have not happened during their lifetime. The forests surrounding our village are gone, so there are no spirits left. Maybe just a few, but not as many as in the old days. Back then, we had forests, vast tracts of forests. Many spirits dwelled in the forests. Now that the forests are gone, it is unlikely that it would happen. When there were many spirits, we could not break taboos.

Seventeen-year-old Habib feels little connection to the spirits of the forests. He says:

It is not instilled in us. Besides, there isn't much of a forest left anyway, just acres of oil palm plantation. I remember when the forests still surrounded our houses when I was young.

Despite the loss of many traditional taboos, certain precautions are still followed, such as one prescribing that children are not to be scolded or teased to the point where they cry uncontrollably. Children are treated gently because many of the younger generations remember or heard of a dangerous storm which followed the breaking of the taboo about teasing children. Twenty-four-year-old Ann, great-granddaughter of the late village *bomoh* (shaman), was there when the storm happened:

Piran, who was then a little boy, was playing with a frog, but then his uncle took the frog away from him. He started crying and was inconsolable. All of a sudden, out of nowhere, there was thunder. The sky became dark and it started to pour. Piran's mother quickly grabbed Piran and ran towards her house, but it was as if the lightning was trailing them from behind. They ran into a local shaman's house who quickly performed jampi *[communication with the spirits]. At once, the rain stopped and the sky became clear and sunny again.*

Sanisah Dep, thirty-eight-year-old granddaughter of the late village *bomoh*, was also there:

I was horrified by what I saw. It was like a storm, but it was different from the usual storms we have here. As she ran, it was as if a group of dark clouds was hovering over her, chasing her. The uncle was teasing the child, so it happened. Now whatever the children want, we try to give or we pacify the child immediately.

In older times, there were *bomohs* who knew how to heal people, how to communicate with the spirits, and how to conduct the necessary rituals. But few of these elders are left. Sanisah lived next door to her grandfather, the village *bomoh*, and is certain that his death in 1997 was a result of his being unable to perform the obligatory ceremony to please the spirits:

Grandfather was an old man, in his eighties. Even so, he was still very strong, and was as fit as a fiddle. He was the village head and shaman, and many people respected him and sought his advice and help. Then early in 1997 the forest surrounding our houses was cleared to make way for Phase 2 of the community oil palm plantation. He was very upset with the village committee for clearing the forest behind his house, as he had asked them to spare a small portion of the forest, for this was where he did the bela kampung *ritual for the wellbeing of his family and the village. He warned them that if they cleared the area where he conducted the* bela kampung, *the spirits would be angry and there could be repercussions later on. No one listened to him and the forest was cleared and the oil palm planted.*

About two to three months after that, Grandfather was still hale and hearty and called all his grandchildren and great-grandchildren

to a small feast in his house. All of a sudden, Grandfather gave a loud cry; he said that his head was very painful. I ran to get help. When I returned, I saw him sprawled on the floor of his house, his face tilted sideways, stiff. Unable to talk, he gestured to us to find his shaman tools so that he could perform jampi. We did not know where he kept them, as he never told us. Unable to help him, we rushed him to the hospital, about 40 kilometers away, but he died upon reaching it. The doctors told us that his kidneys were damaged. I am not convinced, as Grandfather was very healthy. This happened all of a sudden, shortly after failing to perform the bela kampung *when the time was due.*

Now there is no *bomoh* left in Kampung Simpai. There is still a *bomoh* in a nearby village, however, and his help was called for in November 2006 when a twelve-year-old Jakun girl got dengue hemorrhagic fever. The doctors at the nearest hospital said there was little chance of her recovery. To save her, her family took her to the *bomoh*. The girl recovered. She observed all traditional taboos until a special *putus ubat* ceremony was held for the whole extended family, to complete the healing and thank the spirits. Its climax was bathing of the girl and her father with coconut water mixed with water over which the *bomoh* had done *jampi*. In the photo shown here, the girl's maternal aunt is holding a *pelepas* made from coconut leaves, representing the suffering and disease that needed to be purged from the patient's body. The patient tore it into two, marking the end of her illness.

Though earlier generations lived with little chance for work, with even rice a luxury, some of the old people are nostalgic about the past. Abu says:

We Orang Asli open up small portions of the forest for our swidden plots, say ten acres. But now the plantations have opened up thousands of acres of forest. It's so vast that one cannot see anything but oil palm. I remember hearing birds chirping and monkeys making funny noises. Our community was not only a community of people, but also of animals. We do miss the sounds of the animals in the morning. All we hear now is the rumbling of the lorries carrying the oil palm fruit.[39]

In Africa, despite changing social contexts, traditional religion is still strong among some groups, such as the Yoruba, whose priest-diviners are still respected, and to whom the *orisa* reportedly contacted in trance still reveal the nearness and importance of the invisible forces. However, in contemporary urban African areas, the traditional interest in the flow of the past into the present, with value placed on the intensity of present experience, has been rapidly replaced by a Westernized view of time in which one is perpetually anxious about the future. This shift has led to severe psychological disorientation and social and political instability. Those whose spiritual cultures have been merged with world religions such as Islam, Buddhism, or Christianity are now examining the relationship of their earlier tradition to the intercultural missionary traditions. African scholars have noted, for instance, that to put God in the forefront, as Christians do, does violence to the greater social importance of ancestor spirits in African traditional religions.

Indigenous peoples have also been victims of disastrous development projects. In Zimbabwe, thousands of traditional self-sufficient Vaduma people were displaced when their ancestral lands were flooded to create a huge artificial lake for irrigating an area hundreds of miles away. Jameson Kurasha of the University of Zimbabwe describes the effects on the Vaduma:

> When the "idea" of development was imposed on them, families were separated by a massive stretch of water. Now the Murinye Mugabe families are alienated from each other. They are now peoples without a tangible past to guide and unite them because their past [i.e. ancestors] are either buried or washed away by the lake. They are basically a people without a home to point to. The separation has left a cultural damage that will never be restored.[40]

Exploitation by multinational companies of the natural resources on land occupied by indigenous groups has sometimes been cloaked in talk of helping the local economy, but often the results have been devastating for indigenous peoples, spiritually as well as economically. In Nigeria, oil production accounts for eighty-seven percent of the government's foreign revenue. Multinational companies' activities to extract the oil have involved burning the waste gases, leaking oil pipelines, dumping waste products, and oil slicks for decades, causing extensive destruction of animal and plant life, soil damage, air and water pollution, and health problems among the indigenous peoples. The efforts of one severely affected group, the Ogoni, to protest this situation were met with harassment and ultimately the leaders being killed by the government. The Ogoni have continued their opposition nevertheless. Not only have their traditional lifeways been disrupted with the destruction of their environment, but also, more significantly from their point of view, they feel they must try to protect their ancestors' graves on their homesteads, plus their sacred groves and natural holy places. They feel their ancestors will not forgive them if they do not stand up to the oil business's desecration of their graves and sacred sites.

In Malaysia, the indigenous Orang Asli people and anthropologists, sociologists, and development workers who are familiar with their situation feel that the Malaysian government is intentionally but discreetly forcing the people from their traditional homelands so that it can appropriate the timber-rich land. So long as the Orang Asli live in the forests, especially if they were granted land rights to their ancestral lands, the individual state governments cannot get access to the timber revenues. Critics think this is why the government is making efforts to "integrate" the Orang Asli into Malay culture in the name of "development," including relocation, education, and Islamization, in order to detach them from their spiritual affinity to their land.

In the United States, reservations on which thousands of Navajos and Hopis were living were found to be sitting on the largest coal deposit in the country—the 4,000-square-mile "Black Mesa." In 1966, the Navajo and Hopi tribal councils signed agreements allowing Black Mesa to be strip-mined by utility companies to provide electricity for southwestern cities, and, presumably, economic development for the tribes. Since then the sacred land has been devastated, ancient archaeological sites have been destroyed, thousands of Navajos have been displaced, and aquifers are drying up as 1.3 billion gallons of pure water per year have been used to pump the coal slurry to a power plant hundreds of miles away. It is now thought that the government-established tribal councils—themselves not considered genuine representatives of the tribal peoples—were being advised by an attorney who was secretly employed by the coal company. The Black Mesa Trust is pressing for legal action that would impose limits on future damage to the area and curb tactics being used to pressurize the indigenous people. Cherokee attorney Jace Weaver points out that there are difficulties in protecting the rights of indigenous people on religious grounds because the legal definition of "religion" is limited. He writes, "Lacking a concept of the holy, our legal system finally is incapable of comprehending Native religious freedom and land claims."[41]

Modern development schemes—as well as outright plunder of natural resources for profit—are being called into question by land-based traditional peoples around the world, and attempts have begun to re-establish the validity of the ancient wisdom. In India, officials in the Ministry of Environment and Forests are acknowledging that the remaining sacred groves of the indigenous peoples are treasure houses of biodiversity and should not be destroyed. In such areas, it is often the shamans who teach the tribal people the importance of protecting the trees and vegetation.

Some indigenous peoples feel that their traditional sacred ways are not only valid, but actually essential for the future of the world. They see these understandings as antidotes to mechanistic, dehumanizing, environmentally destructive ways of life. Rather than regarding their ancient way as inferior, intact groups such as the Kogi of the high Colombian rainforest feel they are the elder brothers of all humanity, responsible for keeping the balance of the universe and re-educating their younger brothers who have become distracted by desire for material gain.

Differences of opinion and lifestyle between native people who live traditionally and those who have embraced industrial materialistic culture have led to rifts within the communities. There are people for and against selling mineral rights to community land for economic gain. Some indigenous people also question the ethics of developing gambling casinos as a base for economic self-sufficiency. But gaming has interesting precedents in many world religions and was traditionally part of sacred rites in many indigenous cultures. Ceremonial throwing of dice has been symbolically associated with the cycles of death and rebirth, and the movement of the sun, moon, and stars. The chance turn of the dice or wheel of fortune often appears in myths as a metaphor for balance in the continual shifts

myreligionlab
Seeing with
a Native Eye
BARRE TOELKEN

Winona LaDuke

As the narrator of Winona LaDuke's semifictional novel, *Last Standing Woman*, puts it, her clanspeople have a special destiny:

In times past, they were warriors, the ogichidaa, *those who defended the people. Sometimes we still are. We are what we are intended to be when we have those three things that guide our direction—our name, our clan, and our religion.*[42]

Winona herself is a prime example. She is continually in the news as a fighter on behalf of the future of the earth and its disadvantaged peoples. When in 1996 and 2000 she ran as the Green Party candidate for vice-president of the United States, she campaigned for reforms oriented toward long-term survival:

I am interested in reframing the debate on the issues of this society, the distribution of power and wealth, abuse of power, the rights of the natural world, the environment, and the need to consider an amendment to the U.S. Constitution in which all decisions made today would be considered in light of the impact on the seventh generation from now.[43]

Winona now lives on her father's traditional tribal lands in northern Minnesota in the White Earth Reservation. Her father, like many, had left the reservation in search of economic opportunity and for a time became a spiritual teacher called "Sun Bear." Now Winona is trying to re-establish an economic base that will allow her Anishinaabe people to return to their land and to have the legal right to control its use. The land is of spiritual as well as economic importance to her people.

Part of the land on which Winona's Mississippi band of the Anishinaabe had long lived was formally granted to them by an 1867 treaty establishing a reservation of 837,000 acres, in exchange for their giving up their rights to most of Minnesota and Wisconsin. But over time, land slipped away through foreclosures, illegal land transfers, and a 1986 settlement in which Anishinaabe were forced to accept, under pressure from large government agencies and timber companies, sale of remaining lands for only pennies an acre. Now the White Earth Reservation occupies only about one-sixth of the original area. Using part of a Reebok company award for her human rights work, Winona established the White Earth Land Recovery Project to begin to repurchase the land. She says, "We are going to recover our land acre by acre, inch by inch. Our burial grounds must be ours forever, even if we have to buy them back."[44]

The project she initiated has repurchased or received through donations over 1,300 acres of former tribal lands. The lands include burial grounds with undisturbed birch and sugar maple forests, and a 715-acre area encompassing two lakes, nesting sites for waterfowl, wild rice, and many medicinal plants.

Winona, a Harvard-educated journalist, has no fear of fighting against large-scale vested interests. In 1994, for instance, she chained herself to a paper company's gates to protest their clearance of forests including 1,000-year-old trees to make phone books. As a result, she was put in jail for five hours but the publicity led other companies to cancel their contracts with that paper company.

She is now trying to help develop long-range plans for sustainable management of White Earth lands as ecosystems that, if restored, can provide medicines and materials for Anishinaabe traditional culture. Harvest and sale of traditional products such as maple syrup, hominy corn, and wild rice are being used to help people make a living. The goal is to make it possible for people to return to the land. A tribal prophecy indicates that the people of the seventh fire—the current period—will look around and discover the things they had lost. With loss of the land had come loss of traditional spiritual principles. At the end of *Last Standing Woman*, the narrator speaks in the year 2018, describing her culture, which has rediscovered its spiritual traditions:

To understand our relationship to the whole and our role on the path of life. We also understand our responsibility. We only take what we need, and we leave the rest. We always give thanks for what we are given. What carries us through is the relationship we have to the Creation and the courage we are able to gather from the experience of our aanikoobijigan, *our ancestors, and our* oshkaabewisag, *our helpers.*[45]

The International Council of Thirteen Indigenous Grandmothers has been created as a project of the Center for Sacred Studies. The grandmothers form a global alliance for prayer, education, and healing of the earth for the sake of the next seven generations. From left to right, they are Clara Shinobu Iura and Maria Alice Campos Freire (Amazonian rainforest, Brazil), Margaret Behan (Arapaho/Cheyenne, Montana, USA), Rita Pitka Blumenstein (Yup'ik, Alaskan tundra, USA), Beatrice Long Visitor Holy Dance and Rita Long Visitor Holy Dance (Oglala Lakota, Black Hills, South Dakota, USA), Bernadette Rebienot (Omyene, Gabon, Africa), Mona Polacca (Havasupai/Hopi/Tewa, Arizona, USA), Agnes Baker Pilgrim (Takelma Siletz, Grants Pass, Oregon, USA), Julieta Casimiro (Mazatec, Huautla de Jimenez, Mexico), Flordemayo (Mayan, highlands of Central America/New Mexico), Aama Bombo/Buddhi Maya Lama (Tamang, Nepal), and Tsering Dolma Gyaltong (Tibetan).

between happiness and sorrow. Gaming rituals were used by some tribes to help the movement of the seasons and the shifts between night and day, to influence the weather, to assist in hunting, and to restore health. Addictive gambling is a different matter, for it can be disastrous for individuals and their families.

In the 2000 United States census, over four million people said they were at least partly Native American, over twice as many as made that claim during the 1990 census. Why this striking movement toward adopting a previously stigmatized indigenous identity? Possible reasons include the potential for a share in the gambling revenues, scholarships for minority students, the newfound popularity of native spiritual traditions, and the search for roots. There is thus considerable tension over the issue of native credentials, complicated by centuries of intermarriages. Those who consider themselves authentically "Indian" call the newcomers "wannabes" or "pretendians."

While there is a longing for exclusiveness on the part of some elders, others are adopting modern technologies to bring international attention to, and find support for, their causes. Personal visions and ancient prophecies about the dangers of a lifestyle that ignores the earth and the spiritual dimensions of life are leading native elders around the world to gather internationally and raise their voices together. They assert indigenous spiritual insights and observations about the state of the planet, political matters, and contemporary lifestyle issues.

Indigenous elders who are now speaking out seek converts not to their path but to a respect for all of life, which they feel is essential for the harmony of the planet. A respected elder of the Hopi nation, the late Thomas Banyacya, made a stirring appeal to the United Nations in 1992, in which he explained Hopi prophecies about our times. According to the prophecies, the creator made a perfectly balanced world but when humans turned away from spiritual principles for

myreligionlab

Hopi Message
THOMAS BANYACYA

selfish reasons, the world was destroyed by earthquakes. The few survivors developed the second world, but repeated their mistakes, and the world was destroyed by the Ice Age. The few people who survived spoke one language and developed high technologies but when they turned away from natural laws and spiritual principles, the third world was destroyed by a great flood which is remembered in the ancient stories of many peoples. Now we are living in the fourth world. According to Hopi time lines, we are in the final stages of decay. Showing a rock drawing of part of the Hopi prophecy, Thomas Banyacya explained:

There are two paths. The first with high technology but separate from natural and spiritual law leads to these jagged lines representing chaos. The lower path is one that remains in harmony with natural law. Here we see a line that represents a choice like a bridge joining the paths. If we turn to spiritual harmony and live from our hearts we can experience a paradise in this world. If we continue only on this upper path, we will come to destruction.[46]

Many people have said that indigenous peoples are myths of the past, ruins that have died. But the indigenous community is not a vestige of the past, nor is it a myth. It is full of vitality and has a course and a future. It has much wisdom and richness to contribute. They have not killed us and they will not kill us now. We are stepping forth to say, "No, we are here. We live."
Rigoberta Menchú of the K'iché Maya[47]

Suggested reading

Basso, Keith H., *Wisdom Sites in Places: Landscape and Language among the Western Apache*, Albuquerque: University of New Mexico Press, 1996. Interesting first-person ethnographic study of the meanings that Apache people attach to their environment.

Beck, Peggy V. and Anna L. Walters, *The Sacred: Ways of Knowledge, Sources of Life*, Tsaile (Navajo Nation), Arizona: Navajo Community College Press, 1977. A fine and genuine survey of indigenous sacred ways, particularly those of North America.

Bell, Diane, *Daughters of the Dreaming*, second edition, Minneapolis: University of Minnesota Press, 1993. A pioneering study of Australian aboriginal women, by an anthropologist who lived among them.

Berger, Julian, *The Gaia Atlas of First Peoples: A Future for the Indigenous World*, New York: Anchor Books, 1990. An illustrated survey of contemporary survival issues facing the original inhabitants of many lands, with particular reference to threats to their environment from invading cultures.

Brown, Joseph Epes, *The Sacred Pipe*, 1953, New York: Penguin Books, 1971. Detailed accounts of the sacred rites of the Oglala Sioux by Black Elk, a respected holy man.

Eliade, Mircea, *Shamanism: Archaic Techniques of Ecstasy*, trans. Willard Trask, London: Routledge & Kegan Paul, 1964. The first scholarly book to examine shamanism as an authentic religious form rather than as an anthropological oddity.

Erdoes, Richard and Alfonso Ortiz, *American Indian Myths and Legends*, New York: Pantheon Books,1984. A classic collection of stories from eighty North American tribes that offers a wealth of insights into traditional perceptions and lifeways.

Ewen, Alexander, *Voice of Indigenous Peoples*, Santa Fe, New Mexico: Clear Light Publishers, 1994. Speeches and writings from indigenous speakers at the 1992

United Nations Human Rights Day, analyzing the political conditions facing indigenous peoples.

Ford, Clyde, *The Hero with an African Face: Mythic Wisdom of Traditional Africa*, New York: Bantam, 2000. Sensitive exploration of mythological clues to traditional African beliefs.

Gill, Sam D., *Native American Religions*, Belmont, California: Wadsworth, 1982, 2004. A sensitive academic survey of indigenous sacred ways in the United States.

Goulet, Jean-Guy A., *Ways of Knowing: Experience, Knowledge, and Power among the Dene Tha*, Lincoln: University of Nebraska Press, 1998. Honest attempt by an anthropologist to directly experience and then explain to others the contemporary lifeways of these traditional people in northern Canada.

Grim, John, ed., *Indigenous Traditions and Ecology: The Interbeing of Cosmology and Community*, Cambridge: Harvard University Press, 2001. One of the excellent volumes of the series "Religions of the World and Ecology," this volume traces environmental themes across many different indigenous cultures.

Halifax, Joan, *Shamanic Voices: A Survey of Visionary Narratives*, New York: E. P. Dutton, 1979, and Harmondsworth, London: Penguin, 1980. Firsthand accounts of shamanistic visionary experiences.

Harvey, Graham, *Indigenous Religions: A Companion*, London and New York: Continuum International Publishing, 2000. Scholarly articles about specific cultures, attempting to transcend the tendency to understand indigenous religions in terms of concepts taken from other religions.

Lame Deer, John and Richard Erdoes, *Lame Deer: Seeker of Visions*, New York: Pocket Books, 1976. Firsthand accounts of the life of a rebel visionary who tried to maintain the old ways.

Magesa, Laurenti, *African Religion: The Moral Traditions of Abundant Life*, Maryknoll, New York: Orbis Books, 1997. An African Catholic theologian describes African traditional beliefs and practices as teachings about how to live meaningfully and harmoniously.

Mbiti, John S., *African Religions and Philosophy*, second edition, Oxford: Heinemann, 1999. A classic study of traditional African religions from an African point of view, including a strong critique of earlier anthropological perspectives.

Nelson, Richard K., *Make Prayers to the Raven: A Koyukon View of the Northern Forest*, Chicago: University of Chicago Press, 1986. Careful explanations of the close interrelationships between people and the rest of the natural world among these people of the western Canadian forest and tundra.

Olupona, Jacob K., ed., *African Spirituality: Forms, Meanings and Expressions*, New York: The Crossroad Publishing Company, 2000. Studies of spiritual themes in African traditional religions and how they have become integrated with Christian and Muslim influences.

St. Pierre, Mark and Tilda Long Soldier, *Walking in the Sacred Manner*, New York: Simon and Schuster, 1995. First-person accounts of Plains Indian women's spiritual roles.

Weaver, Jace, ed., *Native American Religious Identity: Unforgotten Gods*, Maryknoll, New York: Orbis Books, 1998. A varied collection of essays examining facets of contemporary religious identities among Native Americans.

Key terms

cosmogony A model of the origins of the universe.
Dreaming (Dream Time) The timeless time of Creation, according to Australian aboriginal belief.
indigenous Native to an area.
lifeway An entire approach to living in which sacred and secular are not separate.

medicine person An indigenous healer.

orisa Yoruba term for a deity.

shaman A man or woman who has undergone spiritual ordeals and can communicate with the spirit world to help the people.

vision quest A solitary ordeal undertaken to seek spiritual guidance about one's mission in life.

Review questions

1. How do indigenous sacred ways have an ecological perspective?
2. What effects do indigenous sacred ways' rituals seem to have? For example, consider storytelling, drumming, initiations, healing, self-sacrifice, and vision quests.
3. What are some of the effects of the clashes between indigenous and industrial societies?

Discussion questions

1. In what ways do indigenous approaches to the sacred differ from those of other religions with which you are familiar?
2. What do you see as the benefits and disadvantages of nonindigenous people attempting to adopt indigenous religious practices?
3. Can indigenous sacred ways be reconciled with modern industrial and commercial pressures? Why, or why not?

myreligionlab

For further activities and resources, including access to MyReligionLibrary, please visit MyReligionLab at www.myreligionlab.com

Additional Internet resources

Aboriginal Studies WWW Virtual Library
http://www.ciolek.com/WWWVL-Aboriginal.html

Center for Orang Asli Concerns http://www.coac.org.my

Center for World Indigenous Studies http://www.cwis.org/wwwvl/indig-vl.html

Indian http://www.indians.org/

Isizoh, Chidi Denis, ed., "African Traditional Religion." http://afrikaworld.net/afrel/

Johnson, Kofi. "Understanding African Traditional Religion."
http://organizations.uncfsu.edu/ncrsa/journal/v04/johnson_understanding.htm

Karenga, Maulana, ed. "Kwanzaa." http://www.officialkwanzaawebsite.org/index.shtml

Native Americans http://www.nativeweb.org/

Native Americans: The First People of America http://www.nativeamericans.com/

Native Peoples Magazine http://www.nativepeoples.com

CHAPTER 3

HINDUISM

"With mind absorbed and heart melted in love"

In the Indian subcontinent there has developed a complex variety of religious paths. Some of these are relatively unified religious systems, such as Buddhism, Jainism, and Sikhism. Most of the other Indian religious ways have been categorized together as if they were a single tradition named "Hinduism." This term is derived from a name applied by foreigners to the people living in the region of the Indus River, and was introduced in the nineteenth century under colonial British rule as a category for census-taking.

This labeling and interpretation of Indian religious traditions by non-Indians is currently a hotly debated issue. Some Indians now assert that Western analysis of Hinduism has been carried on by outsiders who were biased against Indian culture, or who presumed that all religions can be studied according to Western religious categories. Even the Hindi word *dharma*, often translated into English simply as "religion," refers to a broad complex of meanings, encompassing duty, natural law, social welfare, ethics, health, and transcendental realization.

The spiritual expressions of Hinduism range from extreme asceticism to extreme sensuality, from the heights of personal devotion to a deity to the heights of abstract philosophy, from metaphysical proclamations of the oneness behind the material world to worship of images representing a multiplicity of deities. According to tradition, there are actually 330 million deities in India. The feeling is that the divine has countless faces.

The extreme variations within Hinduism are reflections of its great age. Few of the myriad religious paths that have arisen over the millennia have been lost. They continue to co-exist in present-day India. Some scholars of religion argue that these ways are so varied that there is no central tradition that can be called Hinduism proper.

In villages, where the majority of Indians live, worship of deities is quite diverse and does not necessarily follow the more reified and philosophical Brahmanic tradition that is typically referred to as "Hinduism." Since it is not possible here to trace all these diffuse, widely scattered strands in their complex historical development, we will instead explore the main facets of the Brahmanic tradition thematically: its philosophical and metaphysical elements, then its devotional and ritual aspects, and, finally, its features as a way of life. These are not in fact totally separate categories, but we will separate them somewhat for clarity. Afterward, we will look at global and political aspects of the contemporary practice of Hinduism.

KEY TOPICS

• PHILOSOPHICAL AND METAPHYSICAL ORIGINS 74

• MAJOR PHILOSOPHICAL SYSTEMS 80

• RELIGIOUS FOUNDATIONS AND THEISTIC PATHS 85

• THE HINDU WAY OF LIFE 97

• HINDUISM IN THE MODERN WORLD 111

Philosophical and metaphysical origins

The Brahmanic tradition can be traced back to the Vedic age, thousands of years ago. The metaphysical beliefs in the Vedas were elaborated into various schools of thought by philosophers and sages. These beliefs were brought forth experientially by various methods of spiritual discipline.

> *Truth is one; sages call it by various names.*
>
> *Rig Veda*

THE INDUS VALLEY CIVILIZATION

Many of the threads of Hinduism may have existed in the religions practiced by the early Dravidian peoples of India. There were also advanced urban centers in the Indus Valley from about 2500 BCE, or even earlier, until 1500 BCE. Major fortified cities with elaborate plumbing and irrigation systems and paved, right-angled streets have been found by archaeologists at Harappa, Mohenjo-Daro, Dholavira, and other sites; the culture they represent is labeled the Indus Valley civilization.

According to theories advanced by eighteenth- and nineteenth-century European scholars, the highly organized cultures of the Indus Valley and other parts of the subcontinent were overrun by lighter-skinned nomadic invaders from some homeland to the north, whose peoples also spread westward and developed European civilizations. The theory argued that the **Vedas**, the religious texts often referred to as the foundations of Hinduism, were the product of the invaders and not of indigenous Indians, or perhaps a combination of both cultures.

myreligionlab
Hymn to Agni
RIG VEDA

The theory of an invasion of, and religious influence on, the Indus Valley civilization by "Aryans" from the north was based largely on linguistic similarities between classical European languages such as Latin and Greek to **Sanskrit**, the ancient language in which the Vedas were composed. The word **"Aryan"** is used in the Vedas to mean a noble person who speaks Sanskrit and practices the Vedic rituals. It is not a racial category. Nevertheless, the idea of an invasion of the Indus Valley by "Aryans" persisted until recent times, when it has become the subject of intense research by scholars of historical linguistics, archaeology, anthropology, and textual analysis. There is as yet no confirmed evidence of what actually happened.

The relationship of the Vedas to the Indus Valley sites is also unclear. The early Vedas seem to have been written by agropastoral people, whereas the Indus Valley civilization was primarily urban centered. Despite claims by some Indian historians that the Vedas may be of great antiquity, Western Indologists generally continue to think that the early Vedas were compiled when the Indus Valley civilization was in decline, approximately 1500 BCE. The Indus script has not yet been deciphered, so there is no way of knowing if it is related to the Sanskrit of the Vedas.

There are, however, some similarities between artifacts of the Indus Valley civilization and religious practices associated with Hinduism. Narrative scenes and figures on seals and pottery include representations of trees with what appear to be deity figures, suggesting that worship may have taken place in natural settings under trees considered sacred—such as the peepul tree, which even in contemporary India is thought to be so sacred that it should not be cut down, even when its great trunk threatens walls and buildings. There are male figures apparently seated in meditation, some of them with horns, which have been interpreted as evidence of ancient practice of yogic postures or worship of the deity Shiva. There are also many decorated female figurines, which may indicate worship of a goddess. Researchers find evidence of many levels of religious practice, from local cults to what may have been established state religions of the elite.

The relationship between ancient Indus Valley spirituality and the Vedas is also not yet clear. And the Vedas themselves are the foundation of upper-caste Brahmanic Hinduism, but not necessarily of all forms of what is called Hinduism.

The Indian subcontinent includes areas that are now politically separate from India. The Indus Valley, for instance, lies in what is now the Muslim state of Pakistan. Another Muslim state was carved out of the eastern portion of India in 1947, and became the independent state of Bangladesh in 1971.

Hinduism

BCE c.8000–6000	According to Indian tradition, Vedas heard by *rishis*, carried orally
c.3102	According to Indian tradition, beginning of Kali Yuga; Vishnu incarnates as Vyasa, who writes down the Vedas
c.2500–1500	Indus Valley civilization
c.1500	Early Vedas first composed
c.900–700	*Brahmanas* written down
c.600–100	*Upanishads* compiled
c.400 BCE–200 CE	*Ramayana* (present form)
c.400 BCE–400 CE	*Mahabharata* (present form)
by 200	Patanjali systematizes Yoga sutras [Indian tradition; yoga practices are ancient, indigenous]
CE 100–300	Code of Manu compiled
c.300	Tantras written down [Indian tradition; Tantras are as old as the *Upanishads*]
500–1500	*Puranas* recorded
c.600–1800	*Bhakti* movement flourishes
711	Muslim invasions begin
c.788–820	or earlier, Shankara reorganizes Vedanta
c.800–900	*Bhagavata Purana* written down
1556–1707	Mogul Empire
1828	Brahmo Samaj revitalization
1836–1886	Life of Ramakrishna
1857–1947	British rule of India
1869–1948	Life of Mahatma Gandhi
1875	Arya Samaj reform
1947	Independence; partition of India and Pakistan
1948	Assassination of Mahatma Gandhi
1992	Demolition of Babri Mosque
2002	Violence erupts again over attempts to build Ram Temple at Ayodhya

The Vedas include hymns praising the cow, which is still beloved and treated as sacred by Hindus: "The cow is our Mother, for she gives us her milk." Bali has its unique ways of carrying on the belief, including this veneration of the cow in a cremation ceremony.

THE VEDAS

Although their origins and antiquity are still unknown, the Vedas themselves can be examined. They are a revered collection of ancient sacred hymns. These sacred teachings seem to have been written down by the middle of the first millennium BCE, though we know that they are much older than their earliest written forms. After being revealed to sages, they were transmitted orally from teacher to student and may then have been written down over a period of 800 or 900 years. According to orthodox Hindus, the Vedas are not the work of any humans. They are considered *shruti* texts—those which have been revealed, rather than written by mortals. They are the breath of the eternal, as "heard" by the ancient sages, or *rishis*, and later compiled by Vyasa. The name "Vyasa" means "Collector." He was traditionally considered to be one person, but some scholars think it likely that many people were acting as compilers.

The Vedas are thought to transcend human time and are thus as relevant today as they were thousands of years ago. The *Gayatrimantra*, a verse in a Vedic hymn, is still chanted daily by the devout as the most sacred of prayers:

> *Aum [the primordial creative sound],*
> *Bhu Bhuvah Svah [the three worlds: earth, atmosphere, and heaven],*
> *Tat Savitur Varenyum,*
> *Bhargo Devasya Dheemahe [adoration of the glory, splendor, and grace that radiate*
>   *from the Divine Light that illuminates the three worlds],*
> *Dhiyo Yo Nah Prachodayat [a prayer for liberation through awakening of the light*
>   *of the universal intelligence].*[1]

myreligionlab

Hymn on Creation
RIG VEDA

The oldest of the known Vedic scriptures—and among the oldest of the world's existing scriptures—is the **Rig Veda**. This praises and implores the blessings of the *devas*—the controlling forces in the cosmos, deities who consecrate every part of life. The major *devas* included **Indra** (god of thunder and bringer of welcome rains), **Agni** (god of fire), Soma (associated with a sacred drink), and Ushas (goddess of dawn). The *devas* included both opaque earth gods and transparent deities of the sky and celestial realms. But behind all the myriad aspects of divinity, the sages perceived one unseen reality. This reality, beyond human understanding, ceaselessly creates and sustains everything that exists, encompassing all time, space, and causation.

The Rig Veda is the first of four collections of which the Vedas are comprised. The other three also contain hymns and sacred sounds to be recited while making offerings to the deities by means of a sacrificial fire. These sounds are thought to carry great power, for they are based on the sound vibrations by which the cosmos was created and sustained.

myreligionlab

Realize the Brahman
UPANISHADS

Other ancient *shruti* texts include the *Brahmanas* (directions about performances of the ritual sacrifices to the deities), *Aranyakas* ("forest treatises" by sages who went to the forests to meditate as recluses), and *Upanishads* (teachings from highly realized spiritual masters). The principal *Upanishads* are thought to have developed last, around 600 to 100 BCE. They represent the mystical insights of *rishis* who sought ultimate reality through their meditations in the forest. Many people consider these philosophical and metaphysical reflections the cream of

Vedic worship with fire is still significant in contemporary rituals. Fire ceremonies may be conducted by Hindu pandits to invoke the blessings of the Unseen.

Indian thought, among the highest spiritual literature ever written. They were not taught to the
masses but rather were reserved for advanced
seekers of spiritual truth. The word "*Upanishad*"
embraces the idea of the devoted disciple sitting
down by the teacher to receive private spiritual
instruction about the highest reality, loosening all
doubts and destroying all ignorance. Emphasis is
placed not on outward ritual performances, as in
the earlier texts, but on inner experience as the
path to realization and immortality.

The *rishis* explain that the bodily senses are
made for looking outward; the eyes, ears, nose,
tongue, and skin are enticed by sensory pleasures.
But ultimately these are fleeting, impermanent.
They pass away and then one dies, never having
experienced what is of greater value because it is
infinite, everlasting. What is real and lasting, they
found, can be discovered only by turning away
from transient worldly things. They taught their
pupils to turn their attention inward and thus discover a transcendent reality from within. This
unseen but all-pervading reality they called
Brahman, the Unknowable: "Him the eye does not
see, nor the tongue express, nor the mind grasp."[2]

From Brahman spring the multiplicity of forms,
including humans. The joyous discovery of the
rishis was that they could find Brahman as the subtle self or soul (**atman**) within themselves. One of
the *rishis* explained this relationship thus:

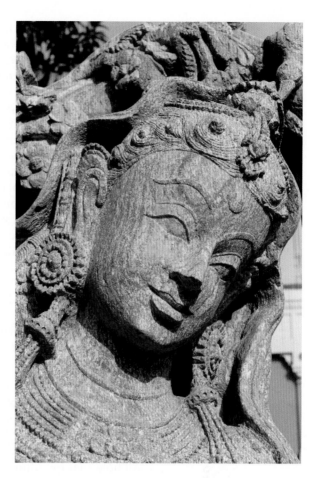

*A Hindu statue conveys
the compassion of the
divine.*

> *In the beginning there was Existence alone—One only, without a second.*
> *He, the One, thought to himself: Let me be many, let me grow forth. Thus*
> *out of himself he projected the universe, and having projected out of himself*
> *the universe, he entered into every being. All that is has its self in him alone.*
> *Of all things he is the subtle essence. He is the truth. He is the Self. And that,*
> *… THAT ART THOU.*

> *Chandogya Upanishad*[3]

When one discovers the inner self, *atman*, and thus also its source, Brahman,
the self merges into its transcendent source, and one experiences unspeakable
peace and bliss.

The *Upanishads* express several doctrines central to all forms of Hinduism. One
is **reincarnation**. In answer to the universal question, "What happens after we
die?" the *rishis* taught that the soul leaves the dead body and enters a new one.
One takes birth again and again in countless bodies—perhaps as an animal or
some other life form—but the self remains the same. Birth as a human being is a
precious and rare opportunity for the soul to advance toward its ultimate goal of
liberation from rebirth and merging with the Absolute Reality.

An important related concept is that of *karma*. It means action, and also the consequences of action. Every act we make, and even every thought and every desire we have, shapes our future experiences. Our life is what we have made it. And we ourselves are shaped by what we have done: "As a man acts, so does he become. ... A man becomes pure through pure deeds, impure through impure deeds."[4] Not only do we reap in this life the good or evil we have sown; they also follow us after physical death, affecting our next incarnation. Ethically, this is a strong teaching, for our every move has far-reaching consequences.

The ultimate goal, however, is not creation of good lives by good deeds, but a clean escape from the *karma*-run wheel of birth, death, and rebirth, or *samsara*. To escape from *samsara* is to achieve *moksha*, or liberation from the limitations of space, time, and matter through realization of the immortal Absolute. Many lifetimes of upward-striving incarnations are required to reach this transcendence of earthly miseries. This desire for liberation from earthly existence is one of the underpinnings of classical Hinduism, and of Buddhism as well.

Major philosophical systems

In addition to the Vedas, elaborate philosophical systems were developed long ago in India. Those associated with Brahmanic Hindu tradition all have certain features in common:

1 All have deep roots in the Vedas and other scriptures but also in direct personal experiences of the truth through meditation;
2 All hold ethics to be central to orderly social life. They attribute suffering to the law of *karma*, thereby suggesting incentives to more ethical behavior;
3 All hold that the ultimate cause of suffering is people's ignorance of the Self, which is omniscient, omnipotent, omnipresent, perfect, and eternal.

Two other major philosophical systems born in India—Jainism and Buddhism—do not acknowledge the authority of the Vedas but nevertheless draw on many of the same currents as Hinduism. Prominent among the philosophical systems that are related to the Vedas are **Samkhya**, **Advaita Vedanta**, and yoga.

SAMKHYA

The Samkhya system, though undatable, is thought to be the oldest in India. Its founder is said to be the semimythical sage Kapila. Its principles appear in Jainism and Buddhism from the sixth century BCE, so the system probably preceded them and may be of pre-Vedic origin.

Samkhya philosophy holds that there are two states of reality. One is the *Purusha*, the Self, which is eternally wise, pure, and free, beyond change, beyond cause. The other is *Prakriti*, the cause of the material universe. All our suffering stems from our false confusion of **Prakriti** with **Purusha**, the eternal Self, pure Consciousness. A **dualistic** understanding of life is essential, according to this system, if we are to distinguish the ultimate transcendent reality of Purusha from the temporal appearances of Prakriti, which bring us happiness but also misery and delusion.

The highly analytical Samkhya system holds that Prakriti consists of three essential qualities. They are *sattva* (fine, illuminated, balanced), *rajas* (active, passionate), and *tamas* (heavy, inert, coarse). Interaction and tension between the equilibrium of *sattva*, the activity of *rajas*, and the resistance to action of *tamas* governs the development of the world.

ADVAITA VEDANTA

Whereas Samkhya is a dualistic system, Advaita ("nondualist") Vedanta is generally **monistic**, positing a single reality. It is based on the *Upanishads*: its founder is said to be Vyasa, systematizer of the Vedas. The eminent philosopher Shankara reorganized the teachings many centuries later, probably between the eighth and ninth centuries CE.

Whereas one view of the *Upanishads* is that the human self (*atman*) is an emanation of Brahman, Shankara insisted that the *atman* and Brahman are actually one. According to Shankara, our material life is an illusion. It is like a momentary wave arising from the ocean, which is the only reality. Ignorance consists in thinking that the waves are different from the ocean. The absolute spirit, Brahman, is the essence of everything, and it has no beginning and no end. It is the eternal ocean of bliss within which forms are born and die, giving the false appearance of being real.

That which makes us think the physical universe has its own reality is **maya**, the power by which the Absolute veils itself. *Maya* is the illusion that the world as we perceive it is real. Shankara uses the metaphor of a coil of rope that, at dusk, is mistaken for a snake. The physical world, like the rope, does actually exist but we superimpose our memories and subjective thoughts upon it. Moreover, he says, only that which never changes is truly real. Everything else is changing, impermanent. In ignorance we think that we exist as individuals, superimposing the notion of a separate ego-self on the underlying absolute reality of pure being, pure consciousness, pure bliss. It is a mistake to identify with the body or the mind, which exist but have no unchanging reality. When a person reaches transcendent consciousness, the oneness of reality is experienced.

YOGA

From ancient times, people of the Indian subcontinent have practiced spiritual disciplines designed to clear the mind and support a state of serene, detached awareness. The practices for developing this desired state of balance, purity, wisdom, and peacefulness of mind are known collectively as **yoga**. It means "yoke" or "union"—referring to union with the true Self, the goal described in the *Upanishads*.

The sages distinguished four basic types of people and developed yogic practices that are particularly suitable for each type, in order that each can attain the desired union with the Self. For meditative people, there is *raja yoga*, the path of mental concentration. For rational people, there is *jnana yoga*, the path of rational

In kundalini *yoga, the body is thought to exist within a field of energy, which is most concentrated at the major chakras—subtle centers along the vertical axis of the body.*

myreligionlab
Desire to Know
the Brahman
SHANKARA

myreligionlab
Yoga Sutras
PATANJALI

inquiry. For naturally active people, there is *karma yoga*, the path of right action. For emotional people, there is *bhakti yoga*, the path of devotion.

Raja yoga Some believe that the *sadhanas*, or practices of *raja yoga*, were known as long ago as the Neolithic Age and were practiced in the Indus Valley culture. By 200 BCE, a yogi named Patanjali (or perhaps a series of people taking the same name) had described a system for attaining the highest consciousness through *raja yoga*—the path of mental concentration. Patanjali's *Yoga Sutras* is a book of 196 terse sayings called *sutras*. These include such observations as:

> *"From contentment comes the attainment of the highest happiness."*
> *"From penance comes destruction of impurities, thence the perfection of the body and the senses."*
> *"From study comes communion with the desired deity."*
> *"From the profound meditation upon Isvara [God] comes success in spiritual absorption."*[5]

Yogis say that it is easier to calm a wild tiger than it is to quiet the mind, which is like a drunken monkey that has been bitten by a scorpion. The problem is that the mind is our vehicle for knowing the Self. If the mirror of the mind is disturbed, it reflects the disturbance rather than the pure light within. The goal of yogic practices is to make the mind absolutely calm and clear.

Patanjali distinguishes eight "limbs" of the yogic path: moral codes (abstentions and observances), physical conditioning, breath control, sense control, concentration, meditation, and the state of peaceful spiritual absorption (*samadhi*).

Yogic adepts have developed extreme control of their bodies to amplify meditation efforts.

The moral and ethical principles that form the first limb of yogic practice are truth, nonviolence, nonstealing, continence, noncovetousness, cleanliness, contentment, burning zeal, self-study, and devotion to God. The second limb consists of *asanas*—physical postures used to cleanse the body and develop the mind's ability to concentrate. Regulated breathing exercises are also used to calm the nerves and increase the body's supply of *prana*, or invisible life energy. Breath is thought to be the key to controlling the flow of this energy within the subtle energy field surrounding and permeating the physical body. Its major pathway is through a series of **chakras**, or subtle energy centers, along the spine. The ideal is to raise the energy from the lowest, least subtle chakra at the base of the spine to the top of the head and open the highest, most subtle chakra there, leading to the bliss of union with the Sublime. This evolved state is depicted as a thousand-petaled lotus, effulgent with light.

In addition to these practices using the body and breath, Indian thought has long embraced the idea that repetition of certain sounds has sacred effects. It is said that some ancient yogic adepts could discern subtle sounds and that **mantras** (sacred formulas) express an aspect of the divine in the form of sound vibration. The sound of the mantras was believed to evoke the reality they named. The language used for these verbal formulas since ancient times was Sanskrit. It was considered a re-creation of the actual sound-forms of objects, actions, and qualities, as heard by ancient sages in deep meditation.

Chanting sacred syllables is thought to still the mind and attune the devotee to the Divine Ground of Existence. Indians liken the mind to the trunk of an elephant, always straying restlessly here and there. If an elephant is given a small stick to hold in its trunk, it will hold it steadily, losing interest in other objects. In the same way, the mantra gives the restless mind something to hold, quieting it by focusing awareness in one place. If chanted with devoted concentration, the mantra may also invoke the presence and blessings of the deity.

Many forms of music have also been developed in India to elevate a person's attunement and may go on for hours if the musicians are spiritually absorbed.

Another way of steadying and elevating the mind is concentration on some visual form—a candle flame, the picture of a saint or guru, the *OM* symbol, or *yantras*. A *yantra* is a linear image with complex cosmic symbolism. Large *yantras* are also created as designs of colorful seeds for ritual invocations of specific deities.

One-pointed concentration ideally leads to a state of meditation. In meditation, all worldly thoughts have dissipated. Instead of ordinary thinking, the clear light of awareness allows insights to arise spontaneously as flashes of illumination.

The ultimate goal of yogic meditation is *samadhi*: a super-conscious state of union with the Absolute. Swami Sivananda attempts to describe it:

> *Words and language are imperfect to describe this exalted state. … Mind, intellect and the senses cease functioning. … It is a state of eternal Bliss and eternal Wisdom. All dualities vanish* in toto. *… All visible merge in the invisible or the Unseen. The individual soul becomes that which he contemplates.*[6]

The OM *symbol, representing the original sound of creation, is topped by the sun and the moon, harmonized opposites. To chant* OM *is to commune with this cosmic sound vibration.*

Classical Indian music is based on inner spiritual communion with the divine.

Jnana yoga The path of rational inquiry—*jnana yoga*—employs the rational mind rather than trying to transcend it by concentration practices. In this path, ignorance is considered the root of all problems. Our basic ignorance is our idea of our selves as being separate from the Absolute. One method is continually to ask, "Who am I?" The seeker discovers that the one who asks the question is not the body, not the senses, not the pranic body, not the mind, but something eternal beyond all these. The guru Ramana Maharshi explains:

> *After negating all of the above-mentioned as "not this," "not this," that Awareness which alone remains—that I am. ... The thought "Who am I?" will destroy all other thoughts, and, like the stick used for stirring the burning pyre, it will itself in the end get destroyed. Then, there will arise Self-realization.*[7]

In the *jnana* path, the seeker must also develop spiritual virtues (calmness, restraint, renunciation, resignation, concentration, and faith) and have an intense longing for liberation. The ultimate wisdom is spiritual rather than intellectual knowledge of the self.

Karma yoga In contrast to these ascetic and contemplative practices, another way is that of helpful action in the world. *Karma yoga* is service rendered without any interest in its fruits and without any personal sense of giving. The yogi knows that the Absolute performs all actions, and all actions are gifts to the Absolute. This consciousness leads to liberation from the self in the very midst of work.

Bhakti yoga The final type of spiritual path is the one embraced by most Hindus. It is the path of devotion to a personal deity, *bhakti yoga*. For the *bhakta* (devotee), the relationship is that of intense love. Bhakta Nam Dev described this deep love in sweet metaphors:

The love between Radha and Krishna is a model for bhaktas' *devotion to the Supreme Person.*

> *Thy Name is beautiful, Thy form is beautiful, and very beautiful is Thy love, Oh my Omnipresent Lord.*
> *As rain is dear to the earth, as the fragrance of flowers is dear to the black bee, and as the mango is dear to the cuckoo, so is the Lord to my soul.*
> *As the sun is dear to the sheldrake, and the lake of Man Sarowar to the swan, and as the husband is dear to the wife, so is God to my soul.*
> *As milk is dear to the baby and as the torrent of rain to the mouth of the sparrow-hawk who drinks nothing but raindrops, and as water is dear to the fish, so is the Lord to my soul.*[8]

Mirabai, a fifteenth-century princess, was married to a ruler at a young age, but from her childhood she had been utterly devoted to the deity Krishna. Her poetry expresses her single-minded love for her beloved:

Everything perishes,
sun, moon, earth, sky, water, wind,
everything.
Only the One Indestructible remains.
Others get drunk on distilled wine,
in love's still I distil mine;
day and night I'm drunk on it
in my Lover's love, ever sunk ...
I'll not remain in my mother's home,
I'll stay with Krishna alone;
  He's my Husband
  and my Lover,
  and my mind is
  at his feet forever.[9]

When Mirabai continued to spend all her time in devotions to Krishna, an infuriated in-law tried to poison her. It is said that Mirabai drank the poison while laughingly dancing in ecstasy before Krishna; in Krishna's presence the poison seemed like nectar to her and did her no harm. The Beloved One is said to respond and to be a real presence in the fully devoted *bhakta*'s life.

In the *bhakti* path, even though the devotee may not transcend the ego in *samadhi*, the devotee's whole being is surrendered to the deity in love. The nineteenth-century saint Ramakrishna explained why the *bhakti* way is more appropriate for most people:

As long as the I-sense lasts, so long are true knowledge and Liberation impossible. ... [But] how very few can obtain this Union [Samadhi] and free themselves from this "I"? It is very rarely possible. Talk as much as you want, isolate yourself continuously, still this "I" will always return to you. Cut down the poplar tree today, and you will find tomorrow it forms new shoots. When you ultimately find that this "I" cannot be destroyed, let it remain as "I" the servant.[10]

myreligionlab
The Way of Devotion
BHAGAVATA PURANA

myreligionlab
Without Krishna
I Cannot Sleep
MIRABAI

Religious foundations and theistic paths

In ancient Vedic times, elaborate fire sacrifice rituals were created, controlled by *brahmins* (priests). Specified verbal formulas, sacred chants, and sacred actions were to be used by the priests to invoke the breath behind all of existence. This universal breath was later called **Brahman**, the Absolute, the Supreme Reality.

After a period when Brahmanic ritual and philosophy dominated, the *bhakti* approach came to prominence around 600 CE. It opened spiritual expression to both *shudras* (a caste of manual laborers and artisans) and women, and has been the primary path of the masses ever since. It may also have been the initial way of the people, as it is difficult to pray to the impersonal Absolute referred to in the *Upanishads*, for it is formless and is not totally distinct from oneself. More personal worship of a Divine Being can be inferred from the goddess and Shiva-like low reliefs found in the archaeological sites of ancient India. Worship of major deities probably persisted during the Vedic period and was later given written expression. Eventually *bhakti*—intense devotion to a personal manifestation of Brahman—became the heart of Hinduism as the majority of people now experience it.

Of all the deities worshiped by Hindus, there are three major groupings: **Shaktas** who worship a Mother Goddess, **Shaivites** who worship the god Shiva, and **Vaishnavites** who worship the god Vishnu. Each devotee has his or her own "chosen deity," but will honor others as well.

Ultimately, some Hindus rest their faith in one genderless deity with three basic aspects: creating, preserving, and destroying, in continuing cosmic cycles.

SHAKTAS

An estimated fifty million Hindus worship some form of the goddess. Some of these Shaktas follow a Vedic path; some are more independent of Vedic tradition. Worship of the feminine aspect of the divine probably dates back to the pre-Vedic ancient peoples of the Indian subcontinent. Her great power is called *shakti*.

The goddess is worshiped in many forms. At the village level, especially in southern India, local deities are most typically worshiped as goddesses. They may not be perceived as taking human-like forms; rather, their presence may be represented by round stones, trees, *yantras*, or small shrines without images. These local goddesses are intimately concerned with village affairs, unlike the more distant great goddesses of the upper class, access to whose temples was traditionally forbidden to those of low caste.

The great goddesses have been worshiped in the plural and also in the singular, when one goddess is seen as representing the totality of deity—eternal creator,

The great goddess Durga is understood as the active principle that can vanquish the demonic forces. (Durga slaying the Buffalo Demon, India, c.1760.)

preserver, and destroyer. The general term **Devi** may be used to refer generically to the goddess in all her forms, understood as the supreme Divine Mother, the totality of all the energy of the cosmos. Sri Swami Sivananda of the Divine Life Society explains that it is quite natural to regard the Divine as Mother:

> To the child, in the mother is centered a whole world of tenderness, of love, of nourishment and of care. It is the ideal world from where one draws sustenance, where one runs for comfort, which one clings to for protection and nourishment; and there he gets comfort, protection and care. Therefore, the ideal of love, care and protection is in the conception of the mother.[11]

Devi is known by many names, and is thought to have many manifestations. Among them are benign, extremely powerful, and even fierce forms. The goddess **Durga** is often represented as a beautiful woman with a gentle face but ten arms holding weapons with which she vanquishes the demons who threaten the *dharma*; she rides a lion. She is the blazing splendor of God incarnate, in benevolent female form.

Kali is the goddess in her fierce form. She may be portrayed dripping with blood, carrying a sword and a severed head, and wearing a girdle of severed hands and a necklace of skulls symbolizing her aspect as the destroyer of evil. What appears as destruction is actually a means of transformation. With her merciful sword she cuts away all personal impediments to realization of truth for those who sincerely desire to serve the Supreme. At the same time, she opens her arms to those who love her. Some of them worship her with blood offerings from animal sacrifices, but some *shakti* temples are now doing away with this practice, at the behest of animal lovers.

Another popular great goddess is **Lakshmi**, who embodies wealth, generosity, good fortune, beauty, and charm. She is often depicted as a radiant woman sitting on a waterborne lotus flower. The lotus floats pristine on the water but has its roots in the mud, thus representing the refined spiritual energy that rises above worldly contamination. The goddess Saraswati is associated with knowledge, the arts, and music and also with the great river Saraswati which once flowed parallel to the Indus River in the cradle of the Indus Valley civilization. The Saraswati River dried up long ago, probably contributing to the decline of that ancient civilization.

myreligionlab
In Praise of Durga
SIVA PURANA

Lakshmi is often pictured standing gloriously upon a lotus flower, bestowing coins of prosperity and flanked by elephants signifying her royal power.

myreligienlab
Worship Him
in Silence
LALLA

From ancient times, worship of the divine female has been associated with worship of nature, particularly great trees and rivers. The Ganges River is considered an especially sacred female presence, and her waters, flowing down from the Himalayas, are thought to be extraordinarily purifying. Pilgrims bathe in Mother Ganga's waters, facing the sun at sunrise, and corpses or the cremated ashes of the dead are placed in the river so that their sins will be washed away.

Sacred texts called **Tantras** instruct worshipers how to honor the feminine divine. Ways of worship include concentration on *yantras*, meditation with the hands in *mudras* (positions that reflect and invoke a particular spiritual reality), **kundalini** practices to raise spiritual energy up the spine, and use of mantras. One such text gives a thousand different "names" or attributes of the Divine Mother as mantras for recitation, such as these: "*Sri mata* (She who is the auspicious Mother), *Sri maha rajni* (She who is the Empress of the Universe) … *Raga svarupa pasadhya* (She who is holding the rope of love in Her hand) … *Nirmada* (She who is without pride), *Mada nasini* (She who destroys pride), *Niscinta* (She who has no anxiety about anything), *Nir ahankara* (She who is without egoism) … *Mahaisvarya* (She who has supreme sovereignty), *Maha virya* (She who is supreme in valor), *Maha bala* (She who is supreme in might), *Maha buddhih* (She who is supreme in intelligence)."[12]

Shakti worship has also been incorporated into worship of the male gods. Each is thought to have a female consort, with whom he is often portrayed in close embrace signifying the eternal unity of male and female principles in the oneness of the divine. Here the female is often conceived as the life-animating force; the transcendent male aspect is inactive until joined with the productive female energy.

Shaivite sadhu *meditating in the Himalayas at the source of the holy Ganges River.*

SHAIVITES

Shiva is a personal, many-faceted manifestation of the attributeless supreme deity. In older systems he is one of the three major aspects of deity: Brahma (Creator), Vishnu (Preserver), and Shiva (Destroyer). Shaivites nevertheless worship him as the totality, with many aspects. As Swami Sivasiva Palani, Shaivite editor of *Hinduism Today*, explains: "Shiva is the unmanifest; he is creator, preserver, destroyer, personal Lord, friend, primal Soul"; and he is the "all-pervasive underlying energy, the more or less impersonal love and light that flows through all things."[13] Shiva is sometimes depicted dancing above the body of the demon he has killed, reconciling darkness and light, good and evil, creation and destruction, rest and activity in the eternal dance of life.

Shiva is also the god of yogis, for he symbolizes asceticism. He is often shown in austere meditation on Mount Kailas, clad only in a tiger skin, with a snake around his neck. The latter signifies his conquest of the ego. In one prominent story, it is Shiva who swallows the poison that threatens the whole world with darkness, neutralizing the poison by the power of his meditation.

Shiva has various *saktis* or feminine consorts. He is often shown with his devoted spouse **Parvati**. Through their union,

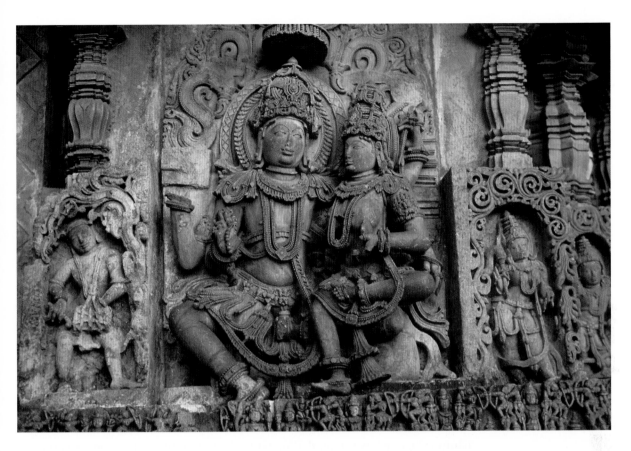

cosmic energy flows freely, seeding and liberating the universe. Nevertheless, they are seen mystically as eternally chaste. Shiva and his *sakti* are also expressed as two aspects of a single being. Some sculptors portray Shiva as androgynous, with both masculine and feminine physical traits. Tantric belief incorporates an ideal of balance of male and female qualities within a person, hopefully leading to enlightenment, bliss, and worldly success as well. This unity of male and female is often expressed abstractly, as a **lingam** within a **yoni**, a symbol of the female vulva.

The lingams used in worship of Shiva are naturally occurring or sculpted cylindrical forms honored since antiquity in India (and apparently in other cultures as well, as far away as Hawaii). Those shaped by nature, such as stones polished by certain rivers, are most highly valued, with rare natural crystal lingams considered especially precious. Tens of thousands of devotees each year undergo dangerous pilgrimages to certain high mountain caves to venerate large lingams naturally formed of ice. While the lingam sometimes resembles an erect phallus, most Shiva-worshipers focus on its symbolic meaning, which is abstract and asexual. They see the lingam as a nearly amorphous, "formless" symbol for the unmanifest, transcendent nature of Shiva—that which is beyond time, space, cause, and form—whereas the yoni represents the manifest aspect.

Shaivism encompasses traditions that have developed outside Vedic-based Brahmanism. These include sects such as the Lingayats, who wear a stone lingam

Shiva and Parvati's embrace symbolizes the unity of masculine and feminine energies.

A large lingam from the 6th century CE honors Shiva as the unmanifest creative force beyond time and space.

Shiva as Lord of the Dance, trampling the demon of evil and bearing both the flame of destruction and the drum of creation. One of his two free hands gestures "Fear not"; the other points to his upraised foot, denoting bliss.

in remembrance of Shiva as the One Undivided Being. Their ancient ways of Shiva worship underwent a strong reform movement in the twelfth century, refusing caste divisions, brahminical authority, and consideration of menstruating women as polluted. They practice strict vegetarianism and regard men and women as equals.

Another branch is represented by the sixty-three great Shaivite saints of Tamil Nadu in southern India, who from the seventh century onward expressed great love for Shiva. They experienced him as the Luminous One, present everywhere in subtle form but apparent only to those who love him. For this realization, knowledge of the scriptures and ascetic practices are useless. Only direct personal devotion will do. The Tamil saint Appar sang:

> *Why chant the Vedas, hear the shastras' lore? …*
> *Release is theirs, and theirs alone,*
> *Whose heart from thinking of its Lord shall never depart.*[14]

Shiva and Parvati's son Ganesh, a deity with the head of an elephant, guards the threshold of space and time and is therefore invoked for his blessings at the beginning of any new venture. Ganesh was the subject of an extraordinary event that happened in temples in many parts of India, as well as in Hindu temples in other parts of the world. On 21 September, 1995, statues devoted to Ganesh began drinking milk from spoons, cups, and even buckets offered by devotees. Scientists suggested explanations such as mass hysteria or capillary action in the stone, but the phenomenon lasted only one day.

VAISHNAVITES

Vishnu is beloved as the tender, merciful deity. In one myth, a sage was sent to determine who was the greatest of the gods by trying their tempers. The first two, Brahma and Shiva, he insulted and was soundly abused in return. When he found Vishnu the god was sleeping. Knowing of Vishnu's good-naturedness, the sage increased the insult by kicking him awake. Instead of reacting angrily, Vishnu tenderly massaged the sage's foot, concerned that he might have hurt it. The sage exclaimed, "This god is the mightiest, since he overpowers all by goodness and generosity!"

The auspicious blessings of Ganesh are invoked for all occasions. Here his image has been painted on a wall before a marriage celebration.

Vishnu has been worshiped since Vedic times and came to be regarded as the Supreme as a person. In Vaishnavite iconography, the world is continually being reborn on a lotus growing out of Vishnu's navel. Vishnu is often associated with his consort, Lakshmi (whom Shaktas worship as a goddess in her own right). According to ideas appearing by the fourth century CE, Vishnu is considered to have appeared in many earthly incarnations, some of them animal forms. Many deities have been drawn into this complex, in which they are interpreted as incarnations of Vishnu. Most beloved of his purported incarnations have been *Rama*, subject of the *Ramayana* (see page 92), and Krishna (see page 94). However, many people still revere Krishna without reference to Vishnu.

Popular devotion to Krishna takes many forms. If Krishna is regarded as the transcendent Supreme Lord, the worshiper humbly lowers himself or herself. If Krishna is seen as master, the devotee is his servant. If Krishna is loved as a child, the devotee takes the role of loving parent. If Krishna is the divine friend, the devotee is his friend. And if Krishna is the beloved, the devotee is his lover. The latter relationship was popularized by the ecstatic sixteenth-century Bengali saint, scholar, and social reformer Shri Chaitanya, who adored Krishna as the flute-playing lover. Following Shri Chaitanya, the devotee makes himself (if a male) like a loving female in order to experience the bliss of Lord Krishna's presence. It is this form of Hindu devotion that was carried to America in 1965, organized as the International Society for Krishna Consciousness, and then spread to other countries. Its followers are known as Hare Krishnas.

THE EPICS AND PURANAS

Personal love for a deity flowered in the spiritual literature that followed the Vedas. Two major classes of scriptures that arose after 500 BCE (according to Western scholarship) were the **epics** and the **Puranas**. These long heroic narratives and poems popularized spiritual knowledge and devotion through national myths and legends. They were particularly useful in spreading Hindu teachings to the masses at times when Buddhism and Jainism—movements born in India but not recognizing the authority of the Vedas—were winning converts.

In contrast to the rather abstract depictions of the Divine Principle in the *Upanishads*, the epics and Puranas represent the Supreme as a person, or rather as various human-like deities. As T. M. P. Mahadevan explains:

> The Hindu mind is averse to assigning an unalterable or rigidly fixed form or name
> to the deity. Hence it is that in Hinduism we have innumerable god-forms and
> countless divine names. And, it is a truth that is recognized by all Hindus that
> obeisance offered to any of these forms and names reaches the one supreme God.[15]

Two great epics, the *Ramayana* and the *Mahabharata*, present the Supreme usually as Vishnu, who intervenes on earth during critical periods in the cosmic cycles. In the inconceivable vastness of time as reckoned by Hindu thought, each world cycle lasts 4,320,000 years. Two thousand of these world cycles are the equivalent of one day and night in the life of Brahma, the Creator god. Each world cycle is divided into four ages, or *yugas*.

Dharma—moral order in the world—is natural in the first age. The second age is like a cow standing on three legs; people must be taught their proper roles in society. During the darker third age, revealed values are no longer recognized, people lose their altruism and willingness for self-denial, and there are no more saints. The final age, **Kali Yuga**, is as imbalanced as a cow trying to stand on one leg. The world is at its worst, with egotism, ignorance, recklessness, and war rampant. According to Hindu time reckoning, we are now living in a Kali Yuga period that began in 3102 BCE. Such an age is described thus:

> When society reaches a stage where property confers rank, wealth becomes
> the only source of virtue, passion the sole bond of union between husband
> and wife, falsehood the source of success in life, sex the only means of
> enjoyment, and when outer trappings are confused with inner religion ...[16]

Each of these lengthy cycles witnesses the same turns of events. The balance inexorably shifts from the true *dharma* to dissolution and then back to the *dharma* as the gods are again victorious over the anti-gods. The Puranas list the many ways that Vishnu has incarnated in the world when *dharma* is decaying, to help restore virtue and defeat evil. For instance, Vishnu is said to have incarnated great **avatars** such as Krishna and Rama to help uplift humanity. It is considered inevitable that Vishnu will continually return in answer to the pleas of suffering humans. It is equally inevitable that he will meet with resistance from "demonic forces," which are also part of the cosmic cycles.

Ramayana   The epics deal with the eternal play of good and evil, symbolized by battles involving the human incarnations of Vishnu. Along the way, they teach examples of the virtuous life—responsibilities to others as defined by one's social roles. One is first a daughter, son, sister, brother, wife, husband, mother, father, or friend in relationship to others, and only secondarily an individual.

The *Ramayana*, a long poetic narrative in the Sanskrit language thought to have been compiled between approximately 400 BCE and 200 CE, is attributed to the bard Valmiki. Probably based on old ballads, it is much beloved and is acted out with great pageantry throughout India every year. It depicts the duties of relationships, portraying ideal characters, such as the ideal servant, the ideal brother, the ideal wife, the ideal king. In the story, Vishnu incarnates as the virtuous prince Rama in order to kill Ravana, the ten-headed demon king of Sri Lanka. Rama is heir to his father's throne, but the mother of his stepbrother compels the king to banish Rama into the forest for fourteen years. Rama, a model of morality, goes willingly, observing that a son's duty is always to obey his parents implicitly, even when their commands seem wrong. He is accompanied into the ascetic life by his wife Sita, the model of wifely devotion in a patriarchal society, who refuses his offer that she should remain behind in comfort.

In the northern Indian festival of Dussehra, giant effigies of Ravana are set on fire and burst with firecrackers to celebrate his defeat by Rama.

Eventually Sita is kidnapped by Ravana, who woos her unsuccessfully in his island kingdom and guards her with all manner of terrible demons. Although Rama is powerful, he and his half brother Lakshman need the help of the monkeys and bears in the battle to get Sita back. Hanuman the monkey becomes the hero of the story. He symbolizes the power of faith and devotion to overcome our human frailties. In his love for the Lord he can do anything. The bloody battle ends in single-handed combat between Ravana and Rama. Rama blesses a sacred arrow with Vedic mantras and sends it straight into Ravana's heart. In what may be a later addition to the poem, when Rama and Sita are reunited he accuses her of infidelity, so to prove her innocence she undergoes an ordeal by fire in which Agni protects her. Another version of the *Ramayana*, perhaps as elaborated by later ballad-singers, has Rama ordering Sita into the forest because his subjects are suspicious of what may have happened while she was in Ravana's captivity. She is abandoned near the ashram of Valmiki. There she takes shelter and gives birth to twin boys. Years later, Valmiki and the sons attend a great ritual

Rama and Lakshman shoot arrows into the breast of the demon Ravana, with Hanuman and the monkeys in the background. (North India, c.19th century.)

conducted by King Rama, and the boys sing the *Ramayana*. There is an emotional reunion of the children with their father. Thereupon Sita, a daughter of the earth, begs the earth to receive her if she has been faithful to Rama. With these words, she becomes a field of radiance and disappears into the ground:

> O Lord of my being, I realize you in me and me in you. Our relationship
> is eternal. Through this body assumed by me, my service to you and your
> progeny is complete now. I dissolve this body to its original state.
>   Mother Earth, you gave form to me. I have made use of it as I ought to.
> In recognition of its purity may you kindly absorb it into your womb.[17]

Mahabharata The other famous Hindu epic is the *Mahabharata*, a Sanskrit poem of more than 100,000 verses. Perhaps partly historical, it may have been composed between 400 BCE and 400 CE. The plot concerns the struggle between the sons of a royal family for control of a kingdom near what is now Delhi. The story teaches the importance of sons, the duties of kingship, the benefits of ascetic practice and righteous action, and the qualities of the gods. In contrast to the idealized characters in the *Ramayana*, the *Mahabharata* shows all sides of human nature, including greed, lust, intrigue, and the desire for power. It is thought to be relevant for all times and all peoples. A serial dramatization of the *Mahabharata* has drawn huge television audiences in contemporary India. The *Mahabharata* teaches one primary ethic: that the happiness of others is essential to one's own happiness. This consideration of others before oneself is a central *dharmic* virtue.

myreligi⊙nlab
Rama, Sita,
and Lakshman
RAMAYANA

myreligi⬤nlab

I am the Beginning
and the End
BHAGAVAD-GITA

The eighteenth book of the *Mahabharata*, which may have originally been an independent mystical poem, is the *Bhagavad-Gita* ("Song of the Supreme Exalted One"). Krishna, revered as a manifestation of the Supreme, appears as the charioteer of Arjuna, who is preparing to fight on the virtuous side of a battle that will pit brothers against brothers, thus occasioning a treatise about the conflict that may arise between our earthly duties and our spiritual aspirations.

Before they plunge into battle, Krishna instructs Arjuna in the arts of self-transcendence and realization of the eternal. The instructions are still central to Hindu spiritual practice. Arjuna is enjoined to withdraw his attention from the impetuous demands of the senses, ignoring all feelings of attraction or aversion. This will give him a steady, peaceful mind. He is instructed to offer devotional service and to perform the prescribed Vedic sacrifices, but for the sake of discipline, duty, and example alone rather than reward—to "abandon all attachment to success or failure ... renouncing the fruits of action in the material world."[18]

Actually, Lord Krishna says those who do everything for love of the Supreme transcend the notion of duty. Everything they do is offered to the Supreme,

TEACHING STORY

Hanuman, the Monkey Chief

Hanuman was of divine origin and legendary powers, but he was embodied as a monkey, serving as a chief in the monkey army. When Rama needed to find his wife Sita after Ravana abducted her, he turned to the monkey king for help. The monkey king dispatched Hanuman to search to the south.

When the monkeys reached the sea dividing India from Sri Lanka, they were dismayed because monkeys do not swim. A vulture brought word that Sita was indeed on the other side of the water, a captive of Ravana. What to do? An old monkey reminded Hanuman of the powers he had displayed as an infant and told him that he could easily jump to Lanka and back if only he remembered his power and his divine origin.

Hanuman sat in meditation until he became strong and confident. Then he climbed a mountain, shook himself, and began to grow in size and strength. When at last he felt ready he set off with a roar, hurling himself through the sky with eyes blazing like forest fires.

When Hanuman landed in Lanka he shrunk himself to the size of a cat so that he could explore Ravana's forts. After many dangerous adventures, he gave Sita the message that Rama was preparing to do battle to win her back, and then he jumped back over the sea to the Indian mainland.

During the subsequent battle of Lanka, Rama and his half brother Lakshman were mortally wounded. Nothing would save them except a certain herb that grew only in the Himalayas. In his devotion to Rama Hanuman flew to the mountains, again skirting danger all the way. But once he got there he could not tell precisely which herb to pick, so he uprooted the whole mountain and carried it back to Lanka. The herb would be effective only before the moon rose. From the air, Hanuman saw the moon about to clear the horizon so he swallowed the moon and reached Lanka in time to heal Rama and Lakshman.

After the victory, Rama rewarded Hanuman with a bracelet of pearls and gold. Hanuman chewed it up and threw it away. When a bear asked why he had rejected the gift from God, Hanuman explained that it was useless to him since it did not have Rama's name on it. The bear said, "Well, if you feel that way, why do you keep your body?" At that, Hanuman ripped open his chest, and there were Rama and Sita seated in his heart, and all his bones and muscles had "Ram, Ram, Ram" written all over them.

Lord Krishna and Arjuna discuss profound philosophical questions in a battle chariot, as represented in this archway above the sacred Ganges River in Rishikesh.

"without desire for gain and free from egoism and lethargy."[19] Thus they feel peace, freedom from earthly entanglements, and unassailable happiness.

This yogic science of transcending the "lower self" by the "higher self" is so ancient that Krishna says it was originally given to the sun god and, through his agents, to humans. But in time it was lost, and Krishna is now renewing his instructions pertaining to "that very ancient science of the relationship with the Supreme."[20] He has taken human form again and again to teach the true religion:

Whenever and wherever there is a decline in religious practice …
   and a predominant rise of irreligion—at that time I descend Myself.
To deliver the pious and to annihilate the miscreants, as well as to re-establish
   the principles of religion, I advent Myself millennium after millennium.[21]

Krishna says that everything springs from his Being:

There is no truth superior to Me. Everything rests upon Me, as pearls are strung
on a thread. …
   I am the taste of water, the light of the sun and the moon, the syllable om *in*
   Vedic mantras; I am the sound in ether and ability in man. …
All states of being—goodness, passion or ignorance—are manifested by My energy.
   I am, in one sense, everything—but I am independent. I am not under the modes
   of this material nature.[22]

This supreme Godhead is not apparent to most mortals. The deity can be known only by those who love him, and for them it is easy, for they remember him at all times: "Whatever you do, whatever you eat, whatever you offer or give away, and whatever austerities you perform—do that … as an offering to Me." Any small act of devotion offered in love becomes a way to him: "If one offers Me with love and devotion a leaf, a flower, fruit, or water, I will accept it."[23]

The Puranas The Puranas, poetic Sanskrit texts that narrate the myths of ancient times, were probably compiled between 500 and 1500 CE. There are a total of eighteen Puranas—six about Vishnu, six about Brahma, and six about Shiva. These narratives popularize the more abstract philosophical teachings found in the Vedas and *Upanishads* by giving them concrete form. Of the Puranas, the most well known and loved is the *Bhagavata Purana*, which includes the life story of Krishna. Most Western Indologists think it was written about the ninth or tenth century CE, but according to Indian tradition it was one of the works written down at the beginning of Kali Yuga by Vyasa.

In the *Bhagavata Purana*, the supreme personality of Godhead is portrayed first in its vast dimensions—the Being whose body animates the material universe:

> *His eyes are the generating centers of all kinds of forms, and they glitter and illuminate. His eyeballs are like the sun and the heavenly planets. His ears hear from all sides and are receptacles for all the Vedas, and His sense of hearing is the generating center of the sky and of all kinds of sound.*[24]

This material universe we know is only one of millions of material universes. Each is like a bubble in the eternal spiritual sky, arising from the pores of the body of Vishnu, and these bubbles are created and destroyed as Vishnu breathes out and in. This cosmic conception is so vast that it is impossible for the mind to grasp it. It is much easier to comprehend and adore Vishnu in his incarnation as Krishna. Whereas he was a wise teacher in the *Bhagavad-Gita*, Krishna of the *Bhagavata Purana* is a much-loved child, raised by cowherds in an area called Vrindavan near Mathura on the Jumna River.

The mythology is rich in earthly pleasures. The boy Krishna mischievously steals balls of butter from the neighbors and wanders garlanded with flowers through the forest, happily playing his flute. Between episodes of carefree bravery in vanquishing demons that threaten the people, he playfully steals the hearts of the *gopis*, the cowherd girls. His favorite is the lovely Radha, but through his magical ways he multiplies himself so that each girl thinks he dances with her alone. Each is so much in love with Krishna that she feels she is one with him and desires only to serve him. Swami Vivekananda explains the spiritual meaning of the *gopis'* divine love for Krishna, which is:

Particular family relationships are extremely meaningful in Hindu traditions. For this ceremony, it is usually the paternal grandfather (otherwise the mother's sister) who offers the child its first solid food.

> too holy to be attempted without giving up everything, too sacred to be understood until the soul has become perfectly pure. Even the Gita, the great philosophy itself, does not compare with that madness, for in the Gita the disciple is taught slowly how to walk towards the goal, but here is the madness of enjoyment, the drunkenness of love, where disciples and teachers and teachings and books ... everything has been thrown away. What remains is the madness of love. It is forgetfulness of everything, and the lover sees nothing in the world except that Krishna, and Krishna alone.[25]

Eventually Krishna is called away on a heroic mission, never returning to the *gopis*. Their grief at his leaving and their intense longing for him serve as models for the *bhakti* path—the way of extreme devotion. In Hindu thought, the emotional longing of the lover for the beloved is one of the most powerful vehicles for concentration on the Supreme Lord.

The Hindu way of life

Although there is no single founder, devotional tradition, or philosophy which can be said to define Hinduism, everyday life is so imbued with spiritually meaningful aspects that spirituality is never far from one's mind. Those we will examine here include rituals, castes and social duties, life stages, home *puja*, homage to the guru, fasting, prayer, auspicious designs, reverence paid to trees and rivers, pilgrimages, and religious festivals.

RITUALS

From the cradle to the cremation ground, the Hindu's life is wrapped up in rituals. There are sixteen rites prescribed in the ancient scriptures to purify and sanctify the person in his or her journey through life, including rites at the time of conception, the braiding of the pregnant mother's hair, birth, name-giving, beginning of solid foods, starting education, investing boys with a sacred thread, first leaving the family house, starting studies of Vedas, marriage, and death. The goal is to continually elevate the person above his or her basically animal nature.

Public worship—*puja*—is usually performed by *pujaris*, or *brahmin* priests, who are trained in Vedic practices and in proper recitation of Sanskrit texts. They conduct worship ceremonies in which the sacred presence is made tangible through devotions employing all the senses. Shiva-lingams may be anointed with precious substances, such as ghee (clarified butter), honey, or sandalwood paste, with offerings of rosewater and flowers. In a temple, devotees may have the great blessing of receiving *darshan* (visual contact with the divine) through the eyes of the images. One hears the sounds of mantras and ringing bells. Incense and flowers fill the area with uplifting fragrances. *Prasad*, food that has been sanctified by being offered to the deities and/or one's guru, is passed around to be eaten by devotees, who experience it as sacred and spiritually charged.

In temples, the deity image is treated as if it were a living king or queen. Fine-haired whisks may be waved before it, purifying the area for its presence. Aesthetically pleasing meals are presented on the deity's own dishes at appropriate intervals; fruits must be perfect, without any blemishes. During visiting hours the deity holds court, giving audience to devotees. In the morning, the image is ritually bathed and dressed in sumptuous clothes for the day; at night, it may be put to rest in bedclothes. If it is hot, the deity takes a nap in the afternoon, so arrangements are made for its privacy. For festivals, the deity is carefully paraded through the streets. In Puri's Ratha Yatra, huge crowds of ecstatic devotees pull and push three massive chariots bearing flower-bedecked deities after their yearly bath with perfumed water. Over a million worshipers seek *darshan* of the colossal statues as their chariots are pulled along the parade route. The largest of these teak chariots bears Lord Jagannath; it is 45 feet (13.7 meters) high, with sixteen wooden wheels. Its ponderous journey has entered English vocabulary, misspelled as "juggernaut."

Loving service to the divine makes it real and present. The statue is not just a symbol of the deity; the deity may be experienced through the statue, reciprocating the devotee's attentions. According to Swami Sivasiva Palani:

> It is thought that the subtle essences of these things given in devotion are actually absorbed by the divine, in an invisible and rather mystical process. It's as though we are feeding our God in an inner kind of way. It's thought that if this is done properly, with the right spirit, the right heartfulness, the right mantras, that we capture the attention of the personal Lord and that he actually communes with us through that process, and we with him. Of course, when I say "us" and "him" I connote a dualism that is meant to be transcended in this process.[26]

Ritual fire ceremonies around a **havan**, or sacred fire place, are also conducted by *brahmin* pandits, following ancient Vedic traditions. The Vedic principle of sacrifice was based on the idea that generous offerings to a deity will be rewarded. Fruits, fragrances, mixtures of herbs and grains, and ghee are placed in the fire as offerings to the deities, invoked and praised by chants, with offerings conveyed by Agni, the god of fire. Sitting before the fire, devotees are also reminded of the brightness of the divine and the power of truth which illuminates the darkness. Such havans may be conducted in celebration of a particular deity, or at the behest of a patron for the sake of his health or good fortune.

Death ceremonies are also carried out by fire, as the body is cremated soon after death. Carefully washed, rubbed with fragrant sandalwood paste, and dressed in fresh clothes, it is wrapped in white sheets and carried on a wooden stretcher to a burning ground. Relatives and well-wishers place flowers on the shrouded body and then logs are stacked around it to make a fierce fire. Pandits may chant Vedic verses designed to cleanse it and assist the soul's release from the body and its passage to the spiritual realm. The senior mourner—usually the eldest surviving son—carries a clay pot of water around the body three times, gradually pouring out the water, then dashes the pot to the ground, a dramatic and emotional moment signifying the end of the earthly body. It is also he who then lights the pyre. Alternatively, the shrouded body may be placed in an electric crematorium. Once the burning of the body is complete, survivors take the remaining bits of bone and ash for ritual immersion in the waters of a holy river. Participating in such a ceremony, the mourners are visually assured that the soul has been set free and the body is no more. Cremation is psychologically satisfying in the context of Brahmanic Hinduism, in which the body is regarded as merely a disposable vehicle for the immortal soul.

In addition to public *puja* ceremonies conducted by pandits, home *puja* is an important aspect of Hindu life.

Even the poorest Hindu families have a special room or place for puja *to their favorite deities.*

Nearly every home in India has a shrine with pictures or small statues of various deities, and many have a prayer room set aside for worship. For *puja*, ritual purity is emphasized; the time for prayer and offerings to the deities is after the morning bath or after one has washed in the evening. *Puja* is an everyday observance, although among orthodox families menstruating women are considered unclean and are not allowed to approach the shrines. Otherwise, women as well as men carry on *puja* in their homes. Typically, a small oil lamp and a smoldering stick of incense are reverently waved before the deities' images to please them with light and fragrance. If the devotee or family has a guru, a picture of him or her is usually part of the shrine.

CASTES, DUTIES, AND LIFE GOALS

The **caste** system which still shapes lives in modern India to a considerable extent goes back to the Vedic age. Because the Vedic sacrifices were a reciprocal communion with the gods, priests who performed the public sacrifices had to be carefully trained and maintain high standards of ritual purity. Those so trained—the *brahmins*—comprised a special occupational group. The orderly working of society included a clear division of labor among four major occupational groups, which later became entrenched as castes. These occupational categories applied to men; women were automatically associated with their father's or husband's caste. The *brahmins* were the priests and philosophers, specialists in the life of the spirit. The next group, later called *kshatriyas*, were the nobility of feudal India: kings, warriors, and vassals. Their general function was to guard and preserve the society; they were expected to be courageous and majestic. *Vaishyas* were the economic specialists: farmers and merchants. The *shudra* caste were the manual laborers and artisans. Lower than these original four castes were those "outcastes" who came to be considered "untouchables." They carried on work such as removing human waste and corpses, sweeping streets, and working with leather from the skins of dead cows—occupations that made their bodies and clothing abhorrent to others.

Over time, Vedic religion was increasingly controlled by the *brahmins*, and contact between castes was limited. Caste membership became hereditary. The caste system became a significant aspect of Indian life until its social injustices were attacked in the nineteenth century. One of its opponents was Mahatma Gandhi, who renamed the lowest caste *harijans*, "the children of God." In 1948 the stigma of "untouchability" was legally abolished, though many caste distinctions still linger in modern India. Marriage across caste lines, for instance, is still usually disapproved of.

Despite its abuses, the division of labor represented by the caste system is part of Hinduism's strong emphasis on social duties and sacrifice of individual desires for the sake of social order. The Vedas, other scriptures, and historical customs have all conditioned the Indian people to accept their social roles. These were set out in religious–legal texts such as the Code of Manu, compiled 100–300 CE. In it are laws governing all aspects of life, including the proper conduct of rulers, dietary restrictions, marriage laws, daily rituals, purification rites, social laws, and ethical guidance. It prescribed hospitality to guests and the cultivation of such virtues as contemplation, truthfulness, compassion, nonattachment, generosity,

myreligionlab
Duties of the Four Castes
MANU SMRTI

myreligionlab
Untouchability
MAHATMA GANDHI

pleasant dealings with people, and self-control. It condemned untouchables to living outside villages, eating only from broken dishes. On the other hand, the code proposed charitable giving as the sacred duty of the upper castes, and thus provided a safety net for those at the bottom of this hierarchical system. And common practice did not necessarily follow the guidelines of the religious–legal texts. Whereas the Code of Manu barred *shudras* from owning land, in South India many *shudras* were apparently wealthy and influential landowners. The code prescribed a subservient status to women, but some ancient temples contain stone carvings commemorating women who had endowed them with money in their own names.

myreligionlab
The Faithful Wife
MANU SMRTI

Hospitality to human guests is a duty for people of all castes. To turn someone away from your door without feeding him or at least offering him a drink of water is a great sin, for every person is the deity incarnate. Ceremonies are often held for making offerings to a deity and feeding the public. The head of the household may, toward the end of his life, engage the services of a number of *brahmins* to help complete the requisite 24,000,000 repetitions of the *Gayatrimantra* during his lifetime. Beggars take advantage of belief in sacrifice by saying that those who give to them will be blessed. But the most important sacrifices are considered to be inner sacrifices—giving one's entire self over to the Supreme Reality.

Hinduism also holds up four major goals that define the good life. One is *dharma*, or carrying out one's responsibilities and duties, for the sake of social and cosmic order. A second is *artha*, or success in worldly activities, including the pursuit of wealth and advantage. A third is *kama*, which refers to love and sensual pleasures, and also to aesthetic expression. Many other religious paths regard eroticism as an impediment to spiritual progress, but the *Mahabharata* proposes that *dharma* and *artha* both arise from *kama*, because without desire and creativity there is no striving. The fourth and ultimate goal of life is *moksha*, or liberation from the cycle of death and rebirth. Its attainment marks the end of all the other goals.

LIFE STAGES

The process of attaining spiritual realization or liberation is thought to take at least a lifetime, and probably many lifetimes. Birth as a human being is prized as a chance to advance toward spiritual perfection. In the past, spiritual training was usually available to upper-caste males only; women and *shudras* were excluded. Women have also become *sannyasins*, however, and today an estimated fifteen percent of the ascetics in India are female. Spiritual training for men has historically been preceded by an initiation ceremony in which the boy received the sacred thread, a cord of three threads to be worn across the chest from the left shoulder.

A *brahmin* male's lifespan was ideally divided into four periods of approximately twenty-five years each. For the first twenty-five years he is a chaste student at the feet of a teacher. Next comes the householder stage, during which he is expected to marry, raise a family, and contribute productively to society. After this period, he starts to detach himself from worldly pursuits and to turn to meditation and scriptural study. By the age of seventy-five, he is able to withdraw totally from society and become a *sannyasin*.

Sacred Thread Ceremony

When a boy from an upper-caste Hindu family reaches a certain age he may be formally initiated into Vedic rites and invested with a sacred thread. Although, according to Hindu canonical texts, the sacred thread is meant to be worn by all three upper castes, today the ceremony is associated only with the *brahmin* community.

The rites involved are lengthy and detailed, for the boy must be taught many ancient Vedic rituals. He is initiated in the presence of his relatives, with his father and several pandits playing the major roles in his training, and his mother and other female relatives playing minor roles. Traditionally, this began the *brahmacharya* (student) stage of life, after which he would enter an ashram to study at the feet of his guru until the next stage of his life, during which he would marry and become a householder. Nowadays it is more likely that he will live at home with his parents, but he will at times be involved in sacred rituals, and will always be aware of his special caste status because beneath his outer clothes he will be wearing his sacred thread.

The ceremony may last four to five hours. Once the sacred thread is placed over the boy's left shoulder by his father and the pandits, his training in Vedic rites begins. For instance, he is taught how to pray using Vedic mantras, how to hold his fingers while eating or doing *pranayama* (the yoga of breathing), and how to carry on *havan* (*homa*) fire rituals. His hair is shaved above his forehead to reveal the shining of his inner third eye. He is bathed and dressed in a new *dhoti*, and then carried to the place of the sacred fire by his maternal uncle, while his aunts wave a tray of red-dyed water before him as an auspicious omen. Three white stripes are painted on his forehead and arms, vertical if

he is a devotee of Vishnu or horizontal to identify him as a devotee of Shiva. He washes his father's feet to show his reverence and affection, and then daubs colored powders on them to seek his father's blessings. After formally requesting his father to give him the ancient Gyatri mantra, he, his father and mother, and the pandit huddle under a cloth so that he can receive the mantra in secret. When they emerge, his relatives throw flowers and rice grains, symbolizing longevity and prosperity, over him.

The boy is then given a branch from a *palaasa* tree, which symbolizes the trees under which the ancient *rishis* used to sit. A *tilak* of vermilion is rubbed on his forehead and he is wrapped in a turmeric-dyed cloth, symbolizing purity. He is taken outside to learn how to look at the sun without having his retinas burned, by interlacing his fingers before his eyes.

After prostrating before the sacred fire, he prostrates before his mother, who blesses him. Then he goes to each of his female relatives with a tray, symbolically begging them for alms, for if he had entered an ashram he would have been begging daily for his food. The net result of his initiation is a strengthening of his identity and confidence as a member of what has traditionally been considered the highest spiritual caste in India, pledged to uphold *dharma* in everything he does.

Left: Ram (Vijay Krishna Ramaswamy), age eight, receives his sacred thread in the ancient math *established by Shankara in the ninth century: Sharada Peetam in Karnataka. Center: Carried by his uncle, Ram is painted with horizontal stripes identifying him as a devotee of Shiva. Right: Ram washes his father's feet with water poured by his mother.*

Living as a renunciate, the *sannyasin* is a contemplative who cuts himself off from wife and family, declaring, "No one belongs to me and I belong to no one." Some *sannyasins* take up residence in comfortable temples. Others wander alone with only a water jar, a walking staff, and a begging bowl as possessions; some of them wear no clothes. In silence, the *sannyasin* is supposed to concentrate on practices that will finally release him from *samsara* into cosmic consciousness.

The majority of contemporary Hindu males do not follow this path to its *sannyasin* conclusion in old age, but many Hindus still become *sannyasins*. Some of them have renounced the world at a younger age and joined a monastic order, living in an **ashram**, a retreat community that has developed around a teacher.

THE GURU

myreligionlab
The World of Illusion
RAVI DAS

Nearly every practicing Hindu seeks to place himself or herself at the feet of a spiritual teacher, or **guru**. The title "guru" is applied to venerable spiritual guides. Gurus do not declare themselves as teachers; people are drawn to them because they have achieved spiritual status to which the seekers aspire. Gurus are often regarded as enlightened or "fully realized" individuals. A guru does not provide academic instruction. Rather, he or she gives advice, example, and encouragement to those seeking enlightenment or realization.

> *Anyone and everyone cannot be a guru. A huge timber floats on the water and can carry animals as well. But a piece of worthless wood sinks, if a man sits on it, and drowns him.*
>
> *Ramakrishna[27]*

Many gurus migrated to the West to spread Hindu teachings there. Paramahansa Yogananda's book Autobiography of a Yogi *continues to attract Western followers to Indian religious traditions.*

The Siddha tradition of southern India specializes in "teaching" by *shaktipat*—the power of a glance, word, touch, or thought. A disciple of the late Swami Muktananda describes the effect, referring to him as "Baba" (Father):

When a seeker receives shaktipat, *he experiences an overflowing of bliss within and becomes ecstatic. In Baba's presence, all doubts and misgivings vanish, and one experiences inner contentment and a sense of fulfillment.[28]*

When seekers find their guru, they love and honor him or her as their spiritual parent. The guru does not always behave as a loving parent; often disciples are treated harshly, to test their faith and devotion or to strip away the ego. True devotees are nevertheless grateful for opportunities to serve their guru, out of love. They often bend to touch his or her feet, partly out of humility and partly because great power is thought to emanate from a guru's feet. Humbling oneself before the guru is considered necessary in order to receive the teaching. A metaphor commonly used is that of a cup and a pitcher of water. If the cup (the disciple, or *chela*) is already full, no water (spiritual wisdom) can be poured into it from the pitcher (the guru). Likewise, if the cup is on the same level as the pitcher, there can be no pouring. What is necessary is for the cup to be empty and below the pitcher; then the water can be freely poured into the cup.

WOMEN'S DUTIES

At the level of spiritual ideals, the female is highly venerated in Hinduism, compared to many other religions. Women are thought to make major contributions to the good earthly life, which includes *dharma* (order in society), marital wealth (by bearing sons in a patriarchal society), and the aesthetics of sensual pleasure. Women are auspicious beings, mythologically associated with wealth, beauty, splendor, and grace. As sexual partners to men, they help to activate the spiritualizing life force. No ceremonial sacrifice is complete unless the wife participates as well as the husband.

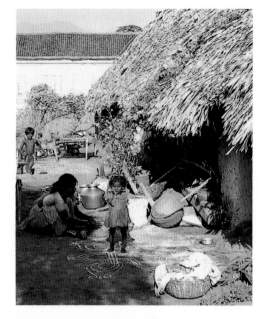

An Indian woman prepares a protective rice-flour pattern on the earth outside her home, honoring the ancient tradition by which her female ancestors created intuitive designs to bring spiritual protection for their families.

In the ideal marriage, husband and wife are spiritual partners. Marriage is a vehicle for spiritual discipline, service, and advancement toward a spiritual goal. Men and women are thought to complement each other, although the ideal of liberation has traditionally been intended largely for the male.

Women were not traditionally encouraged to seek liberation through their own spiritual practices. A woman's role is usually linked to that of her husband, who takes the position of her god and teacher. For many centuries, there was even the hope that a widow would choose to be cremated alive with her dead husband in order to remain united with him after death.

In early Vedic times, women were relatively free and honored members of Indian society, participating equally in important spiritual rituals. But because of social changes, by the nineteenth century wives had become like servants of the husband's family. With expectations that a girl will take a large dowry to a boy's family in a marriage arrangement, girls are such an economic burden that female babies may be intentionally aborted or killed at birth. There are also cases today of women being beaten or killed by the husband's family after their dowry has been handed over.

Nevertheless, many women in contemporary India have been well educated, and many have attained high political positions. As in the past, women are also considered essential to the spiritual protection of their families, for they are thought to have special connections with the deities. Married women carry on daily worship of the deities in their homes, and also fasts and rituals designed to bring good health, prosperity, and long life for their family members.

FASTS, PRAYERS, AND AUSPICIOUS DESIGNS

Orthodox *brahmins* and also common people observe many days of fasting and prayer, corresponding to auspicious points in the lunar and solar cycles or times of danger, such as the four months of the monsoon season. The ancient practice of astrology is so highly regarded that some couples are choosing birth by Caesarean section for the purpose of selecting the most auspicious moment for their child's birth.

Many expressions of Indian spirituality, particularly in rural areas, are not encapsulated within Brahmanic traditions but rather have a timeless existence of their own. Such, for instance, are the homemade designs daily laid out before homes at dawn. They are created by women to protect their household by inviting a deity such as the goddess Lakshmi. Typically made of edible substances, such as rice flour, the designs are soon dismantled by insects and birds, but this is of no concern for they help to fulfill the dharmic requirement that one should feed 1,000 souls every day.

REVERENCE OF TREES AND RIVERS

Practices such as worship under large trees stretch back into prehistory and are apparent in archaeological evidence from the Indus Valley civilization. Such worship continues at countless small shrines today. There is a strong taboo against cutting certain sacred tree species such as the peepul tree, which sprouts wherever it can gain the slightest foothold, often in stone or brick walls, even on the sides of buildings. Whole tracts of virgin forest are kept intact by villagers in some parts of India. There they reverently protect both animal and plant life with the understanding that the area is the home of a deity. These sacred groves are now viewed by environmentalists as important islands of biological diversity.

Not only forests but also hilltops, mountains, and river sources are often viewed as sacred and their natural environment is thus protected to a certain extent. The Narmada River, one of India's most sacred, is regarded by millions of people as a goddess (as are most Indian rivers). Its banks are lined with

A devotee prays before taking a holy bath in the sacred Ganges River.

thousands of temples devoted to Mother Narmada and Lord Shiva. Pilgrims reverently circumambulate the entire 815-mile length of the river, from its source in central India to its mouth in the Gulf of Khambhat, and back again. However, the river and its huge watershed are the subjects of the world's largest water development scheme. The highest of the dams is under construction, creating a reservoir with a final proposed height of 448 feet (136.5 meters). When the reservoir is filled, some 245 villages will be submerged, temples and all. The idea is to capture the water and divert it to drought-ridden areas to benefit people there. However, the inhabitants of the watershed that will be inundated are closely linked to their local sacred landscape. One of them explains, "Our gods cannot move from this place. How can we move without them?"[29] Fierce conflicts have been raging since 1990 between environmentalists and social activists who are fighting the high dams, claiming they will adversely affect at least one million people in the watershed for the sake of vested interests elsewhere, and modernists who regard such high dams, as Nehru said, as "the secular temples of modern India."[30]

An Interview with Somjit Dasgupta

In Hinduism, many forms of dance, song, and instrumental music have evolved as means of spiritual expression. Somjit Dasgupta is a very accomplished Indian musician whose *ragas* softly played on the stringed *sarod* touch a deep place in the soul. His words reflect the importance attached to teacher–pupil lineages in Hindu classical music tradition, and also the reverence that Hindus may feel for their guru:

"My Guru was Radhikamohan Maitreya, whose main instrument was the *sarod*. For music, there has been no distinction between Hindu or Muslim tradition. When the Muslim rulers came here, they preached from the ashrams. Some of the old Hindu musicians were converted and joined the Muslim courts. And some of the Persian musicians who accompanied the sultans learned Indian classical music. By and by, some court instruments were born. But the old instruments were still there, and some of the essence of meditation was carried to the courts.

"In our old Sanskrit texts, it is written, 'There is no education, no learning beyond music.' In the Indian tradition, it is *sangeet*—collective worship and singing.

"Meditation was there in other parts of the world also, but it was very special in this part of the world. Meditation means to sit and see within yourself. Once I asked my Guru, 'What did you achieve in your life? You are highly regarded by almost all the big musicians. They touch your feet, but you are sitting here. You did not play in public concerts. We have our *Gurubhais* [pupils of the same Guru] all over the world, but what I feel is that you are not very famous. What have you achieved?' He said, 'Nobody ever asked me that. But this is a little boy [I was only fourteen at the time]. I will answer that later.'

"After I passed through school and entered college, one day he said 'Acha, Somjit, one day you asked me one thing. I was telling you many things regarding the social status of men and women and such things, but I also told you about this soil, which can give the world the things that come from the spiritual light.'

"Then he told me, 'What do you mean by sound? Sound is some cluster of frequencies that you are hearing. In that way, I am Radhikamohan Maitreya: I am a cluster of frequencies. My body is constructed out of that particular frequency. And you are Somjit Dasgupta. Some other set of frequencies created you. That's why your self and my self are joined in different ways, giving us different personalities. But our aim is to go back to the primordial frequency, through this *sadhana*, this spiritual practice. Everybody in every *sadhana* has to go through music. The *Ramayana* and the *Mahabharat* were sung; all the saints could sing. With our finger touch, by Guru's grace, our aim is to reach that primordial frequency. And there, there is no myself. No self is there. That is eternity. There is no "you" and "other" feeling. This thing my Guru gave me. I cannot say it is an achievement. It is as though you are going back to your father's place. It's a huge joy, joy and joy.' I asked, 'What is there?' Then he said, 'Some day I will tell you. You asked me, and after four years I am saying this to you. I will tell you later what is there.'

"Then he told me about one song, which says, 'The same single *Omkar* [a name referring to the Ultimate Reality as primordial vibration] is spread throughout the world. It has no form, no dimensions. In the primordial frequency there is nothing, nobody, only *Omkar*. When I see That personally, I enjoy That personally, I feel That personally, then only can I think about the Almighty.'

"He also told me about another song from the *drupad* musical tradition, a song which contains the seed, the essence. It says, '*Chaitanya*—the primordial sensations, presence, and sensitivity within me—is eternal, and very calm and quiet. *Bindu* is where you touch to experience that *Chaitanya*. When you are touching your instrument, that is your touching point. Beyond all these things is that same existence, that same primordial frequency.'

"He taught me fourteen songs about the Guru, containing the inner essence of *dharma*. One says, 'There is no knowledge beyond the Guru. There is no spiritual practice, no meditation beyond the Guru. All kinds of inner enlightened knowledge finish in eternity: There my Guru stays, with all the blessings.'

"Our work is not to perform on the stage or anything like that. It is that whatever you get from your Guru, your entire existence is to pass that on, so that this teaching can go on and on and on, and give that essence for the future. Maybe a very worthy person can come who can achieve something much more than me, if I keep this teaching intact. So the main thing is to keep this teaching alive. The rest is up to the Guru, and up to the Almighty."[31]

High dams are not the only threat to sacred rivers. Religious practices themselves may lead to high levels of water pollution. Mass bathing on auspicious occasions is accompanied by wastes, such as butter oil, flowers, and human excreta (contrary to scriptural injunctions about proper behavior in sacred rivers). The remains of dead bodies reverently immersed in the sacred rivers may be incompletely cremated. Immersion of images of Ganesh or Durga on holy days as a symbol of purification has become a major source of water pollution. In one year alone, ritual immersion of idols in Calcutta added to the Hoogli River an estimated seventeen tons of varnish and thirty-two tons of paints, which contained manganese, lead, mercury, and chromium.[32]

PILGRIMAGES

Pilgrimages to holy places and sacred rivers are thought to be special opportunities for personal purification and spiritual elevation. Millions of pilgrims yearly undertake strenuous climbs to remote mountain sites that are thought to be blessed by the divine. One of the major pilgrimage sites is Amarnath Cave. At an altitude of 11,090 foot (3,380 meters) in the Himalayas of Kashmir, ice has formed a giant stalagmite, which is highly revered as a Shiva lingam. Pilgrims may have been trekking to this holy place in the high Himalayas for up to 3,000 years. The 14,800-foot (45-kilometer) footpath over a glacier is so dangerous that 250 people were killed by freak storms and landslides in 1996, but in subsequent years tens of thousands of devotees have continued to undertake the pilgrimage. Similarly, Shaktas trek to *shaktipithas*; these fifty-one pilgrimage spots on the Indian subcontinent are thought to mark abodes of the goddess or places where parts of her body now rest.

Millions of Hindus undertake difficult pilgrimages to worship at mountain shrines each year.

The places where great saints and teachers have lived also automatically become places of pilgrimage, during their lives and after they pass on. It is felt that their powerful vibrations still permeate and bless these sites. One such place is the holy mountain of Arunachala in southern India. The great saint Ramana Maharshi (1879–1951) lived there so absorbed in Ultimate Consciousness that he neither talked nor ate and had to be force-fed by another holy man. But the needs of those who gathered around him drew out his compassion and wisdom, and he spontaneously counseled them on their spiritual needs.

FESTIVALS

Hinduism honors the divine in so many forms that almost every day a religious celebration is being held in some part of India. Sixteen religious holidays are honored by the central government so that everyone can leave work to join in the throngs of worshipers. The holidays are calculated partially on a lunar calendar, so dates vary from year to year. Most Hindu festivals express spirituality in its happiest aspects. Group energy attracts the gods to overcome evils, and humorous abandon helps merrymakers to forget their fears.

On a midwinter night in northern India, people happily celebrate Lohari by building a bonfire and throwing popcorn, peanuts, and sesame candies into it. The feeling is that one is symbolically throwing away evils, and at the same time invoking blessings for the year to come. In particular, families who have given birth to a male child during the past year perform this ceremony for his auspicious future.

Holi is the riotously joyful celebration of the death of winter and the return of colorful spring. Its many attributed meanings illustrate the great diversity within Hinduism (see Box on next page).

In the villages of India, all-night singing of sacred songs often marks special holidays. Women have their own repertoire and improvisations.

Holi

The jolliest of all Hindu festivals is Holi, celebrated at the time of winter's death and the advent of spring. It falls on the first full moon of the lunar month Phagun (late February or early March in the solar calendar). The major activity is throwing colored powder or squirting water paint with wild abandon. This may not seem spiritual when measured by the standards of more staid religions, and people may not even be sure exactly what is being celebrated. Indeed, the same wild flinging of paint is given different meanings in different parts of India, illustrating the great variety of ways that are collectively referred to as "Hinduism."

Apparently Holi has been celebrated since prehistoric times. The earliest colors were made from natural plants that are also used in traditional Ayurvedic medicine to ward off viral fevers and colds, such as yellow-dyeing turmeric powder. Psychologically, Holi's effect is rejuvenating and harmonizing, as social taboos are transcended and people from all levels rub or throw paint on each other. This is a major, albeit temporary, change from the usual taboos according to which males and females, high and low castes, do not touch each other.

Vaishnava devotees relate Holi to the story of Prahlad, a young follower of Vishnu. His father was Hiranyakashipu, king of demons. Hiranyakashipu became so proud that he attacked heaven and earth and demanded that everyone worship him instead of the gods. However, his own son Prahlad persisted in worshiping Vishnu. Hiranyakashipu tried to get him killed by poison, by elephants, and by snakes, but

Prahlad survived all the attacks. Then Hiranyakashipu enlisted the help of his sister Holika, who had a magic shawl that protected its wearer from fire. He ordered Prahlad to sit on his aunt's lap in a fire, expecting his son to burn to death while Holika in her shawl would be unharmed. Instead, the shawl flew off Holika and onto Prahlad, who had prayed to Vishnu for safety. Thus many Vaishnavites begin their Holi celebration by building big fires to rejoice over the burning of the demoness Holika, for whom the festival is named.

Krishna worshipers associate Holi with the love of Radha for Krishna, especially in spring, the season of love. It is thought that Krishna played Holi mischievously with the *gopis*, and when he criticized Radha because her skin was not as dark as his, his mother put Holi colors on her face to darken it.

Yet another Krishna legend has been linked with Holi. According to this, at the time of Krishna's birth his uncle Kans, king of winter, ordered that all babies be murdered to avoid Krishna's future threat to his power. A demoness was sent to suckle Krishna to death, but Krishna, recognizing her, instead sucked out all her lifeblood, whereupon she died. Some Krishna worshipers therefore burn the demoness in effigy as well as spraying colors, singing, and dancing to celebrate Holi at the onset of spring.

To Shiva worshipers, Holi commemorates a story about Shiva. According to this, Kamadeva, god of love, was implored by Parvati to help her get Shiva's attention. Shiva was deep in meditation when Kamadeva shot his weapon at him. At this, Shiva opened his third eye (the all-seeing eye in the center of the forehead), whose gaze was so powerful that Kamadeva was burned to ashes. He was later restored to life at Parvati's request, and Shiva and Parvati were married. In this story, winter is the time of meditation, and the coming of spring signals fertile new life and fulfillment.

Backed by a variety of legends, Holi is celebrated with such vigor that some revelers take it as an excuse for drunken and destructive behavior. Furthermore, environmental groups are now pointing out that the industrial dyes used for Holi powder can be quite toxic. However, like those who are trying to educate the public not to shoot off fireworks on Divali to avoid extreme air pollution, these groups have had little effect on people's exuberant, carefree ways of celebrating the Hindu holidays.

In July or August a special day, Naga Panchami, is devoted to the *nagas*, or snakes. Snakes were considered powerful gods by the indigenous peoples, and the tradition persists. In southern Indian villages, where they are especially honored, thousands of live snakes are caught and exhibited by brave handlers. Worshipers sprinkle vermilion and rice on the hoods of cobras, which are considered especially sacred. On Naga Panchami farmers abstain from plowing to avoid disrupting snake-holes.

In August or September, Vaishnavites celebrate Krishna's birthday (Janmashtami). Devotees fast and keep vigil until midnight, retelling stories of Krishna's life or reading his enlightened wisdom from the *Bhagavad-Gita*. In some places Krishna's image is placed in a cradle and lovingly rocked. Elsewhere, pots of milk, curds, and butter are strung high above the ground to be seized by young men who form human pyramids to get to them. They romp about with the pots, drinking and spilling their contents like Krishna, playful stealer of the milk products he loved.

Janmashtami is often celebrated by placing an image of baby Krishna in a decorated swing. Everyone takes turns to pull the cord and lovingly rock Krishna.

At the end of summer, it is Ganesh who is honored, especially in western and southern India, during Ganesh Chaturti. Special potters make elaborate clay images of the jovial elephant-headed remover of obstacles, son of Parvati who formed him from her body's dirt and sweat, and set him to stand guard while she bathed. When he wouldn't let Shiva in, her angry spouse smashed the boy's head into a thousand pieces. Parvati demanded that the boy be restored to life with a new head, but the first one found was that of a baby elephant. To soothe Parvati's distress at the peculiarity of the transplant, Shiva granted Ganesh the power of removing obstacles. The elephant-headed god is now the first to be invoked in all rituals. After days of being sung to and offered sweets, the Ganesh images are carried to a body of water and bidden farewell, with prayers for an easy year.

At the end of the Durga Puja, images of the ten-armed vanquisher of evil are carried to the river and consigned to the deep, so that she may return to her mate Shiva, who awaits her in the Himalayas.

In different parts of India the first nine or ten days of Asvina, the lunar month corresponding to September or October, are dedicated either to the Durga Puja (in which elaborate images of the many-armed goddess celebrate her powers to vanquish the demonic forces) or to Dussehra (which marks Rama's nine nights of worshiping Durga before killing Ravana on the tenth day). The theme of both Durga Puja and Dussehra is the triumph of good over evil.

Divali, the happy four-day festival of lights, is twenty days later, on the night of the new moon. Variously explained as the return of Rama after his exile, the *puja* of Lakshmi (goddess of wealth, who visits only clean homes), and the New Year of those following one of the Indian calendars, it is a time for tidying business establishments and bringing financial records up to date, cleaning houses and illuminating them with oil lamps, wearing new clothes, gambling, feasting, honoring clay images of Lakshmi and Ganesh, and setting off fireworks, often to the point of severe air pollution.

Initially more solemn is Mahashivaratri, a day of fasting and a night of keeping vigil to earn merit with Shiva. During the ascetic part of the observance, many pilgrims go to sacred rivers or special tanks

Bridges are constructed over the Ganges River at Haridwar to help accommodate huge crowds during the Kumbha Mela.

of water for ritual bathing. Shiva lingams and statues are venerated, and the faithful stay awake throughout the night, chanting and telling stories of their Lord. In one of these, a discussion between Brahma, Vishnu, and Shiva leads to Shiva's manifesting as a pillar of fire and challenging the others to touch its ends, which they will not do. A reformist group, Arya Samaj, decries what it considers superstition and idolatry and honors the day as the end of a week-long celebration of its reform. Its members carry out Vedic fire sacrifices and hold spiritual talks, throwing personal offerings into the fire on the last day.

Every few years, millions of Hindus of all persuasions gather for the immense Kumbha Mela. It is held alternately at four sacred spots where drops of the holy nectar of immortality are said to have fallen. On one day in 2001, in what has been recorded as the largest ever gathering of human beings for a single purpose, over twenty-five million people amassed at the point near Allahabad where the Jumna River meets the sacred Ganges and the invisible Saraswati, the sacred river that dried up long ago but is still considered invisibly present. There they took a purifying bath in icy waters on the most auspicious date, as determined by astrologers. Among the Kumbha Mela pilgrims are huge processions of ascetic *sadhus* from various orders, many of whom leave their retreats only for this festival. They gather to discuss religious matters and also social problems, which sometimes leads to revisions of Hindu codes of conduct. Many of the lay pilgrims are poor people who undergo great hardships to reach the site. A typical pilgrim, an illiterate woman from West Bengal, traveled to Haridwar with her family in a crowded bus, slept in the open in the cold, and was fed free meals in immense tents set up by philanthropical groups and families. She explained, "We are poor, but we have enough. I asked God not for money but for peace and salvation."[33]

Hinduism in the modern world

Hinduism did not develop in India in isolation. Christianity may have put down roots in India as long ago as 70 CE. Muslims began taking over certain areas beginning in the eighth century CE; during the sixteenth and seventeenth centuries a large area was ruled by the Muslim Mogul emperors. Islam and Hinduism generally co-existed, despite periods of intolerance, along with Buddhism and Jainism, which had also grown up within India. Indian traders carried some aspects of Hinduism to Java and Bali, where it survives today with a unique Balinese flavor.

When the Mogul Empire collapsed, European colonialists gradually moved in. Ultimately the British dominated, and in 1857 India was officially placed under direct British rule. Christian missionaries set about correcting abuses they perceived in certain Hindu practices, such as widow-burning and the caste system. But they also taught those who were being educated in their schools that Hinduism was "intellectually incoherent and ethically unsound."[34] Some Indians believed them and drifted away from their ancient tradition.

MODERN MOVEMENTS

To counteract Western influences, Mahatma ("Great Soul") Gandhi (1869–1948) encouraged grassroots nationalism, emphasizing that the people's strength lay in awareness of spiritual truth and in nonviolent resistance to military or industrial oppression. He claimed that these qualities were the essence of all religions, including Hinduism, which he considered the universal religion.

In addition to being made a focus for political unity, Hinduism itself was revitalized by a number of spiritual leaders. One of these was Ramakrishna (1836–1886), who was a devotee of the Divine Mother in the form of Kali. Eschewing ritual, he communicated with her through intense love. He practiced Tantric disciplines and the *bhavanas* (types of loving relationships). These brought him spiritual powers, spiritual insight, and reportedly a visible brilliance, but he longed only to be a vehicle for pure devotion:

> *I seek not, good Mother, the pleasures of the senses! I seek not fame! Nor do I long for those powers which enable one to do miracles! What I pray for, O good Mother, is pure love for Thee—love for Thee untainted by desires, love without alloy, love that seeketh not the things of the world, love for Thee that welleth up unbidden out of the depths of the immortal soul!*[35]

Ramakrishna worshiped the divine through many Hindu paths, as well as Islam and Christianity, and found the same One in them all. Intoxicated with the One, he had continual visions of the Divine Mother and ecstatically worshiped her in unorthodox, uninhibited ways. For instance, once he fed a cat some food

Ramakrishna, the great 19th-century mystic, recognized the divine as being both formless and manifested in many forms, and also as transcending both form and formlessness.

that was supposed to be a temple offering for the Divine Mother, for she revealed herself to him in everything, including the cat. He also placed his spiritual bride, Sarada Devi, in the chair reserved for the deity, honoring her as the Great Goddess.

> *Do not care for doctrines, do not care for dogmas, or sects, or churches, or temples; they count for little compared with the essence of existence in each [person], which is spirituality. ... Earn that first, acquire that, and criticize no one, for all doctrines and creeds have some good in them.*
>
> *Ramakrishna*[36]

Vivekananda was a brilliant spiritual teacher who brought Hinduism to the attention of the West when he spoke at the World Parliament of Religions in 1893. When he returned to India, he founded a mission to spread the teachings of his teacher, Ramakrishna.

The pure devotion and universal spiritual wisdom Ramakrishna embodied inspired what is now known as the Ramakrishna Movement, or the Vedanta Society. A famous disciple, named Vivekananda (1863–1902), carried the message of Hinduism to the world beyond India and excited so much interest in the West that Hinduism became a global religion. He also reintroduced Indians to the profundities of their great traditions. He taught detachment from material perspectives, in favor of evolved spiritual understanding:

> *What we want is neither happiness nor misery. Both make us forget our true nature; both are chains, one iron, one gold; behind both is the Atman, who knows neither happiness nor misery. These are states, and states must ever change; but the nature of the soul is bliss, peace, unchanging.*[37]

Within India Hinduism has also been influenced by reform movements such as Brahmo Samaj and Arya Samaj. The former defended Hindu mysticism and *bhakti* devotion to an immanent deity. The latter advocated a return to what it saw as the purity of the Vedas, rejecting image worship, devotion to a multiplicity of deities, priestly privileges, and popular rituals.

In addition to religious reform movements, Hindu tradition is currently being challenged by social reform movements facing issues of gender, caste, and poverty. Feminists are criticizing the traditional ideal that all women should marry and dedicate themselves to serving and obeying their husbands. Dalit activists are attacking old caste distinctions that tend to keep them marginalized and poor. Since the late twentieth century, the government of India has thus reserved seats in educational institutions and government posts for people of "scheduled castes."

GLOBAL HINDUISM

Hinduism is also experiencing vibrant growth beyond the Indian subcontinent, partly among expatriates and partly among converts from other faiths. For the past hundred years, many self-proclaimed gurus have left India to develop followings in other countries. Some were discovered to be fraudulent, with scandalous private behavior or motives of wealth and power. Despite increased Western wariness of gurus, some of the exported movements have continued to grow.

Many non-Indians discovered Hinduism by reading *Autobiography of a Yogi*, by Paramahansa Yogananda (1893–1952). The book describes his intriguing spiritual experiences with Indian gurus and also explains principles of Hinduism in

myreligionlab
Vision of the Mother
YOGANANDA

Dharmic Principles: The Swadhyaya Movement

Today there are said to be twenty million people in 100,000 villages in India who are beneficiaries of a silent social revolution based on the principles of the ancient Hindu scriptures, especially the *Bhagavad-Gita*. The movement is called Swadhyaya. The term means self-study, using traditional scriptural teachings as a means for critically analyzing oneself in order to improve. On this basis, villagers and village life have profoundly improved.

The work began in the 1950s, as scriptural scholar Pandurang Shastri Athavale, known by his followers as "Dada" (elder brother), determined that the *Gita* was "capable of resolving the dilemmas of modern man and solving the problems of material life, individual and social."[38] He founded a school near Mumbai, refusing until today to accept any financial help from the government or outside funding agency, insisting that "those institutions which depend upon others' favors are never able to achieve anything worthwhile or carry out divine work."[39] He named the buildings for the ancient sages who have inspired people to live according to Vedic principles. It was they who recognized that within each person is a divine spark whose realization gives them the energy and guidance with which to uplift themselves. As Dada once observed, the sage who wrote the *Ramayana* is:

> *virtually urging us to take Ram—the awareness that the Lord is with us and within us all the time—to every home and every heart, as this alone will provide the confidence and the strength to the weakest of the weak and will bring joy and fragrance into the life of every human being.[40]*

Realization of the divine within themselves also leads to realization of the divine within others, which is the beginning of social harmony and cooperation.

The principle upon which Dada's social development work is centered is *bhakti*, or selfless devotion. He inspired his students to pay devotional visits to towns and villages in Gujarat state. They carried their own food and asked for nothing from the people. They simply met the inhabitants one to one and spoke of the divine love which made them reach out to distant places. After years of regular visits and assurance that gratefulness to God and brotherly love was developing among the villagers, they allowed them to build simple hut temples of local materials, devotional places for people of all castes and creeds.

In gratitude toward the in-dwelling God for being present when they go to their farms, giving them energy to work, *swadhyayees* feel that God is entitled to a share in the produce. They therefore bring a portion of their income to the hut temples to be distributed among the most needy, as the benevolence of God.

Believing in work as worship, the villagers were also inspired to set aside a portion of land to be farmed in common, as "God's farm." All give a certain number of days of volunteer service on the farm, in grateful service to God. The harvests are treated as "impersonal wealth." One-third of the money is distributed directly to the needy; two-thirds are put into a community trust for long-term needs to help people stand on their own feet.

The movement spreads from village to village, as missionaries who have seen the positive results of the program voluntarily go to other areas to tell the people there about it. When Swadhyaya volunteers first appeared in fishing villages on India's west coast, they found the people were spending what income they had on gambling and liquor. Now, the same people place a portion of their earnings from fishing and navigation at the feet of God, as it were. They have created such a surplus that they have been able to purchase community fishing boats. These are manned by volunteers on a rotation basis, with everyone eager to take a turn, and the income is distributed impersonally as God's graceful beneficence to those in need.

In addition, *swadhyayees* have created "tree temples," in which trees are planted in formerly barren lands, and have developed cultural programs, sports clubs, family stores, dairy produce centers, children's centers, centers for domestic skills, and discussion centers for intellectuals and professionals. Through water-harvesting by recharging over 90,000 wells and constructing over 500 percolation tanks, *swadhyayees* by their own skill and labor are generating additional annual farm produce worth some 300 million US dollars for small and medium-sized farmers. They have also introduced soakpit systems for disposal of household drainwater and refuse, thus improving village hygiene and health.

Throughout the growing network of *swadhyayees*, there is no hierarchy and no paid staff. Those whose lives have been improved by inner study and devotional service become enthusiastic volunteers and living demonstrations that people are happiest when dharmic principles are placed ahead of self-interest.

loving fashion. Yogananda traveled to the United States and began a movement, the California-based Self-Realization Fellowship, which has survived his death and is still growing, with centers, temples, and living communities in forty-six countries. Their first goal, as set forth by Paramahansa Yogananda, is to "disseminate among the nations a knowledge of definite scientific techniques for attaining direct personal experience of God."[41]

Another still-flourishing example of an exported movement is the Netherlands-based Transcendental Meditation (TM) movement, which was begun by Maharishi Mahesh Yogi (d. 2008) in the 1960s. For $2500, his disciples teach people secret mantras and assert that repeating the mantra for twenty minutes twice each day will bring great personal benefits. These range from enhanced athletic prowess to increased satisfaction with life. By paying $2000 more, advanced practitioners can also learn how to "fly." That is, they take short hops into the air while sitting cross-legged. The organization claims a success rate of sixty-five percent in ending drug and alcohol addiction and asserts that groups of yogic "fliers" temporarily lowered crime rates in Washington, D.C. and conflicts in West Asia, claims that have not been independently verified. TM is now a vast global organization, complete with luxurious health spas in Europe, a Vedic "theme park" near Niagara Falls in Canada, Vedic-based development projects in Africa, colleges, universities, and Maharishi Schools of Management in many countries, an ashram for 10,000 people in India, and ongoing plans to build large "peace palaces" near cities around the world where people could receive training in TM and thus help to bring peace in the collective unconscious of the world, through the "Maharishi effect."

Another rather unlikely success story is found in ISKCON, the International Society for Krishna Consciousness. In 1965, the Indian guru A. C. Bhaktivedanta Swami Prabhupada arrived in the United States, carrying the asceticism and *bhakti* devotion of Shri Chaitanya's tradition of Krishna worship from India to the heart of Western materialistic culture. Adopting the dress and diet of Hindu

Devotees of Lord Krishna ecstatically sing his praises in Western settings—here, in London.

Mata Amritanandamayi comforts a man after he has been operated on for a brain tumor and also embraces his father with her left arm.

monks and nuns, his initiates lived in temple communities. Their days began at 4 a.m. with meditation, worship, chanting of the names of Krishna and Ram, and scriptural study, with the aim of turning from a material life of sense gratification to one of transcendent spiritual happiness. During the day, they chanted and danced in the streets to introduce others to the bliss of Krishna, distributed literature (especially Swami Prabhupada's illustrated and esteemed translation of the *Bhagavad-Gita*), attracted new devotees, and raised funds. Despite schisms and scandals, the movement has continued since Swami Prabhupada's death in 1977, and is growing in strength in various countries, particularly in India and eastern Europe. In England, followers have turned a great mansion into a huge ISKCON temple, which also serves Indian immigrants as a place to celebrate major festivals.

An American devotee who is a descendant of the Ford automobile family is building a large village industries park, tourism hospitality complex, and Vedic planetarium near the global headquarters of ISKCON in India. The planetarium is designed to research and showcase the scientific accuracy of ancient Vedic descriptions of the cosmos.

Some contemporary gurus are also enjoying great global popularity. One of the most famous at present is Mata Amritanandamayi, a seemingly tireless, mother-ly saint from South India who takes people from all walks of life into her arms. In large-scale gatherings around the world, the "hugging saint" may embrace up to 70,000 people at a stretch, through the night and into the next day. She encourages her "children" to find personal solace and compassion for others through worship of the divine in any form. Many of her followers regard "Amma" herself as the personification of the Divine Mother.

myreligionlab

Awakening
of Universal
Motherhood
MATA
AMRITANANDAMAYI

Dr. Karan Singh

Globally active in an extraordinary number of public posts and projects, Dr. Karan Singh is also one of the world's most respected spokesmen for Hinduism. He was born wealthy, as heir to the maharaja of Jammu and Kashmir, but has never retired from a life of intense public service. In fact, he turned over his entire princely inheritance to the service of the people of India and converted his palace into a museum and library, which houses his priceless collection of artworks and his personal library of over 20,000 books.

Dr. Karan Singh's political life began in 1949 when he was only eighteen years old, for his father appointed him regent of Jammu and Kashmir, as requested by Prime Minister Jawaharlal Nehru. Eventually he was elected to the governorship of the area, thus becoming both the last representative of the old hereditary lineage and the first of the new democratic era. In 1967, he became the youngest person ever to become a central cabinet minister in India, in the cabinet of Prime Minister Indira Gandhi. Over the years, he has held three ministerial posts, as well as many other posts, including being the Chancellor of Jammu and Kashmir University, founder of the International Centre of Science, Culture and Consciousness, President of the People's Commission on Environment and Development, Chairman of the Temple of Understanding, and a member of the international steering committee of the Global Forum of Parliamentarians and Spiritual Leaders on Human Survival.

A brilliant orator, Dr. Karan Singh quotes extensively and effectively from the Vedas in his talks and says he has been deeply influenced by them—in particular, the *Upanishads*. He states:

The Upanishads *are the high-water mark of Hindu philosophy. They are texts of tremendous wisdom and power. They represent some of the deepest truths with regard to the all-pervasiveness of the divine. One is the concept that every individual encapsulates a spark of the divine, the* atman. *There is also the concept of the human race as an extended family. Then there is the concept that "The truth is one; the wise call it by many names." That is the ultimate unity of all religions. We also have the concept of the welfare of the many, the happiness of the many. Thus, there are universal*

concepts in the Vedanta which have been of tremendous inspiration to me in all the work that I do in interfaith.

Busy though he is, Dr. Karan Singh always takes time daily to perform his private *puja* (worship ceremonies). He is a worshiper of Lord Shiva. Before Lord Shiva, he also worships the goddess, as is common in Hindu tradition. He feels that acknowledging the feminine aspect of the divine is a very important part of Hindu worship, as is the freedom of choice of one's favorite deity:

My personal devotion is to Lord Shiva; my philosophical background is the Vedanta. As part of my daily routine, I have my own puja. *I do it in the morning, again at night before going to bed, and in the course of the day. Ours is not a religion where you go once a week to a church and that's it. Hinduism is supposed to be something which permeates your entire consciousness. Therefore these* puja *sessions are supposed to be ways of reminding yourself of the Divinity.*

Despite his personal devotion to Lord Shiva, Dr. Karan Singh emphasizes that Hinduism supports acceptance of all manifestations of the divine, and therefore all religions. He asserts:

The exclusivism or monopolistic tendencies in religions who claim that they have the sole agency in the sphere of the divine is not acceptable in this day and age. We have got to accept the fact that there are multiple paths to the divine. We have to not only accept them—we have to respect whoever is traveling on his or her path. That has come to me particularly from the Vedanta tradition.

Although Dr. Karan Singh has often been deeply involved in government, he is free from the taint of corruption and scandal that mars so many political careers. He attributes his clear reputation partly to the fact that the was born into "favorable financial circumstances," and also to his religious upbringing:

Not being corrupt is part of the basic religious teachings around the world. We are brought up on the stories of Raja Harish Chandra, who gave up everything for the sake of truth, and Sri Rama, who gave up everything for the sake of his father's word, and so on. Those sort of mythological stories based on truth and the quest for truth are very strong in wisdom. And if you are pursuing the path of truth, then I presume that automatically rules out your being corrupt.[42]

HINDU IDENTITY

At the same time that Hinduism is reaching around the world, some Hindu groups within India are giving Hinduism a nationalistic thrust. In particular, the RSS—Rashtriya Svayamsevak Sangh—arose early in the twentieth century, espousing Hindu cultural renewal in order to combat the ills of modernity and return to an idealized past referred to as "Ram Rajya," the legendary kingdom of Lord Ram, when Hindu virtues were maintained by a perfect ruler. This movement gave organized expression to the ideals of V. D. Savarkar, who wrote of an ancient Hindu nation and *Hindutva* ("Hinduness"), excluding Muslims and Christians as aliens in India, in contrast to historical evidence that what is called Hinduism is a noncentralized, evolving composite of variegated ways of worship.

Secularism is officially established by India's constitution, which recognizes the multicultural, multireligious fabric of the country and does not confer favored political status on any religion. But according to what could be called Hindu "fundamentalists," in the name of secularism people are being robbed of their religious values and identity, which the RSS, the religious organization Vishva Hindu Parishad (VHP), and political parties such as the Bharatiya Janata Party (BJP) say they are trying to restore.

A major focus of these activities has been the small town of Ayodhya, which according to Hindu mythology is the birthplace of Lord Ram. According to Hindutva belief, Babur, the Muslim Mogul ruler, had the main temple commemorating Ram's birthplace torn down and the Babri Mosque built on its ruins. Firm believers attempted to take matters into their own hands and redress this perceived insult to their holy place. In 1992, some 200,000 Hindus managed to enter Ayodhya and tear down the Babri Mosque. This act was followed by a spate of Hindu–Muslim violence throughout India.

The RSS maintains tens of thousands of branches in Indian villages and cities where Hindu men and boys meet for group games, songs, lectures, and prayers to the Hindu nation, conceived as the Divine Mother. The leader of the RSS has publicly urged throwing all Christian missionaries out of India and has asserted that all Indians are actually Hindus. There are estimated to be 12,000 RSS schools in India in which children are educated according to the Hindutva agenda.

Political affiliates of the RSS—particularly the BJP (Bharatiya Janata Party)—have become very powerful in Indian politics. It was the leading party in the central government in power in 2002 when one coach of a train carrying volunteers who were seeking to illegally construct a new temple in Ayodhya caught fire in the state of Gujarat and was surrounded by a presumably Muslim mob. Inside the coach, fifty-nine Hindus burned to death, a horror that was followed by terrible inter-religious violence. Perhaps 2,000 people, most of them Muslims, were killed by mobs while local officials did little to stop them.

Some Hindu groups are also trying to woo Christian converts back to Hinduism and are actively opposing Christianity in India. Some **"untouchable"** Hindus—who prefer to be called "Dalits"—have converted to Christianity, Buddhism, or Islam because those religions do not make caste distinctions. Christians in particular have offered social services for the poor such as schools and hospitals. An estimated fifty percent of all Christians in India were formerly of low-caste origin.

myreligionlab
Hindu-ness
V. D. SAVARKAR

myreligionlab
The Secular Face
of Hinduism
JOSEPH VELLARINGATT

In recent times, opposition to Christian conversion has sometimes turned quite violent, as it did in 2008, when homes of thousands of Indian Christians were burned in the state of Orissa, apparently by Hindu extremists. Tensions also continue to run high between Hindus and Muslims in Kashmir, where efforts to bring Kashmiri independence from India often pit Hindus and Muslims against each other. Political issues are often obscured by divisions along religious lines, and peace continues to elude the people of the beautiful Kashmir valley.

Such conflicts are not in keeping with the Hindu ideal of tolerance for many ways to the divine. Although tensions between religions exist in many regions of India, what predominates is the spirit of accommodation with which the various communities have lived side by side for hundreds of years.

The Indian Supreme Court has formally defined Hindu beliefs in a way that affirms universality rather than exclusiveness. According to the court's definition, to be a Hindu means:

1 Acceptance and reverence for the Vedas as the foundation of Hindu philosophy;
2 A spirit of tolerance, and willingness to understand and appreciate others' points of view, recognizing that truth has many sides;
3 Acceptance of the belief that vast cosmic periods of creation, maintenance, and dissolution continuously recur;
4 Acceptance of belief in reincarnation;
5 Recognition that paths to truth and salvation are many;
6 Recognition that there may be numerous gods and goddesses to worship, without necessarily believing in worship through idols;
7 Unlike other religions, absence of belief in a specific set of philosophic concepts.[43]

Mahatma Gandhi, the father of independent India, asserted that Hinduism's special identity lies in its inclusiveness, dynamism, and continuing search for truth:

Hinduism is a living organism liable to growth and decay, and subject to the laws of Nature. It is and is not based on scriptures. It does not derive its authority from one book. It takes a provincial form in every province, but the inner substance is retained everywhere. The Vedas, the Upanishads, the Smritis *[authoritative but nonrevealed scriptures], the Puranas, and the* Itihasas *[historical epics] did not arise at one and the same time. Each grew out of the necessities of particular periods. Hinduism abhors stagnation. Every day we add to our knowledge of the power of* Atman, *and we shall keep on doing so.*[44]

Suggested reading

The Bhagavad-Gita, available in numerous translations. Central teachings about how to realize the immortal soul.

Bryant, Edwin, *The Quest for the Origins of Vedic Culture: The Indo-Aryan Migration Debate*, Oxford: Oxford University Press, 2001. Detailed survey of the complex inter-disciplinary, international debates about the origins of Vedic civilization.

Chapple, Christopher Key and Mary Evelyn Tucker, eds, *Hinduism and Ecology*, Cambridge, Massachusetts: Harvard University Press, 2000. Perceptive contemporary essays about the relationship between various Hindu paths and environmental protection.

Eck, Diana, *Darsan: Seeing the Divine Image in India*, second edition, Chambersburg, Pennsylvania: Anima Books, 1985. A lively explanation of deity images and how the people of India respond to them.

Jayakar, Pupul, *The Earth Mother*, New Delhi: Penguin Books, 1989. Explorations of ways of worshiping the goddess in rural India.

Lopez, Donald S., Jr., ed., *Religions of India in Practice*, Princeton, New Jersey: Princeton University Press, 1995. An interesting anthology of popular texts with contemporary rather than stereotypical understandings, primarily from Hinduism but also including Buddhist, Jain, and Sikh material.

Prabhavananda, Swami, *Spiritual Heritage of India*, Madras: Sri Ramakrishna Math, undated. Classic explanation of Indian spirituality and philosophy since the Vedic age by a disciple of Ramakrishna.

Ramaswamy, Krishnan, Antonio de Nicolas, and Aditi Banerjee, *Invading the Sacred: An Analysis of Hinduism Studies in America*, New Delhi: Rupa and Company, 2007. A critique of how Western scholars have portrayed Hinduism.

Ramaswamy, Vijaya, *Walking Naked: Women, Society, Spirituality in South India*, Shimla, India: Indian Institute of Advanced Study, 1997. Groundbreaking study of movements in which women were able to transcend social restrictions and give free expression to their spirituality.

Rinehart, Robin, ed., *Contemporary Hinduism: Ritual, Culture, and Practice*, Santa Barbara, California: ABC/CLIO, 2004. A very accessible, carefully explained introduction to Hindu culture.

Sharma, Veena, *Kailash Mansarovar: A Sacred Journey*, New Delhi: Rol: Books, 2004. Fascinating and informative first-person account of Hinduism's most difficult and sacred pilgrimage.

Singh, Karan, *Essays on Hinduism*, New Delhi: Ratna Sagar, 1987 and 1990. An excellent and concise introduction to the many facets of Hinduism, interpreted in modern terms.

Sondhi, Madhuri Santanam, *Modernity, Morality and the Mahatma*, New Delhi: Haranand Publications, 1997. A brilliant analysis of Indian responses to the challenges of modernity, including the contributions of many religious figures.

Sontheimer, Gunther-Dietz, and Hermann Kulke, *Hinduism Reconsidered*, New Delhi: Manohar, 1997. Provocative articles by Indian and Western scholars on controversial new ways of interpreting many facets of Hinduism.

Thapar, Romila, Jonathan Mark Kenoyer, Madhav M. Deshpande, Shereen Ratnagar, *India: Historical Beginnings and the Concept of the Aryan*, Delhi: National Book Trust, 2006. Essays surveying current archaeological, linguistic, and social research into the Aryan invasion theory.

Key terms

ashram A usually ascetic spiritual community of followers gathered around their guru.

atman The individual soul.

avatar An incarnation of a deity.

bhakti Intense devotion to a personal manifestation of Supreme Reality.

Brahman The Supreme Reality.

brahmin Priest or member of the priestly caste.

caste An occupational category.

chakra A subtle energy center in the body.

darshan Visual contact with the divine.

deva A deity.

dharma Moral order, righteousness, religion.

guru Spiritual teacher.

Kali Yuga The present degraded era.

karma Our actions and their effects on this life and lives to come.

moksha Liberation.

prana The invisible life force.

puja Ritual worship.

reincarnation After death, rebirth in a new life.

rishi A sage.

Shaivite Worshiper of Shiva.

Shakta Worshiper of the divine in female form.

samsara The worldly cycle of birth, death, and rebirth.

sannyasin Renunciate spiritual seeker.

Sanskrit The ancient language of the Vedas.

secularism The constitutional principle of not giving favored status to any religion.

sutra Terse spiritual teaching.

Tantra A sacred esoteric text with spiritual practices honoring the divine in female form.

Vaishnavite Worshiper of Vishnu or one of his manifestations, such as Krishna.

yoga Practices for union with the true Self.

Review questions

1. Describe these major philosophical themes of Hinduism: *atman, karma, samsara, moksha,* Brahman, and yoga.
2. Outline the Hindu ritual practices of *puja, darshan, prasad,* and important festivals and pilgrimages.
3. Describe Hindu views regarding social roles and duties with respect to caste, gender, and life stage, and note some of the challenges leaders such as Gandhi have made to these traditional roles.

Discussion questions

1. Consider the multiple components of the term *dharma* in Hinduism and how they might complicate traditional definitions of the term "religion."
2. Compare and contrast Samkhya, yoga, and Advaita Vedanta.
3. Compare the secular and fundamentalist understandings of Hinduism. Are you aware of similar dynamics in other religions?

Additional Internet resources

myreligionlab

For further activities and resources, including access to MyReligionLibrary, please visit MyReligionLab at www.myreligionlab.com

BBC Religion and Ethics: Hinduism http://www.bbc.co.uk/religion/religions/hinduism

Gazetteer of India http://www.uni-giessen.de/~gk1415/hinduism.htm

Hinduism: The world's third largest religion
http://www.religioustolerance.org/hinduism.htm

Hinduism Website http://www.hinduwebsite.com/hinduindex.asp

Indian religions http://www.sscnet.ucla.edu/southasia/Religions/religions.html

The Indus Civilization http://www.harappa.com/har/har0.html

Internet Sacred Text Archive: Hinduism http://www.sacred-texts.com/hin/index.htm

Puja: expressions of Hindu Devotion http://www.asia.si.edu/pujaonline/puja/start.htm

Understanding Hinduism http://www.hinduism.co.za

CHAPTER 4

JAINISM

"Be careful all the while!"

Although the majority of Indians who are religious continue to follow the Hindu paths, Mother India has given birth to several other religions which are not based on the Vedas. One of them is Jainism, which has approximately six million adherents. Until recently, it has been little known outside India. Even within India it is practiced by only a small minority. Yet its ascetic teachings offer valuable clues to our global survival. It is becoming recognized as a complete and fruitful path with the potential for uplifting human awareness and inculcating high standards of personal ethics. For example, it has never condoned war or the killing of animals for any reason. Jain teachings recognize that we humans are imperfect, but hold out the promise that through careful control of our senses and thoughts we can attain perfection, freedom, and happiness.

KEY TOPICS

• THE TIRTHANKARAS AND ASCETIC ORDERS 121

• FREEING THE SOUL: THE ETHICAL PILLARS 123

• SPIRITUAL PRACTICES 128

• WORLD JAINISM 132

The Tirthankaras and ascetic orders

Jainism's major teacher for this age is Mahavira or Mahavir ("The Great Hero"). He was a contemporary of the Buddha and died approximately 527 BCE. Like the Buddha, he was the prince of a *kshatriya* clan and renounced his position and his wealth at the age of thirty to wander as a spiritual seeker. The austerities he undertook while meditating without clothes in the intense summer heat and winter cold are legendary. He often undertook total fasts of at least two days, not even drinking water. In Jain scriptures it is written that six times he fasted for two months at a time, and once he fasted for six months straight.[1] Swarms of mosquitoes and ants often bit him. Humans also tormented him. He was repeatedly arrested and mistreated by officials who mistook him for a common thief, not recognizing him as the son of their king. In places where he was meditating, often in a standing position, villagers are said to have treated him miserably to make him leave:

> *Once when he [sat in meditation], his body unmoving, they cut his flesh, tore his hair, and covered him with dirt. They picked him up and then dropped him, disturbing his meditational postures. Abandoning concern for his body, free from desire, the Venerable One humbled himself and bore the pain.[2]*

Finally after twelve years of meditation, silence, and extreme fasting, Mahavira achieved liberation and perfection. For thirty years until his death at Pava, he spread his teachings. His community is said to have consisted of 14,100 monks, 36,000 nuns, and 310,000 female and 150,000 male lay followers. They came from all castes, as Jainism does not officially acknowledge the caste system.

The Jain teachings are not thought to have originated with Mahavira, however. He is considered the last of twenty-four **Tirthankaras** ("Fordmakers") of the current cosmic cycle. In Jain cosmology, the universe is without beginning or end. Eternally, it passes through long cycles of progress and decline. At the beginning of each downward cycle, humans are happy, long-lived, and virtuous; they have no need for religion. As these qualities decline, Tirthankaras must create religion in order to steer people away from the growing evil in the world.

The first Tirthankara introduced civilizing social institutions, such as marriage, family, law, justice, and government, taught the arts of agriculture, crafts, reading, writing, and mathematics, and built villages, towns, and cities. Twenty-three more Tirthankaras followed over a vast expanse of time. The twenty-second is generally acknowledged by scholars as an historic figure, Lord Krishna's cousin, renowned for his compassion toward animals. The twenty-third Tirthankara, a prince who became an extreme ascetic and a great preacher, lived from 877 to 777 BCE.

The extreme antiquity of Jainism as a non-Vedic, indigenous Indian religion is well documented. Ancient Hindu and Buddhist scriptures refer to Jainism as an existing tradition that began long before Mahavira.

After Mahavira's death, his teachings were not written down because the monks lived without possessions; they were initially carried orally. In the third century BCE, the great Jain saint Bhadrabahu predicted that there would be a prolonged famine where Mahavira had lived, in what is now Bihar in northeast India. He led some 12,000 monks to southern India to avoid the famine, which lasted for twelve years. When they returned, they discovered that two major changes had been introduced by the monks who had remained. One was relaxation of the requirement of nudity for monks; the other was the convening of a council to edit the existing Jain texts into a canon of forty-five books.

Eventually the two groups split into the **Digambaras**, who had left and did not accept the changes, and the **Svetambaras**, who had stayed near Mahavira's original location. Digambara ("sky-clad") monks wear nothing at all, symbolizing innocence and nonattachment. They do not consider themselves "nude"; rather, they have taken the environment as their clothing. They have only two possessions: a gourd for drinking water and a broom of feathers dropped by peacocks. The broom is used to sweep the ground before they walk on it, to avoid harming any creatures. The Svetambara ("white-clad") monks and nuns wear simple white cloth robes: They do not feel this prevents them from attaining liberation.

The two orders also differ over the subject of women's abilities. Digambaras believe that women cannot become so pure that they could rise to the highest heaven or so impure that they would be reborn in the lowest hell; they cannot renounce clothes and be naked; they cannot be such skillful debaters as men; they are of inferior status in society and in the monastic order. They can be liberated only if they are reborn in a man's body. Svetambaras feel that women are capable of the same spiritual achievements as men, and

myreligi⬤nlab
Mahavir's Stoicism
AKARANGA SUTRA

myreligi⬤nlab
Forsaking
Eternal Bliss
TRADITIONAL
JAIN FABLE

Mahavira is said to have become so detached from worldly concerns that he shed his clothes as well as his royal status.

Jain nuns at the feet of a monolithic fifty-foot (seventeen-meter) tall statue of Bahubali (thought to be the great renunciate son of the first Tirthankara), also shown in miniature in the foreground. During a famous ceremony that takes place once every twelve years a succession of offerings is poured over the statue from a scaffolding above. These include sugarcane juice, milk, turmeric, herbs, sandal, saffron, gold and silver flowers, precious stones, and, at the end, flowers showered from a helicopter.

myreligionlab
The Renunciate Life
SĀDHVI VICAKṢAṆA

that the nineteenth Tirthankara was a woman. In truth, even Svetambara nuns are of lower status than monks, but they still comprise the great majority of Jain nuns. Of today's approximately 6,000 Jain nuns, fewer than 100 are Digambaras. The existence of this thriving order of female ascetics—which includes many skillful teachers and counselors and outnumbers the approximately 2,500 Jain monks—is unique in India. In Brahmanic Hindu tradition, women were never allowed to be mendicants and marriage was considered obligatory.

Freeing the soul: the ethical pillars

In the midst of a world of decline, as they see it, Jains are given great room for hope. The *jiva*—the individual's higher consciousness, or soul—can save itself by discovering its own perfect, unchanging nature and thus transcend the miseries of earthly life. Jains, like Hindus and Buddhists, believe that we are reborn again and again until we finally free ourselves from *samsara*, the wheel of birth and death.

The gradual process by which the soul learns to extricate itself from the lower self and its attachments to the material world involves purifying one's ethical life until nothing remains but the purity of the *jiva*. In its true state, it is fully omniscient, shining, potent, peaceful, self-contained, and blissful. One who has thus brought forth the highest in his or her being is called a **Jina** (a "winner" over the passions), from which the term Jain is derived. The Tirthankaras were Jinas who helped others find their way, by teaching inspiring spiritual principles.

KARMA

Jains believe that the universe is without beginning and that it has no creator or destroyer. Our lives are therefore the results of our own deeds; only by our own efforts can we be saved. Padma Agrawal explains:

In Jainism, unlike Christianity and many Hindu cults, there is no such thing as a heavenly father watching over us. To the contrary, love for a personal God would be an attachment that could only bind Jainas more securely to the cycle of rebirth. It is a thing that must be rooted out.[3]

The world operates by the power of nature, according to natural principles. Jains do believe in gods and demons, but the former are subject to the same ignoble passions as humans. In fact, one can only achieve liberation if one is in the human state, because only humans can clear away karmic accumulations on the soul. Like Hindus and Buddhists, Jains believe that our actions influence the future course of our current life, and of our lives to come. But in Jain belief, *karma* is actually subtle matter—minute particles that we accumulate as we act and think. Until it frees itself from *karmas*, the mundane soul wanders about through the universe in an endless cycle of deaths and rebirths, instantly transmigrating into another kind of being upon death of its previous body. Acharya Shri Kund Kund, a great ancient Jain teacher, asserted, "Nowhere throughout the

The Story of Bahubali

Rishabha, the first Tirthankara of the current cosmic cycle, had 100 sons from one wife and one son, Bahubali, from the other. He gave his eldest son, Bharat, the lion's share of his inheritance. Bharat was eager to be the supreme king, and he wanted his other brothers, who had been given smaller portions of land, to come under his subjugation. All the people surrendered to his sovereignty, except for Bahubali, who refused to surrender his kingdom. He said to Bharat, "You are independent, I am independent. Why should I come under your rule?"

The armies of the two sides were drawn up on the battleground. The wise men from the two sides came forth and said, "In the clash of two brothers, millions of people will be killed. Millions of innocent people will be killed to satisfy the egos of two brothers. Why should this happen?" So it was decided that the two would fight it out between themselves. They would fight in three ways to see who was defeated.

First, they looked into each other's eyes, concentrating until one looked away. Bahubali defeated Bharat in this combat. Then they fought under water, and again Bahubali was victorious. Thirdly, Bahubali picked up Bharat physically and held him overhead, ready to dash him to the ground. That is how he got the name Bahubali—"He whose arms are very powerful."

As Bahubali was holding Bharat aloft, a thought crossed his mind: "Whom am I throwing? My own brother. For what? For this parcel of land? For this kingdom? Only for that, I would kill my brother?" He put Bharat down.

At that point, Bahubali felt like renouncing the world. He ceased to make war, and he went into meditation. For twelve years he meditated, standing. Vines grew on his legs. Snakes made their homes around his body. Many people tried to convince him to come out of his meditation, but he was unmoved. Nevertheless, he could not attain ultimate liberation.

Rishabha, his father, was asked why Bahubali was not attaining liberation. From his omniscient knowledge, Rishabha said that just before Bahubali started his meditation, he had a thought left in his mind: "I am standing on my brother's soil." So Bharat went and prayed to him: "This soil is universal, not yours or mine." The moment that thought entered Bahubali's mind he was liberated.

space in the entire universe is there any place in its course where the mundane soul has not taken birth in many forms, big and small."[4]

Birth as a human is the highest stage of life, short of liberation. One should therefore lose no time in this precious, brief period in human incarnation, for within it lies the potential for perfection.

To perfect and purify themselves as quickly as possible, Jains try to eliminate within themselves any false mental impressions, negative tendencies, or passions, and to develop pure thoughts and actions. Through this process, the veils of *karma* are lifted and the soul experiences more and more of its natural luminosity. In the highest state of perfection, known as *kevala*, the liberated being has "boundless vision, infinite righteousness, strength, perfect bliss, existence without form, and a body that is neither light nor heavy."[5]

The three basic principles that Jains adopt to avoid accumulating *karma* are *ahimsa* (nonviolence), *aparigraha* (nonattachment), and *anekantwad* (non-absolutism).

AHIMSA

The principle of non-violence—*ahimsa*—is very strong in Jain teachings, and through Jainism it also influenced Mahatma Gandhi. Jains believe that every centimeter of the universe is filled with living beings, some of them minute. A single drop of water contains 3,000 living beings. All of them want to live. Humans have no special right to supremacy; all things deserve to live and evolve as they can. To kill any living being has negative karmic effects.

It is difficult not to do violence to other creatures. Even in breathing, Jains feel, we inhale tiny organisms and kill them. Jains avoid eating after sunset, so as not to eat unseen insects that might have landed on the food, and some Jain ascetics wear a cloth over their mouth to avoid inhaling any living organisms.

The higher the life form, the heavier the karmic burden of its destruction. The highest group of beings are those with many senses, such as humans, gods, and higher animals. Lower forms have fewer senses. The "one-sensed" beings have only the sense of touch. They include plants and the earth-bodies in soil, minerals, and stones, the water-bodies in rivers and lakes, fire-bodies in fires and lightning, and wind-bodies in winds and gases. The Jain *sutras* describe the suffering of even these one-sensed beings: it is like that of a blind and mute person who cannot see who is hurting him or express the pain.

The new Jain symbol: ahimsa is inscribed on the open palm. The swastika is an ancient Indian symbol representing the wheel of samsara, *in which beings return to life again and again. The three dots symbolize insight, knowledge, and conduct. The crescent and dot above symbolize the liberated soul in the highest region of the universe.*

> *All breathing, existing, living, sentient creatures should not be slain, nor treated with violence, nor abused, nor tormented, nor driven away. This is the pure, unchangeable, eternal law … Correctly understanding the law, one should arrive at indifference for the impressions of the senses, and not act on the motives of the world.*
>
> *Akaranga Sutra, IV: Lesson 1*[6]

Jains are therefore strict vegetarians, and they treat everything with great care. In Delhi, Jain benefactors have established a unique charitable hospital for sick and wounded birds. Great attention is paid to their every need, and their living quarters are air-cooled in the summer. Jains also go to markets where live animals are usually bound with wire, packed into hot trucks, and driven long distances without water to be killed for meat. Jains buy the animals at any price and raise them in comfort. Even to kick a stone while walking is to injure living beings. Jains are keenly aware that we may cause violence even through the clothes we buy. Many Jains thus eschew both leather and silk. Layman R. P. Jain tells a story of how he felt when he learned how silk is made:

I used to wear silk. On my eighteenth birthday I was telling one of my distant relatives not to eat chocolate because it had egg powder in it. He said, "Turn around—you're wearing silk. What are you preaching? Do you know that to make one yard of silk, nearly fifty thousand to one hundred thousand silkworms are boiled alive? To wear silk is a sin!" When I learned that is the way natural silk is made, I said, "R. P. Jain, what are you doing to your own soul? Shame on you!" From that day, I took a vow never in my life to wear natural silk.[7]

Ahimsa also extends to care in speaking and thinking, for abusive words and negative thoughts can injure another. The revered ascetic Acharya Tulsi (1914–1997) explained:

A non-violent man is he who does not in the least discriminate between rich and poor or between friend and foe. … Non-violence is the best guarantee of humanity's survival and progress. A truly non-violent man is ever awake and is incapable of harbouring any ill will.[8]

One's profession must also not injure beings, so most Jains work at jobs considered harmless, such as banking, education, law, and publishing. Agriculture is considered harmful, for in digging one harms minute organisms in the earth; in harnessing bullocks to plows one harms not only the bullock but also the tiny life forms on its body. Monks and nuns must move slowly with eyes downward, to avoid stepping on any being. In general, they will do the least harm if they devote their time to sitting or standing in meditation rather than moving around.

Global violence is of increasing concern, and here, too, Jains have great wisdom to offer. The late Acharya Tulsi taught that self-restraint is essential for the sake of world peace. He said:

Individual desire and ego are perennial human traits. Whenever they have been conjoined with power, there has been a general increase in war hysteria leading to the repetition of bloody and violent events in history. The reason why moral values have been held in the highest esteem is that they transform this evil combination of desire, ego and power into courteous humility. The history of the human race has been far more honorable and full of freedom during periods of such transformation. … The fact cannot be ignored that the fate of the politicians is finally in the hands of the people. Even though it is generally true that it is the former who ultimately decide war and peace, the awakened conscience of the people is bound to ensure one day that a handful of over-ambitious people are not allowed to play with the future of mankind by imposing wars on them. The way to universal peace lies in our adherence to the precept of self-restraint.[9]

myreligionlab

Remembering our own First Principles
MICHAEL TOBIAS

Jain Purification

A central Jain practice undertaken both by laypeople and by ascetics has for thousands of years been used for freeing the soul from internal impurities. Anger, pride, deceit, and greed are lasting stains that must be completely eradicated if the soul is to realize its true nature: pure consciousness, infinite knowledge, and bliss. Even a momentary realization of this state brings a feeling of great inner purity and calmness and a longing to return to it permanently. The ritual for achieving this inner purification is known as *samayika*.

Jain laypeople usually undertake this practice in the evening, after work and a meal. They sit in a quiet and solitary place, remove excess clothing, sit cross-legged on a mat, and chant formulas to cleanse and pacify their mind. These begin with a pledge to renounce all harmful activities, followed by requesting forgiveness:

> *I ask forgiveness of all beings*
> *may all beings forgive me.*
> *I have friendship with all beings,*
> *and I have hostility with none.*[10]

They reach out mentally to all life forms, saying:

> *Friendship toward all beings,*
> *Delight in the qualities of virtuous ones,*
> *Utmost compassion for affected beings,*
> *Equanimity towards those who are not*
>   *well-disposed towards me,*
> *May my soul have such dispositions forever!*[11]

Then follow verses that commit the person to renouncing food, bodily desires, and passions for the period of the meditation, persisting in equanimity, come what may. The meditation ends with the universal Jain prayer:

> *Cessation of sorrow*
> *Cessation of karmas*
> *Death while in meditation,*
> *Attainment of enlightenment.*
> *O holy Jina! friend of the entire universe,*
>   *let these be mine, for*
> *I have taken refuge at your feet.*

APARIGRAHA

Another central Jain ideal is nonattachment to things and people. One should cut one's living requirements to a bare minimum. Possessions possess us; their acquisition and loss drive our emotions. Digambara monks wear no clothes; the Tirthankaras are always depicted as naked, and therefore free. Even attachments to our friends and relatives bind us to *samsara*. We are to live helpfully and consciously within the world but not be drawn into its snares.

Aparigraha, or nonacquisitiveness, is considered the way to inner peace. If we can let go of things and situations, moment by moment, we can be free. A Jain nun of the Rajasthan desert, Samani Sanmati Pragya, belongs to an order in which the nuns' clothing and bedding is limited to four white saris, one white shawl, and one woolen cloth. She explains:

> *In the winter we do not have a quilt for warmth at night, for it would be too bulky to carry. In the summer we use no fan. It is so hot that we cannot sleep at night. We bear any kind of circumstances. In fact, we remain very happy. Our happiness comes from inside.*[12]

Aparigraha is of value to the world community as well. Contemporary Jains point out that their principle of limiting consumption offers a way out of the global poverty, hunger, and environmental degradation that result from unequal grasping of resources by the wealthy. As His Holiness Acharya Sushil Kumar explained:

myreligionlab

Doctrine of
Manifold Aspects
L. M. SINGHVI

If we live simply, limit our needs and do not try to fulfill every desire, collecting more and more, automatically we will protect the environment. Because we will not need so many things, we will not need big industries to produce unnecessary things. … If we live simply, automatically the environment will stay clean.[13]

ANEKANTWAD

myreligionlab

Blind Men and
the Elephant
TRADITIONAL
JAIN FABLE

The third central principle is *anekantwad*, or "manifold aspects." Jains try to avoid anger and judgmentalism, remaining open-minded by remembering that any issue can be seen from many angles, all partially true. They tell the story of the blind people who are asked to describe an elephant. The one who feels the trunk says an elephant is like a tree branch. The one grasping a leg argues that an elephant is like a pillar. The one feeling the ear asserts that an elephant is like a fan. The one grasping the tail insists that an elephant is like a rope. And the one who encounters the side of the elephant argues that the others are wrong; an elephant is like a wall. Each has a partial grasp of the truth.

In the Jain way of thinking, the fullness of truth has many facets. Shree Chitrabhanu describes the results of eliminating false impressions and allowing the pure consciousness to flow in:

Once you have closed the open gates, dried up the polluted water, and cleaned out all the debris, then you can open them again to receive the fresh, clean rainfall. What is that rainfall? It is the flow of maitri—*pure love, compassion, and communication. You feel free. … See how easily you meet people when there is no feeling of greater or lesser, no scar or bitterness, no faultfinding or criticism.*[14]

Spiritual practices

Jainism is an ascetic path and thus is practiced in its fullest by monks and nuns. In addition to practicing meditation, monks and nuns adopt a life of celibacy, physical penance and fasting, and material simplicity. They may sleep on the bare ground or wooden slabs, and are expected to endure any kind of weather with indifference. At initiation, their hair may be pulled out by the roots. They must learn to accept social disapproval, to depend on others for their food, and to feel no pride at being more spiritually advanced than others.

Jain monks and nuns are celibate ascetics. This 15th-century illustrated text of Mahavira's last teachings shows a monk resisting the attractions of women.

Jain monks and nuns carry *ahimsa* to great extremes in their wariness of injuring one-sensed beings. Among the many activities they must avoid are digging in the ground (because of the earth-bodies there), bathing, swimming, or walking in the rain (because of the water-bodies they might injure), extinguishing or lighting fires (because even to light a fire means that a fire-body will eventually be destroyed), fanning themselves (to avoid sudden changes in air temperature that would injure air-bodies), and walking on vegetation or touching living plants.

In New Delhi, a wealthy sixty-year-old Jain businessman, head of a large construction company, astounded the populace in 1992 by advancing from lay austerities, such as eating and drinking only once in twenty-four hours, to the utterly renunciate life of a naked Digambara monk. Before a huge celebration in which he shed his clothes and his possessions, Lala Sulekh Chand announced:

> *I have no interest in life. I have found that life just means one remains agitated*
> *for twenty-four hours and there is no peace of mind. I have fulfilled all my*
> *responsibilities and obligations in life and handed over my business to my son*
> *and family. I am not taking this path due to some problem.*[15]

He then sat unflinching as his mentor, Muni Amit Sagar, pulled all the hairs from his head, a process that took an hour and a half. Afterward, Muni Amit Sagar admonished the crowd that the way to spiritual liberation lies in nonattachment and patient, indifferent forbearance of all difficulties. "We cannot change anything, but we can change our attitude of expectation," he said. "The peace one gets from renunciation cannot be gained by reading a lot of religious books."[16]

> *Difficult to conquer is oneself; but when that is conquered,*
> *everything is conquered.*
>
> *Uttaradhyayana Sutra 9.34–36*

Most householders cannot carry renunciation as far as monks and nuns, but they can nonetheless purify and perfect themselves. Jain homes and temples are typically scrupulously clean, diets are carefully vegetarian, and medicines are prepared without cruel testing on animals. The mind and passions are also to be willingly controlled. Twelve "limited" vows are to be undertaken by Jain laypeople, the major ones being the first five:

- The vow of nonviolence.
- The vow of truthfulness.
- The vow of not taking anything that has not been given.
- The vow of renouncing any sexual activity outside of marriage.
- The vow of limiting one's possessions.
- The vow of limiting the geographic area of nonvirtuous activities.
- The vow of limiting the quantity of things one will use.
- The vow of abstaining from purposeless harmful activities.
- The vow of meditation and reading scriptures for at least forty-eight consecutive minutes in a day.
- The vow to further reduce for a fixed period the area of nonvirtuous activities.
- The vow of fasting and living like an ascetic for a certain period.
- The vow of giving necessary articles to monks and nuns.

In all spheres of life, Jains are taught to limit the harm they do to themselves, to others, and to the environment. Acharya Mahaprajna points to many facets of

In Jain worship, images of the Tirthankara are ideally to be venerated without expectation of help or a personal response to prayers.

myreligionlab
Righteous Path
ACHARYA KUND-KUND

violence in the world and teaches that violence can only be overcome through profound individual transformation:

Purity of life, peacefulness and compassion are the foremost requirements of a civilized society. Reform cannot come until one achieves the capacity to withstand pain, oppression and hardship.[17]

Practicing strict ethics and self-control, Jains are often quite successful and trusted in their professions. Many Jains have thus become wealthy. Because of the religion's emphasis on nonpossessiveness, wealthy Jains are often philanthropists.

Lay Jains are divided into those who worship at temples and those who do not. For those who worship in temples, Jain philanthropists have built very ornate temples, which are kept immaculately clean. Within the temples, the Tirthankaras are honored through images. They all look alike, for the perfect soul is nonparticularized; symbols such as the bull, always shown with the first Tirthankara, are used to help worshipers identify each of the twenty-four. The worshiper's feeling is one of reverence rather than supplication; the Tirthankaras are elevated beyond the human plane and are not available as helpers. They are instead models for one's own life, and since there can be no divine intervention there is not a great emphasis on priesthood. Laypeople can carry out worship services themselves, either alone or in groups. People pay their respects before images of the Tirthankaras with offerings and by waving lamps, but do not expect any reciprocation from them. Liberation from *samsara* is a result of personal effort, often portrayed by a symbolic diagram laid out with rice grains. Acharya Tulsi expressed the Jain point of view: "The primary aim of *dharma* is to purify character. Its ritualistic practices are secondary."[18]

> *Just as a fire quickly reduces decayed wood to ashes, so does an aspirant who is totally absorbed in the inner self and completely unattached to all external objects shake to the roots, attenuate, and wither away his* karma-*body.*
>
> Samantabhadra, Aptamimamsa 24–7

FESTIVALS AND PILGRIMAGES

With their emphasis on self-discipline and self-perfection, Jains do not celebrate their holy days as jubilantly as Hindus. Even the festival days are characterized by meditation, renunciation, fasting, scriptural study, and hymns. However, these activities are undertaken with enthusiasm and dedication.

Divali, which Hindus celebrate with lights and fireworks, is for Jains an occasion for a three-day fast and an entire night spent reciting hymns and meditating on Mahavir, who is said to have attained liberation on Divali. The fifth day after

An Interview with M. P. Jain

M. P. Jain is the director of Motilal Banarsidass Publishing Company, a venerable publisher of books about Indian religions and culture. He is one of five brothers who live together in New Delhi as an extended family, all involved in the family publishing business along with their married children. He speaks of the difficulty of the lay practice of Jainism:

"Very few people are really practicing the true Jainism—not even the monks. Jain tradition speaks of two aspects: the self and the non-self. Non-self is everything that is destroyable, whether your body, your ideas, your house, your business, or your eatables. Non-self cannot be possessed. The self, the *jivatma*, is eternal. It moves from one body to another body after birth and rebirth. Thus that is the permanent thing, but people do not understand this. They love only those things that are non-self, and non-self is absolutely impermanent.

"To consider all non-self things impermanent and detach yourself from them is very difficult, because in all previous births we have been loving non-self things. This is a habit; there is no habit of concentrating on the self. That requires a lot of spiritual practice. Only then can you divert yourself from non-self to self. The practice is that you have to look upon worldly things as the seer. You are not to be involved in them, because through attachment with worldly things you land up with all those problems that are existing in the world. If you detach yourself, you become only a seer, and then you attach yourself with the self only. Then you can achieve something.

"In business, most people's main purpose is to make money somehow, by wrong or right methods. But I don't agree. One should try to be as fair as possible.

"Renunciation has to be done happily. One must be mentally happy, physically happy, and happy in activities. Only then can one achieve the goal. As a father, I can only tell my family that this is the way, but it is very hard to make them do it. Only through *punye*—good deeds which one has done in previous births—can you renounce. You have to change from the prevalent way. Only one like Mahatma Gandhi, who walked alone, can change from the prevalent way. He had those *punye*, so he could walk alone and thousands of people followed him.

"I have a spiritual teacher. He is an unassuming person, absolutely unknown. He is like a monk, living in the Himalayas. I see him only once a year when he passes through Delhi on his way to meet his mother.

"I go to the temple every day. I worship there, reciting some mantras and doing some rituals. There is a sense of pleasure and a sense of duty. It is essential because I have understood the importance of worshiping those who have attained the highest level of renunciation. If you worship greater people, those who have attained nirvana, you will get the same peace that they have attained. Our guru inspired us to do so. From our family, about twenty percent of us go to the temple every day, including my mother, who is still practicing Jainism to a great extent.

"We support the monks and nuns by providing them the things that they need, like clothes, food, and travel arrangements. They do not travel in vehicles, but when they walk from one station to another, they need a rickshaw for their belongings and a servant to escort them so that they go to the right place. But things are changing. The older monks and nuns have started traveling in wheelchairs; someone pushes them.

"My wife, my mother, and I do not eat after sunset, because in food preparation, drinking water, and so forth there is more death of *jivas* after sunset than before sunset. Some *jivas* cannot be seen; some can be seen. It depends on their size. One should try to save them as much as one can. That is the reason one should not travel during night, because in the night they are many, and in the sunlight they are less.

"As for mosquitoes, I try to keep my room as clean as possible so that the mosquitoes do not show up. If they come, you have to turn on the air-conditioner, take a blanket, and sleep under that. There is no question of killing them. It is better to bear the mosquitoes to be on the safe side, because killing is no answer. If you kill, that is very harmful, because if you kill one soul you kill your own soul also."

Divali is set aside for the worship of pure knowledge. One of the activities is cleaning and worshiping of the books in religious libraries.

Among all Jain festivals, the most important is Paryushan Mahaparva, the annual festival of atonement. Many Jains undertake an eight-day fast, while listening to scriptural readings and lectures about ethical living, particularly the virtue of forgiveness. The final day is celebrated as Forgiveness Day. People seek forgiveness from anyone toward whom they feel hatred or enmity and try to give up these negative karmic burdens, adopting instead feelings such as compassion, contentment, equanimity, and sharing. Jagdish Prasad Jain, president of the Jain Mission in New Delhi, explains:

> One can perform these other activities beneficial to others only when there is renunciation of excessive attachment or sense of mine-ness to material objects, subsidence of the passion of greed, i.e. acquisitiveness and exploitation of others, which are often the cause of enmity and hatred on the part of others. Thus, the virtues of humility, honesty or straightforwardness and purity of mind, including freedom from greed, are dovetailed into forgiveness. One is asked to renounce or minimize the four passions of anger, pride, deceit and greed, which are the real enemies of the purity of the soul and which stand in the way of peace and happiness of the individual as also social well-being.[19]

Pilgrimages to sacred sites are also very popular forms of Jain spiritual practice. Individuals, families, or groups may travel long distances to worship at famous sites, many located on hills or mountains in beautiful natural environments. Many of these are in Bihar, south of the Indian border with Nepal. Bihar is considered the cradle of Jainism, for it was here that twenty of the twenty-four Tirthankaras, including Mahavira, are thought to have achieved liberation. Some areas in western India are also rich in intricately carved Jain temples and pilgrimage places. And in South India there is a colossal statue of Bahubali which was carved out of solid rock in 980 CE. His feet—the most accessible part, as well as the focus of reverence in Indian culture—are daily bathed as a devotional ritual. Every twelve to fifteen years, a huge scaffold is erected so that pots of water, sandalwood fragrance, coconut, and sugar can be poured over the fifty-foot (seventeen-meter) statue. This special ceremony draws enormous crowds of worshipers. Construction of temples continues today, keeping alive ancient traditions of intricate stone-carving.

World Jainism

Through the centuries, Jainism managed to survive as a small minority within largely Hindu India. Today there are approximately six million Jains. Since the twentieth century, Jainism has been carried to the outside world by several teachers. One of them, Shree Chitrabhanu, was for twenty-nine years a monk who walked barefoot over 30,000 miles of Indian soil to teach Jain principles to the populace. When he was invited to address interfaith conferences in Switzerland and the United States in 1970 and 1971, his controversial decision to attend in person marked the first time in Jain history that a Jain monk had traveled outside India. He then established Jain meditation centers in the United States, Brazil, Canada, Kenya, the United Kingdom, and India.

Acharya Shri Sushil Kumar likewise established Jain centers in the United Kingdom and the United States as well as in India. He pointed out that the Jain scriptures consider as "Jains" all those who practice Jain principles:

> If somebody is a real symbol of non-violence, love, compassion, peace, harmony, oneness, then he is the perfect Jain. We can't convert any Jains, but you can convert your habits, your mind.[20]

The revered Acharya Tulsi initiated new orders of "semi-monks" and "semi-nuns" who are allowed to travel abroad in order to spread Jain teachings. He also began the Anuvrat Movement in 1949, to enlist people of all faiths and nationalities to commit themselves to *anuvrats* (small vows). He developed these to help people rejuvenate strong moral standards of self-restraint in the midst of an ethically unhealthy society. The small vows include these: to avoid willful killing of any innocent creature, to refrain from attacks and aggression and to work instead for world peace and disarmament, to avoid discrimination on the basis of caste or race, to eschew religious intolerance, to avoid false business and political practices, to limit acquisition of possessions, to eschew addictive substances, and to avoid wasting water or cutting down trees.

In 1995, Acharya Tulsi renounced even his own position as the leader of his order by installing Acharya Mahaprajna as his successor. Acharya Mahaprajna's self-description is an indication of the internal qualities which keep Jain faith alive:

> I am an ascetic. My asceticism is not bound by inert rituals. ... I follow a tradition, but do not treat its dynamic elements as static. I derive benefit from the scriptures, but do not believe in carrying them as a burden. ... In my consciousness there is no bondage of "yours and mine." It is free from it. My spiritual practice is not to "worship" truth, but to subject it to minute surgery. The only mission of my life is boundless curiosity to discover truth. ... It is not an external accoutrement. Like a seed it is sprouting out of my being.[21]

Suggested reading

Chapple, Christopher, ed., *Jainism and Ecology: Non-violence in the Web of Life*. Cambridge, Massachusetts: Center for the Study of World Religions, 2002. Scholars examine possibilities of bringing Jain principles to bear on contemporary environmental issues.

Chitrabhanu, Gurudev Shree, *Twelve Facets of Reality: The Jain Path to Freedom*, New York: Jain Meditation International Center/Dodd, Mead & Company, 1980. Classic Jain reflections on the realities of life, with many teaching tales.

Jain, Jagdish Prasad "Sadhak," *Fundamentals of Jainism*, New Delhi: Radiant Publishers, 2005. Examination of the ancient roots of Jain tradition, according to literary and archaeological sources, plus Jain ethics and philosophy.

Jaini, Padmanabh S., *The Jaina Path of Purification*, Berkeley: University of California Press, 1979. An appreciative, scholarly analysis of the Jaina path.

Jaini, Padmanabh S., ed., *Collected Papers on Jaina Studies*, Delhi: Motilal Banarsidass Publishers, 2000. In-depth look at contemporary issues in Jain scholarship and practice.

Kumar, Acharya Sushil, *Song of the Soul*, Blairstown, New Jersey: Siddhachalam Publishers, 1987. Insights into Jain mantra practice, as taught by a twentieth-century monk.

Muller, F. Max, ed., *Jaina Sutras*, vols. XLV and XXII of *Sacred Books of the East*, Oxford: Clarendon Press, 1884 and 1895. Engaging translations of various sorts of *sutras*, including both philosophical treatises and rules of conduct for Jain ascetics.

Nyayavijayaji, Munisri, *Jaina Philosophy and Religion*, trans. Nagin J. Shah, Delhi: Motilal Banarsidass Publishers, 1998. A renowned twentieth-century monk's comprehensive tome describing the major aspects of Jain philosophy, liberation practices, logics, metaphysics, and ethics in contemporary terms.

Rankin, Aidan, *The Jain Path: Ancient Wisdom for the West*, Hants, UK: John Hunt Publishing, 2006. Jainism described for a Western audience as clues to a global paradigm shift.

Sangave, Vilas A., *Aspects of Jaina Religion*, New Delhi: Bharatiya Jnanpith, 1990. Concise, accurate discussions of Jain antiquity, principles, practice, relationships to other religions, and cultural contributions.

Suri, Amrtacandra, *The Pravacana-sara of Kund-Kund with the commentary Tattva-dipika*, trans. Barend Faddegon, Fremont, California: Jain Publishing Company, Inc. 1935, reprinted. Terse writings of the ancient Jain sage, Acharya Kund-Kund, with commentaries.

Tobias, Michael, *Life Force: The World of Jainism*, Berkeley, California: Asian Humanities Press, 1991. A highly appreciative and readable account of Jain practices and philosophy by a Western observer.

Key terms

ahimsa Nonviolence, a central Jain principle.
anekantwad The Jain principle of manifold aspects of the truth.
aparigraha Nonacquisitiveness, a major Jain principle.
Digambara A highly ascetic order of Jain monks who wear no clothes.
jiva The soul.
samsara The continual round of birth, death, and rebirth.
Svetambara Jain order of monks who are less ascetic than the Digambara.
Tirthankaras The great enlightened teachers in Jainism, of whom Mahariva was the last in the present cosmic cycle.

Review questions

1. Taking into account *samsara*, caste, *karma*, *kevala*, *jiva*, and Jina, describe the Jain quest for purity.
2. Explain the concepts of *ahimsa*, *aparigraha*, and *anekantwad*.
3. Explain the Jain belief about the Tirthankaras and their role in spiritual liberation.

Discussion questions

1. How might someone put the principle of *ahimsa* into practice in your own society? How would it affect the person's behavior?
2. Compare Jain beliefs about how to live in the world with those of indigenous sacred ways.

myreligionlab
For further activities and resources, including access to MyReligionLibrary, please visit MyReligionLab at www.myreligionlab.com

Additional Internet resources

Ibbotson, Sophie. "Jainism and the legendary Delhi bird hospital." http://www.wildlife extra.com/go/world/bird-hospital.html#cr

Introduction to Jainism http://www.jainnet.com/intro.html

Jain religion, places, festivals http://www.jainuniversity.org

Religion and ethics—Jainism http://www.bbc.co.uk/religion/religions/jainism/

CHAPTER 5

BUDDHISM

"He will deliver by the boat of knowledge
the distressed world"

About the same time that Mahavira was teaching the Jain path, the man who became known as the Buddha preached another alternative to the ritual-oriented Brahmanism of India. The Buddha taught about earthly suffering and its cure. Many religions offer comforting supernatural solutions to the difficulties of earthly life. Early Buddhism was quite different: It held that liberation from suffering depends on our own efforts. The Buddha taught that by understanding how we create suffering for ourselves we can become free.

The effort involved in having to take responsibility for our own happiness and our own liberation may seem daunting and unlikely to attract many followers. On the contrary, the Buddha's teachings spread far and wide from India throughout Asia, becoming the dominant religious tradition in many countries. The Buddha's teachings have been meaningful to some as a profound system of philosophy and to others as a system of religious practice or way of life. As Buddhism spread to new lands, it took new forms, often reflecting earlier local traditions. These new forms might include devotional practices, mystical elements, and appeals to the various Buddhas and bodhisattvas for protection and blessing. Now, more than 2,500 years after the Buddha's death, the path that he taught is attracting considerable interest in Western countries, where its psychological and meditative aspects are often emphasized.

KEY TOPICS

• THE LIFE AND
  LEGEND OF THE
  BUDDHA 135

• THE DHARMA 141

• BRANCHES OF
  BUDDHISM 148

• BUDDHISM IN
  THE WEST 171

• SOCIALLY ENGAGED
  BUDDHISM 177

The life and legend of the Buddha

Although the Buddha was apparently an historical figure, what we know about him is not documented in any way, but is derived from stories passed down over time through generations of followers. His prolific teachings were probably not collected in written form until several hundred years after his death. In the meantime, they were apparently transmitted orally, chanted from memory by monks, groups of whom were responsible for remembering specific parts of the teachings.

Only a few factual details of the Buddha's life have been retained. While stories about his life are abundant in authorized Buddhist texts, these stories were never organized into a unified canonical biography. Extant complete biographies of the Buddha date from four centuries after his passing. These texts venerate the Buddha as a legendary hero, and were written by storyteller poets rather than historians. An example of such a sacred biography is Asvaghosa's famous epic, the *Buddhacarita* (Acts of the Buddha), composed in the first century CE.

The one who became the Buddha (a generic term meaning "Awakened One") was reportedly born near what is today the border between India and Nepal. He was named Siddhartha Gautama, meaning "wish-fulfiller" or "he who has reached his goal." It is said that he lived for over eighty years during the fifth century BCE, though his life may have extended either into the late sixth or early fourth century. His father was apparently a wealthy landowner serving as one of the chiefs of a *kshatriya* clan, the Shakyas who lived in the foothills of the Himalayas. The family name, Gautama, honored an ancient Hindu sage whom the family claimed as ancestor or spiritual guide. His mother Maya is said to have given birth to him in the garden of Lumbini near Kapilavastu. The epics embellish his birth story as a conception without human intercourse, in which a white elephant carrying a lotus flower entered his mother's womb during a dream. He is portrayed as the reincarnation of a great being who had been born many times before and took birth on earth once again out of compassion for all suffering beings.

According to legend, the child was raised in the lap of luxury, with fine clothes, white umbrellas for shade, perfumes, cosmetics, a mansion for each season, the company of female musicians, and a harem of dancing girls. He was also trained in martial arts and married to at least one wife, Yashodara, who bore a son. Despite this life of ease, Siddhartha was reportedly unconvinced of its value. As the legend goes, the gods arranged for him to see "four sights" that his father had tried to hide from him: a bent old man, a sick person, a dead person, and a mendicant seeking lasting happiness rather than temporal pleasure. Seeing the first three sights, he was dismayed by the impermanence of life and the existence of suffering, old age, and death. The sight of the monk piqued his interest in a life

The region where Siddhartha grew up is in full view of the high peaks of the Himalayas.

Buddhism

BCE c.5th century	Life of Gautama Buddha
c.258	King Ashoka begins spreading Buddhism outward from India
c.200 BCE–200 CE	Development of Theravada Buddhism
c.100 BCE–300 CE	Perfection of Wisdom scriptures originally developed
c.80	Pali Canon written down in Sri Lanka
CE c.50	Buddhism transmitted to China and then Southeast Asia
1st century	Development of Mahayana Buddhism
2nd century	Asvaghosha writes *Acts of the Buddha*
c.150–250	Life of Nagarjuna
c.550	Buddhism enters Japan
589–845	Peak of Chinese Buddhism
c.609–650	Life of Songtsan, who declares Buddhism the national religion of Tibet
775	First Buddhist monastery established in Tibet
845	Persecution of Buddhism begins in China
1079–1153	Life of Milarepa
1200–1253	Life of Dogen, who spread Zen Buddhism in Japan
1222–1282	Life of Nichiren
c.1200–1500	Buddhism declines in northern India, then southern India
1893	Buddhist teachers speak at World Parliament of Religions, Chicago
1958	Sarvodaya movement begins in Sri Lanka
1959	Communist Chinese repress Buddhism in Tibet; Dalai Lama escapes to India
1970s on	Dalai Lama teaches widely in the West
1998	Full ordination of 135 nuns from 23 countries

of renunciation. As a result, at the age of twenty-nine Siddhartha renounced his wealth, left his wife and newborn son (whom he had named "Rahul," or "fetter"), shaved his head, and donned the coarse robe of a wandering ascetic. He embarked on a wandering life in pursuit of a very difficult goal: finding the way to total liberation from suffering.

Many Indian *sannyasins* were already leading the homeless life of poverty and simplicity that was considered appropriate for seekers of spiritual truth. Although the future Buddha later developed a new spiritual path that departed significantly from Brahmanic tradition, he initially tried traditional methods. He headed southeast to study with a *brahmin* teacher who had many followers, and then with another who helped him reach an even higher mental state.

Unsatisfied, still searching, Siddhartha reportedly underwent six years of extreme self-denial techniques: nakedness, exposure to great heat and cold, breath retention, a bed of brambles, severe fasting. Finally he acknowledged that this extreme ascetic path had not led to enlightenment. He described his appearance after a long and strenuous period of fasting:

> *Because I ate so little, all my limbs became like the knotted joints of withered creepers; because I ate so little, my protruding backbone became like a string of balls; because I ate so little, my buttocks became like a bullock's hoof; because I ate so little, my gaunt ribs became like the crazy rafters of a tumbledown shed; because I ate so little, the pupils of my eyes appeared lying low and deep in their sockets as sparkles of water in a deep well appear lying low and deep.*[1]

Siddhartha then shifted his practice to a Middle Way that rejected both self-indulgence and self-denial. He revived his failing health by accepting food once more and began a period of reflection. On the night of the full moon in the sixth lunar month, it is said that he sat in deep meditation beneath a tree in a village now called Bodh Gaya, and finally experienced supreme awakening. After passing through four states of serene contemplation, he recalled all his previous lives. Then he had a realization of the wheel of repeated death and rebirth, in which

The Buddha is traditionally thought to have given his first sermon, laying out the basic principles he had realized, in the Deer Park at Sarnath, to ascetics with whom he had previously engaged in severe austerities.

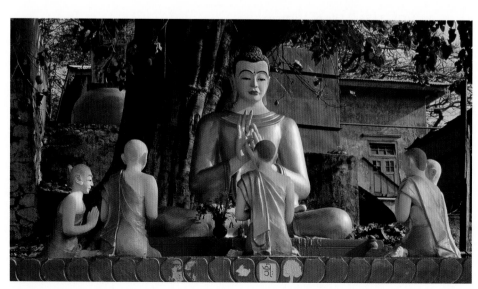

past good or bad deeds are reflected in future lives. Finally, he realized the cause of suffering and the means for ending it. After this experience of awakening or enlightenment, it is said that he was radiant with light.

According to legend, Siddhartha was tempted by Mara, the personification of evil, to keep his insights to himself, for they were too complex and profound for ordinary people to understand. But the Buddha compassionately determined to set the wheel of the Dharma in motion and began by teaching in Sarnath, in the Deer Park. He then spent decades walking and teaching ever-increasing groups of followers all over northern India. The Enlightened One's teachings and personality were apparently so compelling that many people were transformed simply by meeting him. Gradually he became known as "Shakyamuni Buddha," the "sage of the Shakya clan." Out of the abundant and varied scriptures later attributed to Shakyamuni Buddha, historians agree on the validity and centrality of a core of teachings that became known as the **Dharma** (in the Pali dialect: *Dhamma*)* that he taught: the Four Noble Truths, the Noble Eightfold Path, the Three Marks of Existence, and other guidelines for achieving liberation from suffering.

The newly awakened Buddha walked across northern India for forty-five years as a mendicant with an alms bowl, giving teachings and advice to people of all backgrounds and religions. Many young men decided to become monks (*bhikshus*; Pali: *bhikkhus*), emulating his life of poverty and spiritual dedication. Many others adopted his teachings but continued to live as householders.

The **Sangha**—the monastic order that developed from the Buddha's early disciples—accepted people from all castes and levels of society. The Buddha's stepmother Mahaprajapati, who had raised him after the death of his mother, and his wife, Yashodara, became *bhikshunis* (Pali: *bhikkhunis*), members of the order of nuns that the Buddha founded. After the death of his father King Shuddhodana, the Buddha's stepmother requested permission to enter the Sangha. When the Buddha hesitated to admit her, she and 500 women from the court shaved their heads, put on yellow robes, and walked a great distance to Vaishali where he was, and made the same request. At last he agreed, reportedly on the condition that Mahaprajapati observe eight special rules, a story that has been used to justify the subordination of nuns to monks, regardless of seniority. The Buddha's alleged reluctance to admit women to the Sangha is today a matter of much speculation. Some think that later monks may have added the rules or that the eight special rules were laid down with the monks' weaknesses in mind. Be this as it may, in the context of patriarchal Indian society, for women to leave their homes and become itinerant mendicants would probably have been perceived as socially disruptive, as well as difficult for women of the court. According to Hindu social codes, a woman could not lead the renunciate life and could achieve spiritual salvation only through personal devotion, especially devotion to her husband. By contrast, the Buddha asserted that women were as capable as men of achieving enlightenment.

myreligionlab
Defeat of Mara and Enlightenment
ASVAGOSHA

---

* Buddhist terms have come to us both in **Pali**, an Indian dialect first used for preserving the Buddha's teachings (the Buddha himself probably spoke a different ancient dialect), and in Sanskrit, the language of Indian sacred literature. For instance, the Pali *sutta* (aphorism) is equivalent to the Sanskrit *sutra*. In this chapter Sanskrit will be used, as it is more familiar to Westerners, except in the section on Theravada, which uses Pali.

Traditional accounts of the Buddha's death at the age of eighty are evidence of his selfless desire to spare humankind from suffering. His last meal, served by a blacksmith, inadvertently included some poisonous mushrooms or perhaps spoiled pork. Severely ill and recognizing his impending death, the Buddha pushed on to his next teaching stop at Kushinara. He sent word to the blacksmith not to feel remorse or blame himself, for his offering of food accrued great merit. When the Buddha reached his destination he lay down on a stone couch. As his monks came to pay their last respects, he urged them to tend to their own spiritual development:

> *You must be your own lamps, be your own refuges. … A monk becomes his own lamp and refuge by continually looking on his body, feelings, perceptions, moods, and ideas in such a manner that he conquers the cravings and depressions of ordinary men and is always strenuous, self-possessed, and collected in mind.[2]*

The Buddha's final liberation into nirvana when he physically died is symbolized by this enormous Sri Lankan statue that depicts him serenely lying down with eyes closed to the world.

He designated no successor and appointed no one to lead the order. But the Buddhist teachings and the monastic order survived and spread widely. His closest helper, Ananda, explained that before passing away the Buddha made it clear that his followers should take the Dharma and ethical discipline as their support. Followers should study the Dharma, put it into practice, and be able to defend it in the face of criticism.

One way the Buddhist tradition spread was through the dissemination of bone relics remaining after the Buddha's cremation. It is said that relics were given to messengers from seven clans who built dome-shaped reliquaries called **stupas** to commemorate the Buddha's passing, or final liberation (*parinirvana*). The Buddha's death is memorialized by images in which he is serenely lying on his side. These stupas and images became the focus of great devotion to the Buddha. Inscriptions dating back to the third century BCE or even earlier show that both monastics and laypeople made pilgrimages to these sacred sites. Standing before them, followers sense that the Buddha is present there.

The Dharma

Buddhism is often described as a nontheistic religion. There is no personal God who creates the world or to whom prayers can be directed. Buddhists who attended the 1993 Parliament of the World's Religions in Chicago found it necessary to explain to people of other religions that they do not worship the Buddha:

> *Shakyamuni Buddha, the founder of Buddhism, was not God or a god.*
> *He was a human being who attained full Enlightenment through*
> *meditation and showed us the path of spiritual awakening and freedom.*
> *Therefore, Buddhism is not a religion of God. Buddhism is a religion*
> *of wisdom, enlightenment and compassion. Like the worshippers of*
> *God who believe that salvation is available to all through confession*
> *of sin and a life of prayer, we Buddhists believe that salvation and*
> *enlightenment are available to all through removal of defilements*
> *and delusion and a life of meditation. However, unlike those who*
> *believe in God who is separate from us, Buddhists believe that*
> *Buddha which means "one who is awake and enlightened"*
> *is inherent in us all as Buddha nature or Buddha mind.*[3]

Unlike other Indian sages, the Buddha did not focus on descriptions of an unseen reality, the nature of the soul, life after death, or the origin of the universe. He said that curiosity about such matters was like a man who, having been wounded by a poisoned arrow, refused to get it pulled out until he was told the caste and origin of his assailant, his name, his height, the color of his skin, and all details about the bow and arrow. In the meantime, he died.

> *Being religious and following* dhamma *has nothing to do with the*
> *dogma that the world is eternal; and it has nothing to do with the other*
> *dogma that the world is not eternal. For whether the world is eternal*
> *or otherwise, birth, old age, death, sorrow, pain, misery, grief,*
> *and despair exist. I am concerned with the extinction of these.*[4]

The Buddha spoke of his teachings as a raft to take us to the farther shore, rather than a description of the shore or something to be carried around once we get there. The farther shore is **nirvana** (Pali: *nibbana*) or liberation, the goal of spiritual effort; the planks of the raft are insights into the truths of existence and teachings about the path to liberation.

myreligienlab

Speculations
Undeclared
CULAMALUNKYA
SUTTA

THE FOUR NOBLE TRUTHS

In his very first sermon at Sarnath, the Buddha set forth the Four Noble Truths, the foundation for all his later teachings:

1 Life inevitably involves suffering, dissatisfaction, and distress.
2 Suffering is caused by craving, rooted in ignorance.
3 Suffering will cease when craving ceases.
4 There is a way to realize this state: the Noble Eightfold Path.

The Buddha was neither pessimistic nor optimistic about our human condition, but realistic. Sri Lankan monk and scholar Walpola Rahula speaks of the Buddha as "the wise and scientific doctor for the ills of the world."[5] In the Four Noble Truths, the Buddha diagnosed the human condition and proposed a cure, one step at a time. The Buddha's First Noble Truth is the existence of *dukkha*: suffering and dissatisfaction. At some time or another, we all experience grief, unfulfilled desires, sickness, old age, physical pain, mental anguish, and eventually death. We may be happy for a while, but this happiness does not last. Even our personal identity is impermanent. What we regard as a "self" is an ever-changing bundle of fleeting feelings, sense impressions, ideas, and evanescent physical matter. One moment of identity leads to the next like one candle being lit from another, but no two moments are the same.

The Second Noble Truth is that the origin of *dukkha* is craving and clinging—to sensory pleasures, to fame and fortune, for things to stay as they are or for them to be different—and attachment to things and ideas. The Buddha taught that craving leads to suffering because of ignorance: We fail to understand the true, constantly changing nature of the things we crave. We grasp at things and hold onto life as we want it to be, rather than seeing things as they are, in a constant state of flux.

In Buddhism, unhappiness is understood as the inevitable companion of happiness. Sunshine gives way to rain, flowers wilt, friends die, and our bodies eventually age and decay. As the contemporary monk Ajahn Sumedho points out, "trying to arrange, control and manipulate conditions so as to always get what we want, always hear what we want to hear, always see what we want to see, so that we never have to experience unhappiness or despair, is a hopeless task."[6]

To remedy this situation, the Buddha taught awareness of *dukkha*, *anitya* (Pali: *anicca*, impermanence), and *anatman* (Pali: *anatta*). According to this revolutionary and unique doctrine, there is no separate, permanent, or immortal self; instead, a human being is an impermanent composite of interdependent physical, emotional, and cognitive components. Insight into *anatman* is spiritually valuable because it reduces attachment to one's mind, body, and selfish desires. Even suffering is useful, because it helps us to see things as they really are. When we realize that everything changes and passes away, moment by moment, we become aware that nothing in this world is permanent and independently existent. There are only momentary configurations within a continual process of change. As Venerable Ajahn Chah of Thailand explained to a dying woman:

Having been born we get old and sick and then we die, and that's totally natural and normal. As soon as we're born, we're dead. It's a little funny to see how at a death people are so grief-stricken and distracted, fearful and sad, and at a birth how happy and delighted. I think if you really want to cry, then it would be better to do so when someone's born. Just think, "This is the way things are." Right now nobody can help you; there is nothing that your family and your possessions can do for you. All that can help you now is the correct awareness.[7]

Once we have grasped these basic facts of life, we can be free in this life, and free from another rebirth. Ajahn Sumedho explains:

When you open the mind to the truth, then you realize there is nothing to fear. What arises passes away, what is born dies, and is not self—so that our sense of being caught in an identity with this human body fades out. We don't see ourselves as some isolated, alienated entity lost in a mysterious and frightening universe. We don't feel overwhelmed by it, trying to find a little piece of it that we can grasp and feel safe with, because we feel at peace with it. Then we have merged with the Truth.[8]

The Third Noble Truth is that *dukkha* will cease when craving and clinging cease. In this way, illusion ends, insight into the true nature of things dawns, and nirvana is achieved. One lives happily and fully in the present moment, free from self-centeredness and full of compassion. One can serve others purely, without thought of oneself. The Fourth Noble Truth is that craving and suffering can be extinguished by following the Noble Eightfold Path—a path of ethical conduct, concentration, and wisdom.

> *To be free from clinging to thinking and feeling is nirvana—the highest, supreme happiness.*
>
> *Maha Ghosananda[9]*

THE NOBLE EIGHTFOLD PATH TO LIBERATION

The Buddha set forth a systematic approach so that human beings could extricate themselves from suffering and achieve the final goal of liberation. The Noble Eightfold Path offers ways to purify the mind of afflictive emotions and avoid unwholesome actions. By following this path, we can live a happy life and also create the causes for a favorable rebirth. Ultimately, the path leads to freedom from the cycle of death and rebirth, and the peace of nirvana.

The first aspect of the Noble Eightfold Path is right understanding—comprehending reality correctly through deep realization of the Four Noble Truths. Initially, this means seeing through illusions, such as the idea that wealth and possessions can bring happiness. Gradually we learn to question old assumptions in the light of the Four Noble Truths. Everything we do and say is ultimately produced by the mind. The Buddha said that if our mind is defiled and uncontrolled, suffering will follow us just as a chariot follows a horse. If our mind is purified and well trained, then our actions will be wholesome and we will naturally experience happiness and well-being.

The second aspect is right thought or motivation. The Buddha's teachings help us to uncover any afflictive emotions that affect our thinking, such as selfish desires or a tendency to hide our imperfections. As we discover and purify mental defilements such as self-interest, our thinking becomes free from the limitations of self-centeredness—relaxed, clear, and open.

The third aspect is right speech. The Buddha taught his followers to relinquish the propensity to lie, gossip, speak harshly, or engage in divisive speech, and instead to use communication in the service of truth and harmony. He also advised us to speak to ourselves and others in a positive way: "May you be well and happy today."

The fourth aspect is right action, which begins with observing the five basic precepts for ethical conduct: to avoid destroying life, stealing, sexual misconduct, lying, and intoxicants. Beyond these, all actions should be based on clear understanding. "Unwholesome deeds," said the Buddha, are those "done from motives of partiality, enmity, stupidity, and fear."[10]

The fifth is right livelihood—making sure that one's way of making a living does not violate the five precepts. One should choose a profession or line of work that does not cause harm to others or disrupt social harmony.

Right effort, the sixth aspect, means striving continually to eliminate the impurities of the mind and diligently cultivating wholesome actions of body, speech, and mind. Joyful effort is the antidote to laziness.

The seventh aspect, right mindfulness, is a distinctive feature of the Buddhist path. The way to liberation requires discipline and the cultivation of awareness, moment to moment. The *Dhammapada* (Verses on the Path), an early compilation of the Buddha's teachings, includes this pithy injunction:

myreligionlab
The Dhammapada

Check your mind.
Be on your guard.
Pull yourself out
as an elephant from mud.[11]

The eighth aspect, right meditation, applies mental discipline to quiet the mind and develop single-pointed concentration. The Buddha explained that the mind is "subtle, invisible, treacherous."[12] Skillful means are therefore needed to understand and control its restless nature. When the mind is completely stilled, it becomes a quiet pool in which the true nature of things is clearly reflected. The various schools of Buddhism that developed over the centuries have taught different techniques of meditation, but this basic principle remains the same.

Try to be mindful, and let things take their natural course. Then your mind will become still in any surroundings, like a clear forest pool. All kinds of wonderful, rare animals will come to drink at the pool, and you will clearly see the nature of all things. You will see many strange and wonderful things come and go, but you will be still. This is the happiness of the Buddha.
    Ajahn Chah, meditation master, Wat Pa Pong, Thailand[13]

THE WHEEL OF BIRTH AND DEATH

Buddhist teachings about rebirth are significantly different from those of Hindu orthodoxy, for there is no eternal, independently existing soul to be reborn. In

Buddhism, each phenomenon or event acts as a cause that sets another into motion. The central cause in this process of cause and effect is *karma* (Pali: *kamma*)—our actions of body, speech, and mind. The impressions of our virtuous and nonvirtuous actions shape our experience moment-by-moment. When we die, this process continues, passing on the flame to a new life in a realm of existence that reflects our past *karma*.

This wheel of birth and death operates primarily because of the three root afflictions: attachment, aversion, and delusion. The opposites of these afflictions—

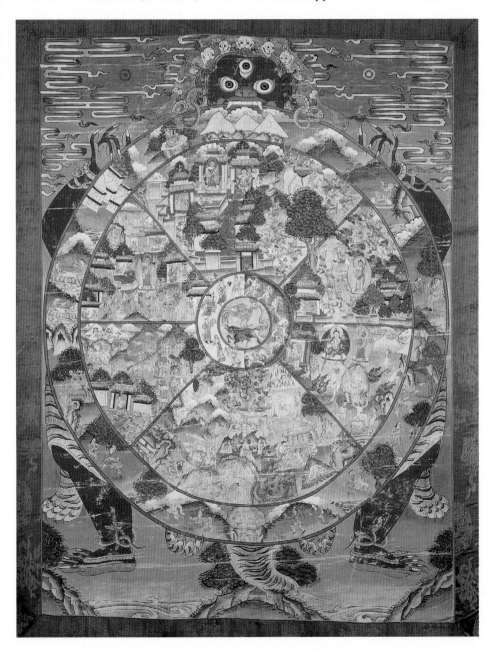

The Wheel of Life: in the center are animals representing the three root afflictions; attachment, aversion, and delusion. The next circle shows the fate of those with good karma *(left) and bad* karma *(right). The third circle represents the six spheres of existence, from the gods to the infernal regions. The outer rim shows the chain of cause and effect. Grasping the wheel is a monster representing death, impermanence.*

non-greed (such as generosity, renunciation for others' sake), non-hate (such as friendliness, compassion, and patience), and non-delusion (such as mental clarity and insight)—act as causes to ultimately leave the circle of birth and death.

In Buddhist thought, not only do sentient beings take birth many times, but they also take on many different forms, creating an interconnected web of life. This has important implications for one's relationships with all life. One text explains:

The Great Ape Jataka Tale

When Brahmadatta was king of Benares, the Buddha took birth among the apes and became the powerful king of the 80,000 monkeys living near the Ganges. Overhanging the river there was a great mango tree, with huge and delicious fruits. When ripe, some fell on the ground and some fell into the river. Eating these mangoes with his monkeys, the Great Being foresaw that those that fell into the water would some day bring danger to the herd. He ordered that all the mangoes growing on branches over the river should be plucked when very small and discarded. However, one fruit was hidden by an ant's nest. When it was ripe, it fell into the nets which the king's fishermen had placed into the river. When they pulled out the ambrosial fruit, they took it to the king in Benares. When he tasted it, he developed a great craving for more and insisted on being taken to the tree from which it came.

A flotilla of boats brought the king to the great mango tree. Camping beneath it, he ate mangoes to his heart's delight. At midnight, the Great Being and his monkeys came and leapt from branch to branch above, eating the mangoes. The king woke up and saw them. He ordered his men to surround the tree and prepare to shoot arrows at the monkeys so that they could feast on mangoes and monkey flesh the following day.

Terrified, the monkeys appealed to the Great Being for help. He told them not to be afraid, for he would save their lives. So saying, he at once climbed to one of the branches over the river and then made a tremendous leap across the wide river to the opposite bank. There he cut a long bamboo shoot which he calculated would be long enough to reach across the river. Lashing it to a bush on the farther shore, he lashed the opposite end of the bamboo to his waist and then made a terrific leap back toward the mango tree where the monkeys were cowering in fear for their lives. The shoot being slightly short, he grabbed an overhanging branch so that his own body's length filled the remaining distance. He signaled to the monkeys that they were to run across his body and then the bamboo shoot in order to escape to the other shore. Paying their obeisances to the Great Being and asking his forgiveness, the 80,000 monkeys ran across him to safety. In the process, one of the monkeys [later reborn as Devadatta, a cousin of the Buddha who repeatedly tried to undermine him] took the opportunity to leap from an upper branch onto the great ape's back, breaking his heart.

After all the monkeys had crossed to safety, the wounded Great Being was left alone, hanging from the tree. The king, who had watched the whole thing, was struck by the greatness of his self-sacrifice for the sake of his monkeys. At daybreak, he ordered his people to gently bring the great ape down from the tree, bathe him, rub his body with fine oil, dress him in yellow, and lay him to rest. Sitting beside the great ape, the king questioned him about his action. The Great Being explained to him that no worry or death could trouble him, and that he had acted for the welfare of all those whom he governed, as an example for the king to emulate. After thus advising the king, the Great Being died. King Brahmadatta ordered funeral ceremonies due to a king for him, and then had a shrine built at the place of his cremation and had his skull inlaid with gold, which he then enshrined at Benares. According to the instructions of the Great Being, Brahmadatta then became a very righteous ruler and a traveler to the Bright World.

When the Buddha told this Jataka Tale, he revealed that the human king was Ananda, and that the ape-king was himself.

In the long course of samsara *[reincarnation], there is not one among living*
beings with form who has not been mother, father, brother, sister, son, or daughter,
or some other relative. Being connected with the process of taking birth, one is kin
to all wild and domestic animals, birds, and beings born from the womb.[14]

It is said that the Buddha remembered all his past lives and told stories about
them to illustrate moral lessons. Hundreds of these stories have been collected as
the Jataka Tales, or birth stories of the Buddha's past lives as a bodhisattva. The
one recounted here, "The Great Ape Jataka Tale" (see Box), illustrates not only
the Buddhist path as a way of personal development but also its importance in
establishing moral guidelines for monastics, laity, and rulers alike.

In Buddhist cosmology, there are multiple possible states of existence, including hell beings, hungry ghosts, animals, humans, and gods. Whether interpreted
as psychological metaphors or metaphysical realities, all these states of rebirth are
imperfect and impermanent. Sentient beings take birth again and again, caught
up in this cycle of *samsara*, repeatedly experiencing birth, aging, suffering, and
death as a result of their actions and mental defilements. Finally, by purifying
their minds of greed, hatred, ignorance, and other delusions, they are able to
achieve nirvana, or liberation from cyclic existence and suffering.

NIRVANA

The Buddha said little about nirvana, the goal of Buddhist practice, but described
it as a desirable state of mind. The only way to end the cycle of suffering is to end
all craving and lead a life free of attachment that has no karmic consequences.
One enters a state that the Buddha called "quietude of heart,"[15] "a state beyond
grasping, beyond aging and dying,"[16] "the unborn, … undying, … unsorrowing,
… stainless, the uttermost security from bonds."[17] For the *arhant* (Pali: *arhat*,
arahat), a worthy one, who has found nirvana in this life:

No suffering for him
who is free from sorrow
free from the fetters of life
free in everything he does.
He has reached the end of his road. …

Like a bird invisibly flying in the sky,
he lives without possessions,
knowledge his food, freedom his world,
while others wonder. …

He has found freedom—
peaceful his thinking, peaceful his speech,
peaceful his deed, tranquil his mind.[18]

When an *arhant* dies, individuality disappears and the being enters the
ultimate state of nirvana. The Buddha remained silent when he was asked what
happens to an *arhant* after death. Why? At one point he picked up a handful of
leaves from the forest floor and asked his disciples which were more numerous,

A nun leaves the meditation hall in Dharamsala, India, after sunrise practices.

the leaves in his hand or those in the forest. When they replied, "Very few in your hand, lord; many more in the grove," he said:

> *Exactly. So you see, friends, the things that I know and have not revealed are more than the truths I know and have revealed. And why have I not revealed them? Because, friends, there is no profit in them; because they are not helpful to holiness; because they do not lead from disgust to cessation and peace, because they do not lead from knowledge to wisdom and nirvana.*[19]

Branches of Buddhism

After the Buddha attracted a group of disciples, he began to send them out in all directions to help teach the Dharma. Two hundred years after the Buddha died, a powerful Indian king named Ashoka led a huge military campaign to extend his empire. After he saw the tremendous loss of life on both sides, he reportedly felt great remorse, became a Buddhist, and began to espouse nonviolence. He had inscriptions written on rocks and pillars throughout his empire teaching the Dharma, with an emphasis on developing an attitude of social responsibility. Under King Ashoka's leadership, Buddhism was disseminated throughout the kingdom and outward to other countries, beginning its development as a global religion. After Ashoka's death, *brahmins* reasserted their political influence and Buddhists were persecuted in some parts of India. By the time of the twelfth-century Muslim invasions of India, Buddhism was in decline and never became the dominant religion in the Buddha's homeland.

As the Buddha's teachings expanded and adapted to local cultures, various schools of interpretation developed. Of the earliest Buddhist schools, only the

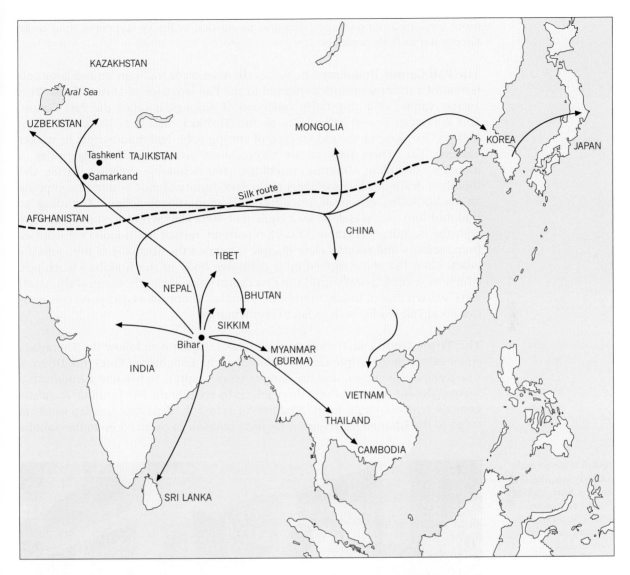

one today known as **Theravada** ("Way of the Elders") survives. This school is prevalent in Southeast Asian countries such as Sri Lanka, Myanmar (formerly Burma), Thailand, Cambodia, and Laos. The schools that developed somewhat later are collectively known as **Mahayana** ("Great Vehicle"). This school gradually became dominant in Nepal, Tibet, China, Korea, Mongolia, Vietnam, and Japan. Followers of all these traditions are in general agreement about the Four Noble Truths, the Noble Eightfold Path, and the teachings about *karma*, *samsara*, and nirvana.

Buddhism spread in all directions from India but had nearly disappeared in India itself by the 13th century CE.

THERAVADA: THE PATH OF MINDFULNESS

Theravadin Buddhists study the early scriptures in Pali, honor the life of renunciation, and follow mindfulness meditation teachings. These characteristics are more obvious among intellectuals and monastics; ordinary laypeople tend to be devotional in their practices.

The Pali Canon Buddhists who follow the Theravada tradition study a large collection of ancient scriptures preserved in the Pali language of ancient India. This ancient **canon**, or authoritative collection of writings, is called the **Pali Canon**. This collection is also referred to as the **Tipitaka** (Sanskrit: *Tripitaka*, "Three Baskets," because of the old practice of storing palm-leaf manuscripts in wicker baskets). The "Three Baskets" are three collections of sacred writings: rules of monastic discipline, Dharma teachings, and scholastic treatises. After the Buddha's death, leading members of the community of monks started compiling an authoritative canon of teachings and monastic discipline. According to Buddhist lore, this was done by a council of 500 elders who had studied directly with the Buddha. Venerable Ananda reportedly recited the Buddha's discourses from memory and another close disciple rehearsed the discipline of the monastic order. Then the elders agreed on a definitive body of the Buddha's teachings, which were recited orally until the first century BCE, when the *sutras* (Pali: *suttas*) were written down. In addition to the Tipitaka, Theravadins accept certain noncanonical Pali works, such as later commentaries.

The Triple Gem Like Buddhists of all schools, those who follow the Theravada go for refuge in the **Triple Gem**: the Buddha (the Enlightened One), the Dharma (the teachings he gave), and the Sangha (community). To become a Buddhist, a person goes for refuge in these three jewels by reciting the Pali formula: *Buddham saranam gacchami* ("I go to the Buddha for refuge"), *dhammam saranam gacchami* ("I go to the Dharma for refuge"), *sangham saranam gacchami* ("I go to the Sangha

Buddhist monks make daily rounds with their begging bowls seeking food from laypeople, who serve them with reverence as in this scene in Laos.

for refuge"). One takes refuge in the Buddha not by praying to him for help, but by honoring him as a supreme teacher and inspiring model. In a sense, taking refuge in the Buddha is honoring the Buddha-wisdom within each of us.

The Dharma is like a medicine that can cure our suffering, but it will not work unless we take it. In the Pali Canon, it is described as immediate, timeless, leading to calmness, and known only through direct experience and personal effort.

The Sangha is ultimately the community of realized beings; on the conventional level, the Sangha is the order of *bhikshus* and *bhikshunis* who have renounced worldly life in order to follow, preserve, and share the Dharma.

The Buddha established one of the world's first monastic orders, and the Sangha remains very strong in Theravada countries. There are presently about half a million Theravadin monks in Southeast Asia. To simplify their worldly lives and devote themselves to studying and teaching the Dharma, monks and nuns shave their heads, dress in simple robes, own only a few basic material items, eat no solid foods after noon, practice celibacy, and depend on the laity for their food, clothing, and medical supplies. Early every morning the monks set forth with an alms bowl, and laypeople regard it as a merit-making opportunity to offer food to them. The monks reciprocate by offering spiritual guidance, chanted blessings, and performing various social services, including offering advice and education.

Buddhist monasteries are at the center of village life, not isolated, as one might imagine. The monasteries are left open, and people come and go throughout the day. The monks hold a revered social position as models of self-control, kindness, and intelligence. In Thailand, it is common for young men to take temporary vows as monks—often for the duration of the rainy season when little farmwork can be done. They wear saffron robes, set forth with shaven heads and alms bowls, and receive religious instruction while practicing a life of simplicity.

In contrast to the monks, there has traditionally been little social support for Buddhist nuns in Southeast Asia. Provisions were made during the time of the Buddha for women monastics to live in their own monasteries, practicing the same lifestyle as monks, but the order of fully ordained nuns (*bhikshunis*) disappeared completely in Theravadin countries about a thousand years ago. Many of the early Buddhist scriptures take an egalitarian position toward women's capacity for wisdom and attainment of nirvana, but spiritual power has remained in the hands of monks and there has been little opportunity for nuns to take positions of teaching and leadership.

myreligionlab
Rejection of Birth Castes
VASETTHA SUTTA

Over time, some of the monks and the texts they edited apparently became somewhat sexist. Because Buddhist monks are celibate, they are not allowed to come into direct contact with women, and many believe that women are hindrances to monks' spiritual development. Feminist scholars object to this interpretation. Thai Buddhist Dr. Chatsumarn Kabilsingh, for instance, asserts:

Newly ordained monks who have not had much experience with practice and are very weak in their mental resolve may be easily swayed by sensual impulses, of which women are the major attraction. Even if no women are present, some monks still create problems for themselves by images of women they have in their minds. Women are not responsible for the sexual behavior or imaginings of men; the monks themselves must cope with their own sensual desires. Enlightened ones are well-fortified against such mental states and are able to transcend gender

Some 135 women from 23 countries received full ordination as Buddhist nuns at Bodh Gaya in 1998, helping to revive orders of bhikshunis.

differences. The Buddha himself found no need to avoid women, because women no longer appeared to him as sexual objects. He was well-balanced and in control of his mental processes.[20]

There are now attempts to revive full ordination for nuns in Theravadin countries. A landmark event occurred in 1998, when 135 nuns from many countries received full ordination in Bodh Gaya. According to the code of discipline, ordination of nuns is possible only if a quorum of both ordained monks and nuns is present. In China, Taiwan, Japan, and Korea orders of fully ordained nuns have continued, and therefore it was possible to assemble the requisite number of ten *bhikshus* and ten *bhikshunis* in Bodh Gaya.

Meditation   The Theravada tradition preserves a wide variety of meditation techniques for cultivating the mind, derived from the early Buddhist teachings. The two major branches of meditation practice are *samatha* (calm abiding) and *vipassana* (insight). The practice begins with increasing one's attentiveness to a specific object to focus the mind and achieve calm abiding. One then proceeds to the practice of *vipassana* to develop insight into *dukkha, anicca,* and *anatta.*

As taught by the famous Burmese meditation master Mahasi Sayadaw (1904–1982), *vipassana* practice begins by simply watching one's breath as it flows in and out, focusing attention on the rise and fall of the abdomen. To keep the mind concentrated on the present movement, rather than being distracted by uncontrolled, conditioned responses, one continually makes concise mental notes of what is happening: "rising" and "falling." Other *vipassana* masters suggest observing a point on the upper lip as the breath goes in and out of the nostrils, posting one's attention like a gatekeeper at that point. Despite the attempt to hold the restless mind to one point, inevitably other thoughts and feelings arise in the restless mind. As they arise, one simply notes these thoughts and feelings—

"imagining," "wandering," "remembering"—and returns one's attention to the rising and falling of the breath. Bodily sensations are handled in the same way, noting "itching," "tight," "tired," and so on, as they arise, but maintaining an observer's attitude rather than letting one's mental equanimity be disturbed by reacting to the sensations. Periods of sitting meditation are alternated with periods of walking meditation, during which one notes the movements of the body in great detail: "lifting," "moving," and "placing." If ecstatic states or visions arise in the process of meditation, one simply notes them and lets them pass away without attachment. In the same way, emotions that arise are simply observed, accepted, and allowed to pass away, without evaluating them as "good" or "bad." As Buddhist teacher Joko Beck mentions, ordinarily it is very easy to get caught up and stuck in our emotions:

> Everyone's fascinated by their emotions because we think that's who we are. We're afraid that if we let our attachment to them go, we'll be nobody. Which of course we are! When you wander into your ideas, your hopes, your dreams, turn back— not just once but ten thousand times if need be, a million times if need be.[21]

The three characteristics of existence that the Buddha described—*dukkha* (suffering and dissatisfaction), *anicca* (impermanence), and *anatta* (no eternal self)— become apparent during the process of meditation. As one continues the practice, the mind becomes calm, clear, attentive, flexible, and free from the disturbances of likes and dislikes. The next step is to carry this same type of mindfulness over into every activity of everyday life.

Devotional practices   In addition to the contemplative and philosophical traditions described above, many lay Buddhists and also many monastic practitioners of Theravada Buddhism in Southeast Asia are likely to turn to the Buddha in devotion, taking refuge in his protective presence and power. Temples, halls, and roadside shrines have been built with images of the Buddha before which people bow, light candles, burn incense, offer flowers, press bits of gold leaf onto the images, and make aspirations and prayers. Some monastics and intellectuals— including Protestant Christians who became interested in Buddhist studies in the late nineteenth century—have labeled such practices antithetical to the spirit of Buddhism, which they understand as rationalistic, philosophical, nonritualistic, noniconic, and nontheistic. Despite the increasing commercialization of Buddhist imagery, some commentators are now trying to trace the history of image-oriented worship. Devotional practices are so widespread and so influential in popular Buddhist practice that scholars have begun to examine them as perhaps being part of the mainstream of Buddhism after all.

A key text in this regard is the *Mahaparinibbana Sutta*, a Pali scripture that describes the Buddha's cremation and the dispersal of his relics. The text also deals with the issue of devotionalism, recounting that, before his death, the Buddha recommended the commemoration of his relics alongside dedicated practice of the Dharma: "Whoever lays wreaths or puts sweet perfumes and colors … with a devout heart, will reap benefit and happiness for a long time."[22] Simultaneously, the text advocates devotion to the Dharma as a way of respecting, revering, and paying homage to the Buddha. When lay Buddhists recite the refuge formula, taking refuge in the Buddha, the Dharma, and the Sangha, they

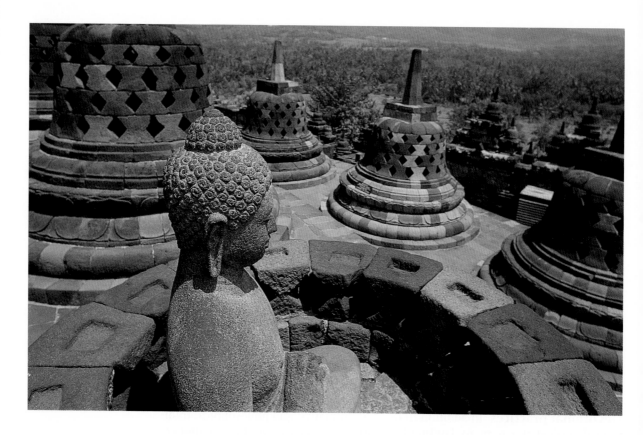

Stupas, such as these bell-shaped monuments in Borobudur, Java, may house relics or statues of the Buddha and are sacred places for pilgrimage. The Buddha's long ears symbolize long life; elders are valued because of their experience and wisdom. The raised upper part of his head represents higher consciousness developed through years of meditation practice. The flame at the top signifies extinction of the flames of anger, hatred, and delusion.

may experience this refuge not merely as a philosophical idea, but as a way of connecting with the timeless presence of the Buddha.

In one popular ritual in northern Thailand, a network of threads attached to a large statue of the Buddha is used in special ceremonies to conduct his spiritual power to the Sangha, holy water, amulets, or new images to be consecrated. The 108 squares formed overhead by the strings are believed to form a magical cosmos whose sacred energy touches the earth through cords hanging downward. People may wrap these cords around their heads during the chanting of *sutras* by monks and thus receive spiritual blessings.

To consecrate new images of the Buddha, monks initially seal them by closing the eyes with beeswax and covering the heads with cloth. Throughout the night, they chant, meditate, and teach about the Buddha and the Dharma as a way to train their minds and also consecrate the images. In the process, the Sangha is also drawn into a strong sense of unity with the Buddha, the Dharma, and each other. At sunrise, the coverings are removed from the images, and they are offered milk and sweet rice; in a sense, they are now living presences.

Similarly, followers may consider the Buddha's power to be present in relics from his cremated body. Images of the Buddha may also be placed in stupas, reliquary mounds reaching toward the sky—a practice perhaps derived from earlier indigenous spiritual traditions. For instance, a tiny bone chip believed to be a relic of the Buddha is enshrined at Doi Suthep Temple in Chiang Mai in Thailand. To share this sacred relic with the people, the ruler is said to have placed it on the

A relic purported to be a tooth of the Buddha is so revered that it is carried on an elephant palanquin in a huge yearly procession in Sri Lanka.

back of a white elephant—a legendary symbol of the Buddha—in the belief that the elephant would choose the best place for the temple. The elephant climbed a nearby hill until it reached the auspicious spot and went down on its knees. Today, flocks of pilgrims climb the 290 steps to the temple and request blessings by acts such as pressing squares of gold leaf onto an image of the Buddha, lighting three sticks of incense to honor the Triple Gem, lighting candles, and offering flowers. So great are the powers associated with relics that huge processions carrying what is thought to be the Buddha's tooth relic have been used by the governments in Sri Lanka and Myanmar to legitimize their claims to temporal power.

Cherished images of the Buddha proliferate in temples and roadside shrines. The shrines are almost identical to the indigenous spirit shrines, which are still quite common in Thailand, where Buddhism is frequently combined with indigenous spirituality and Brahmanism. These physical images are a reminder of the Buddha's teachings and give a sense of his protective, guiding presence. In

The golden feet of a 105-foot (32-meter) high Buddha at Wat Indra Viharn, Bangkok.

Southeast Asia, aspects of Theravada Buddhism are often adopted by shamans for greater efficacy in healing rituals. In Sri Lanka, the *yakeduras* invoke the power of the Buddha and the Dharma to ward off evil spirits and help cure spiritually afflicted people. In the cosmic hierarchy, the Buddha and the Dharma are considered powerful and therefore useful in subduing lesser forces. During healing rituals, patients listen to Buddhist stories to help free themselves from afflictions and obtain protection by the power of the mind. Even monks are regarded as magical protectors of sorts, and followers frequently request chanted blessings for protection.

As in all Buddhist cultures, Buddhist temples are important centers for community identity and integration. There the monks not only teach the Dharma, but also preside over agricultural festivals to improve the harvest, ceremonies to assist the dead to achieve a better rebirth, and ceremonies to invoke the blessings of the deities. All these events generate a festive atmosphere and communal joy. The monks and nuns help the people accumulate merit or spiritual benefits and share them with others. Ashin Nyana Dipa, a monk from Myanmar, explains the idea of transferring merit:

> When we concentrate, our mind is purified. The purified mind can transmit, for it is stable. I can share if I have already done good deeds for the people, such as teaching them *vipassana*. It is like a wire: Without wire, electricity cannot pass. The wire is concentration; the electricity is loving-kindness. We have to use concentration and send benefits with loving-kindness. You have a bank account, so I put something into your bank account to fill it. Like a candle, one gives light to another. Then the light is more and more. My light will not be reduced; it will be more and more. You also get more; I also get more. Sometimes when I meditate, I see your face in my mind. When I see your face, I want to see your face happy, I don't want you to be in trouble. So I'm sending, sending my merits: "Let it be good."[23]

MAHAYANA: THE PATH OF COMPASSION AND WISDOM

Additional Buddhist practices and teachings began to appear in a wide range of scriptures from the early centuries CE. These further developments in thought and practice beyond the Pali scriptures gradually evolved into what is called Mahayana, the Great Vehicle. The Mahayana scriptures emphasize the practice of compassion and wisdom by both monastics and laypeople, toward the goal of liberating all sentient beings from suffering. The Mahayana traditions honor all the teachings set forth in the Pali Canon and, in addition, accept the extensive Mahayana literature originally found in Sanskrit and later translated into Chinese, Tibetan, and other languages. This literature praises the deeds and qualities of innumerable Buddhas and bodhisattvas, and inspires practitioners to develop the compassion and wisdom needed to become bodhisattvas and eventually Buddhas themselves.

The Mahayana scriptures emphasize the importance of religious experience. The Dharma is not embodied only in scriptures; for the Mahayanist it is the source of a transformative experience that awakens the quest for enlightenment as the greatest value in life and seeks to embody the Dharma in every aspect of life. Each school—and there are many branches within Mahayana—offers a special set of methods, or "skillful means," for awakening. These methods are quite varied, in contrast to the uniformity of Theravada, but the Mahayana traditions also share many common characteristics.

Bodhisattvas An early Mahayana scripture, the *Lotus Sutra*, defended its innovative ideas by claiming that earlier teachings were skillful means for those with lower capacities. The idea is that the Buddha geared his teaching to his audience, and that his teachings were presented in different ways and at different levels of completeness in accordance with the readiness of his audience to understand

Map showing the approximate distribution of Theravada and Mahayana Buddhism in the world today.

them. Some researchers explain this as a way to give credit to the earlier teachings while going beyond them. Like other Mahayana texts, the *Lotus Sutra* claimed that there was a higher goal than the *arhant's* achievement of liberation, namely, to aspire to become a **bodhisattva** (a being who is dedicated to liberating others from suffering) and work to achieve the perfect enlightenment of a Buddha. The *Lotus Sutra* says that all beings have the capacity for Buddhahood and are destined to attain it eventually. Both monastics and laity are urged to take the bodhisattva vow and work to become fully enlightened. Today Mahayana Buddhists in East Asia express this commitment in the Four Great Bodhisattva Vows compiled in China in the sixth century CE by Tiantai Zhiyi, founder of the Tiantai School:

Beings are infinite in number, I vow to save them all;
The obstructive passions are endless in number, I vow to end them all;
The teachings for saving others are countless, I vow to learn them all;
Buddhahood is the supreme achievement, I vow to attain it.

His Holiness the Fourteenth Dalai Lama, representing the Tibetan tradition, says:

The motivation to achieve Buddhahood in order to save all sentient beings is really a marvelous determination. That person becomes very courageous, warm-hearted, and useful in society.[24]

Guanyin, "hearer of cries," bodhisattva of mercy, as depicted in a Thai mural.

Soen Nakagawa-roshi, from the Japanese Zen tradition, says:

You are not just here for yourself alone, but for the sake of all sentient beings. Keep your mind pure and warm.[25]

The concept of the selfless bodhisattva is not just an ideal for earthly conduct; numerous bodhisattvas are believed to be present and available to hear the devotees' petitions. As emanations of wisdom and compassion, they are sources of inspiration and blessing on the path to Buddhahood. For karmic purification and removal of inner obstructions to enlightenment and bodhisattvahood, aspirants are taught to practice the Ten Perfections (*Paramitas*): generosity, morality, renunciation, transcendental wisdom, energy and diligent effort, patience and forbearance, truthfulness, determination, loving kindness, and serene equanimity.

The most popular bodhisattva in East Asia is Avalokiteshvara (known as Guanyin in China, Kannon in Japan), who symbolizes compassion and extends blessings to all. Although it is depicted as male in India, the *Lotus Sutra* says that this bodhisattva takes whatever form is needed to help others and lists thirty-two examples. In East Asia, Avalokiteshvara is typically depicted as female, often as the bestower or protector of young children. In one hand, she holds a vase with the nectar of compassion; in the other, she holds a willow branch symbolizing her healing powers. An image of the bodhisattva holding a baby has become especially popular in East Asia as a source of inspiration and blessing for women and children. She may also be depicted standing serenely atop a dragon in a turbulent ocean. The storm-tossed ocean and dragon are symbols of the upheavals of life and within our minds. Guanyin is therefore a model of the inner strength, equilibrium, and self-control with which these turbulences can be mastered.

The Three Bodies of Buddha   The Theravada tradition emphasizes that the Buddha is an historical figure who taught the Dharma as a guide to liberation from suffering, then died like any other human being. By contrast, in the Mahayana tradition, the Buddha came to be regarded as the embodiment of enlightened awareness. Metaphysically, Buddha is said to be an immanent presence in the universe with three aspects, or "bodies." The first aspect is the formless enlightened wisdom of a Buddha; the second is the body of bliss of a Buddha, an aspect that communicates the Dharma to bodhisattvas; and the third is the emanation body, whereby a Buddha manifests in countless forms to help liberate suffering beings. It was in such an emanation body that the Buddha appeared for a time on the earth as the historical figure Shakyamuni Buddha.

In Mahayana, the Buddhas are seen to embody perfect purity, boundless compassion, omniscient wisdom, and many other enlightened qualities. Although some may interpret the Buddhas and bodhisattvas as metaphors for various aspects of enlightened awareness, others regard them as living presences that are able to impart blessings and guidance to those who call on them. Both Theravada and Mahayana are nontheistic, in that the existence or non-existence of gods is not a primary concern, yet ordinary people are inclined to seek help in times of need.

Mahayana scriptures portray Buddhas and bodhisattvas moving swiftly through intergalactic space and time, appearing in multiple forms at different world systems simultaneously. In the Tibetan tradition, for example, the Fourteenth Dalai Lama is regarded as a human emanation of Avalokiteshvara, the bodhisattva of compassion. Many Tibetan monks, nuns, and laypeople followed him into exile after the communist takeover of Tibet and have set up a community in the mountains of northern India, in Dharamsala, to be near him. Practitioners are not to be attached to these appearances, but receive teachings and draw great inspiration from them.

Emptiness As in Theravada, the Mahayana schools understand ultimate reality as the true nature of things. This "suchness" is not an absolute, but the absence of a permanent, independent reality. In accordance with the universal law of cause and effect, all conditioned phenomena arise and perish continuously, and therefore lack true existence. In the Udana scripture from the Pali Canon, the Buddha states, "O monks, there is an unborn, undying, unchanging, uncreated. If it were not so, there would be no point to life, or to training." But here the Buddha is referring to nirvana, a nonregressive state of liberation from mental afflictions, suffering, and rebirth, rather than to an eternal, independently existing reality.

Sunyata, meaning emptiness or voidness, is the most complex and profound of the Mahayana teachings. The concept of *sunyata* was elaborated by the Indian philosopher Nagarjuna around the second and third century CE on the basis of the Perfection of Wisdom scriptures. According to Nagarjuna, compounded things have no independent existence and no eternal reality. All composite phenomena arise and pass away, dependent on causes and conditions. The world of phenomena is therefore empty of true or inherent existence. Insight into emptiness is similar to the insight into no-self that arises when we observe the arising and passing away of the elements of mind and body during *vipassana* meditation. Insight into emptiness also arises by understanding the dependent nature of thought constructs and freeing our minds from fixed concepts.

Everything being empty, there is nothing to cling to, so one who realizes emptiness is free to experience reality directly and to be compassionate without attachment. The concepts of selflessness and emptiness help practitioners understand things "as they are" and also help them overcome attachment to things, including attachment to concepts.

Some people may wonder: If everything is ultimately empty, what's the point of action? The teaching on emptiness does not mean we do nothing, but that we are not attached to the results of our actions. Emptiness is always paired with compassion, skillful means, and the wish to benefit all living beings. Zen teacher Dainin Katagiri advised:

> *Broadly speaking, without desire, how can we survive in this world? Using our knowledge, we consider carefully what to do next. And then whatever we decide to do, let's just do it, do our best to accomplish it from the beginning to the end. That's all we have to do. Immediately, see the result and accept it. Just continue to sow good seeds from moment to moment.[26]*

The Perfection of Wisdom scriptures that celebrate the liberating experience of emptiness are foundational texts for most Mahayana schools. What is distinctive and startling about Mahayana is the application of the idea of emptiness to all things. Even the teachings of the Buddha and emptiness itself are empty of true existence. In the *Heart Sutra*, which is recited in all Mahayana schools, the core

Many Buddhists anticipate the coming of Maitreya, the Buddha of the future, to re-establish the purity of the Dharma.

myreligionlab

Emptiness
NAGARJUNA

myreligionlab

The Heart Sutra

doctrines of traditional Buddhism are also deconstructed. Avalokiteshvara sees that the five aggregates of a person (form, feelings, perceptions, karmic formations, and consciousness) are empty of true existence, because they exist in relation to and dependent on other phenomena. With this realization, the bodhisattva becomes free of delusion. Next, birth and death, purity and defilement, increase and decrease are understood to be empty; the six sense objects, the six sense organs, and the six types of consciousness are empty; life and death are empty; the Four Noble Truths and Eightfold Path are empty. Even knowledge and attainment are proclaimed to be empty. With this "perfection of wisdom," there are no obstacles and no fear. Having seen through the illusion of true existence of even the core Buddhist teachings, one attains nirvana. In the *Heart Sutra*, this realization culminates in the mantra: *Gate, Gate, paragate, parasamgate, bodhi, svaha!* ("Gone, gone, gone beyond, gone completely beyond, awakened, so be it!"). As Professor David Chappell observes:

> The systematic emptying of the central doctrines of the tradition is unparalleled in religious history. (Imagine a Christian saying that the Ten Commandments and Lord's Prayer and Apostles' Creed are empty!) And yet, insight into the impermanence of all things, and their connectedness, gives Mahayana a self-critical profundity and an inclusive acceptance of diversity, which provides balance in the midst of movement, and peace in the midst of compassion.[27]

CHAN AND ZEN: THE GREAT WAY OF ENLIGHTENMENT

Buddhism was transmitted from India to China beginning around the first century CE and thence to Korea, Japan, and Vietnam, absorbing elements of

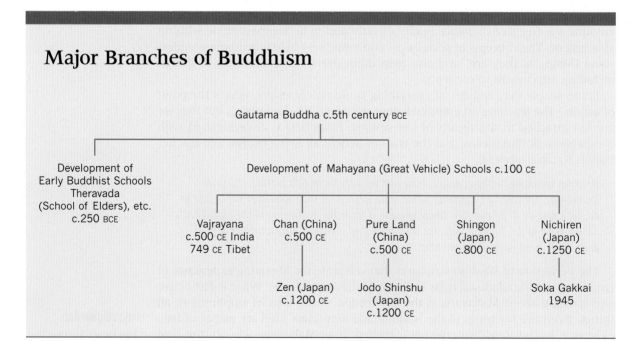

Major Branches of Buddhism

Gautama Buddha c.5th century BCE

Development of Early Buddhist Schools Theravada (School of Elders), etc. c.250 BCE

Development of Mahayana (Great Vehicle) Schools c.100 CE

Vajrayana c.500 CE India 749 CE Tibet

Chan (China) c.500 CE

Pure Land (China) c.500 CE

Shingon (Japan) c.800 CE

Nichiren (Japan) c.1250 CE

Zen (Japan) c.1200 CE

Jodo Shinshu (Japan) c.1200 CE

Soka Gakkai 1945

Daoism along the way. Around the fifth century, according to tradition, a South Indian monk named Bodhidharma traveled to a monastery in northern China, where he reportedly spent nine years in silent meditation, "facing the wall." He became recognized as the first patriarch of the radical path that came to be called Chan Buddhism, from the Sanskrit word *dhyana*, meaning meditation. Although traditional accounts of Bodhidharma's life and contributions may not be completely factual, they illustrate the emphasis on meditation and direct insight that characterize Chan Buddhism, which became the most successful form of Buddhism in China. Bodhidharma's legendary practice became emblematic of a firm determination to reach enlightenment through sitting meditation. In lines attributed to Bodhidharma, Chan Buddhism is described as:

Directly pointing to the human mind,
Achieving Buddhahood by seeing one's nature.[28]

The Chan school was transmitted to Japan, where it is known as **Zen**. Zen claims to preserve the essence of the Buddha's teachings through direct experience, triggered by mind-to-mind transmission of the Dharma. Instead of focusing on scriptures, Buddhas, and bodhisattvas, Zen emphasizes direct insight into the true nature of one's own mind, to reveal one's own Buddha nature. Direct insight results from *zazen* (sitting meditation). "To sit," said the Sixth Zen Patriarch, "means to obtain absolute freedom and not to allow any thought to be caused by external objects. To meditate means to realize the imperturbability of one's original nature."[29]

> *The Great Way is not difficult*
> *for those who have no preferences.*
> *When love and hate are both absent*
> *everything becomes clear and undisguised.*
> *Make the smallest distinction, however,*
> *and heaven and earth are set infinitely apart.*
>
> *Sengtsan*[30]

In Zen, instructions in the manner of sitting are quite rigorous to avoid distracting the mind: One must maintain an upright posture and not move during the meditation period. Skillful means are then applied to make the mind one-pointed and clear. The initial practice is simply to watch and count each inhalation and exhalation from one to ten, starting over from one if anything other than awareness of the breath enters the mind. Although this practice sounds simple, the mind is so restless that many people must work for months before finally getting to ten without having to start over. Getting to ten is not really the goal; the goal is the process itself, the process of recognizing what comes up in the mind and gently letting it go without attachment or preferences.

As one practices *zazen*, undisturbed by phenomena, one becomes inwardly calm and the natural mind is revealed in its original purity. This "original mind" is spacious and free, like an open sky. Thoughts and sensations may float through it like clouds, but they arise and then disappear, leaving no trace. What remains

myreligionlab
Discovering
Universal Emptiness
DOGEN

Zen Oxherding Pictures

The ten Zen oxherding pictures metaphorically illustrate a series of stages along the spiritual path, with the meaning of each picture to be discovered through meditation. The practitioner is the herder (the worldly self, usually portrayed in male form) who is searching for the elusive ox (our true nature) in the wilderness. In the second picture, the herder notices the footprints of the ox. In the third, he catches sight of the ox. In the fourth, he struggles mightily to grasp the ox. In the fifth, he tames the ox with tether and whip, until "well tended and domesticated, the ox grows pure and gentle." In the sixth picture (illustrated upper right), the seeker has found and tamed the ox and leisurely returns home riding high upon it, playing tunes "full of profound meaning." In the seventh, he reaches home, but the ox disappears. In the eighth stage (below left), both ox and herder have disappeared—"Whip, tether, person, ox: all are empty! Blue sky all and all around." In the ninth picture, the herder is shown Returning to the Source: "Inside his hut, he does not see any object outside." In the tenth and final picture (below right), the now-enlightened herder returns to the market-place with helping hands and a wide grin on his face.[31]

Brush and ink drawings by Gyokusei Jikihara

The tea ceremony in Japan, a ritual way of inculcating direct awareness, simplicity, and self-restraint.

is insight into "thusness," the true nature of things. In some Zen schools, this perception of thusness comes in a sudden burst of insight, or *kensho*.

When the mind is calm, action becomes spontaneous and natural. Zen practitioners are taught to rest in the natural simplicity of their own **Buddha-nature**. It is said that two Zen monks, on gaining a glimpse of enlightenment, ran naked through the woods scribbling on rocks. On the other hand, the Zen tradition links spontaneity with intense, disciplined concentration. In the art of calligraphy, the perfectly spontaneous brushstroke is executed with the whole body in a single breath, yet this is the outcome of years of attentive practice. Being fully present in the moment—when pouring tea, being aware only of pouring tea—is simplicity itself. Whether painting, serving tea, sweeping, or simply breathing, the unconditioned "thusness" of life is fully revealed.

Another tool, used in the Rinzai Zen tradition, is the *koan*. Attention is focused ardently on a question that boggles the mind, such as "What was your original face before your parents were born?" As Roshi Philip Kapleau observes, "*Koans* deliberately throw sand into the eyes of the intellect to force us to open our Mind's eye and see the world and everything in it undistorted by our concepts and judgments." To concentrate on a *koan*, one must look closely and experience it directly, without thinking about it. The experience is immediate, beyond abstractions. Roshi Kapleau explains, "The import of every *koan* is the same: that the world is one interdependent Whole and that each separate one of us is that Whole."[32]

The aim of Zen practice is enlightenment, often experienced as the flash of insight known as *satori*. One directly experiences the interrelatedness of all existence, often in a sudden recognition that nothing is separate from oneself. As one Zen master put it:

> *The moon's the same old moon,*
> *The flowers exactly as they were,*
> *Yet I've become the thingness*
> *Of all the things I see![33]*

myreligionlab
Zen and Koans
DAISETZ T. SUZUKI

myreligionlab
Nothing to
Do with Rules
BANKEI

All aspects of life become, at the same time, utterly precious and utterly empty, "nothing special." This paradox cannot be grasped intellectually; it can only be realized through direct intuitive awareness.

PURE LAND: DEVOTION TO AMITABHA BUDDHA

Zen is a practice of inner awareness with close attention given to every action and requires years of disciplined meditation. Other forms of Buddhist practice developed in India and East Asia that had greater appeal. One of the most popular Buddhist schools in East Asia is Pure Land Buddhism. At times of great social upheaval (for instance, when the government became corrupt and society was falling apart), it was widely thought that people had become so degenerate that it was nearly impossible for them to attain enlightenment through their own efforts.

Amida Buddha descends to welcome the faithful to the Western Paradise. Welcoming Descent of Amida Buddha, Anon., 18th century.

Under the circumstances, many became devoted to Amitabha Buddha, the Buddha of Boundless Light. It was believed that Amitabha (**Amida** in Japanese) was previously a prince who vowed to attain enlightenment. After he did so, he used his pure virtue to manifest a Pure Land of Bliss for all those who called his name. In Japan, the original abstract Indian Buddhist concept of a Pure Land in the west to which devotees return after death became more concrete. The Japanese had an ancient tradition of worshiping mountains as destinations which the dead ascend and from which deities descend to earth. They began to depict Amida riding on billowing clouds over the mountains and welcoming his dying devotees.

Jodo Shinshu: The True Pure Land In the thirteenth century, the Japanese religious leader Shinran broke with monastic tradition by marrying. He emphasized the principle that salvation comes through repeating the name of Amida Buddha with sincere trust, not by separating oneself from society. The Jodo Shinshu, or "True Pure Land," school developed by Shrinran's followers became a major Buddhist movement throughout the world. Unlike other Buddhist sects in Japan, it did not mix its beliefs with those of Shinto, nor did its practitioners accept donations for prayers and blessings. It became the most popular form of Buddhism practiced in Japan. It is the most popular Buddhist school among Japanese immigrants and their descendants in North America, with well-established communities also in Europe, Australia, and Africa.

NICHIREN: SALVATION THROUGH THE *LOTUS SUTRA*

While some Buddhists in Japan despaired of achieving enlightenment through their own efforts and therefore relied on the grace of Amdia Buddha, others stressed the importance of striving to enlighten not only ourselves but also society. One example was a thirteenth-century fisherman's son who named himself Nichiren. For Nichiren, the highest truths of Buddhism were embodied in the *Lotus Sutra*, a large compilation of parables, verses, and descriptions of innumerable beings who practiced the Buddha's teachings. Nichiren gave particular attention to two of these beings: the Bodhisattva of Superb Action, who staunchly devotes himself to spreading the Perfect Truth, and the Bodhisattva Ever-Abused, who is persecuted because of his insistence, with unshaken conviction, that each person is potentially a Buddha. Nichiren himself was repeatedly abused by the authorities, but persisted in his efforts to reform Buddhism in Japan and spread what he considered its purified essence, the bodhisattva ideal, to the world. The phrase chanted by Nichiren and his followers, "*Namu myoho rengekyo*," pays homage to the *Lotus Sutra*. Today it is chanted by Nichiren monks, nuns, and laypeople for hours. The chant is thought to slowly reveal the profound meaning of the *Lotus Sutra* and to work inwardly, beyond thought. In our time, some Nichiren followers undertake long peace walks. In one peace effort sponsored by Nipponzan Myohoji in 1995, people walked from Auschwitz in Poland to Hiroshima and Nagasaki in Japan, to commemorate the fiftieth anniversary of the end of World War II, making a plea for nonviolence and respect for all of life. They beat hand-drums while chanting "*Namu myoho rengekyo*," and bowed to the Buddha in each person they met, whether or not they were friendly, as a contribution to world peace. The founder of Nipponzan Myohoji, the Most Venerable Nichidatsu Fujii, strongly influenced Gandhi's doctrine of nonviolence. Before he passed away in 1985 at the age of 100, he explained:

> *We do not believe that people are good because we see that they are good, but by believing that people are good we eliminate our own fear and thus we can intimately associate with them. To believe in the compassionate power of the Supreme Being which we cannot see is a discipline in order to believe in the invisible good in others.*[34]
>
> *Civilization has nothing to do with having electric lights, airplanes, or manufacturing atomic bombs. It has nothing to do with killing human beings, destroying things or waging war. Civilization is to hold one another in mutual affection and respect.*[35]

The chanting of "*Namu myoho rengekyo*" has led to more than seventy Peace Pagodas being built in many countries, with donated materials and labor, by people of all faiths who pray for world peace and the elimination of all weapons.

Soka Gakkai International is another important offshoot of Nichiren's movement, which is based in Japan but has millions of members around the world. Its founders call for a peaceful world revolution through transformation of individual consciousness. They combine the central practice of chanting "*Nam myoho rengekyo*" with modern social activism in areas such as humanitarian relief, environmental awareness, human rights, literacy, and cultural and interfaith exchanges. Members are encouraged to develop their "unlimited potential" for hope, courage, and altruism.

Another new branch of Buddhism inspired by the *Lotus Sutra* is Rissho Koseikai, founded in the 1930s by Rev. Nikkyo Niwano and Myoko Naganuma to bring the message of the *Lotus Sutra* to the world in practical ways in order to encourage happiness and peace. Members meet to discuss ways of applying the Buddha's teachings to specific problems in their own lives. The organization, which is active in international inter-religious activities, asserts that "The Eternal Buddha, invisible but present everywhere, is the great life-force of the universe, which sustains each of us."[36]

> *The Bodhisattva loves all living beings as if each were his only child.*
>
> *Vimalakirtinirdesha Sutra 5*

VAJRAYANA: THE INDESTRUCTIBLE PATH

Of the many branches of Mahayana Buddhism, perhaps the most elaborate is **Vajrayana**. It developed in India, was transmitted to Tibet, and has also historically been practiced in Nepal, Bhutan, Sikkim, and Mongolia. Currently it is practiced throughout the Tibetan diaspora and increasingly in North America and Europe.

Prior to the introduction of Buddhism from India, the mountainous Tibetan region was home to a shamanic religion called Bön. In the seventh century CE a particularly powerful Tibetan king named Songtsan became interested in Buddhism and sent a group of students to India to study it. The journey from Tibet to India was extremely difficult and many of these emissaries died in the searing heat of the Indian plains. Only one member of a second group survived the arduous trip across the Himalayas, returning with many Sanskrit texts. After some of these works were translated into Tibetan, Songtsan declared Buddhism the national religion and encouraged Buddhist virtues in his subjects. Bön proponents are said to have sabotaged the new religion, until finally a tantric adept, Padmasambhava, was invited to Tibet in the eighth century CE. Eventually, it is said, Guru Padmasambhava subdued and converted the local Bön deities and,

Buddhist nuns from Tibet, where a distinctive version of Mahayana developed. Behind them, prayer flags flutter in the wind.

along with his consort Yeshe Tsogyal, firmly established the tantric Buddhist teachings in Tibet. Although the Tibetans' understanding of Buddhism was no doubt influenced by earlier beliefs, and elements such as the use of prayer flags and an emphasis on practices for the dying may reflect Bön concerns, the Tibetans spent many centuries attempting to understand the Indian Buddhist teachings as purely as possible.

After a period of decline in the tenth century, when some misinterpreted the tantric teachings, a teacher named Atisha was invited from the great center of Buddhist learning at Nalanda, India, to set things right. Under Atisha, Tibetan Buddhism became a complex path with three stages, said to have been prescribed by the Buddha. The first stage is quieting the mind and relinquishing attachments through meditation practice, as emphasized in the early Buddhist teachings. The second stage is intensive training in compassion and wisdom, as emphasized in the Mahayana teachings. The third stage is the advanced esoteric path called Vajrayana ("the diamond vehicle") or Tantrayana, a rigorous, accelerated path to nurture enlightenment within a single lifetime that developed in India.

Vajrayana aspirants are guided through a series of tantric practices by qualified teachers, or **lamas**. Some of these teachers are recognized as incarnate bodhisattvas and are carefully trained from a young age to help others advance toward enlightenment.

One of the most beloved of Tibetan Buddhist deities is Tara. She is savior and mother of the world; she protects us and helps us to achieve our spiritual longings. (Detail of Tibetan thangka, 18th/19th century, tempera on cotton.)

> The masses have their heads on backwards. If you want to get things right, first look at how they think and behave, and consider going the opposite way.[37]
> Lama Drom Tonpa, eleventh century

Vajrayana initiates practice **deity yoga**: meditating on themselves in the form of a Buddha or bodhisattva in order to embody the enlightened qualities that the practitioner wishes to manifest. These radiant forms are themselves imagined and therefore lacking true existence, but meditating on them is considered a way to understand one's own true nature. Some of these meditational deities are shown in wrathful form, such as Mahakala, defender of the Dharma, while others, such as Tara, are shown in peaceful form.

The highest Vajrayana practices use the subtle vital energies of the body to transform the mind. A very subtle and profound state of consciousness is produced after lengthy practice; when the "gross mind" is neutralized, the "subtle mind" manifests powerfully as "the clear light of bliss." This innermost subtle mind of clear light is the true empty quality of one's own mind. Once it is realized, one is said to be capable of attaining Buddhahood in a single lifetime. The beloved Seventh Dalai Lama of Tibet (1708–1757) gave this encouraging perspective:

Even the most seemingly evil person has the primordial clear light mind at the heart of his or her existence. Eventually the clouds of distortion and delusion will be cleared away as the being grows in wisdom, and the evil behavior that emanates from these negative mindsets will naturally evaporate. That being will realize the essential nature of his or her own mind, and achieve spiritual liberation and enlightenment.[38]

Tibetan Buddhists' full-length prostrations are so arduous that many have to strap on wooden pads and canvas shields to protect their bodies.

The practices used to transform the mind may also enable supernormal powers such as levitation, clairvoyance, meditating continuously without sleep, and warming the body from within while sitting naked in the snow. Milarepa, the famous Tibetan poet–saint, whose enlightenment was won through great austerities, once sang this song:

Blissful within, I don't entertain
The notion "I'm suffering,"
When incessant rain is pouring outside.

Even on peaks of white snow mountains
Amidst swirling snow and sleet
Driven by new year's wintry winds
This cotton robe burns like fire.[39]

The communist Chinese overran Tibet between 1950 and 1959, destroying countless ancient monasteries and scriptures and killing an estimated one-sixth of the population over decades of occupation. The beloved Fourteenth Dalai Lama, spiritual and political leader of Tibet, escaped to India in 1959. The town of Dharamsala in the mountains of northern India where he established his headquarters has become a magnet for spiritual seekers. Despite persecution, religious practice and meaning still pervade every aspect of Tibetan life, from house-raising to fervent pilgrimages. Monks and laypeople alike meditate on *thangkas* and **mandalas**, visual aids to concentration and illumination, which portray Buddhas and bodhisattvas and representations of an ideal universe. A favorite practice is the chanting of mantras, especially *"Om mani padme hum,"* the mantra of Avalokiteshvara, the bodhisattva of compassion. This mantra evokes an awareness of the sufferings of sentient beings in different states of existence and compassion for all living beings from within the heart of each of us. To help manifest this compassion, mantras are repeatedly recited, written thousands of times, spun in prayer wheels, and printed on prayer flags so that the blessings of the mantra

myreligionlab
Love, Kindness and Universal Responsibility
DALAI LAMA

His Holiness the Dalai Lama

Surely one of the best-known and most loved spiritual leaders in the world, His Holiness the Fourteenth Dalai Lama is a striking example of Buddhist peace and compassion. Wherever he goes, he greets everyone with evident delight. Even when addressing an audience of thousands, he looks around the hall with a broad, childlike grin, which seems directed to each person individually. His example is all the more powerful because he is the leader in exile of Tibet, a small nation that experienced extreme oppression and suffering during the twentieth and twenty-first centuries.

The simplicity of His Holiness's words and bearing belie his intellectual power. His Holiness was a peasant child just two years old in 1937 when he was located and carefully identified as the reincarnation of the thirteenth Dalai Lama. He was formally installed as the fourteenth Dalai Lama when he was only four and a half years old, thus becoming the spiritual and temporal ruler of Tibet. He was raised and rigorously educated in the Potala in Lhasa, capital of Tibet. One of the world's largest buildings, the Potala contained large ceremonial halls, thirty-five chapels, meditation cells, government storehouses, national treasures, a complete record of Tibetan history and culture in 7,000 volumes, plus thousands of illuminated volumes of the Buddhist scriptures. The young Dalai Lama was educated according to the traditional Tibetan Buddhist system, which stressed an extensive and profound method for developing the mind to acquire many kinds of knowledge and also to practice advanced Buddhist meditation techniques.

Such a rigorous grounding in religious education and practice, maintains the Dalai Lama, brings steadiness of mind in the face of any misfortunes. He says:

Humanitarianism and true love for all beings can only stem from an awareness of the content of religion. By whatever name religion may be known, its understanding and practice are the essence of a peaceful mind and therefore of a peaceful world. If there is no peace in one's mind, there can be no peace in one's approach to others, and thus no peaceful relations between individuals or between nations.[40]

The Dalai Lama's equanimity of mind was seriously challenged by the Chinese invasion and oppression of his small country. In 1959, when he escaped from Tibet to India in hopes of preventing bloodshed during a widespread popular revolt against the Chinese, Tibet was home to more than 6,000 monasteries. Only twelve of them were still intact by 1980. It is said that at least one million Tibetans died as a direct result of the Chinese occupation. Violence and suppression of the religion, culture, and people of Tibet continue today as millions of Chinese settlers fill the country.

In the face of the overwhelming military power of the Chinese, and armed with Buddhist precepts, the Dalai Lama has persistently tried to steer his people away from violent response to violence. Asserting that "Non-violence is the only way. … It's a slower process sometimes, but a very effective one," he explains:

Practically speaking, through violence we may achieve something, but at the expense of someone else's welfare. That way, although we may solve one problem, we simultaneously seed a new problem. The best way to solve problems is through human understanding, mutual respect. On one side make some concessions; on the other side take serious consideration about the problem. There may not be complete satisfaction, but something happens. At least future danger is avoided. Non-violence is very safe.[41]

While slowly, patiently trying to influence world opinion so that the voice of Tibet will not be extinguished by Chinese might, the Dalai Lama has established an entire government in exile in Dharamsala, India, in the Himalayas. There he and Tibetan refugees have built schools, orphanages, hospitals, craft cooperatives, farming communities, monasteries, libraries, and institutes for preserving traditional music, drama, dance, painting, and medicine. From this base, he travels tirelessly around the world in an effort to keep the voice of Tibet alive. In the process, he has emerged as one of the greatest moral leaders of our time. His quintessentially Buddhist message to people of all religions is that only through kindness and compassion toward each other and the cultivation of inner peace shall we survive as a species.

extend in all directions as they blow in the wind. In addition to Tibet, Vajrayana is practiced throughout the Himalayan region and beyond: in Nepal, Bhutan, Sikkim, Ladakh, Mongolia, and parts of Russia. Tibetan lamas in exile have also spread the Tibetan Buddhist tradition to Western countries, Southeast Asia, and Taiwan, where it has gained many adherents.

FESTIVALS

Since Buddhism has evolved into different forms in different countries, most of its festivals are not uniformly celebrated. The typical ways that laypeople observe the festivals are to go in the morning to their nearby temple or monastery, make offerings of food to the monks, renew their commitment to the Five Precepts, and listen to a talk about the Dharma. To gain merit, they may then offer food to the poor. In a gesture of respect for the Triple Gem—the Buddha, the Dharma, and the Sangha—they may circumambulate a stupa three times. In the evening, there may be chanted recitations of the Buddha's teachings and meditation practice.

The most important Buddhist festival is *Vesak*, which according to Theravadins marks the Buddha's birth, enlightenment, and death, all of which were said to have miraculously occurred on the same day. For Mahayana Buddhists, *Vesak* marks the day of the Buddha's enlightenment. Vajrayana Buddhists celebrate four distinct days commemorating the Buddha's conception, birth, enlightenment, and death. According to the lunar calendar, the Buddha is said to have been born on the full moon of the month *Vaisakha*, the second month of the Indian calendar, which falls in April and May. In general, devout Buddhists gather at temples or monasteries before dawn to hear stories about the Buddha's life, to wash images of him, to make offerings of flowers, candles, and incense, and carefully to observe the Five Precepts, including refraining from any kind of killing. In several Buddhist-majority countries, slaughterhouses and liquor shops are closed for the holiday by government decree. In Sri Lanka, thousands of insects, birds, and animals are released as a symbolic act of liberation of all beings who are unwillingly imprisoned or tortured.

The monsoon season brings the rainy season retreat for monks and nuns, during a period when it was traditionally difficult to walk through the countryside. In some countries young laymen may temporarily enter the Sangha and live as monks for a while to consecrate their passage into adulthood. What happens during the rainy season retreat varies according to the teacher's instructions, but it is designed to turn one's mind away from worldly concerns and back to calm inner reflection. Vietnamese nun Cue Nguyen describes her rainy season retreat pattern:

I spend most of my day writing in a diary, reflecting upon myself and the world. Only in calm water do things reflect faithfully. I observe nature, people, listen carefully to the crickets and the fallen leaves as if they are the most important things now.[42]

After the rainy season retreat, laypeople may ceremoniously offer new robes and other necessities to the monks and nuns.

On the full moon day of the third lunar month, *Magha* (approximately March), some Buddhists celebrate Magha Puja Day, also known as "Sangha Day." It commemorates a major event early in the Buddha's teachings in which, after giving the sermon to his first disciples at the Deer Park in Sarnath, he went to Rajagaha city to address 1,250 *arhants* who reportedly came on their own to pay their respects and listen to his teachings. They were all ordained by the Buddha.

Many other days are celebrated on local and national levels, such as the Festival of the Tooth in Sri Lanka honoring the Buddha's tooth relic, which is normally hidden within a series of caskets in a special temple but is on this day paraded through the streets on the back of a richly decorated elephant (see page 155). In Thailand, there is a special Festival of Floating Bowls on the full moon night of the twelfth lunar month. Bowls made of leaves and flowers with candles and incense sticks are floated upon the water of rivers and canals, which are then full of water. As people let them go, they feel that their bad luck is floating away.

Buddhism in the West

Images of the Buddha are now enshrined around the world. The path to enlightenment that first gained currency in India has gradually spread to Western countries as well as throughout Asia. Wherever Asian Buddhists traveled, they carried Buddhism into their new surroundings. In the middle of the nineteenth century, Chinese workers migrated to California as the gold rush and railways opened up new opportunities. In their new surroundings they built temples to Guanyin and Amitabha. In the late nineteenth century, Japanese workers migrated to Hawai'i as plantation workers and to California. Wherever they settled, they invited priests of various Buddhist schools from Japan. The largest school, Jodo Shinshu, gradually formed an organization called Buddhist Churches of America.

By the end of the century, Western Orientalists and occultists had developed considerable interest in Buddhism. The landmark 1893 World Parliament of Religions in Chicago included a large delegation of Buddhist teachers from Japan, and some from China, Thailand, and Sri Lanka. One of the leading figures, Angarika Dharmapala from Sri Lanka, announced that just as King Ashoka had twenty-four centuries earlier spread Buddhism from India to teach Asia "the noblest lessons of tolerance and gentleness,"[43] the Buddhists had come bringing the same message to the West. Overflow crowds collected to hear their discourses.

During the twentieth century, North American and European countries became vibrant centers of Buddhism. Scholars are studying Buddhist traditions at a variety of universities and many people are interested in learning Buddhist meditation practices. The exodus of Buddhists from Tibet since 1959, including many high lamas, has led to the establishment of Tibetan Buddhist centers in many Western countries as well as in Southeast Asia and India, the Dalai Lama's home in exile, where over 100,000 Tibetan refugees now live. Several hundred thousand Westerners now have some spiritual involvement with Tibetan Buddhism.

Over 400 Zen meditation centers are also flourishing in North America alone, and there are many Zen monasteries that give training in *zazen* and offer a monastic lifestyle as a permanent or temporary alternative to the stress and confusion of modern life.

Intensive *vipassana* meditation retreats lasting up to three months are held in Theravadin centers such as the Insight Meditation Society in rural Barre, Massachusetts. Theravadin teachers from Southeast Asia and Europe make frequent visits to conduct retreats, and American teachers who have undertaken

Life in a Western Zen Monastery

Side by side in still rows, with birdsong and sunlight streaming in through the tall windows, sit the monks and laypeople of Zen Mountain Monastery. For thirty-five-minute blocks, separated by periods of attentive walking, they support each other by practicing *zazen* together in silence. With this group structure, many find it easier to carry on the rigorous discipline of serious Zen training than they would by themselves.

This particular monastery, located in the Catskill Mountains near Mount Tremper, New York, reflects the changing face of religion in the United States. Over a hundred years ago the main building was handcrafted of stone as a Benedictine monastery; later it became a Lutheran summer camp. Now, back to back with Christ on the cross on the outside of the building is a statue of the Buddha on the altar inside the *zendo*. The monastery houses ordained monastics (including women) who have taken lifetime vows of service, novices and postulants in training (an aspect

adopted from Western monasticism), lay residents who stay for up to a year, and groups of people who come for special retreats and classes. These are primarily professionals and family people from the mainstream culture, rather than the hippies who embraced Buddhism in the 1960s and 1970s. They do not come for a comfortable vacation, for *zazen* is hard work and the teachers are dedicated to creating snags that help people discover the places where they are not free. They are expected to practice intensely and then leave, carrying what they have learned back into the world. As Geoffrey Shugen Arnold, Sensei, vice abbot of the monastery, observes, "If Zen doesn't work in the world, it's not working." In addition to long sessions of silent sitting and walking, Dharma talks by the resident Zen master John Daido Loori Roshi (an American ordained in both authentic Zen lineages), and private coaching by the monks, monastery residents participate in structured nontheistic

John Daido Loori Roshi, abbot of Zen Mountain Monastery.

liturgical services designed to foster attentiveness and appreciation. They chant in Japanese and English, with frequent bowing to each other, to their meditation cushions, and to the Buddha on the altar, in solidarity with all beings and gratitude for the teachings. Zen master Daido notes that liturgy reflects the innards of a religion: "In Catholicism, cathedrals are awe inspiring, the chants expansive; in Zen the form is simple and the chanting is grounded, not otherworldly."

The rest of the day is devoted to taking care of the buildings and 200-acre nature sanctuary, mindfulness practice done in silence, and work practice. Those with office jobs combine ancient and modern skills: They sit cross-legged on low cushions before their computers to prepare news, music, and interviews for their online Zen radio station WZEN.org, and use calligraphic skills to hand-letter signs. Meals are simple and include coarse breads donated by a nearby whole-grain bakery.

Every action—even brushing one's teeth—is treated as practice, in the sense of bringing total attentiveness to the sacredness of even the most "mundane" activity, teaching that enlightenment takes place in one's everyday experience.

Following the lead of their teacher Daido, who is at once highly disciplined in mind-to-mind Dharma transmission and down-to-earth, approachable, compassionate, and married, monastery residents are human, playful, and loving. The women "monks" shave their heads when they get ordained and keep their hair very short thereafter, but that is considered a freedom rather than self-sacrificing asceticism.

From training in flower arranging or Aikido to exploring the relevance of Buddhist principles in the workplace, Zen Mountain Monastery's programs are oriented toward one central goal: the personal experience of enlightenment and its application in the twenty-first-century world.

The stillness of the zendo at Zen Mountain Monastery.

Oriyoki, *a ceremonial meal, at Zen Mountain Monastery.*

Buddhism has spread around the world. Venerable Tenzin Palmo from England, who spent twelve years in a cave in the Himalayas, is standing sixth from the left with Buddhist nuns from Switzerland, India, Nepal, Mongolia, Singapore, Sri Lanka, Australia, Vietnam, the Netherlands, and the United States during a gathering of Daughters of the Buddha in Mongolia.

rigorous training in Southeast Asia under traditional meditation masters are also emerging as respected teachers. An American monk named Venerable Sumedho, who trained in traditional Theravada Buddhism in Thailand, has established monastic forest communities and meditation centers in England, Switzerland, Italy, and the United States. In contrast to the low profile of Buddhist women in Asia, many Buddhist centers in the West are led by women, who are explaining traditional Buddhist teachings to Westerners in fresh, contemporary ways. Some are exemplars of dedicated spiritual practice, such as Tenzin Palmo, a British woman who became a Tibetan Buddhist nun and lived alone for twelve years in a cave located 13,200 feet (4,000 meters) high in the Himalayas, undergoing tremendous austerities in the quest for enlightenment.

The Vietnamese monk Venerable Master Thich Nhat Hanh now lives in exile in southern France, conducting retreats for both women and men in a community called Plum Village. When he travels internationally, large audiences gather and derive inspiration from his teachings. He speaks simply, using familiar examples, and emphasizes bringing the awareness fostered by meditation into everyday life, rather than making spirituality a separate compartment of one's life. He says:

When we walk in the meditation hall, we make careful steps, very slowly. But when we go to the airport, we are quite another person. We walk very differently, less mindfully. How can we practice at the airport and in the market?[44]

Buddhism is often embraced by people in the West because they long for peace of mind in the midst of a chaotic materialistic life.

Many psychotherapists are studying Buddhism for its insights into the mind and human suffering. Richard Clarke, who is both a Zen teacher and a psychotherapist, feels that a discipline such as Zen should be part of the training of counselors and therapists:

Emptiness is ... the source of infinite compassion in working with people: to really feel a person without any agenda, to be spacious to that person, to will that they be the way they are. When a person experiences that in someone's presence, then they can drop away those things that they've invented to present themselves with. Those faces, those armors, those forms of the self become unnecessary.[45]

Are Westerners able to achieve enlightenment by taking Buddhist workshops here and there? Particularly in the case of Tibetan Buddhist practices, Westerners

myreligionlab

Precepts for an Engaged Buddhism
THICH NHAT HANH

often want to be initiated into the most highly advanced teachings without taking time for years of patient practice and being inwardly transformed by the step-by-step foundational teachings. Can teachings developed within a specific cultural context be directly transplanted into the soil of an entirely different culture? Most Westerners who are adopting Buddhist practices are living in highly materialistic societies with different priorities and values, rather than in traditional Buddhist cultures or monastic settings. In their impatience to get results, many shop around from one teacher to the next and experiment with one practice after another, rather than persisting with one path over a long time. As Alan Wallace remarks:

> *In Tibetan society, fickleness is considered to be one of the worst of vices, while reliability, integrity, trustworthiness, and perseverance are held in high regard.*
> *So a few of the finest lamas are now refusing even to come to the West. Some are feeling—given the brevity and preciousness of human life—that devoting time to people with such fickleness and so little faith is time not very well spent.*[46]

Another crucial issue is how to train teachers for the West. Two large Tibetan Buddhist organizations from the Gelukpa order have opened nearly 600 centers for study and meditation around the world but do not have enough fully trained lamas to staff all of them. Traditional training takes up to twenty-five years of rigorous study and debate of the finer points of Buddhist philosophy, logic, meditation, cosmology, psychology, and monastic life. Close guidance by an advanced teacher has traditionally been considered essential, but this is not possible for all Western aspirants, given the shortage of qualified teachers and the language problems entailed.

Given the differences in culture, background, and motivation, are Western students and their teachers in the process of creating new forms of Buddhism adapted to Western ways? How authentic are these new forms? Some observers feel that Western Buddhism, with its emphasis on inner practice rather than outer forms, is actually closer to what they construe as the core of early Buddhism than are later developments in the East. Contemporary Western Buddhists tend to be oriented to the goal of achieving enlightenment by their own efforts, which is reportedly what the Buddha prescribed for his followers, and are searching for ways to achieve that goal, though sometimes hoping to do so with minimum effort. Whether or not Western Buddhism conforms to early patterns, it seems to be evolving in new directions with some people in the West remaking Buddhism in their own image. For instance, the American Buddhist Stephen Batchelor argues in his book *Buddhism Without Beliefs* that the West needs a Buddhism stripped of belief in rebirth and *karma*. He emphasizes instead a secularized version, an "existential, therapeutic and liberating agnosticism."[47] Another important difference between Western Buddhism and historical developments in Asia is the Western tendency to support equal participation of women, as renunciates, teachers, and lay practitioners. In recent years, Buddhists in Asia, confronted by modernization, consumerism, globalization, and new social attitudes, are taking directions similar to those of Western Buddhists.

Since 1987, Buddhist women from Asia and the West have joined hands and held international gatherings to enhance the role of women in Buddhism. Sakyadhita ("Daughters of the Buddha"), the International Association of

myreligionlab
History of Buddhism in America
SERINITY YOUNG

An Interview with Karma Lekshe Tsomo

 Karma Lekshe Tsomo, an American from Hawai'i, has become a very active Tibetan Buddhist nun. Her story illustrates the unusual pathways by which many Westerners come to adopt Buddhism. Lekshe explains, "I was very much attracted to the teachings of Jesus as a child, but there were a lot of unanswered questions for me, especially about the meaning of life and what happens to us after we die. When I asked the ministers they would say, 'If you are good, you go to heaven. If you are bad, you go to hell.' I wanted to know more, so I kept searching.

"My family name was Zenn, so when I was twelve, I read books on Buddhism—*The Way of Zen* by Alan Watts and *Zen Buddhism* by D. T. Suzuki. I thought, 'Wow, home free!' When I was nineteen, I went to Japan to go surfing, then traveled to Thailand, India, and Nepal. On the way I had a clear and beautiful dream that I was a nun. I knew I wanted to be a nun, but where?

"It wasn't until I arrived at the Library of Tibetan Works and Archives in Dharamsala, India, in 1972 that I began a systematic Buddhist education. It was very fortunate that His Holiness the Dalai Lama had just established this institute to preserve Tibetan texts and provide classes on Buddhism with eminent Buddhist teachers and English translation. As I burst into the classroom for the first time, I found a little lama with a yellow pointed hat who was explaining, 'At the second stage after death you will see a faint smoke.' I thought, 'Bingo! This is it!' So I sat at his feet for six years.

"The more I studied Buddhism and the more I practiced, the more I wanted to dedicate my whole life to it. In 1977, I met the Sixteenth Gyalwa Karmapa and told him I wanted to be ordained. Six months later in France, two Tibetan monks cut my long strawberry blonde curls. I felt an indescribable sense of joy when I saw all that hair in my lap. After ordination, I returned to Dharmasala to continue my studies. I knew without question that the best place to study Buddhism was right there. Not only were the teachers some of the greatest scholars the Tibetan tradition has ever produced, but study was also combined with practice—meditation practices. The tenor of the teachings was to transform the mind. I thought, 'I may not know the inner workings of Buddhist philosophy, but I think I am becoming a better person.' I was really determined to continue my study and practice of the Dharma.

"However, life in the Himalayas was tremendously difficult. The climate was icy cold in the winter and boiling hot in the summer. I lived in a mud hut, with no indoor plumbing, at 7,000 to 8,000 feet, and Tibetan monastic robes do not include a sweater or jacket. There were rats living in the walls and scorpions under my pillow. Rats fell down on my head as I meditated. There were fleas, and during the monsoon rains things never got dry. I was very poor and had no support as a nun. The Tibetans were refugees and were having a great deal of trouble taking care of their own community. Tibetans don't have a tradition of going for alms as in the Theravada tradition and Americans who become Buddhists don't have a tradition of supporting renunciants. The third year, things got really difficult. I lived mostly on the offerings I received at *pujas* [offering ceremonies]. The fourth year, an American woman invited me to take lunch with her family for two rupees a day, so I got some sort of a balanced meal once a day. I became really skinny and sick—hepatitis a few times—but somehow I survived.

"As I struggled to acquire a Tibetan Buddhist education, I soon realized that the environment for Buddhist women to study and practice were not the same as for men. Conditions and facilities for education for nuns lagged way behind. It was assumed that men would be the teachers, so they received all the educational opportunities. Fortunately, Buddhism is a rather logical and sensible path. When you question the teachers about whether women have equal capacity for liberation and enlightenment, they have to admit that they do, because the Buddha himself said so. Sometimes, however, social realities for women don't match up to this theoretical equality.

"Today, having completed my studies and full ordination, I work with the Sakyadhita International Association of Buddhist Women to gain equal opportunities for women to study, equal facilities for meditation practice, and also opportunities for women to become ordained, if they wish. Once women get educational opportunities they express a deep concern for the needs of others in their communities, including the children, the old folks, the sick. I strongly feel that Buddhist women can contribute a great deal to society, both on the local and international levels. There are 300 million Buddhist women in the world. They have tremendous potential, goodwill, and energy to work for peace and the benefit of humanity."

Buddhist Women, is working to improve conditions for women's Buddhist education, practice, ordination, and training as teachers of Buddhism. Sakyadhita's biannual conferences bring together women and men, lay and ordained, from different traditions to exchange ideas on meditation, peace-building, and women's roles in contemporary Buddhist practice. The 2008 Sakyadhita conference in Mongolia highlighted Buddhist women's achievements in recent years as well as persistent inequalities in education and ordination. The 2010 Sakyadhita conference in Vietnam paid tribute to eminent Buddhist women in the past and in contemporary society.

Socially engaged Buddhism

An emerging focus in contemporary Buddhist practice is the relevance of Buddhism to social problems. Contrary to popular assumptions, the Buddha did not advise people to permanently leave society to seek their own enlightenment. Sri Lankan Buddhist monk Walpola Rahula explains:

> It may perhaps be useful in some cases for a person to live in retirement for a time in order to improve his or her mind and character, as preliminary moral, spiritual, and intellectual training, to be strong enough to come out later and help others. But if someone lives an entire life in solitude, thinking only of their own happiness and salvation, without caring for their fellow beings, this surely is not in keeping with the Buddha's teaching which is based on love, compassion, and service to others.[48]

Buddhism, like other world religions, has always been engaged with the wider society and political life. In Thailand, for instance, the king is the bearer of the Buddhist heritage, and thus has sacred legitimization. But Thailand also has a tradition of socially conscious lay practice of Buddhism. The renowned Thai monk Buddhadasa Bhikkhu (1906–1993) was a great critic of capitalism, teaching that it increases egoism and selfishness, thus causing distress both to the individual and to society.

In Vietnam, Thich Nhat Hanh and other socially active Buddhists refused to take sides with the governments and military movements of either North Vietnam or South Vietnam during the Vietnam War, for they felt that both were oppressing the common people and also exploiting American soldiers. All were victims of an ideological conflict between communism and anti-communism. Buddhists worked hard to bring a negotiated end to the war, and helped the suffering people as best they could by evacuating villagers caught in the midst of battles, helping to rebuild damaged buildings, taking care of orphans, and providing medical care to people from all sides. They believed that all life is precious and interdependent—violence and suffering affect everyone. Thus they meditated to generate selfless compassion, according to the teachings of the Buddha, who said:

> Hatred is never appeased by hatred. It is appeased by love. This is an eternal law. Just as a mother would protect her only child, even at the risk of her own life, even so let one cultivate a boundless heart towards all beings. Let one's thoughts of boundless love pervade the whole world.[49]

myreligionlab
Engaged
Buddhism in Asia
QUEEN AND KING

However, Buddhism's link with politics has not always been entirely altruistic. In Sri Lanka, a selective interpretation of Theravada Buddhist tradition has been used to bolster nationalistic sentiments among the Sinhalese Buddhist majority against the Tamil (mostly Hindu and Muslim) minority. As in many contemporary fundamentalist movements elsewhere, a chauvinistic, rigid version of religious identity developed in response to rapid colonization, modernization, and Westernization. The reaffirmation of Buddhist identity became a tool of ethnic oppression of the minority, leading to a violent separatist movement among the Tamils and ultimately civil strife which has disrupted life on the lovely island for decades.

In general, however, the Buddha's emphasis on compassion has prevailed, and even when Buddhists have been social activists, they have tended to be guided by Buddhist principles of nonviolence, compassion, and social justice. In this posture, some contemporary Buddhists have tried to correct injustice, oppression, famine, cruelty to animals, nuclear testing, warfare, and environmental devastation. E. F. Schumacher preached what he called "Buddhist economics," to affirm human beings' willingness to live simply, generously, and humanely with each other. Ajahn Pongsak, a Thai Buddhist monk, was so troubled by the devastation of the northern Thai forests that he rallied 5,000 villagers to reforest an area by building a tree nursery, terracing the eroded hillsides, planting nearly 200,000 seedlings, laying irrigation pipes, and fencing the area to protect the new trees. He taught them the importance of a respectful relationship with the forest as their own home, their own parent. He says:

> A mind that feels no gratitude to the forest is a coarse mind indeed—without this basic siladhamma [dharma], how can a mind attain enlightenment? ... The times are dark and siladhamma is asleep, so it is now the duty of monks to reawaken and bring back siladhamma. Only in this way can society be saved.

Cambodians are in the process of recovering from decades of a culture of terror in which the Khmer Rouge murdered over one million people. Buddhists have played major roles in peacemaking and rebuilding the country, promoting nonviolent responses to violence. The monks of Buddhism for Development, for instance, have gone to the villages and cities to carry out community development projects, emphasizing the Dharma of physical development, moral development, spiritual development, and intellectual development. The most instrumental figure has been Venerable Maha Ghosananda (1929–2007), whose entire family was killed during the Pol Pot regime. In addition to political initiatives, he led many peace marches of monks, nuns, and laypeople through areas infested with landmines, and counseled people facing issues such as domestic violence, HIV/AIDS, deforestation, and dire poverty. He urged:

> We must remove the landmines in our hearts which prevent us from making peace—greed, hatred and delusion. We can overcome greed with the weapon of generosity; we can overcome hatred with the weapon of loving kindness; we can overcome delusion with the weapon of wisdom. ...[50]
>
> We must find the courage to leave our temples and enter the temples of human experience, temples that are filled with suffering. If we listen to the Buddha, Christ, or Gandhi, we can do nothing else. The refugee camps, the prisons, the ghettos and the battlefields will then become our temples.[51]

Master Cheng Yen, a Buddhist nun from a poor area in Taiwan, established the Tzu Chi Foundation in 1966 to help the needy, with small donations from 30 housewives. Now its five million members in 45 countries are following and teaching the bodhisattva path by providing volunteer services such as disaster relief, medicine, education, environmental protection, and bone-marrow donor registry.

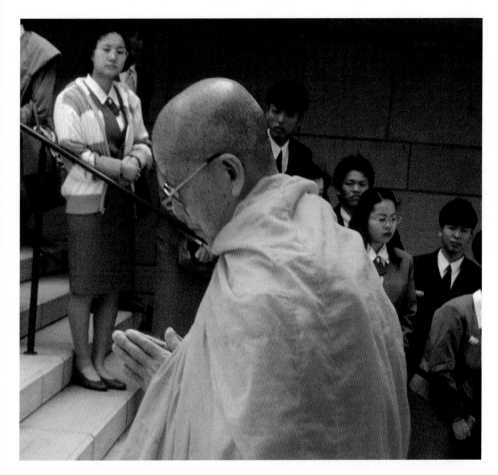

Maha Ghosananda courageously led peace marches through Khmer Rouge territory, and, as leader of the decimated population of Buddhist monks in post-communist Cambodia, helped to revive the religion and the country.

Another notable example of using Buddhist teachings as an antidote to violence is Daw Aung San Suu Kyi, leader of the National League for Democracy in Burma (Myanmar). Her father was assassinated in the attempt to bring democracy to the people, and she has been an outspoken advocate of democratic social change, repeatedly exposing herself to danger and ill health from continual house arrest or imprisonment. Living by Buddhist principles to counteract fear and cope with government oppression, she observes:

It would be difficult to dispel ignorance unless there is freedom to pursue the truth unfettered by fear. With so close a relationship between fear and corruption it is little wonder that in any society where fear is rife corruption in all forms becomes deeply entrenched. The effort necessary to remain uncorrupted in an environment where fear is an integral part of everyday existence is not immediately apparent to those fortunate enough to live in states governed by the rule of law. Where there are no such laws, the burden of holding the principles of justice and common decency falls on the ordinary people. It is the cumulative effect of their sustained effort and steady endurance which will change a nation where reason and conscience are warped by fear into one where legal rules exist to promote man's desire for harmony and justice while restraining the less desirable destructive traits in his nature.[52]

Buddhism was returned to its native India after some 1,000 years' absence by the bold action of a converted Buddhist activist, Dr. B. R. Ambedkar (1891–1956). Born an untouchable Hindu, he was the chief architect of India's new democratic constitution, and built into it many provisions designed to end the oppression of the traditional Hindu caste system. In his personal search for a religion offering freedom and dignity to all human beings, he chose Buddhism. And when he publicly converted shortly before his death, he was the inspiration for almost half a million untouchables to do likewise. Despite this, he openly questioned and changed certain Buddhist teachings. Among them was the emphasis on renunciation and meditation rather than active social engagement, helping the people.

In the midst of the civil strife between the Sinhalese Buddhist majority and the Hindu and Muslim Tamil minority in Sri Lanka, the Buddhist monks of the Sarvodaya Shramadana Sangamaya movement have tried to promote harmony and rural development. The founder, a Buddhist schoolteacher named Dr. A. T. Ariyaratne, asserts that renunciation is not the best path for most people. Rather, they can best realize their spiritual potential in the midst of society, working for its betterment. He and the monks of the Sarvodaya movement have engaged people of all religions, in thousands of villages, in work camps where they come together to eliminate social decadence and poverty by developing schools, nutrition programs, roads, and irrigation canals, and to learn to live by the Four Noble Truths and the Eightfold Path. Dr. Ariyaratne encourages people to look at their own egotism, distrust, greed, and competitiveness and to recognize that these are the cause of their suffering and inability to work together for progress.

Sulak Sivaraksa, founder of the International Network of Engaged Buddhists, explains that socially engaged Buddhism does not mean promoting Buddhism per se:

> The presence of Buddhism in society does not mean having a lot of schools, hospitals, cultural institutions, or political parties run by Buddhists. It means that the schools, hospitals, cultural institutions, and political parties are permeated with and administered with humanism, love, tolerance, and enlightenment, characteristics which Buddhism attributes to an opening up, development, and formation of human nature. This is the true spirit of nonviolence.[53]

Even when one intends to be nonviolent in one's approach to life, difficult ethical questions may still arise. For example, contemporary scholars of Buddhist medical ethics are trying to determine how best to apply Buddhist principles to issues such as abortion, reproductive technologies, genetic engineering, organ transplants, suicide, coma patients, and euthanasia. Although the issues seem modern, some of them were addressed during the time of the Buddha, according to the scriptures. Euthanasia, for instance, is the subject of a number of stories in the texts. The general principle that seems to be applied is to avoid taking human life, even when the person requests help in dying. However, careful reading of the texts seems to allow a dying person to refuse life-extending technology, for death is ultimately one of the realities of life that must be faced.

Buddhism is thus as relevant today, and its insights as necessary, as in the sixth century BCE, when the one who became Shakyamuni Buddha renounced a life of ease to save all sentient beings from suffering.

Suggested reading

Carter, John Ross and Mahinda Palihawadana (trans.), *The Dhammapada: The Sayings of the Buddha*, Oxford: Oxford University Press, 2000. A basic book of sayings attributed to the Buddha that covers the essentials of the Dharma in memorable, pithy verses.

Conze, Edward, I. B. Horner, David Snellgrove, and Arthur Waley, ed. and trans., *Buddhist Texts through the Ages*, Oxford: Oneworld Publications, 1995. A fine collection of Buddhist scriptures translated from Pali, Sanskrit, Chinese, Tibetan, and Japanese.

Eppsteiner, Fred, ed., *The Path of Compassion: Writings on Socially Engaged Buddhism*, Berkeley, California: Parallax Press, 1988. A highly readable and relevant collection of essays by leading contemporary Buddhist teachers about the ways in which Buddhism can be applied to social problems.

Fields, Rick, *How the Swans Came to the Lake: A Narrative History of Buddhism in America*, Boston: Shambhala, 1986. The multifaceted story of Buddhism's transfer to the United States.

Fremantle, Francesca, and Chogyam Trungpa, trans., *The Tibetan Book of the Dead*, Boston and London: Shambhala Publications, 1975. The classic Tibetan Buddhist scripture on the projections of the mind and the practices of deity yoga to attain enlightenment.

Friedman, Lenore, *Meetings with Remarkable Women: Buddhist Teachers in America*, Boston and London: Shambhala Publications, 1987. Wisdom from Buddhist traditions shared in very personal, perceptive interviews.

Ghosananda, Maha, *Step by Step*, Berkeley, California: Parallax Press, 1992. Accessible and touching explanations of basic Buddhist doctrines.

Gross, Rita M., *Buddhism after Patriarchy*, Albany, New York: State University of New York Press, 1993. A feminist reconstruction of Buddhist history, revealing its core of gender equality but later overlays of sexism, plus analysis of key Buddhist concepts from a feminist point of view.

Habito, Ruben, *Experiencing Buddhism: Ways of Wisdom and Compassion*, Maryknoll, New York: Orbis Books, 2005. Clear and sensitive exploration of various ways in which Buddhists are attempting to practice the Buddha's teachings, especially in the contemporary world.

Hanh, Thich Nhat, *The Heart of the Buddha's Teaching: Transforming Suffering into Peace, Joy, and Liberation*, New York: Broadway Books, 1998. In simple, compassionate language, the famous Vietnamese monk explains the efficacy of Buddhist teachings for dealing with today's problems.

Heine, Steven and Charles S. Prebish, *Buddhism in the Modern World: Adaptations of an Ancient Tradition*, New York: Oxford University Press, 2003. Essays examining how specific schools of Buddhism have adapted to contemporary challenges and yet maintained their links with tradition.

Kaza, Stephanie and Kenneth Kraft, *Dharma Rain: Sources of Buddhist Environmentalism*, Boston: Shambhala, 2000. Classic and contemporary texts integrating Buddhist spirituality with environmental awareness and activism.

Levine, Stephen, *A Gradual Awakening*, Garden City, New York: Doubleday, 1979 and London: Rider & Company, 1980. Gentle, poetic presentation of *vipassana* techniques in their relevance to contemporary life.

Lopez, Donald S., Jr., ed., *Buddhism in Practice*, Princeton: Princeton University Press, 1995. Annotated translation of original sources dealing with Buddhist practice around the world, organized around the Triple Jewels of Buddha, the Dharma, and the Sangha.

Lopez, Donald S., Jr., ed., *A Modern Buddhist Bible: Essential Readings from East and West*, Boston: Beacon Press, 2002. An anthology of original writings by modern Buddhist teachers trying to revive original Buddhist traditions of meditation and spirituality.

Lopez, Donald S., Jr. *The Story of Buddhism: A Concise Guide to its History and Teachings*, San Francisco: HarperSanFrancisco, 2001. An introduction incorporating the latest scholarship.

Mackenzie, Vicki, *Cave in the Snow*, London: Bloomsbury Publishing, 1999. Fascinating story of a Western woman who spent twelve years alone in a Himalayan cave to concentrate on intense meditation practices and achieve enlightenment in a woman's body.

Mitchell, Donald W., *Buddhism: Introducing the Buddhist Experience*, New York and Oxford: Oxford University Press, 2002. Detailed descriptions of general and culture-specific manifestations of Buddhism.

Queen, Christopher, Charles Prebish, and Damien Keown, eds, *Action Dharma: New Studies in Engaged Buddhism*, London: Routledge, 2003. Articles on both the theory and practice of Buddhist involvement in contemporary social and political causes.

Queen, Christopher S. and Sallie B. King, eds, *Engaged Buddhism: Buddhist Liberation Movements in Asia*, Albany: State University of New York Press, 1996. A thorough survey of contemporary Buddhist activism in Asian countries.

Rahula, Walpola Sri, *What the Buddha Taught*, New York: Grove Press, 1974. The classic introduction to Buddhist teachings—an accurate and clear guide through the complexities of Buddhist thought and practice, with representative texts.

Reynolds, Frank E. and Jason A. Carbine, eds, *The Life of Buddhism*, Berkeley: University of California Press, 2000. Attempts to analyze Buddhist ways in their cultural and historical contexts.

Sivaraksa, Sulak, *Seeds of Peace: A Buddhist Vision for Renewing Society*, Berkeley, California: Parallax Press, 1992. A renowned Thai social activist examines the "politics of greed" and issues involved in the transformation of society, from the point of view of Buddhist ideals.

Suzuki, Shunryu, *Zen Mind, Beginner's Mind*, New York and Tokyo: Weatherhill, 1970. A beautiful book, leading one gracefully and seemingly simply through the paradoxes of Zen.

Tsomo, Karma Lekshe, ed., *Out of the Shadows: Socially Engaged Buddhist Women*, Delhi: Sri Satguru Publications, 2006. Realistic in-depth expressions of Buddhist women's experiences in many cultures, and their efforts to uphold the Dharma therein.

Key terms

anatman (**Pali:** *anatta*) The principle that there is no eternal self.

anitya (**Pali:** *anicca*) Impermanence.

arhant (**Pali:** *arhat* or *arahat*) A "worthy one" who has followed the Buddha's path to liberation.

bhikshu (**Pali:** *bhikkhu*; feminine: *bhikshuni* or *bhikkuni*) A monk or nun who renounces worldliness for the sake of following the path of liberation and whose simple physical needs are met by lay supporters.

bodhisattva A person who is dedicated to liberating others from suffering.

deity yoga Vajrayana meditation on a deity in order to develop his or her qualities.

Dharma (**Pali:** *Dhamma*) The teachings and laws for conduct given by the Buddha.

dukkha Discomfort, suffering, frustration, disharmony.

karma (**Pali:** *kamma*) Actions; the law of cause and effect.

kensho A sudden experience of enlightened awareness.

koan A question used by Zen teachers to boggle the student's mind and thus liberate direct awareness.

lama A high Vajrayana teacher.

Mahayana The "Great Vehicle," the Buddhist school that stresses the altruistic wish to become perfectly awakened in order to free all living beings from suffering.

nirvana Liberation from mental afflictions, suffering, and rebirth.

Pali Canon Ancient Buddhist scriptures written in Pali and considered authoritative.

samsara Cyclic existence; the continual round of birth, death, and rebirth.

Sangha The monastic community; more broadly, a Dharma community.

stupa Monument containing Buddhist relics or images.

sunyata The doctrine of voidness, emptiness.

Theravada The remaining orthodox school of Buddhism, which adheres to the earliest scriptures.

Triple Gem The Buddha, the Dharma, and the Sangha.

Vajrayana A branch of Mahayana Buddhism practiced in the Tibetan diaspora that incorporates deity yoga, mantras, mudras (hand gestures), and mandalas to achieve awakening.

vipassana Insight. A meditation technique for developing insight into *dukkha*, *anicca*, and *anatta*.

zazen Sitting meditation, in Zen schools.

Zen A Chinese and Japanese school emphasizing that all things have Buddha-nature, which can only be grasped when one escapes from the intellectual mind.

Review questions

1. Tell the story of the Buddha's enlightenment. Examine the Four Noble Truths, the Noble Eightfold Path, and the Middle Way.
2. Describe the major similarities and differences among Theravada, Mahayana, and Vajrayana traditions. Describe their geographical development, and name and quote a main text from each tradition.
3. Explain some of the main trends in Buddhism today, addressing the application of Buddhist principles to social issues, women's roles, and the practice of meditation.

Discussion questions

1. What are the major similarities and differences between Hinduism and Buddhism?
2. What are the Buddhist understandings of time and reality? How do these differ from theistic understandings?
3. What factors do you think may account for the growing popularity of Buddhism in Western societies?

Additional Internet resources

Buddha Education Foundation http://www.buddhanet.net

Buddhist Studies http://www.dharmanet.org/

Buddhist Studies WWW Virtual Library http://www.ciolek.com/WWWVL-Buddhism.html

Daughters of the Buddha http://www.sakyadhita.org

Foundation for Preservation of Mahayana Tradition (Dalai Lama's site)
    http://www.fpmt.org/

Internet Sacred Text Archive: Buddhism http://www.sacred-texts.com/bud/index.htm

Mountains and Rivers Order of Zen Buddhism (Zen Mountain Monastery)
    http://www.mro.org/zmm/

Swearer, Donald K., "Buddhism and Ecology: Challenge and Promise."
    http://fore.research.yale.edu/religion/buddhism/index.html

Tricycle: The Buddhist Review http://www.tricycle.com

Women Active in Buddhism http://members.tripod.com/~Lhamo

myreligionlab
For further activities and resources, including access to MyReligionLibrary, please visit MyReligionLab at www.myreligionlab.com

CHAPTER 6

DAOISM AND CONFUCIANISM

The unity of opposites

KEY TOPICS

• ANCIENT
 TRADITIONS 184

• DAOISM—THE WAY
 OF NATURE AND
 IMMORTALITY 189

• CONFUCIANISM—
 THE PRACTICE OF
 VIRTUE 203

While India was giving birth to Hinduism, Jainism, and Buddhism, three other major religions were developing in East Asia. Daoism and Confucianism grew largely in China, and later spread to Japan and Korea; Shinto is considered distinctively Japanese. In this chapter we will explore the two that developed in China from similar roots but with different emphases: Daoism and Confucianism. Shinto will be the subject of Chapter 7. Buddhism also spread to East Asia, where its encounter with Chinese traditions developed its world-affirming qualities, as we saw in Chapter 5. Buddhism is now the most common religion in China. There are also popular religious practices and beliefs that have persisted alongside, and mixed with, the more formalized religious ways and are still popular even as China becomes highly modernized and economically progressive.

In East Asia religions that will be treated as separate entities in this chapter and the next are, in fact, more subtly blended and practiced. Daoism and Confucianism, though they may seem quite opposite to each other, co-exist as complementary value systems in East Asian societies, and a person's thought and actions may encompass both streams. The idea of distinct religions is not prominent in Chinese thought. Even though scholars may trace the historical threads of Daoism, Confucianism, and Buddhism, Chinese people tend to refer to their religious practices simply as "worshiping," and temples may include images from more than one of the "Three Teachings."

In this chapter we will be transliterating Chinese words according to the contemporary Pinyin system, which has replaced the older Wade-Giles system. Thus "Daoism" is the Pinyin transliteration; "Taoism" was the earlier Wade-Giles transcription of the same word. When terms are first introduced in this chapter, the Wade-Giles equivalent—which is still found in many English books—will be given in parenthesis.

Ancient traditions

Chinese civilization is very old and continuous. By 2000 BCE, people were living in settled agrarian villages in the Yellow River Valley, and also in areas of southern China, with musical instruments and skillful work in bronze, silk, ceramics, and ivory. Interpretations of archeological findings suggest that elements still present in Chinese religious ways, both popular and institutionalized, were practiced there as long ago as this.

WORSHIP AND DIVINATION

There is prehistorical evidence of worship of ancestors. Their graves were lined up in rows near villages and provided with funeral offerings such as ornaments, pottery, and tools, suggesting belief in an afterlife in which they could use them. Perhaps then, as now, the spirits of deceased ancestors were thought to remain closely bonded to their living descendants for some time. Chinese tradition requires that respect must be paid to the ancestors—especially the family's founding ancestor and those recently deceased—through funerals, mourning rites, and then continuing sacrifices. These sacred rituals of ancestor worship are called *li.*

Historic sites of Daoism and Confucianism.

In ancient Chinese tradition the universe arises from the interplay of yin and yang. They are modes of energy commonly represented as interlocking shapes, with dominance continually shifting between the dark, receptive yin mode and the bright, assertive yang mode.

They are essential because the ancestors will help their descendants if treated with proper respect, or cause trouble if ignored.

It appears that in addition to ancestors early Chinese people worshiped a great variety of invisible spirits. Plants, animals, rivers, stones, mountains, stars, cosmic forces—in popular religion, all parts of the natural world are vitalized by cosmic energy and many are personified, honored, and consulted as deities. From the earliest historical dynasty, the Shang (c.1600–1046 BCE), archeological evidence indicates that kings and their priests were making regular sacrifices, not only to ancestors but also to deities living in the earth, water, and air. Wine for them was poured onto the earth, jade thrown into rivers, and grains and animal flesh burned on outdoor altars.

From ancient times, there was also belief in a great variety of demons (such as a thorn demon and a water-bug demon) and the ghosts of people who had not been properly honored after their death. These beings were seen as causing so much mischief that many efforts were made to thwart them, ultimately including evil-deflecting charms, gongs, firecrackers, appeals through spirit mediums, spirit walls to keep them from entering doorways, exorcisms, prayers, incense, and fasts.

The spiritual activities of the common people of the Shang period are not definitely known, but it seems clear that kings played very significant religious roles as chief priests for their kingdoms. They sought the help of their aristocratic ancestors and deities by a process of divination through the medium of oracle bones. These were large flat bones onto which the divining specialist scratched questions posed by the king, such as whether or not the sacrifices had been properly performed, whether hunting or military campaigns would be successful,

This bronze wine vessel from the Shang dynasty is richly ornamented with mystical beings and energies, including dragons, snakes, a tiger, wind, and thunderclouds. According to Professor Minqin Wang of Hunan University, dragons were revered as noble, heavenly animals who helped people by producing clouds and rain. Eventually the dragon became the symbol of the emperor, and Chinese people regarded themselves as descendants of the dragons, who are ready to sacrifice themselves to serve others.

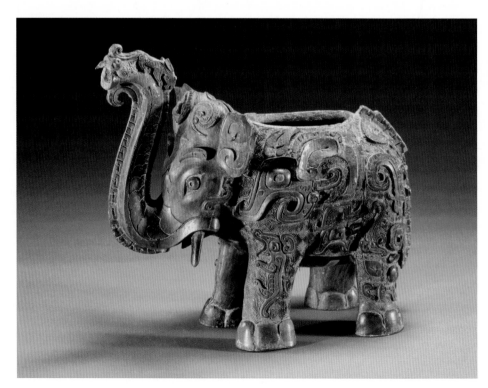

whether or not the coming period would be favorable, and how to interpret dreams. Touching the bones with a hot poker made them crack, forming patterns which the diviner interpreted as useful answers from the ancestors or deities. Kings had the questions and answers inscribed onto the bones, which were maintained as part of the royal archives.

During the reign of the Shang kings, there was a highest god, above deified humans, deities of the local environment, royal ancestors, and gods of the cosmic forces. This highest god was **Shangdi** (Shang Ti) the Lord-on-High. He was understood as a masculine deity who ruled over important phenomena such as the weather, crops, battles, and the king's health. It was the king who was chiefly responsible for maintaining harmony between the transcendent realm of gods and ancestors and the earthly world.

During the Zhou (Chou) dynasty (c.1046–221 BCE), which overthrew the Shang, the rulers continued to play major spiritual roles. However, the focus shifted from Shangdi to Tian (Heaven), a more impersonal power controlling the universe. The emperors of the ruling dynasty then developed the idea of the "Mandate of Heaven" which justified their rule. This was the belief that Heaven responds to human virtue and, specifically, that it endows rulers with the authority to rule based on their virtue. It can also remove the mandate when a ruler's virtue declines. Rulers have a moral duty to maintain the welfare of the people and a spiritual duty to conduct respectful ceremonies for Heaven, Earth, and ancestors. These obligations would later become significant aspects of Confucian thought.

COSMIC BALANCE

In addition to ancestors, gods, and Heaven, there has long existed in China a belief that the cosmos is a manifestation of an impersonal self-generating physical–spiritual substance called *qi* (*ch'i*). It is basically the "stuff" of which all things that exist are composed. It has two aspects whose interplay causes the ever-changing phenomena of the universe. **Yin** is the dark, receptive, "female" aspect; **yang** is the bright, assertive, "male" aspect. Wisdom lies in recognizing their ever-shifting, but regular and balanced, patterns and moving with them. This creative rhythm of the universe is called the **Dao** (Tao), or "way." As traditionally diagramed, yin and yang interpenetrate each other (represented by small circles). As soon as one aspect reaches its fullest point, it begins to diminish, while at the same time its polar opposite increases.

Nothing is outside of this process. As contemporary Confucian scholar Tu Wei-ming explains:

> All modalities of being, from a rock to Heaven, are integral parts of a continuum which is often referred to as the "great transformation." Since nothing is outside of this continuum, the chain of being is never broken. … The continuous presence of qi in all modalities of being makes everything flow together as the unfolding of a single process. Nothing, not even an almighty creator, is external to this process.[1]

To harmonize with the cosmic process, the ancients devised many forms of divination. One system developed during the Zhou dynasty was eventually written down as the *Yijing* (*I Ching*) or *Book of Changes*. It is a common source for both Daoism and Confucianism and is regarded as a classic text in both traditions. The

myreligionlab
Heaven's Gifts
LIEZI

myreligionlab
Doctrine of
the Mean

myreligionlab
Commentary on
Book of Changes

Daoism and Confucianism

	DAOISM	CONFUCIANISM
BCE Legendary Yellow Emperor		
Shang dynasty (c.1600–1046 BCE)	Ancient traditions of worship and divination	Ancient traditions of worship and divination
	DAOISM	**CONFUCIANISM**
Zhou dynasty (c.1046–221 BCE)	c.600–300 Author(s) of *Dao de jing* c.365–290 Life of Zhuangzi	c.551–479 Life of Confucius c.390–305 Life of Mengzi c.340–245 Life of Xunzi
Qin dynasty (221–206 BCE)	Immortality movements Queen Mother of the West cult	Confucian scholars suppressed, books burned
Han dynasty (206 BCE–220 CE)	Early religious Daoist sects Celestial Master tradition begins	Confucian Classics used as training for government officials
CE Tang dynasty (618–907)	Mutual influences between Daoism and Buddhism. 748 Daoist Canon first compiled	Some Buddhist sects reach peak, then are persecuted Confucianism makes comeback
Song dynasty (960–1280)	*Taiji quan* appears Northen Daoist sects flourish	Neo-Confucianism 1130–1200 Life of Zhu Xi
1900	1911 Last imperial dynasty overthrown	1911 Last imperial dynasty overthrown Confucianism rejected as official state ideology
1950	Daoist Association of China (White Cloud Monastery, Beijing)	1949–1976 Mao Zedong and Communist Party take control of China; Mao's "Red Book" replaces Confucian Classics
Cultural Revolution (1966–1976)	Temples and books destroyed	Temples and books destroyed
1980		1989 Students' requests refused at Tiananmen Square
1990–2010	Daoist sects, temples re-established First Daoist Grand Ritual Popular faith and practices Chinese government suppresses Falun Dafa	Confucian Classics reintroduced in schools Confucius's birthday celebrated International Association of Confucians established

Yijing was highly elaborated with commentaries by scholars beginning in the Han dynasty (206 BCE–220 CE). To use this subtle system, one respectfully purifies the divining objects—such as yarrow stalks or coins, whose manipulations will yield either odd numbers signifying yin or even numbers signifying yang. The person asks a question, casts the objects six times, and then consults the *Yijing* for the symbolic interpretation of the yin–yang combinations.

The pattern of throws is diagramed in the *Yijing* as a hexagram, with yin represented as a broken line and yang by a straight line. For example, hexagram number 46, called "Sheng" or "Pushing Upward," has been likened to a tree emerging from the earth, growing slowly and invisibly:

> *Thus the superior person of devoted character*
> *Heaps up small things*
> *In order to achieve something high and great.*[2]

Another set of commentaries is based on the two trigrams within the hexagram. In the case of hexagram 46, the upper pattern of three yin lines can be interpreted as devotion and yielding, and the lower pattern of two yang lines above one yin line suggests gentleness. According to the commentaries, these nonaggressive qualities will ultimately lead to supreme success.

By studying and systematizing the ways of humans and of nature, the ancient Chinese tried to order their actions so that they might steer a coherent course within the changing cosmos. They recognized that any extreme action will produce its opposite as a balancing reaction, and thus they strived for a middle way of discretion and moderation.

From these roots gradually developed two contrasting ways of harmonizing with the cosmos—the more mystically religious ways, which are collectively called Daoism, and the more political and moral ways, which are known as Confucianism. Like yin and yang, they interpenetrate and complement each other, and are themselves evolving dynamically.

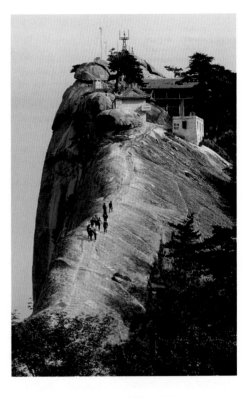

Pilgrimage to holy Mount Huashan. Certain mountains have been revered in China from ancient times to today.

Daoism—the way of nature and immortality

Daoism is as full of paradoxes as the Buddhist traditions it influenced: Chan or Zen Buddhism. It has been adored by Westerners who seek a carefree, natural way of life as an escape from the industrial rat race. Yet beneath its precepts of the simple life in harmony with nature is a tradition of great mental and physical discipline. As developed over time, some Daoist scriptures counsel indifference about birth and death; others teach ways of attaining physical immortality. These variations developed within an ancient tradition that had no name until it had to distinguish itself from Confucianism. "Daoism" is actually a label invented by scholars and awkwardly stretched to cover a philosophical (or "**literati**") tradition, a multitude of self-cultivation and longevity techniques, and an assortment of

The hexagram Sheng is a visual symbol of the various meanings attached to "Pushing Upward."

myreligionlab

Dao de jing
LAOZI

Laozi, one of the major conveyors of the Daoist tradition, is often depicted as a humorous old man riding off into the mountains after reportedly drawing the 5,000 characters of the Dao de jing.

religious sects which probably developed at least in part from the early philosophical texts and practices. Popular religious practices such as home worship of the kitchen god have often mixed with Daoist elements, although institutional Daoism has tried to distance itself from popular religion, seeing itself as a much higher form of religion, with gods who occupy higher heavens.

TEACHINGS OF DAOIST SAGES

Aside from its general basis in ancient Chinese ways, the specific origin of Daoist philosophy and practices is unclear. In China, tradition attributes the publicizing of these ways to the Yellow Emperor, who supposedly ruled from 2697 to 2597 BCE. He was said to have studied with an ancient sage and to have developed meditation, health, and military practices based on what he learned. After ruling for 100 years, he ascended to heaven on a dragon's back and became one of the Immortals.

The classic philosophical or literati form of Daoism has been pursued by intellectuals and artists over the millennia, who explore the concepts about the Dao expressed in ancient texts and perhaps also try to apply them to their social and political environment in the effort to create a condition of harmony known as the Great Peace. The two most salient texts of the classic Daoist tradition are the *Dao de jing* and the *Zhuangzi*.

The *Dao de jing* (*Taõ te Ching*, "The Classic of the Way and its Power") has been translated many times into Western languages, including over 100 English translations, for its ideas are not only fascinating but also elusive for translators. According to tradition, the book was written for a border guard by Laozi (Laotzu), a curator of the royal library of the Zhou dynasty, when he left society for the mountains at the reported age of 160. The guard had recognized Laozi as a sage and begged him to leave behind a record of his wisdom. Laozi reportedly complied by inscribing the 5,000 words now known as the *Dao de jing*. This is traditionally said to have happened during the sixth century BCE, with Laozi somewhat older than Confucius. But archeological finds date the earliest existent version of the *Dao de jing* to 350 BCE and suggest it was an alternative to Confucianism. Many scholars think it was an oral tradition, derived from the teachings of several sages, and question whether there was ever a single person corresponding to the name Laozi ("Old Master").

The book's central philosophy is a practical concern with improving harmony in life. It says that one can best harmonize with the natural flow of life by being receptive and quiet. These teachings were elaborated more emphatically and humorously by a sage named Zhuangzi (Chuang-tzu) (c.365–290 BCE). Unlike Laozi, whose philosophy was addressed to those in leadership positions, Zhuangzi asserted that the best way to live in a chaotic, absurd civilization is to become detached from it.

At the heart of Daoist teachings is the idea of Dao, the "unnamable," the "eternally real."[3] Contemporary Master Da Liu asserts that Dao is so ingrained in Chinese understanding that it is a basic concept that cannot be defined, like "goodness." Moreover, Dao is a mystical reality that cannot be grasped by the mind. The *Dao de jing* says:

> *The way that can be spoken of*
> *Is not the constant way;*
> *The name that can be named*
> *Is not the constant name.*
> *The nameless was the beginning of heaven and earth;*
> *The named was the mother of the myriad creatures.[4]*

Another chapter of the *Dao de jing* is more explicit about the mysterious Unnamable:

> *There is a thing confusedly formed,*
> *Born before heaven and earth.*
> *Silent and void*
> *It stands alone and does not change,*
> *Goes round and does not weary.*
> *It is capable of being the mother of the world.*
> *I know not its name*
> *So I style it 'the way.'*
> *I give it the makeshift name of 'the great.'[5]*

Although we cannot describe the Dao, we can live in harmony with it. Ideally, says Laozi:

> *Humans model themselves on earth,*
> *Earth on heaven,*
> *Heaven on the way,*
> *And the way on that which is naturally so.[6]*

There are several basic principles for the life in harmony with Dao. One is to experience the transcendent unity of all things, rather than separation. This realization can only be attained when one ceases to feel any personal preferences. Daoism is concerned with direct experience of the universe, accepting and cooperating with things as they are, not with setting standards of morality, not with labeling things as "good" or "bad." Zhuangzi asserts that herein lies true spirituality:

> *Such a man can ride the clouds and mist, mount the sun and moon, and wander beyond the four seas. Life and death do not affect him. How much less will he be concerned with good and evil![7]*

The Daoist sage takes a low profile in the world. He or she is like a valley, allowing everything needed to flow into his or her life, or like a stream. Flowing

myreligionlab

Great and
Venerable Teacher
ZHUANGZI

water is a Daoist model for being. It bypasses and gently wears away obstacles rather than fruitlessly attacking them, effortlessly nourishes the "ten thousand things" of material life, works without struggling, leaves all accomplishments behind without possessing them.

This is the uniquely Daoist paradox of *wu wei*—"actionless action," or taking no intentional or invasive action contrary to the natural flow of things. *Wu wei* is spontaneous, creative activity proceeding from the Dao, action without ego-assertion, letting the Dao take its course. Zhuangzi uses the analogy of a butcher whose knife always stays sharp because he lets his hand be guided by the make-up of the carcass, finding the spaces between the bones where a slight movement of the blade will glide through without resistance. Even when difficulties arise, the sage does not panic and take unnecessary action.

> *To know yet to think that one does not know is best;*
> *Not to know yet to think that one knows will lead to difficulty.*
>
> *Laozi*[8]

The result of *wu wei* is noninterference. Much of Laozi's teaching is directed at rulers, that they might guide society without interfering with its natural course. Nothing is evil, but things may be out of balance. The world is naturally in harmony; Dao is our original nature. But according to tradition, the Golden Age of Dao declined as humans departed from the "Way." "Civilization," with its intellectual attempts to improve on things and its rigid views of morality, actually leads to world chaos, the Daoists warn. How much better, Laozi advises, to accept not-knowing, moving freely in the moment with the changing universe.

TEACHING STORY

Three in the Morning

Whether you point to a little stalk or a great pillar, a leper or the beautiful Hsi-shih, things ribald and shady or things grotesque and strange, the Way makes them all into one. ... Only the man of far-reaching vision knows how to make them into one. So he has no use [for categories], but relegates all to the constant. The constant is the useful; the useful is the passable; the passable is the successful; and with success, all is accomplished. He relies upon this alone, relies upon it and does not know he is doing so. This is called the Way.

But to wear out your brain trying to make things into one without realizing that they are all the same—this is called "three in the morning." What do I mean by "three in the morning"? When the monkey trainer was handing out acorns, he said, "You get three in the morning and four at night." This made all the monkeys furious. "Well, then," he said, "you get four in the morning and three at night." The monkeys were all delighted. There was no change in the reality behind the words, yet the monkeys responded with joy and anger. Let them, if they want to. So the sage harmonizes with both right and wrong and rests in Heaven the Equalizer.

Zhuangzi[9]

Daoism places great value on withdrawal from the madding crowd to a contemplative life and love of nature. The classic Daoist seeks to find the still center, save energy for those times when action is needed, and take a humble, quiet approach to life. As asserted in a fourth-century BCE essay on inner training:

> The vitality of all people inevitably comes from their peace of mind.
> When anxious, one loses this guiding thread; when angry,
>   one loses this basic point.
> When one is anxious or sad, pleased or angry, the Way has no place to settle. ...
> That mysterious vital energy within the mind, one moment it arrives,
>   the next it departs.
> So fine nothing can be contained within it, so vast nothing can be outside it.
> The reason we lose it is because of the harm caused by agitation.[10]

The ethical effects of such a philosophy are designed to harmonize humanity with the cosmos. Heaven, earth, and humanity all arise from the same source, the Dao, first cause of the cosmos. Coming from the same source, all things on earth are to be loved and allowed to exist and develop according to their nature. As the sage Ge Hong (283–343 CE) writes in the *Inner Chapters of the Master who Embraces Simplicity*, "Universal Dao acts on non-interference [*wu wei*], that is, lets everything be natural, no matter what relationship among them and how different they are." Along with the motto "Dao follows what is natural," the Daoist feels "I am one with all things."

Chinese artists captured the flows of qi through mountains, water, and trees in their paintings.

The only thing to be pursued is Dao, rather than material gain or fame. Laozi says:

> The five colours make man's eyes blind; ...
> Goods hard to come by
> Serve to hinder his progress.[11]

By contrast, he says:

> I have three treasures
> Which I hold and cherish.
> The first is known as compassion,
> The second is known as frugality,
> The third is known as not daring
>   to take the lead in the empire. ...
> There is no disaster greater than
>   not being content;
> There is no misfortune greater
>   than being covetous.
> Hence in being content, one will
>   always have enough.[12]

Furthermore, according to Daoist ideals, there should not be a great gap between the rich and the poor. Just as Heaven makes adjustments between surpluses and deficiencies, the rich should desire to share with the poor. But as Laozi observes:

Who is there that can take what he himself
   has in excess and offer this to the empire?
Only he who has the way.[13]

POPULAR RELIGION AND ORGANIZED DAOISM

Popular religion and organized Daoism became considerably intertwined over the centuries when Daoist specialists took charge of spiritual tasks such as alchemy, faith healing, and the use of talismans, which seem to have existed from ancient times in China. But some of the folk practices have also survived as independent traditions outside of formal Daoist frameworks.

People may believe in invisible spirits who are involved in their destinies, so out of both fear and respect they want to make sure to worship them properly. Burning incense and making offerings have been ways of communicating with them since antiquity. In temple worship, these practices have become institutionalized, with detailed ritual instructions and a priesthood to carry them out. However, folk practices may transcend the restrictions of classic Daoism, with variations such as making offerings of nonvegetarian foods. Liu Zhongyu, of a branch of the Dragon Gate sect of the Complete Perfection lineage in Hong Kong, pragmatically explains, "In fact, it is forbidden in Daoism to give things such as pig's heads as offerings. But as the people have long been doing so, Daoism has to let things take their own course."[14]

Letting things take their own course has long included the art of *feng shui*, or geomancy—determining natural flows of *qi* through the earth, as revealed by the flows of wind and water. Though awareness of these flows probably arose from shamanistic folk traditions, it sometimes became the province of specialists. By observing the contours of the land and the flows of wind and water, specialists in *feng shui* can reportedly determine the best places for the harmonious placement of a temple, dwelling place, or grave. By examining the flow of *qi* within a dwelling, they decide on the optimal placement of furniture and wall decorations.

Deities arising from folk traditions have in some cases become part of the Daoist pantheon. One of the most familiar deities in popular Chinese traditions is the kitchen god. Although his worship usually takes place at the family level in the home where he lives, he was at one time listed in official Daoist spirit pedigrees as the Great Emperor and Controller of Destinies of the Eastern Kitchen. According to folk belief, the kitchen god sits in a corner of the kitchen watching the family's doings so that he can make an annual report about their virtues and failings to the Jade Emperor. Sometimes, humorous ruses are used to insure that he does not give a bad report. One is to make an offering before he sets off for Heaven that is so intoxicating that he forgets about the family's flaws. Another is to offer him some sweet maltose that is so sticky that he cannot open his mouth to speak when he meets the Jade Emperor.

The ancient practice of worshiping certain people as divine, appointed to heavenly office after they have died, is also encompassed by organized Daoism. For example, a virtuous daughter of the Lin family saved members of her own family and others in distress during the Song dynasty, and is now worshiped as Tianhou (Tien-hou), the Holy Mother in Heaven, especially in coastal regions.

In popular practice, people vow to do a good deed if their prayer request is granted. Accordingly, they may offer incense, candles, or food to the deities to redeem the vow once they feel the deities have blessed them with success. Sometimes the vow-redeeming promises are more elaborate, such as releasing a captive animal, or sculpting a statue of a deity. Many people vow to do some kind of performance to please the deities, often including singing, dancing, music, or beating drums. Some such performances are organized on a large scale, as performance fairs at temples.

As in ancient times, Chinese villages make collective offerings to the local spirits or organize processions in which the spirits visit the local region, bless them, and protect them from harm such as epidemics. The images of the deities from the temple are put in palanquins (or today, trucks) and carried in the procession. Talismans are also made for protection, with the written characters presumed to have magical power to control the spirits.

One of the goals of esoteric Daoist practice is to separate the Immortal Fetus from the body so that the former can operate independently, both before and after death.

INNER ALCHEMY

In contrast to popular practices, an elite thread of ancient traditions that have also become interwoven with Daoism involve inner alchemy: individual spiritual practices for the sake of inner transformation, self-cultivation, longevity, and perhaps immortality. Daoist texts refer to powerful ascetic practices traditionally passed down secretly from teacher to pupil. The teachers lived in the mountains; great Daoist teachers are said to be still hidden in the remote mountains of China and Korea.

The aim of the longevity practices is to use the energy available to the body in order to become strong and healthy, and to intuitively perceive the order of the universe. Within our body is the spiritual micro-universe of the "three treasures" necessary for the preservation of life: generative force (*jing*), vital life force (*qi*), and spirit (*shen*). These three are said to be activated with the help of various methods: breathing techniques, vocalizations, vegetarian diets, gymnastics, absorption of solar and lunar energies, sexual techniques, visualizations, and meditations.

The process of "inner alchemy" begins with the practitioner building a reservoir of *jing* energy in the "cauldron" several inches below the navel, whence it rises up the spine as a vapor, transmuted into *qi* energy. *Qi* is in turn transmuted into *shen* in an upper cauldron in the head, drops down to illuminate the heart center, and then descends to an inner area of the lower cauldron. There it forms what is called the Immortal Fetus, which an adept can reportedly raise through the Heavenly Gate at the top of the head and thus leave their physical body for various purposes, including preparation for life after death. In addition, the adept learns to draw the *qi* of heaven and earth into the micro-universe of the body, unifying and harmonizing inner and outer.

> *The secret of the magic of life consists in using action*
> *in order to attain non-action.*
>
> *The Secret of the Golden Flower*[15]

In contrast to physical practices to lengthen life and lead to immortality, Zhuangzi had counseled indifference to birth and death: "The Master came because it was time. He left because he followed the natural flow. Be content with the moment, and be willing to follow the flow."[19] Laozi referred enigmatically to immortality or long life realized through spiritual death of the individual self, the body and mind transmuted into selfless vehicles for the eternal. As Professor Huai-Chin Han notes, people who are interested in Daoist practices:

> *usually forget the highest principles, or the basis of philosophical theory behind the cultivation of Tao [Dao] and the opening of the ch'i [qi] routes for longevity. ... Longevity consists of maintaining one's health, slowing down the ageing process, living without illness and pain, and dying peacefully without bothering other people. Immortality does not mean indefinite physical longevity; it indicates the eternal spiritual life.*[16]

A quiet contemplative life in natural surroundings, with peaceful mind, health-maintaining herbs, healthy diet, practices to strengthen the inner organs and open the meridians (subtle energy pathways known to Chinese doctors), and meditations to transmute vital into spiritual energy, does bring a marked tendency to longevity. Chinese literature and folk knowledge contain many references to venerable sages thought to be centuries old. They live hidden in the mountains, away from the society of others, and are said to be somewhat translucent. The most famous of the legendary long-lived are the Eight Immortals, humans who were said to have gained immortality, each with his or her own special magical power.

myreligionlab
Story of He Xiangu, Female Immortal

Since ancient times, one of the most revered celestial beings has been the Queen Mother of the West. She guards the elixir of life and is the most wondrous incarnation of yin energy. The Daoist canon also includes the writings of some female Daoist sages who undertook the great rigors of Daoist meditation practices and reportedly mastered its processes of inner transformation. In her mystical poetry, the twelfth-century female sage Sun Bu-er describes the ultimate realization:

> *All things finished.*
> *You sit still in a little niche.*
> *The light body rides on violet energy,*
> *The tranquil nature washes in a pure pond.*
> *Original energy is unified, yin and yang are one;*
> *The spirit is the same as the universe.*[17]

DAOIST SECTS

Institutionalization of such ancient and popular practices into distinctive religious movements, with revealed texts, detailed rituals, and priests serving as ritual specialists, developed as the Han dynasty (206 BCE–220 CE) was declining amidst famine and war. An array of revelations and prophecies predicted the end of the age and finally led to the rise of religious/political organizations.

In 184 CE, inspired by a vision of Great Peace, hundreds of thousands of followers of a leader who was known as a faith healer and advocate of egalitarian ideas rebelled in eight of China's twelve provinces; their rebellion took several years to suppress and presaged the fall of the Han dynasty. Simultaneously, in western China, Zhang Daoling (Chang Tao-ling) had a vision in which he was appointed representative of the Dao on earth and given the title **Celestial Master**. He advocated similar practices of healing by faith and developed a quasi-military organization of religious officials, attracting numerous followers. The older Han religion had involved demons and exorcism, belief in an afterlife, and a god of destinies, who granted fortune or misfortune based on heavenly records of good and bad deeds. These roles were now ascribed to a pantheon of celestial deities, who in turn were controlled by the new Celestial Master priesthood led by Zhang's family. This hereditary clergy performed imperial investitures as well as village festivals, with both men and women serving as libationers in local dioceses. After the sack of the northern capitals early in the fourth century, the Celestial Masters and other aristocrats fled south and established themselves on Dragon-Tiger Mountain in southeast China. Today the Celestial Masters tradition is thriving in Taiwan and Hong Kong, but the movement is also being revived in mainland China.

In approximately 365 CE another aristocratic family in exile in southern China began receiving revelations from a deceased member, Lady Wei. These revelations of the names and powers of newly discovered deities, meditation methods, alchemy, and rituals were recorded in exquisite calligraphy and transmitted to a few advanced disciples. This elite group of celibates, who resided on Mount Mao, called their practices "**Highest Purity Daoism.**" They looked down on the Celestial Master tradition as crude, and they avoided village rituals and commoners. Instead, they focused on meditations for purifying the body with divine energies so as "to rise up to heaven in broad daylight." Although the Highest Purity Daoism did not reach the mass of the people, its texts and influence continue to be revered today as the elite tradition of organized Daoism.

In the late fourth century, another group arose in the wake of Highest Purity: the Numinous Treasure school. It assimilated many elements of Buddhism, creating a medley of new meditation practices, divine beings, rituals, scriptures, heavens, rebirth, and hells. This tradition was in turn succeeded in the twelfth century by **Complete Perfection**, which has been the dominant monastic school ever since. It unites Daoist inner alchemy with Chan Buddhist meditation and Confucian social morality, harmonizing the three religions. Actively monastic, it focuses on meditation and nonattachment to the world. Today its major center is the White Cloud Monastery in Beijing, the headquarters of the government-approved Daoist Association of China. Complete Perfection is also the foundation for most Hong Kong Daoist temples and martial arts groups.

The many revealed scriptures of Daoist movements were occasionally compiled and canonized by the court. The present Daoist canon was compiled in 1445 CE. Containing about 1,500 sophisticated scriptures, it has only recently begun to be studied by non-Daoist scholars. It includes a wealth of firsthand accounts by mystical practitioners—poems of their visionary shamanistic journeys, encounters with deities, advanced meditation practices, descriptions of the perfected human being, methods and elixirs for ascending to heavenly realms and achieving immortality, and descriptions of the Immortals and the heavenly bureaucracies. The rituals and inner cultivation practices of the canon are in use today, and

myreligionlab

Awakening
to Perfection
ZHANG BODUAN

The Lantern Festival

Popular religious practices of ancient origin survive in China today as happy festivals. One of the favorites is the Lantern Festival, the end of Chinese New Year celebrations. These begin on the twenty-third or twenty-fourth day of the twelfth month of the lunar year, which is thought to be the day the gods go to heaven to offer their respects to the supreme deity, the Jade Emperor. One of them is the kitchen god making his report about the family, which will determine their fortunes in the year to come. The New Year begins in the spring, as the earth comes back to life and ploughing and sowing of fields can start again. In preparation for the coming year, houses are thoroughly cleaned to remove any bad luck, and doors and windows may be painted and decorated with auspicious inscriptions. People happily visit each other with offerings of gifts and flowers, and attempt to clear all their debts. Families may wake early on the second or fifth day of the first lunar month to set off firecrackers to welcome the Magic Horse of Wealth to their home.

The climax of the celebrations—the Lantern Festival—occurs on the night of the fifteenth day of the first lunar month. People roam joyfully through the streets carrying, and looking at, a great array of paper lanterns, and enjoying lion dances, dragon dances, parades, plays, fireworks, acrobatics, and sticky sweet rice balls. Owners of the lanterns may write riddles on them, and those who successfully solve them are given small prizes. It is a cultural festival thought to have sacred origins, but there are various understandings of what is being celebrated. Lanterns may illustrate popular subjects or may be decorated with scenes of the Immortals—or else of Buddhas and bodhisattvas.

According to one legend, the Jade Emperor in heaven was so upset because a town had killed his beloved goose that he determined to destroy the town with fire. But the townspeople, warned by a fairy, lit so many lanterns that from above the town appeared to be on fire. Feeling that his anger had already been avenged, the Jade Emperor did not send the firestorm. From then on, people celebrated their rescue by carrying lanterns on the first full moon of the year.

Another explanation features the god of heaven worshiped by people in ancient China. It was he who controlled the fate of the world, as he had sixteen dragons and could therefore send famine, plagues, droughts, or calamities. The emperor would therefore request him to send only good weather and good health to the people of the kingdom. During the Han dynasty, an emperor dedicated a night of great celebrations to the god of heaven, and the tradition has continued.

Yet another story revolves around the Heavenly Official Who Gives Blessings. His birthday is the fifteenth day of the first lunar month. Because he likes all sorts of entertainment, the people decorate lanterns and offer many amusements in the hope of being blessed with good fortune.

Whatever the explanation, people are entertained by great cultural festivals in the name of pleasing the gods. A description of the Lantern Festival from the Song dynasty listed dozens of dancing troupes, including the Cloud Holders, the Sword Players, the Wedding Players, the Clothes Washers' Songs, the Bamboo Horses, the Camels and Elephants, and the Deities and Ghosts, plus twenty-four puppet troupes such as the Land Dragon Boats and the Lantern Kickers. The celebrations and the lanterns became more and more elaborate and now, with the aid of modern electronics, people happily enjoy spectacular entertainments.

the immense pantheon of deities that has evolved is represented by a great variety of images.

At death either Daoist or Buddhist priests may be hired by families to perform rituals to help the deceased. Every temple has a side shrine to Tudi gong (T'u-ti Kung), the local earth god, lowest member of the celestial hierarchy, who can transport offerings to deceased loved ones.

DAOISM TODAY

Historically, whenever the central Chinese government has been strong, it has tended to demand total allegiance to itself as a divine authority and to challenge or suppress competing religious groups. Since the Han dynasty, Chinese emperors were called "Son of Heaven," and their families claimed to have received the Mandate of Heaven when it was taken away from the previous dynasty. Confucian scholars were suppressed and their books were burned by the Qin (Ch'in) dynasty (221–206 BCE), shamans were forbidden during the Han dynasty, Buddhists were persecuted during the Tang dynasty, the Taiping rebellion of the nineteenth century attempted to purge China of Daoism and Buddhism, and during the Cultural Revolution of 1966 to 1976 zealous young Red Guards destroyed Daoist, Buddhist, and Confucian temples and books. However, during the economic liberalization that began in the late twentieth century in mainland China, in spite of an atheistic communist ideology temples were maintained as historic sites, pilgrimages to temples in natural sites and religious tourism have been encouraged, and an explosion of temple building has occurred.

All forms of Daoist practice are still actively undertaken today, in communist mainland China, Taiwan, Hong Kong, and Chinese communities overseas. Chinese temples combine Confucian, Buddhist, and Daoist elements, but the liturgies tend to be Daoist.

myreligionlab

The Way of
Perfect Truth
WANG ZHE

Both Daoist and Buddhist groups continue to be recipients of new revelations and scriptures. These texts, known as "precious scrolls," emanate from deities such as the Golden Mother of the Celestial Pool. It is believed that in the past the Divine Mother sent Buddha and Laozi as her messengers but that now the crisis of the present world requires her direct intervention.

Starting in the 1980s, a few ancient Daoist practitioners in China tried to teach groups of young students so that the disciplines could be continually transmitted. They met with many bureaucratic obstacles within communist China but received considerable support from Chinese communities and scholars abroad. The Communist Party is still officially anti-religious, with the Marxist theory that religion will die out as unnecessary in a socialist state, but in fact there is a great resurgence of religious practice of all sorts, both in the countryside and in the cities. After the violent attempts of the Cultural Revolution to stamp out religion, shrines and halls for worship of clan ancestors are sprouting and many new Daoist and Buddhist temples, Muslim mosques, and Christian churches are being built. Temples are busy with worshipers, including people trying to find clues to their future by casting divining blocks after praying before the image of a deity. Party policy seems to have turned toward the pragmatic view that traditional religious and cultural traditions can perhaps play a "positive role" in building social stability in the midst of rapid social and economic change. Religious organizations must register with the government and operate under government control. There are hundreds of local Daoist associations in the provinces of China, as well as the Daoist Association of China, centered in the White Cloud Monastery in Beijing. Its stated goals include promoting:

the mutual adaptation between Daoism and socialist society. The association is to participate in the building of the socialist modernizations, and devote itself to the maintenance of the stability of society, the unification of the country, and the peace of the world.[18]

Daoist nuns and monks are of equal status. Huang Zhi An, head nun of the Daoist Temple in Hengshan, Hunan Province, collected funds to help rebuild the temple and monastic complex—which also includes a Buddhist monastery and temple of both religions combined—and to build a center for training nuns in the classical arts, including chanting, music, and practices to develop *qi*. Her speech, gestures, and actions are very natural and spontaneous, like those of an energetic child, and yet she presides over solemn, ritualized chanting by the nuns. When asked to explain this combination of opposites, she says simply of Daoist practice, "It's like democracy: There has to be a combination of freedom and also rules for confining freedom, or else there is chaos."[19]

Hong Kong has long been home to many Daoist temples and activities. The Peng Ying Xian Guan (Fung Ying Seen Koon) branch of Complete Perfection Daoism began early in the twentieth century as an attempt by two Dragon Gate priests to develop a secluded holy place for self-cultivation, as a cure for decaying social morality. Now the organization sponsors a free clinic, a school, lectures for teaching the Dao, training classes for priests and study of rites and scriptures, and rituals to pray for blessings and redeem lost souls.

myreligionlab

Significance of Daoist
Ethical Thought
ZHOU ZHONGZHI

Attempting to unite Daoists and promote social welfare, the Hong Kong Taoist Association is developing schools to combine education with Daoist enlightenment and character-building, giving lectures encouraging morality, building and repairing Daoist temples, and organizing festivals observed by all Daoist temples such as Seven-Day-and-Night Rituals for Accumulating Merits for the sake of the prosperity and peace of Hong Kong and harmony in the world. Similar Daoist associations now exist in Taiwan, Malaysia, and Singapore.

Academic study of Daoism is intensifying with the help of such Daoist religious organizations, university scholars, social science research institutes, and cultural and artistic institutions. The Chinese government's Center for Religious Studies carries on activities such as a major project to republish the entire Daoist canon with extensive explanatory material from current research.

Daoist ideas are also being promoted to help curb the environmental and social damage that has resulted in China from rapid industrialization. Zhou Zhongzhi, Director of the Center of Business Ethics Study in Shanghai Normal University, describes the ecological principles embedded in Daoist thought:

Through interaction and interdependence, humans and nature constitute a harmonious and unified system, [but] it is possible to lead to inharmoniousness of human and nature, even burst into ecological crisis, if man becomes insatiable and conscienceless, and impacts on nature become so far-reaching as to go beyond the limit of nature's capability.[20]

On Chinese New Year, Hong Kong temples are filled with worshipers who burn incense sticks to pay homage to the spirits.

According to Zhou, application of Daoist principles would lead people to limit their consumer desires and foster compassionate giving, countering the growing disparities between rich and poor.

Interest in Daoist practices and philosophy has boomed in the West from the middle of the twentieth century. By now there are many masters and centers in the United States. They include organized religious institutions, societies for self-cultivation, and practitioners of techniques for spiritual development, health, and longevity. Many people outside China are now benefiting from acupuncture therapy, which is based on the idea that *qi* flows through the body in channels, or meridians. Needle stimulation or burning of herbs above specific points along the meridians is successfully used to cure or alleviate many ailments. Traditional Chinese herbal medicine is also of increasing interest, as are energy training practices. Of these, *Taiji quan* (T'ai chi ch'uan) was developed in the eighteenth century as a training for martial arts. It is still practiced today by many Chinese at dawn and dusk for their health. It looks like slow swimming in the air, with continual circular movement through a series of dance-like postures. They are considered manifestations of the unobstructed flow of *qi* through the body. According to the *Taiji Quan Classics*, "In any action the entire body should be light and agile and all of its parts connected like pearls on a thread."[21] In combat, the practitioner of *taiji* is advised to "yield at your opponent's slightest pressure and adhere to him at his slightest retreat,"[22] using mental alertness to subtle changes rather than muscular strength in order to gain the advantage. *Taiji quan* is also often physically beneficial in controlling blood pressure, muscular coordination, and balance, and thus is useful to elderly people.

myreligionlab
The Essence of Taiji
AL CHUNG-LIANG HUANG

In the early twentieth century, a sickly tuberculosis patient cured himself by practicing the energy training disciplines from an old Daoist inner alchemical text describing traditional meditation and longevity techniques. He learned to detect the inner movements of *qi* within himself and then wrote about them in contemporary biomedical terms. Others also thence became interested in the traditional health exercises. The self-cultivation systems they popularized are now generally known as *qigong* (ch'i-kung) and are widely used not only in China but also in the West to cure diseases, increase physical vitality, and improve concentration. Some people today claim that the combination of meditation methods, breath control, martial arts, and diet are even helpful in thwarting the ravages of AIDS.

During the 1990s, Chinese masters made the techniques even more popular by advertising that one could attain supernatural powers through them. The most famous of these claims have been made by Li Hongzhi, who in 1992 developed a form of *qigong* that mixed Buddhism with Daoist energy practices, producing a hybrid known as **Falun Gong**. He proposed that he would spiritually install a "falun" or Dharma Wheel in followers' abdomens so that they could perform advanced energy practices. Li, who moved to the United States, claims that practitioners of Falun Gong can attain excellent health, supernatural power, and cosmic enlightenment if they develop the cardinal virtues of truthfulness, benevolence, and forbearance, as well as carrying on the daily exercises. These are taught for free by volunteers at thousands of locations around the world. The movement, **Falun Dafa**, now claims millions of followers. But in China, the movement has been severely curtailed since 1999 by the government, which portrays it as an evil cult using the pretence of religion to practice political and criminal activities. The government has even cracked down on other forms of *qigong* which it once supported, and legislation has been passed that may be used to suppress any mystical Chinese group and any other religious group that has not been sanctioned by the Chinese Communist Party.

Nonetheless, there is general government support for resurgent Daoism and interest in Daoism is running high in many other countries, replete with numerous websites, international Daoist organizations, and international scholarly conferences. In the Western popularization of Daoism, classic Daoist texts are even being used by businesses to teach management practices.

Taiji master Al Huang embodies the fluidity of Taiji quan, practiced both for physical health and for teaching the mind to flow with change so that action is effortless.

Confucianism—the practice of virtue

To trace a different strand of East Asian religion, we return to the sixth century BCE, which was a period of great spiritual and intellectual flourishing in many cultures. It roughly coincided with the life of the Buddha, the Persian Empire, the Golden Age of Athens, the great Hebrew prophets, and in China with the life of another outstanding figure. Westerners call him Confucius and his teaching Confucianism. His family name was Kong; the Chinese honored him as Kong Fuzi (Master Kong) and called his teaching **Rujiao** (the teaching of the scholars). It did not begin with Confucius. Rather, it is based on the ancient Chinese beliefs in Heaven, ancestor worship, and the efficacy of rituals. Confucius developed from these roots a school of thought that emphasizes the cultivation of moral virtues and the interaction between human rulers and Heaven, with political involvement as the way to transforming the world. This philosophy became highly influential in China and still permeates the society, despite great political changes. It exists not only as a school of thought but also as the practice of religious ethics.

For 2,000 years, Daoism, Buddhism, and Confucianism have co-existed in China, contributing mutually to the culture. Both Daoism and Buddhism emphasize the ever-changing nature of things in the cosmos, whereas Confucianism focuses on ways of developing a just and orderly society. This is the Confucian way of connecting human beings to the transcendent—yet also immanent—moral will of Heaven.

Individuals often harmonize the apparently opposite characteristics of Daoism and Confucianism in their own lives. For example, elderly Daoist Master An speaks on one hand of the fact that he and his fellows sweep the temple when they feel like it—"We're not caught up in routines"—and on the other of the ways that his father's teaching of Confucian maxims shaped his life:

> My father was very cultured and adamant about teaching us the true Tao. He mastered the classics, and would write out quotations all the time. Over on the wall there is a quotation by Confucius he wrote:
>
> If I'm not generous with those below me,
> If I'm disrespectful toward the proprieties,
> Or if I do not properly mourn at a funeral,
> How can I have self-esteem?
>
> He'd paste these quotations on our wall above the bed. I'd turn my head and there it was, sinking in my brain. … Confucius also said, "One who seeks the Tao cannot be deficient in manners."[23]

Professor Yu Yingshi explains that Daoism and Confucianism can co-exist because in Chinese tradition there are no major divisions between mind and matter, utopian ideals and everyday life:

> For Chinese, the transcendental world, the world of the spirit, interpenetrates with the everyday world though it is not considered identical to it. If we use the tao to represent the transcendental world and the Confucian ideal of human relationships to represent the human world, we can see how they interface. The tao creates the

character of these human relations. For these relations to exist as such, they must follow the tao, they cannot depart from the tao for a moment. These two worlds operate on the cusp of interpenetration, neither dependent on nor independent of the other. So mundane human relationships are, from the very beginning, endowed with a transcendental character.[24]

MASTER KONG'S LIFE

Confucius was born in approximately 551 BCE, during the Zhou dynasty, into a family whose ancestors had been prominent in the previous dynasty. They had lost their position through political struggles, and his father, a soldier, died when the boy was only three years old. Although the young boy was determined to be a scholar, the family's financial straits necessitated his taking such humble work as overseeing granaries and livestock. He married at the age of nineteen and had at least two children. His mother died when he was twenty-three, and during three years of mourning he lived ascetically and studied ancient ceremonial rites (*li*) and imperial institutions. When he returned to social interaction, he gained some renown as a teacher of *li* and of the arts of governing.

It was a period of political chaos, with the stability of the early Zhou dynasty giving way to disorder. As central power weakened, feudal lords held more power than kings of the central court, ministers assassinated their rulers, and sons killed their fathers. Confucius felt that a return to classical rites and standards of virtue was the only way out of the chaos, and he unsuccessfully sought rulers who would adopt his ideas. He then turned to a different approach: training young men to be wise and altruistic public servants. He proposed that the rulers should perform classical rites and music properly so that they would remain of visibly high moral character and thus inspire the common people to be virtuous. He thus instructed his students in the "Six Classics" of China's cultural heritage: the *Yijing*, poetry, history, rituals, music and dance, and the Spring and Autumn Annals of events in his state, Lu. According to tradition, it was Confucius who edited older documents pertaining to these six areas and put them into the form now known as the Confucian Classics. There are now only five; the treatises on music were either destroyed or never existed. Of his role, Confucius claimed only: "I am a transmitter and not a creator. I believe in and have a passion for the ancients."[25]

Confucius's work and teachings were considered relatively insignificant during his lifetime. After his death in 479 BCE, interstate warfare increased, ancient family loyalties were replaced by large and impersonal armies, and personal virtues were replaced by laws and state control. After the brutal reunification of China by the Qin dynasty, however, rulership required a more cultured class of bureaucrats who could embody the virtues advocated by Confucius. In the second century BCE the Confucian Classics thus became the basis of training for the scholar-officials who were to serve in the government. The life of the gentleman-scholar devoted to proper government became the highest professed ideal. Eventually temples were devoted to the worship of Confucius himself as the model for unselfish public service, human kindness, and scholarship. However, the official state use of the Confucian Classics can be seen as a political device to give the government a veneer of civility.

THE CONFUCIAN VIRTUES

Foremost among the virtues that Confucius felt could save society was *ren* (*jen*). Translations of this central term include innate goodness, love, benevolence, perfect virtue, humaneness, and human-heartedness. In Chapter IV of *The Analects*, Confucius describes the rare person who is utterly devoted to *ren* as one who is not motivated by personal profit but by what is moral, is concerned with self-improvement rather than public recognition, is ever mindful of parents, speaks cautiously but acts quickly, and regards human nature as basically good.

The prime exemplar of *ren* should be the ruler. Rulers were urged to rule not by physical force or coercion but by the example of personal virtue:

> *Confucius said: If a ruler himself is upright, all will go well without orders.*
> *But if he himself is not upright, even though he gives orders they will not be obeyed.*
> *... One who governs by virtue is comparable to the polar star, which remains in its place while all the stars turn towards it.*"[26]

Asked to define the essentials of strong government, Confucius listed adequate troops, adequate food, and the people's trust. But of these, the only true necessity is that the people have faith in their rulers. To earn this faith, the ruling class should "cultivate themselves," leading lives of virtue and decorum. They should continually adhere to *ren*, always reaching upward, cherishing what is right, rather than reaching downward for material gain.

The modern Chinese character for *ren* is a combination of "two" and "person," conveying the idea of relationship. Those relationships emphasized by Confucians are the interactions between parent and child, older and younger siblings, husband and wife, ruler and subject, and friend and friend. In all but the last of these relationships, the first is considered superior to the second. Each relationship is nonetheless based on distinct but mutual obligations and responsibilities. This web of human relationships supports the individual like a series of concentric circles.

At the top, the ruler models himself on Heaven, serving as a parent to the people and linking them to the larger cosmic order through ritual ceremonies. Confucius says that this was the source of the greatness of Yao—a sage king of c.2357 BCE: "It is Heaven that is great and Yao who modeled himself upon it."[27]

In Confucius's ideal world, there is a reciprocal hierarchy in which each knows his place and respects those above him. As the *Great Learning* states it, peace begins with the moral cultivation of the individual and order in the family. This peace extends outward to society, government, and the universe itself like circular ripples in a pond.

The heart of moral rectification is filial piety to one's parents. According to Confucian doctrine, there are three grades of filial piety: the lowest is to support one's

myreligienlab
Analects of Confucius

Confucianism idealized gentleman-scholars, who became the highest class in China until the 20th-century revolution.

parents, the second is not to bring humiliation to one's parents and ancestors, and the highest is to glorify them. In the ancient *Book of Rites*, as revived by Confucius, deference to one's parents is scrupulously defined. For instance, a husband and wife should go to visit their parents and parents-in-law, whereupon:

> On getting to where they are, with bated breath and gentle voice, they should ask if their clothes are (too) warm or (too) cold, whether they are ill or pained, or uncomfortable in any part; and if they be so, they should proceed reverently to stroke and scratch the place. They should in the same way, going before or following after, help and support their parents in quitting or entering (the apartment). In bringing in the basin for them to wash, the younger will carry the stand and the elder the water; they will beg to be allowed to pour out the water, and when the washing is concluded, they will hand the towel. They will ask whether they want anything, and then respectfully bring it. All this they will do with an appearance of pleasure to make their parents feel at ease.[28]

Confucius also supported the ancient Chinese custom of ancestor worship, as an extension of filial piety—indeed, as the highest achievement of filial piety.

Confucius said relatively little about the supernatural, preferring to focus on the here-and-now: "While you are not able to serve men, how can you serve the ghosts and spirits?"[29] He made a virtue of *li* (the rites honoring ancestors and deities), suggesting that one make the sacrifices with the feeling that the spirits were present. According to some interpreters, he encouraged the rites as a way of establishing earthly harmony through reverent, ethical behavior. The rites should not be empty gestures; he recommended that they be outwardly simple and inwardly grounded in *ren*.

Although Confucius did not speak much about an unseen Reality, he asserted that *li* are the earthly expressions of the natural cosmic order. Everything should be done with a sense of propriety. Continually eulogizing the typical gentleman of China's ancient high civilization as the model, Confucius used examples such as the way of passing someone in mourning. Even if the mourner were a close friend, the gentleman would assume a solemn expression and "lean forward with his hands on the crossbar of his carriage to show respect; he would act in a similar manner towards a person carrying official documents."[30] Even in humble surroundings, the proprieties should be observed: "Even when a meal consisted only of coarse rice and vegetable broth, [the gentleman] invariably made an offering from them and invariably did so solemnly."[31]

DIVERGENT FOLLOWERS OF CONFUCIUS

myreligi●nlab
The Book of Mencius

The Confucian tradition has been added to by many later commentators. Two of the most significant were Mengzi (Mencius) and Xunzi (Hsun Tzu), who differed in their approach.

A little over a hundred years after Confucius died, the "Second Sage" Mengzi (Meng Tza, commonly latinized as Mencius) was born. During his lifetime (c.390–305 BCE) Chinese society became even more chaotic. Like his predecessor, the Second Sage tried to share his wisdom with embattled rulers, but to little avail. He, too, took up teaching, based on stabilizing aspects of the earlier feudal system.

Mengzi's major addition to the Confucian tradition was his belief in the inherent goodness of human nature (Xing). Mengzi emphasized the moral duty of rulers to govern by the principle of humanity and the good of the people. If rulers are guided by profit motives, this self-centered motivation will be reflected in all subordinates and social chaos will ensue. On the other hand, "When a commiserating government is conducted from a commiserating heart, one can rule the whole empire as if one were turning it in one's palm."[32] This is a natural way, says Mengzi, for people are naturally good: "The tendency of human nature to do good is like that of water to flow downward."[33] Heaven could be counted on to empower the righteous. The moral potential of human beings is what connects us to Heaven.

Another follower quite disagreed with this assessment. This was Xunzi, who seems to have been born when Mengzi was an old man. Xunzi argued that human nature is naturally self-centered and that Heaven is impersonal, operating according to natural laws rather than intervening on the side of good government or responding to human wishes ("Heaven does not suspend the winter because men dislike cold"[34]). Humans must hold up their own end. Their natural tendency, however, is to envy, to compete, and to desire personal gain and sensual pleasure. The only way to constrain these tendencies is to teach and legally enforce the rules of *li* and *yi* (righteous conduct). Though naturally flawed, humans can gradually attain sagehood by persistent study, patience, and good works and thereby form a cooperative triad with Heaven and Earth.

Xunzi's careful reasoning provided a basis for the new legalistic structure of government. The idealism of Mengzi was revived much later as a Chinese response to Buddhism and became required for the civil service examinations from the thirteenth to the early twentieth centuries. However, their points of agreement are basic to Confucianism: The appropriate practice of virtue is of great value; humans can attain this through self-cultivation; and study and emulation of the ancient sages are the path to harmony in the individual, family, state, and world.

These basic points situate Confucianism within the academic category that can be referred to as "religion," if religion is defined broadly as Frederick Streng did: "a means to ultimate transformation."[35] All things considered, Chinese religions professor Joseph Adler concludes, "In the case of Confucianism, the goal of Sagehood is the endpoint of that transformation, and Heaven symbolizes the ultimacy that makes it religious."[36]

THE STATE CULT

Since ancient times, as we have seen, rulers have been regarded as the link between Earth and Heaven. This understanding persisted in Chinese society, but Confucius and his followers had elaborated the idea that the ruler must be virtuous for this relationship to work. During the Han dynasty, Confucius's teachings were at last honored by the state. The Han scholar Dong Zhongshu (Tung Chungshu, c.179–c.104 BCE) set up an educational system based on the Confucian Classics. He used Confucian ideals to unite the people behind the ruler, who himself was required to be subject to Heaven.

During the Han dynasty, the traditional *Book of Rites* and *Etiquette and Ritual* were reconstructed, with an increased emphasis on offerings, as practiced since ancient times. These rites were thought to preserve harmony between humans,

Heaven, and Earth. At the family level, offerings were made to propitiate the family ancestors. Government officials were responsible for ritual sacrifices to beings such as the gods of fire, literature, cities, mountains, waters, the polar star, sun, moon, and former rulers, and also to Confucius. The most important ceremonies were performed by the emperor, to give thanks and ask blessings from Heaven, Earth, gods of the land and agriculture, and the dynastic ancestors. Of these, the highest ritual was the elaborate annual sacrifice at the white marble Altar of Heaven by the emperor. He was considered Son of Heaven, the "high priest of the world." Both he and his large retinue prepared themselves by three days of fasting and keeping vigil. In a highly reverent atmosphere, he then sacrificed a bull, offered precious jade, and sang prayers of gratitude to the Supreme.

NEO-CONFUCIANISM

Buddhism and Daoism became very popular during the period of disunity that followed the fall of the Han dynasty, and Confucianism declined. But during the Song dynasty (960–1280 CE), Confucianism was revived, on the premise that Buddhism and Daoism had brought moral and thus political weakness into Chinese society. This revised version is referred to as **Neo-Confucianism**.

Under Neo-Confucian influence, the civil service examination system became fully developed as the chief means of attaining government positions. In addition to the five Confucian Classics, the *Four Books* (The *Analects*, the *Mencius*, the *Great Learning*, and the *Centrality and Commonality*) formed the core of Confucian education. Its greatest proponent was the scholar Zhu Xi (Chu Hsi, 1130–1200 CE), who developed a curriculum running from elementary classes to higher education. This approach lasted for centuries, up to the beginning of the twentieth century.

Neo-Confucian thinkers also brought forth a metaphysical basis for Confucianism: the individual is intimately linked with all of the cosmos. According to Zhang Zai's *Western Inscription:*

myreligionlab
The Western
Inscription
ZHANG ZAI

> *Heaven is my father and earth is my mother and even such a small creature as I finds an intimate place in their midst. Therefore, that which extends throughout the universe I regard as my body and that which directs the universe I regard as my nature. All people are my brothers and sisters and all things are my companions. The great ruler [the emperor] is the eldest son of my parents [Heaven and Earth], and the great ministers are his stewards. ... To rejoice in Heaven and to have no anxiety—this is filial piety at its purest.*[37]

By becoming more humane one can help to transform not only oneself but also society and even the cosmos. The Neo-Confucianists thus stressed the importance of meditation and dedication to becoming a sage.

During the Ming and Qing dynasties, women were encouraged to offer themselves in total sacrifice to others. Confucian women had previously been expected to take a subordinate role in the family and in society, but at the same time to be strong, disciplined, wise, and capable in their relationships with their husbands and sons. Eventually, such virtues were subsumed under an extreme ideal of self-sacrifice.

The Hall for Prayer for Good Harvests, part of the Temple of Heaven complex in Beijing, built from 1406 to 1420 for the emperor's annual prayer to Heaven for good crops. The same complex includes the white marble Altar of Heaven, where the emperor made sacrifices for favorable weather each year.

CONFUCIANISM UNDER COMMUNISM

The performance of state rituals was a time-consuming and major part of government jobs, carried out on behalf of the people. But as China gradually opened to the West in recent centuries, a reaction set in against these older ways, and the last of the imperial dynasties was overthrown in 1911. In the 1920s republic, science and social progress were glorified by radical intellectuals of the New Culture movement who were opposed to all the old systems. Under the communist regime established in 1949, communism took the place of religion, attempting to transform the society by secular means. Party chairman Mao Zedong was venerated almost as a god, with the "Little Red Book" of quotations from Chairman Mao replacing the Confucian Classics.

During the Cultural Revolution (1966–1976), Confucianism was attacked as one of the "Four Olds"—old ideas, culture, customs, and habits. The Cultural Revolution attempted to destroy the hierarchical structure that Confucianism had idealized and to prevent the intellectual elite from ruling over the masses. Contrary to the Confucian virtue of filial piety, young people even denounced their parents at public trials, and scholars were made objects of derision. An estimated one million people were attacked. Some were killed, some committed suicide, and millions suffered.

Mao said that he had hated Confucianism from his childhood. What he so disliked was the intellectual emphasis on the study of the Classics, the "superstitious" rituals, and the oppression of the lowest members of hierarchical Chinese society—women and peasants. He urged peasants to overthrow all authoritarian traditions, including religion:

A man in China is usually subjected to the domination of three systems of authority: (1) the state system (political authority) ...; (2) the clan system (clan authority), ranging from the central ancestral temple and its branch temples down to the head of the household; and (3) the supernatural system (religious authority), ranging from the King of Hell down to the town and village gods belonging to the nether world, and from the Emperor of Heaven down to all the various gods and spirits belonging to the celestial world. As for women, in addition to being dominated by these three systems of authority, they are also dominated by the men (the authority of the husband). These four authorities—political, clan, religious and masculine—are the embodiment of the whole feudal-patriarchal system and ideology, and are the four thick ropes binding the Chinese people, particularly the peasants.[38]

Nevertheless, in some respects, Confucian morality continued to form the basis of Chinese ethics. Mao particularly emphasized the (Confucian) virtues of selfless service to the people and of self-improvement for the public good:

All our cadres, whatever their rank, are servants of the people, and whatever we do is to serve the people. How then can we be reluctant to discard any of our bad traits?[39]

For decades, communist China prided itself on being the most law-abiding country in the world. But recently there has been a rise in crime and official corruption. The society has changed abruptly since China opened its doors to the West in 1978, undermining what remained of traditional Confucian virtues. The government blames the influx of materialistic values, resulting from the indiscriminating embrace of the underside of Western culture and the rapid shift toward a free market economy. In 1989, Zhao Ziyang (Chao Tzu-yang), then Communist Party leader, urged officials to maintain Confucian discipline (without naming it that) in the midst of the changes: "The Party can by no means allow its members to barter away their principles for money and power."[40] But when the people picked up this cry, aging leaders chose to suppress popular calls for greater democracy and an end to official corruption; they did so in the name of another Confucian value: order in society.

Chairman Mao is becoming revered as a semi-deified father figure or boddhisatva. Statues of him are on sale at his homestead in Hunan Province, and many people have his image hanging in their cars.

For their part, the intellectuals of the democracy movement had tried to do things in the proper way but were caught on the horns of the poignant Chinese dilemma. Under Confucian ethics, it has been the continuing responsibility of scholars to play the role of upright censors. On the other hand, scholars had to remain loyal to the ruler, for they were subjects and observing one's subservient position as a subject preserved the security of the state. The leaders of the democracy movement tried to deal with this potential conflict by ritualized, respectful action: in 1989 they formally walked up the steps of the Great Hall of the People in Tiananmen

Square to present their written requests to those in power. But they were ignored and brutally suppressed.

Now, in twenty-first-century China, as noted earlier, popular and intellectual interest in various religions is increasing. Evangelical Christianity has grown so vigorous that China is now home to the second largest evangelical Christian community in the world, and there are more Catholics in China than in Ireland. Buddhists account for the majority of religious adherents, with 320,000 nuns and monks in 16,000 Chinese temples and monasteries. Islam is strong in northwest China, home of most of China's eighteen million Muslims. The officially atheistic Communist Party is showing signs of regarding religions as having a certain social usefulness, but it also attempts to control religious activities and beliefs through its Religious Affairs Bureau and police. While Confucianism is not recognized as a "religion"—the five religions officially permitted in China being Buddhism, Islam, Daoism, Protestantism, and Catholicism—its philosophy and ethics are attracting new attention, and the government has sponsored dozens of "Confucian Institutes" in other countries for the study of Chinese culture and language.

Among intellectuals, conferences have recently been held on the mainland in China and also in Taiwan and Singapore to discuss Confucianism. Today it is being analyzed not as an historical artifact but as a tradition that is relevant to modern life, with the potential to contribute significantly to cultural identity, economic progress, social harmony, and a personal sense of the meaning of human life.

Confucianism may inform capitalistic behavior as well as Marxist communism. There is now talk of "Capitalist Confucianism"—business conducted according to Confucian ethics such as humanity, trustworthiness, sincerity, and altruism. As Professor Yao Xinzhong explains:

> Free choice is the foundation of modern society, and the pre-condition of market economy. However, freedom without responsibility would result in the collapse of the social network and in the conflict between individuals and between individuals and society, and would lead to the sacrifice of the future in order to satisfy short-term needs. This has become a serious challenge to human wisdom and to human integrity. In this respect, Confucianism can make a contribution to a new moral sense, a new ecological view and a new code for the global village.[41]

Confucian values are also being reappraised as a significant addition to holistic education. In them is imbedded the motivation to improve oneself and become a responsible and ethical member of one's family and society. Thus the Neo-Confucians developed multistage learning programs that extend beyond the years of formal schooling. Confucianism has always promoted education as a prerequisite to social reform, and further encourages a sense of voluntary service to the community. When a massive earthquake caused tens of thousands of deaths in China in 2008, there was a great outpouring of volunteers to help in clearing debris, locating and treating survivors, and donating money and emergency supplies. Alan Qiu, an investor from Shanghai, explained, "We grew up reciting Confucius saying that all men are born kind, but it takes a disaster like this to bring out the innate kindness of everyday human beings."[42] The government office in charge of promoting socialist ethics, the ministry of education, and the central committee of Chinese communist youth selected fifty children who were given "heroic children" awards for their brave relief efforts.

myreligionlab
Confucianism and the Twenty-First Century
YAO XINGZHONG

myreligionlab
The Great Ultimate
ZHOU DUNYI

An Interview with Ann-ping Chin

 Ann-ping Chin grew up in Taiwan, the daughter of parents from the northern part of mainland China. She teaches Confucianism and Daoism at Wesleyan University and has visited China five times to do research on the continuing changes in that society. Of the contemporary situation there with regard to traditional values she says:

"Lots of things are changing in China. First of all, the economic boom is changing women's perceptions of themselves and of their family. For instance, if a woman is determined to have a profession of her own, in this huge marketplace of China this implies that she would become involved in a private enterprise or begin one herself. If she does that, this means that she would have to consider child-rearing as secondary. Usually these women depend on their parents or in-laws to bring up their children, in their own homes.

"Divorce is very common. Family units are breaking up and children have less security—there are all the problems that we associate with divorce in the West. The woman simply says, 'Look—I'm going to leave or you leave.'

"Making money is now the most important thing for the Chinese. It's finally a free market. Even though it's economic freedom, it's some kind of freedom. 'So,' they feel, 'why not make the most of that sort of freedom? Political freedom can wait. Let's make the most of this that we have, and not ask too much.'

"From an initial impression, perhaps you can say that the fundamental Confucian values are disappearing. Through more than 2,000 years of Chinese history, both in traditional Confucian teachings and in Daoist teachings as well, you find a tremendous deprecation of the idea of making money—of taking advantage or making a profit, be it in money or in human relationships. Now, unless you have the determination to make money, you are not considered a true man in Chinese society.

"On the other hand, if you really delve into their private lives, and try to understand what is really important to the Chinese, I would say that the very basic relationships of parents and children, and of friends to friends are still very strong. The Chinese have given up their relationship with the ruler; that's really a joke. The relationship between husband and wife is much more complicated. Men love the idea of having a very devoted wife. They know that is perhaps impossible, but they still yearn for it. And they still value the traditional qualities that you find in the biographies of virtuous women. If they can find that in their mothers, they still appreciate those values.

"Other values have been abandoned. I'm very disturbed and saddened, pained, by what is happening to the Chinese scholars. They cannot go out and do private enterprise, for they are scholars. They get paid a very pathetic amount of money each month, not enough to make ends meet. Scholars have always been really respected even though people didn't understand them. But now there isn't even that respect since the society is placing so much emphasis on making money.

"My parents both came from very scholarly backgrounds. They passed down to us the traditions without the formalities, without the rigidities, so we were extremely fortunate. I think my father passed down to us his love of students, his love of teaching, and of the very special relationship between teachers and disciples. That relationship is a very special one in Chinese tradition. If you are lucky, you can still see that between an elderly teacher and his disciples. It's not obedience—rather, it's a concern that the disciple expresses toward the teacher.

"In looking at what I've absorbed from my parents, there's also the matter of character. My father's character had a profound effect on me. I just intuitively know that he always tried to do the right thing. And to do the right thing sometimes can be so difficult. This was the only way that he could live—to always try to do the right thing, whether it was for a friend, or for us, for my mom, for his own parents, or for strangers. He would never compromise that."

In the moral and spiritual vacuum left after the demise of fervent Maoism, Confucianism may also help restore a sense of holy purpose to people's lives. The traditional feeling was that the Mandate of Heaven gives transcendent meaning to human life. Professor Tu Weiming, a modern Confucian, explains:

> We are the guardians of the good earth, the trustees of the Mandate of Heaven that enjoins us to make our bodies healthy, our hearts sensitive, our minds alert, our souls refined, and our spirits brilliant. ... We serve Heaven with common sense, the lack of which nowadays has brought us to the brink of self-destruction. Since we help Heaven to realize itself through our self-discovery and self-understanding in day-to-day living, the ultimate meaning of life is found in our ordinary, human existence.[43]

Chinese authorities have reintroduced the teaching of Confucius in elementary schools as a vehicle for encouraging social morality, and the Confucian-based civil service examinations are being partially reintroduced in the selection of public servants. Earlier castigated as "feudal institutions," Confucian academies are being described as fine centers for learning. Chinese authorities are also reviving aspects of the religious cult, such as observance of the birthday of Confucius, perhaps mostly for the sake of tourism. In 1995, the Confucian Temple in Qufu, the home of Confucius, was declared a UNESCO World Heritage site, and in 2004 over three million tourists visited the temple for gala celebrations of Master Kong's birthday.

CONFUCIANISM IN EAST ASIA

Countries near China, which have historically been influenced by China politically and culturally, also show signs of having been influenced by Confucian values. The city-state of Singapore has since 1978 sponsored an annual courtesy campaign to inspire virtuous behavior in the midst of fast-paced modern life. In one recent year, the focus of the campaign was courteous use of mobile phones.

In Korea, where few people now consider themselves adherents of Confucianism as a religion, lectures and special events are nonetheless being sponsored by hundreds of local Confucian institutes to promote Confucian teachings. In some cases, Confucianism is associated with particular clans in East Asia, and thus with political favoritism. Some of the Korean institutes are politically conservative, opposing women's efforts to revise family laws. The Korean Overseas Information Service advocates a flexible, liberal version of the tradition, open to other cultures and to all religions but still providing a firm foundation for social order:

> Confucianism can present contemporary Koreans with a set of practical standards of conduct in the form of rituals and etiquette. Extensive introduction of Western modes of behavior led to the confusion and adulteration of Korea's native behavior pattern. Civility and propriety in speech and deportment enhance the dignity of man. Rites and conduct befitting to a civilized people should be refined and adjusted to the conditions of the time. ... Korea should, through its Confucian heritage, sustain the tradition of propriety and modesty and defend the intrinsically moral nature of man from submergence in economic and materialistic considerations.[44]

Confucian organizations in Hong Kong, Taiwan, and other parts of East Asia are attempting to restore religious versions of Confucianism, such as the worship

Some Confucian rites are still observed today in South Korea. These people making offerings in Chungdak-dong village have maintained a traditional Confucian lifestyle for hundreds of years.

myreligi⊙nlab

Staying Power of Religion in China
PENG LIU

of Confucius himself or study of the Confucian Classics.

Confucian thought has also played a significant role in Japan. It entered Japan during the seventh century when Chinese political thought and religious ideas first began to have significant influence there. It left its mark on the first constitution of Japan, on the arrangement of government bureaucracy, and in the educational system. From the twelfth to the sixteenth century, Confucianism was studied in Zen Buddhist monasteries. Then from the seventeenth to the nineteenth century, Confucianism began to spread more widely among the people of Japan because of its adoption as an educational philosophy in public and private schools. Confucian moral teachings became the basis for establishing proper human relationships in the family and in Japanese society.

Both Confucianism and Shinto were manipulated by the Japanese military in the period before World War II to inculcate a nationalist expansionist ideology. More in keeping with the original motives of Confucianism, some scholars have observed that Japan's notably effective modernization is partly due to values derived from Confucianism. These values include a high regard for diligence, consensus, education, moral self-cultivation, frugality, and loyalty.

Dr. Mary Evelyn Tucker, noted scholar of East Asian studies and the relationships between religions and the environment, concludes that Confucianism is not outdated. Rather, it can be seen as quite relevant now and for the future as well, for, "It aims to promote flourishing social relations, effective educational systems, sustainable agricultural patterns, and humane political governance within the context of the dynamic, life-giving processes of the universe."[45]

Suggested reading

Adler, Joseph A., *Chinese Religious Traditions*, Upper Saddle River, New Jersey: Prentice Hall, 2002. Very clear introduction to the complexes of ancient and popular practices, Confucianism, Daoism, and Buddhism.

Chan, Wing-tsit, *A Source Book in Chinese Philosophy*, Princeton: Princeton University Press, 1963. A large and helpful anthology of Confucian, Daoist, and Buddhist texts.

Ching, Julia, *Chinese Religions*, Maryknoll, New York: Orbis Books, 1993. Survey of the religious dimensions of Chinese traditions, including shamanism.

de Bary, William Theodore, *East Asian Civilizations: A Dialogue in Five Stages*, Cambridge: Harvard University Press, 1988. A masterful overview of 3,000 years of East Asian civilization, including the classical legacy, the Buddhist age, the Neo-Confucian stage, and East Asia's modern transformation.

de Bary, William Theodore and Irene Bloom (vol. 1), and William Theodore de Bary and Richard Lufrano (vol. 2), *Sources of Chinese Tradition*, second edition, New York:

Columbia University Press, 1999. Useful commentaries and extensive texts from Confucian and Daoist schools.

Dao de jing, attributed to Laozi, available in numerous translations, including the English translation by D. C. Lau, London: Penguin Books, 1963, and the English translation by Victor H. Mair, New York: Bantam Books, 1990.

The I Ching, translated into German by Richard Wilhelm and thence into English by Cary Baynes, third edition, Princeton, New Jersey: Princeton University Press, 1967. Insights into the multiple possibilities of the interplay of yin and yang in our lives.

Kindop, Jason and Carol Lee Hamrin, eds, *God and Caesar in China: Policy Implications of Church–State Tensions*, Washington, D.C.: The Brookings Institution, 2004. A survey of China's struggles to control religions throughout history, with particular reference to current Party efforts to compromise with the burgeoning public interest in religion.

Kohn, Livia, *The Taoist Experience*, Albany, New York: State University of New York Press, 1993. Interesting translations of ancient and more recent texts covering the various aspects of Daoism.

Kohn, Livia, *Daoism and Chinese Culture*, Cambridge, Massachusetts: Three Pines Press, second edition, 2004. Concise survey of different forms of Daoism in chronological order, considering comparative aspects and providing additional bibliography.

Lopez, Donald S., ed., *Religions of China in Practice*, Princeton, New Jersey: Princeton University Press, 1996. Excellent articles illustrating the overlap between Confucianism, Daoism, and Buddhism in traditional and contemporary practice, with translations of original texts.

Mencius, trans. D. C. Lau, New York: Viking Penguin, 1970.

Robinet, Isabelle, *Taoist Meditation: The Mao-shan Tradition of Great Purity*, trans. Julian Pas and Norman Girardot, Albany, New York: State University of New York Press, 1993. A careful analysis of the central scriptures and practices used by elite Daoists to become Immortals.

Schipper, Kristofer M., *The Taoist Body*, trans. Karen Duvall, Berkeley: University of California Press, 1992. Explores integration of religious and philosophical Daoism within the Celestial Masters movement, from the Han dynasty to contemporary Taiwan.

Sommer, Deborah, ed., *Chinese Religions: An Anthology of Sources*, New York/Oxford: Oxford University Press, 1995. Interesting primary source material from Daoist, Confucian, Buddhist, and communist writings about religious topics.

Taylor, Rodney, *The Religious Dimensions of Confucianism*, Albany: State University of New York Press, 1990. A collection of essays dealing with the question of whether Confucianism is a religion.

Tu Weiming and Mary Evelyn Tucker, *Confucian Spirituality*, 2 vols, New York: Crossroad Publishing Company, 2003–2004. Eastern and Western scholars analyze Confucianism as a spiritual path.

Tucker, Mary Evelyn and John Berthrong, *Confucianism and Ecology: the Interrelation of Heaven, Earth, and Humans*, Cambridge, Massachusetts: Harvard University Press, 1998. Interesting articles from a major series of conferences probing the relationships between particular religious teachings and the environment.

Watson, Burton, *Chuang Tzu: Basic Writings*, New York: Columbia University Press, 1964. An engaging translation of major writings by Zhuangzi, with an introduction that is particularly helpful in dealing with this paradoxical material.

Wilson, Thomas A., ed., *On Sacred Grounds: Culture, Society, Politics, and the Formation of the Cult of Confucius*, Cambridge: Harvard University Asia Center, 2002. Articles by Chinese and Western scholars tracing factors contributing to the development of Confucianism as a state cult.

Wong, Eva, *The Shambhala Guide to Taoism*, Boston: Shambhala Press, 1996. Introduction to the synthesis of Daoism, Buddhism, and Confucianism in China, Daoist history, techniques, and rites.

Yao, Xinzhong, *Introduction to Confucianism*, Cambridge: Cambridge University Press, 2000. A noted specialist blends traditional and contemporary scholarship to explore the many facets of Confucianism and their relevance today.

Key terms

Dao (Tao) The way or path; the Nameless.

li Ceremonies, rituals, and rules of proper conduct, in the Confucian tradition.

Neo-Confucianism Confucianism stressing the importance of meditation and dedication to becoming a sage, established during the Chinese Song dynasty.

qi (ch'i) The vital energy in the universe and in our bodies according to Chinese cosmology and the Chinese sciences.

ren Humanity, benevolence—the central Confucian virtue.

wu wei In Daoism, "not doing," in the sense of taking no action contrary to the natural flow.

yang In Chinese philosophy, the bright, assertive, "male" energy in the universe.

yin In Chinese philosophy, the dark, receptive, "female" energy in the universe.

Review questions

1. Describe ancient Chinese traditions such as ancestor worship, divination, and the concept of cosmic balance.
2. In what ways might Confucianism be understood as either "religious" or "not religious?"
3. Compare and contrast the practices of Daoism and Confucianism.

Discussion questions

1. Discuss the ways Daoism, Confucianism, and Buddhism may be blended together in practice. Are you aware of similar patterns of blending religion in other areas?
2. Discuss the quotations from the *Dao de jing* in this chapter and what they reveal about the concept of Dao.
3. Discuss the ways in which Confucianism is being adapted to modern concerns in mainland China and other parts of East Asia.

myreligionlab

For further activities and resources, including access to MyReligionLibrary, please visit MyReligionLab at www.myreligionlab.com

Additional Internet resources

Asian Studies WWW Virtual Library http://coombs.anu.edu.au/WWWVL-AsianStudies.html

China Search Engine http://asnic.utexas.edu/asnic/countries/china/index.html

Confucianism and Traditional Chinese Beliefs http://www.sacred-texts.com/cfu/index.htm

Freedom of Religious Belief in China http://chineseculture.about.com/library/china/whitepaper/blsreligion.htm

Internet Guide for Chinese Studies http://sun.sino.uni-heidelberg.de/igcs

Internet Sacred Text Archive: Daoism http://www.sacred-texts.com/tao/index.htm

Daoism Virtual Library http://www.vl-site.org/taoism/intros.html

CHAPTER 7

SHINTO

The way of the *kami*

Japan has embraced and adapted many religions that originated in other countries, but also has its own local traditions closely tied to nature and the unseen world. Under particular historical circumstances, these have been referred to collectively as a religion in themselves, under the label of "Shinto." However, according to current scholarship, Shinto is not a single self-conscious religious tradition but rather an overarching label applied to ways of honoring the spirits in nature. These ways have at times been combined with imperial myths supporting the worldly rulers.

Many modern Japanese combine practices from several religions, for each offers something different. Confucianism informs organizations and ethics, Buddhism and Christianity offer ways of understanding suffering and the afterlife, traditional veneration of ancestors links the living to their family history, and the ways called "Shinto" harmonize people with the natural world and have led to many forms of popular religious culture, such as festivals and visits to shrines.

KEY TOPICS

• THE ROOTS OF "SHINTO" 217

• BUDDHIST AND CONFUCIAN INFLUENCES 227

• STATE SHINTO 228

• "SECT SHINTO" 229

• SHINTO TODAY 230

The roots of "Shinto"

Shinto has no founder, no orthodox canon of sacred literature, and no explicit code of ethical requirements. The meanings of many of its elaborate rituals are unknown by many who practice them. Historically, individual clans apparently worshiped a particular deity as their own ancestor, along with other unseen beings and natural forces, but such worship was localized until the eighth century CE, when the term "Shinto" came into use to distinguish indigenous Japanese ways from Buddhism and other imported religions. The label "Shinto" was formed from the words *shin* (divine being) and *do* (way). The major chronicles of "Shintoism" were written down—the *Kojiki* (compiled 712 CE) and *Nihongi* (720 CE)—but contemporary scholars do not regard them as uniquely Japanese, for they seem to be greatly influenced by Buddhist, Confucian, Korean, and Chinese thought. These chronicles combine myths, historical facts, politics, and literature and are not generally revered as sacred scriptures. The *Kojiki* seems to be aimed at conferring spiritual legitimacy on the Imperial Throne by allegedly documenting the divine origins of the imperial lineage. The legendary founder and first

The Japanese people have traditionally honored the natural beauty of their land and have considered Mount Fuji to be its most sacred peak. Pilgrims have long made the arduous climb up Fuji seeking purification and good fortune.

emperor of Japan, Jimmu, is described as a descendant of Amaterasu, the sun goddess.

During the Tokugawa "Enlightenment" period in Japan (1600–1868), thinkers made another effort to define the "native" Japanese religion, as opposed to foreign incursions, by collating various texts, popular practices, and myths.

Then, in 1868, the Meiji Restoration brought the Emperor Meiji and an imperial state apparatus into power. To confront subjugation by Western colonial powers, the Meiji regime at first tried to copy the West and then turned to conservatism and nationalism, with emphasis on worship of the emperor. The extreme nationalism fostered by this trend, supported by religious veneration of the emperor, came to an end with World War II, with the victors forcing Japan to separate church and state.

Now the priests who run the many shrines in Japan are again promoting the idea that Shinto is a religion unto itself, native to Japan. In this chapter we will examine the characteristics of Japanese culture that are attributed by priests to Shinto religion. Motohisa Yamakage, who retired in 2005 as Seventy-ninth Grand Master of Yamakage Shinto, describes Shinto as "Japan's spiritual heart—an evolving, organic system of spiritual values."[1]

KINSHIP WITH NATURE

Despite industrial pollution and urbanization, Japan is still a country of exquisite natural beauty. The islands marry mountains to sea, and the interiors are laced with streams, waterfalls, and lush forests. Even the agriculture is beautiful, with flowering fruit trees and terraced fields. The people reportedly lived so harmoniously with this environment that they had no separate word for "nature" until they began importing modern Western ideas late in the nineteenth century. Living close to nature, the people organized their lives around the turn of the seasons, honoring the roles of the sun, moon, and lightning in their rice farming. Mount Fuji, greatest of the volcanic peaks that formed the islands, was honored as the sacred embodiment of the divine creativity that had thrust the land up from the sea. The sparkling ocean and rising sun, so visible along the extensive coastlines, were loved as earthly expressions of the sacred purity, brightness, and awesome power at the heart of life.

> *To be fully alive is to have an aesthetic perception of life because a major part of the world's goodness lies in its often unspeakable beauty.*
>
> Rev. Yukitaka Yamamoto, Shinto priest[2]

Although industrialization and urbanization have blighted some of the natural landscape, the sensitivity to natural beauty survives in small-scale arts. In rock gardening, flower arranging, the tea ceremony, and poetry, Japanese artists honor the simple and natural. If a rock is placed "just right" in a garden, it seems alive, radiating its natural essence. In a tea ceremony, great attention is paid to each natural sensual delight, from the purity of water poured from a wooden ladle to the genuineness of the clay vessels. These arts are often linked with Zen Buddhism, but the sensitivities seem to derive from the ancient Japanese ways, and have thus been attached to the idea of Shinto as a religion.

HONORING THE KAMI

Surrounded by nature's beauty and power, the Japanese people found the divine all around them. According to Japanese mythology, as passed down in the *Nihongi*:

> *In primeval ages, before the earth was formed, amorphous matter floated freely about like oil upon water. In time there arose in its midst a thing like a sprouting reedshoot, and from this a deity came forth of its own.*[3]

This deity gave birth to many *kami*, or spirits, two of which—the Amatsu ("heavenly") *kami*—were told to organize the material world. Standing on the Floating Bridge of Heaven, they stirred the ocean with a jeweled spear. When they pulled it out of the water, it dripped brine back into the ocean, where it coagulated into eight islands (interpreted either as Japan or the whole world). To rule this earthly kingdom they created the *kami* Amaterasu, literally "the one who illuminates the sky," or goddess of the sun. The Amatsu *kami* also gave birth to the ancestors of the Japanese. All of the natural world—land, trees, mountains, waters, animals, people—is thus joined in kinship as the spiritual creation of the *kami*.

Although the word *kami* (a way of pronouncing the character *shin*) is usually translated as "god" or "spirit," these translations are not exact. *Kami* can be either singular or plural, for the word refers to a single essence manifesting in many places. Rather than evoking an image, like the Hindu or Mahayana Buddhist deities, *kami* refers to a quality. It means, literally, "that which is above," and also refers to that which evokes wonder and awe in us. The *kami* harmonize heaven and earth and also guide the solar system and the cosmos. It/they tend to reside in beautiful or powerful places, such as mountains, certain trees, unusual rocks, waterfalls, whirlpools, and animals. In addition, it/they manifest as wind, rain, thunder, or lightning. *Kami* also appear in abstract forms, such as the creativity of growth and reproduction. Since the seventh century CE, using the imported Chinese idea of the Mandate of Heaven, the emperor himself came to be revered as a *kami*—a living god, the divinely descended ruler upon whom the well-being of the country depends. In general, explains Sakamiki Shunzo, *kami* include:

> *all things whatsoever which deserve to be dreaded and revered for the extraordinary and preeminent powers which they possess. … [Kami] need not be eminent for surpassing nobleness, goodness, or serviceableness alone. Malignant and uncanny beings are also called* kami, *if only they are the objects of general dread.*[4]

To follow the *kami* is to bring our life into harmony with nature, Shinto adherents feel. *Kannagara*, "the way or nature of the *kami*," can be understood as

"Natural Religion," according to Yukitaka Yamamoto, ninety-sixth Chief Priest of the Tsubaki Grand Shrine:

> *Natural Religion is the spontaneous awareness of the Divine that can be found in any culture. … The Spirit of Great Nature may be a flower, may be the beauty of the mountains, the pure snow, the soft rains or the gentle breeze.* Kannagara *means being in communion with these forms of beauty and so with the highest level of experiences of life. When people respond to the silent and provocative beauty of the natural order, they are aware of* kannagara. *When they respond in life in a similar way, by following ways "according to the* kami," *they are expressing* kannagara *in their lives. They are living according to the natural flow of the universe and will benefit and develop by so doing.*[5]

SHRINES

It is thought that there were no shrines in early Shinto; rather, these may have developed after the sixth-century introduction of Buddhist influences in Japan. At present, there are more than 100,000 shrines in Japan, built to honor the *kami*. Shrines may be as small as beehives or elaborate temple complexes covering thousands of acres. Some honor *kami* protecting the local area; some honor *kami* with special responsibilities, such as healing or protecting crops from insects. The shrines are situated on sites thought to have been chosen by the *kami* for their sacred atmosphere. At one time, every community had its own guardian *kami*.

The greatest number of these shrines are dedicated to Inari, the god of rice. His messengers are foxes, so these shrines are distinguished by statues of foxes, rather than the statues of dogs or lions that are often placed to guard shrine entrances. Other shrines include imperial shrines previously funded and administered by the government, shrines dedicated to Hachiman, the *kami* of war (previously popular among military clans), Tenjin shrines dedicated to the *kami* of a ninth-century scholar (popular among students getting ready for exams), Sengen shrines dedicated to the princess who is considered the guardian deity of Mount Fuji, and shrines dedicated to clan founders.

Most important of all these is the Ise Shrine, which is actually a complex of over 100 shrines. Historians think they were first constructed in their current form in 690 CE. The main shrine is the place of worship of the *kami* Ameraterasu, and its secret inner sanctum, entered only by selected priests, is thought to hold the Sacred Mirror, which is believed to have been given to the first emperor by the gods. This imperial shrine is considered so sacred that the general public is kept at a distance by fences, beyond which they can see only the thatched roofs of the main structures. To always offer the *kami* a clean and fresh place, all the buildings are dismantled every twenty years and then replaced with new buildings constructed in exactly the same ancient way, with massive wooden frames and thick thatched roofs.

The 130,000 Japanese cypresses required for each rebuilding must be over 200 years old and in excellent condition, so new trees are carefully planted in a sacred forest for buildings that will be constructed long after the lives of their caretakers. Wood from the dismantled twenty-year-old buildings is put to use in building *torii* gates, bridges, and such.

Originally, the emperor was responsible both for political administration and also for religious duties, but in time, one of the imperial princesses was given the important task of properly worshiping the *kami* at Ise Shrine on behalf of the kingdom. She was carefully sequestered and purified for this duty. Ise Shrine itself was established by Princess Yamamoto when the emperor decided that Amaterasu could not be properly worshiped within the imperial compound. Having shamanic powers, Princess Yamamoto was instructed in vision by Amaterasu that her shrine was to be constructed at Ise on the southern coast. According to the *Nihongi*, the goddess told Princess Yamamoto:

> *The province of Ise, of the divine wind, is the land whither repair the waves from the eternal world, the successive waves. It is a secluded and pleasant land. In this land I wish to dwell.*[6]

The word *kamikaze*, "divine wind," became one of the aspects of Amaterasu and later, a symbol of divine protection of Japan by the *kami*.

There are tens of thousands of Shinto shrines in Japan. Some of the major ones are shown below.

The earliest places of worship were probably sacred trees or groves, perhaps with some enclosure to demarcate the sacred area. Shrine complexes that developed later also have some way of indicating where sacred space begins: tall gate-frames, known as *torii*, walls, or streams with bridges, which must be crossed to enter the holy precinct of the *kami*. Water is a purifying influence, and basins of water are also provided for washing one's mouth and hands before passing through the *torii*. Statues of guardian lions may further protect the *kami* from evil intrusions, as do ropes with pendants hanging down.

In temple compounds, one first comes to a public hall of worship, behind which is an offering hall where priests conduct rites. Beyond that is the sacred sanctuary, which is entered only by the high priest. Here the spirit of the *kami* is

Amaterasu comes out of the cave

The goddess of the sun, Amaterasu, was born from the left eye of the god Izanagi. The god of the wind, Susanoo, was born from his nose, and the god Tsukiyomi was born from his right eye. Izanagi gave Amaterasu charge of heaven, Susanoo of the sea, and Tsukyomi of the night.

Of these three "august children," Susanoo was known as a wild child. He wanted to see their mother, who had died and was in the land of the dead. Izanagi agreed, but when Susanoo went to heaven on the way to visit his older sister Amaterasu she was suspicious of what mischief he might cause. To check his sincerity, she challenged him to a jewel-spitting contest in which each would spit jewels from the other's collection. Since jewels were associated with fetuses, each jewel they spat out became a child: three daughters from Amaterasu's mouth via Susanoo's sword and five sons from the mouth of Susanoo, via Amaterasu's jewelry. Amaterasu declared that the sons born from her jewelry were hers and the daughters from Susanoo's sword were his. Susanoo pointed out that since "gentle females" had been born from his jewels, his sincerity was proved. Amaterasu accepted his point, and allowed him to stay in heaven for a while. However, Susanoo proved such a wild visitor that he caused great havoc which made it impossible for Amaterasu to carry out her sacred duty: dedicating the first harvest of rice at the sacred altar, wearing a new robe—the chief symbolic duty of the emperor, up to today.

Susanoo's wild actions led to the death of the maidservant of Amaterasu. The goddess was so appalled that she hid in a cavern. The earth became perpetually dark. To lure her out and bring back the sun, the *kami* decided to hold a festival outside her cave. They transplanted a sacred evergreen *sakaki* tree there, hung from its branches sacred jewels, placed a thick straw rope near the mouth of the cave, and prepared a sacred mirror. One of the goddesses began dancing on a wooden tub, making such a loud thumping sound that she went into ecstasy and bared her private parts (symbolic of Mother Earth's fertility). The gods and goddesses began laughing and clapping so hard that Amaterasu peeped out of the cave to see what was happening. One of the deities immediately placed the mirror in front of her face. She was confused to see her own great beauty reflected in it. In her confusion, she was brought out of the cave by one strong god; another barred the entrance with the braided rope. Light returned to the world.

After more adventures on the part of Susanoo, Amaterasu sent her grandson to rule over his land. She sent with him the "three regalia"—the divine mirror, the divine jewel that had been hung in the *sakaki* tree, and the sword that Susanoo had discovered in the tail of an eight-headed serpent, whom he had heroically killed. He had sent the sword to Amaterasu as a peace offering. Her grandson's grandson, Jinmu, became the legendary first emperor of Japan in 660 BCE, and the imperial family has kept the three regalia as revered symbols of its spiritual inheritance up to the present, 126 generations later.

invited to dwell within a special natural object or perhaps a mirror, which reflects the revered light of brightness and purity, considered the natural order of the universe. If there is a spiritually powerful site already present—a waterfall, a crevice in a rock, a hot spring, a sacred tree—the spirit of the *kami* may dwell there. Some shrines are completely empty at the center. In any case, the worshipers do not see the holy of holies; their worship is imageless. As Kishimoto Hideo explains:

> A faithful believer would come to the simple hall of a Shinto sanctuary, which is located in a grove with a quiet and holy atmosphere. He may stand quite a while in front of the sanctuary, clap his hands, bow deeply, and try to feel the deity in his heart. … Shinto being a polytheistic religion, each sanctuary has its own particular deity. But seldom do the believers know the individual name of the deity whom they are worshipping. They do not care about that. … The more important point for them is whether or not they feel the existence of the deity directly in their hearts.[7]

The *kami* of a place may be experienced as energies rather than pictured as forms. At times Shinto has been strongly **iconoclastic** (opposed to images of the divine). In the eighteenth century, for instance, a famous Shinto scholar wrote:

> Never make an image in order to represent the Deity. To worship a deity is directly to establish a felt relation of our heart to the living Divinity through sincerity or truthfulness on our part. If we, however, try to establish a relation between Deity and man indirectly by means of an image, the image will itself stand in the way and prevent us from realizing our religious purpose to accomplish direct communion with the Deity. So an image made by mortal hands is of no use in Shinto worship.[8]

CEREMONIES AND FESTIVALS

To properly encourage the spirit of the *kami* to dwell in a holy sanctuary, long and complex ceremonies are needed. In some temples, it takes ten years for the priests to learn them. The priesthood was traditionally hereditary. One temple has drawn its priests from the same four families for over a hundred generations. Not uncommonly, the clergy may be priestesses. The priests may be assisted by *miko*, young unmarried women dressed in white kimonos. Neither priests nor priestesses live as ascetics; it is common for them to be married, and they are not traditionally expected to meditate. Rather, they are considered specialists in the arts of maintaining the connection between the *kami* and the people.

Everything has symbolic importance, so rites are conducted with great care. The correct materials in temple furnishings, the nine articles held by priests during ceremonies (such as branch, gourd, sword, and bow), the bowing, the sharp clapping of hands, beating of drums, the waving of a stick with paper strips for

Modern Japanese visit Shinto shrines for many purposes, asking the blessing of kami *on the patterns of their lives. Most Shinto shrines are built with an appreciation for simple natural materials, and the larger ones are periodically rebuilt with great ceremony.*

purification—everything is established by tradition and performed with precision. Traditionally, there are no personal prayers to the *kami* for specific kinds of help, but rather a reverent recognition of the close relationship between the *kami*, the ancestors, the people, and nature. When people have made a pilgrimage to a special shrine, they often take back spiritual mementos of their communion with the *kami*, such as a paper symbol of the temple encased within a brocade bag.

Followers of the way of the *kami* may also make daily offerings to the *kami* in their home. Their place of worship usually consists of a high shelf on which rests a miniature shrine, with only a mirror inside. The daily home ritual may begin by greeting the sun in the east with clapping and a prayer for protection for the household. Then offerings are placed before the shrine: rice for health, water for cleansing and preservation of life, and salt for purification and the harmonious seasoning of life. When a new house is to be built, the blessings of the *kami* are ceremonially requested.

Another common feature of Japanese popular culture that is associated with shrine worship is festivals, which are held throughout the year and throughout a person's life. They begin four months before the birth of a baby, when the soul is thought to enter the fetus. Then, thirty-two or thirty-three days after the infant's birth, its parents take it to the family's temple for initiation by the deity. In a traditional family, many milestones—such as coming of age at thirteen, or first arranging one's hair as a woman at age sixteen, marriage, turning sixty-one, seventy-seven, or eighty-eight—are also celebrated with a certain spiritual awareness and ritualism.

The seasonal festivals are reminders to the people that they are descendants of the *kami*. These occasions are exuberant affairs in which the people and the *kami* join in celebrating life. Many have an agricultural basis, ensuring good crops and then giving thanks for them.

*On the nearest Sunday to 15 November, boys of five and girls of three or seven are dressed in traditional clothes and taken to a Shinto shrine by their parents to pray for health and good fortune. This father and daughter are celebrating this Seven-Five-Three (*Shichi-go-san*) festival in Narita, Japan.*

All local shrines celebrate their own *kami* with a festival that usually includes a great parade in which the local *kami* is thought to be taken out of the shrine where it lives and carried through the streets in a portable shrine in order to show it the world outside. The *kami* may be accompanied by elaborate floats and music-makers. During the festivals, offerings of rice, fish, and vegetables may be presented to the *kami*, as well as offerings of music, dance, and praises. Everyone present is blessed by the priests with water flung from *sakaki* tree branches dipped into sanctified water.

One of the biggest annual festivals celebrates New Year. It begins in December with ceremonial house-cleaning, the placing of bamboo and pine "trees" at doorways of everything from homes to offices and bars to welcome the *kami*, and dressing in traditional kimonos. On 31 December, there is a national day of purification. On New Year's Day, people watch the first sunrise of the year and will try to visit a shrine as well as friends and relatives.

On 3 February, the end of winter, people throw beans to toss out bad fortune and invite good, and at shrines the priests shoot arrows to break the power of misfortune. A month-long spring festival is held from March to April, with purification rites and prayers for a successful planting season. The month of June is devoted to rites to protect crops from insects, blights, and bad weather. Fall brings thanksgiving rites for the harvest, with the first fruits offered to the *kami* and then great celebrating in the streets.

There are also many ceremonies honoring those reaching a certain age. For instance, on 15 January, those who are twenty years old are recognized as full-fledged adults, and on 15 November, children who are three, five, or seven years old (considered delicate ages) are taken to a shrine to ask for the protection of the *kami*.

PURIFICATION

In the traditions collectively referred to as Shinto or *kannagara*, the world is beautiful and full of helpful spirits. Sexuality per se is not evil; the world was created by mating deities, and people have traditionally bathed together communally in Japan. However, ritual impurity is a serious problem that obscures our originally pristine nature; it may offend the *kami* and bring about calamities, such as drought, famine, or war.

The quality of impurity or misfortune is called **tsumi**. It can arise through contact with low-level spirits, negative energy from corpses, negative vibrations from wicked minds, hostility toward others or the environment, or through natural catastrophes. In contrast to repentance required by religions that emphasize the idea of human sinfulness, *tsumi* requires purification. The body and mind must be purified so that the person can be connected with *kami* that are clean, bright, right, and straight. One way of removing *tsumi* is paying attention to problems as they arise:

> To live free of obstructing mists, problems of the morning should be solved in
> the morning and those of the evening should be solved by evening. Wisdom and
> knowledge should be applied like the sharpness of an axe to the blinding effect of
> the mists of obstruction. Then may the kami *purify the world and free it of* tsumi.[9]

> After this has been completed, the heavenly kami, *the earthly* kami *and the myriad
> of* kami *can recognize man as purified and everything can return to its original
> brightness, beauty and purity as before since all* tsumi *has wholly vanished from
> the world.*[10]

People may also be purified in a kind of spontaneous movement that washes over them, often in nature, bringing them into awareness of unity with the universe. Hitoshi Iwasaki, a Shinto priest, says that he likes to look at the stars at night in the mountains where the air is clear:

> When I am watching the thoroughly clear light of the stars, I get a pure feeling, like
> my mind being washed. I rejoice to think this is a spiritual misogi [purification

Purification by Waterfall

The cleansing power of water, plentiful in natural Japan, is often used for spiritual purification in Shinto, a practice generally known as *misogi*. One may take a ritual bath in the ocean, source of life. Or, in a lengthy ritual also called *misogi*, a believer may stand beneath a waterfall, letting its force hit his or her shoulders and carry impurities and tensions away. Before even entering the waterfall, those seeking purification must undergo preliminary purification practices because the waterfall itself is *kami*. The women put on white kimonos and headbands, the men white loincloths and headbands.

The *misogi* ritual proceeds with shaking the soul by bouncing the hands up and down in front of the stomach, to help the person become aware of the soul's presence. Next comes a form of warm-up calisthenics called "bird rowing." Following a leader, the participants then shout invocations that activate the soul, affirm the potential for realizing the infinite in their own souls, and unify them with the *kami* of earth, guidance, water, life, and the *ki* energy (which the Chinese know as *qi*).

Before entering the waterfall, the participants raise their metabolism and absorb as much *ki* as possible by practicing a form of deep breathing. They are sprinkled with purifying salt and are given *sake* (rice wine) to spray into the stream in three mouthfuls. The leader counts from one to nine, to symbolize the impurity of the mundane world, and then cuts the air and shouts "*Yei!*" to dispel this impurity. With ritual claps and shouts the participants then enter the waterfall, continually chanting "*Harae-tamae-Kiyome-tamae-ro-kon-sho-jo!*" This phrase requests the *kami* to wash away all *tsumi* from the six elements that form the human being, from the senses, and from the mind. This part of the ritual has been scientifically proven to lower blood pressure.

After this powerful practice, participants dry off, spend time in meditation to calm the soul, and share a ceremonial drink to unify themselves with the *kami* and with each other. The whole ceremony is designed to restore one's natural purity and sense of mission in life. As Yukitaka Yamamoto explains:

> As imperfect beings, we often fail to recognize our mission. These failures come about because we have lost something of our natural purity. This is why purification, or misogi, is so central to Shinto. It enables man to cultivate spirituality and to restore his or her natural greatness.[11]

Misogi, *or ritual purification by standing beneath a waterfall.*

ritual]. … Master Mirihei Ueshiba, the founder of Aikido, is said to have looked
upon the stars one night, suddenly realized he was united with the universe,
and burst into tears, covering his face with his hands. We human beings,
not only human beings but everything existing in this world, are one of
the cells which form this great universe.[12]

In addition to these personal ways of cleansing, there are ritual forms of purification. One is *oharai*, a ceremony commonly performed by Shinto priests, which
includes the waving of a branch from a sacred *sakaki* tree, to which are attached
white streamers (the Japanese version of the shaman's medicine fan of feathers or
the Hindu yak-tail whisk, all used to sweep through the air and thus purify an
area). This ceremony is today performed on cars and new buildings. A version used
to soothe a *kami* that is upset by an impurity was called for in 1978 when there
was a rash of suicides by residents jumping off roofs in a Tokyo housing complex.

Before people enter a Shinto shrine, they will splash water on their hands and
face and rinse their mouth to purify themselves in order to approach the *kami*.
Water is also used for purification in powerful ascetic practices, such as standing
under a waterfall (see Box). Sprinkling salt on the ground or on ritual participants
is also regarded as purifying.

Such ritual practices all have inner meaningfulness. At Tsubaki Grand Shrine
in Japan, priests purify hundreds of new cars every weekend, and the same practice has been adopted at Tsubaki Shrine in the United States. There, the priest
explains to new car owners whose cars are being ritually purified that they themselves must also practice mental purification for the sake of traffic safety.

Buddhist and Confucian influences

Over time, the ways of the *kami* that have been labeled "Shinto" have blended
with other religions imported into Japan, particularly Buddhism, first introduced
into Japan in the sixth century CE, and Confucianism, which has been part of
Japanese culture since its earliest contact with China.

Buddhist monks of medieval times tried to convince the Japanese that the *kami*
were protectors of Buddhist temples, and then that they were actually manifestations of the Buddha essence. During the Heian period (794–1192) Buddhism
and reverence for the *kami* merged to a considerable extent. But during the
Kamakura period (1192–1333), Shinto became more self-conscious and systematic, and the idea was promoted that the *kami* were the original essence and the
Buddhas and bodhisattvas their manifestations. The two religions continued to be
closely interwoven in many ways until the nineteenth century, when the Meiji
government promoted its version of Shinto as part of its program of nationalistic
revival. In the Meiji Restoration, Shinto was distinguished from Buddhism, which
was denounced for its foreign origins.

Today Buddhism is practiced side by side with the ways called Shinto. The
Japanese often go to Shinto shrines for life-affirming events, such as conception,
birth, and marriage, and to Buddhist temples for death rites. A Shinto shrine is
maintained as a clean place for *kami*. Dead bodies would defile the shrine, so

Buddhist temples have long managed funerals. Some villages have stone monuments to the *kami* and statues of Nichiren placed next to each other.

Reverence toward the *kami* is mixed with Buddhist practices in traditions such as ritual ascent of sacred mountains in search of enlightenment. Mountain caves are considered to have special powers in Japan because of the spiritual power of the mountains plus that of the *kami* who are thought to spend the winters there. To reach the cave of Omine-san, a sacred mountain in Nara Prefecture, pilgrims and ascetics climb up a steep trail to the cave mouth while chanting the Buddhist *Heart Sutra*. Small shrines dedicated to various *kami* and also Buddhist figures are encountered on the mountainside. Crawling into the cave and then into an upper chamber, pilgrims find themselves in a dark, wet, womb-like world with secretions dripping from the rocks. This sacred natural space in the deep recesses of the mountain is considered an excellent place for progressing toward full realization of the truth by Buddhist practices such as chanting of the *Heart Sutra*.

As for Confucianism, seventeenth-century Japanese Confucian scholars attempted to free themselves from Buddhism and to tie the Chinese beliefs they were importing to the ancient Japanese ways. One, for instance, likened *li* to the way of the *kami* as a means of social cohesion. Another stressed reverence as the common ground of the two paths and was himself revered as a living *kami*. The Neo-Confucianists' alliance with the ways of the *kami* to throw off the yoke of Buddhism made the somewhat formless Japanese traditions more self-conscious. Scholars began to study and interpret them. The combination of Confucian emphasis on hierarchy and devotion to the *kami* helped pave the way for the establishment in 1868 of the powerful Meiji monarchy.

State Shinto

The Meiji regime took steps to promote Shinto as the spiritual basis for the government. The state cult, amplifying the Japanese traditions of ancestor veneration, had taught since the seventh century that the emperor was the offspring of Amaterasu, the sun goddess. *Naobi no Mitma* (Divine Spirit of Rectification), written in the eighteenth century, expressed this ideal:

> *This great imperial land, Japan, is the august country where the divine ancestral goddess Amaterasu Omikami was born, a superb country. … Amaterasu deigned to entrust the country with the words, "So long as time endures, for ten thousand autumns, this land shall be ruled by my descendants."*
>
> *According to her divine pleasure, this land was decreed to be the country of the imperial descendants … so that even now, without deviation from the divine age, the land might continue in tranquility and in accord with the will of the* kami, *a country ruled in peace.*[13]

It had been customary for the imperial family to visit the great shrine to the sun goddess at Ise to consult the supreme *kami* on matters of importance. But Emperor Meiji carried this tradition much farther. He decreed that the way of the *kami* should govern the nation. This way was labeled "State Shinto" and was administered by government officials rather than Shinto priests, whose objections were silenced, and many of the old rituals were suppressed. State Shinto became the tool of militaristic nationalists as a way to enlist popular support for the throne and the expanding empire.

An illustration of the profound changes in Shinto ushered in by the Meiji Restoration occurs in pre- and post-Meiji versions of the Oracles of the Three Shrines. These are scrolls with sayings attributed to the *kami* of three major shrines. The versions popular before the Meiji Restoration emphasize virtues such as honesty, compassion, and purity. For instance:

> *If you plot and connive to deceive men, you may fool them for a while, and profit thereby, but you will without fail be visited by divine punishment. To be utterly honest may have the appearance of inflexibility and self-righteousness, but in the end, such a person will receive the blessings of sun and moon. Follow honesty without fail.*[14]

A version prepared in the Meiji period, taken from the eighth-century imperial cult, asserts a direct link between the *kami* and the emperor:

> *Amaterasu Sumeomikami commanded her August Grandchild, saying: "This Reed-plain-1500-autumns-fair-rice-ear Land is the region which my descendants shall be lords of. Do thou, my August Grandchild, proceed thither and govern it. Go! and may prosperity attend thy dynasty, and may it, like Heaven and Earth, endure for ever."*[15]

Emperor Hirohito (1901–1989), Meiji's grandson, was held up as a god, not to be seen or touched by ordinary people. But after Japan's surrender in World War II, the emperor officially renounced his hereditary claim to being divine in order to protect the monarchy from being totally disbanded by the occupying powers. The emperor became only a ceremonial figurehead, a role that is now carried on by his son.

"Sect Shinto"

During the social changes of the nineteenth and twentieth centuries, many new religious sects appeared that had their roots in practices of communicating with the *kami*. In rural areas, certain women had long been acting as shamans by falling into trances, in which the *kami* would speak through them. Some of these shamanistic women developed a following of their own, leading to movements that were labeled "Sect Shinto" by the Meiji regime. Some of these movements are still popular today. For example, the Tenrikyo movement was founded by Miki Nakayama in 1838. She was acting as a trance medium for the healing of her son when she was reportedly possessed by ten *kami*. They proclaimed through her, "Miki's mind and body will be accepted by us as a divine shrine, and we desire to save this three-thousand-world through this divine body."[16] It is said that she later spontaneously composed 1,711 poems under divine inspiration, and that these became the sacred scriptures of a new religion. Tenrikyo has continued to be popular since Miki's death, and she is revered as the still-living representative of the divine will.

Another new movement, called "Oomoto," developed from revelations given to Madame Nao Deguchi when she was reportedly possessed by the previously little-known *kami* Ushitora no Konjin in 1892. The revelations criticized the "beastly" state of humanity, with:

> *the stronger preying on the weaker. … If allowed to go on in this way, society will soon lose the last vestiges of harmony and order. Therefore, by a manifestation of Divine Power, the Greater World shall undergo reconstruction, and change into an entirely new creation. … The Greater World shall burst into bloom as plum blossoms at winter's end.*[17]

As developed by Madame Deguchi's relatives and successors, the Oomoto movement survived persecution by the Meiji regime. It has denied that it is a Shinto sect and now has a universalist approach, recognizing founders of other religions as *kami*. Its leaders travel around the world encouraging self-examination, environmental restoration, and global religious cooperation.

Shinto today

In general, the ways attributed to Shinto remain indigenous to Japan. Outside Japan, Shinto beliefs and practices are common only in Hawai'i and Brazil, because many Japanese have settled there. Most Japanese people who visit shrines and pray to the *kami* do not even think of themselves as Shinto adherents. This label is applied mostly by the priestly establishment.

Within Japan, reaction to the horrors of World War II, the elimination of the imperial mythology of State Shinto, and a desire for modernization threatened institutionalized Shinto. After the war, the Japanese Teachers Association began

Participants in a misogi ceremony at Tsubaki Shrine in the United States ritually prepare themselves for the purification.

teaching rejection of the imperial family, of Japanese history, and also of the beliefs and practices associated with Shinto. The Japanese national flag—a red circle on a white background—became a symbol of the past, although its symbolism transcends history. The red circle signifies the rising sun and the white background purity, righteousness, and national loyalty. For a time it was difficult for young people to learn about the ways of the *kami*. But the shrines remain and are visited by more than eighty million Japanese at New Year. People often visit more as tourists than as believers, but many say they experience a sense of spiritual renewal when they visit a shrine. Long-established households still have their *kami* shelf, often next to the Buddhist family altar, which combines tablets memorializing the dead with scrolls or statues dedicated to a manifestation of the Buddha.

Despite the fact that Japan is now one of the most technologically advanced countries in the world, with business its primary focus, there still seems to be a place for ritual—and in some cases, heartfelt—communion with the intangible *kami* that, in traditional belief, permeate all of life.

Modern life, instead of distancing Japanese from their ancient traditions, has ultimately encouraged renewed interest in *kannagara*. Rapid and extreme urbanization, industrial pollution, and despoliation of the natural environment have brought backlashes from concerned citizens who are urging a return to appreciation of the natural beauty of their homeland, traditionally considered the abode of the *kami*.

A great controversy has developed around one of the shrines in Tokyo, now called the "Yasukuni Shrine." It was dedicated during the Meiji Restoration in honor of those who have given their lives in war for the sake of Japan, with the idea that they died to preserve peace in Japan. *Yasukuni* means "peaceful country." Written records of some 2.5 million people who died in various conflicts, including those leading to the Meiji Restoration, up to the Pacific War are enshrined therein. The political controversy concerns the 1978 inclusion of fourteen Class A war criminals, plus visits to the shrine by several Japanese prime ministers. Critics from countries who suffered in the past from Japanese imperialist violence regard the shrine as a symbol of militarism and ultranationalism, and the prime ministers' visits as disregard for the principle of separation of religion from the state. Yasukuni Shrine officials have thus far refused to remove the names of the war criminals from the list of those being honored at the shrine.

Some Shinto adherents now explain their path as a universal natural religion, rather than an exclusively Japanese phenomenon, and try to explain the way of harmony with the *kami* to interested non-Japanese, without striving for conversions. Accordingly, there are now Shinto shrines in Brazil, Canada, France, South Korea, the Netherlands, Taiwan, and the United States. In Washington state, the American branch of Tsubaki Grand Shrine offers a variety of ceremonies including *misogi* in a clear river. The universal application and contemporary relevance of this traditional purification ceremony can be inferred from the shrine's description of it as "a sacred activity meant to teach us how to live every day fully, how to pray sincerely to fulfill your wishes, how to chose the most correct life path, how to work for the benefit of humanity and the world, how to assist in purifying *tsumi/kegare*, how to pray for health of our family, how to find right livelihood, how to pass through critical junctures, how to solve problems."[18]

An Interview with Hitoshi Iwasaki

Hitoshi Iwasaki is a young Shinto priest struggling to educate himself in the suppressed ancient ways of his people. He has officiated at the Shinto shrine in Stockton, California, and at its parent shrine in Japan, Tsubaki Grand Shrine, where a fine waterfall is used for *misogi*.

"We Japanese are very fortunate. We are grateful for every natural phenomenon and we worship the mountain, we worship the river, we worship the sea, we worship the big rocks, waterholes, winds.

"Unfortunately, after World War II, we were prohibited from teaching the Shinto religion in schools. We never learned about Shinto at school. Many young Japanese know the story of Jesus Christ, but nothing about Shinto. The government is not against Shinto. [The silence comes from] newspapers, the media, and the teachers' union, because they were established just after World War II. They have a very left-wing attitude [and associate Shinto with State Shinto]. Ordinary Japanese people don't link Shinto with politics nowadays, but the teachers' union and newspapers never give credence to religion, Shinto, or Japanese old customs.

"Against this kind of atmosphere, we learned in the school that everything in Japan was bad. Shinto and Japanese customs were bad. Many young people are losing Japanese customs. But I went to Ise Shrine University, where I learned that Shinto is not just State Shinto. Some young people like me study Japanese things and they become super-patriots. That's the problem. There is no middle, just super-left or super-right.

"I learned Shinto partly by learning aikido. The founder was a very spiritual person who studied in one of the Shinto churches. In Shinto we don't have services, we don't preach, we don't do anything for people who want to be saved. But I want to introduce the idea of Shinto to the people of the United States and young Japanese and I can do it through aikido. I think I learned the way of nature through aikido practice. We are born as a child of *kami*, which means we are part of the universe, like a tree. People practice aikido not to fight but to be a friend, to unite.

"In Japan some people are going to Shinto. They were all doing Zen before, but Zen is very difficult. In waterfall purification there is no choice, just standing under the waterfall.

"My friend, a Shinto priest, went to the Middle East, in complete desert. He says it was difficult to explain Shinto there. For them, nature is the enemy. They have to fight nature.

"In Japan we have water everywhere. Now the big rivers and streams are polluted. But people come to the shrines. People gather because this is a sacred place from ancient times where people have come to pray. And other people want to go where people are gathered, so some of the shrines become vacation places, surrounded by souvenir shops. Many come to Shinto shrines and pray Buddhist prayers. Why not? Buddha is one of the *kami*. Everything has *kami*."

Within Japan, there are new attempts to teach children the thousands-of-years-old rice cultivation ceremony, and with it, values such as co-existence and "co-prosperity" with the natural environment and with each other. The Association of Shinto Shrines feels that it can play a role in helping people to remember the natural world. The association has stated:

> [Traditionally] the Japanese viewed nature not as an adversary to be subdued, but rather as a sacred space overflowing with the blessings of the kami, *and toward which they were to act with restraint. … While the Japanese have loathed*

environmental destruction, the advance of civilization centered on science and technology, and the rush toward economic prosperity have created a tidal wave of modernization that has frequently resulted in the loss of that traditional attitude handed down from ancestors. … By reconsidering the role of the sacred groves possessed by the eighty thousand or so shrines in Japan, we hope to heighten Japanese consciousness, and expand the circle of active involvement in environmental preservation.[19]

Suggested reading

Bocking, Brian, *A Popular Dictionary of Shinto*, Richmond, Surrey: Curzon Press, 1996. Thorough discussions of ancient and contemporary facets of Shinto, including shrines, festivals, *kami*, new religious movements, historical events, and key figures.

Breen, John and Mark Teeuwen, eds, *Shinto in History: Ways of the Kami*, Honolulu: University of Hawai'i Press, 2000. Scholarly essays distinguishing between unnamed shrine cults and establishment Shinto in historical context.

Carter, Robert E., *The Japanese Arts and Self-Cultivation*, Albany, New York: State University of New York Press, 2008. Examination of aikido, gardening, tea ceremony, flower arrangement, and ceramics as experiential spiritual paths based in ancient Japanese traditions.

Hardacre, Helen, *Shinto and the State, 1868–1988*, 1991, Princeton, New Jersey: Princeton University Press. Detailed analysis of state involvement with Shinto from the Meiji Restoration onward, plus Hardacre's theory that the idea of Shinto has also been used to benefit popular religious movements, individual political ambitions, and local government administrations.

Hori, Ichiro, *Folk Religion in Japan*, Chicago and London: University of Chicago Press, 1968. A lively study of Japanese folk traditions, such as shamanism and mountain worship, which contributed to Shinto.

Kitagawa, Joseph M., *On Understanding Japanese Religion*, Princeton, New Jersey and Guildford, Surrey: Princeton University Press, 1987. A scholarly history including Shinto and "new religions," making distinctions between shrine Shinto, folk Shinto, and sect Shinto.

Nelson, John K., *A Year in the Life of a Shinto Shrine*, Seattle: University of Washington Press, 1995. Both an in-depth description of the ritual cycle at a major Shinto shrine and an accessible introduction to Shinto.

Picken, Stuart D. B., *Essentials of Shinto: An Analytical Guide to Principal Teachings*. Westport, Connecticut and London: Greenwood Press, 1994. A clear introduction by a minister of the Church of Scotland who is also a *misogi* practitioner.

Smith, Robert J., *Ancestor Worship in Contemporary Japan*, Stanford, California: Stanford University Press, 1974. A sociological study of the continuing tradition of venerating family ancestors in contemporary Japan, including historical chapters that are of help in understanding the roots of State Shinto.

Swanson, Paul L. and Clark Chilson, *Nanzan Guide to Japanese Religions*, Honolulu: University of Hawai'i Press, 2006. A collection of articles about the various religious traditions of Japan, including themes that are common to them all.

Yamakage, Motohisa, *The Essence of Shinto: Japan's Spiritual Heart*, Tokyo/New York: Kodansha International, 2006. A Shinto master from a long lineage of masters explains the inner meanings of Shinto practices.

Yamamoto, Yukitaka, *Way of the Kami*, Stockton, California: Tsubaki American Publications, 1987. A highly accessible introduction to Shinto, seen as a universal natural way.

Key terms

kami The invisible sacred quality that evokes wonder and awe in us, the invisible spirits throughout nature that are born of this essence.

kannagara Harmony with the way of the *kami*.

misogi The Shinto waterfall purification ritual.

oharai Shinto purification ceremony.

tsumi Impurity or misfortune, a quality that Shinto purification practices are designed to remove.

Review questions

1. Explain the Shinto approach to nature and environmental concerns, addressing *kami*, mountains, waterfalls, and *kannagara*.
2. Describe the components of some Shinto rituals, such as life cycle and seasonal rites, addressing the role of aesthetic beauty, priests and priestesses, and the shrine.
3. Explain the purpose of personal and collective purification in Shinto, addressing the concepts of *misogi* and *tsumi*.

Discussion questions

1. What elements of Confucianism and Buddhism may be found within Shinto?
2. Why do you think Shinto has been so closely tied to Japanese nationalism? Discuss patriotism, emperor deification, and changes since World War II.
3. Compare and contrast the Shinto view of nature with that of indigenous sacred ways.

myreligionlab

For further activities and resources, including access to MyReligionLibrary, please visit MyReligionLab at www.myreligionlab.com

MyReligionLab

Shinto http://www.religioustolerance.org/shinto.htm

Internet Sacred Text Archive: Shinto and Japanese Religious Texts http://www.sacred-texts.com/shi/index.htm

Shinto: The Way of the Gods http://www.trincoll.edu/zines/tj/tj4.4.96/articles/cover.html

Encyclopedia of Shinto http://eos.kokugakuin.ac.jp/modules/xwords

ZOROASTRIANISM

A bridge between East and West

Zoroastrian priests conduct a ceremony around a sacred fire.

Zoroastrianism, a religion from ancient Iran, at present has perhaps only 124,000 to 190,000 remaining practitioners, but for more than 1,000 years it may have been the official religion of the vast Iranian Empire which extended from Iraq or Turkey to India. It is in some ways a bridge between Eastern and Western religions. Its origins are synchronous with, and similar to, Hinduism, it is thought to have influenced Buddhism, and it introduced beliefs that are similar to those later found in Jewish, Christian, and Muslim religions. Supplanting polytheism, it brought an early form of monotheism, which was subsequently central to those "Western" faiths, as well as to Sikhism, which was born on Indian soil.

However, the extent of Zoroastrianism's direct influence on later faiths is not clear. The theology of ancient Zoroastrianism itself is subject to debate, for over the centuries a large portion of its sacred scriptures was destroyed or forgotten and the meanings of the old language were lost.

In the early faith, people also worshiped a pantheon of gods representing the elements, aspects of nature, and abstract principles such as justice and obedience. These gods often corresponded with those worshiped by Vedic Indians and were similarly named *daevas*, like the Indian *devas*, meaning "Shining Ones," with the highest gods called *Ahuras* ("Lords"). The ritual worship conducted by the priests was designed, as in India, to maintain the natural order, truth, and righteousness of the universe by re-enacting the original sacrifice that led to its creation.

ZARATHUSHTRA'S MISSION

Whereas the faith is known in Iran as Mazdayasna— "the worship of the Wise Lord, Ahura Mazda"—Western scholars refer to the tradition by the name of one of its great reformers, the prophet Zarathushtra (Greek: Zoroaster) who may have lived some time between 1800 and 1500 BCE in Central Asia. The Greeks in the time of Plato mentioned him as an ancient prophet.

It is thought that Zarathushtra was trained as a priest in the Indo-Iranian tradition. He was also apparently a mystical seeker who spent many years in spiritual retreat. At the age of thirty, he is said to have had a stunning vision of a great shining being, Vohu Manah, the embodiment of the good mind. Vohu Manah led him into the presence of Ahura Mazda, the creator god. Ahura Mazda was surrounded by angelic presences manifesting six attributes of the divine. Scholars suggest that these attributes represent earlier Indo-Iranian deities, transformed by Zarathushtra to suit his monotheistic belief but still retaining their association with forces of nature—the earth, the arch of the sky, water, plants, cattle, and fire.

Zarathushtra said he experienced communion with Ahura Mazda and his attributes on many occasions. From these direct contacts with the divine, Zarathushtra reportedly determined that in contrast to the multiplicity of gods worshiped by the Indo-Iranians, Ahura Mazda was the wise Lord, from whom all good things flowed. Zarathushtra denounced all cruelty, selfishness, distortion, and hypocrisy in the name of religion. He insisted that Ahura Mazda creates only goodness and should be worshiped by good thoughts, words, and deeds. There is a cosmic battle between sustaining and destroying forces, and to assure the victory of good over evil, humans must dedicate themselves as spiritual warriors for goodness.

Zarathushtra poured forth his adoration for the Supreme in metric verses called **Gathas**. These hymns are the only words of the prophet that have been retained over centuries of vicissitudes. "Speak to me as friend to friend," he implores Ahura Mazda. "Grant us the support which friend would give to friend."[1] The Gathas are the major existing source of information about Zarathushtra's life and theology, but they are written in an ancient language whose meanings are now obscure. Scholars see linguistic and thematic links between the Gathas and the earliest Rig Vedas.

Zarathushtra was long unable to convince anyone else to follow him in honoring Ahura Mazda above all other gods. At last he journeyed to another kingdom and convinced its king, Vishtapa, of the truth of his understanding. King Vishtapa adopted Zarathushtra's creed and proclaimed it the state religion. Zarathushtra is said to have preached for almost fifty years until his death by assassination at a fire temple at the age of seventy-seven.

SPREAD OF ZOROASTRIAN BELIEFS

It is very difficult to trace the later spread of Zarathushtra's teachings. The Magi—a tribe of priestly specialists in western Iran whose practices included magic and astrology—seem to have become involved with transmission of Zoroastrianism some time after Zarathushtra died, but they may have altered it significantly. They are mentioned in the Book of Matthew in the Christian Bible, in which some Magi reportedly followed a star to present gifts to the infant Jesus, but this may have been a legend written to interest the Magi in converting to Christianity.

Ahura Mazda was apparently revered by the Achaemenid kings of the great Persian Empire. This was set up in the mid-sixth century BCE by King Cyrus, who seems to have been a follower of Ahura Mazda. However, he and the succeeding Achaemenid kings left no written mention of the prophet Zarathushtra. Cyrus's reign was noted for its religious tolerance as well as its power and wealth. The empire Cyrus created by far-reaching conquests stretched from the Indus Valley to what is now Greece. The Jews within this territory were allowed to practice their own religion but may have adopted certain Zoroastrian beliefs, such as the belief that there is an evil aspect in life, an immortal soul, reward or punishment in an afterlife, and final resurrection of the body at the apocalyptic end of the present age—for these beliefs were absent from earlier Judaic religion. From Judaism, they may have passed indirectly into Christianity and Islam.

The spiritual tradition of devotion to Ahura Mazda was severely threatened by the 331 BCE invasion of Alexander, known as "the Great" in the West but "the Accursed" in Iran. According to Zoroastrian belief, he ransacked the beautiful capital of Persepolis, destroying fire temples, burning the library containing the holy scriptures of Zarathushtra, and killing so many Zoroastrian priests that oral transmission of many scriptures was also lost. It is thought that the Gathas of Zarathushtra survived because many people knew them by heart, as they did the most commonly used ritual prayers.

Two centuries later, Zoroastrianism was re-established in a shrunken Iranian Empire by the Parthians, who ruled for almost 500 years to 224 CE. Under the Parthians the surviving revealed teachings of Zoroastrianism were reassembled as the **Avesta**, or "holy texts." Then under the Sassanids of the third to mid-seventh centuries CE, Zoroastrianism came to the fore as the state religion, serving the aristocracy of Iran, and was thus one of the major religions of the ancient world.

However, a major threat to Zoroastrianism came from the spread of Islam after the death of Muhammad in 632 CE. Arabic Muslims defeated the Zoroastrian Iranian forces, and when Mongols invaded from the east they were gradually converted to Islam rather than Zoroastrianism. A number of Persian Zoroastrians avoided conversion to Islam by migrating to western India, whose spiritual origins were similar to their own. In India they were called **Parsis** ("Persians"). The sacred fire they consecrated on reaching India is said to have been kept burning continuously ever since. Some Parsis also migrated to what is now Pakistan.

The numbers of Zoroastrians remaining in Iran dwindled over the centuries under Muslim dominance. Even when Zoroastrians had become a minority in Iran, detailed instructions about the rituals and customs of the faith were preserved in a vast new literature, the **Pahlavi** texts written or translated in Middle Persian from about the ninth century CE. A small community of believers still survives in Iran.

Today, India—particularly the Mumbai area—is the major center of Zoroastrian population, but whether it is also the repository of the purest surviving Zoroastrian teachings is a matter of debate. Zoroastrianism in India seems to have been affected by surrounding religious traditions—such as Hinduism, Buddhism, and Christianity—and, from the nineteenth century onward, by modern spiritual movements such as Theosophy. In its Indian setting, it has nonetheless remained vibrant and meaningful.

ZOROASTRIAN TEACHINGS

After Zarathushtra's death, his teachings seem to have been merged with earlier polytheistic trends. Today there is uncertainty about exactly what he taught, but enough is known for his theology to be sketched, along with its later transformations.

The primacy of Ahura Mazda

Zarathushtra is considered the first of the monotheists of the Western traditions, in the sense that he elevated one god above all others worshiped by the earlier Iranians. His mystical visions convinced him that there is only one divine being who creates and orders the universe. He refers to this god, Ahura Mazda, by the masculine gender. In the Gathas Zarathushtra makes impassioned pleas to Ahura Mazda to make him a more fit spiritual vehicle, so that he can "dedicate to Mazda the life-breath of his whole being."[2] He asks for guidance in the mission of protecting "the poor in spirit, the meek and lowly of heart, who are Thine." He emphasizes the need for clear thought in this mission:

> O Lord of Life, we long for Thy mighty Fire of Thought which is an enduring, blazing Flame bringing clear guidance and joy to the true believer, but as for the destruction-loving, this quickening Flame overcomes his evil in a flash.[3]

Although Zarathushtra perceived Ahura Mazda as the one Eternal Being, he also described six divine powers that radiate from the godhead: The Good Mind, Righteousness, Absolute Power, Devotion, Perfection, and Immortality. After the prophet's death, these six attributes were personified and worshiped as beings, and uttering their names was thought to bring great power. These Holy Immortals, the **Ameshta Spenta**, were described as luminous deities with shining eyes and beautiful forms, guardians of Ahura Mazda's creation who held celestial councils in the heavens and descended to earth on radiant paths. They are chief among the angels, who also include many of the deities worshiped by the earlier Iranians. One of these is the popular Mithra, guardian of the light, protector of the truth, and bestower of wealth. Mithra was worshiped in Hinduism, Manicheanism, and Mithraism, as well as in Zoroastrianism.

The choice between good and evil

Zarathushtra wrestled with the problem of the existence of evil. Many Western scholars describe Zarathushtra's theology as cosmic dualism, with Ahura Mazda opposed by a dark force of equal power. Others feel that this is a later development in Zoroastrianism and that the original teaching was that although there were two opposing forces in the universe, Ahura Mazda was much the stronger. In any case, in

Zoroastrian belief Ahura Mazda is a good creator who creates only perfection and purity.

Zarathushtra did speak of two opposing powers: Spenta Mainyu, the good spirit, and Angra Mainyu, the evil spirit. Spenta Mainyu is life, order, perfection, health, happiness, increase. Angra Mainyu is not-life, chaos, imperfection, disease, sorrow, destruction. The two principles will always actively oppose each other in humans and in creation as a whole until the good spirit is at last victorious. Evil, Zarathushtra asserts, is not all-powerful or eternal, but to assure the victory of good over evil humans must dedicate themselves as spiritual warriors on the side of Spenta Mainyu. Human beings are given the free will and mental capacity to choose between the two powers. In their thoughts, words, and deeds, they can grow in love, devotion, and service, or they can contribute to evil.

Zarathushtra felt that nonloving acts in the name of religion aided the cause of evil. He railed against selfish ritualism and worship of the *daevas*, using the old word for the "shining deities" for what he considered dark forces and magic.

Heaven, hell, and resurrection

At death, Zoroastrians believe, each of us is judged according to the total goodness or evilness of our thoughts, words, and deeds. The greater the goodness, the wider the bridge to heaven, the Kingdom of Light where the souls of the righteous reside. The greater the accumulated evil, the narrower the bridge, until it is so narrow that souls cannot cross. They fall into hell, House of the Lie, a murky, woeful place.

It is not Ahura Mazda who judges and metes out reward or punishment. By natural law, good deeds bring their own reward and evil deeds their just punishment. Zoroastrians feel that the effects of our actions will be felt both in the present and in an afterlife. Tehmurasp Rustamji Sethna explains:

> When a man's actions are good he has self-confidence and usually people say he has nothing to worry about, his road is clear. On the other hand, if a man's actions are bad, it is usually said he is following a precarious path and any moment he will fall.[4]

There is no eternal hell in Zoroastrianism, for good is ultimately victorious. With the help of all individuals who choose goodness over evil, the world will gradually reach a state of perfection in which all souls, living or dead, are liberated forever from evil. This time is the Frashokereti, the "refreshment" of the world in which all of creation is resurrected into perfected immortality. Thenceforth the world will never grow old and never die. This refreshment requires the contributions of many people. Zoroastrianism therefore places great emphasis on the moral responsibility of each person, for the good of the whole.

Religious practices

Rituals are major elements of Zoroastrian practice. One that is particularly important is the act of tying the sacred cord (*kusti*) around one's mid-section, traditionally performed at least five times a day. Symbolically, the faithful are girding themselves as soldiers for Ahura Mazda, strengthening their resolve to follow the spiritual path. The *kusti* is worn by both males and females, in contrast with the male-only Hindu tradition of the sacred thread, for women and men are treated equally in many ways within Zoroastrianism. While tying the *kusti*, the faithful recite a prayer to keep evil at bay.

Zoroastrian rituals also emphasize purification. Water is venerated as a means or symbol of purification. The devout will often dip their fingers into water, apply it to their eyes and forehead, and raise their hands in prayer to Ahura Mazda. It is a great sin to pollute water or to place anything dead in it. Zoroastrians regard the natural world with profound reverence and are taught from childhood to avoid defiling it.

As of old, the other element emphasized in Zoroastrian rituals is fire, long used in Indo-Iranian tradition for its purifying, transformative power. Only Zoroastrians can enter a fire temple, and within the temple certain areas are accessible only to priests in a highly elevated state of purity.

When the physical body dies, Zoroastrians carry it to a Tower of Silence, a special circular building open at the top so that vultures can alight on the corpse to pick the bones clean. This is done to avoid polluting the earth with decaying flesh, which the birds dispose of within an hour or two. The recent near-extinction of vultures in India, perhaps due to their eating the carcasses of animals that had been fed certain medicines, has posed a crisis for this tradition.

The survivors continue to pray for the departed and continue to observe death anniversaries at which the *fravashi*, or eternal principle and guide, of the deceased person is invoked. The *fravashi* is thought to continually evolve toward perfection and to help the living in their good works.

ZOROASTRIANISM TODAY

Few followers remain of this ancient way of combating evil with personal goodness. The number of Zoroastrians is falling toward possible extinction. In Yazd, the central area where Zoroastrianism is still practiced in Iran, a holy flame has been burning continuously for 1,500 years, but there are not enough devotees to keep a Tower of Silence open. If a Zoroastrian living in Iran wants traditional burial rites, the body must be shipped to Mumbai in India, where the last Tower of Silence is still operating.

Conversion to the faith is not emphasized, partly because of a desire not to dilute the teachings or the identity as a distinct faith community. In contemporary Iran, there is little incentive to convert, for Zoroastrians, like Jews and Christians, are tolerated but limited in their privileges under Muslim rule. Historically, however, many Muslims converted to Zoroastrianism during the last years of the Pahlavi dynasty. Some Zoroastrians in North America favor active conversion of non-Zoroastrians to the faith; others are opposed to proselytizing but favor the acceptance of those who are truly moved by personal religious experience. In India, the high priests of the Mumbai Zoroastrian community declared in 2003 that anyone marrying outside the religion would be excommunicated, but this brought such an outcry that they clarified that their statement was only a "guideline" to assure the survival of the Parsi faith.

When the Parsis were influenced by Westernization and Protestant missionary activity, they became somewhat embarrassed about the mystical aspects of their faith. Some began reciting their prayers in English rather than the ancient Avestan language, and interpreting what they were doing as talking to God rather than uttering powerful sacred mantras. They tended to de-emphasize rituals and beliefs in an evil spirit and the end of the temporal world in favor of the more abstract philosophy and ethical standards of the Gathas.

The pendulum now seems to be swinging in the other direction. Training is still available in Iran and India for the hereditary lineage of Zoroastrian priests, and there is now considerable interest in preserving and understanding the tradition. Religious historians, metaphysicians, and linguists have attempted to translate the ancient language, uncover the deep significance behind the rituals, and sift out the origins of the tradition from the thousands of years of later accretions. Such efforts have brought a renewed sense of pride and appreciation within Zoroastrianism.

CHAPTER 8

JUDAISM

A covenant with God

Judaism, which has no single founder and no central leader or group making theological decisions, is the diverse tradition associated with the Jewish people, who may be defined either as a religious group or as an ethnic group.

In religious terms, Jews are those who experience their long and often difficult history as a continuing dialogue with God. In a religious sense, "Israel" refers to all those who answer the call of God and who acknowledge and strive to obey the one God, through the Torah, or "teaching," given to the patriarchs, Moses, and the prophets.

As a nation, "Israel" is an originally nomadic people that throughout its history has been repeatedly dispersed and oppressed. After the horrors of the Holocaust in the twentieth century, some Jews founded a homeland in the land of Israel, the former center of their ancestors' faith. Other Jews live in communities around the world. Many who consider themselves Jews have been born into a Jewish ethnic identity but do not feel or practice a strong connection to Jewish religious traditions.

Given the persecution, dispersion, and even lack of religiosity among many Jews, how have they survived as anything more than fossils? Their survival, and that of Judaism as a whole, has required constant accommodation to changing circumstances. Nonetheless, they have managed to sustain a remarkable degree of cohesiveness and similar practices and beliefs, though Jews have lived throughout the world under very different circumstances, and with little contact between far-flung communities.

In this chapter we will focus on Judaism as an evolving tradition, first by taking an overview of the history of the Jewish people and then by examining the religious concepts and practices that generally characterize the followers of the Torah today.

A history of the Jewish people

The Jewish sense of history begins with the stories recounted in the Hebrew Bible or **Tanakh**. Biblical history begins with the creation of the world by a supreme deity, or God, and progresses through the patriarchs, matriarchs, and Moses who spoke with God and led the people according to God's commandments, and the

KEY TOPICS

- A HISTORY OF THE JEWISH PEOPLE 239
- TORAH 273
- SACRED PRACTICES 278
- HOLY DAYS 282
- CONTEMPORARY JUDAISM 286

myreligienlab
The Jewish Bible:
Tanakh

Judaism

BCE c.1900–1700	Abraham, the first patriarch
c.1300–1200	Moses leads the Israelites out of bondage in Egypt
1207	Israelites present in Canaan
c.1010–970	David, king of Judah and Israel
961–931	King Solomon builds the first Temple of Jerusalem
722	Fall of northern kingdom of Israel to Assyria
586	Fall of southern kingdom of Judah to Babylon; first temple destroyed; Jews exiled to Babylon
c.535	Jews return to Jerusalem and Judaea
515	Second Temple of Jerusalem built
c.430	Torah read to the public by Ezra the Scribe
167	Maccabean Revolt
30 BCE–10 CE	Hillel the Elder
CE 70	Jerusalem falls to the Romans and second temple destroyed
c.90	Jewish Canon of Tanakh set
132–135	Bar Kokhba revolt
c.200	Mishnah compiled
c.500	Babylonian Talmud completed
1095	Crusaders begin massacring Jews in Europe en route to the Holy Land
1135–1204	Life of Maimonides
1478	The Spanish Inquisition begins
1492	Mass expulsion of Jews from Spain
1555 onward	Ghettos of Italy and Germany
1654	Jews begin to settle in North America
1700–1760	The Baal Shem Tov begins Hasidism
c.1720–1780	The Enlightenment in Europe
1881	Large-scale Jewish migrations to North America begin
1933–1945	The Holocaust, reaching its climax in World War II
1935	Nuremberg Laws
1947	Discovery of the Dead Sea Scrolls
1950	Law of Return
1948	Israel declared an independent state
1967	The Six-Day War
1972	First woman rabbi ordained
1982	United Nations supports independent Palestinian state
1990 onward	Israeli–Palestinian conflicts and peace initiatives
2003	Security wall under construction by Israel
2009	First black female rabbi ordained

prophets who heard God's warnings to those who strayed from the commandments. But Jewish history does not end where the stories of the Tanakh end, about the second century BCE. After the holy center of Judaism, the Temple of Jerusalem, was captured and destroyed by the Romans in 70 CE, Jewish history is that of a dispersed people, finding unity in their evolving teachings and traditional practices, which were eventually codified in the great compendium of Jewish law and lore, the Talmud.

BIBLICAL STORIES

Although knowledge of the early history of the Children of Israel is based largely on the narratives of the Tanakh, scholars are uncertain of the historical accuracy of the accounts. Some of the people, events, and genealogies set forth cannot be verified by other evidence, such as archaeological findings or references to the Israelites in the writings of neighboring peoples. It may be that the Israelites were too small and loosely organized a group to be noted by historians of other cultures. No mention of Israel appears in other sources until about 1230 BCE, but biblical narratives and genealogies place Abraham, said to be the first patriarch of the Israelites, at about 1700 to 1900 BCE.

Jews hold the **Pentateuch**, the "five books of Moses" that appear at the beginning of the Tanakh, as the most sacred part of the scriptures. Traditionalists believe

TORAH	The Five Books of Moses	NEVI'IM	The Prophets
בראשית	GENESIS	יהושע	JOSHUA
שמות	EXODUS	שופטים	JUDGES
ויקרא	LEVITICUS	שמואל א	I SAMUEL
במדבר	NUMBERS	שמואל ב	II SAMUEL
דברים	DEUTERONOMY	מלכים א	I KINGS
		מלכים ב	II KINGS
		ישעיה	ISAIAH
		ירמיה	JEREMIAH
		יחזקאל	EZEKIEL
KETHUVIM	The Writings		
תהילים	PSALMS		The Twelve Minor Prophets
משלי	PROVERBS	הושע	HOSEA
איוב	JOB	יואל	JOEL
שיר השירים	THE SONG OF SONGS	עמוס	AMOS
רות	RUTH	עבדיה	OBADIAH
איכה	LAMENTATIONS	יונה	JONAH
קהלת	ECCLESIASTES	מיכה	MICAH
אסתר	ESTHER	נחום	NAHUM
דניאל	DANIEL	חבקוק	HABAKKUK
עזרא	EZRA	צפניה	ZEPHANIAH
נחמיה	NEHEMIAH	חגי	HAGGAI
דברי הימים א	I CHRONICLES	זכריה	ZECHARIAH
דברי הימים ב	II CHRONICLES	מלאכי	MALACHI

The Jewish scriptures consist of the Torah (or Pentateuch), the Prophets, and the Writings. These books date roughly from the 10th to the 2nd century BCE, and were written mostly in classical Hebrew. They are often referred to as Tanakh, an acronym from the first syllables of each division—Torah, Nev'im, Kethuvim.

that these books were divinely revealed to Moses and written down by him as a single document. Some contemporary biblical researchers disagree. On the basis of clues, such as the use of variant names for God, they speculate that these books were oral traditions reworked and set down later by several different sources with the intent of interpreting the formation of Israel from a religious point of view, as the results of God's actions in human history. The Pentateuch seems to have assumed its final form in the days of Ezra the Scribe (fifth century BCE).

Some of the stories in the Pentateuch, such as the Creation, the Garden of Eden, the Great Flood, and the Tower of Babel, are similar to earlier Mesopotamian legends. In the narratives of the continuing history of the Israelites, only the last four books (I and II Samuel and I and II Kings) are thought to be edited directly from contemporary sources. Although the accuracy of many of the stories has not yet been independently documented, they are of great spiritual significance in Christianity and Islam as well as in Judaism. They are also politically important, for along with the Talmud they later gave a scattered people a special sense of group identity and of God's active role in Jewish history.

myreligienlab

In the Beginning
GENESIS

*After eating the fruit of knowledge, Adam and Eve are exiled from paradise. (*The Wandering of Adam and Eve, *Abel Pann, c.1925, Jerusalem.) Colored lithograph.*

From creation to the God of Abraham The Hebrew scriptures begin with a sweeping poetic account of the creation of heaven and earth by God in six days, from the time of "the earth being unformed and void, with darkness over the surface of the deep and a wind from (or: the spirit of) God sweeping over the water."[1] After creating the material universe, God created man and woman in the divine "image" or "likeness," placing them as masters of the earth, rulers of "the fish of the sea, the birds of the sky, and all the living things that creep on the earth."[2] In this account, God is portrayed as a transcendent Creator, without origins, gender, or form, a being utterly different from what has been created. Since Hebrew has no gender-neutral pronouns, God is generally—though not always—described in male singular terms. This creation story (in Genesis 1 and 2:1–4) is attributed by scholars to the "priestly source," thought to be editors writing immediately before or after the exile of the Jews to Babylon in 586 BCE.

A second, probably earlier, version of the creation story follows, beginning in Genesis 2:4. It is thought to be a contribution to the scriptures from the "Yahwist source," which used the word transliterated as "Yahweh" for the supreme deity. Instead of presenting woman as the equal of man, the second account of creation portrays her as an offshoot of Adam, the first man, formed to keep him company. This version has commonly been interpreted as blaming woman for the troubles of humanity, although this reading is not supported in the Hebrew manuscripts. According to the legend of Adam and Eve, originally God placed the first two humans in a garden paradise. The woman Eve ("mother of all the living") was promised wisdom by a serpent (later often interpreted as a symbol of Satan) to encourage her to taste the fruit of the tree of knowledge of good and evil, against God's command. She gave some to Adam as well. According to the legend, this ended their innocence. God cursed the serpent and the land, and banished Adam and Eve from their garden; their lives were no longer paradisical nor were they immortal, for they no longer had access to the "tree of life."

The theme of exile reappears continually in the Hebrew Bible, and in later Jewish history the people are rendered homeless again and again. The biblical narratives emphasize that the people risk God's displeasure every time they stray from God's commands. They are repeatedly exiled from their spiritual home and continually seek to return to it.

A more optimistic interpretation developed later, however. This was the feeling that the Jewish people were spread throughout the world by God's will, for a sacred purpose: to be good citizens of whatever land they reside in, and to help raise the imperfect world back up to the condition of perfection in which God had

The Israelites identified themselves as a people whose ancestors, Abraham and Sarah, moved from Ur and Haran in Mesopotamia to Canaan; Abraham's grandson, Jacob, called "Israel," resettled his large family in Egypt, where the Israelites were eventually treated as slaves.

Abraham's descendants are said to have given birth to the twelve tribes of Israel. They are symbolically depicted here as sitting in the patriarch's lap. (Souvigny Bible, 12th century, France.)

created it. Israel would find its way home only when all of creation was lifted up. The rabbinic tradition, which began in the first century CE and has shaped Jewish theology into the modern period, emphasized that the way out of exile was through study and righteous living. Commandments have their origin in God and, if followed, will lead humanity back to a life in harmony with God.

Covenant   A unique belief introduced into Jewish theology was the idea of a special covenantal relationship between the Jewish people and God. In this contract both are accountable. On the people's side, obedience to God is expected. On the divine side, God grants special favors and is also bound by his own ethical agreements to the people. The paradigm for this special relationship is the covenant between God and Abraham on behalf of the Jewish people. A more universal covenant with humanity as a whole is portrayed in the story of Noah, who was said to be the sole righteous man of his time.

According to the biblical narrator, who attributes thoughts and emotions to God, God despairs of the general wickedness of humans, regrets having created them, and sends a great flood "to destroy all flesh under the sky."[3] The belief that a great flood did occur in Mesopotamia is now supported by nonbiblical evidence from archaeology, geology, and legends of other peoples, grounding at least part of the narrative in historical fact. In the biblical story, God establishes a covenant with Noah and gives directions for the building of an ark, which saves Noah's family and two of each of God's creatures. God promises never again to destroy the created world or to interfere with the established natural order, with the rainbow as a sign of this covenant "between me and all flesh that is on earth."[4]

God does, however, continue to intervene in history, according to the narrators. Ten generations after the legend of Noah, the narrative focuses on Abraham, Isaac, and Jacob (the "patriarchs"), and their wives, Sarah, Rebecca, Leah, and Rachel (the "matriarchs"). According to the biblical narratives, Abraham was born in Ur (now in Iraq), migrated to Haran (now in Turkey), and then was called by God to journey to Canaan. With his wife Sarah and his household, he left the land of his father and also the religion of his father, a worshiper of the old gods.

Abraham is held up as an example of obedience to God's commands. Without hesitation, he is said to undergo circumcision (cutting away of the foreskin of the penis) as an initiatory rite, a sign of the covenant in which God agrees to be the divine protector of Abraham and his descendants, with all males to be likewise circumcised on the eighth day after birth.

Abraham and his wife Sarah were childless for many years. Sarah offered her servant, the Egyptian woman Hagar, as Abraham's concubine. According to social tradition, any child who was born of this relationship was considered to be the offspring of Abraham and Sarah, and if Sarah herself were to give birth to a child, it would carry the inheritance rights of the firstborn. After Hagar conceived a son by Abraham—Ishmael—God blessed Sarah at the age of ninety, saying that she will become the "mother of nations: the kings of many people shall spring from her" (Genesis 17:16). According to the biblical account, Sarah does indeed give birth to a son, Isaac, and then insists that Ishmael and Hagar be banished to the wilderness. God supports this demand, assuring Abraham that he will be father of two nations—one line through Isaac (to become the Israelites) and one through Ishmael (whom Arabs consider their ancestor).

According to the biblical narrative, God tested Abraham by demanding that he sacrifice his most precious possession, which was his beloved son Isaac (see Box). Thinkers have struggled to explain this demand, for human sacrifice was deemed to be very loathsome, but the point of the story seems to be the merit of Abraham's great obedience to God. When Abraham prepares to sacrifice Isaac, the Lord stops him, satisfied that "now I know that you fear God."[5] The Hebrew word *yirah*, usually translated as "fear" of God, also implies "awe of God's greatness," or what Rabbi Lawrence Kushner calls "trembling in the presence of ultimate holiness."[6]

Early monotheism Scholars disagree on whether pure monotheism—the worship of a single God of the universe, exclusive of any other divine beings—was practiced by the early patriarchs. Many names for divinity are used in the early scriptures, and some researchers consider them names of separate gods. It is known that the religion of the Canaanites had some influence on that of the Israelites. The Canaanites were polytheistic, with highly developed mythology

---

TEACHING STORY

Abraham's Willingness to Sacrifice Isaac

God put Abraham to the test. He said to him, "Abraham," and he answered, "Here I am." And He said, "Take your son, your favored one, Isaac, whom you love, and go to the land of Moriah, and offer him there as a burnt offering on one of the heights that I will point out to you." So early next morning, Abraham saddled his ass and took with him two of his servants and his son Isaac. He split the wood for the burnt offering, and he set out for the place of which God had told him. On the third day Abraham looked up and saw the place from afar. Then Abraham said to his servants, "You stay here with the ass. The boy and I will go up there; we will worship and we will return to you."

Abraham took the wood for the burnt offering and put it on his son Isaac. He himself took the firestone and the knife; and the two walked off together. Then Isaac said to his father Abraham, "Father!" And he answered, "Yes, my son." And he said, "Here are the firestone and the wood, but where is the sheep for the burnt offering?" And Abraham said, "God will see to the sheep for His burnt offering, my son." And the two of them walked on together.

They arrived at the place of which God had told him. Abraham built an altar there; he laid out the wood; he bound his son Isaac; he laid him on the altar, on top of the wood. And Abraham picked up the knife to slay his son. Then an angel of the LORD called to him from heaven: "Abraham! Abraham!" And he answered, "Here I am." And he said, "Do not raise your hand against the boy, or do anything to him. For now I know that you fear God, since you have not withheld your son, your favored one, from Me." When Abraham looked up, his eye fell upon a ram, caught in the thicket by its horns. So Abraham went and took the ram and offered it up as a burnt offering in place of his son. …

The angel of the LORD called to Abraham a second time from heaven, and said, "By Myself I swear, the LORD declares: Because you have done this and have not withheld your son, your favored one, I will bestow My blessing upon you and make your descendants as numerous as the stars of heaven and the sands on the seashore; and your descendants shall seize the gates of their foes. All the nations of the earth shall bless themselves by your descendants, because you have obeyed My command."

Genesis 22:1–18

Statue of the Canaanite high god El, 13th century BCE.

and ritual directed largely to agricultural fertility. They were settled agricultural peoples who paid homage to a high male god called El, and a Great Mother Goddess named Asherah, whose worship may be more ancient. The goddess, associated with vegetation, agricultural knowledge, and abundance, was worshiped at *asherahs*, sacred tree-symbol altar poles.

Although the Israelites destroyed the *asherahs*, they apparently incorporated or adapted elements of the older faiths of the area into their own. The hymns recorded in the biblical book of Psalms, for example, may have roots in Canaanite traditions. However, the ultimate thrust of Judaism was the rejection of the gods of surrounding peoples. The Israelites came to see themselves as having been chosen by a single divine patron. In their patriarchal culture, this God was perceived as a ruler in a close relationship to the people, like a parent to children, or a sovereign to vassals. At first Israel's God may have been perceived as a private tribal god, later known as the supreme and only deity of the universe.

Israel's birth in struggle It is also unclear who the people of the biblical narratives were. Some scholars think the word "Hebrew" is derived from the generic term *habiru*, used for the low-class, landless people who lived as outlaws and were often hired as mercenaries. Another derivation may relate to the Hebrew word *ivrim*, which means nomads or wanderers. Others point to *'ibri* as the biblical word for Hebrew, meaning "children of Eber," an ethnic term. But because of frequent moving and intermarrying, the Israelites were actually of mixed ethnic stock, including Hebrew, Aramaean, and Canaanite. The word **Semite** is a modern linguistic term applied to Jews, Arabs, and others of eastern Mediterranean origin whose languages are classified as Semitic; it is often inaccurately used as an ethnic designation.

According to the genealogies set forth in the Pentateuch, the people who became known as Israelites were the offspring of Israel (first called Jacob), grandson of Abraham. Jacob received the new name after wrestling all night with a being who turned out to be an angel of God. "Israel" means "the one who struggled with God."

This story in which a human being struggles and finally is reborn at a higher level of spirituality has been taken as a metaphor for the spiritual evolution of the people of Israel. As a result of the struggle, Israel the patriarch receives not only a new name but also the promise that many nations will be born from him. The nation Israel—"the smallest of peoples"[7]—is perceived as the spiritual center for the world to grow toward God. This is its destiny, though Jews do not feel that it has yet been fulfilled.

myreligionlab
The Mosaic Covenant
EXODUS

Egypt: bondage and exodus Jacob/Israel is said to have had one daughter and twelve sons by his two wives and their two maidservants. The twelve sons became the progenitors of the twelve tribes of Israel. The whole group left Canaan for Goshen in Egypt during a famine. Exodus, the second book of the Tanakh, opens about four centuries later with a statement that the descendants of Israel had become numerous. To keep them from becoming too powerful, the reigning pharaoh ordered that they be turned into slaves for massive construction projects. To further curb the population, the pharaoh ordered midwives to kill all boy babies born to the Israelite women.

One who escaped this fate was Moses, an Israelite of the tribe of Levi, who was raised in the palace by the pharaoh's own daughter. He is said to have fled the country after killing an Egyptian overseer who was beating an Israelite worker. While he lived in exile in Midian, the oppression of the Israelites in Egypt grew worse and worse.

According to the scriptural Book of Exodus, Moses was chosen by God to defy the pharaoh and lead the people out of bondage, out of Egypt. On a mountain, an angel of God appeared to him from within a bush blazing with fire but not consumed by it. God called to him out of the bush and yet cautioned, "Do not come closer. Remove your sandals from your feet, for the place on which you stand is holy ground."[8] When God told Moses to go and rescue "My people, the Israelites, from Egypt,"[9] Moses demurred, but God insisted:

> I will be with you … Thus you shall say to the Israelites, "Ehyeh [I Am] sent me to you. … The LORD, the God of your fathers, the God of Abraham, the God of Isaac, and the God of Jacob, has sent me to you."[10]

The word given in this biblical translation as "LORD" is considered too sacred to be pronounced. In the Hebrew scriptures it is rendered only in consonants as YHWH or YHVH; the pronunciation of the vowels is not known.

With his brother Aaron to act as spokesperson, Moses did indeed return to Egypt. Many chapters of Exodus recount miracles used to convince the pharaoh to let the people go into the wilderness to worship their God. These signs included a rod that turned into a serpent, plagues of locusts, flies, and frogs, animal diseases, a terrible storm, lasting darkness, and finally the killing by the Lord of all first-born children and creatures. The Israelites were spared this fate, marking their doors with the blood of a slaughtered lamb so that the Lord would pass over them. (The holiday Passover commemorates this story.) At this, the pharaoh at last let the Israelites go. The redemption from bondage by the special protection of the Lord has served ever since as a central theme in Judaism.

According to the scriptural account, the Lord's presence led the Israelites, manifesting as a pillar of cloud by day and a pillar of fire by night. The armies of the deceitful pharaoh pursued them until the famous scene in which Moses stretched his staff toward the sea and God caused an east wind to blow all night, dividing the waters so that the Israelites could pass through safely on a dry seabed. As the Egyptians tried to follow, God told Moses again to hold out his arm over the sea, and the walls of water came crashing down on them, drowning every one. Miriam the prophetess, sister of Moses and Aaron, took a timbrel and danced in triumph, and all the women joined her.

From the wilderness to Canaan According to the Pentateuch, God told Moses that he would lead the people back to Canaan. First, however, it was necessary to travel to the holy Mount Sinai to re-establish the covenant between God and the people. The Lord is

God speaks to Moses from a burning bush, as depicted by Marc Chagall (1887–1985). (Stained-glass window, detail, Cathedral of St. Etienne, Metz, France.)

Miriam's triumphant dance. Engraved by H. Bourne from a painting by W. Hensel.

said to have descended to its summit in a terrifying show of lightning, thunder, fire, smoke, and trumpeting. God is said to have then given the people through Moses a set of rules for righteous living, later called the Torah. Among them were the utterances that Christians call "The Ten Commandments" (see Box), on stone tablets. God also gave a set of social norms, prescribed religious feasts, and detailed instructions for the construction of a portable tabernacle with a holy ark, the **Ark of the Covenant**, in which to keep the stone tablets on which God inscribed the commandments.

During the forty days that Moses was on the mountain receiving these instructions, the people who had just agreed to a holy covenant with God became disturbed and impatient. The biblical account says that under Aaron's reluctant supervision they melted down their gold jewelry and cast it into the form of a golden calf, practicing what the authors of the biblical narratives considered idol-worship, which had been explicitly forbidden by God. Moses is said to have been so outraged by their idolatry that he smashed the stone tablets and destroyed the idol. He ordered the only people still siding with YHWH, the Levites, to slay 3,000 of those who had strayed.

After another forty-day meeting with God on the summit of Mount Sinai, Moses again returned with stone tablets on which God had inscribed the commandments. Moses' face was said to be so radiant from his encounter with God that he had to veil it. Aaron and his sons were invested as priests, the tabernacle

The Ten Commandments

I am the LORD your God who brought you out of the land of Egypt, the house of bondage:

You shall have no other gods besides Me.

You shall not make for yourself a sculptured image, or any likeness of what is in the heavens above, or on the earth below, or in the waters under the earth. You shall not bow down to them or serve them. For I the LORD your God am an impassioned God, visiting the guilt of the parents upon the children, upon the third and upon the fourth generations of those who reject Me. But showing kindness to the thousandth generation of those who love Me and keep My commandments.

You shall not swear falsely by the name of the LORD your God; for the LORD will not clear one who swears falsely by His name.

Remember the Sabbath day and keep it holy. Six days you shall labor and do all your work, but the seventh day is a Sabbath of the LORD your God: you shall not do any work. ... For in six days the LORD made heaven and earth and sea, and all that is in them, and He rested on the seventh day; therefore the LORD blessed the Sabbath day and hallowed it.

Honor your father and your mother, that you may long endure on the land that the LORD your God is assigning to you.

You shall not murder.

You shall not commit adultery.

You shall not steal.

You shall not bear false witness against your neighbor.

You shall not covet your neighbor's house: you shall not covet your neighbor's wife, or his male or female slave, or his ox or his ass, or anything that is your neighbor's.

Exodus 20:2–14

was constructed as directed, and the people set off for the land of Canaan, with the Presence of the Lord filling the tabernacle.

Acceptance of the laws given to Moses at Mount Sinai brought a new dimension to the covenant between God and Israel. God had freed the Jews from slavery and extinction at the hands of the Egyptians, and now the Jews freely agreed to accept the Torah. As Rabbi Irving Greenberg explains:

> The teaching that guides the way of the Jews, the Torah, became the constitution of the ongoing relationship of God and the Jewish people. Israel promises to walk the way of the Lord. In faithfulness to that commitment, the people of Israel pledge to teach the way of justice and righteousness as best they can, to remain distinctive and unassimilated in the world and thus hold up the message for all people to see, to create a model community showing how the world can go about realizing the dream, and to work alongside others to move society toward the end goal of redemption. Thus, the Jewish covenantal mission will be a blessing for all families of the earth.
>
> For its part, the Divine is pledged never to abandon Israel, to protect and safeguard the people, to help in the realization of the dream.[11]

Carrying the ark representing this covenant, the Israelites had to wander for forty years through the desert before they could re-enter the promised land, fertile Canaan, which at that time belonged to other peoples. The long sojourn in the wilderness is a familiar metaphor in the spiritual search. Faith is continually tested by difficulties. But even in the wilderness, the Israelites' God did not forsake them. Every day they found their daily bread scattered on the ground, in the form of an unknown food, which they named *manna*.

Moses presents the Ten Commandments of God to his people. Detail of Michal Meron, The Ten Commandments.

A stone inscription, the Merneptah Stele, written for the Egyptian pharaoh Merneptah, places the Hebrews as being in Canaan about 1207 BCE. Through what was described as the miraculous help of God, they fought many battles against the kings and tribes of Canaan. Archaeological evidence indicates that every Canaanite town was destroyed from one to four times between the thirteenth and eleventh centuries BCE, though the identity of the conquerors is not known. At Sinai, God had vowed to oust the inhabitants of the lands into which the Israelites advanced, warning them against adopting the local spiritual practices: "No, you must tear down their altars, smash their pillars, and cut down their sacred posts."[12] The editors of the scriptures clearly considered the Canaanite religion spiritually invalid and morally inferior to their own. But the Israelites' attention to their God was not absolute. According to the scriptures, whenever they turned away from YHWH, forgetting or worshiping other gods, surrounding peoples found them easy prey.

The first Temple of Jerusalem David, the second king of Israel, is remembered as Israel's greatest king. An obscure shepherd, David was chosen by the prophet Samuel to be anointed on the head with oil, for thus were future kings found and divinely acknowledged in those times. Composer and singer of psalms, David was summoned to the court of the first Israelite king, Saul, to play soothing music whenever an evil spirit seized the king. When Saul and his son were killed in

myreligionlab
The Davidic Covenant
II SAMUEL

battle, David was made king. By defeating or making allegiances with surrounding nations, David created the beginnings of a secure, prosperous Israelite empire. He made the captured city of Jerusalem its capital and brought the Ark of the Covenant there.

Under the reign of King Solomon (son of David), a great temple was built in Jerusalem. It was to be a permanent home for the Ark of the Covenant, which was housed in the innermost sanctum, and a place for making the burned offerings of animals, grain, and oil to the divine. There already existed an ancient practice among pre-Israelite peoples of using high places for altars where sacrifices were made to the gods. After centuries of wandering worship, the Israelites now had a central, stationary place where God would be most present to them. God is said to have appeared to Solomon after the fourteen-day temple dedication ceremony and pledged: "I consecrate this House which you have built and I set My name there forever. My eyes and My heart shall ever be there."[13]

The temple became the central place for sacrifice in Judaism. But its builder, Solomon, also accumulated great personal wealth, at the expense of the people, and built altars to the gods of his wives, who came from other nations. This so angered the Lord, according to the scriptures, that he divided the kingdom after Solomon's death. An internal revolt of the ten northern tribes established a new kingdom of Israel, which was independent of Jerusalem and the dynasty of David. The southern kingdom, continuing in its allegiance to the house of David and retaining Jerusalem as its capital, renamed itself Judah, after David's tribe.

Prophets such as Elijah warned the people against worshiping gods other than the Lord, and exhorted them to end their evil ways. Over the centuries, these prophets were men and women who had undergone transformational ordeals that made them instruments for the word of God. The "early prophets," such as Elijah, focused on the sin of idolatry; the "later prophets" warned that social injustice and moral corruption would be the ruin of the Jewish state.

By the reign of King Hoshea of Israel, the kingdom was so corrupt and idolatrous that, in the scriptural interpretation, God permitted the strong kingdom of Assyria to overtake what was left of the small country. To sustain the population needed for its empire-building and to keep Israel from rising again as a nation, Assyria carried off most of the Israelites to exile among the **Gentiles** (non-Jewish people). Most of the Israelites became dispersed within Assyria; these people who thenceforth lost a distinct ethnic identity are known as the "Ten Lost Tribes of Israel." This destruction of the northern kingdom took place in 722 BCE and is attested in Assyrian annals.

Judah maintained its independence, declining and continually warned of impending doom by its prophets. In graphic terms, the eighth-century BCE prophet Micah described the coming divine punishment of the chiefs of the House of Israel, "For you ought to know what is right, But you hate good and love evil" (Micah 3:7). Indeed, King Nebuchadnezzar of Babylonia (which by 605 BCE had taken over the Assyrian Empire) captured Jerusalem. In 586 BCE the great walls of Jerusalem were battered down and its buildings put to the torch by the Babylonians. The great temple was emptied of its sacred treasures, the altar dismantled, and the building destroyed. Many Judaeans were taken to exile in Babylonia, where they were thenceforth known as "Jews," since they were from Judah. The psalmist describes the feeling of exile from Zion, God's chosen place:

myreligionlab

The Prophecies of Isaiah
ISAIAH

By the waters of Babylon there we sat, sat and wept, as we thought of Zion.
There on the poplars we hung up our lyres,
for our captors asked us there for songs, our tormenters, for amusement,
"Sing us one of the songs of Zion."
How can we sing a song of the Lord on alien soil?

Psalms 137:1–4

The prophets interpreted these events as reasonable punishment by God for Judah's idolatry and misbehaviors. In exile among foreigners, the Jews nonetheless remained loyal to their God. They transformed the taunt of their captors into a spiritual challenge. This faithfulness in the midst of difficulties, without the security and support for community provided by territory, was an important development in the history of Western religions. Remembering the terrestrial Zion, maintaining communities of Jews in the land of Israel, and turning in the direction of Zion three times a day in prayer helped preserve the Jews as a scattered people through what they experienced as their thousands of years of exile. It pushed the expectation of God's covenantal accountability into the future. Isaiah and a later anonymous prophet prophesied that God would soon usher in a new era of peace and justice among all peoples, from his holy temple in Jerusalem.

I never could forget you.
See, I have engraved you
On the palms of My hands …

Isaiah 49:15–16

RETURN TO JERUSALEM

After fifty years of exile in Babylon, a small group of devoted Jews, probably fewer than 50,000, returned to their holy city and land, now called Judaea. They were allowed to return by the Persian king, Cyrus. But most of the Jews did not return to Jerusalem from Babylon, which was now their home. They were thenceforth said to be living in the **diaspora**, from the Greek word for "disperse." They always remembered Zion as a central part of their faith, but also learned to establish their creative lives in the diaspora.

King Cyrus authorized the rebuilding of the Temple of Jerusalem, which was completed in 515 BCE. The second temple became the central symbol to a scattered Jewish nation. A new emphasis on temple rites developed, with an hereditary priesthood tracing its ancestry to Aaron.

The priestly class, under the leadership of Ezra, a priest and a scribe, also undertook to revise, or redact, the stories of the people, editing the Pentateuch to reveal the hand of God. Some scholars think that it was these priestly editors who wrote the creation account in Genesis 1, glorifying the greatness and omnipotence of their God as creator of the universe.

The Torah was now established as the spiritual and secular foundation of the dispersed nation. In approximately 430 BCE, Ezra the scribe set the precedent of reading for hours from the Torah scrolls in a public square. These "five books of Moses" were accepted as a sacred covenant.

myreligionlab
The Earth will
Teach You
JOB

As the Jews lived under foreign rule—Persian, Greek, Parthian, and then Roman—Judaism became somewhat open to cross-cultural religious borrowings. Concepts of Satan, the hierarchy of angels, reward or punishment in an afterlife, and the final resurrection of the body on the Day of Judgment are thought by some scholars to have made their way into Jewish belief from the Zoroastrianism of the Persian Empire, for these beliefs were absent from earlier Judaic religion. However, they were not uniformly accepted. Greek lifestyle and thought were introduced into the Middle East by Alexander the Great in the fourth century BCE. The rationalistic, humanistic influences of Hellenism led many wealthy and intellectual Jews, including the priests in Jerusalem, to adopt a Hellenistic attitude of scepticism rather than unquestioning belief.

Tension between traditionalists and those embracing Greek ways came to a head during the reign of Antiochus IV Epiphanes, a Hellenistic ruler of Syria (175–164 BCE), the nation that then held political sovereignty over the land of Israel. Antiochus seems to have tried to achieve political unity by forcing a single Hellenistic culture on all his subjects, abolishing the Torah as the Jewish constitution, burning copies of the Torah, killing families who circumcised their sons, building an altar to Zeus in the Temple of Jerusalem, and sacrificing a hog on it (in defiance of the Mosaic law against eating or touching dead pigs as unclean). The Maccabean rebellion, a revolt led by the Hasmon family of priests, called in Hebrew the Maccabees ("Hammers"), won a degree of independence for Judaea in 164 BCE. The successful rebellion established a new and independent kingdom, once again called Israel, once again centered around Jerusalem, and ruled by the Hasmonean family.

Under the Hasmonean kings, three sects of Jews formed in Judaea. One was the **Sadducees**, priests and wealthy businesspeople, conservatives intent on preserving the letter of the law. The **Pharisees** were more liberal citizens from all classes who sought to study the applications of the Torah to everyday life. A third general movement was uncompromising in its piety and its disgust with what it considered a corrupted priesthood. The Jewish historian Josephus describes one of these groups: the **Essenes**. Its initiated members were males who dressed in white, shared their property communally, avoided luxury, and placed great emphasis on ritual purity. What may have been a similar or related group retreated to the desert soon after the Hasmonean takeover of the high priesthood in 152 BCE, and there developed a fortified compound at Qumran, near the Dead Sea. Their leader was the "Teacher of Righteousness," a priest, reformer, and mystic whose name was not uttered. The extensive library of this community, now known as the Dead Sea Scrolls, was discovered near Qumran in 1947.

Scholars are engaged in intense study of these scrolls for clues to the period between biblical Judaism and rabbinic Judaism (to be discussed in the next section). It is possible that members of the dissident sect that collected and wrote the scrolls were scattered throughout Palestine, with Qumran as their center for study and initiation into states of higher ritual purity and thus closer contact with God. They apparently maintained an intense loyalty to Jerusalem as the holy city and were preparing themselves for a cosmic battle in which the "Sons of Light" would be victorious over the "Sons of Darkness" and establish a reign of utmost purity centered in Jerusalem.

*Ruins of the
Qumran settlement.*

Eventually the conflicts among the Hasmoneans erupted into civil war. The Roman general Pompey was called in from Syria in 63 BCE to choose between contenders to the Hasmonean throne, but he took over the country instead. There followed four centuries of oppressive Roman rule of Judaea.

Under Roman rule, belief grew among Jews—including the sects living in the desert—about a messianic age in which the people would at last be rescued from their sufferings and Jews would return to their homeland. This belief had been voiced by earlier prophets. For instance, the prophet Ezekiel received a vision in which God showed him a valley of scattered, dry human bones, which God then reunited and brought back to life, explaining:

> *O mortal, these bones are the whole House of Israel. They say; "Our bones are dried up, our hope is gone; we are doomed." Prophesy, therefore, and say to them: "Thus said the Lord GOD: I am going to open your graves and lift you out of the graves, O My people, and bring you to the land of Israel." ... I am going to take the Israelite people from among the nations they have gone to, and gather them from every quarter, and bring them to their own land. I will make them a single nation in the land, on the hills of Israel, and one king shall be king of them all. ... My servant David shall be king over them; there shall be one shepherd for all of them. They shall follow My rules and faithfully obey My laws. Thus they shall remain in the land which I gave to My servant Jacob and in which your fathers dwelt; they and their children and their children's children shall dwell there forever, with My servant David as their prince for all time. ... And when My Sanctuary abides among them forever, the nations shall know that I the LORD do sanctify Israel.*
>
> *Ezekiel 37:11–28*

In addition to anticipating this national redemption of Israel, with the ingathering of the Jewish people back to the land of Israel, the classical prophets had foreseen a universal destiny for Israel. Combining the particular and universal orientations of Judaism, they had prophesied a coming "End of Days" in which disaster would be followed by universal redemption, in which all nations, going up to the "mountain of the Lord, to the house of the God of Jacob" (Micah 4:2), would recognize the one God. In the books of both Isaiah and Micah appears a famous passage about the coming reign of world peace:

Instruction shall come forth from Zion,
The word of the Lord from Jerusalem.
Thus He will judge among the many peoples,
And arbitrate for the multitude of nations,
However distant;
And they shall beat their swords into plowshares
And their spears into pruning hooks.
Nation shall not take up
Sword against nation;
They shall never again know war;
But every man shall sit
Under his grapevine or fig tree
With no one to disturb him.

Micah 4:2–4

Although the second Temple of Jerusalem was largely destroyed in 70 CE, what is thought to be a section of its western supporting wall remains intact. It is considered the most sacred place in Judaism because of its proximity to the Holy of Holies in the former temple.

Under oppressive Seleucid Greek rule of Palestine, **apocalyptic** literature became very popular. Such literature sees the world in stark terms of good and evil, predicts the coming of God's victory over evil, asserts that God will then reward good people and punish evil people, and thus urges people to live righteous lives now in preparation for that time. Among some Jews, the belief grew that there would be a person, a **Messiah**, who would come to bring evil times to an end and establish the reign of peace. In the biblical book of Daniel, probably written while Jews were being persecuted by the Seleucid emperor Antiochus IV (who had ruled from 175 until 164 BCE), the chief character Daniel describes a symbolic vision of "one like a human being" who would come on heavenly clouds, and on him the white-haired, fiery-throned "Ancient of Days" would confer "everlasting dominion" over all people, a kingship "that shall not be destroyed."[14] By the first century CE, expectations had developed that through this Messiah, God would gather the chosen people and not only free them from oppression but also reinstate Jewish political sovereignty in the land of Israel. Then all nations would recognize that Israel's God is the God of all the world. The messianic end of the age, or end of the world, would be heralded by a period of great oppression and wickedness. Many felt that this time was surely at hand. There were some who felt that Jesus was the long-awaited Messiah.

Spurred by anti-Roman militias called **Zealots**, some Jews rose up in armed rebellion against Rome in 66 CE. The rebellion was suppressed, and after heroic resistance, the Jewish defenders were slaughtered in the holy walled city of Jerusalem in 70 CE. The Roman legions destroyed the Jewish temple in Jerusalem, leaving only a course of foundation stones still standing. This temple has never been rebuilt; the remaining foundation stones, called the Western Wall, have been a place of Jewish pilgrimage and prayer for twenty centuries. The Essene movement was apparently annihilated in this uprising.

A second ultimately disastrous revolt followed in 132 CE. Its leader was Simon bar Kokhba. His initial success against the Romans brought short-lived excitement over what some considered the long-awaited Messianic Age, and coins were minted announcing "the first year of the redemption of Israel." Bar Kokhba's rule over the independent state lasted only three years, however, for the Romans committed one-third to one-half of their entire army to reconquer the area. A Roman historian of the time reported that 580,000 Jews were killed. Jerusalem was reduced to ruins, along with all Judaean towns. Those remaining Jews who had not been executed were forbidden to read the Torah, observe the Sabbath, or circumcise their sons. None was allowed to enter Jerusalem when it was rebuilt as the Roman city Aelia Capitolina, except on the anniversary of the destruction of the temple, when they could pay to lean against all that remained of it—the Western Wall—and lament the loss of their sacred home. Judaea was renamed Palestine after the ancient Philistines. Judaism no longer had a physical heart or a geographic center.

RABBINIC JUDAISM

Judaism could have died then, as its people scattered throughout the Mediterranean countries and western Asia. One of the groups who survived the destruction of Judaea were the **rabbis**, inheritors of the Pharisee tradition. They are the founders of rabbinic Judaism, which has defined the major forms of Jewish practice over the last 2,000 years. Another was the messianic movement that had formed around Jesus of Nazareth, later known as Christianity. Between them they have kept the teachings of the Tanakh vibrantly alive. Both Christianity and rabbinic Judaism used the Hebrew Bible as a foundation document, but from it they have developed in their own ways.

The rabbis were teachers, religious decision-makers, and creators of liturgical prayer. No longer were there priests or temple for offering sacrifices. The substitute for animal sacrifice was liturgical prayer and ethical behavior. Without the Jerusalem temple, the community itself gained new importance. The people met in **synagogues**, which simply means "meeting places," to read the Torah and to worship communally, praying simply and directly to God. Synagogue services did not involve animal sacrifices, but rather prayer, song, and readings from the Torah. A *minyan*—a quorum of ten adult males—had to be present for community worship.

Everyone was taught the basics of the Torah as a matter of course, but, from the age of five or six, many men also occupied themselves with deep study of the

A rabbi studying the Talmud.

myreligionlab

Midrash

myreligionlab

The Passover Story
SEDER MEAL
CEREMONY

scriptures. Women were excluded or exempted from formal Torah study. Women's family responsibilities at home were considered primary for them. They were responsible for keeping the strict dietary laws, preparing for the Sabbath and other home-centered aspects of Jewish religious life, lighting the Sabbath candles, caring for young children, teaching their daughters the commandments they would be expected to fulfill as women, and regulating sexual expression in the marriage according to rabbinic laws in order to maintain ritual purity in their homes. Although they were under sacred obligation to pray, women did not receive much religious education. By contrast, literacy was highly valued for men, and this characteristic persisted through the centuries even in the midst of largely illiterate societies. It is said that in the afterlife one can see the Jewish sages still bent over their books studying. This is Paradise.

The revealed scriptures were closed; what remained was to interpret them as indications of God's word and will in history. This process continues to the present, giving Judaism a continually evolving quality in tandem with unalterable roots in the ancient books of Moses. Centering the religion in books and teachings rather than in a geographical location or a politically vulnerable priesthood has enabled the dispersed community to retain a sense of unity across time and space, as well as a common heritage of law, language, and practice.

The rabbis set themselves the task of thoroughly interpreting the Hebrew scriptures. Their process of study, called **Midrash**, yielded two types of interpretation: legal decisions, called *halakhah* ("proper conduct"), and non-legal teachings, called *haggadah* (folklore, sociological and historical knowledge, theological arguments, ritual traditions, sermons, and mystical teachings).

In addition to delving into the meanings of the written Torah, the rabbis undertook to apply the biblical teachings to their contemporary lives, in very different cultural circumstances from those of the ancients, and to interpret scripture in ways acceptable to contemporary values. The model for this delicate task of living interpretation had been set by Hillel the Elder, who taught from about 30 BCE to 10 CE, probably overlapping with the life of Jesus. He was known as a humble and pious scholar, who stressed loving relationships, good deeds, and charity toward the less advantaged. He also established a valuable set of rules for flexible interpretation of the Torah.

> *What is hateful to you, do not do to your neighbor:*
> *that is the entire Torah;*
> *the rest is commentary;*
> *go and learn it.*
>
> *Hillel the Elder[15]*

Another of the early founders of rabbinic Judaism was Rabbi Akiva (c.50–135 CE). From humble beginnings, he became revered as a supporter of the poor who was at the same time a powerful intellectual influence upon systematization of the *halakhah*.

This process of Midrash yielded a vast body of legal and spiritual literature, known in Jewish tradition as the oral Torah. According to rabbinical tradition, God gave Moses two versions of the Torah at Sinai: the written Torah, which appears in the five books of Moses, and the oral Torah, a larger set of teachings, which was memorized and passed down through the generations all the way to the early rabbis. After the fixing of the Jewish canon—the scriptures admitted to the Tanakh in about 90 CE under the leadership of Rabbi Akiva—the rabbinical schools set out to systematize all the commentaries and the oral tradition, which was continually evolving on the basis of expanded and updated understandings of the original oral Torah. In about 200 CE, Judah the Prince completed a terse edition of legal teachings of the oral Torah, which was thenceforth known as the **Mishnah**.

The Mishnah's method of deriving legal principles for social order is based on logical analysis of how things are and why they are so. It systematically sets up hierarchical classifications, such as levels of women's status and domestic responsibilities according to the number of slave girls they bring when married. If, for instance, she brings one slave girl, the wife does not have to grind flour, bake bread, or do laundry, but she must prepare the meals, feed her child, make the bed, and work in wool. This detailing of the woman's obligations to the household economy makes clear her status within the family: She enjoys rights and protection from her husband and benefits from the expectations that she be creative and a moral beacon.

Despite the subordination of women to men in traditional Jewish legal codes, there are also directives in the Mishnah regarding men's responsibility to women—such as a husband's obligation to give sexual pleasure to his wife—and, in general, the responsibility of rulers and privileged members of society to insure legal justice for people of all classes and to provide for the material well-being of the lower classes, widows, orphans, and resident aliens. Accordingly, Jews have often been prominent in movements for social justice.

The ultimate point in the hierarchy is God, but God's role is often implicit rather than explicit in the Mishnah. Professor Jacob Neusner explains:

> *The cases are particular, the principles universal. … God in the form, God in the order, God in the structure, God in the heights, God at the head of the great chain of hierarchical being. True, God is premise, scarcely mentioned. But it is because God's name does not have to be mentioned when the whole of the order of being says that name, and only that name, and always that name, the name unspoken because it is always in the echo, the silent, thin voice, the numinous in all phenomena.[16]*

The Mishnah became the basic study text for rabbinic academies in Judaea and Babylonia, and after several centuries, the Mishnah and the rabbis' commentaries on it were organized into the **Talmud**. This is a vast compendium of law, Midrash, and argument. It does not have a beginning, middle, and end in any traditional sense. It records disagreements among rabbis and sometimes leaves them standing. Drawing on "prooftexts" from the Torah, the rabbis came to different and often inventive conclusions.

There are actually two authorized Talmuds. Both have the same Mishnah; what differs is the additional commentaries, or **Gemara**. The Jerusalem Talmud is the earlier one, written down about 400 CE. It emphasizes continual study of the Torah as a spiritual practice, a primary way of coming to know the will and ways of God. Studying the Torah is said to increase one's holiness and spiritual power.

myreligionlab
Talmud

In the Jerusalem Talmud it is written, for instance, that a river parted at the word of a rabbi who was intent on studying the Torah:

> *Once Rabbi Phinehas was going to the house of study, and the river Ginai which he had to pass was so swollen that he could not cross it. He said, "O river, why do you prevent me from getting to the house of study?" Then it divided its waters, and he passed over. And his disciples said, "Can we too pass over?" He said, "He who knows that he has never insulted an Israelite can pass over unharmed."*[17]

The Babylonian Talmud grew out of the other major center of rabbinical study: Babylonia. Completed about 500 CE, it is more developed as an encyclopedia of the Torah, for Jewish life in Babylonia was less precarious. The Babylonian Talmud was also better preserved than the Jerusalem Talmud, and it has thus become the dominant version in Jewish theology and law. It, too, describes study of the Torah as essential to Israel's destiny as a nation upholding God's laws.

Midrash is still open-ended, for significant commentaries and commentaries on commentaries have continued to arise over the centuries. No single voice has dominated this continual study of the Torah and its interpretations. Rabbis have often disagreed in their interpretations, and these disagreements, sometimes between rabbis from different centuries, are presented together. This continual interweaving of historical commentaries, as if all Jewry were present at a single marathon Torah-study event, has been a significant unifying factor for the far-flung, often persecuted Jewish population of the world.

In the process of **exegesis**, the rabbis have actually introduced new ideas into Judaism, while claiming that they were merely revealing what already existed in the scriptures. Notions of the soul are not found in the Tanakh, but they do appear in the Talmud and Midrash. The ways in which God is referred to and perceived also change. In the early biblical narratives, the Lord appears to the patriarchs and Moses in dramatic forms, such as the burning bush and the smoking mountain. Later, the prophets are visited by angelic messengers, and they sometimes hear a divine inner voice speaking to them. In the rabbinical mystical literature, God is presented in even more transcendent, less anthropomorphic ways. God's presence in the world, in relationship to the people, is called the **Shekhinah**, a feminine noun that often represents the nurturing aspect of God. Sometimes the loving protection of the Shekhinah is depicted as a radiant, winged presence.

The Throne of the Shekhinah, as depicted by contemporary artist Hannah Omer and cyber-architect Yitzhak Hayut-Man.

The rabbis also developed prayers that over time replaced sacrifices in the temple. These are still used in contemporary Jewish liturgy. For instance, the *Kaddish*, exaltation of God's name recited repeatedly in Jewish prayer services, is preserved in Aramaic, the language of Babylonia, the great center of early rabbinical Judaism.

> *May His great name be praised to all eternity.*
> *Hallowed and honored, extolled and exalted, adored and acclaimed be the name*
> *of the Holy One, though He is above all the praises, hymns, and songs of*
> *adoration which men can utter.*
>
> *Excerpt from the Kaddish[18]*

At the same time that rabbinical Judaism was further developing beliefs and liturgy for public worship, Christianity was also developing as an institution. Contemporary scholars think that Jesus, a Jew who can be seen within the context of the movements of his time, was influenced by the Essenes and may even have lived with them for a while, but that he was more closely related to the Pharisees and the school of Hillel. That is, he emphasized holiness in worldly life and, like the Jewish prophets, observance of the spirit and the full and often complex ethical implications of the law, not merely fulfillment of the letter of the law. The early apostles of Jesus emphasized rabbinic traditions holding that, with the arrival of the Messiah and the age of messianic redemption, observance of the ritual laws would be abrogated. The apostle Paul, who became the major missionary of the Christian sect, preached to both Jews and Gentiles in the diaspora that with the advent of Jesus, God would accept them without their practicing circumcision (which Greeks and Romans considered barbaric) and Mosaic laws governing many aspects of daily life and hygiene. Belief or disbelief in Jesus and the launching of the messianic age now had very practical implications as to whether they observed Jewish law in their daily lives. Both monotheistic and from common stock, Judaism and Christianity grew farther and farther apart.

JUDAISM IN THE MIDDLE AGES

In the early centuries of the Common Era, the Jewish population of the land of Israel declined, though it never disappeared, nor did the land of Israel ever lose its spiritual centrality in Jewish consciousness. Some Jews settled in other regions of the Roman Empire, and larger numbers established themselves beyond the boundaries of Rome among the Zoroastrian Persians in Mesopotamia. The city of Babylon, which already had a sizable Jewish population dating back to the biblical exile, became the major center of Jewish intellectual activity, a position it would hold well into the tenth century. The authoritative Babylonian Talmud received its final editing in the middle of the sixth century CE.

Even when the Talmud was complete, the rabbinic enterprise continued. The two great Babylonian rabbinic academies were often appealed to with difficult questions from far-flung Jewish communities. Their answers, which were considered binding on all Jews, and the questions themselves, became a new and enduring form of legal writing, *Responsa* literature, which continues to the present.

When Baghdad became the capital city of the great Abbasid Empire in the eighth century, Jewish life concentrated around that city as well. Jews were treated relatively well under Islamic rule. Like Christians, they were recognized as a "People of the Book," and were allowed to maintain their religious traditions and run their communities autonomously as long as they paid a substantial head tax in acknowledgment of their subordinate status. In Baghdad, as throughout the Islamic Middle East, many Jews were prosperous merchants, professionals, and craftsmen. In the early Middle Ages, in fact, Jews tended to dominate international trade between Muslim and Christian realms because of their facility with languages and their ability to find supportive co-religionists in virtually any community.

Life under Islamic rule was also intellectually exciting for the Jewish community, which had rapidly adopted Arabic as its spoken language. During its early centuries, Islam was far advanced beyond Christian Europe in its explorations of science, medicine, philosophy, poetry, and the fine arts. Jews living in Muslim countries benefited from an atmosphere of cultural creativity and tolerance, and themselves developed Jewish religious philosophy and Hebrew secular poetry. Many Jews were well-known physicians. Muslim Spain, in particular, where some Jews rose to high political position in Muslim courts, is renowned for its outstanding Hebrew poets and major philosophical and scientific Jewish writers.

From time to time, however, Jews were threatened by intolerant Muslim rulers and were forced to flee to other territories. The great scholar and physician Maimonides (1135–1204) was forced to leave his ancestral home of Córdoba, Spain, in the mid-twelfth century; he and his family eventually settled in Egypt. Considered one of the greatest of all Jewish intellectuals, Maimonides is particularly famous for his synthesis between reason and faith. In writings such as *The Guide of the Perplexed* he spoke on behalf of the rationality that had characterized Judaism since the dawning of the rabbinic age:

> *What is man's singular function here on earth? It is, simply, to contemplate abstract intellectual matters and to discover truth. ... And the highest intellectual contemplation that man can develop is the knowledge of God and his unity.*[19]

Jews who lived in Christian countries were less exposed to the vibrant intellectual energy of the Islamic world between the seventh and twelfth centuries. Christian Europe in those centuries was primarily a feudal agricultural society in which literacy mainly belonged to the Church. Jews, who were primarily merchants, were among the few town dwellers, and generally lived under charters of protection from the ruler of the area. Jews became expendable, and throughout the later Middle Ages there was a steady pattern of expulsions of Jews from countries in which they had long lived.

Prejudice against Jews had long been simmering among Christians. While Jews and Christians, like all humans, suffered from hatred and unwarranted attacks and often directed the vitriol against each other, Jews were hated all the more because Jesus was a Jew but many of his own people never accepted Christian claims that he was the Messiah. Jews were also blamed for his murder and for preventing his messianic successes ever after by refusing to believe in him.

myreligionlab
Thirteen Principles
of Faith
MAIMONIDES

Beginning in 1095, Jews became victims of mobs of Christian crusaders traveling through Europe with the intention to defend the Holy Land. They had been provoked by rumors that Christians were being harmed there by Muslims, with Jews as their accomplices. Believing in the holiness of their mission, crusaders and orders of knights also attacked Jews as nonconformists who did not agree with the doctrines of the Christian church. They massacred so many Jews that many formerly prosperous Jewish communities in Germany were wiped out.

In the twelfth century, superstitious rumors were spread in England that Jews were engaged in ritual murders of Christians, and many were subsequently slaughtered. Then, in thirteenth-century Germany, Jews were accused of stealing the consecrated bread used by Christians for communion with Jesus, and then torturing it. Such strange rumors were never verified, but they spread rapidly, and with them, killings of Jews. In the fourteenth century, Jews were blamed for the plague and thus were either killed or forced out of many countries. In 1492, tens of thousands of Jews were forced to leave Spain, where they had lived for over a thousand years. Some Jews fled to safety in Portugal or Italy, or the Muslim realms of North Africa and the Ottoman Empire of Turkey. Others chose to convert to Christianity rather than to leave their homeland even though staying in Spain as *conversos* (converted Jews) would expose them to the dreaded Inquisition, which had been established in Spain in 1478. The Inquisition represented the Roman Catholic Church, and its mission was to discover perceived heretics within the Christian community. It had no power over Jews, but it did have jurisdiction over the large numbers of Jews who had converted to Christianity, whether voluntarily or by force, and who might be practicing their former religion in secret. The Inquisition, which had the power to torture the accused and to execute the convicted, continued to function in Spain and in Spanish territories well into the eighteenth century.

There was further deterioration of Jewish life in western Europe in the sixteenth and seventeenth centuries. After 1555, those Jews who remained in some cities of Italy and Germany were forced to live in **ghettos**, special Jewish-only quarters, which were often walled in and locked at night and during Christian holy days, to limit mixing between Christians and Jews.

During the later Middle Ages, Poland had become a haven for the expelled Jews of western Europe. Jews were welcomed by Poland's feudal leaders who needed a middle class for the economic development of their agricultural country. Jews were allowed freedom of residence and occupation, and they rapidly grew in numbers, finding in their new home an enclave of peace and prosperity. By the sixteenth and early seventeenth centuries eastern Europe had become the major European center of Jewish life and scholarship. Jews lived an intensely religious life in villages and towns that were almost completely Jewish, speaking Yiddish, a distinctive Jewish language that was based on the medieval German they had spoken in western Europe. Among the devotional additions to Jewish literature in Yiddish were *tkhines*, or supplicatory prayers, including private prayers composed by women reflecting the concerns of their domestic lives.

In 1648, the flourishing of the Ashkenazi Jewish communities of central and eastern Europe suffered a great setback when the Cossack peasants of the Ukraine revolted against Polish rule. Associating Jewry with their Roman Catholic Polish oppressors, Greek Orthodox people led terrible massacres against the Jews, which were followed by even more killing as Poland collapsed.

In this time of despair in both eastern and western Europe, Jews were heavily taxed and ill-treated. Their longing for deliverance from danger, poverty, and oppression fueled the old messianic dream. Among the "pseudo-Messiahs" who rose to the occasion, the most famous was Shabbatai Tzevi (1626–1676) of Smyrna, a Turkish port. A rather unstable personality, he became convinced that it was his calling to be the Messiah. A young man named Nathan, who became his enthusiastic prophet, sent letters to Jews throughout Europe, Asia, and Africa announcing that the Messiah had at last appeared in his master. Many believed him and prepared for their return to the Holy Land. However, when Tzevi entered the Ottoman Empire he was arrested and put in jail. Given the choice of converting to Islam or being executed, he chose conversion and was given a government position. The shock to his supporters was terrible.

KABBALAH AND HASIDISM

A central Kabbalistic image is the Tree of God, a representation of the emanation of the qualities of the infinite Ein Sof *into revealed aspects, the* sephiroth. *The topmost circle represents Will; the tenth represents the Shekhinah—the presence of God.*

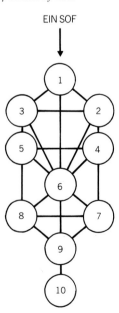

Mystical yearning has always been a part of Jewish tradition. The fervent experience of, and love for, God is an undercurrent in several writings of the biblical prophets, and is incorporated into the Talmud as well. Mystical encounter with indescribable sanctity is recorded by the prophet Isaiah (Isaiah 6), and includes the chant of the heavenly court, "*Kadosh, Kadosh, Kadosh*" ("Holy, Holy, Holy"), which is included in all Jewish communal prayer. The Merkabah ("chariot") mystical traditions from the late Hellenistic period are based on the account attributed to the prophet Ezekiel of a vision of "the semblance of the Presence of the LORD"—a radiant "semblance of a human form" on a "semblance of a throne" in the heavens above a fiery chariot made of winged angels and sparkling wheels within wheels (Ezekiel 1:26–28). Some mystical writings are found in the extra-biblical collections of texts known as the Apocrypha and the Pseudepigrapha. The apocryphal Book of Enoch describes the ascent to God as a journey through seven heavenly spheres to an audience with the King of the celestial court. Some texts from the Qumran settlement also seem to concern mystical experiences.

In the Middle Ages, esoteric teachings developed known as **Kabbalah**. The most important book in this genre is the Zohar ("Way of Splendor"). The Zohar is a massive and complex offering of stories, explanations of the esoteric levels of the Torah, and descriptions of visionary practice and experiences. It depicts the world we perceive with our senses as but a lower reflection of a splendid higher world. During the sixteenth century Kabbalah's most influential leader was Isaac Luria (1534–1572). He explained creation as the beaming of the divine light into ten special vessels, some of which were shattered by the impact because they contained lower forces that could not bear the intensity of the light. The breaking of the vessels spewed forth particles of evil as well as fragments of light into the world. Humans have a great responsibility to help end chaos and evil in the world by regathering the "sparks of holiness" in the unclean realms to repair the holy vessels. This concept of *tikkun olam* (repairing the world) has continued to be very important in Jewish thought, emphasizing the relationship between God and humans as a covenantal one with reciprocal responsibilities in which both are working together to uplift the world, and where every human act, both good and

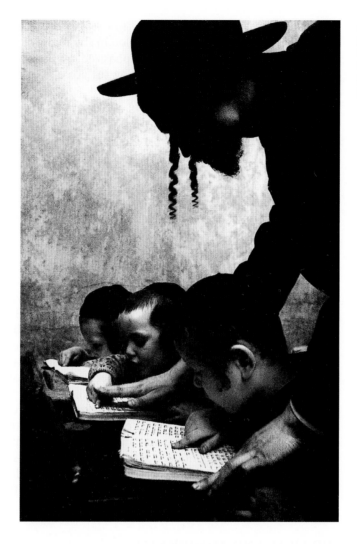

In a Hasidic school, preservation of traditional ways is maintained in the teacher's dark dress, beard, and side curls.

bad, has ultimate significance. To this end, Luria asked his followers to follow strict ascetic purification practices, prayer, and observance of the commandments of the Torah, and to chant sacred formulas.

Lurianic Kabbalism resurfaced in a very different form in the eighteenth century as **Hasidism**, the path of ecstatic piety. It developed in Ukraine and Poland, where Jews had become subject to legal limitations, poverty-stricken, and fearful for their lives from riots and murders. The rabbis had little to offer them, retreating into academic debates about legal aspects of the Torah.

Into this grim setting came the Baal Shem Tov (1700–1760), a beloved healer and Hasidic teacher, who offered a joyful version of Jewish holiness. He believed that Torah study and obedience to the letter of the law were not superior to deep-felt, pure-hearted prayer; everyone is capable of the highest enlightenment. He asserted that the divine could be found everywhere, in the present, thereby de-emphasizing the perennial waiting for a future Messiah. "Leave sorrow and sadness," he cried, "man must live in joy and contentment, always rejoicing in his

myreligionlab

From Strength to Strength
BAAL SHEM TOV

lot."[20] Followers of the Baal Shem Tov worshiped through joyous songs and ecstatic, swaying prayer, and found God in the midst of the ghetto.

God can be found everywhere, emphasized the Baal Shem Tov, but can be seen only by those who are not taken in by surface appearances. God is here in the midst of even the most mundane everyday activities; if carried out in remembrance of God, even eating, drinking, and working become holy acts. The highest goal is *devekut*, "cleaving" to God, free of the egotism and vanity that separate humans from the Holy One.

> *As the hand held before the eye conceals the greatest mountain, so the little earthly life hides from the glance the enormous lights and mysteries of which the world is full, and he who can draw it away from before his eyes, as one draws away a hand, beholds the great shining of the inner worlds.*
>
> *Attributed to Reb Nachman of Bratislava*

Soon an estimated half of all eastern European Jews were followers of the Hasidic path. Spread of the teachings is credited to Dov Ber, who emphasized the importance of the *tzaddik*, or enlightened saint and teacher, called *rebbe* (or Reb) when ordained as a Hasidic spiritual guide. Dov Ber urged Hasidim to take spiritual shelter with a *tzaddik*, whose prayers and wisdom would be more powerful than their own because of the *tzaddik*'s personal relationship with God. This idea stirred enormous opposition from non-Hasidic leaders, who believed that each Jew should be his or her own *tzaddik*. While the position of *tzaddik* became hereditary and was sometimes subject to exploitation by less-than-holy lineage carriers, such charismatic leadership remains a central element and perhaps one of the enduring attractions of modern Hasidism. The religious fervor associated with Hasidism clearly continues as an influence within Judaism, and many of the Hasidic movements themselves still thrive, despite the devastation of the Holocaust and the challenges of modernity.

JUDAISM AND MODERNITY

In the late eighteenth and nineteenth centuries, the great majority of Jews lived in eastern European countries such as Poland and Russia, which were little affected by the eighteenth-century European movement called the Enlightenment. The Enlightenment, however, provided new opportunities and better conditions for the Jews in western Europe. It played down tradition and authority in favor of tolerance, reason, and material progress. In such a rational atmosphere, restrictions on Jews began to decrease. The French Revolution (1789–1799) brought equality for the masses, including Jews living in France, and in the course of the nineteenth century this trend slowly spread to other European nations. Ghettos were torn down, and some Jews even ascended to positions of prominence in western European society. The Rothschild family, for instance, became international financiers, benefactors, and patrons of the arts.

Inspired by Enlightenment views and liberated from the social restrictions that had kept them isolated as a religious community, some "Enlightenment Jews" of

Europe also embarked on a path of secularization and acculturation that has brought a sea change in Judaism in the modern world. Baruch Spinoza (1632–1677) went so far as to question the divine source of the Torah, the authority of rabbis, and the sacredness of ritual. Moses Mendelssohn (1729–1786), adopting the Enlightenment ideal of the universalism of humanity, urged his fellow Jews to learn German and to dress and comport themselves as non-Jews. At the same time he urged the governments of his time to separate church and state, and to tolerate differences in beliefs among their citizens.

Opponents of these trends warned that in the name of Enlightenment Judaism could lose its distinctive position at the center of Jewish life, and that in adapting to the surrounding culture, Jews would inevitably cease to observe their traditional rituals. Reformers, for their part, insisted that those very halakhic observances were standing in the way of Jews' integration into modern life. In the face of this threat to the integrity of their received religious traditions, some scholars and rabbis asserted the validity of the oral law as the word of God, the proper framework for all life, and encouraged Jews not only to live by *halakhah* but also to segregate themselves from non-Jewish secular culture. This position led to what came to be called **Orthodox Judaism**. One of its staunchest advocates was Moses Sofer (1762–1839), the leader of central European traditional Judaism. His testament is still read by today's ultra-Orthodox Jews. In part:

> *May your mind not turn to evil and never engage in corruptible partnership with those fond of innovations, who, as a penalty for our many sins, have strayed from the Almighty and His law! ... Be warned not to change your Jewish names, speech, and clothing—God forbid. ... Never say: "Times have changed!" We have an old Father—praised be His name—who has never changed and never will change. ... The order of prayer and synagogue shall remain forever as it has been up to now, and no one may presume to change anything of its structure.*[21]

Meanwhile, the reform movement—which became known as **Reform Judaism**—was moving farther and farther away from its traditional moorings. In the second decade of the nineteenth century, the New Israelite Temple Association in Hamburg, Germany, adopted the changes that were already beginning to appear elsewhere: hymns and sermons in the vernacular instead of Hebrew, a shorter version of the liturgy, emphasis on the weekly Saturday service rather than the traditional prayers three times every weekday, and choirs and organ music as in Christian churches. These reformers also prepared a new prayerbook omitting references to Jews' longing for a personal Messiah and return to Zion.

Judaism was also evolving in the Americas. In 1654 a small group of Sephardic Jews who had emigrated to Brazil sought to enter the colony of New Amsterdam as refugees. During their twenty-four years in Brazil as the first organized Jewish community in the "New World," the emigrants had enjoyed a period of legal equality and economic freedom. In the New Amsterdam colony as well, they were protected by a 1663 directive from the Dutch West India Company that the colony should allow people to pursue their own religions, so long as they did not cause any trouble.

With the independence of the United States and the framing of its Constitution, Jews as well as other minorities were automatically granted equal

myreligionlab
Branches of Judaism

rights, under the ideals of equality of all humans and separation of church and state. As the new country became a haven for persecuted minorities, it was a descendant of the first Sephardic immigrants, Emma Lazarus (1849–1887), who wrote the famous poem inscribed on the Statue of Liberty: "Give me your tired, your poor, your huddled masses yearning to breathe free. ..." America was perceived as a land of economic opportunity as well as religious freedom, and substantial Jewish immigration to the United States began in the mid-nineteenth century.

Today, the United States, with approximately six million Jews, has the largest Jewish population in the world. It continues to be a highly diverse population, consisting of both Jews who are religiously affiliated and those who are not. The German immigrants brought their emerging reformist versions of Judaism with them, and in the rapidly changing American milieu these became more extreme and distinctive than in Europe. We will return later to the modern development of various branches of Judaism, but first will look at another major influence on the shape of modern Judaism: the Holocaust, the overwhelmingly tragic event of Jewish history.

THE HOLOCAUST

For many Jews the defining event of the twentieth century was the **Holocaust**, the murder of almost six million European Jews by the Nazi leadership of Germany during World War II. These Jews constituted over a third of the Jewish people in the world and half of all Jews in Europe.

Anti-Judaism had been part of Greco–Roman culture, and had been present in Europe since the Roman Empire first adopted Christianity as its state religion in the fourth century CE. New and virulent strains of this disease appeared in western Europe at the end of the nineteenth century as **anti-semitism**, with the idea that there is a racial, ethnic, genetic component of Judaism. Racist theories spread that those of "pure" Nordic blood were genetically ideal, while Jews were a dangerous "mongrel" race.

Reactionary anti-Jewish feelings also resurfaced late in the nineteenth century in Russia and in eastern Europe, where Jews formed a sizable minority of the population and where they were accumulating wealth and establishing a presence in higher educational circles. Jews were increasingly associated with left-wing movements pushing for social change, even though many Jewish socialists such as Leon Trotsky were non-observant Jews. Trotsky's leadership in the violent Bolshevik Revolution, and the Red Army, brought terrible reprisals, called **pogroms**, against Jewish communities by White Russians in the civil war. In 1,000 separate incidents, up to 70,000 Jews were killed by unrestrained rioting mobs.

In the aftermath of Germany's defeat in World War I and the desperate economic conditions that followed, Adolf Hitler's Nazi Party bolstered its popular support by blaming the Jews for all of Germany's problems. Germany, the Nazis claimed, could not regain its health until all Jews were stripped of their positions in German life or driven out of the country. Demands to eliminate the Jews for the sake of "racial hygiene" were openly circulated. Seeing the writing on the wall, many Jews, including eminent professionals, managed to emigrate, leaving

As pogroms occurred, many Jewish families left their homes to try to escape further oppression. Maurycy Minkowski, After the Pogrom, 1910.

their homes, their livelihoods, and most of their possessions behind. Others stayed, hoping that the terrifying signs would prove to be short-lived.

With Hitler's rise to power, acts of violence against Jews in Germany were instigated by his Nazi thugs and laws were passed that separated Jews from the rest of the population and deprived them of their legal and economic rights. When Hitler annexed Austria in 1938 and then invaded Poland, Denmark, Norway, Belgium, Holland, and France, several million more Jews fell under Nazi control.

Immediately after World War II began with the German invasion of Poland in 1939, systematic oppression started, with orders to all Polish Jews to move into the towns, where walled ghettos were created to confine them. Jews were made to wear a yellow or white badge with the Star of David on it to reveal their stigmatized status, and since all other jobs were taken away from them, they could do only menial labor.

Along the Russian front, special "action groups" were assigned to slaughter Jews, gypsies, and commissars (heads of government departments) as the German troops advanced, and to incite the local militia to do the same. One cannot comprehend the numbers of men, women, and children killed in these mass murders—34,000 at Babi Yar, 26,000 at Odessa, 32,000 at Vilna—probably totaling hundreds of thousands.

By 1942, large-scale death camps had been set up by the Nazis to facilitate the "final solution"—the total extermination of all Jews in Europe. From the ghettos Jews were transported by cattle cars (in which many died) from all over Europe to concentration camps. There they were starved, worked to death as slaves, tortured, "experimented" on, and/or shipped to extermination camps. Industrial-scale gas chambers were found to be the most efficient means of killing.

myreligionlab
Surviving Auschwitz
VIKTOR FRANKL

The anguish of the Holocaust, suggested in a sculpture in Miami, Florida, by Kenneth Treister.

The governments of some countries, to a greater or lesser extent, tried to protect their Jews; also some individuals, at great personal risk, in every part of Europe, hid Jews or tried to help them escape. For example, Chiune Sugihara, a Japanese diplomat, managed to issue Japanese transit visas to some 10,000 Jews, ignoring all risks to himself in order to help them quickly escape from danger. But there was little outcry against Hitler's genocidal actions from the outside world. In hindsight, many historians have concluded that Hitler's hideous policy could have been slowed by determined resistance from free Allied countries.

No modern Jewish thinker can ignore the challenge that the Holocaust poses to traditional Jewish beliefs of an omnipotent and caring God. Elie Wiesel (b. 1928), who as a boy survived a Nazi death camp in Poland, but lost all his other family members and was witness to, and suffered great atrocities, was so embittered against God that he could not bring himself to utter the traditional prayers:

> *Why should I bless Him? In every fiber I rebelled. Because He had had thousands of children burned in His pits? Because He kept six crematoria working night and day, on Sundays and feast days? Because in His great might He had created Auschwitz, Birkenau, Buna, and so many factories of death? How could I say to Him: "Blessed art Thou, Eternal, Master of the Universe, Who chose us from among the races to be tortured day and night, to see our fathers, our mothers, our brothers, end in the crematory?"*[22]

Wiesel says that we cannot turn away from the questions about how it could happen, for genocidal actions are being undertaken against other minority groups in our times as well.

ZIONISM AND CONTEMPORARY ISRAEL

Zionism is the Jewish movement dedicated to the establishment of a politically viable, internationally recognized Jewish state in the biblical land of Israel. While political Zionism was a reaction to increasing anti-semitism in Europe in the late nineteenth century, it is a movement with deep roots in Judaism and Jewish culture. The desire to end the centuries-long exile from Zion (the site of the Jerusalem temples) was a central theme in all Jewish prayer and in many religious customs. Jewish messianism is focused around a descendant of King David who will return his united people to the land of Israel, where Jewish sovereignty will be eternally re-established in an atmosphere of universal peace. Professor Aviezer Ravitzky describes the Zionist ideal:

It was a dream of utter perfection: the day would come when the entire Jewish people, the whole Congregation of Israel, would reassemble as one in an undivided Land of Israel, reconstituting its life there according to the Torah in all its aspects. The Jewish people would free itself completely from its subjugation to the great powers. It would then be a source of blessing for all nations, for its redemption would bring about the redemption of the world as a whole. [23]

Hitler's final solution was to herd Jews into concentration camps throughout Nazi-occupied Europe and then ship the survivors east into extermination camps in Poland. The pie charts show the number of Jews in each country who were left after the Holocaust, compared to their previous populations.

myreligi●nlab
Choose Life
DEUTERONOMY

Zionism became an organized international political movement under the leadership of the journalist Theodor Herzl (1860–1904), who believed that the Jews could never defend themselves against anti-semitism until they had their own nation. Herzl worked to provide political guarantees for the Jewish settlement that existed in Palestine through the nearly 2,000 years of exile and to offer institutional support to encourage Jews from around the world to immigrate to Palestine through the formation of various Zionist organizations. Simultaneously, pioneers, mainly secular Jews from eastern Europe, began increasing the Jewish presence on the land. In 1917, as the Allies prepared to carve up the former Ottoman Empire at the end of World War I, Great Britain's foreign secretary, Lord Balfour, sent a letter to Lord Rothschild, a leader of the British Jewish community, advising him that the British government would support the creation in Palestine of a "national home for the Jewish people…, it being clearly understood that nothing shall be done which may prejudice the civil and religious rights of existing non-Jewish communities in Palestine." The existing non-Jewish communities in Palestine at the time were primarily Muslims, plus some Christians. Out of Palestine's total estimated population of 600,000, some 85,000 to 100,000 were Jews living there[24] when Lord Balfour wrote this brief note which ultimately had a tremendous impact on the history of West Asia. It became known as the Balfour Declaration. Its language was replicated in a 1922 League of Nations mandate giving the United Kingdom administrative control of Palestine. Neither document offered any clarity about how the rights of Arabs living in Palestine were to be protected. To date, a viable two-state option in the land of Palestine remains elusive.

Zionist leader Henrietta Szold discusses plans with pioneers of the kibbutz system in about 1940.

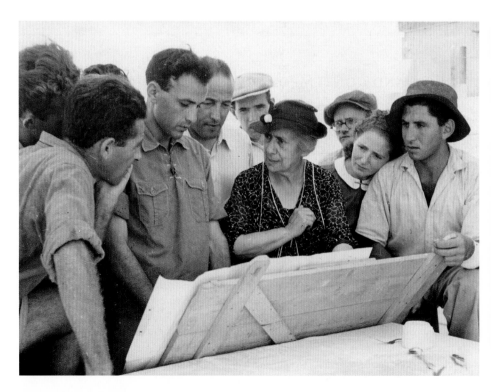

Not all Jews supported the Zionist movement. Most Reform Jews of that time believed the destiny of Jews was to be lived out among the Gentiles, where the Enlightenment had fueled hopes of a freer future and where Jews hoped they could be recognized as legitimate citizens of the countries in which they lived. Some support for Zionism came from traditional Orthodox Jews, but not all of the traditional community embraced the idea. Many felt it was God who had punished the people for their unfaithfulness by sending them away from the promised land and that only God would end the exile. They rejected active political initiative in favor of passive waiting for miraculous divine intervention.

Nonetheless, by a United Nations decision in 1947, Palestine was partitioned into two areas, one to be governed by Jews and the other by Arabs, with Jerusalem an international zone. The Jews accepted the plan, and in 1948 declared Israel an independent Jewish state with full rights for minorities. However, the Arabs did not accept the partition and as soon as British troops moved out, Israel was attacked by its Arab neighbors—Jordan, Iraq, Syria, Lebanon, and Egypt. Outnumbered, Israel nonetheless managed to control a larger area than was allotted to it in the partition plan, thus bringing many Arabs under its rule. Those Arabs who fled to avoid violence were not allowed into the surrounding countries; they were instead kept in refugee camps, in which for generations people have continued to live in distress and growing hatred for Israel. Egypt and Jordan kept sending guerrilla troops, known as *fedayeen*, to attack the Israelis, whose sovereignty they refused to recognize.

When an attack by Arab neighbors and Palestinians seemed imminent in 1967, Israel launched a stunningly successful pre-emptive strike—the Six-Day War. Nevertheless, the Arab countries still refused to recognize Israel's nationhood and Palestinian resistance grew. Despair over attaining any lasting peace with the surrounding Arabs brought hardliners to the fore in Israeli politics. They saw in expanded settlements a fulfilment of biblical prophecy and a defense against Palestinian terrorism.

From time to time, a negotiated peace has seemed almost possible, but it has not yet happened. Informal frameworks for Palestinian–Israeli settlement such as the Geneva Accords of 2003 have offered some hope of decreasing hostilities in the region by creating two independent states of Palestine and Israel, but they have not satisfactorily dealt with major sticking points. One of these is the "right of return" sought by Palestinian refugees from the 1948–1949 war and their descendants. Countering this demand, some Jews point out that over 600,000 Jews likewise had to flee their homes in Arab countries where they were severely persecuted after the creation of Israel. There is also Palestinian concern that the new state of Palestine would consist only of isolated, dependent enclaves under Israeli control. Yet another problem is control of, and access to, sites which are holy to both Muslims and Jews such as the Temple Mount in Jerusalem, known to Muslims as the place from which the Prophet Muhammad began his Night Journey to the seven heavens.

One attempt of Jews to protect themselves from Palestinians has been the building of massive security fences and walls up to 25 feet (7.6 meters) high that impede the mixing of the two communities. Palestinian communities thus live in isolated cages in which farmers are cut off from their own fertile land and water, and in some cases, even from the other side of their now-divided villages.

Palestinians and Israelis are now separated in many areas by a massive wall which Israelis have built to protect themselves from suicide bombers.

However, efforts persist to keep person-to-person contacts open between Israeli Jews and those who have been historically pitted as their opponents. For instance, an Israeli organization—the Interfaith Encounter Association—sponsors religious gatherings among Jews, Muslims, Christians, and other groups who live in the Holy Land, so that they may meet "the other," developing interfaith friendships that transcend the political violence and separation.

Tensions also exist within the Jewish community in Israel. Jewish settlers have come to Israel from many divergent backgrounds. Those who are of eastern European origin—the Ashkenazi who founded the state—tend to regard themselves as superior to Jewish settlers from other areas. Ultra-Orthodox religious authorities insist on strict observance of religious rituals, assert considerable control over education and politics in the nation, and claim that converts consecrated by Reform and Conservative rabbis in the United States are not really Jews at all. The Orthodox rabbis generally favor hardline political policies in Israel, and yet Orthodox Jews are exempted from military service. The Orthodox rabbis do not represent the majority of Israeli citizens in religious terms either, for only an estimated fifteen percent of Israelis claim to live completely according to religious laws. The majority are non-Orthodox or not religiously observant. There is also internal dissension over relationships with the Palestinians. Some sympathize with the Palestinians' situation, while Religious Zionists believe that the land has been promised to them by God for the redemption of the Jewish people and eventually the entire world. The ancient Zionist vision remains unfulfilled. Aviezer Ravitzky comments, "As the rabbis said, the End of Days continues to 'tarry.'"[25]

Although the dream of a sovereign Torah-based nation is still elusive, Israel is nonetheless a unique home or place of pilgrimage for Jews, and many immigrants are still arriving from countries such as India, Yemen, Morocco, Ethiopia, and the former Soviet Union. According to the Law of Return passed in 1950, any Jew is granted automatic citizenship in Israel. Even though most Israeli Jews describe themselves as "nonreligious," Israel is a country in which businesses close and buses stop running on the Jewish Sabbath, Jewish holidays are national holidays, and most people celebrate Passover, marry other Jews, and light the Chanukah menorah if not the Sabbath candles. Jewish identity in Israel thus retains something of its religious roots even among the secular-minded.

Torah

It is difficult to outline the tenets of the Jewish faith. As we have seen, Jewish spiritual understanding has changed repeatedly through history. Rationalists and mystics have often differed. Since the nineteenth century, there has been disagreement between liberal and traditional Jews, to be discussed later.

Nevertheless, there are certain major themes that can be extricated from the vast history and literature of Judaism. Jewish teachings are known as the **Torah**. In its narrowest sense, the Torah refers to the "five books of Moses." On the next level, it means the entire Hebrew Bible and the Talmud, the written and the oral law. For some, "Torah" can refer to all sacred Jewish literature and observance. At the highest level, Torah is God's will, God's wisdom.

THE ONE GOD

The central Jewish belief is monotheism. It has been stated in different ways in response to different cultural settings (emphasizing the divine unity when Christians developed the concept of the Holy Trinity, for instance, and emphasizing that God is formless and ultimate holiness in opposition to the earthly local gods). But the central theme is that there is one Creator God, the "cause of all existent things."[26]

God is everywhere, even in the darkness, as David sings in Psalms:

Where can I escape from Your spirit?
Where can I flee from Your presence?
If I ascend to Heaven, You are there:
if I descend to Sheol [the underworld],
You are there too.

If I take wing with the dawn
to come to rest on the western horizon,
even there Your hand will be guiding me,
Your right hand will be holding me fast.

Psalm 139:7–14

This metaphysical understanding of God's oneness is difficult to explain in linear language, which refers to the individual objects perceived by the senses. As the eleventh-century Spanish poet and mystical philosopher Ibn Gabirol put it, "None can penetrate ... the mystery of Thy unfathomable unity."[27]

One of the most elegant attempts to "explain" God's oneness has been offered by the great twentieth-century thinker Abraham Joshua Heschel (1907–1972). He linked the idea of unity to eternity, explaining that in eternity, "past and future are not apart; here is everywhere, and now goes on forever." Time as we know it is only a fragment, "eternity broken in space." According to Heschel:

> *The craving for unity and coherence is the predominant feature of a mature mind. All science, all philosophy, all art are a search after it. But unity is a task, not a condition. The world lies in strife, in discord, in divergence. Unity is beyond, not within, reality. ... The world is not one with God, and this is why his power does not surge unhampered throughout all stages of being. Creature is detached from the Creator, and the universe is in a state of spiritual disorder. Yet God has not withdrawn entirely from this world. The spirit of this unity hovers over the face of all plurality, and the major trend of all our thinking and striving is its mighty intimation. The goal of all efforts is to bring about the restitution of the unity of God and world.[28]*

Plurality is incompatible with the sense of the ineffable.
You cannot ask in regard to the divine: Which one?
There is only one synonym for God: One.

Abraham Joshua Heschel[29]

In traditional Judaism, God is often perceived as a loving Father who is nonetheless infinitely majestic, sometimes revealing divine power when the children need chastising.

LOVE FOR GOD

The essential commandment to humans is to love God. The central prayer in any Jewish religious service and the inscription on the *mezuza* at the doorpost of every traditional Jewish home is the *Shema Israel*:

> *Hear, O Israel! The Lord is our God, the Lord alone. You shall love the Lord your God with all your heart and with all your soul and with all your might. Take to heart these instructions with which I charge you this day. Impress them upon your children. Recite them when you stay at home and when you are away, when you lie down and when you get up. Bind them as a sign on your hand and let them serve as a symbol on your forehead; inscribe them on the doorposts of your house and on your gates.*
>
> *Deuteronomy 6:4–9*

Even Maimonides, the great proponent of reason and study, asserted the primacy of love for God. He emphasized that one should not love God from selfish or fearful motivations, such as receiving earthly blessings or avoiding problems in the life after death. One should study the Torah and fulfill the commandments out of sheer love of God.

THE SACREDNESS OF HUMAN LIFE

Humans are the pinnacle of creation, created in the "image" of God, according to the account of Creation in Genesis 1. Jews do not take this passage to mean that God literally looks like a human. It is often interpreted in an ethical sense: That humans are so wonderfully endowed that they can mirror God's qualities, such as justice, wisdom, righteousness, and love.

All people are potentially equal; they are said to be common descendants of the first man and woman. But they are also potentially perfectible, and in raising themselves they uplift the world. God limited the divine power by giving humans free will, involving them in the responsibility for the world's condition, and their own. If we are suffering, according to the Talmud, we should examine our own deeds.

The German scholar Martin Buber (1878–1965) described the relationship between God and humans as reciprocal:

Jewish theology has been shaped by the most compelling thinkers of each era. In the 20th century, Martin Buber described the cherished human–divine encounter as an I–Thou relationship, in which the self experiences its wholeness.

You know always in your heart that you need God more than everything; but do you not know too that God needs you—in the fulness of His eternity needs you? How would man exist, how would you exist, if God did not need him, did not need you? You need God, in order to be—and God needs you, for the very meaning of your life. ... There is divine meaning in the life of the world ... of human persons, of you and of me. ... We take part in creation, meet the Creator, reach out to him, helpers and companions.[30]

Human life is sacred, rather than lowly and loathsome; Judaism celebrates the body. Sexuality within marriage is holy, and the body is honored as the instrument through which the soul is manifested on earth. Indeed, according to some thinkers, body and soul are an inseparable totality.

> *I praise You, for I am awesomely, wondrously made.*   Psalm 139:14

LAW

Because of the great responsibility of humankind, traditional Jews give thanks that God has revealed in the written and oral Torah the laws by which they can be faithful to the divine will and fulfill the purposes of Creation by establishing a Kingdom of God here on earth, in which all creatures can live in peace and fellowship. In the words of the biblical prophet Isaiah, speaking for God:

The wolf and the lamb shall graze together,
And the lion shall eat straw like the ox,
And the serpent's food shall be earth.
In all my sacred mount
Nothing evil or vile shall be done.[31]

To the extent that traditional Jews act according to the Torah, they feel they are upholding their part of the ancient covenant with God.

An Interview with Eli Epstein

Eli Epstein, an Orthodox Jew, is a successful international businessman living in New York. In accordance with the teaching of his ancestors, he is also a philanthropist. His particular interest is in promoting interfaith understanding, having noted surprising similarities between Judaism and Islam during his many trips to West Asia. One of the projects he has initiated and supported is "Children of Abraham," which he co-directs with a Muslim philanthropist, to develop dialogue between Jewish and Muslim teenagers through the Internet. He explains the attitude toward giving that he has been taught:

"Jewish philanthropy has its antecedents in scripture. The Torah speaks about the fact that the farmers, for example, have to leave some of their crop for the poor to be able to take the droppings and the things that are extra. It has been inculcated into our tradition, to every home and every family. It gives us firstly the sense that what we have is not necessarily our own. And if we are blessed with things that are beyond our own needs, it is because God wants us to effectively be his partner in helping the world, in repairing the world, and in improving the condition of people and civilization around us, Jewish and non-Jewish.

"Jewish people who believe in the giving of charity, which is called *tzedakah*, know that it is based on the word meaning 'justice'. So it's not something we do out of the amazing ability of our hearts. It's because God says it's a form of justice, to equal out to people around us that which they can't do for themselves, for reasons which we never really understand. We don't have to ask why God gave us more than we need. But when we do have it, we shouldn't be attached to it. We should feel like it's an important thing to do, just to give. In fact, the sages say that the more you give, the more you will be blessed with being able to give more afterwards.

"We want to be able to give with an open heart, to everyone who comes and asks. Sometimes you do more, sometimes you do less. But the notion of giving is very much part of our lives and in fact, almost all Jewish homes will have something which is called a 'charity box' in English. We will use it even for small coins. So we show our young children that giving is very much part of our lives.

"[In our family life], there was almost no occasion in which you wouldn't give. Even in families such as mine which comes from eastern Poland, which was very poor and impoverished, the poor people themselves gave. It's almost as if nobody was excused from giving. The truth is that beggars have the responsibility to give as well. These people who were asking for money because they don't have enough to even feed themselves are responsible to give. It's not always in the form of money. You can give of your time and your efforts. You should give all different kinds and forms. The highest form is when you give a person a job, so you're not giving him anything but his own dignity. And the most perfect form of charity is when you clean a body before burial. It's called in Hebrew *'chesed shel emet.' Chesed* means 'kindness', *emet* being 'of truth.' It is the most pristine form of giving, because there is no one who will say, 'Thank you.' So when you are cleaning the body of nobody you will ever see again, you wash it, you purify it, you dress it in shrouds. Even when you finish that act of ultimate kindness, you can't even tell people you did it, because in the acknowledgment that you did it, they will see you as a higher person, and you can't even have that. The family can't pay you, the family can't thank you. You just walk away. You don't even say 'Good night' to the person you worked with, because 'Good night' is a blessing. So you say, 'You should be worthy of doing more acts of kindness,' and you walk away."[32]

The Torah, as indicated through rabbinic literature, is said to contain 613 commandments, or **mitzvot** (singular: **mitzvah**). Jewish law does not differentiate between sacred and secular life, so these include general ethical guidelines such as the Ten Commandments and the famous saying in Leviticus 19:18—"Love your fellow as yourself"—plus detailed laws concerning all aspects of life, such as land ownership, civil and criminal procedure, family law, sacred observances, diet, and ritual slaughter. The biblical Book of Genesis also sets forth what is called the Noahide Code of seven universal principles for a moral and spiritual life: idolatry (worshiping many gods or images of God), blasphemy against God, murder, theft, sexual behaviors outside of marriage, and cruelty to animals are all prohibited, and the rule of law and justice in society is affirmed as a positive value.

From the time of its final editing in Babylonia in the mid-sixth century CE, the Talmud, together with its later commentaries, has served as a blueprint for Jewish social, communal, and religious life. Through the rabbinic tradition, law became the main category of Orthodox Jewish thought and practice, and learned study of God's commandments one of the central expressions of faith.

From a contemporary point of view, Ismar Schorsch notes that many of the ancient commandments are ecologically useful, for they restrain humanity's ways of using the natural environment. They are addressed to humans not as wise masters of the earth, as envisioned in the first account of Creation in Genesis, but as the Adam and Eve of the second Creation story, who are disobedient and must be saved from themselves lest they destroy the planet, "for as the Bible so often avers: the land ultimately belongs to its Creator and we mortals are but His tenants."[33]

A Sabbath prayer, *Ahavat Olam*, expresses Jews' profound gratitude for God's laws:

> *With everlasting love You have loved Your people Israel. You have taught us the Torah and its* Mitzvot. *You have instructed us in its laws and judgments.*
>
> *Therefore, O Lord our God, when we lie down and when we rise up we shall speak of Your commandments and rejoice in Your Torah and* Mitzvot.
>
> *For they are our life and the length of our days; on them we will meditate day and night.*[34]

SUFFERING AND FAITH

Jewish tradition depicts the universe as being governed by an all-powerful, personal God who intervenes in history to reward the righteous and punish the unjust. Within this context, Jews have had considerable difficulty in answering the eternal question: Why must the innocent suffer? This question has been particularly poignant since the Holocaust.

The Hebrew Bible itself brings up the issue with the challenging parable of Job, a blameless, God-fearing, and wealthy man. The story involves Satan, depicted as an angel beneath God, who, in a conversation with God, predicts that Job will surely drop his faith and blaspheme the Lord if he is stripped of all his possessions. With God's assent, Satan tests Job by destroying all that Job has, including his children and his health. On hearing the news of his children's deaths:

Job arose, tore his robe, cut off his hair, and threw himself on the ground and worshiped. He said, "Naked came I out of my mother's womb, and naked shall I return there; the Lord has given, and the Lord has taken away, blessed be the name of the Lord."[35]

myreligionlab

Where were you?
JOB

With an itchy inflammation covering him from head to foot, Job begins to curse his life and to question God's justice. In the end, Job acknowledges not only God's power to control the world but also his inscrutable wisdom, which is beyond human understanding. God then rewards him with long life and even greater riches than he had before the test.

Debate over the meanings of this ancient story has continued over the centuries. One rabbinical interpretation is that Satan was cooperating with God in helping Job grow from fear of God to love of God. Another is that faith in God will finally be rewarded in this life, no matter how severe the temporary trials. Another is that those who truly desire to grow toward God will be asked to suffer more, that their sins will be expiated in this life so that they can enjoy the divine bliss in the life to come. Such interpretations assume a personal, all-powerful, loving God doing what is best for the people, even when they cannot understand God's ways. In such belief, God is seen as always available, like a shepherd caring for his sheep, no matter how dark the outer circumstances.

> *Though I walk through a valley of deepest darkness,*
> *I fear no harm, for You are with me;*
> *Your rod and Your staff—they comfort me.*
>
> *Psalm 23:4*

On the other hand, oppression and then the Holocaust have led some Jews to complain to God in anguish. They, too, feel close to God, but in a way that allows them to scream at God, as it were. In questioning the justice of history, they hold God responsible for what is inexplicably monstrous. But even in the Holocaust, there were those who held fast to hope for better times. As they walked to their death in Nazi gas chambers, some were reciting the hymn *Ani maamin*: "I believe with complete faith in the coming of the Messiah, and even though he may delay, nevertheless I anticipate every day that he will come."[36]

Sacred practices

Since the rabbinic period began, a major Jewish spiritual practice has been daily scriptural study. Boys were traditionally taught how to read and write ancient Hebrew and how to interpret scripture through the process of exegesis, by means of the oral Torah. This required extensive knowledge of the scriptures and concentrated intellectual effort. This classical pattern continues today even in the Diaspora, where some children continue to be trained in special schools to carry on the study of the Torah, thus encouraging them not only to learn and obey the commandments but also through rational analysis to delve into deeper understanding of truth.

In addition to study, a Jew is urged to remember God in all aspects of life, through prayer and observance of the commandments. These commandments are not otherworldly. Many are rooted in the body, and spiritual practices often engage all the senses in awareness of God.

Boys are ritually circumcised in the *brit milah* ceremony when they are eight days old, to honor the seal of God's commandment to Abraham. Orthodox Jews consider women ritually impure during their menstrual periods and for seven blood-free days afterwards, during which time they and their husbands are prohibited from having sexual intercourse with each other. At the end of this forbidden period Orthodox Jewish women undertake complete immersion in a *mikva*, a special deep bath structure, symbolizing their altered state. Marital sex is sacred, with the Sabbath night the holiest time for making love. By contrast, adultery is strictly forbidden as one of the worst sins against God, for Jewish tradition is extremely concerned with maintaining pure lines of descent.

What one eats is also of cosmic significance, for according to the Torah some foods are definitely unclean. For example, the only ritually acceptable, or **kosher**, meats, are those from warmblooded animals with cloven hoofs, such as cows, goats, and sheep, which chew their cuds. Poultry is kosher, except for birds of prey, but shellfish is not. Meat is kosher only if it has been butchered in the traditional way, with an extremely sharp, smooth knife by an authorized Jewish slaughterer. Great pains are taken to avoid eating blood; meat must be soaked in water and then drained on a salted board before cooking. Meat and milk cannot be eaten together, and separate dishes are maintained for their preparation and serving.

These dietary instructions are laid out in the biblical Book of Leviticus, which quotes God as saying to Moses and Aaron, "For I the Lord am He who brought you up from the land of Egypt to be your God: you shall be holy, for I am holy."[37] The rules of diet, if strictly followed, give Jews a feeling of special sacred identity and link them to the eternal authority of the Torah.

Some contemporary Jews feel that consciousness about what they eat should be extended to environmental considerations. To them, the styrofoam box in which a cheeseburger is sold at fast-food places is as much a problem as the mixing of meat and milk. Nuclear power-generated electricity used for cooking might itself be non-kosher, as long as there is no safe provision for disposing of nuclear waste.

For traditional observant Jews, the morning begins with a prayer before they open their eyes to thank God for restoring the soul. The hands must then be washed before reciting blessings and, for all traditional male Jews, putting a special fringed rectangle of cloth around the neck. It is usually worn under the clothes as a reminder of the privilege of being given divine commandments. For weekday morning prayers men also put *t'fillin*, or phylacteries, small leather boxes containing biblical verses about the covenant with God, on the forehead and the upper arm, held against the heart, in fulfillment of the Shema commandment, as literally understood: "Bind them [the Shema's words about the primacy of love for God]

Before praying, traditional Jewish men bind t'fillin *to their arms and foreheads in remembrance of their covenant with God.*

as a sign on your hand and let them serve as a symbol on your forehead." Traditional Jewish men also wear a fringed prayer shawl, or *talit*, whose fringes act as reminders of God's commandments, and keep their heads covered at all times, if possible.

Traditionally, prayers are recited on waking and at bedtime. In addition, three prayer services are chanted daily in a synagogue by men if there is a *minyan* (quorum of ten). Women can say them also, but they are excused from rigid schedules partly because of their household responsibilities, and partly because of the belief that women have a more intuitive sense of spirituality.

Jews are also expected to give thanks continually. One should recite a hundred benedictions to God every day. To this end, there is a blessing to be said every time one takes a drink of water. There is even a blessing to be recited after using the toilet:

> *Blessed art thou, our God, Ruler of the universe, who hast formed (human) beings in wisdom, and created in them a system of ducts and tubes. It is well known before thy glorious throne that if but one of these be opened, or if one of those be closed, it would be impossible to exist in thy presence. Blessed art thou, O God, who healest all creatures and doest wonders.[38]*

The Jewish **Sabbath** is observed as an eternal sign of the covenant between the Jews and God. The Sabbath runs from sunset Friday night to sunset Saturday night, because the Jewish "day" begins with nightfall. The Friday night service welcomes the Sabbath as a bride and is often considered an opportunity to drop away the cares of the previous week so as to be in a peaceful state for the day of rest. Just as God is said to have created the world in six days and then rested on the seventh, all work is to cease when the Sabbath begins. Rabbi Nina Beth Cardin explains Sabbath as:

> *a magical, holy place that opens its doors to us once a week. ... Shabbat is a weekly dose, a megadose, of holiness. For on Shabbat, we are invited to enter God's dream for our world, a place of wholeness and fullness, a place of caring and peace. We wish each other Shabbat shalom, a day full of the peace we hope one day to find.[39]*

Ruth Gan Kagan describes the Sabbath experience:

> *I am aware of a wave of peace flooding my heart and that transparent veils of tranquility are covering the World around me. A moment before I would probably be rushing around trying to finish all the preparations, ... but all this tension and rush vanishes when the fixed moment arrives; not a second earlier nor a second later. The moment I light the Sabbath candles and usher in the Sabbath spirit everything undergoes a magical transformation.*
>
> *The Queen has arrived. In Her presence there are not even talks of weekday matters. The mind quiets down leaving business, plans and worries behind as one quietly walks to the synagogue for services; the sky is aglow with the colours of sunset; the bird-song is suddenly more present; the people of the congregation gather to welcome in the Sabbath in song, prayer and silence.*
>
> *Coming home, the stars are out; in a religious neighborhood, no traveling cars break the descended peace; children are holding their parents' hands, walking in the middle of the road without fear of death.[40]*

California family praying over challah *before the Sabbath meal.*

The Saturday morning service incorporates public and private prayers, singing, and the reading of passages from the Pentateuch and Prophets sections of the Hebrew Bible. Torah scrolls are kept in a curtained ark on the wall facing Jerusalem. They are hand-lettered in Hebrew and are treated with great reverence. It is a great honor to be "called up" to read from the Torah.

More liberal congregations may place emphasis on an in-depth discussion of the passage read. Often it is examined not only from an abstract philosophical perspective but also from the point of view of its relevance to political events and everyday attempts to live a just and humane life. Torah study, and study of all Jewish literature, is highly valued as a form of prayer in itself, and synagogues usually have libraries for this purpose.

In Hasidic congregations, the emphasis falls on the intensity of praying, or *davening*, even in saying fixed prayers from the prayer book. Some sway their bodies to induce the self-forgetful state of ecstatic communion with the Loved One. Others quietly shift their attention from earthly concerns to "cleave to God." The rabbinical tradition states the ideal in prayer: "A person should always see himself as if the Shekhinah is confronting him."[41]

In addition to, or instead of, going to a service welcoming the Sabbath, observant families usually begin the Sabbath eve with a special Friday night dinner. The mother lights candles to bring in the Sabbath light; the father recites a blessing over the wine. Special braided bread, *challah*, is shared as a symbol of the double portions of manna in the desert. The rituals help to set a different tone for the day of rest, as do commandments against working, handling money, traveling except by foot, lighting a fire, cooking, and the like. The Sabbath day is set aside for public prayer, study, thought, friendship, and family closeness, with the hope that this renewed life of the spirit will then carry through the week to come.

It is customary to recognize coming of age, at thirteen, in Jewish boys by the **Bar Mitzvah** ("son of the commandment") ceremony. The boy has presumably undertaken some religious instruction, including learning to pronounce Hebrew, if not always to understand it. He is called up to read a portion from the Torah scroll and recite a passage from one of the books of the Prophets, in Hebrew, and then perhaps to give a short teaching about a topic from the reading. Afterwards there may be a simple *kiddush*, a celebration with blessing of wine and sweet bread or cake, but a big party is more likely. This custom of welcoming the boy to adult responsibilities has been extended to girls in non-Orthodox congregations in the **Bat Mitzvah** ("daughter of the commandment").

Holy days

Judaism follows an ancient lunar calendar of annual holidays and memorials linked to special events in history. The spiritual year begins with the High Holy Days of Rosh Hashanah and Yom Kippur. Rosh Hashanah (New Year's Day) is a time of spiritual renewal in remembrance of the original creation of the world. It is celebrated on the first two days of the seventh month (around the fall equinox). For thirty days prior to Rosh Hashanah, each morning synagogue service brings the blowing of the *shofar* (a ram's horn that produces an eery, unearthly blast) to remind the people that they stand before God. At the service on the eve of Rosh Hashanah, a prayer is recited asking that all humanity will remember what God has done, that there will be honor and joy for God's people, and that righteousness will triumph while "all wickedness vanishes like smoke."[42]

Rosh Hashanah includes the blowing of the shofar *in a note of alarm, three wails, and nine sobbing blasts of contrition.*

The ten Days of Awe follow Rosh Hashanah. People are encouraged to change inwardly, by looking at their mistakes of the past year. It is said that during this period God makes it easier for a person to be repentant, and is also more likely to accept repentance. A biblical passage from the prophet Isaiah is cited: "Seek ye the Lord while He may be found, Call ye upon Him while He is near."[43]

Yom Kippur completes the High Holy Days, renewing the sacred covenant with God in a spirit of atonement and cleansing. Historically, this was the only time when the high priest entered the Holy of Holies in the Temple of Jerusalem, and the only time that he would pronounce the sacred name of the Lord, YHWH, in order to ask for forgiveness of the people's sins. Today, there is an attempt at personal inner cleansing, and individuals must ask pardon from everyone they may have wronged during the past year. If necessary, restitution for damages should be made. Congregations also confess their sins communally, ask that their negligence be forgiven, and pray for their reconciliation to God in a new year of divine pardon and grace.

Sukkot is a fall harvest festival. A simple outdoor booth (a *sukkah*) is built and decorated as a dwelling place of sorts for seven days. Usually this is done as a ritual act, but seeking a deeper experience of the meaning of Sukkot, some contemporary Jews are actually attempting to live in the *sukkah* they construct. The fragile home reminds the faithful that their real home is in God, who sheltered their ancestors on the way from Egypt to the promised land of Canaan. Some contemporary groups also pray for peace amid our vulnerability to nuclear war. Participants hold the *lulav* (a bundle made of a palm branch, myrtle twigs, and willow twigs) in one hand and the *etrog* (a citrus fruit) in the other and wave them together toward the four compass directions and to earth and sky, praising God and acknowledging him as the unmoving center of creation. Traditionally there was an offering of water, precious in the desert lands of the patriarchs, and great merrymaking. During the second temple days, the ecstatic celebration even included burning of the priests' old underclothes. The day after the seven-day Sukkot festival is Simhat Torah ("Joy in Torah"), ending the yearly cycle of Torah readings, from Creation to the death of Moses, and beginning again.

Near the winter solstice, the darkest time of the year, comes Hanukkah, the Feast of Dedication. Each night for eight nights, another candle is lit on a special candle holder. The amount of light gradually increases like the lengthening of sunlight. Historically, Hanukkah was a celebration of the victory of the Maccabean rebellion against the attempt by Antiochus to force non-Jewish practices on the Jewish people. According to legend, when the Jews regained access to the temple, they found only one jar of oil left undefiled, still sealed by the high priest. It was enough to stay alight for only one day, but by a miracle the oil stayed burning for eight days. Many Jewish families also observe the time by nightly gift-giving. The children have their own special Hanukkah pastimes, such as spinning the *dreidel*, a top with four letters on its sides as an abbreviation of the sentence "A great miracle happened there."

As the winter rainy season begins to diminish in Israel, some Jews celebrate the reawakening of nature on Tu B'shvat.

Repentance and inner renewal are central themes of the High Holy Days. (Rothschild MS, c.1470.)

Observances lavish appreciation on a variety of fruits and plants. In Israel, the time is now marked by the planting of trees to help restore life to the desert.

On the full moon of the month before spring comes Purim. It commemorates the legend of Esther, queen of Persia, and Mordecai, who saved their fellow Jews from destruction by the evil viceroy Haman. It has been linked to Mesopotamian mythology about the goddess Ishtar, whose spring return brings joy and fertility. Purim is a bawdy time of dressing in costumes and mocking life's seriousness, and the jokes frequently poke fun at sacred Jewish practices. As the story of Esther is read from an ornate scroll, the congregation responds with noisy stomping, rattles, horns, and whistles whenever Haman's name is read. Purim is also celebrated with gifts of money to the poor and gifts of food to friends and family.

The next major festival is Pesach, or Passover, which celebrates the liberation from bondage in Egypt and the springtime advent of new life. It was the tenth plague, death to all firstborn sons of the Egyptians, that finally brought the pharaoh to relent. The Israelites were warned to slaughter a lamb for each family and mark their doors with its blood so that the angel of death would pass over them. They were to roast the lamb and eat it with unleavened bread and bitter herbs. So quickly did they depart that they didn't even have time to bake the bread, which is said to have baked in the sun as they carried it on their heads. The beginning of Pesach is still marked by a **Seder** dinner, with the eating of unleavened bread (*matzah*) to remember the urgency of the departure, and bitter herbs as a reminder of slavery, so that they would never impose it on other peoples. Also on the table are *charoset* (a sweet fruit and nut mixture, a reminder of the mortar that the enslaved Israelites molded into bricks) and salt water (a reminder of the tears of the slaves) into which parsley or some other plant (a reminder of spring life) is dipped and eaten. Children ask ritual questions about

Simhat Torah is a joyous celebration of the Torah, with dancing and singing. Here the Torah scrolls are being carried in a celebration in Tel Aviv.

Passover Innovations

In the United States, the most widely practiced and loved Jewish holiday is Passover. Not only do a great majority of American Jews, whether otherwise observant or not, celebrate a Passover Seder, but they are actively engaged in creating new ways of doing so. While reminding Jews of their past, the new Seders are also designed to keep the traditions fresh, relevant, and personally meaningful. Since the Seder is often celebrated at home, people are free to choose or put together their own Haggadah liturgy, perhaps incorporating events from the recent past, homemade rituals honoring deceased relatives, or new ideas found on the Internet. There are apparently thousands of versions of the Passover Haggadah now in existence, including interactive services for children, feminist Haggadahs, secular humanist Haggadahs, transgender Haggadahs, interfaith Haggadahs, Haggadahs in remembrance of the Holocaust, Haggadahs in support of victims of domestic violence, and egalitarian Haggadahs. The innovative rituals are immediately available to others through blogs, podcasts, and YouTube.

Each item of the Seder service is intended to be rich in symbolic meaning. Contemporary Seder tables may include a goblet of water and an orange—apparently ordinary objects, but packed with significance for those in attendance. The water has been added by feminists in honor of the prophetess Miriam, who reportedly led the women in dancing in jubilation after the Israelites had safely crossed through the Sea of Reeds. Inspired by her story, some contemporary women decorate tambourines for joyous dancing during the Seder celebration. "Miriam's cup" on the Seder table is a reminder of the well of water that, according to Midrash, was created by God on the sixth day of creation and appeared wherever the Israelites sojourned in the wilderness, so long as Miriam the prophetess was with them. Placing a goblet of water on the Seder table may be considered symbolic evocation of her healing and rejuvenating presence, or it may be used to affirm the wisdom of women in general.

An orange may be placed on the Seder plate in solidarity with Jewish lesbians and gay men, as well as others who are considered marginalized. This tradition seems to refer back to the occasion in 1979 when a Berkeley, California, Jewish women's group asked the wife of their rabbi to comment on the position of lesbians in Judaism. She reportedly replied something to the effect that, "There's as much room for a lesbian in Judaism as there is for a crust of bread on the Seder plate."[44] Some lesbians thence engaged in symbolic protest by actually putting bread on their Seder plates. Other people were uncomfortable with this flouting of tradition, for the Seder plate had always included only unleavened *matzah*, since all products made from leavened grain flour are *chometz* (forbidden by the Torah in Jewish households during Passover). Feminist scholar Susannah Heschel thus began using an orange instead to signify solidarity with all those who felt marginalized by traditional Judaism, including widows as well as lesbians and gay men. Heschel explains:

> Bread on the Seder plate brings an end to Pesach— it renders everything chometz. And its symbolism suggests that being lesbian is being transgressive, violating Judaism. I felt that an orange was suggestive of something else: the fruitfulness for all Jews when lesbians and gay men are contributing and active members of Jewish life. In addition, each orange segment had a few seeds that had to be spit out—a gesture of spitting out, repudiating the homophobia that poisons too many Jews.[45]

why these things are done, as basic religious instruction. A movement for contemporary liturgical renewal has yielded many new **Haggadahs**, scripts for the Seder—such as special Haggadahs for feminists, for secular Zionists, and for co-celebration of Pesach with Muslims.

A new holy day may be celebrated in April or May: Holocaust Memorial Day. Observances often include the singing in Yiddish of a song from the Jewish Resistance Movement. In part:

> *Never say that you are*
> *going your last way,*
> *though leaden skies*
> *blot out the blue of day.*
> *The hour for which we*
> *long will certainly appear.*[46]

In Israel, Holocaust Remembrance Day is observed with a countrywide minute of silence, in which all traffic, speaking, and movement stop entirely. This is a powerful secular ritual that enables secular and religious Jews to remember the Holocaust together.

Early summer brings Shavuot, traditionally identified with the giving of the Torah to Moses on Mount Sinai and the people hearing the voice of God. It is likely that Shavuot was initially a summer harvest festival that later was linked with the revelation of the Torah. In Israeli kibbutzim, the old practice of bringing the first fruits to God has been revived. Elsewhere, the focus is on reading the Ten Commandments and on presenting the Torah as a marriage contract between God and Israel. In some congregations, Shavuot is a time to celebrate children's graduation from religious school.

Then come three weeks of mourning for the temples of Jerusalem, both of which were destroyed on the ninth day of the month of Av (July or August), Tisha Be-av. This is traditionally a time of fasting and avoidance of joyous activities. Some feel that there is no longer cause for mourning because even though the temples have not been rebuilt, the old city of Jerusalem has been recaptured. Others feel that they are all still in exile from the state of perfection.

Contemporary Judaism

Within the extended family of Judaism, there are many groups, many different focuses, and many areas of disagreement. Currently disputed issues include the degree of adherence to the Torah and Talmud, requirements for conversion to Judaism, the extent of the use of Hebrew in prayer, and the full participation of women.

MAJOR BRANCHES TODAY

To a certain extent, contemporary Jews may be divided along historic ethnic lines. The majority—at least sixty-five percent—are descendants of the **Ashkenazim**, who originally migrated to Italy from West Asia during the first and second centuries CE, and then spread through central and eastern Europe, and thence to the

Americas. The second largest grouping is the **Sephardim**, descendants of those who migrated to Spain from West Asia in the eighth and ninth centuries, and thence to North Africa, the Americas, and back to West Asia. These ethnic distinctions account for certain cultural, linguistic, and dietary differences.

As we saw earlier, other distinctions among Jews who are religiously observant have developed as Judaism has encountered the modern world. Judaism, like all modern religions, has struggled to meet the challenge of secularization: the idealization of science, rationalism, industrialization, and materialism. The response of the Orthodox has been to stand by the Torah as the revealed word of God and the Talmud as the legitimate oral law. Orthodox Jews feel that they are bound by the traditional rabbinical *halakhah*, as a way of achieving closeness to God. But within this framework there are great individual differences, with no central authority figure or governing body. Orthodoxy includes mystics and rationalists, Zionists and anti-Zionists. The Orthodox also differ greatly in their tolerance for other Jewish groups and in their degree of accommodation of the surrounding secular environment. **Modern Orthodoxy** values secular knowledge and integration with non-Jewish society so that its members can be enriched by interaction with the

Major Branches of Judaism Today[*]

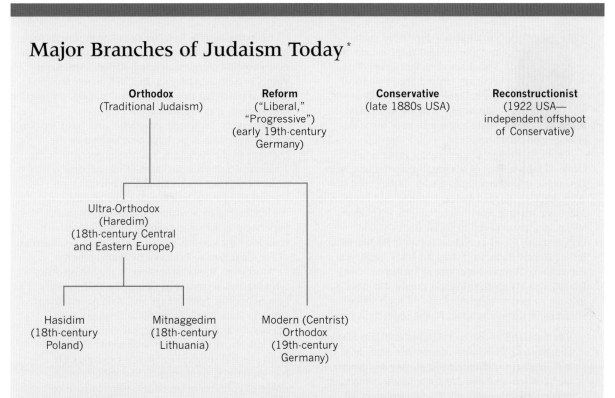

| Orthodox (Traditional Judaism) | Reform ("Liberal," "Progressive") (early 19th-century Germany) | Conservative (late 1880s USA) | Reconstructionist (1922 USA— independent offshoot of Conservative) |

Ultra-Orthodox (Haredim) (18th-century Central and Eastern Europe)

Hasidim (18th-century Poland)   Mitnaggedim (18th-century Lithuania)   Modern (Centrist) Orthodox (19th-century Germany)

*Places and approximate dates of origin are indicated. In Israel, most of the fifteen percent who consider themselves religiously observant are either the equivalent of Modern Orthodox or identify themselves as Haredim. The Haredim (Strict or Ultra-Orthodox) remain divided over worship, with the Hasidim following Isaac Luria's mostly Sephardi prayerbook, and the Mitnaggedim using the traditional Ashkenazi Polish rites. The Masorti (traditional) movement in Israel is most closely related to the American Conservative movement. The Progressive movement in Israel is related to the American Reform movement.

modern world and also help to uplift it; at the same time, Modern Orthodoxy, which first developed in nineteenth-century western Europe, is dedicated to the national and religious significance of Israel and to Jewish law as divinely given. **Religious Zionism**, which is based on the teachings of Rabbi Abraham Isaac Kook (1864–1935), places central emphasis on resettlement of the Jewish people in Israel as the working out of a divine plan for the salvation not only of Jews but also for the whole world. Involvement with secular society is permissible only when such involvement is beneficial for the state of Israel. **Haredi (Ultra-Orthodox)** Judaism—which may overlap with Religious Zionism, especially in Israel—is generally in favor of a degree of detachment from non-Jewish culture, so that the community can focus on study of the Torah. Some Haredi groups practice complete withdrawal from the secular world and the rest of the Jewish community, while others, such as the **Lubavich Hasidim** (originally from Lithuania,

---

RELIGION IN PUBLIC LIFE

Rabbi David Saperstein

Judaism has produced many notable philanthropists and also social activists. In twenty-first-century United States political arenas, the voice of Rabbi David Saperstein is heard again and again as an advocate for social change and social justice.

Rabbi Saperstein comes from a large family circle of rabbis. Two of his great-grandfathers were Orthodox rabbis, his great-uncles, father, and uncle were highly regarded Reform rabbis, and his brother Marc is a leading Jewish scholar. His wife, Ellen Weiss, is also involved in social issues as Vice President for News at National Public Radio. His father Harold Saperstein was for forty-eight years the rabbi of Temple Emanuel in Lynbrook, Long Island, and his mother Marcia taught a course in current events to generations of high school students in the synagogue. Rabbi Saperstein recalls:

The popularity of that course helped keep kids involved in synagogue; its insightfulness opened many of us to a sense of responsibility for this hurting and broken world. It was then that I began to see the connections between tikkun olam *and Jewish identity; to see* tikkun olam *as a gateway to shaping Jewish lives, a powerful organizing principle of Jewish identity.*[47]

His parents fully lived by their commitment to social justice, continually undertaking projects such as organizing clergy to register African American voters in Selma, Alabama, in 1965, when tensions were so high that one of their co-workers, a Christian seminarian, was murdered.

Extremely dedicated, energetic, and hard-working, Rabbi Saperstein is perhaps best known as the Director of the Religious Action Center of Reform Judaism. Under his direction, it has become a powerful center for social justice advocacy on Capitol Hill in Washington, D.C. In addition to his leadership in Jewish organizations, Rabbi Saperstein is active in helping to build interfaith coalitions for various causes and is the Co-Chairman of the Coalition to Preserve Religious Liberty.

Moreover, Rabbi Saperstein is also an attorney who teaches seminars at Georgetown University Law School in Jewish Law and First Amendment Church-State Law. He writes and speaks very effectively and often appears on television news and talk shows, basing his arguments about controversial subjects in biblical teachings. He has something significant to say about a great range of contemporary issues, from torture of political prisoners to global warming. For instance, in lobbying the United States Senate with reference to proposed legislation on hate crimes, he said:

with strong communities in many countries), are devoted to extending their message to as many Jews as possible, using all the tools of modern technology for their sacred purpose. The Lubavich, who offer highly structured and nurturing communities in which male–female roles are strictly defined and an all-embracing piety and devotion to a charismatic leader are universally shared, have had considerable success in attracting young Jews to their way of life.

The **Reform** (or Liberal) movement, at the other end of the spectrum, began in nineteenth-century Germany as an attempt to help modern Jews appreciate their religion rather than regarding it as antiquated, meaningless, or even repugnant. In imitation of Christian churches, synagogues were redefined as places for spiritual elevation, with choirs added for effect, and the Sabbath service was shortened and translated into the vernacular. As we have seen, the liturgy was also changed to eliminate references to the hope of return to Zion and animal

As it is written in Leviticus 19:16, "You cannot stand idly by when your neighbor's blood is being shed." We cannot stand idly by while our brothers and sisters, parents and children live in fear that racism, bigotry, homophobia, misogyny, and xenophobia continue to go unchecked. We cannot stand idly by while hate crimes destroy the sense of community that we and so many others have worked so hard to build. This is an issue that hits especially close to home for the Jewish people. We have watched in horror as anti-semitism has terrorized Europe and nations across the globe over the last few months. Hundreds of hate crimes against Jews have created an atmosphere of fear and intimidation. … More than that, though, we are ever mindful that Jews are far from the only victims of senseless hatred. It is a painful bond we share with all too many others. … Hate crimes are more than mere acts of violence. … Hate crimes are nothing less than attacks on those values that are pillars of our republic and the guarantors of our freedom. They are a betrayal of the promise of America.[48]

Social action is at the heart of lived Jewish faith, according to Rabbi Saperstein:

Is it not self-evident that we cannot fulfill our destiny to be a light to the nations, that we cannot respond to God's central call to us to be a holy people, if we retreat from struggles for justice, peace, and equality in our nation and in our world? This work of tikkun olam must play a powerful role in our Jewish life, simply because it is right—and God calls us to that task of righteousness.

Three thousand years of our mothers and fathers have insisted that we Jews do not continue for continuity's sake alone, do not exist for existence's sake alone—but are called for a holy purpose and a holy mission: to be God's partners in shaping a better and more hopeful world. "You shall be holy, for the Eternal your God is holy," God commands in Leviticus. And how, does God tell us, can we strive to be like God, can we manifest that holiness? By feeding the hungry, and removing the stumbling block before the blind; speaking out against injustice and paying the laborer a fair and timely wage; by creating courts of justice and a marketplace that is fair and honest.

This vision resonates through the entire prophetic tradition, the rabbinic creation of the world's first social welfare system, the immense charitable undertakings of organized Jewish communities in the Diaspora for over 1,000 years —and in Judaism's magnificent contributions to the evolution of contemporary democracy and human rights.

As the great Orthodox Jewish scholar Isadore Twersky concluded: One cannot claim to be a God-intoxicated Jew without having an unquenchable thirst for social justice.[49]

sacrifices in the temple. Women and men were allowed to sit together in the synagogue, in contrast to their traditional separation. Halakhic observances were reevaluated for their relevance to modern needs, and Judaism was understood as an evolving, open-ended religion rather than one fixed forever by the Torah. Reform congregations are numerous in North America, where they are continually engaged in a "creative confrontation with modernity." Rather than exclusivism, Reform rabbis cultivate a sense of the universalism of Jewish values.

Given this approach, it is not surprising that Reform Judaism, particularly in North America, has been at the forefront in the establishment of interfaith dialogue and faith-based social activism, in cooperation with non-Jewish groups. Rabbi Maria Feldman of the Religious Action Center of Reform Judaism affirms:

> To be a Reform Jew is to hear the voice of the prophets in our head; to be engaged in the ongoing work of tikkun olam; to strive to improve the world in which we live. The passion for social justice is reflected in the ancient words of our prophets and sages and in the declarations of our Movement's leaders throughout its history. The ancient command "Tzedek, Tzedek Tirdof! Justice, justice shall you seek!" constantly reverberates in our ears.[50]

Reform Judaism is not fully accepted in Israel, where the Israeli rabbinate, which has considerable civil and political power, does not recognize the authority of non-Orthodox rabbis.

The liberalization process has also given birth to other groups with intermediate positions. With roots in mid-nineteenth-century responses to the liberal Reform movement in Germany, **Conservative** Judaism sought to maintain ("conserve") traditional Jewish laws and practices while also using modern means of historical scholarship, sponsoring critical studies of Jewish texts from all periods. In the United States, Conservative Judaism received a great boost in 1902 when the famous scholar Solomon Schechter became President of the Jewish Theological Seminary, which thenceforth became one of the major centers of Jewish scholarship. Conservative Jews believe that Jews have always searched and added to their laws, liturgy, Midrash, and beliefs to keep them relevant and meaningful in changing times. Conservative women have long served as cantors and have been ordained as rabbis since 1985. To avoid confusion with political conservatism, Conservative Judaism is now in many places called "Masorti" Judaism, from the Hebrew word meaning "traditional."

Rabbi Mordecai Kaplan, an influential American thinker who died in 1983, branched off from Conservatism and founded a movement called **Reconstructionism**. Kaplan held that the Enlightenment had changed everything and that strong measures were needed to preserve Judaism in the face of rationalism. Kaplan asserted that "as long as Jews adhered to the traditional conception of the Torah as supernaturally revealed, they would not be amenable to any constructive adjustment of Judaism that was needed to render it viable in a non-Jewish environment."[51] He defined Judaism as an "evolving religious civilization," both cultural and spiritual, and asserted that the Jewish people are the heart of Judaism. The traditions exist for the people, and not vice versa, he said. Kaplan denied that the Jewish people were specially chosen by God, an exclusivist idea. Rather, they had chosen to try to become a people of God. Kaplan created a new prayer book, deleting traditional portions he and others found offensive, such as derogatory references to women and Gentiles, references to physical resurrection of the body, and passages describing God as rewarding or punishing Israel by manipulating natural phenomena.

In the United States, now home of the largest Jewish community in the world, there has been a great shift in leadership within Orthodox, Conservative, and Reform organizations. For example, the seminaries of all three movements now have "baby boomers" as their presidents, and in 2007 neither the President of Yeshiva University—where mostly Orthodox male students study the Torah, Mishnah, and Talmud—nor the Chancellor of the Jewish Theological Seminary were rabbis.

In addition to those who affiliate with a religious movement, there are many Jews who identify themselves as secular Jews, affirming their Jewish origins and maintaining various Jewish cultural traditions while eschewing religious practice. There are also significant numbers of people of Jewish birth, particularly in North America and western Europe, whose Jewish identity is vestigial at best, and unlikely to survive in future generations. The possibilities for total assimilation into Western culture are evident in statistics indicating that over fifty percent of Western Jews marry non-Jews. In most cases, neither spouse in such a marriage converts, and research indicates that it is highly unlikely that their children will identify as Jews. Thus, one of the great ironies of the liberty offered to the Jewish people by democratic secular societies is the freedom to leave Judaism as well as to affirm it.

JEWISH FEMINISM

In contrast to the option of leaving Judaism, some feminists are coming back to religious observance, but not in the traditional mold, which they regard as patriarchal and sexist. Since the mid-twentieth century, women have taken an active role in claiming their rights to full religious participation—for instance, to be counted as part of a *minyan*, to be called up to read from the Torah, and to be ordained as rabbis. They are also redefining Judaism from a feminist perspective. Part of this effort involves trying to reconstruct the history of significant biblical women, for the Torah was written down by men who devoted far more space to the doings of men than of women. There are hints, for instance, that there were powerful prophetesses, such as Miriam and Huldah, but little information is given about them. There have also been post-biblical women scholars, writers, and teachers, women who supported synagogues and Jewish publications from their earnings as businesswomen, and women who were active in social reform, and their stories and names are being uncovered.

In the past half-century, Jewish feminists have also tackled liturgical issues, changing language to gender-neutral and gender-inclusive terms for worshipers and for God. The Hebrew scriptures describe God as both female and male, validating translations from the Hebrew that use gender-neutral language. There was initial resistance and even shock over feminists' attempts to replace references to God as "He" or "King." But decades after these initial attempts, Rabbi Karyn D. Kedar asks:

So did we go too far in seeking new ways of thinking about and addressing God, or not far enough? … As the metaphors become literal, our perception of God is

myreligionlab

Women in Jewish Life
ELLEN UMANSKY

Rabbi Alysa Stanton, first black female rabbi in mainstream Judaism, in the synagogue of Hebrew Union College, where she was ordained in 2009, many years after her conversion to Judaism from Christianity. She has been called to serve in a North Carolina synagogue whose president says the congregation needs someone with her magnetism, warmth, scholarship, and rapport with children and various kinds of people.

weakened, and, thus, our experience of God becomes limited. As Jewish feminists, the greatest service we can give is to call upon the poets of our generation to teach us once again that metaphor is symbolic, that God is beyond reach and can only be understood in whispers of meaning through images, and in pictures that are diverse and rich. God is "like" father and "like" mother. God is "like" king and "like" the womb. Above all, God is none of these. And beyond the metaphor of gender, God is my light, Adonai ori *(Psalms 27:1), and God is wind,* ruach Elohim merachefet *(Genesis 1:2), and God is a silent whisper,* kol damma daka *(1 Kings 19:12), and God is the shadow beneath the wings,* b'tzel kanfefecha *(Psalms 63:8).*[52]

As a result of feminist efforts, gender-neutral liturgy and women's participation in synagogue worship have become quite common in contemporary Judaism. In Reform, Conservative, and Reconstructionist synagogues, women may now be counted in the *minyan* and called up to recite blessings and read from the Torah. Many women have been ordained as rabbis, invested as cantors who lead the prayer service, and installed as presidents of synagogues as well as heads of philanthropical organizations. Many liberal congregations use prayer books with gender-neutral language. Many couples are making egalitarian commitments to each other in their wedding vows, as in this contemporary sample:

In the spirit of Jewish tradition, I will be your loving friend as you are mine. …
I will respect you and the divine image within you. May our hearts be united
forever in faith and hope. Let our home be built on Torah and loving-kindness,
rich in wisdom and reverence. May we always keep these words in our hearts
as a symbol of our eternal commitment to each other: I am my beloved's and
my beloved is mine.[53]

Reform and Conservative denominations in the United States now allow their rabbis to officiate at same-sex weddings. Even in Orthodox congregations, the Jewish Orthodox Feminist Alliance is serving as a resource "for a community constantly balancing tradition and modernity, … guided by the principle that *halakhic* Judaism offers many opportunities for observant Jewish women to enhance their ritual observance and to increase their participation in communal leadership."[54]

Having achieved considerable success in bringing about these changes, Jewish feminists are now expanding their perspective to consider global problems such as the threats of terrorist violence and ecological disaster. Since solutions to such problems will require transformation in human thinking, some Jewish feminists have turned to the ongoing process of Midrash—interpretation of the deeper meanings of traditional texts. Rabbi Tirzah Firestone reports:

I am a teacher of Jewish texts—Tanach, Chasidut, Zohar—that have a unique
power to engage and call us into discovery and wisdom. Rarely have I witnessed
more eagerness and excitement than when I invite women to enter the text itself. …
With more aplomb than ever before, today's women are entering the stories and
changing them, breaking them open to reveal the places of both wounds and
opportunity. They are seizing the chance to transform the stories that guide
our lives, and in so doing, they are rewriting the maps that determine the
paths we will travel.[55]

An example of new feminist Midrash revolves around the interwoven stories of Sarah and Hagar, the mothers of the sons of Abraham who are said to be the founders of Judaism and Islam, respectively. Rabbi Firestone explains:

> *Once intimates, Hagar and Sarah were later divided by issues of competition*
> *for prestige and honor, and the Torah offers no story of their reconciliation.*
> *The story of Hagar and Sarah and their sons lies deep in our collective unconscious*
> *and affects our beliefs about the entrenched relationship with our Arab cousins.*
> *To change the rigid story lines requires that we first collectively re-vision and*
> *humanize the story of these two women. Many female midrashists have taken up*
> *the task of plumbing their relationship. ... [In a musical exploration by Linda*
> *Hirshchhorn] they understand that to survive they must finally speak each other's*
> *name, hear each other's prayers, share each other's dream of a homeland. I have*
> *witnessed hundreds of people weeping as they hear this musical midrash, the*
> *reaching out in longing and regret of Sarah and Hagar becoming their own,*
> *the pain of the centuries and the possibility for healing alive, palpable, urgent.*[56]

There is also a feminist critique of women's position in the state of Israel. Women among the early Zionist settlers envisioned a society in which men and women would work side by side and each apply their full capabilities to the creation of a new society. Even though laws were created that supported gender equality, traditional sexual divisions of labor were perpetuated, especially once the Orthodox parties took a major role in the formation and governance of the state. However, some progress toward women's equality and empowerment is occurring within all denominations in Israel, including Orthodoxy. As in the United States, new Hebrew texts have been prepared using gender-inclusive language to refer to worshipers, adding female characters, offering new ritual opportunities for women, and incorporating gender-inclusive or gender-balanced metaphors of God (such as alternating male names for God with invocations of God as "Shekhinah"). Yet because the liturgy is in the language spoken by the people, any such changes in the traditional Hebrew texts stand out very prominently, and even secular Jews in Israel may not be comfortable with changes that seem "unnatural" to their ears.

JEWISH RENEWAL

Both men and women from varied backgrounds are being attracted to newly revitalized expressions of Jewish spirituality, and conversions to Judaism seem to be increasing. Although anti-semitism continues to flare up here and there, many non-Jews object to negative stereotyping of Jews. The Evangelical Lutheran Church in America has issued an historic public apology for the anti-Jewish writings of Martin Luther, the father of Protestant Christianity. In part, they declared:

> *We recognize in anti-Semitism a contradiction and an affront to the Gospel,*
> *a violation of our hope and calling, and we pledge this church to oppose the*
> *deadly working of such bigotry.*[57]

In post-Soviet Russia, where under Stalin Jews had been so persecuted that only a few rabbis remained in all of Russia, there are now Jewish seminaries and universities, schools, and kindergartens.

Celebrations of life-cycle events, such as this baby naming ceremony for a girl child, are bringing many Jews back to Jewish practice.

myreligi●nlab
The Ten
Commitments
MICHAEL LERNER

Contemporary Jewish renewal is not just an absence of fear. It is an active search for personal meaning in the ancient rituals and scriptures, and the creation of new rituals for our times. There are now numerous small *havurot*, or communities of Jews, who are not affiliated with any formal group but get together on a regular basis to worship and celebrate the traditions. They favor a democratic organization and personal experience, choosing what parts of the traditions to use and how. Some incorporate study groups, continuing the ancient intellectual tradition of grappling with the ethical, philosophical, and spiritual meanings of the texts. Some are bringing fresh ideas to traditional celebrations, so that they are actively transformational rather than simply matters of habit.

From highly conservative to highly liberal quarters, there are now attempts to renew the ancient messianic ideal of Judaism, that by its practice the world might be healed.

Suggested reading

Ariel, David S., *The Mystic Quest: An Introduction to Jewish Mysticism*, Northvale, New Jersey: Jason Aronson, 1988. An accessible introduction to mystical Jewish thinking.

Baskin, Judith R., ed., *Jewish Women in Historical Perspective*, Detroit: Wayne State University Press, second edition, 1998. Fifteen pioneering essays by modern scholars explore Jewish women and their activities in a variety of times and places.

Berger, Alan L., ed., *Judaism in the Modern World*, New York: New York University Press, 1994. Articles by leading contemporary Jewish scholars on facets of the changing identities and paradoxes of modern Jewry.

Cardin, Rabbi Nina Beth, *The Tapestry of Jewish Time*, Springfield, New Jersey: Behrman House, 2000. Material about Jewish festivals and life-cycle celebrations.

Encyclopedia Judaica, New York: Macmillan Press, 2006. The authoritative, multivolume reference on all aspects of Judaism, as seen from a broad spectrum of points of view.

Goldstein, Rabbi Elyse, ed., *New Jewish Feminism: Probing the Past, Forging the Future*, Woodstock, Vermont: Jewish Lights Publishing, 2009. An anthology of contemporary feminist writings from many different denominations, assessing the past and future of Jewish feminist theology, rituals, Torah interpretation, religious leadership, and gender, age, and social justice issues.

Goldstein, Rabbi Elyse, ed., *The Women's Torah Commentary: New Insights from Women Rabbis on the 54 Weekly Torah Portions*, Woodstock, Vermont: Jewish Lights Publishing, 2000. Scholarship and Midrash about portions of the Five Books of Moses drawing on women's personal perspectives.

Greenburg, Blu, *On Women and Judaism: A View from Tradition*, Philadelphia: The Jewish Publication Society of America, 1998. An intimate personal attempt to reconcile Jewish feminism and the practice of Orthodox Judaism.

Grossman, Susan and Rivka Haut, eds, *Daughters of the King: Women and the Synagogue*, Philadelphia: Jewish Publication Society, 1992. An excellent anthology of history, *halakhah*, and contemporary testimonies concerning women and synagogue participation.

Henry, Sondra and Emily Taitz, *Written out of History: Our Jewish Foremothers*, New York: Biblio Press, 1990. The stories of significant Jewish women rediscovered and placed within their historical context.

Heschel, Abraham J., *Between God and Man: An Interpretation of Judaism*, ed., Fritz A. Rothschild, New York: The Free Press, 1959. An intimate exploration of the relevance of traditional Judaism for today's world, by a great twentieth-century theologian.

Holtz, Barry, *Back to the Sources*, New York: Schocken Books, 1984. Excellent introduction to classical Jewish religious texts. Each chapter takes the reader through a step-by-step approach on how to read representative selections of the Bible, Talmud, Midrash, the Zohar, liturgical texts, and others.

Johnson, Paul, *A History of the Jews*, New York: HarperCollins, 1987. Informative, balanced, and thoughtful presentation of the many facets of the great span of Jewish history.

Lerner, Michael, *Jewish Renewal: A Path to Healing and Transformation*, New York: HarperCollins, 1994. Profound and moving analyses of why Jews left Judaism and the revitalization that is drawing them back to faith.

Levine, Hillel, *Economic Origins of Antisemitism: Poland and its Jews in the Early Modern Period*, New Haven: Yale University Press, 1991. Brilliant insights into the relationships between anti-semitic trends and failed modernization in Poland when it was home to half of the world's Jews.

Liebman, Charles S., *Religion, Democracy and Israeli Society*. The Netherlands: Harwood Academic Publishers, 1997. A case study of Israel with reference to the problems of trying to manifest the vision of a religious state, and the problems raised by religious fundamentalism in a democratic society.

Mendes-Flohr, Paul and Jehuda Reinharz, *The Jew in the Modern World: A Documentary History*, second edition, New York/Oxford: Oxford University Press, 1995. A wealth of historical documents from the seventeenth to the twentieth centuries tracing the many facets of Judaism as it encountered modernity.

Ochs, Vanessa L., *Inventing Jewish Ritual*, Philadelphia: Jewish Publication Society, 2007. Exploration of new forms of ritual appearing in popular culture in twenty-first-century America.

Plaskow, Judith, *Standing Again at Sinai: Judaism from a Feminist Perspective*, San Francisco: Harper San Francisco, 1991. Studies of all aspects of Jewish feminism, including the reconstruction of women's history, women in Israel, gender-equal God-language, sexuality in feminist religious context, and women's role in the repair of the world.

Ravitzky, Aviezer, *Messianism, Zionism, and Jewish Religious Radicalism*, Chicago: University of Chicago Press, 1996. Extensive analysis of varying Orthodox religious responses to Jewish statehood in Israel.

Robinson, George, *Essential Judaism*, New York: Pocket Books, 2000. Concise guide to Jewish beliefs, customs, and rituals.

Sarna, Jonathan D., *American Judaism*, New Haven: Yale University Press, 2004. Detailed history of the development of Judaism in the United States as the largest Jewish community in the world.

Schachter-Shalomi, Zalman, with Donald Gropman, *The First Step: A Guide for the New Jewish Spirit*, New York: Bantam Books, 1983. A modern explanation of the essence of Judaism, of special interest to non-observant Jews who want to find their way back into the faith.

Schiffman, Lawrence H., *Reclaiming the Dead Sea Scrolls: Their True Meaning for Judaism and Christianity*, New York: Doubleday, 1995. Re-examination of the Dead Sea Scrolls as clues to Jewish history.

Scholem, Gershom G., *Major Trends in Jewish Mysticism*, New York: Schocken Books, 1974. The classic scholarly work on the development of mystical Judaism.

Seltzer, Robert, *Jewish People, Jewish Thought: The Jewish Experience in History*, New York: Macmillan, 1980. An excellent, comprehensive, one-volume history of the Jewish people, with a particular emphasis on philosophy, mysticism, and religious thought.

Strassfeld, Michael, *A Book of life: Embracing Judaism as a Spiritual Practice*, Woodstock, Vermont: Jewish Lights Publishing, 2002. Jewish life presented as everyday possibilities for connecting with the sacred.

Tanakh: The Holy Scriptures, The New JPS Translation according to the Traditional Hebrew Text, Philadelphia: The Jewish Publication Society, 1988. The preferred translation of the Hebrew scriptures, in graceful and spiritually sensitive modern English.

Umansky Ellen M. and Dianne Ashton, *Four Centuries of Jewish Women's Spirituality: A Sourcebook*, Boston: Beacon Press, 1992. Firsthand accounts of the spiritual lives of a great variety of Jewish women.

Wiesel, Elie, *Night*, New York: Bantam, 1960. Short, searing memoir of a teenage boy's Holocaust experience.

Key terms

anti-semitism Although "Semitic" properly refers to Arab and other peoples as well as Jews, the term "anti-semitism" has come to be applied to expressions of prejudice against Jews in general.

apocalypse In Judaism and Christianity, the dramatic end of the present age.

Ashkenazim An ethnic grouping of the Jews that migrated first to Italy, spread throughout central and eastern Europe and thence on to the Americas.

ghetto An urban area occupied by those rejected by a society, such as quarters for Jews in some European cities.

haggadah The nonlegal part of the Talmud and Midrash.

halakhah Jewish legal decision and the parts of the Talmud dealing with laws.

Hasidism Ecstatic Jewish piety, dating from eighteenth-century Poland.

Kabbalah The Jewish mystical tradition.

kosher Ritually acceptable, applied to foods in Jewish Orthodoxy.

Messiah The "anointed," the expected king and deliverer of the Jews; a term later applied by Christians to Jesus.

Midrash The literature of delving into the Jewish Torah.

minyan The quorum of ten adult males required for Jewish communal worship.

mitzvah (plural: *mitzvot*) In Judaism, a divine commandment or sacred deed in fulfillment of a commandment.

Orthodox Judaism Observing the traditional rabbinical *halakhah*; the strictest form of Judaism.

Pentateuch The five books of Moses at the beginning of the Hebrew Bible.

rabbi Teacher; the ordained spiritual leader of a Jewish congregation.

Reform or **Liberal Judaism** Movement that began in the nineteenth century as a way of modernizing the religion and making it more accessible and open-ended.

Sabbath The day of the week set aside for rest and worship; in Judaism running from sunset Friday night to sunset Saturday night.

Sephardim An ethnic grouping of the Jews who migrated first to Spain and then to North Africa, the Americas, and back to West Asia.

Shekhinah God's presence in the world, in Judaism.

synagogue Meeting place for Jewish study and worship.

Talmud Jewish law and lore, as finally compiled in the sixth century CE.

Tanakh The Jewish scriptures.

Torah The Pentateuch; also, the whole body of Jewish teaching and law.

Zionism Movement dedicated to the establishment of a politically viable, internationally recognized Jewish state in the bibilical land of Israel.

Review questions

1. Describe the Tanakh, Torah, and Talmud, and name at least one other Jewish text, noting each text's significance in religious practice.
2. What is the significance of the term "covenant" in Jewish tradition? What are the major covenants?
3. What role has history played in the development of Jewish identity? How are historical events commemorated in religious practice? Give specific examples.

Discussion questions

1. Discuss the major branches of contemporary Judaism. What issues have led to the development of new branches? How do they differ on issues such as interpretation of sacred texts, religious practice, and women's roles?
2. Describe the evolving role of women in Judaism, as illustrated by biblical figures such as Eve and Sarah, statements about women in the Talmud and other Jewish texts, and changes in contemporary Judaism.
3. Discuss the origins of Zionism and the creation of the modern state of Israel. What are some of the key topics debated within Israel today?

Additional Internet resources

The Abraham Fund Initiatives http://www.abrahamfund.org

Articles on Jewish Studies http://jnul.huji.ac.il/rambi

Commentary Magazine http://commentarymagazine.com

Jewish Films http://www.jewishfilm.com

Jewish life http://www.myjewishlearning.com/

Jewish Links http://www.jewishlink.net

Jewish Virtual Library http://www.jewishvirtuallibrary.org

Jewish Women's Archive http://jwa.org

Jewishnet http://www.jewishnet.net

Internet Sacred Text Archive: Judaism http://www.sacred-texts.com/jud/index.htm

Tikkun Magazine http://www.tikkun.org

myreligionlab
For further activities and resources, including access to MyReligionLibrary, please visit MyReligionLab at www.myreligionlab.com

CHAPTER 9

CHRISTIANITY

"Jesus Christ is Lord"

KEY TOPICS

• HISTORICAL
EVIDENCE 298

• EVIDENCE OF THE
BIBLE 299

• THE LIFE AND
TEACHINGS OF JESUS
301

• THE EARLY CHURCH
318

• CHURCH
ADMINISTRATION 326

• INTELLECTUAL
REVIVAL AND
MONASTICISM 330

• MEDIEVAL
MYSTICISM 331

• THE PROTESTANT
REFORMATION 334

• THE ROMAN
CATHOLIC
REFORMATION 339

• LIBERAL TRENDS 340

• THE SECOND VATICAN
COUNCIL 341

• THE ORTHODOX
WORLD TODAY 342

• CENTRAL BELIEFS IN
CONTEMPORARY
CHRISTIANITY 347

• SACRED PRACTICES
349

• CONTEMPORARY
TRENDS 360

Christianity is a faith based on the life, teachings, death, and resurrection of Jesus. He was born as a Jew about 2,000 years ago in Roman-occupied Palestine. He taught for fewer than three years and was executed by the Roman government on charges of sedition. Nothing was written about him at the time, although, some years after his death, attempts were made to record what he had said and done. Yet his birth is now celebrated around the world and since the sixth century has been used as the major point from which public time is measured, even by non-Christians. The religion centered around him has more followers than any other.

In studying Christianity we will first examine what is known or inferred about the life and teachings of Jesus. We will then follow the evolution of the religion as it spread to all continents and became theologically and liturgically more complex. This process continues in the present, in which there are not one but many different versions of Christianity.

Historical evidence

There is very little historical proof of the life of Jesus, but extensive scholarly research has turned up some shreds of evidence. The Jewish historian Josephus (born in approximately 37 CE), who was captured by the Romans and then defected to their side, wrote extensively about other details of Jewish history that have been confirmed by archaeological discoveries. He made two brief references to Jesus that may have been given a positive slant by Christian copyists, but are nonetheless now regarded as proof that Jesus did exist. In addition, the *Baraitha* and *Tosefta*, supplements to the Jewish Mishnah, contain a few references to "Yeshu the Nazarene" who was said to practice "sorcery" (healings) and was "hanged."

While historical evidence of the life of Jesus is very skimpy, more is known about the milieu into which he was born. He was born as a Jew in the land of Israel, which had been subject to various foreign influences for centuries, during which it had been exposed to Egyptian, Babylonian, Persian, Hellenistic, Roman, and Parthian cultures. Though influenced by these streams, Jews also maintained their allegiance to one God and worship in the temple of Jerusalem. They were experiencing a degree of political freedom since the Maccabean revolt of 167 BCE, although the king of the Judaeans, Herod "the Great," was a half-Jew who had been installed with Roman backing. Matters of Torah interpretation were under dispute between the Sadducees and Pharisees, while a third party, the Essenes, seem to have rejected the priesthood as corrupt and engaged in ascetic practices while awaiting divine intervention and restoration of spiritual purity. Expectations of a messiah who would save the people from foreign oppression were running high. Many **apocalyptic** texts were circulating that announced the imminent end of the present age, with evil giving way to a reign of righteousness. Unrest over increased taxes and economic difficulties under Roman rule was also brewing, and would eventually spawn various urban terrorist movements and armed resistance in the countryside, such as the 66–70 CE revolt involving the Zealots and the Bar Kokhba revolt of 132–135 CE. By contrast, the Jesus movement did not advocate violence or political activism.

We do not know what Jesus, the founder of the world's largest religion, looked like. Rembrandt used a young European Jewish man as his model for this sensitive "portrait" of Jesus.

Evidence of the Bible

Many Christians feel that the true story of Jesus can be found in the Bible. Traditionally, the holy scriptures have been reverently regarded as the divinely inspired Word of God. Furthermore, in Eastern Orthodox Christianity, "the Gospel is not just Holy Scripture but also a symbol of Divine Wisdom and an image of Christ Himself."[1] Bibles used by various Christian groups are not uniform. All use a version of the Hebrew Bible called the Old Testament, which is organized differently from the Bible of the Jews, plus the twenty-seven books of the New Testament written after Jesus' earthly mission. Some Bibles also include noncanonical Jewish texts called the Apocrypha and Deuterocanonical books, such as "Maccabees" (books that purport to give the history of the Maccabean revolt, interwoven with religious allusions) and "The Wisdom of Solomon," from the long-standing "wisdom tradition" in which a sage imparts wise teachings about life.

Given the textual complexity of the Bible, some Christians have attempted to clarify what Jesus taught and how he lived, so that people might truly follow him. The field of theological study that attempts to interpret scripture is called **hermeneutics**. In Jewish tradition, rabbis developed rules for interpretation. In the late second and early third centuries CE, Christian thinkers developed two highly different approaches to biblical hermeneutics. One of these stressed the literal meanings of the texts; the other looked for allegorical rather than literal meanings. Origen, an Egyptian theologian (c.185–254 CE) who was a major proponent of the allegorical method, gave this example from the Book of Genesis:

> *When God is said to "walk in the paradise in the cool of the day" and Adam to hide himself behind a tree, I do not think anyone will doubt that these are figurative expressions which indicate certain mysteries through a semblance of history and not through actual events (Gen. 3:8).[2]*

During medieval times, allowance was made for interpreting scriptural passages in at least four ways: literal, allegorical, moral (teaching ethical principles), and heavenly (divinely inspired and mystical, perhaps unintelligible to ordinary

myreligienlab

How to Interpret Scripture
ORIGEN

thinking). This fourfold approach was later followed by considerable debate on whether the Bible should be understood on the basis of its own internal evidence or whether it should be seen through the lens of Church tradition. During the eighteenth century, critical study of the Bible from a strictly historical point of view began in western Europe. This approach, now accepted by many Protestants, Catholics, and some Orthodox, is based on the literary method of interpreting ancient writings in their historical context, with their intended audience and desired effect taken into account. In the nineteenth and twentieth centuries, emphasis shifted to questions about the process of hermeneutics, such as how to understand ancient texts that came from other cultures, how individual passages relate to the whole text, how the biblical message is conveyed through the medium of language, and how it is grasped by people in modern contexts.

Christian beliefs about the life and teachings of Jesus are especially founded on biblical texts, particularly the first four books of the New Testament, which are called the **gospels** (good news). On the whole, they seem to have been originally written about forty to sixty years after Jesus' death. They are based on the oral transmission of the stories and discourses, which may have been influenced by the growing split between Christians and Jews. The documents, thought to be pseudonymous, are given the names of Jesus' followers Matthew and John, and of the apostle Paul's companions Mark and Luke. The gospels were first written down in Greek and perhaps Aramaic, the everyday language that Jesus spoke, and then copied and translated in many different ways over the centuries. They offer a composite picture of Jesus as seen through the eyes of the Christian community.

Three of the gospels, Matthew, Mark, and Luke, are so similar that they are called the **synoptic** gospels, referring to the fact that they can be "seen together" as presenting rather similar views of Jesus' career, though they are organized somewhat differently. Most historians think that Matthew and Luke are largely based on Mark and another source called "Q." This hypothesized source would probably be a compilation of oral and written traditions. According to historical-critical analysis, the author of Mark probably put together many fragments of oral tradition in order to develop a connected narrative about Jesus' life and ministry, for the sake of propagating the faith.

The other two synoptic gospels often parallel Mark quite closely but include additional material. The gospel according to Matthew (named after one of Jesus' original disciples, a tax collector) is sometimes called a Jewish Christian gospel. It represents Jesus as a second Moses as well as the Messiah ushering in the Kingdom of Heaven, with frequent references to the Old Testament. Matthew's stories emphasize that the **Gentiles** (non-Jews) accept Jesus, whereas the Jews reject him as savior.

Luke, to whom the third gospel is attributed, is traditionally thought to have been a physician who sometimes accompanied Paul the apostle. The gospel seems to have been written with a Gentile Christian audience in mind. Luke presents Jesus' mission in universal rather than exclusively Jewish terms and accentuates the importance of his ministry to the underprivileged and lower classes.

The Gospel of John, traditionally attributed to "the disciple Jesus loved," is of a very different nature from the other three. It concerns itself less with following the life of Jesus than with seeing Jesus as the eternal Son of God, the word of God made flesh. It is seen by many scholars as being later in origin than the synoptic gospels, perhaps having been written around the end of the first century CE. By this time, there was apparently a more critical conflict between Jews who believed in Jesus as the Messiah, and the majority of Jews, who did not recognize him as the Messiah they were awaiting. The Gospel of John seems to concentrate on confirming Jesus' Messiahship, and also to reflect Greek influences, such as a dualistic distinction between light and darkness. It is also more mystical and devotional in nature than the synoptic gospels.

> *The light shines on in the dark, and the darkness has never mastered it.*
> *The Gospel of John 1:5*

Other gospels circulating in the early Christian Church were not included in the canon of the New Testament. They include magical stories of Jesus' infancy, such as an account of his making clay birds and then bringing them to life. The Gospel of Thomas, one of the long-hidden manuscripts discovered in 1945 in a grave near Nag Hammadi, Egypt, is of particular interest. Some scholars feel that its core may have been written even earlier than the canonical gospels. It contains many wise sayings of Jesus in common with the other gospels but also others which were unknown until the Nag Hammadi discovery, such as this mystical statement:

Jesus said:
I am the Light that is above them all.
I am the All,
The All came forth from me
And the All attained to me.
Cleave a (piece of) wood, I am there.
Lift up the stone and you will find Me there.[3]

Jesus is often pictured as a divine child, born in a humble stable, and forced to flee on a donkey with his parents. (Monastère Bénédictin de Keur Moussa, Senegal, Fuite en Egypte.)

The life and teachings of Jesus

It is not possible to reconstruct from the gospels a single chronology of Jesus' life nor to account for much of what happened before he began his ministry. Nevertheless, the stories of the New Testament are important to Christians as the foundation of their faith. And after extensive analysis most scholars have concluded on grounds of linguistics and regional history that many of the sayings attributed to Jesus by the gospels may be authentic.

BIRTH

According to the Christian doctrine of the **incarnation**, Jesus is the divine Son of God who "became flesh" by being conceived and born as a human being. The biblical Book of Colossians states, "In him the whole fullness of deity dwells bodily" (Colossians 2:9).

Most historians think Jesus was probably born a few years before the first year of what is now called the **Common Era**. When sixth-century Christian monks

myreligionlab

The Annunciation
LUKE

"The Nativity," Jesus' humble birth depicted in a 14th-century fresco by Giotto. (Scrovegni Chapel, Padua, Italy.)

began figuring time in relationship to the life of Jesus, they may have miscalculated slightly. Traditionally, Christians have believed that Jesus was born in Bethlehem. This detail fulfills the rabbinic interpretation of the Old Testament prophecies that the Messiah would be born in Bethlehem, the home of David the great king, and in the lineage of David. The Gospel of Matthew offers a genealogy tracing Jesus through David back to Abraham; the gospel of Luke traces his lineage all the way back to Adam, the son of God. However, some scholars suggest that Jesus was actually born in or near Nazareth, his own home town in Galilee. This region, whose name meant "Ring of the Gentiles," was not fully Jewish; it was also scorned as somewhat countrified by the rabbinic orthodoxy of Judaea.

According to the gospels, Jesus' mother was Mary, who was a virgin when she conceived him by the Holy Spirit; her husband was Joseph, a carpenter from Bethlehem. Luke states that they had to go to Bethlehem to satisfy a Roman ruling that everyone should travel to their ancestral cities for a census. When they had made the difficult journey there was no room for them in the inn, so the baby was born in a stable among the animals. He was named Jesus, which means "God saves." This well-loved birth legend exemplifies the humility that Jesus taught. According to Luke, those who came to pay their respects were poor shepherds to whom angels had appeared with the glad tidings that a Savior had been born to the people. Matthew tells instead of Magi, sages from "the east," who may have been Zoroastrians and who brought the Christ child symbolic gifts of gold and frankincense and myrrh, confirming his divine kingship and his adoration by Gentiles.

PREPARATION

No other stories are told about Jesus' childhood in Nazareth until he was twelve years old, when, according to the Gospel of Luke, he accompanied his parents on their yearly trip to Jerusalem for Passover. Left behind by mistake, he was said to have been discovered by his parents in the temple discussing the Torah with the rabbis; "all who heard him were amazed at his understanding and his answers." When scolded, he reportedly replied, "Did you not know that I must be in my Father's house?"[4] This story is used to demonstrate his sense of mission even as a boy, his knowledge of Jewish tradition, and the close personal connection between Jesus and God. In later accounts of his prayers, he spoke to God as "Abba," a very familiar Aramaic and Hebrew word for father.

The New Testament is also silent about the years of Jesus' young manhood. What is described, however, is the ministry of John the Baptist, a prophet citing Isaiah's apocalyptic prophecies of the coming Kingdom of God. He was conducting baptism in the Jordan River in preparation for the Kingdom of God.

According to all four gospels, at the age of about thirty Jesus appeared before John to be baptized. John was calling people to repent of their sins and then be spiritually purified and sanctified by immersion in the river. He felt it improper to perform this ceremony for Jesus, whom Christians consider sinless, but Jesus insisted. How can this be interpreted? One explanation is that, for Jesus, this became a ceremony of his consecration to God as the Messiah. The gospel writer reports:

> When he came up out of the water, immediately he saw the heavens opened
> and the Spirit descending upon him like a dove; and a voice came from heaven.
> "Thou art my beloved Son; with thee I am well pleased."[5]

Another interpretation is that Jesus' baptism was the occasion for John to announce publicly that the Messiah had arrived, beginning his ministry. A third interpretation is that by requesting baptism Jesus identified himself with sinful humanity. Even though he had no need for repentance and purification, he accepted baptism on behalf of all humans.

After being baptized, Jesus reportedly undertook a forty-day retreat in the desert wilderness, fasting. During his retreat, the gospel writers say he was tempted by Satan to use his spiritual power for secular ends, but he refused.

John the Baptist is said to have baptized Jesus only reluctantly, saying he was unworthy even to fasten Jesus' shoes. When he did so, the Spirit allegedly descended upon Jesus as a dove. (Painting by Esperanza Guevara, Solentiname, Nicaragua.)

MINISTRY

myreligionlab

Jesus' Ministry
Begins
MATTHEW

In John's gospel, Jesus' baptism and wilderness sojourn were followed by his gathering of the first disciples, the fisherman Simon (called Peter), Andrew (Peter's brother), James, and John (brother of James), who recognized him as the Messiah. Jesus warned his disciples that they would have to leave all their possessions and human attachments to follow him—to pay more attention to the life of the spirit than to physical comfort and wealth. This call to discipleship continues to be experienced by Christians today, and a person's response makes all the difference. The great German theologian Dietrich Bonhoeffer (1906–1945), who, opposing the Nazis, ultimately gave his life for his beliefs, wrote that to follow

From north to south, the area covered by Jesus during his ministry was no more than 100 miles. Yet his mission is now worldwide, with more followers than any other religion.

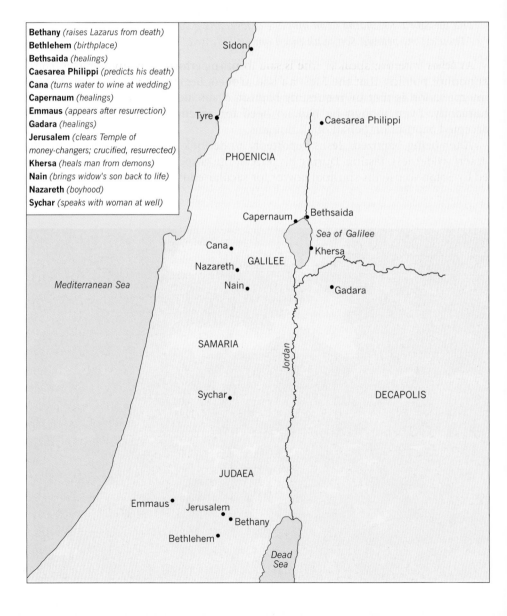

Bethany (raises Lazarus from death)
Bethlehem (birthplace)
Bethsaida (healings)
Caesarea Philippi (predicts his death)
Cana (turns water to wine at wedding)
Capernaum (healings)
Emmaus (appears after resurrection)
Gadara (healings)
Jerusalem (clears Temple of money-changers; crucified, resurrected)
Khersa (heals man from demons)
Nain (brings widow's son back to life)
Nazareth (boyhood)
Sychar (speaks with woman at well)

Sidon

Tyre

Caesarea Philippi

PHOENICIA

Capernaum Bethsaida

Sea of Galilee

Cana Khersa

Nazareth GALILEE

Nain Gadara

Mediterranean Sea

SAMARIA

Jordan

Sychar DECAPOLIS

JUDAEA

Emmaus Jerusalem

Bethany

Bethlehem

Dead Sea

Jesus one must leave worldly ties and self-centered ways of thinking behind: "Only the man who is dead to his own will can follow Christ."[6]

Jesus said that it was extremely difficult for the wealthy to enter the kingdom of heaven. God, the Protector, takes care of physical needs, which are relatively unimportant anyway:

> *Is not life more than food, and the body more than clothing? Look at the birds of the air; they neither sow nor reap nor gather into barns, and yet your heavenly Father feeds them. Are you not of more value than they? And which of you by being anxious can add one cubit to his span of life?*[7]

Jesus taught that his followers should concentrate on laying up spiritual treasures in heaven, rather than material treasures on earth, which are short-lived. Because God is like a generous parent, those who love God and want to follow the path of righteousness should pray for help, in private: "Ask, and it will be given you; seek, and you will find; knock, and it will be opened to you."[8]

As Jesus traveled, speaking, he is said to have performed many miracles, such as turning water into wine, healing the sick, restoring the dead to life, walking on water, casting devils out of the possessed, and turning a few loaves and fish into

Jesus is said to have brought Lazarus back to life four days after he died and was laid in a tomb. (Fresco by Giotto, Scrovegni Chapel, Padua, Italy.)

enough food to feed a crowd of thousands, with copious leftovers. Jesus reportedly performed these miracles quietly and compassionately; the gospels interpreted them as signs of the coming Kingdom of God.

The stories of the miracles performed by Jesus have symbolic meanings taken from the entire Jewish and early Christian traditions. In the sharing of the loaves and fishes, for instance, it may have been more than physical bread that Luke was talking about when he said, "and all ate and were satisfied."[9] The people came to Jesus out of spiritual hunger, and he fed them all, profligate with his love. Bread often signified life-giving sustenance. Jesus was later to offer himself as "the bread of life."[10] On another level of interpretation, the story may prefigure the Last Supper of Jesus with his disciples, with both stories alluding to the Jewish tradition of the Great Banquet, the heavenly feast of God, as a symbol of the messianic age. The fish were a symbol of Christ to the early Christians; what he fed them was the indiscriminate gift of himself.

Theological interpretations of the biblical stories are based on the evidence of the Bible itself, but people also bring their own experiences to them. To William, a twentieth-century Nicaraguan peasant, the miracle was not the multiplication of the loaves but the sharing: "The miracle was to persuade the owners of the bread to share it, that it was absurd for them to keep it all while the people were going hungry."[11]

Jesus preached and lived by truly radical ethics. In contrast to the prevailing patriarchal society and extensive proscriptions against impurity, lepers and a bleeding woman touched him and were healed. In his inclusive "table fellowship," he ate with people of all sorts, including those designated as impure by Jewish law in order to preserve temple purity. These marginalized people included all women because of menstruation and childbirth, most poor and uneducated people because they could not understand or observe the laws of purity, as well as the sick, blind, deformed, lame, people with skin diseases and secretions, people who earned their living in ways that were regarded as sinful or polluting, and Gentiles, for they were not worshipers of the God of Israel. Feminist scholar Rosemary Radford Ruether explains that the Jesus movement brought:

> the joyful good news that these separations had been overcome in an overflowing graciousness of God. All these would be collectively referred to by the Jesus movement simply as "the poor," a group whose deprivation was of many kinds, but united in their "unholy" status vis-à-vis "the righteous." The liberation that Jesus expressed was not that of a military uprising, a political campaign, or a strategy for economic or social change, but an immediately experienced liberation of the blind, the lame, lepers, those with bodily fluxes, those possessed by demons that caused madness and "fits," all those healed and restored to mental and physical health; also the "sinners," the prostitutes, tax collectors, and various impoverished people, all affirmed as God's beloved children.[12]

In a culture in which the woman's role was strictly circumscribed, Jesus welcomed women as his disciples. Mary Magdalene, Mary the mother of James the younger and Joses, Salome the mother of the disciples James and John, Mary of Bethany, Martha, Susanna, and Joanna are among those mentioned in the gospels. Some of them traveled with Jesus and even helped to support him and his disciples financially, a great departure from orthodox Jewish tradition. In

myreligionlab

The Last Supper
MARK

An Interview with David Vandiver

 Born into a devout small-town Southern Baptist family, David Vandiver became the manager of a wilderness camp in the Appalachian Mountains near Washington, D.C., for inner-city African American children whose backgrounds were very different from his own. Now he and his wife and daughters are living in voluntary simplicity in rural Maine, trying to maximize their family time and minimize their impact on the environment. Here he describes the evolution of his understanding and practice of Christianity, and his hope for its future:

"The primary values as I grew up were ones of honesty, fairness, and caring for others. The great sins were the ones most affecting families—divorce, adultery, and irresponsible parenting. It was not until much later in my life that the vast scope of values held by Christians in differing places in the world came to my attention. I was not aware, for example, that there were Christians who believed God wanted them to influence politics for justice, work for equal rights for all people, protect the natural environment, or make peace with other nations and peoples of differing faiths. We had no cause to practice tolerance because we were all so similar, except for the African Americans in our town—about twenty percent of the population—who were already Christian and from whom we, as Anglo-Americans, wished to stay separated. I grew up with racism all around me.

"Nonetheless, as a high school youth in the early 1970s, I joined my friends in dragging my church into the foray of the U.S. Civil Rights Movement because I couldn't see Jesus as one who would keep any group of people powerless and poor. Christianity was a voice for the downtrodden and oppressed of the world, and if I was to follow Jesus, I would have to take up their cause for justice in some way.

"The most accessible way for me to take up this cause was to enter an educational path that would lead to a paid vocation as a Christian minister. In my studies I began to consider the teachings of Jesus the Christ more deeply. What did it mean to 'love my neighbor as myself'? In practical terms, it came to mean that I could not simply spend the rest of my life pursuing a comfortable living while ignoring the

fact that millions are living in poverty and oppression. I saw that following Jesus would take me out of the mainstream of the world in order to love it fully. On the other hand, I was painfully aware of the impossibility of loving others unconditionally.

"Vocationally and geographically, I found a home as the manager of a wilderness camp for inner-city children from Washington. Many of the children who came to our camp had never been out of the city. As I watched and listened to them entering this environment that was foreign to them, they became my teachers, helping me to understand the fears with which they faced the wilderness, and the fears they confronted at home in the city. I was reminded of how I grew up, unaware of the larger world around me. I worked to help them find the tools that would assist them in loving their enemies, abusers, oppressors, and those who ignore them.

"Now I have become a minister due to a growing sense of historical urgency. Evidence has accumulated that our planet is reaching carrying capacities for population, atmospheric carbon, and extraction of certain resources such as petroleum. As Rob McCall, our local Congregational minister says, 'If we ignore the laws of Mother Nature, she will sweep up our species, hair and bone, with neither malice nor discrimination, and we will inhabit this world no more.' The suffering resulting from our greed-based decision-making is already real, both for the rich and the poor.

"I am turning my energies toward the contributions that could be made by a healthy faith. Since the Protestant Reformation, Western Christianity has become increasingly focused on the individual. We have an underdeveloped ability to make life-affirming decisions as a group. In the North American context of gross overconsumption, the time has come for a new Reformation that would recover—among other things—widespread respect for the laws of nature. Christianity can make a great contribution, but alone could never bring the changes necessary to change life. An unprecedented level of mutual understanding between all faiths, each one enriching respect for life, is being called forth.

"As for my civil rights experiences, I now see them as an example of how the whole world needs to operate, judging all species as worthy of dignity and respect. My faith supports that."

addition, wives of some of the married men among Jesus' first disciples apparently accompanied them as they traveled with Jesus (1 Corinthians 9:5). His was a radically egalitarian vision.

He also extended the application of Jewish laws: "You have heard that it was said to the men of old," Jesus began, "You shall not kill; and whoever kills shall be liable to judgment. But I say to you that every one who is angry with his brother shall be liable to judgment."[13] Not only should a man not commit adultery; it is wrong even to look at a woman lustfully. Rather than taking revenge with an eye for an eye, a tooth for a tooth, respond with love. If a person strikes you on one cheek, turn the other cheek to be struck also. If anyone tries to rob you of your coat, give him your cloak as well. And not only should you love your neighbor, Jesus says:

> Love your enemies and pray for those who persecute you, so that you may be sons of your Father who is in heaven; for he makes his sun rise on the evil and on the good, and sends rain on the just and on the unjust.[14]

The extremely high ethical standards of the Sermon on the Mount (Matthew 5–7) may seem impossibly challenging. Who can fully follow them? And Jesus said these things to people who had been brought up with the understanding that to fulfill incompletely even one divine commandment is a violation of the Law. But when people recognize their helplessness to fulfill such commandments, they are ready to turn to the divine for help. Jesus pointed out, "With man this is impossible, but not with God; all things are possible with God."[15]

TEACHING STORY

The Good Samaritan

On one occasion a lawyer came forward to put this test question to Jesus: "Master, what must I do to inherit eternal life?" Jesus said, "What is written in the Law? What is your reading of it?" He replied, "Love the Lord your God with all your heart, with all your soul, with all your strength, and with all your mind; and your neighbor as yourself." "That is the right answer," said Jesus; "do that and you will live."

But he wanted to vindicate himself, so he said to Jesus, "And who is my neighbor?" Jesus replied, "A man was on his way from Jerusalem down to Jericho when he fell in with robbers, who stripped him, beat him, and went off leaving him half dead. It so happened that a priest was going down by the same road; but when he saw him, he went past on the other side. So too a Levite came to the place, and when he saw him went past on the other side. But a Samaritan [a person from a region against whom the Jews of Judaea had developed religious and racial prejudice] who was making the journey came upon him, and when he saw him was moved to pity. He went up and bandaged his wounds, bathing them with oil and wine. Then he lifted him on to his own beast, brought him to an inn, and looked after him there. Next day he produced two silver pieces and gave them to the innkeeper, and said, 'Look after him; and if you spend any more, I will repay you on my way back.' Which of these three do you think was neighbor to the man who fell into the hands of the robbers?" He answered, "The one who showed him kindness." Jesus said, "Go and do as he did."[16]

The main thing Jesus taught was love. He stated that to love God and to "love your neighbor as yourself"[17] were the two great commandments in Judaism, upon which everything else rested. To love God means placing God first in one's life, rather than concentrating on the things of the earth. To love one's neighbor means selfless service to everyone, even to those despised by the rest of society. Jesus often horrified the religious authorities by talking to sinful prostitutes and tax-collectors, and the poorest and lowliest of people. He set an example of loving service by washing his disciples' feet. This kind of love, he said, should be the mark of his followers, and at the Last Judgment, when the Son of Man judges the people of all time, he will grant eternal life in the kingdom to the humble "sheep" who loved and served him in all:

> *Then the righteous will answer him, "Lord, when did we see thee hungry and feed thee, or thirsty and give thee drink? And when did we see thee a stranger and welcome thee, or naked and clothe thee? And when did we see thee sick or in prison and visit thee?" And the King will answer them, "Truly, I say to you, as you did it to one of the least of these my brethren, you did it to me."[18]*

Jesus preached that God is forgiving to those who repent. He told a story likening God to the father who welcomed with gifts and celebration his "prodigal son" who had squandered his inheritance and then humbly returned home. He told story after story suggesting that those who considered themselves superior were more at odds with God than those who were aware of their sins. Those who sincerely repent—even if they are the hated toll-collectors, prostitutes, or ignorant common people—are more likely to receive God's forgiveness than are the learned and self-righteous. Indeed, Jesus said, it was only in childlikeness that people could enter the kingdom of heaven. In a famous series of statements about supreme happiness called the **Beatitudes**, Jesus is quoted as promising blessings for the "poor in spirit,"[19] the mourners, the meek, the seekers of righteousness, the pure in heart, the merciful, the peacemakers, and those who are persecuted for the sake of righteousness and of spreading the gospel.

myreligionlab
The Beatitudes
MATTHEW

Jesus' stories were typically presented as **parables**, in which earthly situations familiar to people of his time and place were used to make a spiritual point. He spoke of parents and children, of masters and servants, of sowing seeds, of fishing. But even though the subject matter was familiar, the outcomes often contained paradoxes that turned conventional thinking upside-down. For example:

> *The kingdom of heaven is like treasure hidden in a field,*
> *which someone found and hid; then in his joy he goes and sells*
> *all that he has and buys that field.*

[Matthew 13:44]

Such radical teachings about what is of true value were not easy for wealthy people to embrace. To give up everything for a life of surrender to God flies in the face of conventional value placed on earning and acquiring.

As we have seen, messianic expectations were running very high among Jews of that time, oppressed as they were by Roman rule. They looked to a time when the people of Israel would be freed and the authority of Israel's God would be recognized throughout the world. Jesus reportedly spoke to them again and again about the fulfillment of these expectations: "The time is fulfilled, and the kingdom of God is at hand; repent, and believe in the gospel"[20]; "I must preach the good news of the kingdom of God … for I was sent for this purpose."[21] He taught them to pray for the advent of this kingdom: "Thy kingdom come, Thy will be done on earth as it is in heaven."[22] However, in contrast to expectations of secular deliverance from the Romans, Jesus seems to refer to the kingdom as a manifestation of God's full glory, the consummation of the world.

> *Every one who drinks of this water will thirst again, but whoever drinks of the water that I shall give him will never thirst; the water that I shall give him will become in him a spring of water welling up to eternal life.*
>
> *Jesus, as quoted in the Gospel of John 4:13–14*

Jesus' references to the kingdom, as reported in the gospels, indicate two seemingly different emphases: one that the kingdom is expected in the future, and the other that the kingdom is already here. In his future references, as in the apocalyptic Jewish writings of the time, Jesus said that things would get much worse right before the end. He seemed to foretell the destruction of Jerusalem by the Romans that began in 70 CE. But:

> *then will appear the sign of the Son of man in heaven, and then all the tribes of the earth will mourn, and they will see the Son of man coming on the clouds of heaven with power and great glory; and he will send out his angels with a loud trumpet call, and they will gather his elect from the four winds, from one end of heaven to the other.*[23]

It was his mission, he said, to gather together everyone who could be saved.

CHALLENGES TO THE AUTHORITIES

As Jesus traveled through Galilee, many people gathered around him to be healed. Herod Antipas, a Jew who had been appointed by the Romans as ruler of Galilee, had already executed John the Baptist and may have been concerned that Jesus might be a troublemaker, perhaps one of the Zealots of Galilee who were stirring up support for a political uprising against the Romans. Jesus therefore moved outside Herod's jurisdiction for a while, to carry on his work in Tyre and Sidon (now in Lebanon).

According to the gospels, Jesus was also regarded with suspicion by prominent Jewish groups of his time—the emerging **Pharisees** (the shapers of rabbinic Judaism), **Sadducees** (the temple priests and upper class), and the scribes (specially trained laymen who copied the written law and formulated the oral law of Judaism). Jesus seems not to have challenged Mosaic law but, rather, its interpretations in the evolving rabbinic traditions and the hypocrisy of some of those who claimed to be living by the law. It is written in the Gospel of Matthew that the Pharisees and scribes challenged Jesus' disciples for not washing their hands before eating. Jesus responded:

Christianity

c.4 BCE–0 CE	Jesus born
c.27–33 CE	Jesus crucified
c.37–100	Josephus
c.50–60	St. Paul organizes early Christians
c.70–95	Gospels written down
c.150	Last of New Testament writings
c.185–254	Life of Origen, who supports allegorical interpretation of Bible
306–337	Constantine emperor of Roman Empire
325	Nicene Creed; Council of Nicaea affirms divinity of Jesus
354–430	Life of St. Augustine, influential formulator of Christian doctrines
379–395	Christianity becomes state religion under rule of Emperor Theodosius
c.480–542	Life of St. Benedict and creation of his monastic rule
800–1300	Middle Ages in Europe; centralization of papal power
1054	Split between Western and Eastern Orthodox Church
1182–1226	Life of St. Francis of Assisi
1225–1274	Thomas Aquinas
1232	The Inquisitions begin suppressing and punishing heretics
1300s	Proliferation of monastic orders
1412–1431	Joan of Arc
1453	Gutenberg Bible published
1478	Spanish Inquisition set up
1509–1564	Life of John Calvin
1517	Martin Luther posts ninety-five theses; Protestantism begins
1534	Church of England separates from Rome
1545–1563	The Council of Trent; Roman Catholic Reformation
1624–1691	Life of George Fox, English founder of Quakers
1703–1791	Life of John Wesley, founder of Methodist Church
c.1720–1780	The Enlightenment in Europe
1859	Charles Darwin's *On the Origin of Species* challenges beliefs in creation by God
1906–1909	Asuza Street Revival
1945	Discovery of the Nag Hammadi manuscripts
1947	First Dead Sea Scrolls discovered
1948	World Council of Churches formed
1962–1965	The Second Vatican Council
1988	Churches reopened in Russian Federation
2000	Pope John Paul II asks forgiveness for sins of the Roman Catholic Church
2002	Boston's Roman Catholic bishop resigns in growing scandal over sexual abuse by priests; seven women claim ordination as Roman Catholic priests
2005	Pope Benedict XVI's papacy inaugurated

*"What goes into the mouth does not make a man unclean; it is what comes
out of the mouth that makes him unclean. ..."[24]*

*"Alas for you, scribes and Pharisees, you hypocrites! You who are like
whitewashed tombs that look handsome on the outside, but inside are full
of dead men's bones and every kind of corruption. In the same way you
appear to people from the outside like good honest men, but inside you
are full of hypocrisy and lawlessness."[25]*

Despite such critical remarks about the Pharisees appearing in the New
Testament, scholars have noted many similarities between Pharisees and the
beliefs of early Christians. For instance, the Pharisees did not see God as belonging only to Israel, but rather as the parent watching over, and taking care of,
every individual. They addressed God by new names, such as *Abinu she-
Bashamayim* ("Our Father Who art in Heaven"), the same form of address by
which Jesus reportedly taught his followers to pray to God (Matthew 6:9).

Many seemingly anti-Jewish statements in the New Testament are suspected
by some modern scholars to be additions or interpretations dating from the
period after Jesus' death, when rabbinic Judaism and early Christianity were
competing for followers. Nevertheless, more universal teachings are apparent in
such stories attributed to Jesus. For instance, in all times and all religions there
have been those who do not practice what they preach when claiming to speak
with spiritual authority.

Jesus is said to have also confronted the commercial interests in the Temple of
Jerusalem, those who were making a living by charging a profit when exchang-
ing money for temple currency and selling animals for sacrificial offerings:

*So they reached Jerusalem and he went into the Temple and began driving
out those who were selling and buying there; he upset the tables of the money
changers and the chairs of those who were selling pigeons. Nor would he allow
anyone to carry anything through the Temple. And he taught them and said,
"Does not scripture say; 'My house will be called a house of prayer for all the
peoples?'[26] But you have turned it into a robbers' den."[27] This came to the ears
of the chief priests and the scribes, and they tried to find some way of doing
away with him; they were afraid of him because the people were carried
away by his teaching.[28]*

According to the gospel accounts, Jesus appropriated to himself the messianic
prophecies of Second Isaiah. It is written that he privately asked his disciples, "Who
do you say that I am?" Peter answered, "You are the Christ."[29] "Christ" is Greek for
"anointed one," a translation of the Aramaic word *M'shekha* or **Messiah**, which
also means "perfected" or "enlightened one." His disciples later spoke of him as the
Messiah after he died and was resurrected. And his follower Martha, sister of
Lazarus whom Jesus reportedly raised from the dead, is quoted as having said to
Jesus, "I now believe that you are the Messiah, the Son of God who was to come
into the world."[30] Some contemporary biblical scholars have concluded, however,
that Jesus rejected the title of Messiah, for it might have been misunderstood.

According to the gospel tradition, a transcendental phenomenon, the
"Transfiguration," was witnessed by three disciples. Jesus had climbed a mountain to pray, and as he did:

He was transfigured before them, and his face shone like the sun, and his
garments became white as light. And behold, there appeared to them Moses
and Elijah, talking with him. … When lo, a bright cloud overshadowed them,
and a voice from the cloud said, "This is my beloved Son, with whom I am
well pleased; listen to him."[31]

The presence of Moses and Elijah (who in Jewish apocalyptic tradition were expected to return at the end of the world) placed Jewish law and prophecy behind the claim that Jesus is the Christ. They were representatives of the old covenant with God, by which the Jewish people agreed to obey the laws of God and to regard God as their sole ruler. Jesus brought a new dispensation of grace.

Jesus claimed that John the Baptist was Elijah come again. The authorities had killed John the Baptist, and, Jesus prophesied, they would attack him, too, not recognizing who he was. John quotes Jesus as saying things like "My teaching is not mine, but his who sent me"; "I am the light of the world"; "You are from below, I am from above; you are of this world, I am not of this world"; and "Before Abraham was, I am."[32] Jesus characterized himself as a good shepherd who is willing to lay down his life for his sheep. Foreshadowing the **Crucifixion**, he said he would offer his own flesh and blood as a sacrifice for the sake of humanity. His coming death would mark a "new covenant" in which his blood would be "poured out for many for the forgiveness of sins."[33]

It is possible that such passages defining Jesus' role were later interpolations by the early Christians as they tried to explain the meaning of their Master's life and death in new terms during the decades when the New Testament was in the process of formation.

CRUCIFIXION

The anti-institutional tenor of Jesus' teachings did not endear him to those in power, who were wary of incipient revolts. Jesus knew that to return to Jerusalem would be politically dangerous. But eventually he did so, at Passover. He reportedly entered the town in a humble way, riding on a donkey and accompanied by supporters who waved palm branches and announced him as the Messiah, crying:

"Hosanna! Blessed be he who comes in the name of the Lord! Blessed be
the kingdom of our father David that is coming! Hosanna in the highest!"[34]

However, Jesus warned his disciples that his end was near. At the Last Supper, a Jewish Seder meal during the Passover season, he is said to have given them instructions for a ceremony with bread and wine to be performed thenceforth to maintain an ongoing communion with him. However, one of the disciples would betray him, he said. This one, Judas, had already done so, selling information leading to Jesus' arrest for thirty pieces of silver.

Jesus took three of his followers to a garden called Gethsemane, on the Mount of Olives, where he is said to have prayed intensely that the cup of suffering would pass away from him, if it be God's will, "yet not what I will, but what thou wilt."[35] The gospels often speak of Jesus' spending long periods in spontaneous prayer addressing God very personally as "Abba." It is possible to interpret Jesus'

*At the Last Supper, Jesus foretold his death and instructed his disciples to maintain mystical communion with him through a ceremony with bread and wine. (*The Last Supper, *attributed to Francisco Henriques, fl. 1500–1518 [detail].)*

prayer at Gethsemane as a confirmation of his great faith in God's mercy and power. In the words of New Testament theologian Joachim Jeremias:

> *Jesus takes into account the possibility that God may rescind his own holy will … The Father of Jesus is not the immovable, unchangeable God who in the end can only be described in negations. He is not a God to whom it is pointless to pray. He is a gracious God, who hears prayers and intercessions, and is capable in his mercy of rescinding his own holy will.*[36]

Nevertheless, after this period of prayer Jesus said, according to Mark's gospel, "It is all over. The hour has come."[37] A crowd including Judas approached with swords and clubs; they led Jesus away to be questioned by the chief priest, elders, and scribes.

All four gospels include "**passion narratives**" describing Jesus' sufferings during his betrayal, trial, and execution by crucifixion. Matthew and Mark report a hearing before the high priest, Joseph Caiaphas. According to the Gospel of Matthew, the high priest asked Jesus if he was the Messiah, the Son of God. Jesus reportedly answered:

> *You have said so. But I tell you, hereafter you will see the Son of man seated at the right hand of Power, and coming on the clouds of heaven.*[38]

Caiaphas pronounced this statement blasphemy, meaning attributing divinity to oneself and thus showing a lack of reverence for God, a crime punishable by death according to Jewish law. However, under Roman occupation the Sanhedrin (supreme Jewish court made up of chief priests, elders, and law teachers) was forbidden to pass the death sentence. Therefore Jesus was taken to Pontius Pilate, the Roman governor, for sentencing. To Pilate's leading question, "Are you King of the Jews?" Jesus is said to have replied, "You have said so."[39] According to the biblical accounts, Pilate seems to prefer to let Jesus off with a flogging, for he sees no reason to sentence him to death. Nevertheless, the crowd demands that he be killed on the grounds that he is a challenger to the earthly king, Caesar. The Gospel of John reports extraordinary dialogues between Pilate and Jesus as the crowd clamors for his execution. For instance, according to the Gospel of John, Pilate asks Jesus, "What have you done?" and Jesus reportedly replies:

myreligionlab
The Crucifixion
MARK

> My kingdom does not belong to this world. My kingly authority comes from elsewhere." "You are a king then?" said Pilate. Jesus answered, "King is your word. My task is to bear witness to the truth. For this was I born; for this I came into the world, and all who are not deaf to truth listen to my voice." Pilate said, "What is truth?" and with those words went out again to the Jews.[40]

At last, unable to pacify Jesus' critics, Pilate turns him over to his military guard for execution by crucifixion, a form of death by torture widely used within the Roman Empire. In this method, the victim was typically tortured or beaten brutally with whips and then hung or nailed onto a wooden cross to die as a hideous example to intimidate the public. The guards put a crown made of thorns

Jesus' crucifixion was interpreted by many later Christians as the sacrifice of an innocent lamb as atonement for the sins of humanity. Another interpretation was that God gave "himself or herself" in love, drawing the world into a loving relationship with the divine. (Rembrandt, The Three Crosses, 1653.)

on Jesus' head and paraded him and his cross to the hill called Golgotha ("Place of the Skull"). It was probably used frequently for such executions. The accusation—"This is Jesus, King of the Jews"—was set over his head, and two robbers were crucified alongside him. The authorities, the people, and even the robbers (one of them, at least, according to Luke) mocked him for saying that he could save others when he could not even save himself.

Jesus hung there for hours until, according to the gospels, he cried out, "My God, my God, why hast thou forsaken me?"[41] This is the first line of Psalm 22, which is actually a great proclamation of the faith in God of one who is persecuted. Then Jesus died. This event is thought to have happened on a Friday some time between 27 and 33 CE. A wealthy Jewish disciple named Joseph of Arimathea asked Pilate for Jesus' body, which Joseph wrapped in a linen shroud and placed in his own tomb, with a large stone against the door. A guard was placed at the tomb to make sure that no followers would steal the body and claim that Jesus had risen from the dead.

RESURRECTION AND ASCENSION

That seemed to be the end of it. Jesus' disciples were terrified, so some of them hid, mourning and disheartened. The whole religious movement could have died out, as did other messianic cults. However, what is reported next in varying gospel accounts seemed to change everything. Some of the women who had been close to Jesus and had traveled with him from Galilee—Mary Magdalene, plus, according to different gospels, Mary mother of James, Joanna, Salome, and perhaps others—visited the tomb on Sunday to prepare the body for a proper burial, a rite that had been postponed because of the Sabbath. Instead, they found the tomb empty, with the stone rolled away. Angels then appeared and told them that Jesus had risen from death. The women ran and brought two of the male disciples, who witnessed the empty tomb with the shroud folded.

Then followed numerous reports of appearances of the risen Christ to various disciples. He dispelled their doubts about his **Resurrection**, having them touch his wounds and even eating a fish with them. He said to them, as recounted in the Gospel of Matthew:

> *All authority in heaven and on earth has been given to me. Go therefore and make disciples of all nations, baptizing them in the name of the Father and of the Son and of the Holy Spirit, teaching them to observe all that I have commanded you; and lo, I am with you always, to the close of the age.*[42]

The details of the appearances of the resurrected Jesus differ considerably from gospel to gospel. However, some scholars think that to have women as the first witnesses to the empty tomb suggests that there must be some historical truth in the claims of Jesus' Resurrection, for no one trying to build a case would have rested it on the testimony of women, who had little status in a patriarchal society. Feminist scholar Elisabeth Schüssler Fiorenza finds deep meaning in the presence of women disciples at the time of Jesus' death and resurrection:

> *Whereas according to Mark the leading male disciples do not understand this suffering messiahship of Jesus, reject it, and finally abandon him, the women*

myreligienlab
The Resurrection
MARK

disciples who have followed Jesus from Galilee to Jerusalem suddenly emerge as the true disciples in the passion narrative. They are Jesus' true followers who have understood that his ministry was not rule and kingly glory but diakonia, *"service" (Mark 15:41). Thus the women emerge as the true Christian ministers and witnesses. The unnamed woman who names Jesus with a prophetic sign-action in Mark's Gospel [by anointing him as a sign that she recognized him as the Messiah] is the paradigm for the true disciple. While Peter had confessed, without truly understanding it, "you are the anointed one," the woman anointing Jesus recognizes clearly that Jesus' messiahship means suffering and death.*[43]

It was the Resurrection that turned defeat into victory for Jesus, and discouragement into hope for his followers. As the impact of all they had seen set in, the followers came to believe that Jesus had been God present in a human life, walking among them. According to the book of Acts of the Apostles, Peter later accused the Israelites of having Jesus killed, but pointed to the greater power of God, who raised him from the dead. Jesus was no longer seen as a victim but a victor. The Resurrection became the basis for the Christian hope of salvation through belief in Jesus. Peter explained:

This Jesus is the stone that was rejected by you,
*   the builders;*
It has become the cornerstone.
There is salvation in no one else,
For there is no other name under heaven given
*   among mortals by which we must be saved.*[44]

According to two gospel accounts, after the resurrected Jesus appeared to his disciples, encouraging them to carry the gospel to the whole world, he ascended into heaven. The end of the gospel of Mark, which is thought to be a later addition to the chapter, adds, "and sat down at the right hand of God" (Mark 16:19). Some Christians believe that Jesus miraculously ascended bodily into the highest heaven, an invisible realm in the sky where God is sitting with Jesus beside him, as an advocate for his faithful followers. Whether understood metaphorically or literally, the **Ascension** is an article of Christian faith. It is further extended in the Acts of the Apostles into belief that Jesus will return bodily to the earth in the future:

As they were watching, he was lifted up, and a cloud took him out of their sight. While he was going and they were gazing up toward heaven, suddenly two

Books of the New Testament

Gospels
Matthew
Mark
Luke
John

The Acts of the Apostles

The Letters of Paul
Romans
1 and 2 Corinthians
Galatians
Ephesians*
Philippians
Colossians*
1 and 2* Thessalonians
1 and 2 Timothy*
Titus*
Philemon

The General Epistles
Hebrew
James
1 and 2 Peter
1, 2, and 3 John
Jude

Revelation

*Scholars question whether these letters were written by Paul or by others using his name as a pseudonym, in the custom of the times.

men in white robes stood by them. They said, "Men of Galilee, why do you stand looking up toward heaven? This Jesus, who has been taken up from you into heaven, will come in the same way as you saw him go into heaven."[45]

Jesus' Resurrection and Ascension give rise to the Christian belief in life after death for those who believe in God. Greek Orthodox Professor Christos Yannaras explains:

Many religions and philosophies proclaim the 'immortality of the soul,' but the Church is differentiated from all these, because she understands immortality, not as an uninterpreted form of 'survival' after death, but as a transcendence of death by means of the relationship with God. Death is, for the Church, separation from God, the denial of the relationship with Him, the refusal of life as love and intimate communion. … Faith in eternity is the trust that this love will not stop but will always constitute my life whether my psychosomatic capacities function or do not function.[46]

The early Church

Testing their faith, persecution became the lot of Jesus' followers. But by 380 CE, despite strong opposition, Christianity became the official religion of the vast Roman Empire. As it became the establishment, rather than a tiny, scattered band of dissidents within Judaism, Christianity continued to define and organize itself.

FROM PERSECUTION TO EMPIRE

The earliest years of what became the mainstream of Christianity are described in the New Testament books that follow the gospel accounts of the life of Jesus. "The Acts of the Apostles" was presumably written by the same person who wrote the Gospel of Luke, and Acts refers back to the Gospel of Luke as an earlier part of a single history of the rise of Christianity. Acts is followed by letters to some of the early groups of Christians, most of them apparently written by Paul, a major organizer and **apostle** (missionary), in about 50 to 60 CE.

Like the gospel accounts, the stories in these biblical books are examined by many contemporary scholars as possibly romanticized, idealized documents, used to convert, to increase faith, to teach principles, and to establish Christian theology, rather than to accurately record historical facts.

According to Acts, an event called **Pentecost** galvanized the early Christians into action. At a meeting of the disciples, something that sounded like a great wind came down from the sky, and what looked like tongues of fire swirled around to touch each one's head. The narrative states that they all began speaking in different languages, so that all who listened could understand in their own language. Some mocked them, saying they were drunk, but Peter declared that they had been filled with the Spirit of God, as the Old Testament prophet Joel had prophesied would happen in the last days before the onset of the kingdom of God. He testified that the Jesus whom the people had crucified had been raised up by God, who had made him "both Lord and Christ."[47] Reportedly, 3,000 people were so convinced that they were baptized that day.

One of the persecutors of Christians was Saul. He was a Pharisee tentmaker who lived during the time of Jesus but never met him. Instead, after Jesus died, he helped to throw many of his followers into prison and sentence them to death. Acts relates that on the way to Damascus in search of more heretics, he saw a light brighter than the sun and heard the voice of Jesus asking why Saul was persecuting him. This resistance was useless, said the vision of Jesus, who then appointed him to do the opposite—to go to both Jews and Gentiles:

> to open their eyes, that they may turn from darkness to light and from the power of Satan to God, that they may receive forgiveness of sins and a place among those who are sanctified by faith in me.[48]

This meeting with the risen Christ, and through him, God, was an utterly transformational experience for Saul. He wrote about his previous life:

> I count everything sheer loss, because all is so far outweighed by the gain of knowing Christ Jesus my Lord, for whose sake I did in fact lose everything. I count it so much garbage, for the sake of gaining Christ and finding myself incorporate in him, with no righteousness of my own, no legal rectitude, but the righteousness which comes from faith in Christ, given by God in response to faith. All I care for is to know Christ.[49]

Saul was baptized and immediately began promoting the Christian message under his new name, Paul. His indefatigable work in traveling around the Mediterranean was of great importance in shaping and expanding the early Christian Church. He was shipwrecked, stoned, imprisoned, and beaten, and probably died as a martyr in Rome, but nothing short of death deterred him from his new mission.

Paul tried to convince Jews that Jesus' birth, death, and Resurrection had been predicted by the Old Testament prophets. This was the Messiah they had been waiting for, and now, risen from death, he presided as the cosmic Christ, offering God's forgiveness and grace to those who repented and trusted in God rather than in themselves. Some Jews were converted to this belief, and the Jewish authorities repeatedly accused Paul of leading people away from Jewish law and tradition. There was a major difference between Jews and Christians over the central importance given to Jesus. It is possible that Jesus himself may not have claimed that he was the Messiah, and that it was Paul who developed this claim. To this day, Jews tend to feel that to put heavy emphasis on the person of Jesus takes attention away from Jesus' message and from God.

myreligionlab
Paul's Conversion
ACTS

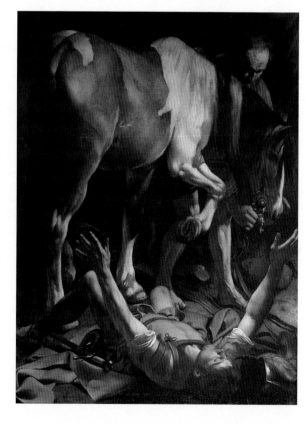

Caravaggio's painting, The Conversion of St. Paul, *focuses on the light falling on Paul, a spiritual experience that totally transformed his life.*

myreligienlab
Paul's letters to
the new Christian
churches

In Paul's time, those Jews who emphasized that Jews had been especially chosen by God were offended by interpretations of Jesus' life and teachings that saw Christianity as a universal mission of salvation for all peoples. These interpretations made the new sect, Christianity, seem irreconcilable with exclusive versions of Judaism, and the gap between the two became deep and bitter. The New Testament writings reflect the criticisms of the early Christians against the large Jewish majority who did not accept Jesus as their Messiah. Only in Jerusalem did Jewish leaders have the authority to persecute them as dissidents. Opposition in Israel led to Christians spreading out to carry the gospel elsewhere, thus helping to expand their mission, but Christian animosity toward Jews lingered, to resurface in virulent forms from time to time.

Paul also tried to sway **Gentiles**: worshipers of the old gods whose religion was in decline, supporters of the emperor as deity, ecstatic initiates of mystery cults, and followers of dualistic Greco–Roman philosophers who regarded matter as evil and tried to emancipate the soul from its corrupting influence. He taught them that God did not reside in any idol but yet was not far from them, "For in him we live and move and have our being."[50] For Gentiles embracing Christianity, Paul and others argued that the Jewish tradition of circumcision

Places visited by the apostle Paul during his far-reaching missionary journeys, 46–60 CE.

The Nag Hammadi manuscripts found in Egypt were buried about 400 CE. They contain copies and translations of early Christian texts condemned as heretical by the Church.

should not be required of them (as for example in Romans 2:29). As Paul interpreted the gospel, salvation came by repentant faith in the grace of Christ, rather than by observance of a traditional law. In Paul's letter to the Church in Rome, he argues that even Abraham was **justified**, or accepted by God in spite of sin, because of his great faith in God rather than by his circumcision. Greco–Romans had idealized the male human body, with great athletic spectacles performed by nude men, so the necessity of altering the human form would have been a barrier to their acceptance of Paul's teachings. Shifting away from circumcision as a traditional requirement was a significant example of the enculturation of Christianity as it evolved in various contexts and began to distinguish itself from Judaism.

Christianity spread rapidly and soon became largely non-Jewish in membership. By 200 CE, it had spread throughout the Roman Empire and into Mesopotamia, despite fierce opposition. Many Christians were subjected to imprisonment, torture, and confiscation of property, because they rejected polytheistic beliefs, idols, and emperor worship in the Roman Empire. They were suspected of being revolutionaries, with their talk of a Messiah, and of strange cultic behaviors, such as their secret rituals of symbolically drinking Jesus' blood and eating his flesh. Persecution did not deter the most ardent of Christians; it united them intimately to the passion and death of Christ. In addition to martyrdom, many early Christians embraced a life of ascetic self-denial by fasting, wearing coarse clothes, renouncing sexuality, spending hours in prayer and contemplation, and serving others. They sought to be living sacrifices, giving up the pleasures of the material world for the sake of loving and serving God.

With the rise of Constantine to imperial rule early in the fourth century CE, opposition turned to the official embracing of Christianity. Constantine said that in 312 CE God showed him a vision of a cross to be used as a standard in battle. After he used it and won a major victory, he instituted tolerance of Christianity alongside the state cult, of which he was the chief priest. Just before his death, Constantine was baptized as a Christian.

By the end of the fourth century CE, people of other religions were stripped of all rights, and ordered into Christian churches to be baptized. Some paid outward service to Christianity but remained inwardly faithful to their old traditions. As Christianity became the favored religion, many converted for secular reasons.

By the end of the fifth century CE, Christianity was the faith claimed by the majority of people in the vast former Roman Empire. It also spread beyond the empire, from Ireland in the west to India and Ceylon (Sri Lanka) in the east.

EVOLVING ORGANIZATION AND THEOLOGY

During its phenomenal growth from persecuted sect to state religion throughout much of the ancient world, Christianity was developing organizationally and theologically. By the end of the first century CE, it had a bureaucracy that carried on the rites of the Church and attempted to define mainstream Christianity, denigrating trends that it judged heretical.

One form that was judged to be outside the mainstream was Gnostic Christianity, which appeared as a movement in the second century CE. **Gnosticism** means mystical perception of knowledge. The Nag Hammadi library found in Egypt presents Jesus as a great Gnostic teacher. His words are interpreted as the secret teachings given only to initiates. "He who is near to me is near to the fire," he says in the Gospel of Thomas.[51] The Gnostics held that only spiritually mature individuals could apprehend Jesus' real teaching: that the Kingdom of Heaven is a present reality experienced through personal realization of the Light.

myreligionlab

The Formation
of the Canon
ATHANASIUS

When New Testament texts were translated into Latin in the fourth century, the Gnostic gospels were not included. Instead, the Church treated possession of Gnostic texts as a crime against Church law because the Christian faith community felt that Jesus had not taught an elitist view of salvation and had not discriminated against the material aspect of creation.

What became mainstream Christianity is based not only on the life and teachings of Jesus, as set forth in the gospels selected for the New Testament, but also on the ways that they have been interpreted over the centuries. One of the first and most important interpreters was Paul. His central contribution—which was as influential as the four gospels in shaping Christianity—was his interpretation of Jesus' death and Resurrection.

Paul spoke of *agape*—altruistic, self-giving love—as the center of Christian concern. He placed it above spiritual wisdom, asceticism, faith, and supernatural "gifts of the Spirit," such as the ability to heal, prophesy, or spontaneously speak in unknown tongues. Love was applied not only to one's neighbors but also to one's relationship with the divine. It was love plus gnosis—knowledge of God, permeated with love—that became the basis of contemplative Christianity, as it was shaped by the "Fathers" of the first centuries.

Let all that you do be done in love.

1 Corinthians 16:14

The cross, with or without an image of Jesus crucified on it, became a central symbol of Christianity. It marked the path of suffering service, rather than political domination, as the way of conquering evil and experiencing union with a compassionate God. To participate in Jesus' sacrifice, people could repent of their sins, be baptized, and be reborn to new life in Christ. In the early fifth century CE the bishop Augustine, one of the most influential theologians in the history of Western Christianity, described this spiritual rebirth thus:

Where I was angry within myself in my chamber, where I was inwardly pricked, where I had sacrificed, slaying my old man and commencing the purpose of a new life, putting my trust in Thee—there hadst Thou begun to grow sweet unto me and "hadst put gladness in my heart."[52]

myreligionlab
The Confessions of Augustine
AUGUSTINE OF HIPPO

Rowan Williams, the twenty-first-century theologian and Archbishop of Canterbury, leader of the Anglican Church, explains this repentance and spiritual resurrection as:

the refusal to accept that lostness is the final human truth. Like a growing thing beneath the earth, we protest at the darkness and push blindly up in search of light, truth, home—the place, the relation where we are not lost, where we can live from deep roots in assurance. "Because I live, you will live also."[53]

The expectation of the coming of God's kingdom and final judgment of who would go to heaven and who to hell, so fervent in the earliest Christianity, began to wane as time went by and the anticipated events did not happen. The notion of the Kingdom of God began to shift to the indefinite future, with emphasis placed on a preliminary judgment at one's death. There was nevertheless the continuing expectation that Christ would return in glory to judge the living and the dead and bring to fulfillment the "new creation." This belief in the "Second Coming" of Christ is still an article of faith today for some Christians; others regard it as symbolic of a pointing to the certainty of God's coming rule of love and peace.

The Holy Trinity is a distinctively Christian view of God. God is One as a communal plurality, an endless circle sharing the love intrinsic to the Godhead, inviting all to be healed and saved by this love.

Reflecting on the life of Jesus and their experience of the risen Christ, Christians believed that the transcendent and invisible God had become immanent and visible in Jesus. This led to the early development of the doctrine of the **Holy Trinity**, which speaks of three equal "persons" within one divine being: Father, Son, and Holy Spirit. The Father is the one who sends the Son to become incarnate in Jesus with the mission to reveal God's love to the world. The Son or Word manifests God in the world in many ways, but the incarnation in Jesus is a culmination of that revelation. The Holy Spirit, or Holy Ghost, who Jesus promises will be sent after his death, is the power and presence of God, actively guiding and sustaining the faithful.

Although Jesus had spoken in parables with several levels of meaning, the evolving Church found it necessary to articulate some of its beliefs more openly and systematically. A number of **creeds**, or professions of faith, were composed for use in religious instruction and baptism, to define who Jesus was and his relationship to God, and to provide clear stands in the face of various controversies. The emperor Constantine was particularly concerned to bring doctrinal unity among the Christian churches which he had legalized and whose beliefs he was promoting throughout his widespread empire. One major controversy concerned the teachings of Arius, a leader of the congregation in Alexandria. The issue was the relationship between God and Jesus. The Christians worshiped Jesus, but at the same time came from monotheistic Jewish tradition, in which God alone is worshiped. Was Jesus therefore somehow the same as God? To Arius, the "Son of God" is a metaphor; it does not mean that Jesus has the same status as God, for Jesus was a human being. Opponents of this belief argued that Jesus is properly worshiped as the incarnation of God.

myreligionlab
The Nicene Creed

Constantine convened a general council of the bishops of all area churches in Nicaea in 325 CE to settle this critical issue. After decades of controversy, Arius's beliefs were ultimately rejected in the framing of the **Nicene Creed**, traditionally dated to another council held in Constantinople in 381 CE (and thus sometimes referred to as the Niceno-Constantinopolitan Creed). It is still the basic profession of faith for many Christian denominations in both East and West, including all Orthodox churches, and has been proposed as a basis for unifying all Christians:

> *We believe in one God, the Father, the almighty, maker of heaven and earth,*
> *of all that is, seen and unseen. We believe in one Lord, Jesus Christ, the only*
> *Son of God, eternally begotten of the Father, God from God, Light from Light,*
> *true God from true God, begotten not made, of one Being with the Father.*
> *Through him all things were made. For us men and for our salvation he*
> *came down from heaven; by the power of the Holy Spirit he became incarnate*
> *of the Virgin Mary, and was made man. For our sake he was crucified under*
> *Pontius Pilate; he suffered death and was buried. On the third day he rose again*
> *in accordance with the Scriptures; he ascended into heaven and is seated at the*
> *right hand of the Father. He will come again in glory to judge the living and*
> *the dead, and his kingdom will have no end. We believe in the Holy Spirit,*
> *the Lord, the giver of life, who proceeds from the Father (and from the Son).*
> *With the Father and the Son he is worshiped and glorified. He has spoken*
> *through the Prophets. We believe in one holy, catholic, and apostolic Church.*
> *We acknowledge one baptism for the forgiveness of sins. We look for the*
> *resurrection of the dead, and the life of the world to come. Amen.*

As we will see later, the small phrase "and from the Son" was added to the creed by the Western part of the Church in the early Middle Ages and became a major point of disagreement between the Western Church and the Eastern Christian churches, which did not add it.

Christology—the attempt to define the nature of Jesus and his relationship to God—received further official clarification during the Council of Chalcedon in 451. This council issued a statement that allows considerable leeway in Christological interpretations by declaring that Jesus is of "two natures"—perfectly divine and also perfectly human. The Council of Chalcedon defined Jesus as:

*perfect in divinity and humanity, truly God and truly human, consisting
of a rational soul and a body, being of one substance with the Father in
relation to his divinity, and being of one substance with us in relation to
his humanity, and is like us in all things apart from sin (Hebrews 4:15).
He was begotten of the Father before time in relation to his divinity,
and in these recent days was born from the Virgin Mary, the Theotokos
[Mother of God], for us and for our salvation.*

EARLY MONASTICISM

Alongside the development of doctrine and the consolidation of Church structure, another trend was developing. Some Christians were turning away from the
world to live in solitary communion with God, as ascetics. There had been a
certain amount of asceticism in Paul's writings. He himself was celibate, as
he believed that avoiding family entanglements helped one to concentrate
on the Lord.

By the fourth century CE, Christian monks—and apparently also some remarkable ascetic women referred to as *ammas* (mothers)—were living simply in caves
in the Egyptian desert with little regard for the things of the world. They had no
central organization but tended to learn from the examples of other ascetics.
Avoiding emphasis on the supernatural powers that often accompany the ascetic
life, they told stories demonstrating the virtues they valued, such as humility,
submission, and the sharing of food. For example, an earnest young man was said
to have visited one of the desert fathers and asked how he was faring. The old
man sighed and said, "Very badly, my child." Asked why, he said, "I have been
here forty years doing nothing other than cursing my own self each day, inas-
much as in the prayers I offer, I say to God, 'Accursed are those who deviate from
Your commandments.'"[54] The young seeker was moved by such humility and
made it his model.

The desert fathers and mothers were left to their own devices at first. In
Christian humility, they avoided judging or trying to teach each other and
attempted to be, at best, harmless. But by the fifth century CE, the monastic life
shifted from solitary, unguided practice to formal spiritual supervision. Group
monasteries and structures for encouraging obedience to God through an abbot
or abbess were set up, and rules devised to help monks persevere in their calling.
The Rule of St. Benedict became a model for all later monastic orders in the West,
with its emphasis on poverty, chastity, and obedience to the abbot, and its insistence that each monastery be economically self-sufficient through the labor of
the monastics. The Benedictines have been famous over the centuries for their
practice of hospitality to pilgrims and travelers, and are today active participants
in inter-religious monastic dialogue.

myreligionlab
Grief and Joy
GREGORY OF SINAI

---

*The carefree man, who has tested the sweetness of having no personal
possessions, feels that even the cassock which he wears and the jug
of water in his cell are a useless burden, because these things, too,
sometimes distract his mind.*

A Desert Father[55]

Church administration

During the late first and early second centuries CE, some men and women had followed a charismatic Christian life, leaving home to preach, baptize, prophesy, and perhaps die as martyrs; others had moved toward an institutionalized patriarchal Church. By the beginning of the second century CE, a consolidation of spiritual power had begun with the designation of specific people to serve as clergy and bishops (superintendents) to administer the Church affairs of each city or region. While some women served as deacons ministering to women, the clergy and bishops had to be male, with wife and children. The bishops of the chief cities of the Roman Empire had the greatest responsibilities and authority, with the greatest prestige being held by the Bishop of Rome, eventually known as the **pope**.

Politically, late in the third century CE, the Roman Empire had been divided into two: an eastern section and a western section. In the fourth century CE, Constantine established a second imperial seat in the east, in Constantinople (now Istanbul, Turkey). It was considered a "second Rome," especially after the sack of Rome by the Goths in 410. The two halves of the Christian world grew apart from each other, divided by language (Latin in the west, Greek in the east), culture, and religious differences.

In the western half, religious power was becoming more and more centralized in the Roman pope and other high officials. The Byzantine east was organized into a number of **sees**. The five major sees were those of Rome, Constantinople,

Map showing the approximate distribution of Christians in the world today.

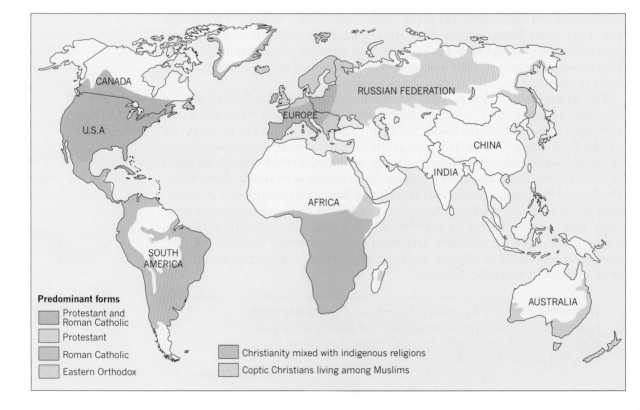

Predominant forms

- Protestant and Roman Catholic
- Protestant
- Roman Catholic
- Eastern Orthodox
- Christianity mixed with indigenous religions
- Coptic Christians living among Muslims

Alexandria, Antioch, and Jerusalem. But this distinction was for organizational purposes; spiritually, all bishops, regardless of the status of the cities with which they are associated, are to today thought to be equal as successors to the original apostles, equally empowered to perform the sacraments and teach the faith. Rome was accorded a "primacy of honor" but not supreme jurisdiction. The East did not recognize the Roman pope's claim to universal authority in the Church.

By the fifth century CE, Pope Leo I argued that all popes were apostolic successors to Peter, the "rock" on which Jesus in Matthew's gospel said he would found his Church. The Roman emperor passed an edict that all Christians were to recognize the authority of the Bishop of Rome.

The strongest of Church administrators during these early centuries was Gregory I ("the Great"), who died in 604 CE. Wealthy by birth but ascetic by choice, he devoted his personal fortune to founding monasteries and feeding the poor. At a time of pestilence, floods, and military invasions, he promoted the discipline of the clergy, including the Western ideal that priests should be celibate in order to concentrate on piety and ministry without family obligations. He revamped the liturgy (Gregorian chanting is named after him), and re-established the Church as a decent, just institution carrying high spiritual values.

Pope Gregory also sent missionaries to convert England to Christianity. They were ultimately successful in gradually turning the people from worship of indigenous deities to worship of Jesus and the saints of the Church, partly because of the royal protection the missionaries and converts won and partly because rather than destroying the old religious shrines, Gregory instructed the missionaries to replace the old idols with relics of martyrs and saints—bits of bone, cloth, even dirt from their graves—which they carried to England. Worship of goddesses of the area was thus deflected to devotion to holy women from far away, whose deep spirituality was thought to be so strong that it was present in their relics.

The papacy began to wield tremendous secular power. Beginning in the eighth century, the approval of the papacy was sought as conferring divine sanction on feudal kings. In the ninth century the Church produced documents old and new believed to legitimate the hierarchical authority of the papacy over the Church, and the Church over society, as the proper means of transmitting inspiration from the divine to humanity. Those who disagreed could be threatened with **excommunication**. This exclusion from participation in the sacraments was a dread ban, cutting a person off from the redemption of the Church (blocking one's entrance to heaven in the afterlife), as well as from the benefits of the Church's secular power.

Late in the eleventh century, Pope Gregory VII set forth unprecedented claims for the papacy. The pope, he asserted, was divinely appointed and therefore could be ruled by no human. The pope had the right to depose emperors; the princes of the world should kiss his feet.

EAST–WEST DIVISION

The eastern part of Christendom did not accept the absolute claims of the papacy. By the early Middle Ages, there were also doctrinal disagreements. In its version of the Niceno-Constantinopolitan Creed, for example, the Western Church added the *filioque*, a formula professing that the Holy Spirit came from the Father *"and from the Son"*; the Eastern Church retained what is considered the more original text, professing that the Holy Spirit proceeds only from the Father.

In 1054, leaders of the eastern and western factions excommunicated each other over the disagreement about the Holy Spirit, and also over the papal claim, celibacy for priests (not required in the Eastern Church, which requires celibacy for bishops only), and whether the eucharistic bread should be leavened or unleavened. To the Eastern Church, the last straw was its treatment by crusaders.

From 1095 to about 1290, loosely organized waves of Christians poured out of Europe in what were presented as "Holy **crusades**" to recapture the holy land of Palestine from Muslims, to defend the Byzantine Empire against Muslim Turks, and in general to wipe out the enemies of Christianity. It was a tragic and bloody time. One of the many casualties was the already tenuous relationship between the Eastern and Western Churches. When crusaders entered Constantinople in 1204, they tried to intervene in local politics. Rebuffed, they were so furious that they ravaged the city. They destroyed the altar and sacred icons in Hagia Sophia, the awesome Church of the Holy Wisdom (later taken over as a Muslim mosque), and placed prostitutes on the throne reserved for the patriarch of the region. Horrified by such profanity, the Orthodox Church ended its dialogue with Rome and proceeded on its own path, claiming to be the true descendant of the apos-

After Jerusalem fell in 1077 to Turkish forces, who then denied Christian pilgrims access to the city, Western popes launched a series of crusades to recover what Christians considered their holy land, where Jesus had walked. These military expeditions were considered holy missions, and crusaders carried the cross and the Bible.

Priests chant and beat drums in the Ethiopian Orthodox Church of St. George, carved out of rock in Lalibela, Ethiopia, in the 12th century.

tolic Church. Despite periodic attempts at reconciliation the Eastern and Western Churches are still separate.

The Eastern Church itself also became divided over doctrinal and political issues at the time of the Council of Chalcedon in 451 CE. Bishops who refused to accept the dogma established by the council that Jesus is of two natures—one divine and one human—were declared to be "out of communion" with the bishops both of Rome and of Constantinople, and were thus excommunicated. These Non-Chalcedonian Churches or Oriental Orthodox Churches remain distinct from the Eastern Orthodox Church in general. They include Syriac Orthodox, Coptic Orthodox, Ethiopian Orthodox, Eritrean Orthodox, Malankara Orthodox Syrian Church (India), and Armenian Apostolic Churches. The Ethiopian Orthodox Church is the largest of these.

SOCIAL CHAOS AND THE PAPACY

In the Western Church, centralization of power under the pope became a major unifying element in the Europe of the Middle Ages. Kingdoms broke up between 800 and 1100 as Vikings invaded from the north and Magyars from the east. For the sake of military protection, peasants gave up their freedom to feudal lords. The feudal lords in turn began to war among themselves. In the midst of the ensuing chaos, people looked to the pope as an orderly wielder of power.

Church and states were at times locked in a mutual struggle for dominance, with popes alternately supporting, dominating, and being deposed by secular rulers. The power of the papacy was also somewhat limited by the requirement that the pope be elected by a council of cardinals. The position could not become hereditary. But it was nonetheless open to intrigue, scandal, and power-mongering.

The thirteenth century saw the power of the papacy placed behind the **Inquisition**, an ecclesiastical court set up during the 1230s to investigate and suppress heresy. This court was based on Augustine's concept that heretics should be controlled for the sake of their own eternal salvation, out of love for their souls. But whereas Augustine saw fines and imprisonment as reasonable coercion to help people change their minds, in some cases the medieval inquisitors had them tortured and burned to deter others from dangerous views. For example, in northern Italy and southern France a sect arose that was later called Cathari ("the pure"), for its members lived ascetically, emphasizing poverty and mutual aid. Though similar to Christianity in organization and worship, the movement denied that Jesus was the incarnation of God, and saw spirit as good but matter as bad. Such beliefs were proclaimed heretical by the papacy; the Cathars, attacked by the Inquisition, disappeared.

Though strong, the papacy was often embroiled in its own political strife. During the fourteenth century, the popes left their traditional seat in turbulent Rome for the more peaceful climate of Avignon, France. There they built up an elaborate administrative structure, increasingly involved in worldly affairs. After the papacy was persuaded to return to Rome, a would-be reformer, Pope Urban VI, got so embroiled in power politics that at one point he had five cardinals tortured and killed. In the Great Western Schism that followed, starting in 1378, several rival lines of "anti-popes" began, including one sitting in Avignon, creating divisions that lasted for decades.

Intellectual revival and monasticism

Although the papacy was subject to abuses, mirrored on a lesser scale by the clergy, Christian spirituality was vigorously revived in other quarters of medieval society. During the twelfth and thirteenth centuries great universities developed in Europe, often from cathedral schools. Theology was considered the greatest of the sciences, with Church ideals permeating the study of all areas of life. Soaring Gothic cathedrals were built to uplift the soul to heavenly heights, for God was perceived as being enthroned in the heavens, far above the workaday world.

The yearning for spiritual purity was particularly pronounced in monasticism. It was largely through monks and nuns that Christian spirituality survived and spread. Monasteries also became bulwarks of Western civilization. In Ireland, particularly, they were the centers of larger communities of laypeople and places of learning within illiterate warring societies.

During the twelfth century many new monastic orders appeared in the midst of a massive popular reinvigoration of spiritual activity. A major influence was a community in Cluny, France. Its monks specialized in liturgical elaborations and prayer, leaving agricultural work to serfs. An alternative direction was taken by the Cistercians, Gregorians, and Carthusians. They returned to St. Benedict's rule of combining manual work and prayer; "to labor is to pray," said the monks. The Carthusians lived cloistered lives as hermits, meeting each other only for worship and business matters. Despite such austere practices, people of all classes flocked to monastic life as a pious refuge from decadent society.

myreligionlab

A Medieval Argument for the Existence of God
ANSELM OF CANTERBURY

> *It is not only prayer that gives God glory but work. … He is so great that all things give Him glory if you mean they should.*
>
> *Gerard Manley Hopkins*[56]

In contrast to monks and nuns living cloistered lives, mendicant friars, or brothers, worked among the people. In 1215, the Dominican Order was instituted primarily to teach the faith and refute heresies. A famous Dominican scholar, Thomas Aquinas, created a monumental work, *Summa Theologiae,* in which rational sciences and spiritual revelations were joined in an immense, consistent theological system. Aquinas was much influenced by the recovery of the classical writings of Aristotle that had been preserved by Muslims and returned to Europe through Spain.

Franciscans, following the lead of the beloved St. Francis of Assisi (see below), wandered about without personal property or established buildings, telling people about God's love and accepting charity for their meager needs. The mendicant Dominicans and Franciscans, still noted as missionaries today, became one of the major features of medieval Christianity.

In addition to organized orders of nuns, there was a grassroots movement among thirteenth-century German and Flemish women to take private vows of chastity and simplicity. These women, who were called "beguines," lived frugally by their own work. Because they were not organized into a religious order, they chose their own lifestyles, intending simply to live "religiously." At times persecuted because it did not fit into any traditionally sanctioned pattern, the movement persisted, drawing tens of thousands of women. Eventually they built small convents for themselves; by the end of the fourteenth century, there were 169 beguine convents in Cologne, the heart of the movement.

Medieval mysticism

Mysticism also flowered during the Middle Ages, renewing the spiritual heart of the Church. Especially in cloistered settings, monks and nuns sat in contemplation of the meanings of the scriptures for the soul. Biblical stories of battles between heroes and their enemies were, for instance, interpreted as the struggle between the soul and one's baser desires. Beyond this rational thought, some engaged in quiet nonconceptual prayer, simply resting receptively in the presence of God.

One remarkable mystic was the German abbess Hildegard of Bingen (1098–1179). Founder of two monasteries on the Rhine, from a young age she experienced frequent visions, which she recorded in several books of revelations. She wrote treatises on medical and scientific matters as well as much fine spiritual poetry, and achieved considerable fame as a composer. Corresponding with popes, emperors, and kings, she remained privately devoted to mystical thought and to prophecy.

In thirteenth-century Italy, there was the endearing figure of St. Francis of Assisi (1182–1226). The carefree, dashing son of a merchant, he underwent a

myreligi●nlab
Everything Lives
in God
HILDEGARD OF BINGEN

Statues of St. Francis often show birds perched on him, representing his kinship with the natural world.

radical spiritual transformation. He traded his fine clothes for simple garb and "left the world"[57] for a life of total poverty, caring for lepers and rebuilding dilapidated churches, since in a vision Jesus spoke to him from the cross, saying: "Repair my Church." Eventually Francis understood that his real mission was to rebuild the Church by re-emphasizing the gospel and its commands of love and poverty. A band of brothers, and then of sisters led by the saintly Clare, gathered around him. The friars preached, worked, begged, tended lepers, and lived a simple life of penance and prayer while wandering from town to town. This ascetic life was permeated with mystical joy, one of St. Francis's hallmarks. He was also known for his rapport with wild animals and is often pictured with birds resting lovingly on his shoulders. Two years before his death, Francis received the "stigmata," replicas on his own body of the crucifixion wounds of Jesus. This miracle was interpreted as a sign of the saint's union with Christ by suffering, prayer, holiness, and love.

The flowering of English mysticism during the fourteenth century was exemplified by Julian of Norwich (1342–c.1416). As a girl, she had prayed that when she reached the age of thirty (the age at which Jesus began his public mission) she would have an illness that would bring her an understanding of his Passion (the sufferings of his final days). As requested, she did indeed become so ill when she was thirty that she almost died. During this crisis she had visions and conversations with Christ, which revealed the boundless love with which he continually offers himself for humanity. Her writings delve into the perennial problem of reconciling the existence of evil with the experience of a loving God, whom she sometimes referred to as "God our Mother."

An anonymous fourteenth-century English writer contributed a volume entitled *The Cloud of Unknowing*. Christianity then and now largely follows what is called the affirmative way, with art, liturgy, scriptures, and imagery to aid devotion. But the author of *The Cloud* spoke to those who were prepared to undertake the negative way of abiding in sheer love for God, with no thoughts. God cannot be known through ideas or physical images; "a naked intent toward God, a desire for him alone, is enough."[58] In the silence of wordless prayer, the light of God may pierce the cloud of human unknowing that obscures the divine from the seeker.

Fourteenth-century Italy witnessed a period of unprecedented degradation among the clergy, while the papacy occupied itself with organizational matters in

The young Catherine of Siena, "mother of thousands of souls," had a vision in which Christ, in the company of the Virgin Mary and other saints, gave her a wedding ring, the sign of the mystical marriage.

Russian Orthodox Kenoticism

A great mystical spiritual tradition emerged on Russian soil. The **kenotic** pattern of loving and world-directed monastic work was set by the eleventh-century saint Theodosius, who attempted to imitate the poverty and self-sacrificing humility of Jesus. He ate nothing but dry bread and herbs, spent his nights in prayer and his days in work. He dressed in the rough clothes of a peasant, patiently bore insults, worked with his own hands—chopping wood, spinning thread, baking bread, comforting the sick—and refused to present himself as an authority, even though he became the revered leader of this monastic community.

It is recorded that once, after Theodosius had visited a distant prince, the prince sent his own coach to take the saint home in comfort. The coachman, seeing Theodosius's crude clothing, assumed he was a beggar, and asked him to mount the horse so that the coachman could sleep. The saint humbly did so and thus drove the coach all night, with the coachman sleeping inside. When St. Theodosius became too sleepy to drive,

he dismounted and walked; when he became weary of walking, he rode again. As the morning sun rose, the noblemen of his area recognized him, dismounted, and bowed to him, whereupon the saint gently said to the coachman, "My child, it is light. Mount your horse." The coachman was amazed and terrified as he saw the great reverence paid to the saint as they proceeded. Rather than chastizing him, Theodosius led him by the hand to the refectory, ordered that he should be given all the food and drink that he wanted, and paid him for the journey.

In the thirteenth century, Russia suffered from Mongolian invasions. Even though the Tartar Mongol khans nominally protected the Christians' freedom of religious practice when they themselves adopted Islam, spiritual and social life were in disarray. Monasticism shifted from urban settlements to the wilderness of the great forests of northern Russia. Hermit monks lived there in silence and solitary prayer until so many of the faithful gathered that thriving communities developed around them.

One of the most celebrated of the forest monks was St. Sergius. As a boy, Sergius retreated to the forest and built a small chapel for his intense devotions. Despite his noble lineage, he dressed like a peasant and did manual work. Even when he was abbot of the community that grew up around him, he was asked by one of his monks to build a cell, for which labor he was given a bit of moldy bread. In his contemplations, Sergius was said to be graced with visions of Mary, Mother of Christ, and of angels, fire, and light. He was nonetheless socially engaged with the national effort to resist foreign rule, and his blessing of the first victorious battle of Russians against Tartars set the precedent for the future close links between church and state in Russia. The relics of St. Sergius's body still lie undecayed in the huge and ornate Holy Trinity Lavra near Moscow, in Zagorsk where once he had built his simple chapel. Among his followers were seventy famous saints of Russia.

St. Sergius and the bear.

Avignon. In this spiritual vacuum, laypeople gathered around saintly individuals to imbibe their atmosphere of genuine devotion. One of the most celebrated of these was the young Catherine of Siena. In her persistent efforts to restore spiritual purity and religious discipline to the Church, she gained the ear of Pope Gregory XI, helping to convince him to return to Rome. She was called "mother of thousands of souls," and people were said to be converted just by seeing her face.

The Protestant Reformation

myreligionlab
Lutheran Church

Despite the genuine piety of individuals within the Catholic Church, some who clashed with its authority claimed that those in power seemed often to have lost touch with their own spiritual tradition. With the rise of literacy and printing in the late fifteenth century, many Christians were rediscovering early Christianity and comparing it unfavorably with what the Roman Catholic Church had made of it. Roman Catholic fundraising or church-building financial activities were particularly criticized. These included **indulgences** (remission of the punishment for sin by the clergy in return for services or payments), the sale of relics, purchases of masses for the dead, spiritual pilgrimages, and the earning of spiritual "merit" by donating to the Church.

Salient among the reformists was Martin Luther (1483–1546). Luther was a monk, priest, and Professor of Biblical Studies at the University of Wittenberg. He struggled personally with the question of how one's sins could ever be totally atoned for by one's own actions. The Roman Catholic Church's position was that to be forgiven of post-baptismal sins, people should repent and then confess their sins to a priest and be pardoned. In addition, after death punishment for sins could be remitted either by the performance of prescribed penances or through being granted an indulgence. Indulgences could even be purchased to make sure that the souls of those who had died repentant were freed from **Purgatory** (the intermediate place of purifying suffering for those who died in a state of repentance and grace but who were not yet sufficiently stainless to enter heaven). The Castle Church at Wittenberg housed an immense collection of relics, including what were believed to be hairs from the Virgin Mary and a thorn from the "crown" of thorns placed on Jesus' head before he was crucified. This relic collection was deemed so powerful that those who viewed them on the proper day and contributed sufficiently to the Church could receive indulgences from the pope freeing themselves or their loved ones from almost two million years in Purgatory.

By intense study of the Bible, Luther began to emphasize a different approach. Both Paul and Augustine could be interpreted as saying that God, through Jesus, offered salvation to sinners in spite of their sins. This salvation was offered by God's grace alone and received solely by repentant faith. The good works and created graces prescribed by Catholics to earn merit in heaven were not part of original Christianity, Luther argued. Salvation from sin comes from faith in God, which itself comes from God, by grace. This gift of faith brings justification (being found righteous in God's sight) and then flowers as unselfish good works, which characterize the true Christian:

Martin Luther's political influence and prolific writings led to a deep split in the Western Church, severing Protestant reformers from the Roman Catholic Church. (Lucas Cranach the Elder, Martin Luther, 1533.)

From faith flows love and joy in the Lord, and from love a joyful, willing and free
mind that serves one's neighbor willingly and takes no account of gratitude or
ingratitude, of praise or blame, of gain or loss. ... As our heavenly father has in
Christ freely come to our help, we also ought freely to help our neighbor through
our body and its works, and each should become as it were a Christ to the other.[59]

In 1517 Luther invited the university community to debate this issue with him,
by the established custom of nailing his theses to the door of the church. He
apparently had no intention of splitting with the Church. Nevertheless, he
refused to recant passages from his theses when threatened with excommunication. He was thence excommunicated by a papal bull (decree) in 1521.

Cut off from Rome, Luther sought support from the secular princes of
Germany. For reasons sometimes more political than spiritual, many came over
to his side and helped to enforce his ideas. Although there were some attempts at
compromise by followers of both Luther and Rome, conciliatory efforts collapsed.

Major Divisions of Christianity Today*

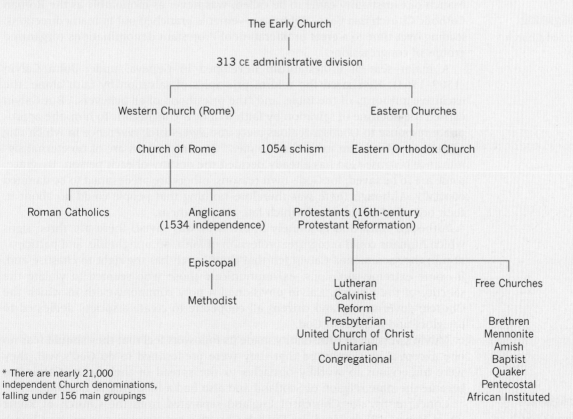

The Early Church

313 CE administrative division

Western Church (Rome)   Eastern Churches

Church of Rome   1054 schism   Eastern Orthodox Church

Roman Catholics   Anglicans   Protestants (16th-century
                    (1534 independence) Protestant Reformation)

Episcopal

Methodist

Lutheran   Free Churches
Calvinist
Reform
Presbyterian
United Church of Christ   Brethren
Unitarian   Mennonite
Congregational   Amish
                            Baptist
* There are nearly 21,000   Quaker
independent Church denominations, Pentecostal
falling under 156 main groupings   African Instituted

Luther's evolving theology took him farther and farther from the institutions of the Roman Catholic Church. He did not think that the Bible supported the Roman Catholic tradition that pope, bishops, priests, and monks should have spiritual authority over laypeople; instead, he asserted that there is "a priesthood of all believers." He also felt that the sacred rites, or **sacraments**, of the Church were ways of nourishing faith instituted by Jesus and that they included only **baptism** and the **Eucharist** (also known as the Lord's Supper, Holy Communion, or Mass).

Another major reformer who eventually broke with Rome was the Swiss priest Ulrich Zwingli (1484–1531). He rejected practices not mentioned in the Bible, such as abstaining from meat during Lent, veneration of relics and saints, religious pilgrimages, and celibacy for monks and priests. Zwingli asserted that the Lord's Supper should be celebrated only as a memorial of Jesus' sacrifice; he did not believe in the mysterious presence of Jesus' blood and body in the consecrated wine and bread. He even questioned the spiritual efficacy of rituals such as masses for the dead and confession of one's sins to a priest:

> *It is God alone who remits sins and puts the heart at rest, so to Him alone ought we to ascribe the healing of our wounds, to Him alone display them to be healed.*[60]

The ideals of these reformists were adopted by many Christians. The freedom of scriptural interpretation opened numerous options. Protestantism, as the new branch of Christianity came to be called, was never as monolithic as the Roman Catholic Church had been. Reform movements branched out in many directions, leading over time to a great proliferation of Protestant **denominations** (organized groups of congregations).

myreligienlab
Reformed Church

A major seat of Protestantism developed in Geneva, under John Calvin (1509–1564). He shared the reform principles of salvation by faith alone, the exclusive authority of the Bible, and "the priesthood of all believers." But Calvin carried the doctrine of salvation by faith to a new conclusion. To him, the appropriate response to God is a zealous piety and awe-struck reverence in which one "dreads to offend him more than to die."[61] Human actions are of no eternal significance because God has already decided the destiny of each person. By grace, some are to be saved; for God's own reasons, others are predestined to be damned eternally. Although there was therefore nothing that people could do about it, their behavior would reveal which fate awaited them.

Although only God absolutely knew who was saved, there are three signs which humans could recognize: profession of faith, an upright life, and participation in the sacraments. Calvin felt that the Church has the right to chastise and, in some extreme situations, excommunicate those who seemed to violate the sanctity of the Church. Calvin envisioned a holy commonwealth in which the Church, government, and citizens all cooperate to create a society dedicated to the glory and mission of God.

Calvin's version of Christianity made its followers feel that they should fear no one except God. Convinced that they were predestined to do God's will, they were impervious to worldly obstacles to the spread of their faith. **Calvinism** became the state religion of Scotland and also had a following in England.

myreligienlab
Anglican Church

Concurrently, the Church of England separated from the Church of Rome when Henry VIII declared the English Church's independence from the Church of Rome. His daughter Elizabeth I finalized the breach with Rome in the

Elizabethan Settlement of 1559. Now called **Anglicanism**, this form of Christianity is in communion with Old Catholics and also shares some similarities with the Protestant churches, but it is now generally considered a separate, independent Church. The Anglican Church retains many of the Roman Catholic rituals but rejects the authority of the Roman Catholic pope (referring instead to its Archbishop of Canterbury as its spiritual leader) and allows priests to marry. One of its thirty-seven autonomous churches is the Episcopal Church in the United States, a name referring to it being a Church with bishops.

John Wesley, founder of Methodism, rode thousands of miles every year on horseback as an evangelist.

Another offshoot of the Church of England is Methodism. It originated with the evangelist John Wesley (1703–1791), who emphasized personal holiness and methodical devotions. He traveled an average of 8,000 miles a year by horseback to urgently call people to wake up to a life of repentance and faith in Jesus' intercession:

> *Repentance frequently means an inward change, a change of mind from sin to holiness. But we now speak of it in a quite different sense, as it is one kind of self-knowledge, the knowing ourselves sinners, yea, guilty, helpless sinners, even though we know we are children of God. … 'I sin in every breath I draw, Nor do Thy will, nor keep Thy law on earth, as angels do above: But still the fountain open stands, Washes my feet, my heart, my hands, Till I am perfected in love.'[62]*

Martin Luther's reformation of the German Church led directly to present-day **Lutheranism**. It maintains a strong emphasis on liturgy and sacraments and is currently practiced mostly in Germany, Scandinavia, the Baltics, and the northeastern United States. As the Protestant Reformation progressed, political entities in Europe chose specific forms of Christianity as their official religions. Spain, France, and Italy remained largely Roman Catholic. Northern Germany was largely Lutheran. Ireland split between Catholicism and Protestantism, leading to wars that continue today. The two major Reformed Churches that sprang from Calvinism were the Scottish movement called **Presbyterianism** (in which the congregation is governed by presbyters, who rank second below bishops, ministers, and elders) and **Congregationalism** (which emphasizes the independence of each local church and the "priesthood" of all members). Some Polish and Hungarian communities adopted a form of **Unitarianism**, which rejected original sin, the Trinity, and Jesus' divinity in favor of a simple theism and imitation of Jesus.

Some Protestant groups that were outlawed by the Church of England emigrated to new colonies in North America. These are sometimes referred to as "Free Churches," being independent of government endorsement. One of the largest of these groups is the **Baptists**, a denomination in which people are baptized as conscious adult believers rather than as infants. **Quakers** (formally known as the Religious Society of Friends) date from the seventeenth-century followers of George Fox (1624–1691). They traditionally worshiped without any liturgy or minister, in the hope that as they sat in worshipful silence God would speak through any one of their members.

myreligionlab
Free Churches

During the nineteenth and twentieth centuries, yet more Protestant churches sprang up in the United States, including evangelical churches—those emphasizing salvation by personal faith in Jesus, personal conversion, the importance of the Bible, and preaching instead of ritual. **Seventh Day Adventists** believe that

Quaker meeting in Leeds, England.

the Second Coming of Christ will soon occur, and they regard the Bible as an absolute guide to faith and spiritual practice in anticipation of his return. **Jehovah's Witnesses** criticize other Christian Churches as having developed false doctrines from the second century onward, and they urge people to leave these "false religions" and prepare for a coming time when all who do not hold true belief will be destroyed.

Protestant missionary societies and evangelists were also active in carrying the gospel to Asia and Africa, where many independent denominations have evolved, and to South America, where Protestant groups are gaining strongholds in areas that had formerly been largely Roman Catholic since the Spanish conquests of these countries. This multiculturalism and contemporary evangelism will be examined in detail at the end of this chapter.

Despite the great diversity among Protestant denominations, most share several characteristics that distinguish them somewhat from Orthodoxy and Roman Catholicism, though the Catholic Church's positions are now much closer to those of Protestants as a result of the profound changes introduced in 1962 by the Second Vatican Council. Both take the Bible as their foundation, but differ on how it is to be interpreted. Protestants tend to follow Martin Luther in believing that the individual's conscience and reason are the ultimate guides to understanding the scripture. This is in contrast to Roman Catholics who assert the authority of Church tradition and the infallibility of the Vatican's pronouncements about essentials of the faith, and Orthodox, who regard the Bible as a "verbal icon" of Christ and thus tend to focus more on venerating it than on interpreting it. A second point that has divided Protestants and Roman Catholics is the Protestant belief that we can achieve salvation only by God's grace, through repentance and faith; Roman Catholics support the doctrine of salvation by both faith and good works. A third divisive issue is that of spiritual authority.

Protestantism asserts the "priesthood of all believers" and the individual's direct relationship to God and Jesus, in contrast to Roman Catholicism, which stands on mediation of God's grace through the officials of the Church. The officials themselves differ in many respects, such as the provision that Protestant ministers can be married, unlike Catholic priests, who are expected to remain celibate in the belief that restraint of physical desires enhances spirituality. Fourth, Protestants have radically redefined the Roman Catholic and Orthodox concept of sacraments; Luther and Zwingli insisted that the only holy sacraments are those instituted by Jesus and regarded even those as instructive or commemorative rather than as mystical vehicles for God's grace. The sacraments and their meanings for Protestants, Roman Catholics, and Orthodox believers will be examined in depth later in this chapter.

The Roman Catholic Reformation

As the Protestant reformers were defining their positions, so was the Roman Catholic Church. Because reform pressures were under way in Catholicism before Luther, Catholics refer to the movement as the Catholic Reformation, rather than the "Counter-Reformation," as Protestants call it. However, the Protestant phenomena provoked the Roman Catholic Church to clarify its own position through councils of bishops, especially the Council of Trent (1545–1563). It attempted to legislate moral reform among the clergy, to tighten the Church administration, and to recognize officially the absolute authority of the pope as the earthly vicar of God and Jesus Christ. The council also took historic stands on a number of issues, emphasizing that its positions were **dogmas**, or authoritative truths. For example, one of the fundamental doctrines of the Roman Catholic Church is the dogma of **original sin**. All humans are said to be morally defective, or "fallen," having inherited a sinful nature from the first human ancestors. They can be saved from this condition only by the grace of God, as mediated through the death and Resurrection of Jesus, and the cleansing sacrament of baptism.

The Council of Trent reiterated that salvation requires "good works" as well as faith. These works include acts of mercy, veneration of the saints, relics, and sacred images, and participation in the sacraments. In the sacrament of the Eucharist, the Council reiterated the doctrine of **transubstantiation**: what appear to be ordinary bread and wine are mysteriously transformed into the body and blood of Christ.

In addition to the actions of the Council of Trent, the Roman Catholic Church gradually chose popes who were more virtuous than some in the past, and several new monastic orders grew out of the desires for reform. The Jesuits offered themselves as an army for God at the service of the pope. The Society of Jesus, as the order was formally called, was begun by Ignatius Loyola (1491–1556) in the sixteenth century. His *Spiritual Exercises* is still regarded as an excellent guide to meditation and spiritual discernment. However, it was as activists and educators in the everyday world that Jesuits were highly influential in the Reformation, and they were among the first to carry Roman Catholicism to Asia.

Roman Catholicism was also carried to the Western hemisphere and the Philippines by Spanish *conquistadores*. At home, Spain was host to a number of

Another Theresa, St. Thérèse of Lisieux (1873–1897), the "Little Flower," lived as a cloistered Carmelite nun for ten years of her short life. Her journal is full of small, secret sacrifices. Published posthumously as Story of a Soul, *it brought so much fame to this "little one" that she was soon declared a saint.*

outstanding mystics during the sixteenth and seventeenth centuries. St. Teresa of Avila (1515–1582), a Carmelite nun, became at mid-life a dynamo of spiritual activity, in an order of ascetic discalced ("barefooted") Carmelite nuns and monks. The order continues its deep spiritual practices today, with two hours of silent prayer daily as well as observance of the full Liturgy of the Hours—daily prayer services of hymns and scriptural readings that punctuate the day and night. Despite her organizational activity, St. Teresa was able to maintain a calm sense of deep inner communion with God. In her masterpiece entitled *The Interior Castle*, she described the state of "spiritual marriage":

> *Here it is like rain falling from the heavens into a river or a spring; there is nothing but water there and it is impossible to divide or separate the water belonging to the river from that which fell from the heavens.*[63]

St. Teresa's great influence fell onto a young friend, now known as St. John of the Cross. He became a member of one of the Carmelite houses for men; when imprisoned by other Carmelites who opposed the reforms, he experienced visions and wrote profound spiritual poetry. For John, the most important step for the soul longing to be filled with God is to surrender all vestiges of the self. This state he called the "dark night of the soul," a relinquishing of human reasoning into a state of not-knowing into which the pure light of God may enter without resistance. He is still considered one of the great masters of the spiritual life.

Liberal trends

Major potential threats to Christianity arose during the eighteenth-century Enlightenment in Europe. Intellectual circles exalted human reason and on this basis rejected faith in biblical miracles and revelations. As discussed in Chapter 1, some people felt that nineteenth-century scientific advances undermined the biblical story of the creation of the world. However, many nineteenth-century scientists were devout Christians who viewed the truth of science as supporting the truth of faith. There emerged two opposing trends: a liberal one, trying to join faith with modern knowledge, and a conservative one, emphasizing the conflict between faith and science.

Undaunted, and in some cases invigorated, by rationalist challenges to traditional faith, Protestantism developed a strong missionary spirit, joining Roman Catholic efforts to spread Christianity to every country, along with colonialism. As John Wesley, the founder of Methodism, had explained:

> *I looked upon all the world as my parish; … that in whatever part of it I am, I judge it meet, right, and my bounden duty to declare unto all that are willing to hear, the glad tidings of salvation.*[64]

In the late nineteenth and early twentieth centuries, Protestant Churches came to the forefront of efforts at social and moral reform. Women, long excluded from important positions in the Church, played major roles in Church-related missionary and reform efforts, such as the abolition of slavery; they cited certain biblical passages as supporting equality of the sexes. When Sarah Grimke (1792–1873) and other women were criticized by their Congregational Church for speaking publicly against slavery, Grimke asserted, "All I ask of my brethren is that they will take their feet from off our necks and permit us to stand upright on that ground which God has designed us to occupy."[65]

Liberal trends in Protestant theology led to efforts to analyze the Bible as literature. What, for instance, were the earliest texts? Who wrote them? How did they relate to each other? Who was the historical Jesus? Such questions were unthinkable in earlier generations. However, now in New Testament scholarship there is an interest in studying the texts as they are, receiving them as a whole, rather than analyzing and pulling them apart, in Enlightenment fashion, as if dissecting a frog.

The Second Vatican Council

In the meantime, the Roman Catholic and Eastern Orthodox Churches had continued to defend tradition against the changes of modern life. A general council of the Roman Catholic hierarchs was held in 1869–1870. It found itself embroiled chiefly in the question of papal infallibility, a doctrine it ultimately upheld. The pope, proclaimed the bishops of the council, can never err when he speaks from the seat of his authority (*ex cathedra*), on matters of faith and morals.

In 1962, Pope John XXIII, known for his holiness and friendliness, convened the Second Vatican Council for the express purposes of updating and energizing the Church and making it serve the people better as a living force in the modern world rather than being an old, embattled citadel. When questioned about his intentions, he demonstrated them by opening a window to let in fresh air. With progressives and traditionalists often at odds, the majority nevertheless voted for major shifts in the Church's mission.

Many of the changes involved the liturgy of the mass, or the Eucharist. Rather than celebrate it in Latin, which most people did not understand, the liturgy was to be translated into the local languages. Rites were to be simplified. Greater use of sacred music was encouraged, and not just formal, traditional organ and choir offerings.

For the first time the laity were to be invited to participate actively. After Vatican II thus unleashed creativity and simplicity in public worship, entirely new forms appeared, such as informal folk masses—with spiritual folk songs sung to guitar accompaniment.

Another major change was the new emphasis on **ecumenism**, in the sense of rapprochement among all branches of Christianity. The Roman Catholic Church acknowledged that the Holy Spirit is active in all Christian Churches, including Protestant denominations and the Eastern Orthodox Churches. It pressed for a restoration of unity among all Christians, proclaiming that each could preserve its traditions intact. It also extended the concept of revelation, increasing the hope of dialogue with Jews, with whom Christians share "spiritual patrimony,"[66] and with Muslims, upon whom the Church "looks with esteem," for they "adore one God" and honor Jesus as a prophet. Appreciative mention was also made of other world religions as ways of approaching the same One whom Christians call God.

Vatican II clearly marked major new directions in Catholicism. Its relatively liberal, pacifist characteristics are still meeting with some opposition within the Church decades later. In the late twentieth century, conservative elements in the

Vatican began to reverse the direction taken by Vatican II to some extent, to the dismay of liberal Catholics. In the final section of this chapter, concerning current trends in Christianity, we will note several ways in which the renewed conservatism in the Vatican is being expressed.

The Orthodox world today

The Holy Trinity Lavra, one of the greatest monasteries of the Russian Orthodox Church, grew up in Sergeyev Posad near Moscow, where St. Sergius used to live as an ascetic in the forest. It is now a popular tourist attraction.

After its 1054 split with the Western Church, the Eastern Orthodox Church had spread throughout the Slavic and eastern Mediterranean countries. After the Muslim Ottoman Turks took Constantinople in the fifteenth century, Russia became prominent in the Orthodox Church, calling itself the "third Rome."

There are now fifteen self-governing Orthodox Churches worldwide, each having its own leader, known as patriarch, metropolitan, or archbishop. The majority of Orthodox Christians now live in Russia, the Balkan states, and eastern Europe, in formerly communist countries where the teaching and propagation of

Eastern Orthodox Church

- Patriarchate of Constantinople (Turkey, Mount Athos)
- Patriarchate of Alexandria (Egypt, Africa)
- Patriarchate of Antioch (Syria, Lebanon)
- Patriarchate of Jerusalem
- Self-governing local Churches (Russia, Serbia, Romania, Bulgaria, Georgia, Cyprus, Greece, Poland, Albania, Czech lands and Slovakia)
- Plus archbishops or metropolitans in the Americas, Australia, India, and European countries

Christianity had been severely restricted. Autocephalous (independent) churches there include the large Church of Russia, which is dominated by the Patriarchate of Moscow, plus the Churches of Serbia, Bulgaria, Romania, Albania, Poland, and the Czech Republic. The original and still central Patriarchate of Constantinople is based within Turkey, as a small minority within a Muslim country, which now has no Orthodox seminaries. The Patriarchate of Constantinople nonetheless tries to play a central role in maintaining Orthodox unity and the historical continuity of Orthodox sacred practices, dating back to the Desert Fathers.

The Patriarchate of Constantinople also includes islands in the Aegean and the precipitous Mount Athos peninsula. The latter was historically a great center of Orthodox monasticism, but its population of monks declined considerably in the twentieth century when emigration of monks was prohibited by communist regimes. Now women have agitated to be allowed to enter Mount Athos, where even the presence of female animals is banned. Traditionalists maintain that Mount Athos is the only truly monastic community left in the world and should continue its antique ways unchanged and undistracted; women counter that the ban on women is degrading, a "sexist, anti-democratic decision taken by men, not by God."[67]

The Patriarchate of Alexandria is based in Egypt and includes all of Africa, where Orthodoxy arose independently in Uganda and has been embraced with considerable enthusiasm. The Patriarchate of Antioch consists mostly of Orthodox Christian Arabs in Syria and Lebanon. The Patriarchate of Jerusalem is charged with guarding the Holy Places of Christianity.

The Greek Orthodox Church dominates religious life in Greece and is assisting in the revival of interest in the classical books and arts of Orthodox spirituality. In the Church of Cyprus, the archbishop is also traditionally the political leader of the people.

Extensive emigration, particularly from Russia during the first few years of communist rule, also created large Orthodox populations in Western countries. Some retain direct ties to their home patriarchate, such as the New York-based Archdiocese of the Greek Orthodox Church in North and South America. Alongside that, the Orthodox Church in America was granted its independence

myreligionlab
Eastern Orthodox Church

in 1970, and now claims over four million members in a country where Protestantism and Roman Catholicism are the predominant forms of Christianity. Missionary activity by the Russian Orthodox Church also established Orthodoxy in China, Korea, Japan, and among the indigenous peoples in Alaska.

THE RUSSIAN ORTHODOX CHURCH

Largest of the Eastern Orthodox Churches is the Russian Orthodox Church. It was closely associated with Russian national history since its adoption by Vladimir I in 988. But it was severely repressed by the Soviet government during the twentieth century. Lenin saw institutionalized religion as a divisive, backward force in society, an apology for oppression, which should wither away in the socialist state. During the 1917 Revolution, thousands of monasteries and churches were taken over, and in the early 1920s thousands of priests, nuns, and lay Christians were killed. During the 1930s more monasteries and churches were closed, and great numbers of clergy were imprisoned.

The bishops were imprisoned in the Solovky labor camp; many were killed there. It is estimated that some 40,000 priests were killed from 1918 to 1940. Out of almost 80,000 churches and chapels in the Russian Empire in 1914, only a few hundred or a thousand remained by the beginning of World War II. Under Khrushchev, a new campaign against religion was unleashed, and perhaps two-thirds of the remaining Orthodox churches were closed.

Nevertheless, the Russian Orthodox Church did not die, for it was deeply rooted in the minds and hearts of the people, and was closely linked to national identity. In the mid-1980s, it had an estimated fifty million members.

The Russian Orthodox Church witnessed a great change in government policy

Orthodox priests conduct Easter Mass in Moscow.

in 1988, the celebration of its first millennium in Russia and Ukraine. Mikhail Gorbachev's government approached the Orthodox Church leaders, asking their help with *perestroika* and returning some church buildings, which had been turned into museums or warehouses. Some 1,700 churches were reopened in 1988 and 1989, and each was immediately filled with worshipers again. Now the Russian Orthodox Church has very powerful influence in government policy and is strongly supported by political leaders from all parties, including communists.

Since the early days of the Soviet Union, there have also been Orthodox Christians who refused to collaborate or compromise with the government. At the risk of their jobs and lives, some Christian laypeople and priests began to worship secretly in what became known as catacomb churches, just as the early Christians had worshiped in underground catacombs to evade persecution.

Even today, some Orthodox Christians continue to worship in secret rather than subject their congregations to the registration requirements of the state and disapproval of the official Church. Bishop Feodor, bishop of underground Christians in Moscow, Riga, and the Far East, objects to the assertive power of the Russian Orthodox Church:

> If the Church has pride, it has no holy power. We are all brothers in Adam
> and in Christ. We are all baptized by God. This is true for each Christian.
> If you cannot love your brother who is next to you, how can you love one you
> cannot see, such as Christ, who has not been with us for two thousand years?[68]

DISTINCTIVE FEATURES OF ORTHODOX SPIRITUALITY

Over the centuries, the individual Orthodox Churches have probably changed less than have the many descendants of the early Western Church. There is a strong conservative tradition, attempting to preserve the pattern of early Christianity. Even though the religious leaders can make local adaptations suited to their region and people, they are united in doctrine and sacramental observances. Any change that will affect all churches is decided by a **synod**—a council of officials trying to reach common agreements, as did the early Church. Although women are important in local Church affairs, they cannot be ordained as priests or serve in hierarchical capacities.

In addition to the Bible, Orthodox Christians honor the writings of the saints of the Church. Particularly important is a collection called the *Philokalia*. It consists of texts written by Orthodox masters between the fourth and fifteenth centuries. "Philokalia" means love of the exalted, excellent, and beautiful, in other words, the transcendent divine source of life and truth. The *Philokalia* is essentially a Christian guide to the contemplative life for monks, but it is also for laypeople. A central practice is called "unceasing prayer": the continual remembrance of Jesus or God, often through repetition of a verbal formula that gradually impresses itself on the heart. The most common petition is the "Jesus prayer": "Lord Jesus Christ, Son of God, have mercy on me, a sinner." The repetition of the name of Jesus brings purification of heart and singularity of desire. To call upon Jesus is to experience his presence in oneself and in all things.

The Orthodox Church has affirmed that humans can approach God directly. Some may even see the light of God and be utterly transformed by it:

He who participates in the divine energy, himself becomes, to some extent, light: he is united to the light, and by that light he sees in full awareness all that remains hidden to those who have not this grace; ... for the pure in heart see God ... who, being Light, dwells in them and reveals Himself to those who love Him, to His beloved.[69]

Another distinctive feature of Orthodox Christianity is its veneration of **icons**. These are stylized paintings of Jesus, his mother Mary, and the saints. They are created by artists who prepare for their work by prayer and ascetical training. There is no attempt at earthly realism, for icons are representations of the reality of the divine world. They are beloved as windows to the eternal. In addition to their devotional and instructional functions, some icons are reported to have great spiritual powers, heal illnesses, and transmit the holy presence. Believers enter into the grace of this power by kissing the icon reverently and praying before it.

Some of the major icons in an Orthodox church are placed on an iconostasis, a screen separating the floor area for the congregation from the Holy of Holies, the sanctuary that can be entered only by the clergy. On either side of the opening to the altar are icons of Jesus and the Virgin Mary ("Mother of God," often venerated as Protectress and Ruler of Russia).

Orthodox choirs sing the divine liturgy in many-part harmony, producing an ethereal and uplifting effect as the sounds echo and re-echo around each other. Everything strives toward that beauty to which the *Philokalia* refers. Archimandrite Nathaniel of the Russian Orthodox Pskova-Pechorsky Monastery, which has been a place of uninterrupted prayer for almost 600 years despite 800 attacks on its walls and numerous sieges, speaks of the ideal of beauty in Orthodox Christianity:

Most icon painters, such as this monk at Mount Athos, Greece, use the ancient Byzantine style in creating sacred icons, which represent Christian stories and open windows to the divine.

Christians lighting candles around a Christmas tree in Bucharest, Romania, 25 December, 1989, as communism collapsed.

The understanding of God is the understanding of beauty. Beauty is at the heart of our monastic life. The life of prayer is a constant well of beauty. We have the beauty of music in the Holy Liturgy. The great beauty of monastic life is communal life in Christ. Living together in love, living without enmity, as peaceful with each other as one dead body is peaceful with another dead body, we are dead to enmity.[70]

Central beliefs in contemporary Christianity

The history of Christianity is characterized more by divisions than by uniformity among Christian groups. The Church is vast and culturally diverse, and Christian theologies are complex and intricate. Nevertheless, there are a few basic motifs on which the majority of faithful Christians would probably agree today.

A central belief is the divine Sonship of Jesus—the assertion that Jesus is the incarnation of God. According to the Gospel of John, before Jesus' death he told his disciples that he would be going to "my Father's house … to prepare a place for you." When they asked how they would find the way to that place, Jesus reportedly said:

I am the way, I am the truth and I am life. No one comes to the Father except by me. … Anyone who has seen me has seen the Father. … It is the Father who dwells in me doing his own work.[71]

Throughout most of Christian history, there has been the belief that Jesus was the only incarnation of God. Interestingly, Thomas Aquinas argued that although God could become incarnate in multiple incarnations (as in Hindu belief), in fact he chose to do so only once, in Christ. Theologian Paul Knitter, co-editor of *The*

Myth of Christian Uniqueness, is one of the contemporary voices calling for a less exclusive approach that still honors the unique contribution of Jesus:

> *What Christians do know, on the basis of their praxis of following Jesus, is that his message is a sure means for bringing about liberation from injustice and oppression, that it is an effective, hope-filled, universally meaningful way of realizing* Soteria *[human welfare and liberation of the poor and oppressed] and promoting God's kingdom. ... Not those who proclaim "only Lord, only Lord," but those who do the will of the Father will enter the kingdom (Matthew 7:21–23).[72]*

For Christians, Jesus is the Savior of the world, the one whom God sent to redeem people from their sins and reconcile them with God. Matthew reports that Jesus said he "did not come to be served, but to serve, and to give up his life as a ransom for many."[73] His own suffering and death are regarded as a substitute sacrifice on behalf of all those who follow and place their faith in him. According to the Gospel of John:

> *God loved the world so much that he gave his only Son, that everyone who has faith in him may not die but have eternal life. It was not to judge the world that God sent his Son into the world, but that through him the world might be saved.[74]*

According to one strand of Christian belief, humanity has a sinful character, illustrated metaphorically in the Old Testament by the fall of Adam and Eve. We have lost our original purity. Given free will by God, we have chosen disobedience rather than surrender to the will of God. We cannot save ourselves from our fallen condition; we can only be forgiven by the compassion of a loving God. However, some Christians such as Methodists and Quakers are more optimistic about human nature.

Through fully surrendered faith in Jesus, Christians hope to be washed of their egotistical sinfulness, regenerated, made righteous, adopted by God, sanctified, and glorified in the life to come. These are the blessings of salvation, which Christians feel Jesus won for them by his sacrifice.

Although Christians worship Jesus as Savior, as the incarnation of a merciful God, they also see him as a human being showing fellow human beings the way to God. His own life is seen as the perfect model for human behavior. Archbishop Desmond Tutu of South Africa emphasizes Jesus' identification with the human condition:

> *God does not occupy an Olympian fastness, remote from us. He has this deep, deep solidarity with us. God became a human being, a baby. God was hungry. God was tired, God suffered and died. God is there with us.[75]*

This is the central mystery of Christianity: that God became human in order to lead people back to God.

The human virtue most often associated with Jesus is love. Many Christians say they experience Jesus' love even though he is no longer walking the earth in human form. And in turn, they have deep love for Jesus. Those who are experiencing problems are comforted to feel that Jesus is a living presence in their lives, supporting them spiritually, loving them even in the darkest of times. Reverend Larry Howard, the African American pastor of Hopps Memorial Christian Methodist Episcopal Church in Syracuse, New York, declares:

We found a Jesus. A Jesus who came in the midnight hour. A Jesus that was able to rock babies to sleep. A Jesus that stood in the midst and walked the miles when the freedom train rode through the South all the way through Syracuse. Jesus brought us through the mighty trials and tribulations. Why did Jesus do that? Jesus loved us and through that love and because of that love we stand here today. Not because the world has been so good to us. Not because we have been treated fair. Not because we have been able to realize the dream that God has given every man, woman, and child. But we stand here because we love Jesus. We love him more and more and more each day.[76]

> *The basic thrust of Jesus' message is to invite us into divine union, which is the sole remedy for the human predicament.*
>
> *Father Thomas Keating*[77]

In addition to being the paragon of love, Jesus also provides a model of sinlessness. To become like God, humans must constantly be purified of their lower tendencies. This belief has led some Christians to extremes of penance, such as the monks who flogged themselves and wore hairshirts so that their conscience might always be pricked. In a milder form, confession of one's sinfulness is a significant part of Christian tradition. There is an emphasis on self-discipline to guard against temptations, on examination of one's own faults, and on rituals, such as baptism, that help to remove the contamination that is innate in humanity. Although one must make these efforts at purification, most Christians believe that it is only through the grace of God—as mediated by the saving sacrifice of Jesus—that one can be delivered from sin and rise above ordinary human nature toward a divine state of sinlessness.

Sacred practices

Imitation of the model set by Jesus in his own life is the primary practice of Christians. In the widely read fourteenth-century book, *The Imitation of Christ*, people are encouraged to aspire to Jesus' own example as well as his teachings:

> *O how powerful is the pure love of Jesus, which is mixed with no self-interest, nor self-love! … Where shall one be found who is willing to serve God for naught?*[78]

In addition to the inner attempt to become more and more like Jesus, Christians have developed a variety of spiritual practices. Although forms and understandings of the practices vary among the branches of Christendom, they may include public worship services with sermons and offering of the sacraments, celebrations of the liturgical year, private contemplation and prayer, and devotions to Mary and the saints.

WORSHIP SERVICES AND SACRAMENTS

Christian worship typically takes place in a church building, which may be revered as a sacred space. The late-nineteenth-century Russian Orthodox saint Ioann Kronshtadtsky (d. 1908) explained:

Entering the church you enter some special realm which is not like the visible one. In the world you hear and see everything earthly, transient, fragile, liable to decay, sinful. In the church you see and hear the heavenly, the non-transient, the eternal, the holy. A temple is the threshold of heaven. It is like the heaven itself, because here is God's throne, the service of angels, the frequent descent of the Holy Spirit. … Here everything from icons to censer and the priests' robes fills you with veneration and prayer; everything tells you that you are in God's shrine, face to face with God himself.[79]

myreligi⊙nlab
The Eucharistic
Prayer
ROMAN CATHOLIC
MASS

The word sacrament can be translated as "mystery." In Roman Catholicism and Orthodoxy, the sacraments are the sacred rites that are thought capable of transmitting the mystery of Christ to worshipers. Roman Catholic and Eastern Orthodox churches observe seven sacraments: baptism (initiation and symbolic purification from sin by water), confirmation (of membership in the Church), Eucharist (the ritual meal described below), penance (confession and absolution of sins), extreme unction (anointing of the sick with oil, especially before death), holy orders (consecration as a deacon, priest, or bishop), and matrimony. In general, Protestant churches recognize only baptism and the Eucharist as sacraments and have a somewhat less mystical understanding of their significance.

The ritual of public worship, or liturgy, usually follows a set pattern, though in some churches the actions of the Holy Spirit are thought to inspire spontaneous expressions of faith.

In most forms of Christianity, the central sacrament is the Holy Eucharist (also called Holy Communion, mass, or Lord's Supper). It is a mystery through which the invisible Christ is thought to grant communion with himself. Believers are given a bit of bread to eat, which is received as the body of Christ, and a sip of

The sacrament of the Eucharist, celebrated here in Ghana, engages believers in a communal mystical encounter with the presence of Christ.

wine or grape juice, understood as his blood. The priest or minister may consecrate the bread and wine in ritual fashion and share them among the people. For Protestants, these are symbols of Jesus' presence. In Roman Catholic or Orthodox masses, the cup of wine and the bread are thought to be mystically transformed by the Holy Spirit into the blood and body of Christ. They are treated with profound reverence. In sharing the communion "meal" together, the people are united with each other as well as with Christ. The traditional ideal was to take communion every day and certainly every Sunday (the day set aside as the Sabbath).

Jesus is pictured in the Bible as having set the pattern for this sacrament at what is called the Last Supper, the meal he shared with his inner circle before his capture by the authorities in Jerusalem. The body and blood of Christ are seen as the spiritual nourishment of the faithful, that which gives them eternal life in the midst of earthly life.

Mother Julia Gatta, an Anglican priest in Connecticut, describes this sacred experience from the point of view of the clergy who preside at the liturgy:

> To be the celebrant of Eucharist is, I think, the most wonderful experience on earth. In a sense, you experience the energy flowing both ways. … One experiences the Spirit in them offering their prayer through Christ to the Father. But at the same time, you experience God's love flowing back into them. When I give communion to people, I am aware that I am caught in that circle of love.[80]

The partaking of sacred bread and wine is the climax of a longer liturgy of Holy Communion. The communion service, often called a mass in Catholicism, begins with liturgical prayers, praise, and confession of sinfulness. A group confession chanted by some Protestant congregations enumerates these flaws:

> Most merciful God, we have sinned against you in thought, word, and deed, by what we have done and by what we have left undone. We have not loved you with our whole heart; we have not loved our neighbors as ourselves.[81]

Catholics were traditionally encouraged to confess their sins privately to a priest before taking communion, in the sacrament of **penance**, or "reparation for guilt" (also called "reconciliation"). After hearing the confession, the priest pronounces forgiveness and blessing over the penitent, or perhaps prescribes a penance. Orthodox Christians were also traditionally expected to spend several days in contrition and fasting before receiving communion. The reason for the emphasis on purification is that during the service the church itself is perceived as the Kingdom of God, in which everything is holy. In Orthodox services, the clergy walk around the church, swinging an incense censer to set apart the area as a sacred space and to lift the prayers of the congregants to God.

In all Christian churches, passages from the Old and New Testaments may be read and the congregation may sing several hymns, songs of praise or thanksgiving to God. The congregation may be asked to recite a credal statement of Christian beliefs, and to make money offerings. There may be an address by the priest or minister (called a sermon or a homily) on the readings for the day. These parts of the liturgy constitute the Liturgy of the Word, in which Christ is thought to be present as the living Word, addressing the people through scripture and preaching. In Protestant churches, the Liturgy of the Word is often offered by itself, without the communion service.

In both Protestantism and Roman Catholicism, there are now attempts at updating the liturgy to make it more meaningful and personally relevant for contemporary Christians. One innovation that seems to have taken hold everywhere is the "sharing of the peace." Partway through the worship service, congregants turn to everyone around them to hug or shake hands and say, "The Peace of Christ be with you"—"and also with you."

myreligionlab

Baptism
BOOK OF COMMON
PRAYER

In addition to regular liturgies and the sacrament of the mass or communion, there are special events treated in sacred ways. The first to be administered is the sacrament of baptism. Externally, it involves either immersing the person in water or, more commonly, pouring sanctified water (representing purification) on the candidate's head, while invoking the Holy Trinity. In a recent ecumenical document, the World Council of Churches defined the general meaning of the practice:

> *By baptism, Christians are immersed in the liberating death of Christ where their sins are buried, where the "old Adam" is crucified with Christ, and where the power of sin is broken. … They are raised here and now to a new life in the power of the resurrection of Jesus Christ.*[82]

Aside from adult converts to Christianity, the rite is usually performed on infants, with parents taking vows on their behalf. There are arguments that infant baptism has little basis in the Bible and that a baby cannot make the conscious repentance of sin and "conversion of heart" implied in the ceremony. Baptists and several other Protestant groups therefore reserve baptism for adults.

A second ceremony—**confirmation**—is often offered in early adolescence in Roman Catholicism and Protestantism. After a period of religious instruction, a group of young people are allowed to make a conscious and personal commitment to the Christian life.

Some Christians observe special days of fasting. Russian Orthodox Old Believer priest Father Appolinari explains fasting as a way of *soprichiastna*, of becoming part of something very large, the spiritual aura of the Lord. He says:

> *More and more ordinary people are seeking a comfortable life. More and more we leave spirituality. We try to fill this vacuum with material things. I told my students that there was a fast coming up. They groaned, "Why?" I said that we fast for spiritual reasons. The rule is that you should fast not with a spirit of suffering but with such elevated spirit that your soul sings.*
>
> *When we limit our physicality, as in limiting our food intake, then we grow in our spirituality. I advise my students to notice whether their brain works better when their stomach is full or when it is almost empty. Monks refuse physical things in order to get spiritual benefits. We look at them and see their lives as dark, but for them, it is light.*[83]

THE LITURGICAL YEAR

Just as Christians repeatedly enact their union with Christ through participation in the Eucharist sacrament, Christian churches celebrate a yearly cycle of festivals, leading the worshiper through the life of Jesus and the gift of the Spirit. As the faithful repeat this cycle year after year, they hope to enter more deeply into the mystery of God in Christ, and the whole body of believers in Christ theoretically grows toward the kingdom of God.

Christmas and Epiphany   First of the major periods in the Church calendar, each associated with a series of preparatory celebrations, is the season of light: Christmas and **Epiphany**. Christmas is the celebration of Jesus' birth on earth as the incarnation of God. Epiphany means "manifestation" or "showing forth." It celebrates the recognition of Jesus' spiritual kingship by the three Magi (in the Western Church), his acknowledgement as the Messiah and the beloved Son of God when he is baptized by John the Baptist, and his first recognized miracle, the turning of water into wine at the wedding in Cana.

In early Christianity, Epiphany was more important than the celebration of Jesus' birth. The actual birth date is unknown, but the setting of the date near the winter solstice allowed Christianity to take over the older "pagan" rites celebrating the return of longer periods of daylight at the darkest time of year. In the Gospel of John, Jesus is "the true light that enlightens every man,"[84] the light of the divine appearing amid the darkness of human ignorance.

Advent, the month preceding Christmas, is supposed to be a time of joyous anticipation. But in industrialized countries, it is more likely a time of frenzied marketing and buying of gifts, symbolizing God's gift of Jesus to the world.

In some countries churches stage pageants re-enacting the birth story, with people taking the parts of Mary, Joseph, the innkeeper who has no room, the shepherds, and the three Magi. Since the nineteenth century, it has been traditional to cut or buy an evergreen tree (a symbol of eternal life, perhaps borrowed from indigenous ceremonies) and erect it in one's house, decorated with lights and ornaments. On Christmas Eve some Christians gather for a candlelit "watch-

Young children re-enact the Christmas story, adoring Jesus as a baby.

night" service, welcoming the turn from midnight to a new day in which Christ has come into the world. On Christmas Day, Catholic and Protestant children are sometimes told that presents have been magically brought by St. Nicholas, a fourth-century bishop noted for his great generosity. The exchange of gifts may be followed by a great feast.

Easter   In terms of religious significance, the most important event of the Christian liturgical year is Easter. This is the commemoration of Jesus' death (on "Good Friday") and Resurrection (on Easter Sunday, which falls in the spring but is celebrated at different times by the Eastern and Western Churches). Like Christmas, Easter is a continuation of earlier rites—those associated with the vernal (spring) equinox, celebrating the regeneration of plant life and the return of warm weather after the cold death of winter. It is also related to Pesach, the Hebrew Passover, the Jewish spring feast of deliverance.

Liturgically, Easter is preceded by a forty-day period of repentance and fasting, called **Lent**. Many Christians perform acts of asceticism, prayer, and charity, to join in Jesus' greater sacrifice. In the Orthodox Church, the last Sunday before Lent is dedicated to asking forgiveness. People request forgiveness from each other, bowing deeply. In the West, Lent begins with Ash Wednesday, when many Christians have ash smudges placed on their foreheads by a priest who says, "Remember, man, thou art dust and unto dust thou shalt return." On the Sunday before Easter, Jesus' triumphal entry into Jerusalem is honored by the waving of palm or willow branches in churches and the proclaiming of Hosannas. His death is mourned on Good Friday. The mourning is jubilantly ended on Easter Sunday, with shouts of "Christ is risen!"

In Russia, the Great Vigil welcoming Easter morning lasts from midnight until dawn, with the people standing the entire time. Jim Forest describes such a service in a church in Kiev, with 2,000 people crowding into the building and as many more standing outside:

> The dean went out the royal doors into the congregation and sang out, "Christos Voskresye!" [Christ is risen!] Everyone responded in one voice, "Veyeastino voskresye!" [Truly he is risen!] It is impossible to put on paper how this sounds in the dead of night in a church overheated by crowds of people and hundreds of candles. It is like a shudder in the earth, the cracking open of the tomb. Then there was an explosion of ringing bells.[85]

Ascension   Ascension may also be celebrated as one of the major holy days in the Christian liturgical calendar, honoring the bodily Ascension of Jesus to heaven. It is celebrated on the Thursday that occurs forty days after Easter, or on the following Sunday. Apparently this event has been celebrated since the early centuries of Christianity. Solemn liturgical observances focus on readings from biblical accounts and credal statements regarding the religious significance of the Ascension. In medieval England, the Ascension was celebrated by a triumphal torchlight procession with a banner portraying a lion above a dragon, symbolizing the ascended Christ's triumph over Satan.

Pentecost   Fifty days after the Jewish Passover (which Jesus is thought to have been celebrating with a Seder meal as the Last Supper with his disciples) comes the Jewish celebration Shavuot (which commemorates the giving of the Torah to Moses, as well as the first fruits of the harvest). Jews nicknamed it Pentecost, which is Greek for "fiftieth." Christians took over the holiday but gave it an entirely different meaning.

In Christianity, Pentecost commemorates the occasion described in Acts when the Holy Spirit descended upon the disciples after Jesus' death, Resurrection, and Ascension, filling them with the Spirit's own life and power and enabling them to speak in foreign tongues they had not known. In early Christianity, Pentecost was an occasion for baptisms of those who had been preparing for admission to the Church.

The Transfiguration and Assumption Some Christian Churches also emphasize two other special feast days. On 6 August, people honor the Transfiguration of Jesus on the mountain, revealing his supernatural radiance. On 15 August, they celebrate the Assumption of Mary, known as "The Falling Asleep of the Mother of God," in which she was thought to ascend body and soul into heaven at the end of her physical life. These feasts are prominent in the Eastern Church, which generally places more emphasis on the ability of humanity to break out of its earthly bonds and rise into the light, than on the heaviness and darkness of sin.

CONTEMPLATIVE PRAYER

The contemplative tradition within Christianity is beginning to re-emerge. The hectic pace and rapid change of modern life make periods of quietness essential, if only for stress relief. Many Christians, not aware of a contemplative way within their own Church, have turned to Eastern religions for instruction in meditation.

One of the most influential twentieth-century Christian contemplatives was the late Thomas Merton (1915–1968). He was a Trappist monk who received a special dispensation to live as a hermit in the woods near his abbey in Kentucky. Merton lived simply in nature, finding joy in the commonplace, experienced attentively in silence. He studied and tried to practice the great contemplative traditions of earlier Christianity and reintroduced them to a contemporary audience through his writings. In meditative "prayer of the heart," or "contemplative prayer," he wrote:

> We seek first of all the deepest ground of our identity in God. We do not reason about dogmas of faith, or "the mysteries." We seek rather to gain a direct existential grasp, a personal experience of the deepest truths of life and faith, finding ourselves in God's truths. … Prayer then means yearning for the simple presence of God, for a personal understanding of his word, for knowledge of his will and for capacity to hear and obey him.[86]

Before he became a Christian monk, Merton had studied Eastern mysticism, assuming that Christianity had no mystical tradition. He became friends with a Hindu monk who advised him to read St. Augustine's *Confessions* and *The Imitation of Christ*. These classic works led Merton toward a deep appreciation of the potential of the Christian inner life, aligned with a continuing openness to learn from Eastern monasticism. He died in an accident while in Asia visiting Buddhist and Hindu monastics.

The Christian monk Thomas Merton and the Tibetan Buddhist Dalai Lama, two great ecumenical figures of the 20th century, met shortly before Merton died in 1968 during a trip to visit the monks of the Eastern traditions.

Spiritual renewal through inner silence has become an important part of some Christians' practice of their faith. Syrian Orthodox bishop Paulos Mar Gregorios of India, past President of the World Council of Churches, concluded from the Bible evidence that Jesus himself was a contemplative:

> *Christ spent seventy percent of his whole life in meditation. He would sleep rarely. All day he gave himself to healing the sick. At night he would pray, sometimes all night. He was not seeking his own self-realization. His meditation and prayer were not for himself but for the world—for every human being. He held the world in his consciousness through prayer, not with attachment but with compassion. He groaned and he suffered with humanity. To follow Jesus in the way of the cross means to say, "I lay aside all personal ambition and dedicate myself to God: 'Here I am, God. I belong to you. I have no idea where to go. It matters not what I am, so long as You lead me.'"*[87]

A form of Christian meditation instituted by the Franciscans and still practiced in many Catholic and Anglican churches is the Stations of the Cross. These are fourteen plaques or paintings placed on the walls of the church, depicting scenes from the death of Jesus. As one sees him taking up the cross, falling three times under its weight, being stripped of his clothes and being nailed to the cross, one becomes painfully and humbly aware of the suffering that God's Son experienced in manifesting as a human redeemer.

Contemplation of the humanness of Jesus is used to help believers identify with him and thence to aspire to his divine model. Theology professor and spiritual director Kathleen Dugan says that when she teaches devotions on the deep humanity of Jesus:

*My students have difficulty assimilating it. "You mean to say that he felt sorrow
like I do?" "Yes." "That he cried?" "Yes." "That he felt joy?" "Yes." The Gospel
examples show that he wept before Lazarus's tomb. He wept at the sorrow of
Martha and Mary over their brother. He rejoiced with the couple that were being
married at the wedding of Cana. He felt terrible isolation; so many things in the
Gospels speak of that. He said on the cross, "My God, my God, why have you
forsaken me?" There is no human emotion that he did not experience. He did suffer.
Crucifixion was a long, lingering death, with great agony. Jesus is our brother, our
spouse, our son. When students think about these things, it is often transforming.*

*Here is a living, breathing image of what it means to be God. We are called to
imitate the saints, but primarily we are called to imitate Jesus.[88]*

In Orthodoxy, the central contemplative practice is repetition of the Jesus
Prayer: "Lord Jesus Christ, have mercy on me" (and some add, "a sinner").
Eventually its meaning embeds itself in the heart and one lives in a state of
unceasing prayer. An unknown nineteenth-century Russian peasant who lived
with continual repetition of the Jesus Prayer described its results:

*The sweetness of the heart, warmth and light, unspeakable rapture, joy, ease,
profound peace, blessedness, and love of life are all the result of prayer of the heart.[89]*

DEVOTION TO MARY

Thus far in this chapter, little has been said about Mary, the mother of Jesus, for
she has not been in the forefront of historical theological disputes. Veneration of
Mary has come as much from the grassroots as from the top. Drawings of her
were found in the catacombs in which the early Christians met; explicit devotion
to her was well developed by the third or fourth century CE.
Despite the absence of detailed historical information, she
serves as a potent and much-loved spiritual symbol. She is
particularly venerated by Roman Catholics, Eastern
Orthodoxy, and Anglicans.

Some researchers feel that devotion to Mary is derived from
earlier worship of the Mother Goddess. They see her as representing the feminine aspect of the Godhead. She is associated
with the crescent moon, representing the receptive willingness
to be filled with the Spirit. In the story of the **Annunciation**—
the appearance of an angel who told her she would have a
child conceived by the Holy Spirit—her reported response was
"Behold, I am the handmaid of the Lord; let it be to me according to your word."[90] This receptivity is not seen as utter pow-
erlessness, however. Mary, like Christ, embodies the basic
Christian paradox: that power is found in "weakness."

Whether or not devotion to Mary is linked to earlier
Mother Goddess worship, oral Christian traditions have given
her new symbolic roles. One links her with Israel, which is
referred to as the daughter of Zion or daughter of Jerusalem in
Old Testament passages. God comes to her as the overshad-

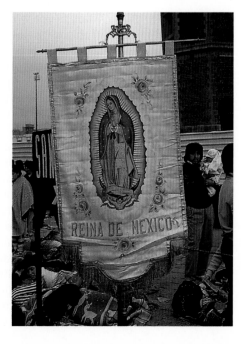

*The Virgin of
Guadalupe, who
reportedly appeared in
the 16th century to an
indigenous convert to
Catholicism, speaking
the native language
Nahuatl, has been
embraced as patron
saint of the Americas.*

owing of the Holy Spirit, and from this love between YHWH and Israel, Jesus is born to save the people of Israel.

Mary is also called the New Eve. The legendary first Eve disobeyed God and was cast out of the Garden of Eden; Mary's willing submission to God allows birth of the new creation, in which Christ is in all.

In the Orthodox and Catholic traditions, she is referred to as the Mother of God. In Russia, she is also revered as the protectress of all humanity, and especially of the Russian people. Before he died on the cross, Jesus is said to have told John, the beloved disciple, that thenceforth Mary was to be his Mother. The story is interpreted as meaning that thenceforth all humanity was adopted by Mary.

Another symbolic role ascribed to Mary is that of the immaculate virgin. According to the gospels of Matthew and Luke, she conceived Jesus by heavenly intervention rather than human biology. Roman Catholicism asserts that at the Immaculate Conception she herself was conceived without any of the "original sin" exhibited by the rest of humanity. Even in giving birth to Jesus, she remained a virgin. Orthodoxy does not insist on these doctrines, nor on the Catholic dogma that Mary ascended bodily to heaven after her physical death. The emphasis on virginity is a spiritual sign of being dedicated to God alone, rather than to any temporal attachments.

According to the faithful, Mary is not just a symbol but a living presence, like Christ. She is appealed to in prayer and is honored in countless paintings, statues, shrines, and churches dedicated to her name. Catholics are enjoined to repeat the "Hail Mary" prayer:

> *Hail, Mary, full of grace, the Lord is with thee. Blessed art thou among women, and blessed is the fruit of thy womb, Jesus. Holy Mary, Mother of God, pray for us sinners, now and at the hour of our death.*

Theologians point out that veneration of Mary is really directed toward God; Mary is not worshiped in herself but as the mother of Christ, reflecting his glory. If this were not so, Christians could be accused of idolatry.

Be this as it may, Mary has been said to appear to believers in many places around the world. At Lourdes, in France, it is claimed that she appeared repeatedly to a young peasant girl named Bernadette in the nineteenth century. A spring found where Mary indicated it would be has been the source of hundreds of medically authenticated healings from seemingly incurable diseases. In 1531, in Guadalupe (within what is now Mexico City), Mary appeared to a converted Aztec, Juan Diego. She asked him to have the bishop build a church on the spot. To convince the sceptical bishop, Juan filled his cloak with the out-of-season roses to which she directed him. When he opened the cloak before the bishop, the petals fell away to reveal a large and vivid image of Mary, with Indian features. The picture is now enshrined in a large new church with moving walkways to handle the crowds who come to see it, and the Virgin of Guadalupe has been declared Celestial Patroness of the New World.

Sightings of Mary continue around the world. Ever since 1981, six people who were then children have been witnessing an apparition of a beautiful lady who calls herself "Queen of Peace" in Medjugorje, a village in western Herzegovina. They say she appears indescribably beautiful, amid brilliant flashes of light. Others who have visited the site claim to have been healed and spiritually affected. Thousands of people and thirty or more priests continue to assemble at the site every evening for three-hour prayer and Eucharist services. The visionaries report that Mary gives them messages in which she urges people toward peace, faith, conversion, prayer, and fasting, to ward off evil and war and to save humanity. Despite disapproval from the communist government when the apparitions began and despite caution on the part of church authorities, the Vatican and Yugoslavian bishops have now adopted a stance of "Informal Approval" with reference to the reported apparitions and messages.

VENERATION OF SAINTS AND ANGELS

Roman Catholics and Orthodox Christians honor their spiritual heroes as saints. These are men and women who are recognized as so holy that the divine life of Christ is particularly evident in them. After their death, they are carefully judged by the Church for proofs of exalted Christian virtue, such as tolerance under extreme provocation, and of miraculous power. Those who are canonized by this process are subject to great veneration.

> *Each saint is a unique event, a victory over the force of evil. So many blessings can pour from God into the world through one life.*
>
> *Father Germann, Vladimir, Russia*[91]

Orthodox Christians are given the name of a saint when they are baptized. Each keeps an icon of this patron saint in his or her room and prays to the saint

The lives of saints are considered inspiring models of devotion. Here Carmelite nuns in California view the relics of the beloved young 19th-century French nun, St. Thérèse of Lisieux ("The Little Flower"), which were taken on a worldwide tour.

daily. Icons of many saints fill an Orthodox church, helping to make them familiar presences rather than names in history books. Saints are often known as having special areas of concern and power. For instance, St. Anthony of Padua is invoked for help in finding lost things. **Relics**, usually parts of the body or clothes of saints, are felt to radiate the holiness of the saints' communion with God. They are treasured and displayed for veneration in Catholic and Orthodox churches. It is said that saints' physical bodies were so transformed by divine light that they do not decay after death, and continue to emit a sweet fragrance.

Roman Catholics and Orthodox Christians also pray to **angels** for protection. Angels are understood as spiritual beings who serve as messengers from, and adoring servants of, God. They are usually pictured as human figures or faces with wings. In popular piety, each person is thought to have a guardian angel for individual protection and spiritual help.

Contemporary trends

At this time, Christianity is gaining membership and enthusiastic participation in some quarters and losing ground in others.

The fall of communism in the former Soviet Union and its satellites has brought reopening and renovation of many churches and a renewed interest in spirituality throughout that large area. Orthodox Christianity has also received a boost from the activist approach of Ecumenical Patriarch Bartholomew, Archbishop of Constantinople, whose position makes him the leading voice in Orthodoxy. He is known as the "Green Patriarch" for his environmental activism, and has also taken an active role in improving Orthodox relations with Roman Catholics and Protestants, and in conflict resolution in areas where people of different religions are at war with each other.

myreligionlab
The Green Patriarch
MELBA NEWSOME

> *There will be an effective, transformative change in our world only when we are prepared to make sacrifices that are radical, painful, and genuinely unselfish.*
> *Ecumenical Patriarch Bartholomew*[92]

The contemporary Coptic Cross. The circle symbolizes the eternal love of God, as manifested in the sacrificial offering of the Son of God.

In Egypt, Orthodox Coptic Christians, heirs to the ancient tradition of the Desert Fathers, have long been submerged under Muslim rule, but the monasteries have begun to flourish again. The sixteen million Coptic Christians have their own pope.

Roman Catholicism is experiencing divisions between conservatives and liberals. After the liberal tendencies of Vatican II, Pope John Paul II reaffirmed certain traditional stands and strengthened the position of the right wing of the Church. In 2000, Cardinal Joseph Ratzinger, then head of the Vatican's highly conservative Congregation for the Doctrine of the Faith (the successor to the Inquisition), delivered "*Dominus Jesu,*" a thirty-six-page document proclaiming, "There exists a single Church of Christ, which subsists in the Catholic Church," which has been entrusted with "the fullness of grace and truth." Other Christian communities "are not churches in the proper sense" and non-Christians are in a "gravely deficient situation" regarding salvation.[93]

In an historic gesture, Pope Benedict XVI stood facing Mecca as he prayed alongside Muslim clerics in the Blue Mosque in Istanbul, November 2006.

The conservative trend in the Vatican was continued with the election of Cardinal Ratzinger in 2005 as the new pope, Benedict XVI. He is known for his defense of traditional Catholic doctrines and values. He has cautioned against overuse of technologies such as mobile phones and the Internet, if they mean that people pay less attention to their inner lives, and he has described the global financial crisis as proof that desire for material wealth is ultimately meaningless. He has spoken out against both capitalism and Marxism for "marginalizing" God. Nevertheless, he has reached out to young people by setting up his own Facebook profile on the Internet, made historic trips to Muslim and Jewish holy sites, and, in contrast to earlier cautions about charitable work, has stated, "Is there anything more tragic, is there anything more opposed to belief in the existence of a good God and a Redeemer of mankind, than world hunger?"[94]

In spite of the public attention paid to the pope as a person, the priesthood is dwindling considerably in most Western countries, partly because of the requirement that Catholic priests be celibate. In recent years, revelations of sexual abuses by some priests of their parishioners—often innocent children—have rocked people's confidence in the priesthood. In the United States, thousands of people have come forward with complaints of sexual abuse by their priests. American bishops have tried to repair the damage by apologizing, declaring "zero tolerance" for such behaviors, and paying large amounts of money to those who claim to have been abused, but at the same time, they have refused to deny the Catholic tradition of expecting priests to be celibate males. Catholic theologian Father Joe Mannath explains the potential for good or bad in the institutionalized celibacy of Catholic priests, monks, and nuns:

myreligionlab
Child Abuse Struggles
THOMAS REESE

The Catholic Church has the largest body of full-time, life-long celibates, a veritable force for doing good, if love is the fuel behind our celibate commitment. Our structures, rules and routine can be used in the service of love, if we are men and women of inner freedom, who have found meaning and joy, who radiate enthusiasm and transparent goodness. In the hands of unloving or power-hungry (or sexually frustrated) men and women, these same structures and rules can become instruments of oppression. If not "maintained" (like a good road) as a channel of God's love, celibacy degenerates to a barren state of being merely unmarried. Then, our unhealthy drives will easily take over, undeterred by the balancing elements of family love and care of children.[95]

There is increased interest in participation by women (who are not allowed by the Vatican to be priests), and widespread disregard of papal prohibitions on effective birth control, abortion, test-tube conception, surrogate motherhood, genetic experimentation, divorce, and homosexuality.

While cautioning against a recreational view of sexuality, Sean McDonagh of the Columban Fathers (SSC) emphasizes that the environmental and social consequences of unlimited population growth require a rethinking of the traditional Catholic ban on birth control:

The pro-life argument needs to be seen within the widest context of the fragility of the living world. Is it really pro-life to ignore the warnings of demographers and ecologists who predict that unbridled population growth will lead to severe hardship and an increase in the infant mortality rate for succeeding generations? Is it pro-life to allow the extinction of hundreds of thousands of living species which will ultimately affect the well-being of all future generations on the planet?[96]

The Vatican has responded to these trends by insisting on the value of tradition and authority. Acting as a group, Roman Catholic bishops in the United States have issued statements deploring sexism as a "sin" (recommending that spiritual positions of responsibility and authority be opened to women and that non-sexist language be used in liturgy), supporting peace efforts, and insisting on the morality of economic social justice.

In Protestantism, traditional denominations in Europe and the United States are declining in membership. According to a Gallup poll, only a minority of the "unchurched" actually disagree with their denomination's teachings. They are more likely to drop away because of apathy, a lack of services, or a lack of welcome on the part of the minister.

On the other hand, "megachurches" have witnessed phenomenal growth, with congregations of over 2,000 attending friendly services by charismatic preachers with attractions such as video clips and lively "Christian rock" music, plus add-ons such as restaurants, job training classes, fitness centers, schools, and support groups for parents, children, families, addicts, people living with HIV/AIDS, people suffering from depression, and so on. Rick Warren's Saddleback Church and his own dress and mannerisms are designed to be "seeker-sensitive" in order to attract the "unchurched."

The Anglican Church is in the midst of lively discussions, but they threaten to split the global Anglican Communion, which encompasses seventy-nine million people. Conservative Anglican leaders are strongly opposed to liberals' support for the ordination of women as bishops and ordination of homosexuals as clergy.

Approximately 20,000 people attend weekend services at Pastor Rick Warren's Saddleback Church in Lake Forest, California, one of the signature "megachurches" in North America.

Although many traditional Christian churches are losing members, other groups and trends are taking vigorous root. These include evangelical and charismatic groups, non-Western Christian churches, liberation theology, feminist theology, creation-centered Christianity, and the ecumenical movement.

EVANGELICALISM

A highly active segment of contemporary Christianity falls under the umbrella term **evangelicalism**. This dynamic movement encompasses a large group of people who place the "born-again" experience as the central component in a Christian's life. The definition of Scotch historian David Bebbington is often used to define the movement. He proposed that its four defining characteristics are:

myreligionlab
An Evangelical
Manifesto of 1989

1. Biblicism (a particular and constant regard for the Bible).
2. Crucicentrism (a stress on the atoning sacrifice of Jesus on the cross).
3. Conversionism (conviction that lives need to be changed).
4. Activism (the expression of the gospel in effort).

Over time, this tradition has flowered into different groups, including fundamentalists, mainline Protestant evangelicals, the Holiness movement, and Pentecostals.

Contemporary manifestations of evangelicalism are related to the work of eighteenth- and nineteenth-century evangelists, such as the itinerant Methodist preacher John Wesley (1703–1791), George Whitefield (1714–1770), who preached dramatically to large open-air crowds in England and the United States, and Charles Grandison Finney (1792–1875), whose preaching reportedly led hundreds of thousands of people to conversion experiences.

In the United States, dramatic preaching in the 1730s and 1740s by figures such as the Calvinist Jonathan Edwards brought a religious revival called "The First Great Awakening." Edwards' most famous sermon was "Sinners in the Hands of an Angry God" (1741), in which he exhorted a Connecticut congregation to be wary of God's power "to cast wicked men into hell at any moment." He used vivid imagery to evoke anxiety in listeners about the state of their souls:

> The wrath of God burns against them, their damnation does not slumber;
> the pit is prepared, the fire is made ready, the furnace is now hot, ready to
> receive them; the flames do now rage and glow. The glittering sword is whet,
> and held over them, and the pit hath opened its mouth under them.[97]

Another influential factor was the fundamentalist-modernist controversy of the early twentieth century. As discussed earlier, the **fundamentalists** were reacting against the liberal or modern movement in Christianity that sought to reconcile science and religion and to use historical and archaeological data to understand the Bible. This movement had an optimistic view of human nature and stressed reason, free will, and self-determination. In response, a group of Christians called for a return to what they considered the "fundamentals" of Christian faith. In 1911, "fundamentalists" in the United States published as their uncompromising tenets the total inerrancy of the Bible, and Christ's literal virgin birth, substitutionary atonement, bodily resurrection, and anticipated second coming. The controversy between fundamentalism and modernism received its most famous public expression in the Scopes trial in 1925 when John Thomas Scopes, a high school teacher in Tennessee, challenged a state law forbidding the teaching of Darwin's theory of evolution in schools.

During the twentieth century the fundamentalist movement in the United States developed into a powerful political and social force that now rejects much of what it considers secular: public education, big government, and social programs run by the government. An attitude of withdrawing from the negative influence of the modern world dominates this movement.

myreligionlab

The Rise of the Megachurch
THE WEEK MAGAZINE

Many evangelicals and other conservative Protestants anticipate the **rapture**—a time when Christians will be transported up to heaven to live with Jesus in immortal bodies. Popular Christian media in the United States have fanned the belief that the end times are imminent and one should be ready, a belief that has serious ramifications in political decision-making.

Like all Protestants, evangelicals practice the two sacraments of baptism and the Lord's Supper, but they are much more concerned that the sacrament be personal and meaningful than that it be correctly done according to a book of worship. Evangelicals' messages now enjoy widespread visibility through international electronic media. Television programs and websites offer enthusiastic preaching, videotapes, audiotapes, CDs, books, prayers for those in need, and the inevitable appeals for financial contributions to support these huge organizations, each centered on a persuasive charismatic speaker.

On the ground, evangelicalism is also growing around the world. In South America, in areas that were largely Roman Catholic as a result of colonization by Spain centuries ago, in the early 1990s an average of five evangelical churches were being established each week in Rio de Janeiro. Most of them were in the slum areas, offering to the very poor food, job training, day care, and perhaps conversion.

SPIRIT-ORIENTED MOVEMENTS

Overlapping somewhat with the evangelical surge, there is a rising emphasis on **charismatic** experience—that is, divinely inspired powers—among Christians of all classes and nations. While Christian fundamentalists stress the historical Jesus, charismatics feel they have also been touched by the "third person" of the Trinity, the Holy Spirit. These include members of Protestant Pentecostal churches but also Roman Catholics, members of mainline Protestant denominations, and Orthodox churches who are caught up in a widespread contemporary spiritual renewal that harks back to the biblical descent of the Holy Spirit upon the disciples of Jesus, firing them with spiritual powers and faith.

This movement encompasses all those who look for the spiritual gifts mentioned numerous times in the letters attributed to Paul, suggesting that these were common manifestations in the early Church. In I Corinthians, Paul writes:

> *To each is given the manifestation of the Spirit for the common good. To one is given through the Spirit the utterance of wisdom, and to another the utterance of knowledge according to the same Spirit, to another faith by the same Spirit, to another gifts of healing by the one Spirit, to another the working of miracles, to another prophecy, to another the discernment of spirits, to another various kinds of tongues, to another the interpretation of tongues. All these are activated by one and the same Spirit, who allots to each one individually just as the Spirit chooses.*[98]

There is no typical pattern to the charismatic experience of being endowed with divine powers. Vazhayil Babu is from South India, a Christian by birth, but a nominal Christian. He says he experienced a great void in his life, even as he married and became a successful businessman in the United States. He felt inwardly so desperate that he became sick. He prayed, asking, "What should I do?" Then he reportedly experienced a Power in the room and heard a voice say, "Get out from the house now!" He thus took his wife and got on a Caribbean cruise ship. He sat in the hold praying until, he says, "God told me, 'Go to Bible college. Study the Word.'" Being over fifty years old, poor in English, and running a business to support his family, he struggled to obey that command, but at last finished his degree and began preaching. He reports:

> *When I speak the word of God, the Bible, when I speak about Jesus, I tell them to come to the altar, and I pray for them. They're blind—they are healed. There are lame and crippled—they walk. I see with my two eyes. Sometimes I speak before 20,000 people. I pray a lot and then speak the word of God. I see miracles after miracles.*[99]

One of the streams feeding the charismatic tradition was the nineteenth-century Holiness movement in the United States. It was an outgrowth of John Wesley's concept of "Christian perfection" through a transformational conversion experience. This opened doors to religious empowerment of the poor, women, and minorities. It also brought the element of emotional involvement into worship, in contrast to more formal worship in mainstream Protestant churches.

A Holiness preacher in Kansas, Charles Parham (1873–1929), was healed of rheumatic fever and thence began a healing ministry and a school in which he proposed to train people for world evangelization, with the Bible as their only

William Joseph Seymour founded the Azusa Street Revival, one of the major sources of Pentecostalism.

textbook. He challenged his students to wait in expectation for the spiritual gift of speaking in tongues, as evidence of baptism by the Holy Spirit.

One who was influenced by Parham was an African American preacher, William Joseph Seymour (1870–1922), whose parents were freed slaves. Given the segregation of races in the South, Seymour was only allowed to listen to Parham's talks through a half-opened door. Seymour was invited to be the pastor of a small African American Holiness church in Los Angeles, but he was locked out of it when he preached that speaking in tongues was a sign of baptism by the Spirit. Several members of the church invited him to pray with them in one of their homes. When the host asked Seymour to lay his hands on him, the man fell to the floor, seemingly unconsciousness, and began speaking in unknown languages. Seymour and others then had the same experience. For three days and nights they kept praying and rejoicing loudly. As more people joined them, including white people, the house was too small, so they rented an unused church building at 312 Azusa Street. Sitting on planks for benches, they held spontaneous, emotional meetings from morning until late at night. There was no planned worship. People sang in tongues and fell to the ground as they were "slain in the Spirit." These inter-racial revival meetings on Azusa Street eventually drew people from all over the United States and abroad, and as new centers were opened, the movement became known as **Pentecostalism**. Seymour himself was a humble, gracious, prayerful person, and without racial or gender discrimination he developed a core team of leaders who were both male and female, black and white.

The Holiness/Pentecostal movement brought spiritual women to the foreground even in times when women were otherwise excluded from church leadership. For instance, Aimee Semple McPherson (1890–1944) was told by an inner voice, "Preach the Word!" and had several powerful experiences of the Holy Spirit. But how to preach? With no institutional framework, she simply stood on a chair in the street and prayed silently for an hour, with her arms held in the air. Curious people gathered around her. When she spoke to them afterward, her speech was so compelling that many followed her. This went on until crowds grew so huge that she had to set up an immense tent—her "canvas cathedral." Then she outfitted a large car as her "Gospel car" and traveled around the United States, calling people to Jesus. When she built the Angelus Temple in Los Angeles, her services became so popular that they caused traffic jams. During the Great Depression, she organized a soup kitchen that fed 80,000 people a month, as well as giving blankets and shelter to thousands of homeless people. The International Church of the Foursquare Gospel that she founded has grown to encompass over five million people in eighty-three countries. It has not, however, emphasized gender equality; there are few women in its leadership roles.

Pentecostalism is now a rapidly growing world movement. Its adherents generally look for a second experience of the Holy Spirit after the initial experience of salvation by belief in Jesus as Savior for the forgiveness of their sins; they require speaking in tongues as a sign of this "second grace" of baptism by the Holy Spirit. Adherents to this tradition affirm that they are under the influence of the Spirit when they speak in tongues (a phenomenon known as glossolalia), stand and gesture as they lovingly sing praises of Jesus and God, pray and utter praises, spontaneously heal by the laying on of hands and prayer, and bear witness to spiritual miracles.

The Pentecostal–charismatic movement has brought spontaneous spiritual expressiveness into previously restrained cultures, such as this congregation in Kent, England.

Speaking of the descent of the Holy Spirit, Roman Bilas, Moscow head of the Union of Pentecostal Christians of Evangelical Faith, says passionately:

This moment when you really feel God's power in yourself brings so much peace and joy within you. It transforms you and society. There comes a sense of total forgiveness for your sins, and the ability in you to forgive others. At that moment, you start to speak in different languages, maybe such that no one can understand.

We may also receive the gift of prophecy. ... We check to see if the message is consistent with the Bible. If it is, then we will listen. Otherwise, the person is told not to speak publicly because he would create confusion in the Church.

The main thing is that the person should be filled with God's Power. A nice-looking car will not move unless it is fueled. God's Power will only fill those who are pure. That is why in the early Church people went into the wilderness to fast and repent. Then God could fill them with His Power. Each sermon should have this Power of God; then the people will really listen and repent of their sins.[100]

The Pentecostal–Charismatic movement is now said to be the fastest-growing religious movement throughout the world. Asia, Africa, and Latin America are experiencing explosive growth of Pentecostal–Charismatic churches. Many of these churches are carrying on extensive social work, such as running relief services, feeding the poor, and building hospitals and schools. In Korea, Pastor David Yonggi Cho has developed the immense Yoido Full Gospel Church, which with over 800,000 members and hundreds of pastors is the world's biggest Christian congregation. His "five-fold message of the Gospel" consists of renewal, experience of the Spirit, healing, belief in the Second Coming, and the blessings of salvation: "soul prosperity," "prosperity in all things," and "a healthy life."[101]

Some Pentecostal churches are linked to "classical Pentecostalism," with roots in the nineteenth-century revivals in the United States. Others are denomina-

The Yoido Full Gospel Church in South Korea houses one of the largest Protestant Christian congregations in the world, with at least 830,000 members.

tions colored by regional cultural traditions, such as the vibrant African Instituted Churches, which are usually oriented toward healing and protection from evil, the most prominent aspects of African indigenous religions. There are also independent "Neo-Pentecostal" churches whose leaders' business sense has helped to market Spirit-oriented traditions to young people and upwardly mobile professionals. Whatever the type, Pentecostals tend to follow a strict code of personal ethics. Because of their conversion experiences, having become "a new creature in Christ," they typically do not drink, gamble, indulge in sex outside of marriage, or spend money and time carelessly.

Mainstream Christian churches, which have often rejected emotional spiritual experience in favor of a more orderly piety, are gradually becoming more tolerant of it. Among Roman Catholics the movement is often called "Charismatic Renewal," for it claims to bring true life in the Spirit back to Christianity. By broad definition, one-fourth of all Christians today could be considered members of this Spirit-oriented movement,[102] and the percentage is growing.

THE GREAT REVERSAL

Although contemporary Christianity was largely shaped in Europe and its North American colonies, the largest percentage of the Christian Church now lies outside these areas. It has great numerical strength and vigor in Africa, Latin America, and parts of Asia and its strength in these areas is changing the face of Christianity. In 1970, Christianity was about forty-three percent non-Western, whereas today it is about sixty-five percent non-Western. In this short span of time, many independent, indigenous churches have arisen in the world. Tens of millions of Chinese Christians are now worshiping in their homes and in non-church buildings; hundreds of millions of Africans are members of **African Instituted Churches**. As soon as the Western colonial supports were taken away, Christianity exploded in Africa as an indigenous religion. To wit: Africa was twenty-five percent Christian in 1950, whereas it is forty-eight percent Christian today. Some of the most active areas in terms of outreach are now Brazil, Korea, China, India, southern Africa, and the United States. Lamin Sanneh of Gambia, Professor of Missions and World Christianity at Yale Divinity School, describes the geographic shifts characterizing Christian resurgence:

"World Christianity" is the movement of Christianity as it takes form and shape in societies that previously were not Christian, societies that had no bureaucratic tradition with which to domesticate the gospel. In these societies Christianity was received and expressed through the cultures, customs, and traditions of the people affected. World Christianity is not one thing but a variety of indigenous responses through more or less effective local idioms, but in any case without necessarily the European Enlightenment frame. ...

What is at issue now is the surprising scale and depth of the worldwide Christian resurgence, a resurgence that seems to proceed without Western organizational structures, including academic recognition, and is occurring amidst widespread political instability and the collapse of public institutions, part of what it means to speak of a post-Western Christianity. Even church leaders have been unable to comprehend fully, still less to respond effectively to, the magnitude of the resurgence. In some areas it's like being hit by a tidal wave and unable to hold your footing.[103]

Some signs of the times: instead of the old pattern in which the West sent missionaries to spread Christianity to Asia, Africa, and South America, congregations in those areas are now being asked to send volunteers to the West to help spread the gospel in new missionary efforts there. Catholic prayer requests are now being "outsourced" through the Vatican to India from the United States, Canada, and Europe, where there are not enough clergy to handle the requests. Churches in Europe are becoming empty of worshipers as the people become more and more secular in their approach to life.

The vigor of Christianity in the United States can be explained partly by the growth of evangelical and charismatic churches and a linking of fundamentalist Christianity with right-wing political claims to patriotism and a defense of traditional American values. An equally important contribution to the vigor of Christianity in the United States is immigration. Today, as in the past, the majority of those who migrate to the United States are Christians, and migrants tend to build vital churches. Contemporary Christian migrants include Roman Catholic or Pentecostal Latin Americans, Presbyterian or Methodist Koreans, plus Christians from Africa, China, India, and West Asia. By contrast, most of the contemporary immigrants to Europe are Muslims.

Some of the most active remnants of Christianity in Europe are involved in peace and reconciliation movements and, like many Christian denominations in the United States, tried to oppose the US-led attack on Iraq. Not only in the United States but around the globe, many fundamentalists feel they are fighting a cultural war against liberalism, secularism, and materialism—within as well as beyond Christianity. Spiritually diverse, Christianity is also politically and culturally diverse.

When Western missionaries spread Christianity to other regions, they often assumed that European ways were culturally superior to the indigenous ways and peoples. But some of these newer Christians have come to different conclusions. Theologians of the African Instituted Churches, for instance, reject the historical missionary efforts to divorce them from their traditions of honoring their ancestors. This effort tore apart their social structure, they feel, with no scriptural justification:

> As we became more acquainted with the Bible, we began to realise that there was nothing at all in the Bible about the European customs and Western traditions that we had been taught. What, then was so holy and sacred about this culture and this so-called civilisation that had been imposed upon us and was now destroying us? Why could we not maintain our African customs and be perfectly good Christians at the same time? ...
>
> We have learnt to make a very clear distinction between culture and religion. ... [For instance], the natural customs of any particular nation or race must never be confused with the grace of Jesus Christ our Saviour, Redeemer and Liberator.[104]

Contemporary perceptions of Jesus have been deeply enriched by those from the inhabitants of poor Third World countries who have brought personal understanding of Jesus' ministry to the outcasts and downtrodden. In Asia, where Christians are usually in the minority, there is an emphasis on a Christ who is present in the whole cosmos and who calls all people to sit at a common table to partake of his generous love. In Latin America, Jesus is viewed as the liberator of the people from political and social oppression, from dehumanization, and from sin. In Africa, the African Instituted Churches have brought indigenous traditions of drumming, dancing, and singing into community worship of a Jesus who is seen as the greatest of ancestors—a mediator carrying prayers and offerings between humans and the divine, and watchful caretaker of the people.

LIBERATION THEOLOGY

myreligionlab
I've Seen the Promised Land
MARTIN LUTHER KING, JR.

Although many Christians make a distinction between the sacred and the secular, some have involved themselves deeply with social issues as an expression of their Christian faith. For instance, the Baptist preacher, Martin Luther King, Jr. (1929–1968), became a great civil rights leader, declaring: "It was Jesus of Nazareth that stirred the Negroes to protest with the creative weapon of love."[105] This trend is now called **liberation theology**, a faith that stresses the need for concrete political action to help the poor. Beginning in the 1960s with Vatican II and the conference of Latin American bishops in Colombia in 1968, Roman Catholic priests and nuns in Latin America began to make conscious, voluntary efforts to understand and side with the poor in their struggles for social justice. A biblical basis for this approach is found in the Acts of the Apostles:

> The group of believers was one in mind and heart. No one said that any of his belongings was his own, but they all shared with one another everything they had. ... There was no one in the group who was in need. Those who owned fields or houses would sell them, bring the money received from the sale and turn it over to the apostles; and the money was distributed to each one according to his need.[106]

Archbishop Desmond M. Tutu

During the years of struggle against apartheid in South Africa, one voice that refused to be silenced was that of the Anglican Archbishop of Cape Town, Desmond Mpilo Tutu (b. 1931). Afterward, he served his country as Chairperson of the Truth and Reconciliation Commission, "looking a beast in the eye" to investigate abuses from all sides that were perpetrated during the apartheid era. In this capacity, he still refused to mute his criticisms of those wielding power, no matter what their race and stature. In 1995 he proclaimed:

The so-called ordinary people, God's favourites, are sick and tired of corruption, repression, injustice, poverty, disease and the violation of their human rights. They are crying out "enough is enough!" It is exhilarating when you are able to say to dictators everywhere: You have had it! You have had it! This is God's world and you will bite the dust! They think it will not happen but it does, and they bite the dust comprehensively and ignominiously.

We will want to continue to be the voice of the voiceless. It is the role of the church to be the conscience of society.[107]

The "Arch's" fearless stance on behalf of truth and justice for the oppressed earned him the Nobel Peace Prize in 1984. He confronted not only those in power but also those who sought change through violence and those in the Church who witnessed the horrors of apartheid but kept silent. He explains, "Our task is to be agents of the Kingdom of God, and this sometimes requires us to say unpopular things."[108]

The former archbishop feels that faith requires one to be actively engaged in politics because government affects the people, but at the same time to remain independent of political factionalism in order to freely stand for truth. He says of the link between religion and politics:

Faith is a highly political thing. At the centre of all that we believe as Christians is the incarnation— the participation of God in the affairs of this world. As followers of that God we too must be politically engaged. We need inner resources, however, in order to face the political demands of our time.[109]

How has Archbishop Tutu developed his inner resources? Through meditation, prayer, and fasting. He observes the traditional daily devotions of the Anglican Church, always starts meetings with prayer, and annually takes a long spiritual retreat. He regularly prays for others, and many are also praying for him; he asserts that intercessory prayer has practical effects. His spiritual confessor, Francis Cull, describes Archbishop Tutu's inner life as rooted in the Benedictine monastic discipline that underlies Anglican spirituality. He explains:

As I ponder on the prayer life of Desmond Tutu I see the three fundamental Benedictine demands that there shall be: rest, prayer, and work and in that order. It is a remarkable fact, and it is one reason at least why he has been able to sustain the burdens he has carried, that he has within him a stillness and a need for quiet solitude. ... The "rest" of which St. Benedict speaks is not a mere switching off; it is a positive attempt to fulfill the age-old command to rest in God. ... The pattern of Jesus which he follows here: "Come apart and rest awhile," is an urgent need for all those who are caught up in the busyness of church and world.[110]

Desmond Tutu himself insists that spiritual practice is essential in order to know and follow the will of God:

God's will has to do with what is right, just, decent and healing of the wounds of society. To know what this means we need to cleanse ourselves of ourselves— of our fears, greed, ambitions and personal desires. ... We must be vigilant in ensuring that the good that is within all people triumphs over the evil that is also there. ... We must commit ourselves to tell the truth. We must identify evil wherever we see it.[111]

myreligionlab

Not Development,
but Liberation
GUSTAVO GUTIÉRREZ

The Peruvian theologian Gustavo Gutiérrez (b. 1928), who coined the expression "theology of liberation," explains the choice of voluntary poverty as:

a commitment of solidarity with the poor, with those who suffer misery and injustice. … It is not a question of idealizing poverty, but rather of taking it on as it is—an evil—to protest against it and to struggle to abolish it.[112]

For their sympathetic siding with those who are oppressed, Catholic clergy have been murdered by political authorities in some countries. They have also been strongly criticized by conservatives within the Vatican. When Pope Benedict headed the Congregation for the Doctrine of the Faith, he decried liberation theology. He said that it inappropriately emphasizes liberation from material poverty rather than liberation from sin. The movement has nevertheless spread to all areas where there is social injustice. Bakole Wa Ilunga, Archbishop of Kananga, the Democratic Republic of Congo (formerly Zaire), reminds Christians that Jesus warned the rich and powerful that it would be very difficult for them to enter the kingdom of heaven. By contrast, writes Ilunga:

Jesus liberates the poor from the feeling that they are somehow less than fully human; he makes them aware of their dignity and gives them motives for struggling against their lot and for taking control of their own lives.[113]

Maryknoll Sister Jocelyn Fenix assists farmers in a hothouse in Panama.

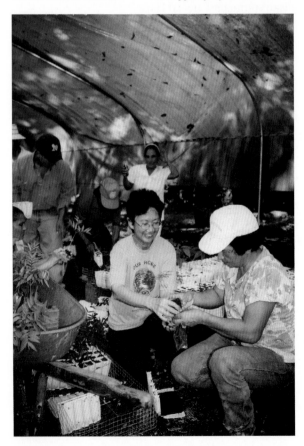

Taking control is not easy for those who are oppressed minorities. In the United States, the Church offers the large African American community of Christians a way of developing an alternative reality in the midst of poverty, urban violence, and discrimination. As theologian Dwight Hopkins observes:

The black community has a long tradition of practicing faith as a total way of life. … Within worship, especially, the church is noted for its uplifting preaching, singing, shouting, dancing, and recognition of individual achievements and pain. … The rituals of individual healing and celebration serve to recharge the worshipers' energy to deal with the rigors and racism of a "cruel, cruel world" from Monday through Saturday.[114]

The practical activities of the Black Church range from building shelters and arranging jobs to treatment for addiction, campaigns against police brutality, voter registration drives, and leadership training. Even without social empowerment, people often feel inwardly empowered and cherished by the presence of Jesus in their lives.

Other Christian denominations are also deeply engaged in social service ministries. For example, Kenyan Pentecostal Florence Muindi undertook training as a doctor because when she was praying she had a shocking vision of sick, starving, and deaf and dumb people. When she went to a very poor village in Ethiopia to serve in conjunction with the local Baptist church, she found health problems so endemic there that she trained a team of "health evangelists" to help eradicate the underlying causes: poor sanitation and hygiene. As they worked with families to improve sanitation in their environment, ministering to people's physical as well as spiritual needs, they also brought greater social cohesion in the community. Florence explains, "We are the hands of Jesus Christ. The church is the representative of Christ in a suffering world. "[115] It is through serving the poor and disenfranchised that people feel connected to Jesus, as they try to carry on his mission.

FEMINIST THEOLOGY

The issue of taking control of one's life and defining one's identity has also been taken up by feminists within the Christian Church. The Church institution has historically been dominated by men, although there is strong evidence that Jesus had active women disciples and that there were women leaders in the early churches. Reconstructing their history in the early Christian movement and the effects of patriarchical domination is a task being addressed by considerable in-depth scholarship. The effect of the apostle Paul in shaping attitudes toward women as he guided the developing Christian communities is one area of particular concern. Some of the statements attributed to him in the biblical Epistles seem oppressive to women; some seem egalitarian. He argues, for example, that men should pray or prophesy with their head uncovered but that women should wear a veil:

> For a man ought not to have his head veiled, since he is the image and reflection of God; but woman is the reflection of man. Indeed, man was not made from woman, but woman from man. Neither was man created for the sake of woman, but woman for the sake of man.[116]

Contemporary scholars are trying to sort out the cultural and historical as well as the theological contexts of such statements. Feminist theologian Rosemary Radford Ruether suggests that Paul was trying to preserve something of the status quo, and establish himself as a higher authority than other apostles who had apparently been teaching the Corinthians that, with Christian baptism, all the old separations between people had been erased:

> For these Corinthians the new life in Christ, begun in baptism, overcame the old world of sin and brought the believer into a present experience of resurrected life. This new life in Christ was experienced particularly in Spirit-filled assemblies in which all members, women and men, could participate in spontaneous testimonies of prayer and prophecy that combined "intelligible" and ecstatic forms of speech or "tongues." ... The Corinthian opponents of Paul practiced dissolution of gender and other status hierarchies within their community, and open boundaries between themselves and the world around them. These practices were not arbitrary but reflected a theological belief that the evil powers that lay behind a world divided by gender, social status, and clean and unclean spheres had already been overcome in the new life in Christ.[117]

myreligionlab

Why Can't We Talk about Religion and Politics?
JIM WALLIS

Reverend Catherine Rumen blesses the communion cup in London.

myreligionlab
Roman Catholic Womenpriests

Another area of feminist theological scholarship is the role models for women offered by the Bible. A central female figure in the New Testament is Mary, mother of Jesus. Ivone Gebara and Maria Clara Bingemer of Brazil look at Mary from the perspective of "the great masses of Latin America, the overwhelming majority of whom are poor, enjoy no adequate quality of life, and lack respect, bread, love, and justice." While acknowledging that the dogmas developed by the Catholic Church about Mary may be inflated, they nonetheless reveal a well-spring of hope for women and other oppressed humans:

> *The exaltation that understandably comes out in dogma cannot ... hide what is essential in God's salvation, that is, making God's glory shine on what is regarded as insignificant, degrading or marginal. ... In exalting her they exalt precisely her poverty, her dispossession, and her simplicity. This is the only key for understanding the mystery of God's incarnation in human history, of which Jesus and Mary are the protagonists. This is, moreover, the only key for understanding the mystery of the church as a community of salvation, holy and sinful, striving amid the most diverse kinds of limitations and problems to be a sign of the Kingdom in the midst of the world.[118]*

A third major area of Christian feminist theology is the concept of God. The divine is commonly referred to as "He" or "Father," but scholarship reveals that this patriarchal usage is not absolute; there also existed other models of God as Mother, as Divine Wisdom, as Justice, as Friend, as Lover. Sally McFague points out that to envision God as Mother, for instance, totally changes our understanding of our relationship to the divine:

rest of the world passed it by, aside from contact through trading caravans. The Arabs of the area were mostly nomadic cattle-breeders, shifting their herds through the desert in search of areas that had some greenery. Robbing caravans and settlements also helped them to sustain themselves, except during three months of the lunar year when raids were forbidden according to tribal religion. Drinking, gambling, and prostitution were apparently commonplace activities. There was no high civilization throughout the area. Mecca was situated along trade routes and was a trading center, but apparently it consisted only of simple palm-branch huts.

The most powerful of the tribes there were the Quraysh, comprising approximately a dozen clans who lived as merchants. Nomadic tribal rules mandated that clan chiefs should take care of their weaker and poorer clan members, but this social rule was not necessarily followed by the merchant clans.

Because of their nomadic traveling, the Arabic tribes were in contact with each other and had a relatively uniform culture and a common language. They worshiped many deities and felt that people's lives were controlled by an impersonal force, called Fate or Time. Their tribal code of ethics held an entire clan responsible for its members' misdoings, and often took a life for a life. Long-lasting blood feuds were therefore common. But violence was prohibited within a large area surrounding the Ka'bah. Before Islam, the Ka'bah is thought to have contained 360 idols of Arabian tribal deities, perhaps including the Daughters of God and Hubal, one of the primary deities worshiped by the Quraysh. Statues of Jesus and Mary were also enshrined there.

The Ka'bah in Mecca is Islam's holiest place of worship.

The Prophet Muhammad

In this unpromising pre-Islamic setting which Muslims call "the age of ignorance," a child named Muhammad ("the praised one") was born into a poor clan of the Quraysh tribe. His father died during a trading journey before he was born. After his mother also died when he was six, and then his grandfather, who had been chief of the clan, Muhammad became the ward of his uncle, who put him to work as a shepherd.

Although Muhammad is not to be worshiped by Muslims, whose faith resides only in God, his life story is considered important as a model of the teachings of the Qur'an. Even in his youth, he was known for his thoughtful and trustworthy character. The stories of Muhammad's life and his sayings are preserved in literature called the **Hadith**, which reports on the Prophet's **Sunnah** (sayings and actions). As a young man, Muhammad managed caravans for a beautiful, intelligent, and wealthy woman named Khadijah. When she was forty and Muhammad was twenty-five, she appreciated his good qualities and offered to

myreligionlab
Hadith

According to tradition, Muhammad undertook spiritual retreats in this cave on Mount Hira outside Mecca. It was here that he received the first revelations of the Qur'an.

myreligionlab

The Beginning
of Muhammad's
Revelation
SAHIH MUSLIM

marry him. Khadijah became Muhammad's strongest supporter during the difficult and discouraging years of his early mission.

With Khadijah's understanding of his spiritual propensities, Muhammad began to spend periods of time in solitary retreat. These retreats were not uncommon in his lineage. They provided opportunities for contemplation, away from the world.

When Muhammad was forty years old, he made a spiritual retreat during the month called Ramadan. An angel in human-like form, Gabriel, reportedly came to him and insisted that he recite. Three times Muhammad demurred that he could not, for he was unlettered, and three times the angel forcefully commanded him. In desperation, Muhammad at last cried out, "What shall I recite?" and the angel began dictating the first words of what became the Qur'an:

> *Proclaim! (or Recite!)*
> *In the name*
> *Of thy Lord and Cherisher,*
> *Who created—*
> *Created man, out of*
> *A (mere) clot*
> *Of congealed blood:*
> *Proclaim! And thy Lord*
> *Is Most Bountiful,—*
> *He Who taught*
> *(The use of) the Pen,—*
> *Taught man that*
> *Which he knew not.*[1]

Muhammad returned home, deeply shaken. Khadijah comforted him and encouraged him to overcome his fear of the responsibilities and ridicule of prophethood. The revelations continued intermittently, asserting the theme that it was the One God who spoke and who called people to **Islam** (which means complete, trusting surrender to God). According to tradition, Muhammad described the form of these revelations thus:

> *Revelation sometimes comes like the sound of a bell; that is the most painful way. When it ceases I have remembered what was said. Sometimes it is an angel who talks to me like a human, and I remember what he says.*[2]

The Prophet shared these revelations with the few people who believed him: his wife, Khadijah; his young cousin, 'Ali; his friend, the trader Abu Bakr; and the freed slave, Zayd.

After three years, Muhammad was instructed by the revelations to preach publicly. He was ridiculed and defamed by the Qurayshites, who operated the Ka'bah as a polytheistic pilgrimage center and organized profitable trading caravans through Mecca. While Muhammad was somewhat protected by the influence of his uncle, his followers were subject to persecution. A dark-skinned Abyssinian slave named Bilal, who was among the first converts, was imprisoned and brought out daily under the hot sun, pinned to the ground with a heavy stone on his chest, and ordered to deny the Prophet and worship the old gods. He staunchly refused, saying, "One, one." Once bought by the Prophet's friend Abu Bakr, Bilal became the first **muezzin** (one who calls the people to prayer from a high place), illustrating the Prophet's discarding of racial and social class distinctions. Finally, according to some accounts, Muhammad and his followers were banished for three years to a desolate place where they struggled to survive by eating wild foods such as tree leaves.

Faithful Muslims pray five times a day, no matter where they are. The prayer rug provides a sacred precinct from which one can turn toward Mecca, the center of the faith.

Representations of humans, including himself, were forbidden by the Prophet to avoid idolatry, but Persian artists later gave imaginative expression to stories such as the Miraj, or Ascension, of the Prophet.

myreligionlab

The Night Journey
SAHIH MUSLIM

The band of Muslims was asked to return to Mecca, but the persecution by the Qurayshites continued. Muhammad's fiftieth year, the "Year of Sorrows," was the worst of all: he lost his beloved wife Khadijah and his protective uncle. With his strongest backers gone, persecution of the Prophet increased.

According to tradition, at the height of his trials Muhammad experienced the Night of Ascension. He is said to have ascended through the seven heavens to the far limits of the cosmos, and thence into the Divine Proximity. There he met former prophets and teachers from Adam to Jesus, saw paradise and hell, and received the great blessings of the Divine Presence.

Pilgrims to Mecca from Yathrib, an oasis to the north, recognized Muhammad as a prophet. They invited him to come to their city to help solve its social and political problems. Still despised by the Qurayshites as a potential threat, Muhammad and his followers left Mecca secretly. Their move to Yathrib, later called al-Medina ("The City [of the Prophet]"), was not easy. The Prophet left last, accompanied (according to some traditions) by his old friend Abu Bakr. To hide from the pursuing Meccans, it is said that they took refuge in a cave, where the Prophet taught his friend the secret practice of the silent remembrance of God.

This *hijrah* (migration) of Muslims from Mecca to Medina took place in 622 CE. The Muslim era is calculated from the beginning of the year in which this event took place, for it marked the change from persecution to appreciation of the Prophet's message.

In Medina, Muhammad drew up a constitution for the city of Yathrib/Medina that later served as a model for Islamic social administration. The departure of Muslims from Mecca was viewed with hostility and suspicion by the leaders of Mecca. Their assumption was that Medina had become a rallying point for enemies of the Meccans who, under Muhammad's leadership, would eventually attack and destroy Mecca. To forestall this, Mecca declared war on Medina, and a period of open conflict between the two cities followed.

Muhammad himself directed the first raid against a Meccan caravan. The battle between Muslim emigrants and Meccans took place at Badr near Medina; the small group of Muslims was victorious. According to the Qur'anic revelations, God had sent thousands of angels to help Muhammad. Furthermore, Muhammad threw a handful of pebbles at the Meccans and this turned the tide, for it was God who threw, and "He will surely weaken the designs of the unbelievers."[3] Enraged by the Islamic victory, Mecca made a surprise attack against Medina and routed the Muslims, injuring Muhammad and scattering his forces. Within two years, Mecca had mounted a much larger force, including cavalry and numerous archers, for a siege intended to subdue Medina permanently. Warned by spies, the Muslims defended Medina with a large trench encircling the city. The Meccans were forced to retreat, but rather than continue hostilities Muhammad negotiated a truce between the two warring cities.

In 630 CE the Prophet returned triumphant to Mecca with such a large band of followers that the Meccans did not resist. Reportedly, only thirty people were killed in the historic conquest of Mecca. The Ka'bah was purged of its idols, and from that time it has been the center of Muslim piety. Acquiescing to Muhammad's political power and the Qur'anic warnings about the dire fate of those who tried to thwart God's prophets, many Meccans converted to Islam. Muhammad declared a general amnesty. Contrary to tribal customs of revenge, the Prophet showed his unusual gentleness by forgiving those who had been his opponents.

The Prophet then returned to Medina, which he kept as the spiritual and political center of Islam. From there, a number of campaigns were undertaken. In addition to northern Africa, the Persian states of Yemen, Oman, and Bahrain came into the fold. As the multicultural, multiracial embrace of Islam evolved, the Prophet declared that the community of the faithful was more important than the older tribal identities that had divided people. The new ideal was a global family, under God. In his "Farewell Sermon," Muhammad stated, "You must know that a Muslim is the brother of a Muslim and the Muslims are one brotherhood."[4]

In the eleventh year of the Muslim era, Muhammad made a final pilgrimage to the Ka'bah in Mecca to demonstrate to the faithful the rites that were to be followed thenceforth. After his return to Medina, he became very ill. As he recognized that the end was near, he gave final instructions to his followers, promising to meet them at "the Fountain" in paradise. Muhammad died in 632 CE. In the circumstances that followed Muhammad's death, his steadfast friend Abu Bakr was elected the first **caliph** (successor to the Prophet). Another possible successor was the trustworthy and courageous 'Ali, the Prophet's cousin and husband of his favorite daughter, Fatima. One tradition has it that the Prophet Muhammad actually transferred his spiritual light to Fatima before his death, but that in the midst of funeral arrangements, neither she nor 'Ali participated in the selection of the first caliph. The Shi'ite faction would later claim 'Ali as the legitimate heir.

Muhammad's own life has continued to be very precious to Muslims, and it is his qualities that a good Muslim tries to emulate. He always denied having any superhuman powers, and the Qur'an called him "a human being like you," just "a servant to whom revelation has come," and "a warner."[5] The only miracle he ever claimed was that, though unlettered, he had received the Qur'anic revelations in extraordinarily eloquent and pure Arabic. He did not even claim to be a teacher—"God guides those whom He will,"[6] he was instructed to say—although Muslims consider the Prophet the greatest of teachers.

Nevertheless, all who saw the Prophet remarked on his touching physical beauty, his nobility of character, the fragrance of his presence, his humility, and his kindness. Many stories are told of his affectionate compassion toward animals, children, women, widows, and orphans, contrary to prevailing customs. When asked the short cut to heaven, he reportedly said that Paradise lies under the feet of the mother. In his devotion to God, he quietly endured poverty so extreme that he tied a stone over his stomach to suppress the pangs of hunger. He explained, "I eat as a slave eats, and sit as a slave sits, for I am a slave (of God)." Although the Qur'an says that the Prophet is the perfect model for humanity, the purest vehicle for God's message, he himself perpetually prayed for God's forgiveness. When he was asked how best to practice Islam, he said, "The best Islam is that you feed the hungry and spread peace among people you know and those you do not know."[7]

Muhammad's mystical experiences of the divine had not led him to forsake the world as a contemplative. Rather, according to the Qur'an, the mission of Islam is to reform society, to actively combat oppression and corruption, "inviting to all that is good, enjoining what is right, and forbidding all that is wrong."[8] The Prophet's task—which Muslims feel was also undertaken by such earlier prophets as Moses and Abraham—is not only to call people back to faith but also to create a just moral order in the world as the embodiment of God's commandments.

The Qur'an

The heart of Islam is not the Prophet but the revelations he received. Collectively they are called the Qur'an ("reading" or "reciting"). He received the messages over a period of twenty-three years, with some later messages replacing earlier ones. At first they were striking affirmations of the unity of God and the woe of those who did not heed God's message. Later messages also addressed the organizational needs and social lives of the Muslim community.

Reading the Qur'an in Java.

After the *hijrah*, Muhammad heard the revelations and dictated them to a scribe; many of his companions then memorized them. They are said to have been carefully safeguarded against changes and omissions. Recited, the passages have a lyrical beauty and power that Muslims believe to be unsurpassed; these qualities cannot be translated. The recitation is to be rendered in what is sometimes described as a sad, subdued tone, because the messages concern God's sadness at the waywardness of the people. Muhammad said, "Weep, therefore, when you recite it."[9]

Recitation of the Qur'an is thought to have a healing, soothing effect, but can also bring protection, guidance, and knowledge, according to Islamic tradition. It is critical that one recite the Qur'an only in a purified state, for the words are so powerful that the one who recites it takes on a great responsibility. Ideally, one learns the Qur'an as a child, when memorization is easiest and when the power of the words will help to shape one's life.

During the life of the Prophet, his followers attempted to preserve the oral tradition in writing as an additional way of safeguarding it from loss. The early caliphs continued this effort until a council was convened by the third caliph around 650 CE to establish a single authoritative written text. This is the one still used. It is divided into 114 *suras* (chapters). The first is the **Fatiha**, the opening *sura*, which reveals the essence of the Qur'an:

> *In the name of God, Most Gracious, Most Merciful.*
> *Praise be to God,*
> *The Lord of the Worlds;*
> *Most Gracious, Most Merciful;*
> *Master of the Day of Judgment.*
> *Thee do we worship,*
> *And Thine aid we seek.*
> *Show us the straight way,*
> *The way of those on whom*
> *Thou has bestowed Thy Grace*
> *Those whose portion*
> *Is not wrath,*
> *And, who go not astray.*

The verses of the Qur'an are terse, but are thought to have multiple levels of meaning. These may not survive translation into other languages, particularly in the case of idiomatic expressions, subtle implications of Arabic grammatical structures, and historic references, unless there are extensive footnotes or bracketed explanations. Translator and commentator Abdullah Yusuf Ali notes that in the mystical early passages there are often three layers: (1) a reference to a particular person or situation; (2) a spiritual lesson; and (3) a deeper mystical significance. He offers interpretation of these three levels in the first two verses of Sura 74 ("O thou wrapped up / [In a mantle]! / Arise and deliver thy warning!"):

> *As to 1, the Prophet was now past the stage of personal contemplation, lying down or sitting in his mantle; he was now to go forth boldly to deliver his Message and publicly proclaim the Lord ... As to 2, similar stages arise in a minor degree in the life of every good man, for which the Prophet's life is to be a universal pattern. As to 3, the Sufis understand, by the mantle and outward wrappings, the circumstances of our phenomenal existence, which are necessary to our physical comfort up to a certain stage; but we soon outgrow them, and our inner nature should then boldly proclaim itself.[10]*

The Qur'an makes frequent mention of figures and stories from Jewish and Christian sacred history, all of which is considered part of the fabric of Islam by Muslims. Islam is the original religion, according to the Qur'an. Submission has existed as long as there have been humans willing to submit. Adam was the first prophet. Abraham was not exclusively a Jew nor a Christian; he was a monotheistic, upright person who had surrendered to God. Jesus was a very great prophet.

Muslims believe that the Jewish prophets and Jesus all brought the same messages from God. However, the Qur'an teaches that God's original messages have been added to and distorted by humans. For instance, Muslims do not accept the idea developed historically in Christianity that Jesus has the authority to pardon or atone for our sins. The belief that this power lies with anyone except God is considered a blasphemous human interpolation into what Muslims understand as the basic and true teachings of all prophets of the Judeo-Christian-Islamic tradition: belief in one God and in our personal moral accountability before God on the Day of Judgment. In the Islamic view, the Qur'an was sent as a final corrective in the continuing monotheistic tradition. Muslims, citing John 14:16 and 14:26 from the Christian New Testament, believe that Jesus prophesied the coming of Muhammad when he promised that the **Paraclete** (advocate) would come to assist humanity after him.

The Qur'an revealed to Muhammad is understood as a final and complete reminder of the prophets' teachings, which all refer to the same one God, known in Arabic as **Allah** ("The God"). For example, in Sura 42, Muhammad is told:

> Say: "I believe in whatever Book Allah has sent down; and I am commanded to judge justly between you. Allah is our Lord and your Lord! For us is the responsibility for our deeds, and for you for your deeds. There is no contention between us and you. Allah will bring us together, and to Him is our final goal."[11]

The central teachings

On the surface, Islam is a very straightforward religion. Its teachings can be summed up very simply, as in this statement by the Islamic Society of North America:

> Islam is an Arabic word which means peace, purity, acceptance and commitment. As a religion, Islam calls for complete acceptance of the teachings and guidance of God.
>
> A Muslim is one who freely and willingly accepts the supreme power of God and strives to organize his life in total accord with the teachings of God. He also works for building social institutions which reflect the guidance of God.[12]

This brief statement can be broken down into a number of articles of faith.

THE ONENESS OF GOD AND OF HUMANITY

The first sentence chanted in the ear of a traditional Muslim infant is the **Shahadah**—"*La ilaha illa Allah Muhammad-un Rasul Allah*" ("There is no god but God, and Muhammad is the Messenger of God"). Exoterically, the Shahadah supports absolute monotheism. As the Qur'an reveals in Sura 2:163:

> Your God is One God:
> There is no god but He,
> Most Gracious, Most Merciful.

Esoterically, the Shahadah means that ultimately there is only one Absolute Reality; the underlying essence of life is eternal unity rather than the apparent separateness of things in the physical world. Muslims think that the Oneness of

myreligionlab
Allah
THE QUR'AN

Muslims express their belief in the Oneness of the divine by saying the Shahadah ("There is no god but God, and Muhammad is the Messenger of God"), the sentence emblazoned on this Turkish plaque.

God is the primordial religion taught by all prophets of all faiths. Muhammad merely reminded people of it.

It has been estimated that over ninety percent of Muslim theology deals with the implications of Unity. God, while One, is referred to by ninety-nine names. These are each considered attributes of the One Being, such as *al-Ali* ("The Most High") and *ar-Raqib* ("The Watchful"). Allah is the name of God that encompasses all the attributes. Each of the names refers to the totality, the One Being.

Unity applies not only to the conceptualization of God, but also to every aspect of life. In the life of the individual, every thought and action should spring from a heart and mind intimately integrated with the divine. Islam theoretically rejects any divisions within itself; all Muslims around the globe are supposed to embrace as one family. All humans, for that matter, are a global family; there is no one "chosen people," for all are invited into a direct relationship with God. Science, art, and politics are not separate from religion in Islam. Individuals should never forget Allah; the Oneness should permeate their thoughts and actions. Abu Hashim Madani, an Indian Sufi sage, is said to have taught: "There is only one thing to be gained in life, and that is to remember God with each breath; and there is only one loss in life, and that is the breath drawn without the remembrance of God."[13]

> The "remembrance of God" is like breathing deeply in the solitude of high mountains: here the morning air, filled with purity of the eternal snows, dilates the breast; it becomes space and heaven enters our heart.
>
> *Frithjof Schuon*[14]

PROPHETHOOD AND THE COMPASS OF ISLAM

myreligionlab

Messengers
THE QUR'AN

Devout Muslims feel that Islam encompasses all religions. Islam honors all prophets as messengers from the one God:

Say ye: We believe
In God, and the revelation
Given to us, and to Abraham,
Isma'il, Isaac, Jacob,
And the Tribes, and that given
To Moses and Jesus, and that given
To (all) Prophets from their Lord:
We make no difference
Between one and another of them:
And we bow to God in surrender.[15]

Muslims believe that the original religion was monotheism, but that God sent prophets from time to time as religions decayed into polytheism. Each prophet came to renew the message, in a way specifically designed for his culture and time. The Qur'anic revelations declared Muhammad to be the "Seal of the Prophets," the last and ultimate authority in the continuing prophetic tradition. The prophets are mere humans, although holy and powerful; none of them is divine, for there is only one Divinity.

Islam is thought to be the universal religion in its pure form. All scriptures of all traditions are also honored, but only the Qur'an is considered fully authentic, because it is the direct, unchanged, untranslated word of God. Whatever exists in other religions that agrees with the Qur'an is divine truth.

myreligionlab
People of the Book
THE QUR'AN

HUMAN RELATIONSHIP TO THE DIVINE

We are nearer to [a person] than his jugular vein.
                                                            The Holy Qur'an, Sura 50:16

In Muslim belief, God is all-knowing and has intelligently created everything for a divine purpose, governed by fixed laws that assure the harmonious and wondrous working of all creation. Humans will find peace only if they know these laws and live by them. They have been revealed by the prophets, but the people often have not believed. To believe is to surrender totally to God. As the Qur'an states:

None believes in Our revelations save those who, when reminded of them, prostrate themselves in adoration and give glory to their Lord in all humility; who forsake their beds to pray to their Lord in fear and hope; who give in charity of that which We have bestowed on them. No mortal knows what bliss is in store for these as a reward for their labors.[16]

The Qur'an indicates that human history provides many "signs" of the hand of God at work bestowing mercy and protection on believers. Signs such as the great flood, which was thought to have occurred at the time of Noah, illustrate that nonbelievers and evildoers ultimately experience great misfortune in this life or the afterlife. None is punished without first being warned by a messenger of God to mend his or her ways. Creation itself is a sign of God's compassion, as well as of God's omnipotent will.

According to Islam, the two major human sins involve one's relationship to God. One is *shirk* (associating anything else with divinity except the one God). The Qur'an instructs,

Say: "Oh People of the book!
Come to common terms as between us and you:
That we worship none but Allah;
That we associate no partners with Him;
That we erect not from among ourselves
Lords and patrons other than Allah."[17]

In other words, in Islam's pure monotheism one is enjoined not to worship anything but God—not natural forces, or mountains, or stones, or incarnations of God, or lesser deities, or human rulers. Idol worship is vigorously denounced, as is worship of natural phenomena: "Adore not the sun nor the moon, but adore Allah Who created them."[18]

The other major sin is *kufr* (ungratefulness to God, unbelief, atheism). Furthermore, a major human problem is forgetfulness of God. God has mercifully sent us revelations as reminders. The veils that separate us from God come from us, not from God; Muslims feel that it is ours to remove the veils by seeking God and acknowledging the omnipresence, omniscience, and omnipotence of the divine. For the orthodox, the appropriate stance is a combination of love and fear of God. Aware that God knows everything and is all-powerful, one wants to do everything one can to please God, out of both love and fear. This paradox was given dramatic expression by the Caliph 'Umar ibn al-Khattab:

> *If God declared on the Day of Judgment that all people would go to paradise except one unfortunate person, out of His fear I would think that I am that person. And if God declared that all people would go to hell except one fortunate person, out of my hope in His Mercy I would think that I am that fortunate person.*[19]

THE UNSEEN LIFE

Muslims believe that our senses do not reveal all of reality. In particular, they believe in the angels of God. These are nonphysical beings of light who serve and praise God day and night. They are numerous, and each has a specific responsibility. For instance, certain angels are always with each of us, recording our good and bad deeds. The Qur'an also mentions archangels, including Gabriel, highest of the angelic beings, whose main responsibility is to bring revelations to the prophets from God. But neither he nor any other angel is to be worshiped, according to strict monotheistic interpretation of Islam, for the angels are simply utterly submissive servants of God. By contrast, according to Islamic belief, there is a nonsubmissive being called Satan. He was originally one of the *jinn*—immaterial beings of fire, whose nature is between that of humans and angels. He proudly refused to bow before Adam and was therefore cursed to live by tempting Adam's descendants—all of humanity, in other words—to follow him rather than God. According to the Qur'an, those who fall prey to Satan's devices will ultimately go to hell.

Popular Muslim piety also developed a cult of saints. The tombs of mystics known to have had special spiritual powers have become places of pilgrimage. Many people visit them out of devotion and desire for the blessings of the spirit, which is thought to remain in the area. This practice is frowned upon by some reformers, who assert that Muslim tradition clearly forbids worship of any being other than God.

THE LAST JUDGMENT

myreligionlab
The Day of Judgment
THE QUR'AN

In the polytheistic religion practiced by Arabs before Muhammad, the afterlife was only a shadow, without rewards or punishments. People had little religious incentive to be morally accountable. By contrast, the Qur'an emphasizes that after a period of repose in the grave, all humans will be bodily resurrected and assembled for a final accounting of their deeds. At that unknown time of the Final Judgment, the world will end cataclysmically: "The earth will shake and the mountains crumble into heaps of shifting sand" (Sura 73:14). Then comes the terrible confrontation with one's own life:

> *The works of each person We have bound about his neck. On the Day of Resurrection, We shall confront him with a book spread wide open, saying, "Read your book."*[20]

According to Muslim belief, angels are everywhere; they come to our help in every thought and action. A group of angels is here shown helping the 8th-century Sufi ascetic, Ibrahim ibn Adham.

Hell is the grievous destiny of unrepentant nonbelievers—those who have rejected faith in and obedience to God and His Messenger, who are unjust and who do not forbid evil. Hell also awaits the hypocrites who even after making a covenant with God have turned away from their promise to give in charity and to pray regularly:

> It is a flaming Fire. It drags them down by their scalps; and it shall call him who turned his back and amassed riches and covetously hoarded them.[21]

Muslim piety is ever informed by this belief in God's impartial judgment of one's actions, and of one's responsibility to remind others of the fate that may await them.

Basically, Islam says that what we experience in the afterlife is a revealing of our tendencies in this life. Our thoughts, actions, and moral qualities are turned into our outer reality. We awaken to our true nature, for it is displayed before us. For the just and merciful, the state after death is a Garden of Bliss. Those who say, "Our Lord is God … shall have all that your souls shall desire. … A hospitable gift from One Oft-Forgiving, Most Merciful!" (Sura 41:30–32). The desire of the purified souls will be for closeness to God, and their spirits will live in different levels of this closeness. For them, there will be castles, couches, fruits, sweetmeats, honey, houris (beautiful virgin women), and immortal youths serving from goblets and golden platters. Such delights promised by the Qur'an are interpreted metaphorically to mean that human nature will be transformed in the next life to such an extent that the disturbing factors of this physical existence will no longer have any effect.

People are asleep, but when they die, they wake up.
Hadith of the Prophet Muhammad

By contrast, sinners and nonbelievers will experience the torments of hell, fire fueled by humans, boiling water, pus, chains, searing winds, food that chokes, and so forth. It is they who condemn themselves; their very bodies turn against them "on the Day when their tongues, their hands, and their feet will bear witness against them as to their actions" (Sura 24:24). The great medieval mystic al-Ghazali speaks of spiritual torments of the soul as well: the agony of being separated from worldly desires, burning shame at seeing one's life projected, and terrible regret at being barred from the vision of God. Muslims do not believe that hell can last forever for any believer, though. Only the nonbelievers will be left there; the others will eventually be lifted to paradise, for God is far more merciful than wrathful.

The Five Pillars

The basic spiritual practices incumbent on all Muslims are known as the Five Pillars of Islam. A Muslim must do his or her best to fulfill the Five Pillars because they are considered God's commandments.

BELIEF AND WITNESS

The first pillar of Islam (the Shahadah) is believing and professing the unity of God and the messengership of Muhammad: "There is no god but God, and Muhammad is the Messenger of God," to which Shi'ites add "and 'Ali is the Master of the believers." The Qur'an requires the faithful to tell others of Islam, so that they will have the information they need to make an intelligent choice. However, it rules out the use of coercion in spreading the message:

Let there be [or: There is] no compulsion
In religion: Truth stands out

Around the world, many Muslim scholars are meeting to delve into the tenets of Islam. These scholars are attending the Women's Islamic Initiative in Spirituality and Equality. Second from the left is Dr. Amina Wadud, a renowned feminist author and scholar.

Clear from Error: whoever
Rejects Evil and believes
In God hath grasped
The most trustworthy
Hand-hold, that never breaks.[22]

The Qur'an insists on respect for all prophets and all revealed scriptures.

DAILY PRAYERS

The second pillar is the performance of a continual round of prayers (*salaat*). Five times a day, the faithful are to perform ritual ablutions with water (or sand or dirt if there is no water), face Mecca, and recite a series of prayers and passages from the Qur'an, bowing and kneeling. Around the world, this joint facing of Mecca for prayer unites all Muslims into a single world family. When the prayers are recited by a congregation, all stand and bow shoulder to shoulder, with no social distinctions. In a mosque, women and men usually pray separately, with the women in rows behind the men, to avoid sexually distracting the men. There may be an imam, or prayer-leader, but no priest stands between the worshiper and God. On Friday noon, there is usually a special prayer service in the mosque. Remembrance of God is an everyday obligation; such remembrance continually polishes the rust from the heart.

Prayer is thought to strengthen one's belief in God's existence and goodness and to carry this belief into the depths of the heart and every aspect of external life. Praying thus is also expected to purify the heart, develop the mind and the conscience, comfort the soul, encourage the good and suppress the evil in the per-

myreligionlab
How to Perform Salaat

At a Muslim mosque, there are no social distinctions, as all worshipers line up shoulder to shoulder to pray together. These men are praying at Mahmoud mosque in Cairo.

Salaat

The practice of *salaat* (formal prayer) varies somewhat between men and women and by local custom, but nonetheless follows rather standard patterns around the world. No matter what the local language, *salaat* is always performed in Arabic.

According to references in the Holy Qur'an, the five obligatory daily prayer times are usually understood to be (1) early morning after dawn and before sunrise; (2) early afternoon; (3) late afternoon; (4) immediately after sunset; and (5) night before going to bed. Each consists of a certain number of *rak'ahs*, or complete acts of devotion, some of which are congregational (*fardz*) and some of which are individual (*sunnah*). The morning prayer, for instance, consists of two individual *rak'ahs* and then two congregational *rak'ahs*. During the congregational *rak'ahs*, the whole congregation prays side by side, with their movements matching each other, but during the individual *rak'ahs*, people may be praying at their own pace.

There are four parts to each *rak'ah*. The first part is done in standing position, facing the Ka'bah in Mecca. Hands are first raised with open palms, thumbs touching the edge of the ears, and then folded reverently over the waist or breast, with the right hand covering the left. Inwardly, the person should feel that he or she is standing before the Divine Presence. The open palms mean, "I have come empty-handed into this world and I shall leave empty-handed." Hands crossed over the breast or waist may be understood as a gesture to subdue desires and worldly thoughts, so that all attention can be given to God. The worshipper utters *Allahu Akbar* ("God is great," or "God is the greatest"), followed by the Fatiha, and perhaps a traditional prayer and a passage chosen from the Qur'an, all recited softly to avoid disturbing others, who may be reciting different passages at their own speed. In the congregational part of the prayer, however, the imam who leads the prayers recites any passage from the Qur'an audibly while the others listen and perhaps quietly praise or make requests to God according to the content of the passage.

For the second part of each *rak'ah*, the worshiper bows over, standing with hands on knees and praises the glory of the divine by a phrase such as *Subhana Rabbiy-al-Azim* ("Glory to my Lord, the Great"), repeated three times. A prayer may also be added thereafter.

In the third part of each *rak'ah*, the worshiper first rises up to standing position with hands hanging down freely, while saying *Sami' Allahu li-man hamidah* ("Allah listens to him who praises Him") and *Rabbana wa la-k-al-hamd* ("Our Lord! All praise is due to Thee."). Then the worshiper drops down to his knees in humble prostration with forehead touching the ground while saying *Allahu Akbar*. Rising briefly to sitting position, he then prostrates himself again in a gesture of surrender.

The fourth part is a period of sitting with feet tucked under, a posture assumed after two *rak'ahs* have been completed. In this position, the worshiper utters several prayers, such as the following: "My Lord! Make me and my offspring keep up prayer, our Lord! And accept my prayer, our Lord! Grant protection to me and my parents and the believers on the day when the reckoning will take place." Turning his head to the right and then the left, the person then says to the angels on each shoulder, *As-salamu 'ali-kum wa rahmatu-llah* ("Peace be on you and the mercy of Allah").

The final prayers usually include the famous *Ayat al-Kursi* ("Verse of the Throne") from Surah 2:255, "Allah! There is no god but He: the Living, the Self-subsisting, Supporter of all." The worshiper may also repeat *subhan-Allah* ("Glory be to Allah"), *al-hamduli-ilah* ("Praise be to Allah"), and *Allahu Akbar* ("God is the greatest") several times. Variations in choice of prayers and utterances of praises during the individual *rak'ahs* allow the worshiper to express inner feelings of reverence and submission, while the congregational *rak'ahs* uttered together give a powerful feeling of unity with the global Muslim community.

Sufism

In addition to the two orthodox traditions within Islam—Sunni and Shi'a—there is also an esoteric tradition, which is said to date back to the time of the Prophet. He himself was at once a political leader and a contemplative with a deep prayer life. He reportedly said that every verse of the Qur'an has both an inner and an outer meaning. Around him were gathered a group of about seventy people. They lived in his Medina mosque in voluntary poverty, detached from worldly concerns, praying night and day.

After the time of the first four caliphs, Muslims of this deep faith and piety, both Sunni and Shi'a, were distressed by the increasingly secular, dynastic, wealth-oriented characteristics of Muhammad's Umayyad successors. The mystical inner tradition of Islam, called **Sufism** (Arabic: *tasawwuf*), also involved resistance to the legalistic, intellectual trends within Islam in its early development.

Sufis have typically understood their way as a corrective supplement to orthodoxy. For their part, some orthodox Sunnis do not consider Sufis to be Muslims. Sufis consider their way a path to God that is motivated by longing for the One. In addition to studying the Qur'an, Sufis feel that the world is a book filled with "signs"—divine symbols and elements of beauty that speak to those who understand. The intense personal journeys of Sufis and the insights that have resulted from their truth-seeking have periodically refreshed Islam from within. Much of the allegorical interpretation of the Qur'an and devotional literature of Islam is derived from Sufism.

The early Sufis turned to asceticism as a way of deepening their piety. The Prophet had said: "If ye had trust in God as ye ought He would feed you even as He feeds the birds."[28] Muhammad himself had lived in poverty, reportedly gladly so. Complete trust in and surrender to God became an essential step in the journey. **Dervishes** (poor mendicant mystics) with no possessions, no attachments in the world, were considered holy people like Hindu *sannyasins*. But Sufi asceticism is based more on inner detachment than on withdrawal from the world; the ideal is to live with feet on the ground, head in the heavens.

To this early asceticism was added fervent, selfless love. Its greatest exponent was Rabi'a (c.713–801). A famous mystic of Iraq, she scorned a rich man's offer of marriage, saying that she did not want to be distracted for a moment from God. All her attention was placed on her Beloved, which became a favorite Sufi name for God. Rabi'a emphasized disinterested love, with no selfish motives of hope for paradise or fear of hell. "I have served Him only for the love of Him and desire for Him."[29] Any other motivation is a veil between lover and Beloved. When no veils of self exist, the mystic dissolves into the One she loves.

myreligi⬤nlab
The Rarest Treasure
RABI'A

> The Beloved is all, the lover just a veil.
> The Beloved is living, the lover a dead thing.
>
> *Jalal al-Din Rumi*[30]

In absolute devotion, the lover desires *fana*, total annihilation in the Beloved. This Sufi ideal was articulated in the ninth century CE by the Persian Abu Yazid al-Bistami. He is said to have fainted while saying the Muslim call to prayer.

Hajji Waris Ali Shah (1819–1905) of Deva Sharif near Lucknow, India, was a great shaykh *revered by people of all religions. Understanding Islam as ideally encompassing every religion, he said, "All are equals in my eyes."*

When he awoke, he observed that it is a wonder that some people do not die when saying it, overwhelmed by pronouncing the name Allah with the awe that is due to the One. In his desire to be annihilated in God, al-Bistami so lost himself that he is said to have uttered pronouncements such as "Under my garment there is nothing but God,"[31] and "Glory be to Me! How great is My Majesty!"

The authorities were understandably disturbed by such potentially blasphemous statements. Sufis themselves knew the dangers of egotistical delusions inherent in the mystical path. There was strict insistence on testing and training by a sufficiently trained, tested, and illumined *murshid* (teacher) or *shaykh* (spiritual master). Advanced practices were taught only to higher initiates. It was through the *shaykh* that the *barakah* (blessing, sacred power) was passed down, from the *shaykh* of the *shaykh*, and so on, in a chain reaching back to Muhammad, who is said to have transmitted the *barakah* to 'Ali.

A number of *tariqas* (esoteric orders) evolved, one of which traced its spiritual lineage back to Junayd of Baghdad (who died in 910 CE). He knew that it was dangerous to speak openly of one's mystical understandings; the exoteric-minded might find them blasphemous, and those who had not had such experiences would only interpret them literally and thus mistakenly. He counseled veiled speech, and much Sufi literature after his time is couched in metaphors accessible only to mystics.

Despite such warnings, the God-intoxicated cared little for their physical safety and exposed themselves and Sufism to opposition. The most famous case is that of Mansur al-Hallaj (c.858–922). After undergoing severe ascetic practices, he is said to have visited Junayd. When the master asked, "Who is there?", his disciple answered, *"ana'l-Haqq"* ("I am the Absolute Truth," i.e., "I am God"). After Junayd denounced him, al-Hallaj traveled to India and throughout the Middle East, trying to open hearts to God. He introduced into the poetry of divine love the simile of the moth that flies ecstatic into the flame and, as it is burned up, realizes Reality.

Authorities imprisoned and finally killed al-Hallaj for his *"ana'l-Haqq."* Now, however, al-Hallaj is considered by many to be one of the greatest Muslim saints, for it is understood that he was not speaking in his limited person. Like the Prophet, who had reportedly said, "Die before ye die,"[32] al-Hallaj had already died to himself so that nothing remained but the One.

> *What's in your head—toss it away! What's in your hand—give it up! Whatever happens—don't turn away from it. … Sufism is the heart standing with God, with nothing in between.*
>
> *Abu Sa'id Abu al-Khayr*[33]

myreligionlab
Mysticism
AL-GHAZALI

A more moderate Sufism began to make its way into Sunni orthodoxy through Abu Hamid al-Ghazali (1058–1111). He had been a prominent theologian but felt compelled to leave his prestigious position for a life of spiritual devotion. Turning within, he discovered mystical truths, which saved him from his growing scepti-

Pilgrimage to the tombs of Sufi saints is a popular form of piety. People of all religions pay their respects at the tomb of the revered Indian Sufi saint, Nizamuddin Aulia.

cism about the validity of religion. Like mystics of all religions, he urged awareness of the certainty of death as an antidote to entanglements in worldly concerns:

> *Death does not come upon us at a specified time or in a specified way or at a specified age; but come upon us he does, and so preparation for death is better than preparation for this world. You know that you remain here for only a brief space—perhaps there remains but a single day in your allotted span, perhaps but a single breath. Imagine this in your heart every day and impose upon yourself patience in obeying God daily.*[34]

Al-Ghazali's persuasive writings combined accepted Muslim theology with the assertion that Sufism is needed to keep the mystical heart alive within the tradition. By the fourteenth century, mysticism was generally accepted by the orthodoxy as one of the sciences of religion, along with theology and jurisprudence.

Over the centuries, other elements have been added to Sufism. Some Sufis have embraced teachings from various religions, emphasizing that the Qur'an clearly states that the same Voice has spoken through all prophets. Shihabuddin Suhrawardi (1153–1191), for instance, combined many currents of Islam with spiritual ideas from the Zoroastrians of ancient Iran and the Hermetic tradition from ancient Egypt. His writings are full of references to the divine light and hierarchies of angels. We humans have descended from the angels and realms of light, he wrote; we are in exile here on earth, longing for our true home, searching for that radiant purity, dimly remembered, in this dark world of matter.

Although Sufi teachings and practices have been somewhat systematized over time, they resist doctrinal, linear specification. They come from the heart of mystical experiences which defy ordinary logic. Paradox, metaphor, the world of creative imagination, of an expanded sense of reality—these characteristics of Sufi thought are better expressed through poetry and stories. A favorite character in Sufi teaching tales is Mulla Nasrudin, the wise fool. An example, as told by Idries Shah:

*Sufi dancers and
musicians in Gaza City.*

*One day Nasrudin entered a teahouse and declaimed, "The moon is more
useful than the sun." Someone asked him why. "Because at night we need
the light more."*[35]

These "jokes" boggle the mind, revealing the limitations of ordinary thinking at
the same time that they offer flashes of metaphysical illumination for those who
ponder their deeper significances.

myreligienlab

The Sound of Love
RUMI

Poetry has been used by Sufis as a vehicle for expressing the profundities and
perplexities of relationship with the divine. The Turkish dervish Jalal al-Din Rumi
(c.1207–1273), by whose inspiration was founded the Mevlevi Dervish Order in
Turkey (famous for its "Whirling Dervishes" whose dances lead to transcendent
rapture), was a master of mystical poetry. He tells the story of a devotee whose
cries of "O Allah!" were finally answered by God:

*Was it not I that summoned thee to service?
Did not I make thee busy with My name?
Thy calling "Allah!" was My "Here am I,"
Thy yearning pain My messenger to thee.
Of all those tears and cries and supplications
I was the magnet, and I gave them wings.*[36]

The aim of Sufism is to become so purified of self that one is a perfect mirror
for the divine attributes. The central practice is called *dhikr*, or "remembrance." It
consists of stirring the heart and piercing the solar plexus, seat of the ego, by
movements of the head, while continually repeating *"la ilaha illa Allah,"* which
Sufis understand in its esoteric sense: "There is nothing except God." Nothing in
this ephemeral world is real except the Creator; nothing else will last. As the seventy thousand veils of self—illusion, expectation, attachment, resentment, egocentrism, discontent, arrogance—drop away over the years, this becomes one's
truth, and only God is left to experience it.

The spread of Islam

In the time of Muhammad, Islam combined spiritual and secular power under one ruler. This tradition, which helped to unify the warring tribes of the area, was continued under his successors. Islam expanded phenomenally during the centuries after the Prophet's death, contributing to the rise of many great civilizations. The *ummah* became a community that spread from Africa to Indonesia. Islam was not usually spread by the sword. The Qur'an forbids coercion in religion, recommending instead that Muslims invite others to the Way by their wisdom, beautiful teaching, and personal example. Islam spread mostly by personal contacts: trade, attraction to charismatic Sufi saints, appeals to Muslims from those feeling oppressed by Byzantine and Persian rule, unforced conversions. There were some military battles conducted by Muslims over the centuries, but they were not necessarily for the purpose of spreading Islam, and many Muslims feel that wars of aggression violate Muslim principles. Non-Muslim citizens of newly entered territories were asked to pay a poll tax entitling them to Muslim defense against enemies and exempting them from military service.

Muhammad's nonviolent takeover of Mecca occurred only two years before he died. It was under his successors that Islam spread through West Asia and far beyond. Only a year after Muhammad died, a newly converted Qurayshite, Khalid ibn al-Walid (d. 642), commanded a series of campaigns that within seven years had claimed the entire Arabian peninsula and Syria for Islam. Newly Islamic Arab armies quickly swept through the Sassanian Persian Empire, which had

Only 100 years after Muhammad's death, Islam had spread around the Mediterranean. Its diffusion continued for centuries and the numbers of converts are still increasing, making Islam the fastest-growing religion today. Of areas previously converted to Islam, all remain Muslim except Spain, Greece, and the Mediterranean islands.

Life of Muhammad 622–632 CE

Expansion 632–661 CE

Expansion 661–750 CE

The spread of Islam to 1500 CE

stood for twelve centuries. Defeated in battle in 637 CE, the Persian emperor fled, leaving the capital in Arab hands. Within ten years of the Prophet's death, a mere 4,000 horsemen commanded by Amr ibn al-As took the major cities of Egypt, centers of the Byzantine Empire. Another wave of conquest soon penetrated into Turkey and Central Asia, North Africa, and north through Spain, to be stopped in 732 CE in France at the battle of Tours. At this point, only 100 years after Muhammad died, the Muslim *ummah* under the Umayyad caliphs was larger than the Roman Empire had ever been.

Muslims cite the power of the divine will to establish a peaceful, God-conscious society as the reason why this happened. By contrast with their strong convictions, the populations they approached were often demoralized by border fighting among themselves and by grievances against their rulers. Many welcomed them without a fight. For example, the Christians of Damascus expected Muslim rule to be more bearable than Byzantine rule, so they opened the city

---

TEACHING STORY

Transformation by Islam

From the beginning, Islam ended old tribal conflicts and racial discrimination, and radically changed individuals. The Prophet put the freed black slave Zayd in command of the Qurayshi chiefs. Another freed slave, Tariq ibn Ziyad, led the army of 90,000 warriors who conquered Spain and established one of the greatest civilizations in world history. When he entered the defeated king's treasury, he was not tempted to take anything, for he said to himself:

> Be careful, Tariq. Yesterday you were a slave with a chain around your neck. God emancipated you, and today you are a victorious commander. However, you will change tomorrow into flesh rotting under earth. Finally a day will come when you will stand in the Presence of God.[37]

He continued to live simply. His greatest victory was not his conquest of Spain, but his defeat of his own desires.

'Abd Allah ibn Mas'ud was a weak little shepherd. Nobody paid any attention to him until he converted to Islam. Soon he became one of the greatest of the Companions of the Prophet. The Caliph 'Umar sent him to Kufa in Iraq as a teacher. He helped to create such a thriving intellectual climate there that Kufa became one of the major centers of Islamic jurisprudence, Qur'anic interpretation, and even a beautiful script for the writing of Arabic.

Among many other examples of personal transformation, perhaps none is greater than that of 'Umar, who became the second caliph. He was a Meccan who firmly and cruelly opposed Muhammad's monotheistic path as a threat to Quraysh unity. It is said that he intended to kill the Prophet. According to one traditional account, on the way to do so he met a Muslim who told him to first put his own house in order, since his own sister and brother-in-law were secret converts to Islam. On entering their house, he found them reciting the Qur'an. He began brutally beating his brother-in-law, and then his sister as well when she tried to protect her husband. When they bore his blows patiently, he asked to see what they were reading. His sister showed him a portion of the Surat Ta Ha, which describes the Qur'an as "A revelation from Him Who created the earth and the heavens on high ..." [Holy Qur'an 20:4]. 'Umar was so struck by the beauty of the passage they had been reading that he proceeded to find the Prophet, offered him the sword with which he had planned to kill him, and accepted Islam on the spot. He became one of the most powerful Muslim leaders and was so renowned for his justice toward both Muslims and non-Muslims that he was called *Al-Farooq* ("the one who distinguishes between good and bad").

gates to the Muslim armies. Jerusalem and Egypt accepted the Muslims in similar fashion. Syrian Christians at Shayzar under Byzantine rule reportedly went out to meet the Muslim commander and accompanied him to their city, singing and playing tambourines. In Spain, Visigoth rule and taxation had been oppressive; the persecuted Jews were especially glad to help Islam take over. Both Christians and Jews often converted to Islam.

Some historians cite economic factors as an underlying motive for Arabs' expansion beyond their original territory. However, although Islamic civilization did become quite opulent, the central leadership did not always support the far-reaching adventures. The conquered peoples were generally dealt with in the humane ways specified in the Qur'an and modeled by Muhammad in his negotiations with tribes newly subjected to Muslim authority. The terms offered by Khalid to the besieged Damascans were these:

> *In the name of God, the merciful, the compassionate. This is what Khalid would grant the inhabitants of Damascus when he enters it. He shall grant them security for their lives, properties and churches. Their city wall shall not be demolished, neither shall any Moslem be quartered in their homes. Thereunto we give them the pact of God and the protection (*dhimmah*) of His Messenger, upon whom be God's blessing and peace, the caliphs and the Believers. So long as they pay poll-tax nothing but good shall befall them.*[38]

Monotheistic followers of revealed traditions, Christians and Jews, who like Muslims were "people of the book," were treated as *dhimmis*, or protected people. They were allowed to maintain their own faith, but not to try to convert others to it. The Dome of the Rock was built on the site of the old temple of the Jews in Jerusalem, honoring Abraham as well as Muhammad in the city that is still sacred to three faiths: Judaism, Christianity, and Islam.

The Umayyad caliphs had their hands full administering this huge *ummah* from Damascus, which they had made its capital. They tended to focus more on organizational matters than on the spiritual life. Some were also quite worldly; Walid II, for example, is said to have enjoyed a pool filled with wine so that he could swim and drink at the same time. In 747 CE a rival to the caliphate is said to have invited eighty of the princes of the line to a banquet, where he had them all killed. Three years after "the bloodshedder," a new series of caliphs took over: the Abbasids. They held power until 1258 CE.

ISLAMIC CULTURE

Under the Abbasids, who took over the caliphate in 750 CE, Muslim rule became more Persian and cosmopolitan and Islamic civilization reached its peak. The capital was moved to the new city of Baghdad. No more territories were brought under centralized rule, and merchants, scholars, and artists became the cultural heroes. A great House of Wisdom was built, with an observatory, library, and an educational institution where Greek and Syriac manuscripts on subjects such as medicine, astronomy, logic, mathematics, and philosophy were translated into Arabic. In Cairo, under the Fatimid Ismaili Caliphate, Muslims built in 972 CE the great university and mosque, Al-Azhar, still important in Muslim scholarship and legal decisions.

myreligionlab
Rationalism
IBN SINA (AVICENNA)

myreligionlab
Two Truths
IBN RUSHD (AVERROES)

In its great cities, Islam went through a period of intense intellectual and artistic activity, absorbing, transmitting, and expanding upon the highest traditions of other cultures. For instance, from Persia, which was to become a Shi'ite stronghold, it adopted a thousand-year-old tradition of exquisite art and poetry. To these avid cultural borrowings Islam added its own innovations. The new system of nine Arabic numerals and the zero derived from Indian numbers revolutionized mathematics by liberating it from the clumsiness of Roman numerals. A love of geometry and a spiritual understanding of numbers, from the One to infinite divisions, provided the basis for beautifully elaborated art and architectural forms. Muslim philosophers were highly interested in Aristotelian and Neo-Platonic

Court of the Lions in the Alhambra, Granada, an example of the heights to which architecture evolved in Muslim Spain.

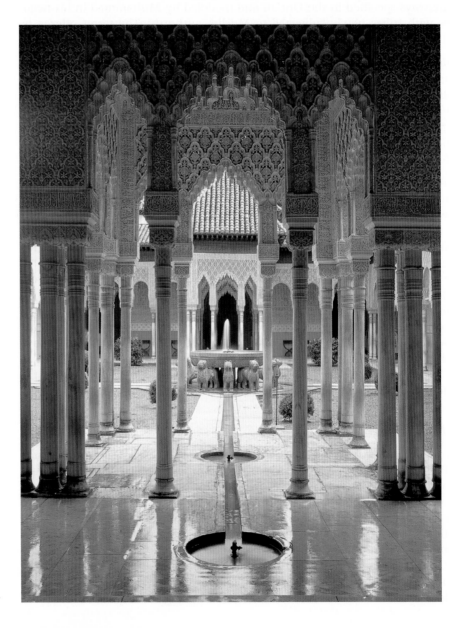

thought, but in their unique synthesis these intellectual ways were harmonized with revealed religion. Muslim scholars' research into geography, history, astronomy, literature, and medicine lifted these disciplines to unprecedented heights.

The pivotal institution of Islamic society was the *ulama*, whose primacy and influence were unchallenged. The *ulama* were not only guardians of the faith but were also the pervasive force holding together Islamic society. They were *qadis* (judges), *muftis* (jurisconsultants), guides and pastors of the artisans' guilds, spiritual leaders, mosque imams, the sole teachers of the civil and military schools, state scribes, and market inspectors. The major sources of their economic power and their independence from the state were religious endowments and private endowments, run and controlled by the *ulama*.

Although Baghdad was the capital of the Abbasids, independent caliphates were declared in Spain and Egypt. Muslim Spain was led by successors to the Umayyads and became a great cultural center. Córdoba, the capital, had 700 mosques, seventy libraries, 300 public baths, and paved streets. Europe, by contrast, was in its Dark Ages; Paris and London were only mazes of muddy alleys. Spanish Muslim scientists developed a prototype of a flying machine, mechanical clocks, and highly accurate astronomical clocks, many centuries before such inventions were introduced into Europe through translations of Arabic manuscripts.

Tunisia and Egypt comprised a third center of Islamic power: the Shi'ite Fatimid caliphate (so named because they claimed to be descendants of Muhammad's daughter Fatima). While otherwise known for their brilliant cultural and scientific accomplishments, under the troubled Fatimid caliph, al-Hakim (985–c.1021), the Fatimids broke with Islamic tradition and persecuted *dhimmis*; they also destroyed the Church of the Holy Sepulcher in Jerusalem, provoking European Christian crusades to try to recapture the Holy Lands.

Crusading Christians fought their way to Jerusalem, which they placed under siege in 1099. When the small Fatimid garrison surrendered, the crusaders slaughtered the inhabitants of the holy city. Eyewitnesses recount the beheading of 70,000 captives at the al-Aqsa mosque, near the altar site of the ancient Jewish temple. Severed hands and feet were piled everywhere. Anti-crusading Muslims led by the famous Salah-al-Din (known in the West as Saladin) retook Jerusalem in 1187 and treated its Christian population with the generous leniency of Islam's highest ideals for the conduct of war. But widespread destruction remained in the wake of the crusaders, and a reservoir of ill-will against Christians lingered, to be exacerbated centuries later by European colonialism in Muslim lands.

The Islamic period in Spain was known for its tolerance of Judaism. But during the twelfth and thirteenth centuries, Christians took Spain and later instituted the dread Inquisition against those not practicing Christianity. By the beginning of the sixteenth century, an estimated three million Spanish Muslims had either been killed or had left the country.

EASTWARD EXPANSION

Its westward advance stopped at Europe, Islam carried its vitality to the north, east, and south. Although Mongol invasions from Central Asia threatened, the Mongols were converted to Islam; so were the Turks. While Uzbek Khan, Mongol leader from 1313 to 1340, zealously desired to spread Islam throughout Russia, he nonetheless maintained tolerance toward the Christians in the conquered lands. He granted a charter to the Orthodox Metropolitan concerning the treatment of Christians: "Their laws, their Churches; their monasteries and chapels shall be respected; whoever condemns or blames this religion, shall not be allowed to excuse himself under any pretext but shall be punished with death."[39]

Similar tolerance toward other religions was practiced by the Muslim Turks, but in 1453 the Turks conquered Constantinople, the heart of the old Byzantine Empire, and renamed it Istanbul; Hagia Sophia was turned into a mosque even though it did not face Mecca. At its height, the Turkish Ottoman Empire dominated the eastern Mediterranean as well as the area around the Black Sea.

Farther east, Islam was carried into northern India, where Muslim conquerors destroyed some Hindu idols and temples but allowed the Hindu majority a pro-

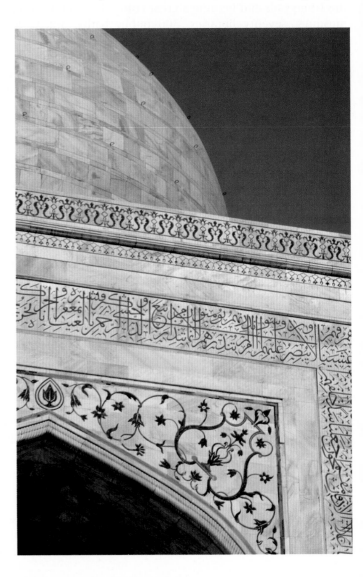

Arch of the Taj Mahal, Agra, India, surrounded by verses from the Qur'an in intricate marble inlay. From 1632 to 1654, the finest masons and 20,000 laborers worked under the Mogul emperor Shah Jahan to create this mausoleum for his beloved wife, Mumtaz Mahal.

tected *dhimmi* status. The Chishti Sufi saints drew people to Islam by their great love for God. "The heart of a mystic is a blazing furnace of love which burns and destroys everything that comes into it because no fire is stronger than the fire of love," declared Khwaja Muinuddin Chishti.[40]

Under the Muslim Moguls, the arts and learning flourished in India. In the ecumenical spiritual curiosity of the emperor Akbar, who rose to the Mogul throne in 1556, representatives from many traditions—Hindu, Zoroastrian, Jain, Christian—were invited to the world's first interfaith dialogues. Eventually Akbar devised a new religion that was a synthesis of Islam and all these other religions, with himself as its supposedly enlightened head, but it died with him, and Muslim orthodoxy gained ascendancy with his grandson, Aurangzeb.

Under British colonization of India, tensions between Hindus and Muslims were inflamed, partly to help Britain divide and rule. India gained its independence under the influence of Mahatma Gandhi, who was unable to devise a political solution to the concerns of Muslims fearing domination by a Hindu-majority government. In 1947, West and East Pakistan (the East section now the independent nation of Bangladesh) were partitioned off to be Muslim-ruled and predominantly populated by Muslims, while India was to be run by Hindus. The creation of Pakistan was one of the major contemporary attempts to create a model nation based on the principles of Islam. Mohammed Ali Jinnah, the London-educated lawyer who is regarded as the founder of Pakistan, conceived of Pakistan as a modern and democratic state in which women, minorities, and human rights would be respected, according to Islam's true tenets of tolerance, compassion, and justice. However, the entrenched powers and ethnic and cultural divisions within the country have prevented realization of his dream. At its inception, the partition of India into Muslim majority and Hindu majority nations turned into a violent and chaotic nightmare. Millions lost their lives trying to cross the borders. The strife between the two faiths continues despite recurrent attempts to renew peaceful relationships between the peoples of Pakistan and India, who, though divided into different religions, actually share one culture. In India, Hindus and Muslims had long lived side by side in relative harmony, but in December 1992, militant Hindus set off renewed communal violence by destroying a mosque in Ayodhya, India, in the belief that it had been built by the Moguls on the site of an ancient temple to Lord Rama. Another terrible wave of Hindu violence against Muslims occurred in the state of Gujarat in 2002, in retaliation for the burning of a train illegally carrying Hindu volunteers to build a new Ram temple on the disputed Ayodhya site.

The greatest concentration of Muslims developed even farther east, in Indonesia, where Muslim traders and missionaries may have first landed as early as the tenth century CE. Nearly ninety percent of the people are now Sunni Muslims, but despite recent violence between Muslims, Hindus, and Christians, the government has attempted to preserve a secular, pluralistic society rather than establish Islam as the state religion. In 1989, then-President Suharto stated: "We want each and all religions existing and developing in our country to achieve progress in an atmosphere of unity and mutual respect."[41]

China and the former Soviet Union encompass tens of millions of Muslims. To the south, Islam spread into Africa along lines of trade. In competition with Christianity, Islam sought the hearts of Africans and eventually won in many areas. Many converted to Islam; many others maintained some of their indigenous ways in combination with Islam. The prosperous Mali Empire was headed by a Muslim, who made an awe-inspiring pilgrimage to Mecca with a gold-laden retinue of 8,000 in 1324. As the spread of Islam encompassed an increasing diversity of cultures, *hajj* became important not only for individuals but also for the religion as a whole, holding its center in Mecca in the midst of worldwide variations.

Relationships with the West

Although Islam honors the prophets of all traditions, its own religion and prophet were denounced by medieval Christian Europe. Some people fear that the medieval "clash of civilizations" may be replayed in our times if ignorance, distrust, and fear lead to exclusivist, simplistic, and violent responses to the rapid changes in the modern globalized world. Christianity had considered itself the ultimate religion and had launched its efforts to bring the whole world under its wings. Islam felt the same way about its own mission. In the struggle for souls, the Church depicted Muhammad as an idol-worshiper, an anti-Christ, the Prince of Darkness. Islam was falsely portrayed as a religion of many deities, in which Muhammad himself was worshiped as a god (thus the inaccurate label "Muhammadanism"). Europeans watched in horror as the Holy Lands became Muslim and the "**infidel**" advanced into Spain and elsewhere in Europe. Even though Muslim scholars and artists preserved, shared, and advanced the classic civilizations while Europe was benighted, the wealth of Arabic culture was interpreted in a negative light.

By the nineteenth century, Western scholars began to study the Arabic classics, but the ingrained fear and loathing of Muhammad and Muslims remained. The ignorance about, and negative stereotyping of, Muslims continues today. Annemarie Schimmel, late Professor of Indo-Muslim Culture, Harvard University, explained:

> The idea that the Muslims conquered everything with fire and sword was unfortunately deeply ingrained in the medieval mind. All these misconceptions about Islam as a religion and the legends and lies that were told about it are really unbelievable. I have often the feeling that this medieval image of Islam as it was perpetuated in ever so many books and even scholarly works is part of our subconscious. When someone comes and says, "But real Islam is something completely different," people just will not believe it because they have been indoctrinated for almost fourteen hundred years with the image of Islam as something fierce and something immoral. Unfortunately, some of the events of our century have revived this medieval concept of Islam.[42]

> Borrow the Beloved's eyes. Look through them and you'll see
> the Beloved's face everywhere. ...
> Let that happen, and things you have hated will become helpers.
>
> Jalal al-Din Rumi[43]

Although it had enjoyed great heights of culture and political power, the Muslim world fell into decline. It seems that the Mongol invasions were at least partly responsible, for they eradicated irrigation systems and libraries and killed scholars and scientists, erasing much of the civilization that had been built up over 500 years. Some Muslims today feel that spiritual laxness was the primary reason that some of the previously glorious civilizations became impoverished Third World countries. Another theory is that Muslims were simply overtaken by stronger military and economic powers better equipped than they were, such as the Mongols in the thirteenth century, and subsequently the Europeans.

During the late eighteenth and early nineteenth centuries, many Muslim populations fell under European domination. From the mid-twentieth century onward, most gained their independence as states that had adopted certain Western ideals and practices. In many cases, they had let go of some aspects of their Muslim heritage, considering it a relic that prevented them from success in the modern world. Arabic was treated as an unimportant language; Western codes of law had replaced the Shari'ah in social organization. But yet they were not totally Westernized, and they resumed local rule with little training for self-government and participation in a world economy dominated by industrial nations.

Societies that had been structured along traditional lines fragmented from the mid-nineteenth century onward, as wide-ranging programs of reforms and modernization were unleashed throughout the Muslim world. The local autonomy of the traditional Islamic society was swept away and replaced by centralized regulations of Western origin. Traditional schools, markets, guilds, and courts into which the societies had been organized lost much of their reason for being.

Before the colonial forces moved out, foreign powers led by Britain helped to introduce a Jewish state in West Asia. After long and terrible persecution in many countries, Jewish Zionists sought resettlement in Palestine, which they considered their ancient homeland. But some historians allege that the chief motive of the countries supporting this claim was to protect European interests. Lord Palmerston of Britain suggested that a wealthy Jewish population transplanted to Palestine, and highly motivated to protect itself, would

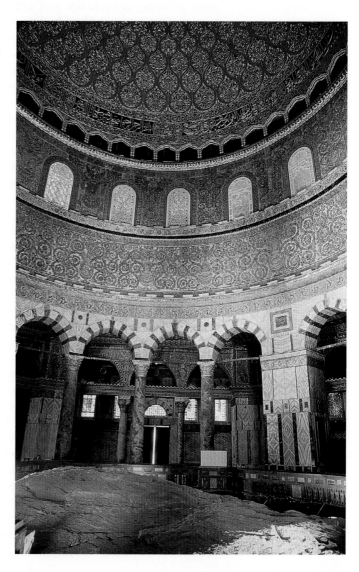

Dome of the Rock, Jerusalem. In an area held sacred by Jews, Christians, and Muslims, the dome was completed in 691–692 as the first major Muslim monument. The rock had been associated with Abraham's sacrifice of his son. Muslim tradition identified it as the place of the Prophet's ascension to heaven during his Night Journey.

prop up the decaying Ottoman Empire so that it could serve as a bulwark against Russian imperialism; the new Jewish presence in Palestine would also serve as a check against the attempts of Egypt to create a pan-Islamic state encompassing Egypt, Syria, and the Arabian peninsula. In 1948 Jordan and Egypt annexed twenty-two percent of Palestinian territory—the West Bank and the Gaza Strip; in 1967, this territory was occupied by Israel. Decades of violence and counterviolence have followed, with Palestinians in the disputed area suffering from appropriation of their lands, destruction of their houses, severe curtailing of their material supplies, and restrictions on their movements, and Israelis living in fear of terrorist attacks.

ISLAM IN THE WEST

Even as Muslims were feeling humiliated by foreign domination elsewhere, they were growing in numbers and self-pride within the United States. Islam is the fastest growing religion in the United States, and may now be the second largest religion in the country. Two-thirds of American Muslims are immigrants; one-third of American Muslims are converts, most of them African Americans.

Conversion to Islam by African Americans was encouraged early in the twentieth century as a form of separatism from white oppression. Awareness grew that many of the slaves who had been brought from West Africa had been of Muslim faith. A number of movements developed to bring the former slaves back to their suppressed ancestral faith. For instance, in 1913 Noble Drew Ali (1886–1929) began a movement that was designed to begin teaching the elements of the faith to African Americans and thus give them a strong sense of their own identity. Members were encouraged to adopt Noble Drew Ali's understanding of Muslim lifestyles, with modest dress, gender separation, traditional family structure, and community solidarity.

Some other early Muslim communities in the United States were based on missionary efforts, such as that of the Ahmadiyyah Movement from India, which was active in publishing tracts and English translations of the Qur'an and in helping African American converts learn Arabic. By the end of the twentieth century, the Ahmadiyyah Movement had established branches in thirty-eight cities in the United States as part of its global family of ten million members, complete with social service programs. However, most Muslims do not accept the Ahmadiyyah Movement as Muslim, for the movement's prophet proclaimed himself the Mahdi and Messiah, contrary to mainstream understanding of Muhammad as the "seal of the prophets."

Other movements had a strong nation-building character. In particular, under the leadership of Elijah Muhammad, who proclaimed himself a messenger of God, tens of thousands of African Americans became "Black Muslims," calling themselves the Nation of Islam. However, faith in Elijah Muhammad himself was shaken by allegations about his sexual relationships with his secretaries. Some followers—especially the influential leader Malcolm X and Warith Deen Muhammad, son of Elijah Muhammad—developed contacts with mainstream Muslims in other countries and came to the conclusion that Elijah Muhammad's version of Islam was far removed from Muslim orthodoxy. They steered converts toward what they perceived as the true traditions of Islam and alliance with the world Muslim community.

Others of African American heritage, especially Minister Louis Farrakhan, current leader of the Nation of Islam, maintain Elijah Muhammad's more political focus on unifying against white oppression, despite Islam's strong tradition of nonracism. However, politicization of Islamic identity is probably not the main aspect of the growth of Islam. Many American Muslims embrace their religion as a bulwark of discipline and faith against the degradations of materialism.

The homes of African American Muslims become places of refuge from the surrounding culture, with Qur'anic inscriptions, provisions for prayer spaces, cleanliness and lack of clutter, and windows covered as privacy screens. Soon after birth, children are placed with their mothers on their prayer rugs and gradually learn to recite portions of the Qur'an. They are carefully trained in politeness to elders, modest dress, and proper behavior. The environment these children encounter in public schools is a great contrast to this traditional upbringing. Young Muslim girls are taunted about their headscarves, and sex education classes, which begin at an early age, are offensive to Muslim parents who do not accept dating and extramarital sexuality for their children. Some African American Muslim parents thus attempt to home-school their children.

In Europe, decades of immigration from formerly French and British colonies in Africa and Asia have expanded the Muslim presence considerably. There are now over twenty million Muslims in western Europe. There they have often maintained their traditional cultures rather than adopting European behaviors. The secular policies of the French government have prompted a legal ban on overt display of religious symbols, including the headscarves traditionally worn by Muslim women. Refusal to allow wearing of headscarves in school has led some Muslim girls to leave public schools and pursue education through home schooling or religious schools, causing further separation between Muslim and non-Muslim populations. Resentment is also growing in European welfare states that Muslim immigrants are benefiting from their welfare systems.

Muslim resurgence

The Muslim world had lost its own traditional structure and was also generally helpless against manipulations by foreign nations until it found its power in oil. In the 1970s, oil-rich nations found that by banding together they could control the price and availability of oil. OPEC (the Organization of Petroleum Exporting Countries) brought greatly increased revenues into previously impoverished countries and strengthened their self-image as well as their importance in the global balance of power. Most of the oil-rich nations are predominantly Muslim.

As the wealth suddenly poured in, it further disrupted established living patterns. Analysts feel that some people may have turned back to a more conservative version of Islam in an effort to restore a personal sense of familiarity and stability amid the chaos of changing modern life; the increase in literacy, urbanization, and communications helped to spread revived interest in Islam. There was also the hope that Islam would provide the blueprint for enlightened rule, bringing spiritual values into community and politics as Muhammad had done in Medina. It is thought that the Prophet had intentionally tried to create a united community in which each Muslim is responsible for his fellow human beings, in

A woman in Bamiyan, Afghanistan, wears a burqa *over her clothes in order to go to the market.*

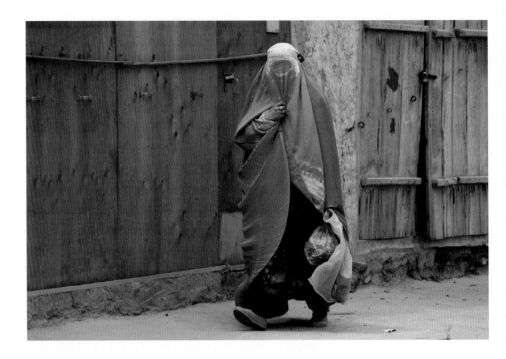

which no one should be hungry or unfairly treated, and in which the leader of the community is a just and religious person. This ideal has perhaps never been fully realized, but it continues to inspire committed Muslims today as the best defense against social decadence and, perhaps, as the salvation of the world.

Traditionally, Muslims have seen the world as divided into *dar al-Islam*, "the abode of Islam" (those places where Muslims are a majority and Shari'ah governs worldly life), *dar al-sulh*, "the abode of peace" (where Muslims are a minority but can live in peace and freely practice Islam), and *dar al-harb*, "the abode of conflict" (where Muslims are in the minority, struggling to practice Islam).

As overt colonialism wanes, the world has become divided into autonomous nation-states with strong central governments. In this process, forty-three primarily Islamic nation-states have been created. They differ greatly in culture and in the degree to which each society is ruled by Islamic ethics. But all are now being reconsidered as possible frameworks for *dar al-Islam*, within which the Muslim dream of religion-based social transformation might be accomplished. Those who seek to establish Islamic states in which the sovereignty of God is supreme are often now referred to as **Islamists**.

In the past few centuries, modern industrial societies separated religion from politics. Social, political, and economic issues have been treated without any reference to a higher authority or to the values taught by the prophets; religion has been considered a largely private matter, even within some Muslim-majority states such as Turkey, where separation of religion from government became law after reformist President Ataturk led his people in abolishing the Ottoman sultanate and establishing the secular Republic of Turkey in 1923. By contrast, a re-emerging ideal among some contemporary Muslim social reformers is that, as Professor Muhammad Mashuq ibn Ally explains:

The human being, the servant, is the trustee of creation under the sovereignty of God, capable of transforming it within the framework of the divine will. Humankind's obedience to, and fulfillment of, the divine command results in happiness and thus unites worldly and cosmic justice. This visionary paradigm in the unity of religious and cultural consciousness enables the assembly of a formidable force to spearhead a new world order, where the consensus is salam—*peace.*[44]

TRADITION AND MODERN LIFE

The resurgence of Islam takes several forms. One is a call for a return to Shari'ah rather than secular law derived from European codes. The feeling of the orthodox is that the world must conform to the divine law, rather than diluting the law to accommodate it to the material world. In Iran, for instance, an attempt has been made to shape every aspect of life according to Shari'ah. Fasting during Ramadan is strictly enforced in Saudi Arabia and Iran, and restaurants in many Muslim countries close during the fasting hours. In Muslim-dominated northern Nigeria, a 1999 Shari'ah ruling barred men and women from traveling in the same public vehicles, in an effort to combat immorality and crime.

Private behaviors are also becoming more traditional. In particular, to honor the Qur'anic encouragement of physical modesty to protect women from being molested, many Muslim women have adopted *hijab* (veiling), covering their bodies except for hands, face, and feet, as they had not done for decades. In Saudi Arabia, where women have been ordered to be "properly covered" outside their homes, some wear not only head-to-toe black cloaks but also full veils over their faces without even slits for their eyes. Some Muslim women assert that they like dressing more modestly so that men will not stare at them. Others feel that men are simply treating women as slaves.

In some Muslim-majority countries, women are allowed to join the workforce only if they are veiled. In Iran, the replacement of more Westernized customs with Muslim moral codes, including veiling of women, has allowed women from conservative backgrounds to leave their homes and enter public life without antagonizing their families. Now that a great number of Iranian Muslim women have been educated and have entered the workforce and politics, they are a formidable part of reformist efforts to challenge the control of the male clerical elite over social life. They have also become active participants in contemporary Iranian attempts to reconcile Islam with human rights and democracy.

Women's rights to divorce and to choose their own marriage partners are among the hotly debated issues in contemporary attempts to define Shari'ah. Shari'ah has been locally adapted to various societies over the centuries; to attempt to restore its original form is to deny the usefulness of its flexibility. Some customs thought to be Muslim are actually cultural practices not specified in the basic sources; they are the result of Islamic civilization's assimilation of many cultures in many places. Muhammad worked side by side with women, and the Qur'an encourages equal participation of women in religion and in society. Veiling and seclusion were practices absorbed from conquered Persian and Byzantine cultures, particularly their upper classes; peasant women could not carry out their physical work under encumbering veils or in seclusion from public view.

myreligionlab

Rights of Women
RIFFAT HASSAN

Muslim women scholars are now carefully re-examining the Qur'an and Hadith to determine the historical realities and principles of women's issues that have long been hidden behind an exclusively male interpretation of the traditions. Qur'anic scholar Amina Wadud, for instance, asserts that the Qur'an is potentially a "world-altering force" that offers universal moral guidance for all believers, be they male or female:

> The more research I did into the Qur'an, ... the more affirmed I was that in Islam a female person was intended to be primordially, cosmologically, eschatologically, spiritually, and morally a full human being, equal to all who accepted Allah as Lord, Muhammad as Prophet, and Islam as din [religious way]. ... Conservative thinkers read explicit Qur'anic reforms of existing historical and cultural practices as the literal and definitive statement on these practices for all times and places. What I am calling for is a reading that regards those reforms as establishing precedent for continual development toward a just social order.[45]

Another problem with applying Shari'ah as civil law is that some ethical issues that arise today either did not exist in their present form at the time the legal codes were created or were not specifically addressed by the Qur'an or Hadith. Artificial birth control methods, for example, were not available then. However, infanticide was mentioned by the Qur'an: "Do not kill your children for fear of poverty. We will provide for them and for you." Does this mean that all forms of population control should be considered forbidden by Islam, or should the over-population of the earth be a major contemporary consideration? According to Islamic legal reasoning, the accepted method for determining such ambiguous issues is to weigh all the benefits and disadvantages that might result from a course of action and then discourage it if the likely disadvantages outweigh the advantages. For those Muslim intellectuals who want to retain their faith within the context of modern life, the process of *ijtihad* (reasoned interpretation, independent judgment by a qualified scholar) is critical.

The global family of Islam is not a political unit; its unity under Arab rule broke up long ago. There is as yet no consensus among Muslim-majority states about how to establish a peaceful, just, modern society based on basic Muslim principles. But there is widespread recognition that there are problems associated with modern Western civilization that should be avoided, such as crime, drug abuse, corruption of values, and unstable family life.

> Today everyone cries for peace but peace is never achieved, precisely because it is metaphysically absurd to expect a civilization that has forgotten God to possess peace.
>
> Seyyed Hossein Nasr[46]

OUTREACH AND EDUCATION

Another sign of Muslim resurgence is the increase in outreach, as Muslims become more confident of the value of their faith. Islam is the fastest growing of all world religions, with over 1.2 billion followers. New mosques are going up

Shirin Ebadi

In 2003, Iranian lawyer Shirin Ebadi became the first Muslim woman to win the prestigious Nobel Peace Prize, which is awarded annually for extraordinary efforts for the sake of peace and social improvement. In her work and in her speeches, Ebadi is fighting to convince people that Iran can be at the same time a democracy in which leaders are fairly elected and accountable to the citizenry, and also a nation observing Islamic values.

Ebadi was born in 1947 as the daughter of a progressive professor and lawyer. She became Iran's first woman judge, President of the City Court of Tehran during the rule of Shah Pahlavi, who tried to increase women's rights and decrease the power of Islamic religious leaders, amidst the harshness of his own rule. When the shah was deposed by the 1979 revolution, Iran was declared an Islamic state with Ayatollah Khomeini as its leader. Khomeini cancelled the shah's reforms and instituted strict observance of Shari'ah. Women lawyers were forbidden to practice independently, so Ebadi lost her position. Rather than leave the country, as many intellectuals did, she chose to remain in Iran and try to bring transformation in consonance with Islamic law, particularly with respect to human rights.

After the 1989 death of the ayatollah, women were again allowed to practice law, and Ebadi began to defend people whose rights had been denied by the government. She founded the Association for Support of Children's Rights in Iran and also the Center for the Defense of Human Rights. Her position is that while Shari'ah can serve as the basis for law, it can be interpreted in ways that support freedom and equality. She maintains that Islam is a religion of peace and justice, and that the Qur'an includes many references to ideals such as respect for others' opinions. For speaking thus, she has been arrested, imprisoned in solitary confinement, attacked in newspapers, criticized by protestors while speaking, and subjected to death threats. Nevertheless, she continues to speak and write, emphasizing the need for education and justice if terrorism is to be stopped, rather than using the war on terrorism as a pretext for violation of human rights. In her acceptance of the Nobel Peace Prize, she explained:

"I am a Muslim. In the Qur'an the Prophet of Islam has been cited as saying: 'Thou shalt believe in thy faith and I in my religion.' That same divine book sees the mission of all prophets as that of inviting all human beings to uphold justice. Since the advent of Islam, too, Iran's civilization and culture has become imbued and infused with humanitarianism, respect for the life, belief, and faith of others, propagation of tolerance and compromise and avoidance of violence, bloodshed, and war. ... The people of Iran have been battling against consecutive conflicts between tradition and modernity for over a hundred years. By resorting to ancient traditions, some have tried and are trying to see the world through the eyes of their predecessors and to deal with the problems and difficulties of the existing world by virtue of the values of the ancients. But many others, while respecting their historical and cultural past and their religion and faith, seek to go forth in step with world developments and not lag behind the caravan of civilization, development, and progress. The people of Iran, particularly in the recent years, have shown that they deem participation in public affairs to be their right, and that they want to be masters of their own destiny.

"This conflict is observed not merely in Iran, but also in many Muslim states. Some Muslims, under the pretext that democracy and human rights are not compatible with Islamic teachings and the traditional structure of Islamic societies, have justified despotic governments, and continue to do so. ...

"Islam is a religion whose first sermon to the Prophet begins with the word 'Recite!' The Qur'an swears by the pen and what it writes. Such a sermon and message cannot be in conflict with awareness, knowledge, wisdom, freedom of opinion and expression, and cultural pluralism. ...

"If the twenty-first century wishes to free itself from the cycle of violence, acts of terror and war, and avoid repetition of the experience of the twentieth century—that most disaster-ridden century of humankind—there is no other way except by understanding and putting in practice every human right for all mankind, irrespective of race, gender, faith, nationality, or social status."[47]

A class of women in Izmir, Turkey, are learning to read the Qur'an in Arabic so that they can understand it themselves.

everywhere. Some Muslims who constitute a minority in their countries are trying to assert their rights to practice their religion by praying five times a day, leaving work to attend Friday congregational prayer at noon, and wearing traditional head-coverings. Special Islamic satellite channels offer alternatives to Western-oriented programming that Muslims find offensive, and also act as a force for international Muslim unity. The channel Iqra, for instance, is financed by a Saudi Arabian millionaire, offering free broadcasting of what it describes as "entertaining programmes that are devoid of decadence and impropriety and are appropriate for viewing by Muslim families."[48]

A third sign of Muslim resurgence is the increasing attention being given to developing educational systems modeled on Islamic thought. Islam is not anti-scientific or anti-intellectual; on the contrary, it has historically bridged reason and faith and placed a high value on developing both in order to tap into the fullness of human potential. Western education has omitted the spiritual aspects of life, so Muslims consider it incomplete and imbalanced.

While there are many excellent Muslim educational institutions, the numerous *madrasas*, traditional religious schools, typically teach a narrow version of Islam, ignoring its sophisticated cultural and scientific heritage and nuanced philosophy. Because some of these schools have proved to be breeding grounds for militants, fanning hatred of the West, particularly among the poor rural students, they are now coming under closer scrutiny. The Sustainable Development Policy Institute in Islamabad released a report in 2003 which identified a number of troubling features of textbooks and curricula in Pakistan:

- inaccuracies and omissions of facts that lead to distorted interpretations of national history
- insensitivity to the diversity of religions in the country

- glorification of violence
- encouragement of prejudices toward women, religious minorities, and other countries
- omission of material and perspectives for developing critical thinking
- outdated teaching practices that fail to stimulate interest and insight.[49]

Pakistan is now revising its textbooks to correct such points. Similarly, Saudi Arabia, the homeland of fifteen of the nineteen airplane hijackers of 11 September, has come under criticism for giving distorted religious messages through its schools, and is now revising its curricula and textbooks to promote peace and harmony.

At the same time, efforts are being made in some countries to increase the accuracy and sensitivity of portrayals of Islam in the education of non-Muslims. Western textbooks have tended to present history as the progress of Western civilization, from which perspective Islam is described mainly as an adversary rather than a high civilization in its own right which has made great contributions to science and culture, not to mention philosophy.

Philanthropic projects funded by Muslims are also on the increase. Most notably, the Ismaili Shi'a Muslim community, under the contemporary direction of its current imam, His Highness the Aga Khan, has organized many award-winning public service projects under the aegis of the Aga Khan Development Network, one of the world's largest development networks. Noordin Kassam, a chartered accountant from England who serves as a regional officer in the network, explains:

> The impetus that spurred this development derives from the Muslim ethic to serve one's fellow man in the spirit of brotherhood. The Aga Khan Development Network is a network of agencies that work in the social sector, finance and industrial services, cultural and tourism promotion for the welfare of not just Ismailis but for the communities in which they find themselves. Two considerations are paramount in the work of the AKDN: that development is only a meaningful and purposive activity if it is conceived holistically; that is, to develop not just oneself but those whom one lives with as well. And second, that we serve because we want to. Over ninety-five percent of the work of the network across twenty-five countries is undertaken by volunteers—people of all walks of life. ... Additionally, I should add an adage of the Aga Khan, which allows contemporary Ismailis to live without contradiction in the modern world. He says: To seek wealth is not against Islam. But what one does with that wealth is the important thing. If you have excess, then share it. The possibilities to serve and to volunteer what one has are unlimited and provide a constant source of gratification to many members of my community.[50]

ISLAM IN POLITICS

At present, the facet of Islam that is of greatest concern around the world to both Muslims and non-Muslims is its association with politics. Many governments are becoming Islamicized. Political leaders are referring more frequently to Islam and Qur'anic statements. Some use this approach to support the status quo and glorify Islam's past heights. In Arabic countries, others have used Muslim idealism to rally opposition to ruling elites who are perceived as being corrupt or tied to the

West. Some charismatic leaders have used their own interpretations of Islam to ignite violent political expressions of frustration and hatred against Western global domination. These include suicidal terrorist attacks against civilian targets by those who have been assured that their self-sacrifice for the cause will earn them quick entry to paradise, contrary to Quranic passages refusing suicide and upholding the value and sanctity of each human life.

myreligionlab

Islam and the West
SAMUEL HUNTINGTON

A major issue at stake is the understanding of **jihad**. All Muslims are enjoined by the Qur'an to carry on jihad. Commonly mistranslated as "holy war," it means "striving." The Prophet Muhammad is said to have distinguished between two types of jihad. Of these, he said, the Greater Jihad is the struggle against one's lower self. It is the internal fight between wrong and right, error and truth, selfishness and selflessness, hardness of heart and all-embracing love. This inner struggle to maintain peaceful equilibrium is then reflected in outer attempts to keep society in a state of harmonious order, as the earthly manifestation of Divine Justice. The Lesser Jihad is an external effort to protect the Way of God against the forces of evil. This jihad is the safeguarding of one's life, faith, livelihood, honor, and the integrity of the Muslim community. The Prophet Muhammad reportedly said that "the preferred jihad is a truth spoken in the presence of a tyrant."[51]

myreligionlab

God in a World
of Christians
and Muslims
MARTIN FORWARD

Jihad is not to be undertaken for personal gain. The Qur'anic revelations that apparently date from the Medina period when the faithful were being attacked by Meccans make it clear that:

> *To those against whom*
> *War is made, permission*
> *Is given (to fight), because*
> *They are wronged;—and verily,*
> *God is Most Powerful*
> *For their aid;*
>
> *(They are) those who have*
> *Been expelled from their homes*
> *In defiance of right,*
> *(For no cause) except*
> *That they say, "Our Lord*
> *Is God."*[52]

The Qur'an gives permission to fight back under such circumstances, and Islamic Shari'ah law gives detailed limitations on the conduct of war and the treatment of captives, to prevent atrocities.

Muhammad is considered the prototype of the true *mujahid*, or fighter in the Path of God, one who values the Path of God more than life, wealth, or family. He is thought to have had no desire for worldly power, wealth, or prestige. By fasting and prayer, he continually exerted himself toward the One, in the Greater Jihad. In defending the Medina community of the faithful against the attacking Meccans, he was acting from the purest of motives. It is believed that a true *mujahid* who dies in defense of the faith goes straight to paradise, for he has already fought the Greater Jihad, killing his ego.

The absolute conviction that characterizes jihad derives from the recognition of the vast disparity between evil and the spiritual ideal, both in oneself and in society. Continual exertion is thought necessary in order to maintain a peaceful equilibrium in the midst of changing circumstances. Traditionalists and radicals have differed in how this exertion should be exercised in society.

In terms of the Lesser Jihad, support can be found in the Qur'an both for a pacifist approach and for active opposition to unbelievers. The Qur'an asserts that believers have the responsibility to defend their own faith as well as to remind unbelievers of the truth of God and of the necessity of moral behavior. In some passages, Muslims are enjoined simply to stand firm against aggression. For example, "Fight for the sake of Allah those that fight against you, but do not be aggressive. Allah does not love the aggressors."[53] In other passages, the Qur'an suggests active opposition to people who do not believe in the supremacy of the one God:

> *Tumult and oppression are worse than slaughter.*
> *Nor will they cease fighting you*
> *Until they turn you back from your faith*
> *If they can. ...*
> *Fight them on*
> *Until there is no more tumult or oppression*
> *And there prevail justice and faith in God.*[54]

In addition to varying interpretations of Quranic passages regarding jihad, contemporary use of violence in the name of Islam involves a complex of varying historical, cultural, and political circumstances in different countries. There is as yet no political unity among Muslim states, but growing antagonism toward the West is tending to create a certain political unity in opposition to pre-emptive use of American military power against Muslim countries in the "war against terror."

One of the leading radical voices that emerged in the twentieth century was that of the Egyptian scholar and activist Sayyib Qutb (1906–1966). After World War II, he saw most Muslim countries being controlled either by corrupt monarchies or by cruel military dictatorships. He had also visited the United States, but was disgusted by its culture. Devoutly religious, he saw the sex, violence, and selfish greed in Western culture as the headwaters of evil that was spreading around the world. His writings during years of imprisonment by the Egyptian government before they eventually executed him have been pivotal in the thinking of all later Islamists. Compared to the ideal example of the life of the Prophet Muhammad, he described Westernization thus:

> *Humanity today is living in a large brothel! One has only to glance at its press,*
> *films, fashion shows, beauty contests, ballrooms, wine bars, and broadcasting*
> *stations! Or observe its mad lust for naked flesh, provocative postures, and sick-*
> *suggestive statements in literature, the arts and the mass media! And add to all this,*
> *the system of usury which fuels man's voracity for money and engenders vile*
> *methods for its accumulation and investment, in addition to fraud, trickery, and*
> *blackmail dressed up in the garb of law.*[55]

Similar thinking later came to the fore in Iran, one of the first Muslim-majority countries in which violence was used in recent times as a political tool to advance the cause of Islam. In predominantly Shi'ite Iran, the Pahlavi shahs had tried to rapidly modernize their country, turning it into a major military and industrial power. In the process, they eroded the authority of the *ulama*, the clerics and expounders of the Shari'ah. A revolutionary leader emerged from this disempowered group, the Ayatollah Khomeini (c.1900–1989), and swept the shah from power in 1979. Khomeini insisted that social transformation should be linked with spiritual reformation, but made some drastic changes in the interpretation of Islam in order to justify violent revolutionary behavior. He also attempted to export his revolution to other Muslim countries with Shi'ite populations that could carry on the work. Khomeini's call for governmental change was not heeded, so radicals resorted to sabotage and terrorism as their most powerful weapons, in what Khomeini described as a great world battle between Islam and the Satanic forces of Western imperialism and Zionism. The radicals' surprise attacks on civilians tended to turn world opinion against Islam, rather than promoting its ideals. Reformers such as Shirin Ebadi (see Box, p. 425) propose that the government should be founded on Islamic law, but that this law should be interpreted in ways that allow a considerable degree of individual freedom and free expression rather than authoritarianism. In 2009 Iran's unique blend of theocracy and democracy witnessed unprecedented citizen protests over a contested presidential election in which eighty-five percent of the population had voted. The protests themselves have been interpreted as a sign of the growing freedom and confidence of Iran's educated citizenry.

Iraq has also seen Islam used as a rallying point for political power. Islam was cast as a political football by both sides in the Gulf War, in which Iraq's president Saddam Hussein tried to reannex Kuwait, using references to Islam as a means of mass mobilization against what he saw as Western intrusion in the Gulf. After the Gulf War, years of economic sanctions by the United Nations against Iraq over continuing suspicion of its military intentions created such hardships for the populace that Iraqis referred to the sanctions as a means of genocide.

Then the United States launched massive bombings of Iraq in 2003 in a campaign it said would "shock and awe" the Iraqi regime and liberate the people from the tyrannical rule of Saddam Hussein, as well as saving the world from what it claimed were Iraq's massive stockpiles of weapons of mass destruction. By contrast, many Muslims around the world perceived the American-led attacks and

Remembrance of Ayatollah Khomeini is still encouraged in Iran.

occupation of the country as an unprovoked attack on innocent Muslim civilians as well as an attempt to control its oil resources. No such weapons of mass destruction were found. Terrorist activity increased in Iraq and elsewhere in protest at the American-led invasion, and perhaps hundreds of thousands of Iraqi civilians have been killed in the chaotic aftermath of the U.S. intervention, including casualties of Sunni–Shi'a conflicts in the destabilized country. When Saddam Hussein was hanged at the end of 2006, many Muslims regarded him as a martyr for his resistance to American power.

In Afghanistan during the 1980s, the United States supported armed Muslim militants—including Osama bin Laden, the Saudi leader who ran terrorist-training camps in rural Afghanistan—to help them drive out the Soviet Union. When the Russian troops left, Afghanistan collapsed into factional fighting and chaos, from which emerged oppressive control by the Taliban from 1996 to 2001. Theirs was an extreme and exclusivist view of the ideal Muslim state. Originally Islamists trained in a particular school in Kandahar, the ardent Taliban discarded all secular laws and replaced them with their interpretation of Shari'ah. To deter crime, for instance, they organized public spectacles in which the hands of thieves were amputated and adulterers were whipped, contradicting the Prophet's insistence on compassion and tolerance. They bombed the huge ancient cliff-hewn statues of Buddha at Bamiyan with the understanding that they were idolatrous, and severely restricted women, keeping them out of the workplace, denying them education, and insisting that they wear head-to-toe *burqas*. The tenacious Revolutionary Association of the Women of Afghanistan resisted the anti-women regimes of both the Taliban and other ruling factions in Afghanistan, documenting the raping, killing, and kidnapping of women by militia members as an instrument of social repression. Law professor Azizah Y. al-Hibri analyzed the issue of how the Taliban were interpreting and using Shari'ah:

> While there is no central interpretive authority in Islam, an acceptable interpretation must satisfy a minimum number of requirements. For example, the interpretation must be based on the Qur'an and Sunnah. It must be based on knowledge and motivated by Piety. It must also serve (rather than harm) maslaha, the public interest of Muslims in particular and humanity in general. ... The Taliban seems to have no such concerns. This is consistent with their rejection of other basic Islamic principles, such as shura (consultation with other Muslims) and bay ah (a system of elective non-authoritarian governance). It is also consistent with their rejection of the Islamic injunction that the pursuit of education is the duty of every Muslim, male and female. Finally, it is consistent with their rejection of the overarching Islamic model of harmonious gender, racial, religious, and general human relations.[56]

Under military attack by the United States, the Taliban's political power in Afghanistan was broken. Hundreds of women in the capital city of Kabul shed their *burqas* publicly, demanding the right to work, education for their daughters, and a voice in politics. While a coalition backed by the United States tries to maintain order, based on a constitution that attempts to combine the teachings of the Qur'an with democracy, the country is still torn and poverty-stricken. Talibanism spilled over into neighboring Pakistan, but its extremist version of Islam is not supported by the majority of the country's citizens, some two million of whom have reportedly been displaced and thousands killed in fighting between the Taliban and the Pakistani government in 2009 in areas which the Taliban had taken over.

Since 1932, Saudi Arabia has been under the absolute monarchical control of the huge al-Sa'ud family. Friendly to the West and using its oil wealth lavishly, the regime is often criticized for exposing the populace to the corrupting influence of Western culture by allowing Western troops on its soil. Despite the plush modern lifestyles and technologies of the elite, the country is religiously conservative, harkening to the ideas of the eighteenth-century legal scholar and reformer Muhammad ibn 'Abd al-Wahhab, who urged discarding of all practices not specifically approved by the Qur'an and Sunnah. Whereas **Wahhabism** has been recently blamed as a source of everything from fundamentalist interpretations of the Qur'an to violent terrorist movements, study of Ibn 'Abd al-Wahhab's voluminous writings shows that he did not use the Qur'an as justification for holy war; rather, he was very careful to explore the historical context of all passages in the Qur'an relating to jihad and then interpret them only in that context, with an emphasis on limiting violence and preserving human lives and dignity. Wahhabism has also been blamed for severe oppression of women, including Saudi Arabia's insistence that women be covered by a full *burqa* from head to toe and its ban on women driving cars or leaving home unless accompanied by a close male relative. But current scholarship suggests that such restrictions stem from local customs and laws rather than from Ibn 'Abd al-Wahhab's life and writings, which in fact reflect Muhammad's own concern for women's rights. In 2008, Saudi Arabia sponsored an interfaith conference in Mecca to showcase Islam's message of tolerance and encouragement of peaceful coexistence.

The most well-known self-styled jihadi in the world is Osama bin Laden, an exiled member of the Saudi aristocracy. In his extremist mixture of religion with politics, martyrdom is an heroic cult, the world is strictly divided into good and evil sides, destruction of property and lives is justified, and the faithful are urged to undertake jihad on a global scale. Bin Laden's militant organization, Al Qaeda, is thought to be responsible for many acts of terrorism around the globe, including the devastating 11 September, 2001 attacks on the World Trade Center and Pentagon in the United States which set in motion a sea change in relationships between Muslims and non-Muslims everywhere. Al Qaeda's agenda is to strike back at the United States for its support for Israel and its intrusive presence in the Arabian peninsula, which bin Laden and others interpret as non-Muslim control over Muslim lands. Shortly after the 11 September attacks, for which Al Qaeda claimed responsibility, Bin Laden issued a videotaped address that included the following insights into his way of thinking:

> *What America is tasting now is only a copy of what we have tasted. Our Islamic nation has been tasting the same for more than eighty years of humiliation and disgrace, its sons killed and their blood spilled, its sanctities desecrated. …*
> *They have been telling the world falsehoods that they are fighting terrorism. In a nation at the far end of the world, Japan, hundreds of thousands, young and old, were killed and this is not a world crime. … But when a few more than ten were killed in Nairobi and Dar es Salaam, Afghanistan and Iraq were bombed and hypocrisy stood behind the head of international infidels: the modern world's symbol of paganism, America, and its allies.*

I tell them that these events have divided the world into two camps, the camp
of the faithful and the camp of infidels. May God shield us and you from them.
Every Muslim must rise to defend his religion. The wind of faith is blowing
and the wind of change is blowing to remove evil from the Peninsula of
Muhammad, peace be upon him.[57]

Although Al Qaeda's operatives are continuing to risk their lives in countries around the world in violent attacks protesting Western cultural and political domination, it appears that they are losing public support and funding, and suicide bombers are being paid less for their self-sacrifices.

In the continuing struggle of Palestinians to reclaim a secure homeland in the face of Israeli settlement, various Palestinian movements have developed, often with help from other countries who contribute to the confusion in West Asia. The two major factions are Fatah and Hamas. Fatah was founded in the 1950s to end Israeli control of Palestine. More recently, it has supported a "two-state" solution through a peace process. Hamas means "zeal" in Arabic. It was formed in 1987 as the Palestinian branch of the Muslim Brotherhood, an Islamist organization based in Egypt. Hamas was initially supported by Israel in the late 1970s as a counter to the Palestine Liberation Organization, under the umbrella of doing religious and social work. But its charter calls for the destruction of Israel, and it has supported suicide attacks against Israeli settlements. Internal struggles between Hamas and Fatah erupted into fratricidal war from 2006 onward. Palestinians call this conflict *Wakseh*, which means humiliation and ruin through damage that is self-inflicted. There is some movement toward reconciliation between the two factions, but around a hardline stance toward Israel.

Turkey, long home to Ataturk's secular vision, is now engaged in power struggles between secularists, devout Muslims, and hardline Islamists. This conflict leads to paradoxical situations. For instance, women are prohibited from wearing traditional headscarves in universities. Religiously observant women who do not want to give up their headscarves and expose their hair publicly are now resorting to an unusual protest measure: Some students are wearing their headscarves and then jamming wigs over them when they attend classes.

As a result of civil wars such as the devastating internal fighting in Sudan, wars between nations, military attacks led by the United States in Iraq and Afghanistan, natural disasters, and climate change, millions of Muslims now live as refugees or internally displaced persons. Muslims account for almost half of all refugees and internally displaced persons in the world. The human misery is staggering.

At the same time, even where Muslims have sought refuge, there is increasing tension between Muslims and non-Muslims. Terrorist activities that have killed civilians have brought a backlash of anti-Muslim sentiments, with growing perception of Islam as a religion encouraging violence and fanaticism. The United States's "war on terrorism" has brought an increase in acts of terrorism and made it more difficult for moderate Muslim leaders to hold their ground against critics within their countries. As Islamophobia grows among non-Muslims, many leading Muslims are trying to explain to them that Islam does not equal violence.

The Qur'an permits the jihad of violence only under very specific conditions. To fight, people must have been deprived of their right to live and support themselves. The action must be undertaken not by individuals but by the collective

Because they are involved in conflicts around the world, many Muslims are mourning the loss of their loved ones, becoming refugees, or being attacked or killed. This scene of grief occurred in Falluja, Iraq.

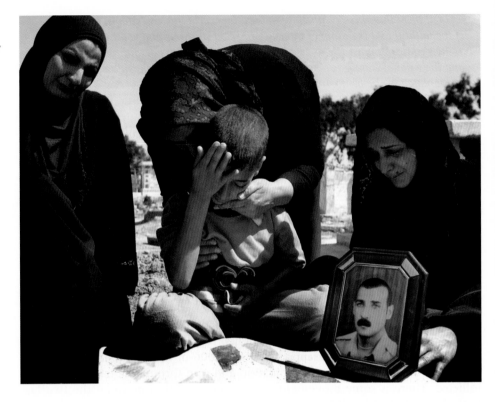

wisdom of the Muslim community. *Jihadis* are never allowed to harm women, children, or unarmed civilians. They cannot wilfully destroy property. The tactics of terrorists are therefore not permitted by the Qur'an. In general, relations with people of other religions are to be as tolerant as possible. It is written in the Qur'an:

> *Do not argue with the followers of the earlier revelations otherwise than in a most kindly manner—unless it be such of them as are bent on evil-doing—and say: We believe in that which has been bestowed from on high upon us, as well as that which has been bestowed upon you; for our God and your God is one and the same, and it is unto Him that we all surrender ourselves. (Holy Qur'an 29:46)*

Nevertheless, particularly after 11 September, 2001, and terrorist bombings in Madrid in 2004 and London in 2005, there have been hate crimes against Muslims as a result of a renewed idea among non-Muslims that Islam breeds violence and fanaticism. Some people suspect that there has been a deliberate Western policy of portraying political conflicts as religion-based struggles in order to fan fear of a threat to the Western way of life from Islam, thus steering Western electorates to support a "war on terror," with an underlying agenda of controlling oil-rich lands belonging to Muslims. Be this as it may, suspicion of Muslims has grown to the extent that imams have been removed from airline flights for performing their prayers, France has outlawed Muslim headscarves in public schools in fear of Muslims' different communal identity, and the British government has proposed forbidding Muslim students to wear full-face veils in class, on the grounds that seeing a woman with a veiled face makes non-Muslims "feel uncomfortable" and even fear that an intruder might be hiding behind the veil.[58]

Alongside such reactions, there are also attempts on the part of both Muslim and non-Muslim scholars at deeper understanding of the complex mixtures of religion with politics. John Esposito, American Professor of Religion and International Affairs and Director of the Center for Muslim–Christian Understanding, writes:

> If we are to understand and respond to the challenge of political Islam, its diverse manifestations must be seen within the multiplicity of intellectual and political contexts in which it occurs. While the threats of extremism and violence must be countered forcefully and effectively, the long-term relations of the West with the Muslim world—like the legitimacy of governments within the Muslim world—will hinge on its response to the emergence of new social and political forces and its respect for their legitimate aspirations for greater political participation, social justice, and human rights.[59]

ISLAM FOR THE FUTURE

Challenged to explain Islam to its critics, Muslim scholars and intellectuals are meeting at global conferences to formulate unified responses to current issues. There is a tendency toward rapprochement between Sunnis and Shi'as at some levels, with the understanding that their differences are not so much matters of religious doctrine as of historical conflicts over leadership. Religious modernists, Islamists, and secularists are all trying to understand the roots of extremism and to seek new ways of relating to and even shaping the rapidly changing world. They feel that extremism is undermining Islam by contradicting its principles and spreading hatred for the religion.

myreligionlab

Ecology: A Sacred Science
SEYYED H. NASR

While media attention is centered on sensational manifestations of Islamism in present-day societies, these deeper currents of thought are forward-looking, exploring how Islam can help to shape a new social order in the world. Professor Asaf Hussain of the University of Leicester, England, points out that the goal of a just society inspires but still eludes Muslim resistance movements:

> Today many Islamic fundamentalist movements have declared war on their own people and are trying to transform their states on the model of the First Islamic state. But the conditions of the seventh century do not obtain today. A new model of the Islamic state has to be devised. The dominating civilization of the present day is Western and its models control the Third World, including the Muslim world. Islamic movements have revolted against this but their strategies have not been well thought out. They do not have to dominate Western civilization but create a parallel which excels it. This will be a long, arduous task but the struggle has just begun.[60]

Mahmoon-al-Rasheed, founder of the Comprehensive Rural Educational, Social, Cultural and Economic Center in Bangladesh, maintains that there is violence within and between nations because people have not developed a sense of duty toward each other and have not recognized how inseparably all people of the earth are related to each other. He proposes that Islamic values are not aimed at creating a political state but rather a harmoniously integrated world society, for:

We cannot begin to realize our full potential until we have achieved a community
which knows no limit but that of human society and renders all obedience to a
Law common to all.[61]

Dr. Ahmad Kamal Abu'l Majd, an ex-Minister of Culture in Egypt, looks
toward the future:

I'm glad and proud I'm a Muslim. I carry on my shoulders a scale of values,
a code of ethics that I genuinely believe is good for everybody. … I even venture
sometimes to say that Islam was not meant to serve the early days of Islam when
life was primitive and when social institutions were still stable and working.
It was meant to be put in a freezer and to be taken out when it will be really
needed. And I believe that time has come. But the challenge is great because
not all Muslims are aware of this fact: That the mission of Islam lies not in
the past but in the future.[62]

Suggested reading

Ahmed, Akbar S., *Discovering Islam: Making Sense of Muslim History and Society*, London and
New York: Routledge, revised edition, 2002. A well-known Pakistani diplomat and
scholar teaching in the United States offers keen insights into the spirituality and
history of modern Muslim cultures.

Ahmed, Akbar, S., *Islam Under Siege*, Cambridge: Polity Press, 2003. Careful explanation
of Islamic ideals and concerns in the context of contemporary violence in the name of
Islam.

Ahmed, Leila, *Women and Gender in Islam: Historical Roots of a Modern Debate*, New Haven,
Connecticut: Yale University Press, 1992. Detailed analysis of historical conditions
within which oppression of Muslim women developed.

Ali, Maulana Muhammad, *The Religion of Islam*, sixth edition, Columbus, Ohio:
Ahmadiyya Anjuman Isha'at Islam, 1994. A classic reference explaining all aspects of
Muslim belief and practice, from the Ahmadiyya perspective.

Armstrong, Karen, *The Battle for God*, New York: Alfred A. Knopf, 2000. A monumental
study of the development of fundamentalism in the United States, Israel, and Egypt in
response to modernity.

Capan, Ergu, ed., *Terror and Suicide Attacks: An Islamic Perspective*, Somerset, New Jersey:
The Light, Inc., 2006. Turkish scholars carefully examine written and oral traditions
which clearly refute terrorism in the name of Islam.

Delong-Bas, Natana J., *Wahhabi Islam: From Revival and Reform to Global Jihad*, Oxford:
Oxford University Press, 2004. Careful examination of the writings of Ibn 'Abd al-
Wahhab, with the thesis that they do not fit the stereotypical notion of Wahhabism as
a major source of extremist movements.

Esposito, John L., *Islam: The Straight Path*, third edition, New York and Oxford: Oxford
University Press, 2004. A scholarly, clear introduction to historical and contemporary
Islam.

Gülen, M. Fethullah, *The Messenger of God: Muhammad*, Somerset, New Jersey: The Light,
Inc., 2006. A loving spiritual analysis of the life of the Prophet.

Hefner, Robert W. and Patricia Horvatich, eds, *Islam in an Era of Nation-states: Politics and
Religious Renewal in Muslim Southeast Asia*, Honolulu: University of Hawaii Press, 1997.
Detailed analyses of Muslim reformist movements in Southeast Asia with reference to
modern governmental structures.

The Holy Qur'an. Although the Qur'an is considered untranslatable, numerous
translations from the Arabic have been attempted. Many Muslims' favorite English

translation is by Abdullah Yusuf Ali (Durban, South Africa: Islamic Propagation Center International, 1946). Thomas Ballantine Irving (Al-Hajj Ta'lim'Ali) has prepared "The First American Version" of the Qur'an (translation and commentary, Brattleboro, Vermont: Amana Books, © 1985).

Lawrence, Bruce, *The Qur'an: A Biography*, New York: Atlantic Monthly Press, 2007. Insightful exploration of the life of the Qur'an, as it has been transmitted, recorded, translated, and understood during its 1,400-year history.

Lings, Martin, *Muhammad*, London: George Allen & Unwin, and Islamic Text Society, 1983. A highly regarded biography of the Prophet.

McCloud, Aminah Beverly, *African American Islam*, New York and London: Routledge, 1995. An accessible inside view of contemporary African American Muslim communities and issues they face in a contrasting cultural context.

Nasr, Seyyed Hossein, *Ideals and Realities of Islam*, second edition, London: Unwin Hyman Ltd., 1985. Thoughtful presentation of both esoteric and exoteric features of Islam.

Nasr, Seyyed Hossein, ed., *Islamic Spirituality I: Foundations*, New York: Crossroad Publishing Company, 1987 and London: SCM Press, 1989. Excellent chapters on key features of Muslim spirituality, from fasting to angels, with sections on Sunnism, Shi'ism, and Sufism.

Nasr, Seyyed Hossein, *Traditional Islam in the Modern World*, London and New York: Kegan Paul International, 1990. Religiously sensitive discussions of varied topics in attempts to bring forth traditional Muslim values within contemporary social settings.

Nasr, Seyyed Hossein, Hamid Dabashi, and Seyyed Vali Reza Nasr, *Shi'ism: Doctrines, Thought, and Spirituality*, Albany, New York: State University of New York Press, 1988. A set of thoughtful essays on aspects of Shi'ite spirituality.

Paige, Glenn D., Chaiwats Satha-Anand, and Sarah Gilliatt, *Islam and Nonviolence*, Honolulu: University of Hawaii, Center for Global Nonviolence Planning Project, 1993. Strong essays on theories and practice of nonviolence stemming from Muslim values.

Pinault, David, *The Shiites: Ritual and Popular Piety in a Muslim Community*, New York: St. Martin's Press, 1992. Sensitive discussions of Shi'ite interpretations of Muslim history and how these inform communal life and action.

Rashid, Ahmed, *Taliban: Militant Islam, Oil and Fundamentalism in Central Asia*, New Haven, Connecticut: Yale University Press, 2000. A Pakistani journalist chronicles the Taliban's rise to power, including global politics and economics as well as religion.

Ruthven, Malise, *Islam in the World*, third edition, Oxford: Oxford University Press, 2006. Explanations of mixtures of Islam with politics and culture throughout history, especially modern history.

Safi, Omid, ed., *Progressive Muslims: On Justice. Gender, and Pluralism*, Oxford: Oneworld Publications, 2003. Scholars and activists explore progressive ways of interpreting Islam in the context of modern issues.

Sajoo, Amyn B., ed., *Civil Society in the Muslim World: Contemporary Perspectives*, London: I. B. Tauris, 2004. Essays exploring the intimate relationships between secular, sacred, and state realms in Muslim society, both existing and ideal.

Schimmel, Annemarie, *And Muhammad is His Messenger: The Veneration of the Prophet in Islamic Piety*, Chapel Hill, North Carolina: University of North Carolina Press, 1985. Extensive exploration of Muslims' love for the Prophet.

Schimmel, Annemarie, *Mystical Dimensions of Islam*, Chapel Hill, North Carolina: University of North Carolina Press, 1975. A classic survey of Sufi history, teachings, and saints.

Tibi, Bassam, *The Challenge of Fundamentalism: Political Islam and the New World Disorder*, Berkeley: University of California Press, 1998, 2002. A Syrian scholar analyzes Islamist movements as manifestations of Islam's confrontation with modernity.

Wadud, Amina, *Qur'an and Woman*, New York and Oxford: Oxford University Press, 1999. Probing hermeneutic analysis of the Qur'an, revealing its principles of social justice, including gender equality.

Webb, Gisela, *Windows of Faith: Muslim Women Scholar-Activists in North America*, Syracuse, New York: Syracuse University Press, 2000. Articles revealing the depth of feminist scholarship within Islam, particularly with reference to the ideal of social justice as seen from the point of view of women of faith.

Zaman, Muhammad Qasim, *The Ulama in Contemporary Islam*, Princeton, New Jersey: Princeton University Press, 2002. Study of the evolution and contemporary importance of the *ulama* in several countries where these religious scholars have re-emerged as a significant factor in religiopolitical activism.

Key terms

Allah The one God, in Islam.

caliph In Sunni Islam, the successor to the Prophet.

fatwa A legal opinion issued by an authority according to a particular school of law; often erroneously defined as an edict against someone or something.

hajj The holy pilgrimage to Mecca for Muslims.

Hadith Traditional report about the sayings and actions of the Prophet Muhammad.

hijab The veiling of women for the sake of modesty.

hijrah Muhammad's migration from Mecca to Medina.

Imam In Shi'ite Islam, the title for the person carrying the initiatic tradition of the Prophetic Light.

Islam In its original meaning, complete, trusting surrender to God.

Islamist A person seeking to establish Islamic states in which the rule of God is supreme.

jihad The Muslim's struggle against the inner forces that prevent God-realization and the outer barriers to establishment of the order.

madrasa Traditional religious school teaching a narrow version of Islam.

muezzin In Islam, one who calls the people to prayer from a high place.

Shahadah The central Muslim expression of faith: "There is no god but God, and Muhammad is the Messenger of God."

Shari'ah The divine law in Islam.

Shi'a The minority branch of Islam which tells that Muhammad's legitimate successors were 'Ali and a series of Imams; a follower of this branch.

Sufism The mystical path in Islam.

Sunnah The behavior of the Prophet Muhammad, used as a model in Islamic law.

Sunni A follower of the majority branch of Islam which tells that successors to Muhammad are to be chosen by the Muslim community.

sura A chapter of the Holy Qur'an.

ummah The Muslim community.

Review questions

1. Outline Muhammad's life story, and describe how his life influenced aspects of Islamic practice and belief.
2. Explain the Five Pillars of Islam, noting the purpose of each pillar and how each is put into practice.
3. Describe the role of the Qur'an, as well as Hadith and Sunnah in Islam.
4. Describe the differences between Sunni and Shi'a Islam, and the nature of Sufism in Islam.

Discussion questions

1. What are the most important religious themes and people that Islam, Judaism, and Christianity have in common?
2. Discuss aspects of Islamic tradition that relate to gender roles within society and the ways these aspects have been interpreted.
3. Discuss the concept of jihad and how it has been interpreted throughout the history of Islam. Do you think that jihad has been oversimplified or stereotyped in the media?

Additional Internet resources

Al-Islam http://www.al-islam.org

Hadith http://www.searchtruth.com/hadith_books.php

Internet Sacred Text Archive: Islam http://www.sacred-texts.com/isl/index.htm

Islam and Islamic Studies Resources http://www.uga.edu/islam/

Islam.com http://www.islam.com

Islamicity http://www.islamicity.com

Islam World http://www.islamworld.net

Mevlevi Sufi Order http://www.hayatidede.org

Religious Tolerance: Islam http://www.religioustolerance.org/islam.htm

Universal Islamic Declaration of Human Rights. Islamic Council of London, 1981

http://www.alhewar.com/ISLAMDECL.html

myreligionlab

For further activities and resources, including access to MyReligionLibrary, please visit MyReligionLab at www.myreligionlab.com

CHAPTER 11

SIKHISM

"By the Guru's grace shalt thou worship Him"

KEY TOPICS

• THE *SANT*
  TRADITION 440

• GURU NANAK 441

• THE SUCCESSION
  OF GURUS 444

• CENTRAL BELIEFS
  450

• SACRED
  PRACTICES 453

• SIKHISM TODAY 457

Another great teacher made his appearance in northern India in the fifteenth century CE: Guru Nanak. His followers were called Sikhs, meaning "disciples, students, seekers of truth." In time, he was succeeded by a further nine enlightened Gurus, ending with Guru Gobind Singh (1666–1708). Despite the power of these Gurus, the spiritual essence of Sikhism is little known outside India and its **diaspora** (dispersed communities), even though Sikhism is the fifth largest of all world religions. Many Sikhs understand their path not as another sectarian religion but as a statement of the universal truth within, and transcending, all religions. Their beliefs and practices have been interpreted as an offshoot of Hinduism or a synthesis of the Hindu and Muslim traditions of northern India, but Sikhism has its own unique quality, independent revelation, and history. As awareness of Sikh spirituality spreads, Sikhism is becoming a global religion, although it does not actively seek converts. Instead, it emphasizes the universality of spirituality and the relevance of spirituality in everyday life.

The *sant* tradition

myreligionlab
Guru Nanak at Mecca

Before Guru Nanak, Hinduism and Islam had already begun to draw closer to each other in northern India. One of the foremost philosophers in this trend was the Hindu saint Ramananda, who held theological discussions with teachers from both religions. But a deeper marriage occurred in the hearts of *sants*, or "holy people," particularly Sufi mystics, such as Shaikh Farid, and Hindu *bhaktas*, such as Sri Caitanya and Bhagat Namdev (1270–1350). They shared a common cause in emphasizing devotion to the Beloved above all else. Many of them were from lower castes, but their spiritual realization was of great heights. They were basically nonsectarian monotheists who did not accept ritualism or casteism.

The most famous of the bridges between Hindu and Muslim is the fifteenth-century weaver Kabir (1440–1518). Legend describes Kabir as the son of Muslim parents and as a disciple of Ramananda. Rather than taking the ascetic path, he remained at work at his loom, composing songs about union with the Divine that are at once earthly and sublime. He could easily transcend theological differences between religions, for he was opposed to outward forms, preferring ecstatic personal intimacy with God. Speaking for the One, he wrote:

O human, where dost thou seek Me?
Lo! I am beside thee.
I am neither in temple nor in mosque:
   I am neither in Kaaba nor in Kailash:
Neither am I in rites and ceremonies; nor in yoga and renunciation.
If thou art a true seeker, thou shalt at once see Me: thou shalt meet Me in a moment
   of time.
Kabir says, "O Sadhu! God is the breath of all breath."[1]

Guru Nanak

When Guru Nanak (1469–c.1539) was born, the area of northern India called the Punjab was half-Muslim, half-Hindu, and ruled by a weak Afghan dynasty. For centuries, the Punjab had been the lane through which outer powers had fought their way into India. In 1398, the Mongolian leader Tamerlane had slaughtered and sacked Punjabis on his way both to and from Delhi. During Guru

Guru Nanak holding spiritual dialogue with Hindu ascetics. (Illustration from Biography of Guru Nanak *by Kartar Singh.)*

Nanak's time, it was the Mogul emperor Babur who invaded and claimed the Punjab. This casting of the Punjab as a perpetual battle-ground later became a crucial aspect of Sikhism.

What Sikhs believe about the life of Guru Nanak is based not so much on historic records as on *janam-sakhis*—traditional stories about his life. The earliest collection of these was probably written down in the seventeenth century; others were written from the eighteenth to twentieth centuries. From historians' point of view, they reflect the biases and concerns of their times, such as early seventeenth-century opposition to the ritualism of Brahmanic Hinduism, and they recount many miraculous happenings that cannot be historically verified. The picture of Guru Nanak that has been handed down is thus a record of how he has been remembered by the faithful.

According to the *janam-sakhis*, Nanak was little concerned with worldly things. As a child he was of a contemplative nature, resisting the formalities of his Hindu religion.

Even after he was married, it is said that he roamed about in nature and gave away any money he had to the poor. At length he took a job as an accountant, but his heart was not in material gain.

When Nanak was thirty, his life was transformed after immersion in a river, from which it is said he did not emerge for three days. Some people now think he was meditating on the opposite side, but in any case he could not be found until he suddenly appeared in town, radiant. According to one account, he had been taken into the presence of God, who gave him a bowl of milk to drink, saying that it was actually nectar (*amrit*) which would give him "power of prayer, love of worship, truth and contentment."[2] The Almighty sent him back into the world to redeem it from Kali Yuga (the darkest of ages). Later Nanak sang:

> Me, the worthless bard, the Lord has blest with Service.
> Be it night or day, many a time He gives His call,
> And calls me verily into His presence.
> And there I praise Him and receive the robe,
> And the Nectar-Name [of God] becomes my everlasting food.[3]

According to the *janam-sakhis*, after Nanak's disappearance in the river in 1499, he began traveling through India, the Himalayas, Afghanistan, Sri Lanka, and Arabia, teaching in his own surprising way. When people asked him whether he would follow the Hindu or Muslim path, he replied, "There is neither Hindu nor Mussulman [Muslim], so whose path shall I follow? I shall follow God's path. God is neither Hindu nor Mussulman."[4] Nanak mocked the Hindu tradition of throwing sacred river water east toward the rising sun in worship of their ancestors—he threw water to the west. If Hindus could throw water far enough to reach their ancestors thousands of miles away in heaven, he explained, he could certainly water his parched land several hundred miles away near Lahore by throwing water in its direction. Another tradition has it that he set his feet toward the Ka'bah when sleeping as a pilgrim in Mecca. Questioned about this rude conduct, he is said to have remarked, "Then kindly turn my feet toward some direction where God is not."

Guru Nanak emphasized three central teachings as the straight path to God: working hard in society to earn one's own honest living (rather than withdrawing into asceticism and begging); sharing from one's earnings with those who are needy; and remembering God at all times as the only Doer, the only Giver. Encouraging people to stay in the world and to help others rather than renounce the world in search of spiritual fulfillment, Guru Nanak himself settled with his family as a farmer at the end of his travels. The multitudes of *sikhs* who came to him contributed foods or labor to a free community kitchen in which there were no caste distinctions. The Guru encouraged them to live a disciplined life of rising early in the morning to praise God and working hard to support themselves and share with those in need. To a society that stressed distinctions of caste, class, gender, and religions, Guru Nanak introduced the idea of a social order based on equality, justice, and service to all, in devotion to the One God whom Guru Nanak perceived as formless, pervading everywhere.

Nanak's commitment to practical faith, as opposed to external adherence to religious formalities, won him followers from both Hinduism and Islam. Before he died, they argued over who would dispose of his body. According to the *janam-*

Sikhism

CE 1469–c.1539	Life of Guru Nanak, the first Sikh prophet
1563–1606	Life of the Fifth Guru, Arjun Dev
c.1621–1675	Life of the Ninth Guru, Tegh Bahadur
1666–1708	Life of the Tenth Guru, Guru Gobind Singh
1699	Guru Gobind Singh founds the order of Khalsa
1708	Guru Granth Sahib installed as Eternal Guru
1780–1839	Maharaja Ranjit Singh rules the Sikh kingdom, respecting all religions
1849	British rule in Punjab; Sikh rule comes to an end
1947	Partition of India and Pakistan; 2.5 million Sikhs forced to leave Pakistani territory for India
1984	The Indian army, seeking to overthrow Sikh separatists, takes the Golden Temple at Amritsar; Indira Gandhi, Indian prime minister, assassinated by her Sikh bodyguards, triggering Hindu violence against Sikhs
1999	Millions of Sikhs converge on Anandpur Sahib to celebrate the 300th anniversary of the founding of the Khalsa
2000	Quadricentenary of installation of Adi Granth in Golden Temple
2008	Celebrations of 300 years of Guru Granth Sahib as Eternal Guru

sakhis, he told Muslims to place flowers on one side of his body, Hindus on the other; the side whose flowers remained fresh the next day could bury or cremate him. The next day they raised the sheet that had covered his body and reportedly found nothing beneath it; all the flowers were still fresh, leaving only the fragrance of his being.

> *Oh my mind, love God as a fish loves water:*
> *The more the water, the happier is the fish,*
> *   the more peaceful his mind and body.*
> *He cannot live without water even for a moment.*
> *God knows the inner pain of that being without water.*
>
> *Guru Nanak[5]*

The succession of Gurus

There were eventually a total of ten Sikh Gurus, all of whom were thought to be transmitting the spiritual light of Nanak. Before he passed away, Guru Nanak passed his spiritual authority to Lehna, previously a devotee of the goddess Durga. Lehna had become so dedicated to Guru Nanak's mission that the Guru gave him the name Angad—a part of his body (*ang*). Although the spiritual transmission from Guru Nanak reportedly made him so powerful that he became famous for healing incurable diseases such as leprosy, Guru Angad (1504–1552) was a model of humility and service to the poor and needy. He continued the tradition of *langar* and served the people with his own hands. One of the many stories told of his humility concerns an ascetic who was jealous of the Guru's popularity. The monsoon rains which were essential for the crops had not come, so the ascetic used the opportunity to turn the poor farmers against Guru Angad. He taunted them that if the Guru was so powerful, he should call for rain. The desperate villagers begged Guru Angad to do so, but he peacefully replied that one should not interfere with God's ways; rain would come only when God so willed. The ascetic persisted in turning the people against Guru Angad, telling them that he himself would magically bring the rains if they would get rid of the Guru. Thus the simple people drove Guru Angad away. Agreeably, he left the village. Refused shelter anywhere nearby, he settled in a forest. Thereafter the ascetic fasted and tried all his mantras, but the rains did not come. At last, Amar Das, who later became the third of the Sikh Gurus, learned of the situation and reproached the villagers for forsaking the sun for the light of a small lamp. Recognizing their mistake, the villagers begged Guru Angad to forgive them and return to the village. He did so, amid great rejoicing, and the rains came.

The Third and Fourth Gurus, Amar Das and Ram Das, developed organizational structures for the growing Sikh **Panth** (community) while also setting personal examples of humility. Ram Das founded the holy city of Amritsar, within which the Fifth Guru, Guru Arjun Dev (1563–1606), built the religion's most sacred shrine, the Golden Temple. The Fifth Guru also compiled the sacred scriptures of the Sikhs, the **Adi Granth** (original holy book, now known as the **Guru Granth Sahib**), from devotional hymns composed by Guru Nanak, the other Gurus, and Hindu and Muslim saints, including many spiritual figures from social castes considered lowly. Among the latter are holy people such as Bhagat Ravi Das, a low-caste Hindu shoemaker who achieved the heights of spiritual realization. His powerful poetry incorporated into the Guru Granth Sahib includes this song:

> When I was, You were not.
> When You are, I am not.
> As huge waves are raised in the wind in the vast ocean,
> But are only water in water,
> O Lord of Wealth, what should I say about this delusion?
> What we deem a thing to be,
> It is not, in reality.
> It is like a king falling asleep on his throne
> And dreaming that he is a beggar.
> His kingdom is intact,
> But separating from it, he suffers. …
> Says Ravi Das, the Lord is nearer to us than our hands and feet.[6]

myreligionlab
Hymns of the
Sikh Gurus

myreligionlab
Hymns of the Hindu
and Muslim Saints

Emperor Akbar visited the Third and Fourth Gurus and was very pleased with the teachings of the Gurus. But his son and successor, Jehangir, was jealous of Guru Arjun Dev's popularity among Muslims, and thus had him tortured and executed in 1606 on a false charge. It is said that Guru Arjun Dev remained calmly meditating on God as he was tortured by heat, with his love and faith undismayed. His devotional hymns include words such as these:

> *Merciful, merciful is the Lord.*
> *Merciful is my master.*
> *He blesses all beings with His bounties.*
> *Why waverest thou, Oh mortal? The Creator Himself shall protect you.*
> *He who has created you takes care of you. …*
> *Oh mortal, meditate on the Lord as long as there is breath in your body.*[7]

To protect Sikhism and to defend the weak of all religions against tyranny, the Sixth Guru, Hargobind (1595–1644), established a Sikh army, carried two swords

---

TEACHING STORY

Guru Arjun Dev's Devotion

Throughout his life, Guru Arjun Dev, the Fifth Sikh Guru, responded with calm faith in God to jealous plots against him.

The Mogul emperor Jehangir was incited to claim that the Adi Granth—the sacred scripture that Guru Arjun Dev had compiled—was negative toward Hindus and Muslims, even though both were becoming followers of the gentle Guru. The appearance of the emperor's rebellious son Khusro in the Guru's court to seek his blessings precipitated the matter. Jehangir ordered that all references to Hinduism and Islam be deleted from the holy book and that the Guru be fined 200,000 rupees. The Guru reportedly replied that the hymns of the Sikh Gurus and Muslim and Hindu saints were inspired praises of God and that no one could change them. Furthermore, monies were not his own property but rather belonged to the Sikh community, to be used for the welfare of those in need. Even though his Sikhs started collecting money to pay the fine, the Guru stopped them, saying that he had not done anything wrong and that compromising with wrong is irreligious.

Ostensibly for his refusal to follow the emperor's orders—but more likely to end his popular influence—the Guru was subjected to torture by heat, during the already terrible heat of summer. He was made to sit on a hot iron sheet. Hot sand was dumped onto his body and he was placed into boiling water.

As these tortures were being inflicted, Mian Mir, an established saint of Islam who reportedly laid the foundation stone of the Golden Temple at Amritsar, pleaded with the Guru to let him use his mystical power against the persecutors. Guru Arjun Dev refused, telling Mian Mir to patiently accept the reality that everything is under God's control; every leaf that moves does so by God's will.

The daughter-in-law of Chandu, the rich man of Lahore who had turned the emperor against the Guru, tried to offer sherbet to the Guru to ease his agony. But just as he had refused attempts to wed his son to Chandu's daughter, saying that a rich man's daughter would not be happy in the home of a dervish, he refused her food, saying that he would accept nothing. Nonetheless, he blessed her for her devotion.

Through five days of torture, Guru Arjun Dev persisted in calm faith in God. His torturers then forced him to bathe in the river alongside the Mogul fort. His followers wept to see the blisters covering his body. As he walked on blistered feet, he repeated again and again, "Your will is sweet, Oh God; I only seek the gift of Your Name." Calmly, he walked into the water and breathed his last.

(one symbolizing temporal power, the other, spiritual power), and taught the people to defend their religion. The tenderhearted Seventh Guru, Har Rai (1630–1661), was a pacifist who never used his troops against the Moguls. He taught his Sikhs not only to feed anyone who came to their door, but also to:

> *do service in such a way that the poor guest may not feel he is partaking of some charity but as if he had come to the Guru's house which belonged to all in equal measure. He who has more should consider it as God's trust and share it in the same spirit. Man is only an instrument of service: the giver of goods is God, the Guru of us all.*[8]

The Eighth Guru, Har Krishan (1656–1664), became successor to Guru Nanak's seat when he was only five years old and died at the age of eight. When taunted by Hindu pandits (learned men) the "Child Guru" reportedly touched a lowly deaf and dumb Sikh watercarrier with his cane, whereupon the watercarrier expounded brilliantly on the subtleties of the Hindu scripture, *Bhagavad-Gita*.

The ninth master, Guru Teg Bahadur (c.1621–1675), was martyred. According to Sikh tradition, he was approached by Kashmiri Hindu pandits who were facing forced conversion to Islam by the Mogul emperor, Aurangzeb. The emperor viewed Hinduism as a totally corrupt, idolatrous religion, which did not lead people to God; he had ordered the destruction of Hindu temples and mass conversion of Hindus throughout the land, beginning in the north with Kashmir. Reportedly, one of the Kashmiri pandits dreamed that only the Ninth Guru, the savior in Kali Yuga, could save the Hindus. With the firm approval of his young son, Guru Teg Bahadur told the Hindu pandits to inform their oppressors that they would convert to Islam if the Sikh Guru could be persuaded to do so. Imprisoned and forced to witness the torture and murder of his aides, the Ninth Guru staunchly maintained the right of all people to religious freedom. Aurangzeb beheaded him before a crowd of thousands. But as his son later wrote, "He has given his head, but not his determination."[9]

myreligienlab
Writings of the
Tenth Guru
DASAM GRANTH

The martyred Ninth Guru was succeeded by his young son, who became the tenth master, Guru Gobind Singh (1666–1708). It was he who turned the intimidated Sikhs into saint–soldiers. In 1699 he reportedly told an assembly of Sikhs that the times were so dangerous that he had developed a new plan to give the community strength and unity. Total surrender to the master would be necessary, he said, asking for volunteers who would offer their heads for the cause of protecting religious ideals. One at a time, five stepped forward. Each was escorted into the Guru's tent, from which the Tenth Guru emerged alone with a bloody sword. According to the story, after this scene was repeated five times the Guru brought all the men out of the tent, alive and dressed in new clothes. Some say the blood was that of a goat, in a test of the people's loyalty; others say that Guru Gobind Singh had killed the men and then resurrected them.

Whatever actually happened that day, Sikhs believe that the reported willingness of the five men to sacrifice themselves for the Guru's mission was dramatically proven, and the *amrit* (nectar-like holy water) prepared by Guru Gobind Singh is thought to have turned his followers into heroes, with sugar added by his wife symbolizing the ideal that they would also be compassionate. The Guru called them his Five Beloved Ones (*Panj Piaras*). The Five Beloved Ones became models for Sikhs. It is noteworthy that they came from the lowest classes and from different geographic areas.

After initiating the first five, the Guru (whose name up to that time was Gobind Rai) established a unique Guru–Sikh relationship by asking that they initiate him—thus underscoring the principle of equality among all Sikhs. The initiated men were given the surname *Singh* ("lion"); the women were all given the name *Kaur* ("princess") and treated as equals. Guru Gobind Rai took the name of Guru Gobind Singh. He called the initiates **Khalsa** (Pure Ones), a community pledged to a special code of personal discipline.

Khalsa women praying: left to right, Malika Preet Kaur, Amardeep Kaur, Gur Ramandeep Kaur. Whether to cover one's long hair with a veil or a turban, and what color this should be, is a woman's personal choice. There are no degrees of initiation in Sikhism. Traditionally, the emphasis falls on inner spirituality.

According to Sikh belief about what happened in 1699, they were sworn to wear five distinctive symbols of their dedication: unshorn hair, a comb to keep it tidy, drawstring underbreeches for modesty, a small sword in a sheath symbolizing dignity and the willingness to stand up for justice and protection of the weak, and an iron bracelet worn as a personal reminder that one is a servant of God, and perhaps also offering some protection to the wrist in hand-to-hand combat.

These "**Five K's**" (so called because all the words begin with a "k" in Punjabi) have been interpreted as proud hallmarks of Sikh identity dating from the birth of the Khalsa in 1699. They clearly distinguished Sikhs from Muslims and Hindus, supporting the assertion that Sikhism constituted a third path with its own right to spiritual sovereignty. All of these innovations are thought to have turned the meek into warriors capable of shaking off Mogul oppression and protecting freedom of religion; the distinctive dress made it impossible for the Khalsa to hide from their duty by blending with the general populace. In Sikh history, their bravery was indeed proven again and again.

However, to interpret the Five K's only as symbols of power and separate identity is to overlook the spiritual and egalitarian aspects of Sikhism. By mandating the same symbolic dress for people of all castes, both women and men, Sikhs gave both genders and all castes equal importance, contrary to Indian cultural traditions. There may also be significant spiritual symbols embedded in the Five K's. The sword, for instance, is often used in the Guru Granth Sahib as a metaphor for divine wisdom that cuts through ignorance and egocentrism. The devotee who wields it—and even the sword itself—is commonly referred to in female terms. For example, "By taking up the sword of knowledge, she fights against her mind and merges with her self."[10] Feminist scholar Nikky-Guninder Kaur Singh sees the iron bracelet (*kara*) as a metaphorical reminder of the total integration of material and spiritual realities:

> *With neither a beginning nor an end, the circular bracelet is a reminder of the Infinite One. Like the sword, it is a means of centering the self as the person is*

engaged in various activities; like her, it is not a means for high-handed aggression. Worn around the right wrist, the kara *participates in all physical functions and gestures, thereby reminding men and women that the timeless moment touches upon each moment, that sacred action touches upon every action. Dressing up, hugging, cooking, reading the holy book, working in the farm or at a computer— all actions are equally validated by the* kara.[11]

Uncut hair is important to observant Sikhs because through it they feel a close inner relationship to Guru Gobind Singh, who called it his "divine stamp."

It is thought that Guru Gobind Singh also commanded his Khalsa to follow a particular disciplinary code, including eschewing hair-cutting, adultery, tobacco, and the meat of animals slowly bled to death in Muslim fashion. Scholars debate the historicity of various versions of the code of conduct now in use, some of which contain hundreds of rules.

Guru Gobind Singh ended the line of bodily succession to Guruship. As he was passing away in 1708, he transferred his authority to the Adi Granth rather than to a human successor. Thenceforth, it was called the Guru Granth Sahib—the living presence of the Guru embodied in the sacred scripture, to be consulted by the congregation for spiritual guidance and decision-making.

As the Mogul Empire began to disintegrate and Afghans invaded India, the Sikhs fought for their own identity and sovereignty, as well as to protect Hindu and Muslim women from the attackers, and to protect freedom of religion in the country. At the end of the eighteenth century and beginning of the nineteenth century under Maharaja Ranjit Singh, they formed the Sikh Empire, a non-sectarian government noted for its generous tolerance toward Muslims, despite the earlier history of oppression by the Muslim rulers. Maharaja Ranjit Singh is said to have been unusually kind to his subjects and to have humbly accepted chastisement by the Sikh religious authorities for moral lapses on his part. The Sikh Empire attempted to create a pluralistic society, with social equality and full freedom of religion. It also blocked the Khyber Pass against invaders. The empire lasted only half a century, for the British subdued it in 1849.

Resistance to oppression became a hallmark of Sikhism, for the times were grim for India's people. Despite heavy losses, Guru Gobind Singh's outnumbered Sikhs began the protection of the country from foreign rule, a process that continued into the twentieth century. During the Indian struggle against British rule Sikhs set heroic examples of nonviolent resistance to oppression, despite their military abilities. One famous story concerns Guru ka Bagh, a garden and shrine that had been used by Sikhs for cutting wood for the community's free kitchen. British police began arresting and then beating and killing Sikhs who went to the garden to collect firewood. Every day a new wave of 100 Sikhs would come voluntarily to suffer fierce beatings and perhaps even be killed, without a murmur except for the Name of God on their lips, to resist injustice.

At one point, Sikh political prisoners arrested at Guru ka Bagh were being shifted by train. The Sikh community in Hasanavdal asked the stationmaster there to stop the train so they could offer food to the prisoners. He refused, saying that it was a special train and would not stop at Hasanavdal. Determined to care for the prisoners, three leading Sikhs told the *sangat* (congregation) to bring food, and then they courageously lay down on the tracks to force the train to stop. The driver being unable to brake in time, the train ran over them, crushing their bodies, and then stopped. As the *sangat* tried to help the dying martyrs one of them ordered, "Don't care for us. Feed the prisoners." Thus the *langar* (community meal) was served to the prisoners on the train, and the Sikhs who had laid their bodies on the track died.

High praise for Guru Gobind Singh's military effect has been offered by Dr. S. Radhakrishnan, the respected second president of India:

> *For one thousand years, after the defeat of Raja Jaipal, India had lain prostrate. The raiders and invaders descended on India and took away the people, to be sold as slaves. … Guru Gobind Singh raised the Khalsa to defy religious intolerance, religious persecution and political inequality. It was a miracle that heroes appeared out of straws and common clay. Those who groveled in the dust rose proud, defiant and invincible in the form of the Khalsa. They bore all sufferings and unnamable tortures cheerfully and unflinchingly. … India is at long last free. This freedom is the crown and climax and a logical corollary to the Sikh Guru's and Khalsa's terrific sacrifices and heroic exploits.*[12]

Baba Siri Chand, elder son of Guru Nanak, combined the power of intense meditation with the power of hard work.

In addition to the bravery evident in Sikh history, stories of the Gurus are full of miracles that reportedly happened around them, such as the Eighth Guru's empowering a lowly watercarrier to give a profound explanation of the *Bhagavad-Gita*. Neither age, nor caste, nor gender is thought to have any relevance in Sikh spirituality. In contrast to the restricted position of women in Indian society, the Sikh Gurus accorded full respect and freedom of participation to women.

> *God is like sugar scattered in the sand. An elephant cannot pick it up. Says Kabir, the Guru has given me this sublime secret:*
> *"Become thou an ant and partake of it."*
>
> *Kabir, Guru Granth Sahib p. 1377*

Although the Sikh Gurus gave their followers no mandate to convert others, their message was spread in a nonsectarian way by the **Udasis**, renunciates who do not withdraw from the world but rather practice strict discipline and meditation while at the same time trying to serve humanity. Their missionary work began under Baba Siri Chand, the ascetic elder son of Guru Nanak. He had a close relationship with the Sikh Gurus and was highly respected by people of all castes and creeds because of his spiritual power, wisdom, and principles. During the reign of the Mogul emperor Shah Jahan, a census showed that Baba Siri Chand had the largest following of any holy person in India. Nevertheless, he directed all attention and praise to his father, and never claimed to be a Guru himself. Udasi communities and educational institutions are still maintained in the subcontinent, and old Udasi inscriptions have been discovered in Baku, Azerbaijan.

Central beliefs

Sikhism's major focus is loving devotion to one God, whom Sikhs recognize as the same One who is worshiped by many different names around the world. God is formless, beyond time and space, the only truth, the only reality. This boundless concept was initially set forth in Guru Nanak's *Mul Mantra* (basic sacred chant), which prefaces the Guru Granth Sahib, and *Jap Ji*, the first morning prayer of Sikhs:

> *There is One God*
> *Whose Name is Truth,*
> *The Creator,*
> *Without fear, without hate,*
> *Eternal Being,*
> *Beyond birth and death,*
> *Self-existent,*
> *Realized by the Guru's grace.*[13]

Following Guru Nanak's lead, Sikhs often refer to God as *Sat* ("truth") or as *Ik Onkar*, the One Supreme Being. God is pure being, without form.

Guru Gobind Singh, a great custodian of scholars who kept many poets in his court, offered a litany of praises of this boundless, formless One. His inspired composition, *Jaap Sahib*, includes 199 verses such as these:

> *Immortal*
> *Omnipotent*
> *Beyond Time*
> *And Space*
> *Invisible*
> *Beyond name, caste, or creed*
> *Beyond form or figure*
> *The ruthless destroyer*
> *Of all pride and evil*
> *The Salvation of all beings …*
> *The Eternal Light*
> *The Sweetest Breeze*
> *The Wondrous Figure*
> *The Most Splendid.*[14]

The light of God is thought to shine fully through the Guru, the perfect master. In Sikh belief, the light of God is also present in the Guru Granth Sahib, the Holy Word of God, and in all of creation, in which **Nam**, the Holy Name of God, dwells. God is not separate from this world. God pervades the cosmos and thus can be found within everything. As the Ninth Guru wrote:

> *Why do you go to the forest to find God? He lives in all and yet remains distinctly detached. He dwells in you as well, as fragrance resides in a flower or the reflection in a mirror. God abides in everything. See him, therefore, in your heart.*[15]

Sikhism does not claim to have the only path to God, nor does it try to convert others to its way. It has beliefs in common with Hinduism (such as *karma* and reincarnation) and also with Islam (such as monotheism). It is said that the

An Interview with Inderpreet Kaur

 Inderpreet Kaur is a thirteen-year-old student in New Delhi, studying in an English-language, Christian-based school, as is the ideal of many middle- and upper-class families in India. She nonetheless maintains her family's Sikh traditions and tries to live by the essence of the teachings of the Sikh Gurus, as she understands them. She explains:

"We respect the Almighty. We just love Him infinitely. We don't seem to do external practices or rituals. But we should have a connection with the Divine Power, God. That is the main thing. Our Gurus say that if we love God with a pure heart, if we pray to Him with all our concentration, and meditate on Him, if we praise God and thank Him, God will surely help us.

"If I remember God with a pure heart, there is just God and me. Miracles happen every minute. God is always there to help me. If we thank God, praise Him, and we love Him dearly, I think we can even cross a mountain. It is written in our holy book, the Guru Granth Sahib, that there are no boundaries. The house of God is without walls. It doesn't exclude any people. It is open for all. God asks for love and not anything else.

"There are many religious paths, but they are all leading to the one goal. I personally go to a [Hindu] temple, my school has a church, and I offer prayers to Lord Jesus. I may not know the rituals or the practices, how to offer prayers to Lord Jesus, but I love God with a pure heart, I really do love Jesus, and I think God helps us if we love Him. He also wants us not to create distinctions between the people. He just wants us to be good, to do good things in life, so that our sins can be washed away.

"The problems we face, the bad things that happen to us, are the result of our bad *karmas*,

reborn. I think the main goal in our life should be to respect every human being, to do good, and live by the principles of the religion which we follow, because every religion says one thing: The main thing is to love God with a pure heart.

"In Sikhism, we offer prayers every morning and evening, and we do *prakash* in the morning—we open our holy book, the Guru Granth Sahib. We have ten Gurus, and Guru Granth Sahib, the holy book, is our Eternal Guru. After reading from the holy scripture, we take *hukam*, that is, the teaching of the day, from the holy book. Our Gurus told that we should imbibe the teaching that is written in the book. They tell us what to do, how to lead a life, and we should follow those teachings. We see that every time we should always keep remembering God, we should take His Name, and we should always thank Him for whatever He has given us. Whatever He shall do, that will be given for our benefit. The problems which come in our life are for our own good, because we learn from them, and God will surely help us.

"It seems that we should also work hard. Hard work is the main principle. We should recite God's Name, work hard for a living, and share with others, as Guru Nanak taught us. In the evening after our day's work, again we read our holy scripture, and then in the nighttime, we close the book and we offer prayers to the Lord. And then again in the morning, we open it.

"*Seva* means service. All beings are the creation of God, so we should help each other, but without expecting anything, and we should offer service to God. We should do good things in life and avoid crying for everything here. That is according to our Gurus' teachings. We wear an iron bracelet, *kara*, on our wrist. Whenever we are doing a wrong thing, as soon as we see it, it reminds us that, yes, we are dedicated to God and God is watching us. We can't hide anything from God."[16]

respected Muslim mystic Mian Mir was invited to lay the cornerstone of the Golden Temple in Amritsar. It was constructed with four doors, inviting people from all traditions to come in to worship. When Guru Gobind Singh created an army to resist tyranny, he advised Sikhs not to feel enmity toward Islam or Hinduism. The enemy, he emphasized, was oppression and corruption.

Sikh soldier–saints are pledged to protect the freedom of all religions. Sikhism is, however, opposed to empty ritualism, and Guru Nanak and his successors sharply challenged hypocritical religious practices. "It is very difficult to be called a Muslim," said Guru Nanak. "A Muslim's heart is as soft as wax, very compassionate, and he washes away the inner dirt of egotism."[17] By contrast, said Guru Nanak, "The Qazis [Muslim legal authorities] who sit in the courts to minister justice, rosary in hand and the name of *Khuda* (God) on their lips, commit injustice if their palm is not greased. And if someone challenges them, lo, they quote the scriptures!"[18]

According to the Sikh ideal, the purpose of life is to realize God within the world, through the everyday practices of work, worship, and charity, of sacrificing love. All people are to be treated equally, for God's light dwells in all and ego is a major hindrance to God-realization. From Guru Nanak's time on, Sikhism has refused to acknowledge the traditional Indian caste system. In their social services, such as hospitals, leprosariums, and free kitchens, Sikhs observe a tradition of serving everyone, regardless of caste or creed. A special group of Sikhs, known as Seva Panthis, place great emphasis on this aspect of Sikhism, refusing to accept any offerings to support their services to the needy. They are inspired by the example of Bhai Kanahia, who in the time of Guru Gobind Singh was found offering water to the fallen opponents as well as to Guru Gobind Singh's wounded soldiers. The Guru's people complained about his behavior to the Guru, who questioned Bhai Kanahia about what he was doing. Bhai Kanahia reportedly said that he was obeying the Sikh Gurus' teaching that one should look upon all with the same eye, whether friend or foe. Guru Gobind Singh praised him and gave him ointment, with the instruction not only to give water but also to soothe the wounds of soldiers from both armies.

In contrast to the low status of women in Indian society, the Gurus accorded considerable respect to women. Guru Nanak asked: "Why denounce her, who even gives birth to kings?"[19] Many women are respectfully remembered in Sikh history. Among them are Guru Nanak's sister Bibi Nanaki, who first recognized her brother's great spiritual power and became his first devotee. A group of Guru Gobind Singh's soldiers deserted him in the face of seemingly impossible odds when his citadel at Anandpur was being besieged, but their women refused to allow them to return to their homes. The women threatened to dress in the men's clothes and return to fight for the Guru, to expunge the shame of the men's cowardice. One woman—Mai Bhago—did so and helped to lead forty of the deserters back to battle on the Guru's side against Aurangzeb's army. The men all died on the battlefield, asking the Guru to forgive them, but Mai Bhago survived and remained in the Guru's personal security guard, dressed as a man, with his permission. When *amrit* was first prepared for Khalsa initiation, it was Guru Gobind Singh's wife who added sugar crystals to make the initiates sweet-tempered as well as brave. In Brahmanic Hindu tradition, such an action by a woman would have been considered a defilement. Women were active as missionaries carrying

Guru Gobind Singh's program. During the terrible Mogul persecutions of the eighteenth century, Sikh women were noted for their courage and steadfast faith.

A preference for sons nonetheless persisted, in part because of the heavy dowry burden traditionally expected of females in India. To counter this trend, Guru Gobind Singh reportedly forbade female infanticide, and in 2001 the chief Sikh authorities issued an order that anyone practicing female feticide would be excommunicated from the faith.

In developing the military capabilities of his followers in order to protect religious freedom, Guru Gobind Singh set forth very strict standards for battle. He established five stringent conditions for "righteous war": (1) Military means are a last resort to be used only if all other methods have failed; (2) Battle should be undertaken without any enmity or feeling of revenge; (3) No territory should be taken or captured property retained; (4) Troops should be committed to the cause, not mercenaries fighting for pay, and soldiers should be strictly disciplined, forswearing smoking, drinking, and abuse of opponents' women; and (5) Minimal force should be used and hostilities should end when the objective is attained.

Like Hinduism, Sikhism conceives a series of lives, with *karma* (the effects of past actions on one's present life) governing transmigration of the soul into new bodies, be they human or animal. The ultimate goal of life is mystical union with the Divine, reflected in one's way of living.

> *I was separated from God for many births, dry as a withered plant,*
> *But by the grace of the Guru, I have become green.*
>   *Guru Arjun, Guru Granth Sahib, p. 102*

Sacred practices

To be a true Sikh is to live a very disciplined life of surrender and devotion to God, with hours of daily prayer, continual inner repetition of the Name of God (Nam), and detachment from negative, worldly mind-states. In Sikh belief, Nam carries intense spiritual power, capable of making a person fearless, steady, inwardly calm and strong in the face of any adversity, willing to serve without any reward, and extending love in all directions without any effort. Why is it so powerful? It comes from the Guru as a transmission of spiritual blessing that automatically transforms people and links them with God. Some feel that Nam is the essence of creation, the sound and vibration of which the cosmos is a material manifestation. The mystics and Gurus whose writings are included in the Guru Granth Sahib refer to many Names of God, such as *Murari* (a reference to Krishna), *Narain* (the One present in water), *Allah*, and *Râm*. Some Sikhs recite "*Wahe Guru*" (God wondrous beyond words), some say "*Ik Onkar Sat nam Siri Wahe Guru*" (God is One, the Truth Itself, Most Respectful, Wondrous beyond words), some recite the whole *Mul Mantra*, a key verse by Guru Nanak summarizing his philosophy, used at the beginning of the Guru Granth Sahib and in many other places in it.

In the Sikh path, at the same time that one's mind and heart are joined with God, one is to be working hard in the world, earning an honest living, and helping those in need. Of this path, the Third Sikh Guru observed:

The way of devotees is unique; they walk a difficult path.
They leave behind attachments, greed, ego, and desires, and do not speak much.
The path they walk is sharper than the edge of a sword and thinner than a hair.
Those who shed their false self by the grace of the Guru are filled with the fragrance
of God.[20]

The standards set by Guru Gobind Singh for the Khalsa are so high that few people can really meet them. In addition to outer disciplines, such as abstaining from drugs, alcohol, and tobacco, the person who is Khalsa, said the Guru, will always recite the Name of God:

The Name of God is light, the Light which never extinguishes, day or night. Khalsa
recognizes none but the One. I live in Khalsa; it is my body, my treasure store.[21]

The one who is Khalsa renounces anger and does not criticize anybody. He fights on the front line against injustice and vanquishes the five evils (lust, anger, greed, attachment, and ego) in himself. He burns his *karmas* and thus becomes egoless. Not only does he not take another person's spouse, he doesn't even look at the things that belong to others. Perpetually reciting Nam is his joy, and he falls in love with the words of the Gurus. He faces difficulties squarely, always attacks evil, and always helps the poor. He joins other people with the Nam, but he is not bound within the forts of narrow-mindedness.[22]

The Sikh Gurus formed several institutions to help create a new social order with no caste distinctions. One is *langar*, the community meal, which is freely offered to all who come, regardless of caste. This typically takes place at a *gurdwara*, the building where the Guru Granth Sahib is enshrined and public worship takes place. The congregation is called the *sangat*, in which all are equal; there is no priestly class or servant class. During community worship as well as *langar*, all

Langar, *a free meal, is provided daily at some* gurdwaras *and all visitors are expected to partake. Rich and poor must sit side by side, with no distinction.*

strata of people sit together, though men and women may sit separately, as is the Indian custom. People of all ethnic origins, ideologies, and castes, including untouchables, may bathe in the tank of water at Sikh holy places. Baptism into the Khalsa is thought to do away with one's former caste and make a lowly person a chief. At least one-tenth of one's income is to be contributed toward the welfare of the community. In addition, the Sikh Gurus glorified the lowliest forms of manual labor, such as sweeping the floor and cleaning shoes and dirty pots, especially when these are done as voluntary service to God.

The morning and evening prayers take about two hours a day, starting in the very early morning hours. The first morning prayer is Guru Nanak's *Jap Ji. Jap*, meaning "recitation," refers to the use of sound, especially the Name of God (Nam), as the best way of approaching the Divine. Like combing the hair, hearing and reciting the sacred word is used as a way to comb all negative thoughts out of the mind. Much of the *Jap Ji* is devoted to the blessings of Nam. For example,

> *The devotees are forever in bliss, for by hearing the Nam their suffering and sins are destroyed.*
> *Hearkening to the Nam bestows Truth, divine wisdom, contentment.*
> *By hearing the Nam, the blind find the path of Truth and realize the Unfathomable.*[23]

"*The Lord is stitched into my heart and never goes out of it even for a moment.*"
Guru Arjun Dev, Guru Granth Sahib, p. 708

The second morning prayer is Guru Gobind Singh's universal *Jaap Sahib*. It names no prophet, nor creates any religion. It is sheer homage to God. The Guru addresses God as having no form, no country, and no religion but yet as the seed of seeds, song of songs, sun of suns, the life force pervading everywhere, ever merciful, ever giving, indestructible. Complex in its poetry and profound in its content, *Jaap Sahib* asserts that God is the cause of conflict as well as of peace, of destruction as well as of creation; God pervades in darkness as well as in light. In verse after verse, devotees learn that there is nothing outside of God's presence, nothing outside of God's control.

In addition to recitation of these and other daily prayers, passages from the Guru Granth Sahib are chanted or sung as melodies, often with musical accompaniment. This devotional tradition of *kirtan* was initiated by Guru Nanak. But great discipline is required to attend the predawn hymns and recitations every day, and in contrast to the self-respect developed by Guru Gobind Singh in the Khalsa, worshipers humble themselves before the sacred scriptures. The Guru Granth Sahib is placed on a platform, with a devotee waving a whisk over the sacred book to denote the royalty of the scripture. Worshipers bow to it, bring offerings, and then sit reverently on the floor before it. Every morning and evening, the spirit of God reveals its guidance to the people as an officiant opens the scripture at random, intuitively guided, and reads a passage that is to be a special spiritual focus for the day. For many occasions, teams of people carry out *Akhand Path*, reading the entire Guru Granth

Guru Gobind Singh writing Jaap Sahib, *a hymn praising the attributes of God, "without form, beyond religion." (Painting by Mehar Singh)*

His Holiness Baba Virsa Singh

 For decades, His Holiness Baba Virsa Singh (c.1934–2007) developed farms and communities in India in which people are trying to live by the teachings of the Sikh Gurus. Not only Sikhs but also Hindus, Muslims, and Christians, literate and illiterate, live and work side by side as brothers and sisters there. Baba Virsa Singh himself, the son of a village farmer, had no formal education. From childhood he had an intense yearning for communion with God. He related:

> *From childhood, I kept questioning God, "In order to love Jesus, must one become a Christian or just love?" He told me, "It is not necessary to become a Christian. It is necessary to love him."*
>
> *I asked, "To believe in Moses, does one have to observe any special discipline, or just love?" The divine command came: "Only love." I asked, "Does one have to become a Muslim in order to please Muhammad, or only love?" He said, "One must love." "To believe in Buddha, must one become a monk or a Buddhist?" He replied, "No. To believe in Buddha is to love." God said, "I created human beings. Afterward, human beings created sectarian religions. But I created only human beings."*[24]

Intense spirituality is the base of Baba Virsa Singh's communities, which are known collectively as Gobind Sadan ("The House of God"). Volunteers work hard to raise record crops on previously barren land. The harvests are shared communally and also provide the basis for Gobind Sadan's continual free kitchens (*langar*) for people of all classes, free medical services, and celebrations of the holy days of all religions. Devotions are carried on around the clock, with everyone from gardeners and pot-washers to governors and professors helping to clean the holy areas and maintain perpetual reading of the Sikh scriptures. Everyone of all ages and conditions is encouraged to do useful work. Thus under Baba Virsa Singh's guidance, a living example has been developed of the power of Guru Nanak's straightforward, nonsectarian spiritual program: Work hard to earn your own honest living, share with others, and always remember God.

Another social effect of the work of Baba Virsa Singh is an easing of the tensions that have arisen between people of different religions. Even the most rigid proponents of their own religions have been gently convinced to open their eyes toward the validity of other faiths. He taught Sikhs that their own scripture repeatedly praises and invokes the "Hindu" gods and goddesses. He taught Hindu extremists that there is no one tradition that can be called "Hinduism" and that to take the name of Ram is to invoke the heights of moral character and selfless service to humanity. He taught Muslims to appreciate the spiritual depths of their religion.

To religious leaders, he highly recommended the method used at Gobind Sadan—celebrating the holy days of all prophets with great enthusiasm—as a way to combat religious intolerance. The blame, he said, lies with religious leaders:

> *When religious leaders speak, the issue is not whether they have read books. The question is whether or not they themselves have awakened spiritually. Dharma is very powerful. It transforms people's minds, transforms their lives, and transforms their inner habits. It is only spirituality that changes people.*
>
> *If priests, pujaris, or granthis are sitting in temples, mosques, churches, or gurdwaras, it does not necessarily mean that they have realized God. They are managers. Religious leaders will know whether they themselves are spiritual or not. Do we have the forgiveness of Jesus, who from the cross prayed, "Forgive them, for they know not what they do"? When the prophets were here, they had no gold-covered buildings. They built a beautiful inner temple where peace prevailed. If we are spiritual, we will be contemplating all prophets, loving their messages, loving their commandments, loving their ethical codes.*
>
> *Throughout the world, religion has become a great fort made of hatred. All the prophets have taught us otherwise. All prophets, messiahs, and nabis have come in love, and all have in common the same thing: Love.*[25]

Another area in which Baba Virsa Singh influenced public life is his effect on government officials. He urged them to attend to the practical needs of the people and to uphold order and justice in society.

Baba Virsa Singh also gave people spiritual hope for a new world order. To a Russian magazine, he explained:

> *Truth is always tested. Who tests it? Evil—evil attacks the truth. But truth never stops shining, and evil keeps falling back. Truth's journey is very powerful, with a very strong base. It never wavers. It is a long journey, full of travails, but evil can never suppress the truth.*[26]

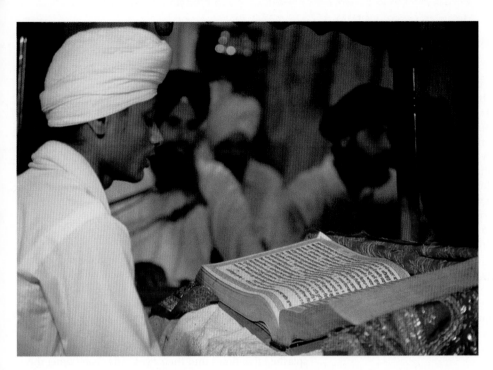

Sikhs young or old may read from the Guru Granth Sahib, in which are enshrined the writings of Hindu and Muslim saints as well as Sikh Gurus.

Sahib from start to finish within approximately forty-eight hours, taking turns of two hours each.

Some *gurdwaras*, including the Golden Temple in Amritsar, have previously allowed only men to read publicly from the Guru Granth Sahib, to preach, to officiate at ceremonies, or to sing sacred hymns. This has been a cultural custom, however, for nothing in the Sikh scriptures or the Code of Conduct bars women from such privileges. Indeed, Guru Gobind Singh initiated women as well as men into the Khalsa and allowed women to fight on the battlefield. In 1996, the central body setting policies for Sikh *gurdwaras* ruled that women should be allowed to perform sacred services.

In addition to group chanting, singing, and listening to collective guidance from the Guru Granth Sahib, devout Sikhs are encouraged to begin the day with private meditations on the name of God. As one advances in this practice and abides in egoless love for God, one is said to receive guidance from the inner Guru, the living word of God within each person.

Sikhism today

An enterprising and adventurous community, the Sikhs have done well at home and abroad. Though they constitute less than two percent of India's population, they have played a leading role in government of the nation. Dr. Manmohan Singh became the country's first Sikh prime minister in 2004, and his economic expertise has been sought after in world forums since the global financial meltdown.

The center of Sikhism remains the Punjab. The area of this territory, which is under Indian rule, was dramatically shrunk by the partition of India in 1947, for

myreligionlab
The Sikh Gurus' Vision of an Ideal Society
DHARAM SINGH

Amrit Ceremony on Baisakhi

Kirtan *on Baisakhi by a* sangat *from Gurdaspur, Punjab.*

The natural exuberance of Punjabis bursts forth every spring in the festival of Baisakhi. Traditionally this was a harvest festival, celebrating the wheat harvest on the first day of the solar month of Baisakh (or Vaisakh), on 13 or 14 April. In anticipation of a happy period of plenty, and reportedly also to protect the crop from damage by ill fortune, the people of the Punjab used to gather and perform folk dances. Of these, the most well-known is the *bhangra* dance—a jubilant, athletic dance by men wearing colorful long wrapped skirts and costume jewelry, stamping their feet to the strong backbeat of drums, raising their arms overhead, and shaking their shoulders independently of their torsos. In the time of Guru Amar Das, this jubilant harvest festival became the occasion for a gathering of the Sikh community around the Guru. It was when many Sikhs had gathered in Anandpur Sahib around Guru Gobind Singh for the Baisakhi festival in 1699 that the Guru is said to have dramatically initiated the first Khalsa members.

Sikhs now celebrate Baisakhi with great enthusiasm every year as the birthday of the Khalsa. In *gurdwaras* around the world, *Akhand Paths*—continuous reading of the Guru Granth Sahib—are held, culminating in a community prayer, *kirtan*, and special *langar*. There may also be displays of martial arts, such as adept swordplay.

Baisakhi is also a favorite occasion for initiation of new Khalsa members, via the *Amrit* ceremony. In some private area, in the presence of the Guru Granth Sahib, those to be inducted appear in clean dress, wearing the Five K's. They may or may not be Sikhs, but they agree to follow the principal teachings of the Gurus and to live according to a strict code of outer discipline. Initiates may also dedicate themselves to developing the inner qualities defining Khalsa, such as defeating the five evils within themselves. Formerly initiated Khalsa who have lapsed from the disciplinary code may also appear to be reinitiated after carrying out some specified spiritual punishment.

The ceremony is conducted by five baptized people representing the first Five Beloved Ones (*Panj Piaras*) who offered their heads to Guru Gobind Singh. They are expected to be exemplary members of the Khalsa who know the daily prayers by heart. The ceremony begins with a prayer to the Guru Granth Sahib and reading of guidance from it for the would-be initiates. The officiants then recite the five daily prayers—a process which may take up to two hours—while slowly stirring sugar-sweetened water in an iron bowl to turn it into *amrit* (nectar). The *amrit* is stirred with a *khanda*, a double-edged sword symbolizing the disintegration of egotism and demolishing of social barriers such as caste and gender discrimination. When the *amrit* is prepared and prayed over, five handfuls are given to each initiate to drink, it is sprinkled five times on their hair, and it is splashed five times into their eyes. After each time, the initiate is told to say, "The Khalsa is God's, and the victory is God's." Each then drinks from the bowl, turn by turn. Drinking from the same bowl by people of all castes was a revolutionary practice in 1699, and to a certain extent it still is, because of strong caste prohibitions in India and taboos about contamination of food. After *amrit* initiation, the Khalsa are considered to be in such a pure state that they can share food with each other, but not with anyone else. At the end of the ceremony they are told that they are all children of the same family, with Guru Gobind Singh as their father and his wife Mata Sahib Kaur as their mother, and that they are spiritual residents of Anandpur Sahib.

The *Amrit* ceremony ends as it began, with the central prayer of Sikhs, but now with new meaning for the initiates. In part:

Bestow upon the Sikhs the boon of Sikhism, of preserving hair, of observing Sikh code of conduct, of divine wisdom, of firm faith, of unshakable belief, the supreme boon of the Name of God, and of the holy bath in the pool of nectar in Amritsar. May the kirtan *choirs, flags, and shrines last till eternity, and may righteousness triumph. … May the mind of the Sikhs be humble and their wisdom profound. … In the name of [Guru] Nanak, may everyone be in high spirits! By Thy will, may all prosper. The Khalsa is of God; all victory is the victory of God!*[27]

two-thirds of the Punjab was in the western area thenceforth called Pakistan. The two million Sikhs living in that part were forced to migrate to the eastern side of the border under conditions of extreme hardship. Through emigration, there are also large Sikh communities in Britain, Canada, the United States, Malaysia, and Singapore.

In India, Sikhs and Hindus lived side by side in mutual tolerance until 1978 to 1992, when violent clashes occurred over some of the policies of the Indian government. Sikh separatists wanted to establish an independent Sikh state, called Khalistan, with a commitment to strong religious observances and protection for Sikhs from oppression and exploitation by the much larger Hindu community. In 1984, Prime Minister Indira Gandhi chose to attack the Golden Temple, Sikhism's holiest shrine, for Sikh separatists were thought to be using it as a shelter for their weapons. The attack seemed an outrageous desecration of the holy place, and counterviolence increased. The prime minister herself was killed later in 1984 by her Sikh bodyguards. In retribution, terrible mob killings of thousands of Sikhs followed.

Many Sikhs "disappeared" in the Punjab, allegedly at the hands of both separatists and police terrorists. Violence has now ended, but tensions are kept alive by Sikhs living outside India who persist in demanding the formation of Khalistan and promoting a militant, rigid version of the religion.

Historical tensions have also arisen within Sikhism as it has been institutionalized and used by some factions for their own ends, such as acquiring the landholdings of the *gurdwaras*. Leadership of *gurdwaras* is democratic, by elected committees, but this provision has not stopped fractiousness within the organizations.

The Punjab at the end of the reign of the Mogul emperor, Akbar. The 1947 partition of India left two-thirds of the Punjab, including many of its Sikh temples, inside Pakistan, a Muslim state.

- 1947 partition
- The Punjab at the end of Mughal Emperor Akbar reign (1605)
- The Punjab as it was before the partition of India and Pakistan

Surrounded by a sacred pool, the Golden Temple at Amritsar houses the Guru Granth Sahib. It has a door on each of its four sides, symbolizing its openness to people of all faiths.

In 1998, factions of a Canadian *gurdwara* had a bloody fight over the issue of using chairs and tables in the *langar* rather than the tradition of sitting in rows on the ground.

From time to time, self-styled Sikh "saints" or "gurus" have claimed to have special powers and have set themselves up as spiritual guides, thus antagonizing mainstream Sikhs, who believe that the Tenth Sikh Guru turned over the role of guru to the Guru Granth Sahib, and that there will therefore be no more worldly successors to the position. Some of the new gurus have split off from—or been ostracized by—the mainstream tradition and have formed their own new religious movements, such as Nirankaris, Namdharis, and Radhasoamis.

There is also growing tension between orthodox Sikhs and *deras* (communities) composed largely of lower-class *dalits* who have converted to Sikhism but worship their own leaders as gurus and perhaps also saints from lower classes whose hymns are included in the Guru Granth Sahib. Such tensions are inflamed by political rivalries and sometimes erupt into violence. In 2007 a newspaper published a photograph of the leader of the Sacha Sauda *dera* apparently dressed to look like Guru Gobind Singh. He had hundreds of thousands of followers and was reportedly claiming spiritual authority and giving his followers *amrit* in his own way. A widespread conflict ensued between outraged mainstream Sikhs, who considered his actions blasphemous toward Guru Gobind Singh, and his followers. The clash was seemingly fanned by rivalry between political parties. Again in 2009, Dera Sach Khand followers who worship Bhagat Ravi Das were embroiled in violence with mainstream Sikhs after Dera Sach Khand leaders were attacked in a Vienna *gurdwara*. Rioting occurred across Punjab as a result.

Another issue is authority over the Sikh community. The Sixth Guru started a tradition of sitting on a high platform or *takht* ("throne") in Amritsar opposite the Golden Temple and issuing *hukamnamahs* (edicts) to Sikhs. This place, the Akal Takht ("Eternal Throne"), remains the highest seat of both worldly and spiritual authority for Sikhs. In time, four more *takhts* associated with the life of Guru Gobind Singh were recognized as additional seats of authority, as wielded by their *jathedars* (leaders), but the *jathedar* of the Akal Takht is still the most eminent. This system of control over the affairs of the Sikh Panth is being challenged by some Sikhs as contrary to the original spirit of Sikhism. The challengers argue that Sikhism rejects clergy and rigid authoritarianism in favor of the direct relationship between the devotee, the Guru, and God.

There are also tensions between those Sikhs who favor a more spiritual and universal understanding of their religion and those who interpret it more rigidly and exclusively. During the years when Sikhs were asserting their distinct identity, lest they be subsumed under Hinduism, the ecumenical nature of Sikhism was downplayed. There were no forcible attempts to convert anyone else to Sikhism, but Sikhs became proud of their heroic history and tended to turn inward.

In the diaspora, many Sikhs have attempted to resist assimilation to the surrounding cultures and to raise their children according to their Indian traditions. Whenever communities of Sikhs have collected in the diaspora, they have tried to build a *gurdwara* for their own worship services. One of the chief personal issues over assimilation—not only outside India but also within India, in modern society—is the dilemma over keeping long hair and wearing a turban or veil. The French government's 2004 ruling against wearing of religious symbols in schools has meant that Sikh boys cannot attend public schools wearing their turbans. Some Sikh men feel that they cannot fit into the modern world while wearing a turban, but their families may feel strongly that they should not break with sacred tradition, and put great pressure on them not to cut their hair.

Wearing the *kirpan* on a sling openly is also perceived as a problem in some non-Sikh environments, where others would view it with alarm, so some Khalsa initiates wear miniature symbols of the **kirpan**, comb, and *khanda* (symbolic

The Guru Granth Sahib arrives in state atop an elephant for the 300th anniversary of the Khalsa in 1999 at Anandpur Sahib, which drew together millions of Sikhs from around the world.

double-edged sword) on a necklace, while nonetheless wearing their drawstring underwear and keeping their long hair bound under a turban or veil. In the wake of terrorist attacks in the United States and London, many Sikhs in the diaspora who had kept their traditional dress and long hair with beards and turbans found themselves the mistaken victims of hate crimes, since they were confused with Muslims. The Sikh community found it necessary to explain their religion publicly, and inevitably stressed its universality, democratic nature, and spirit of religious tolerance. Proponents of the traditional symbols were encouraged by a bill unanimously passed in California in 2009 by the state legislature mandating training of policemen about the religious meaning of the *kirpan*.

A strain of exclusivism continues among contemporary scholars and internet bloggers who deny the historic spiritual closeness of Sikhism to Hindu and Muslim traditions. In this strain, some scholars have insisted that the **Dasam Granth**, the purported writings of Guru Gobind Singh, was not entirely written by Guru Gobind Singh because it contains many positive references to Hindu deities and moreover is sexually explicit in places.

Another academic issue is that some Western scholars of Sikhism have come to conclusions that are rejected by many Sikh scholars as being academically unsound, as well as offensive to the faithful. These conclusions include the work of the New Zealand scholar Hew McLeod (1932–2009), who asserted that stories about some of the journeys of Guru Nanak are fictitious and questioned the traditional history of the creation of the Khalsa.

Major conflicts have also arisen over calendar dates for Sikh holidays, with rejection by some factions of the traditional—and somewhat inaccurate—Hindu way of accommodating differences between solar and lunar calendars. Such complex debates get mixed up with politics, with the elected *gurdwara* committee leadership issuing controversial rulings that are presented as authoritative and binding on all Sikhs.

Without going so far as to deny the uniqueness or continuing tradition of Sikhism, many contemporary Sikh and non-Sikh scholars are appreciating the message of the Sikh Gurus as supporting the underlying unity of people of all religions. Baba Virsa Singh (see Box, p. 456) expressed the universality of the Gurus' teachings:

> That which we call dharma, that which we call Sikhism, that which we call the religion of Guru Nanak, that which we call the command of Guru Gobind Singh is this: That we should not forget God even for one breath.
> Guru Nanak prepared a lovely ship, in which all the seats were to be given to those who were doing both manual work and spiritual practice.
> The religion of Guru Gobind Singh, of Guru Nanak was not given to those of one organization, one village, one country. Their enlightened vision was for the whole cosmos. Guru Granth Sahib is not for some handful of people. It is for everyone.[28]

In the words of Guru Gobind Singh:

> Same are the temple and the mosque
> And same are the forms of worship therein.
> All human beings are one though apparently many,
> Realize, therefore, the essential unity of mankind.[29]

Suggested reading

Cole, W. Owen, and Piara Singh Sambhi, *The Sikhs: Their Religious Beliefs and Practices*, second edition, Sussex, England: Academic Press, 1995. A clearly written survey of the Sikh tradition.

Duggal, K. S., *Secular Perceptions in Sikh Faith*, New Delhi: National Book Trust, revised edition, 1999. Clear and touching presentation of aspects of Sikh history and belief promoting universalist thought.

Macauliffe, Max Arthur, *The Sikh Religion: Its Gurus, Sacred Writings, and Authors*, Oxford: Oxford University Press, reprinted in Delhi: S. Chand and Company, 1963. The most respected general account of Sikhism in English, even though its author was not Sikh.

McLeod, W. H., *Exploring Sikhism: Aspects of Sikh Identity, Culture, and Thought*. Oxford: Oxford University Press, 2000. An influential non-Sikh scholar brings historical method and skepticism to bear on traditional Sikh beliefs.

McLeod, W. H., trans. and ed., *Textual Sources for the Study of Sikhism*, Totowa, New Jersey: Barnes and Noble Books, 1984 and Manchester: Manchester University Press, 1984. Interesting compilation of Sikh literature, from selections from the Adi Granth to rules for the Khalsa initiation ceremony, all with explanatory comments.

Nesbitt, Eleanor, *Sikhism: A Very Short Introduction*. Oxford: Oxford University Press, 2005. Accessible explanations of Sikh practices and beliefs in contemporary context.

Singh, Dharam, *Sikhism: Norm and Form*, New Delhi: Vision and Venture, 1997. Discussion of Sikhism as a vision of a new social order: a classless and casteless brotherhood of enlightened humans.

Singh, Guru Gobind, *Jaap Sahib*, English translation by Surendra Nath, New Delhi: Gobind Sadan Publications, 1997. Powerful praises of the formless, ultimately unknowable God, without reference to any particular religion.

Singh, Dr. Gopal, *A History of the Sikh People 1469–1978*, New Delhi: World Sikh University Press, 1979. Thorough and scholarly history of the Sikhs to modern times.

Singh, Harbans, ed., *The Encyclopedia of Sikhism*, Patiala: Punjabi University, 1992–1999. Four volumes on all aspects of Sikhism, prepared by leading scholars.

Singh, Khushwant, trans., *Hymns of Guru Nanak*, New Delhi: Orient Longmans Ltd, 1969. Stories about Guru Nanak's life and selections from his sacred songs.

Singh, Manmohan, trans., *Sri Guru Granth Sahib*, eight volumes, Amritsar: Shromani Gurdwara Parbandhak Committee, 1962. A good English translation of the Sikh sacred scripture.

Singh, Dr. Mohinder, *Guru Granth Sahib: The Guru Eternal*, New Delhi: Himalayan Books, 2008. A splendidly illustrated history and analysis of the Guru Granth Sahib.

Singh, Nikky-Guninder Kaur, *The Birth of the Khalsa: A Feminist Re-Memory of Sikh Identity*, Albany: State University of New York Press, 2005. Unique feminist interpretations of the birth and significance of the Khalsa.

Singh, Nikky-Guninder Kaur, *The Name of My Beloved: Devotional Poetry from the Guru Granth and the Dasam Granth*, San Francisco: HarperSanFrancisco, 1995. Daily devotional hymns in contemporary English translation.

Singh, Trilochan, Jodh Singh, Kapur Singh, Bawa Harkishen Singh, and Khushwant Singh, trans., *The Sacred Writings of the Sikhs*, New York: Samuel Weiser, 1973. Selections from the Adi Granth and hymns by Guru Gobind Singh in English translation.

Key terms

amrit Nectar made with sugar and water, symbolizing the sweetness of compassion.

Dasam Granth The collected writings of Guru Gobind Singh.

Five K's The symbols worn by Khalsa members.

gurdwara A Sikh temple.

Guru Granth Sahib (Adi Granth) The sacred scripture compiled by the Sikh Gurus.

Jaap Sahib The second morning prayer of Sikhs, written by Guru Gobind Singh.

janam-sakhis Traditional biographies, especially stories of the life of Guru Nanak.

Jap Ji The first morning prayer of Sikhs, written by Guru Nanak.

Khalsa Order of Sikhs who have undergone special initiation and observe a strict code of conduct.

kirpan Small sword worn by Khalsa initiates.

kirtan Singing of sacred hymns from Guru Granth Sahib.

langar Community meal for all, regardless of caste or position.

Nam The holy Name of God, as recited by Sikhs.

Panth The religious community in Sikhism.

sangat A Sikh congregation.

Udasi An ascetic Sikh order.

Review questions

1. Describe the central beliefs of the Sikhs and how they compare to those of other Indian religions such as Hinduism, Buddhism, and Jainism.
2. Describe the life and teachings of Guru Nanak, the significance of the Guru in Sikhism, and the role of the Guru Granth Sahib.
3. Describe how the teachings of Sikhism are expressed and put into practice in the *gurdwara*, in *langar*, and in the Khalsa.

Discussion questions

1. Discuss how Sikhism developed in, and responded to, the social, religious, and political situation in north India during the time of the Gurus.
2. Discuss the challenges faced by Sikhs who wear long hair, a turban, and a sword.
3. Discuss the role of women in Sikhism, addressing recent areas of change and debate, and compare women's roles in Sikhism to those in other religions.

myreligionlab

For further activities and resources, including access to MyReligionLibrary, please visit MyReligionLab at www.myreligionlab.com

MyReligionLab

All About Sikhs http://www.allaboutsikhs.com

Gateway to Sikhism http://www.sikh-history.com/main.shtml

Gobind Sadan http://www.gobindsadan.org

Internet Sacred Text Archive: Sikhism http://www.sacred-texts.com/skh/index.htm

Shiromani Gurdwara Parbandhak Committee http://www.sgpc.net/index-nm.html

Sikh Foundation International http://www.sikhfoundation.org/

Sikhism Home Page http://www.sikhs.org/topics.htm

Sikh Women http://www.sikhwomen.com

C H A P T E R   1 2

NEW RELIGIOUS MOVEMENTS

"That yielding of the human mind to the divine"

The history of religions is one of continual change. Each religion changes over time, new religions appear, and some older traditions disappear. Times of rapid social change are particularly likely to spawn new religious movements, for people seek the security of the spiritual amidst worldly chaos. In the period since World War II, thousands of new religious groups have sprung up around the world. In sub-Saharan Africa, there are now over 7,000 different religions; every Nigerian town of several thousand people has up to fifty or sixty different kinds of religion.[1] In Japan, an estimated thirty percent of the population belongs to one of hundreds of new religious movements. Imported versions of Eastern traditions, such as Hinduism and Buddhism, have made many new converts in areas such as North America, Europe, and Russia, where they are seen as "new religions." Websites now offer global opportunities for new religious movements to explain themselves and attract new followers.

To move into a new religious movement may be a fleeting experience or it may signal a deep change in one's life. In religion, as in other life commitments such as marriage, there are potential benefits in dedication and obedience. Many religions, including the largest world religions, teach self-denial and surrender as cardinal virtues that help to vanquish the ego and allow one to approach ultimate reality. The question for a spiritual person is where to place one's faith.

KEY TOPICS

- SOCIAL CONTEXT OF NEW RELIGIOUS MOVEMENTS 465

- CHARISMATIC LEADERSHIP 468

- OFFSHOOTS OF OLDER RELIGIONS 471

- COMBINATIONS OF OLDER RELIGIONS 477

- SOCIAL TRENDS 484

- OPPOSITION TO NEW RELIGIOUS MOVEMENTS 494

- WILL NEW RELIGIOUS MOVEMENTS LAST? 497

Social context of new religious movements

New religious movements are often popularly referred to as "cults" or "sects." These words have specific, neutral meanings: a **cult** represents a distinct break from other traditions, while a **sect** is a splinter group or a subgroup associated with a larger tradition. Both words have sometimes been used imprecisely and pejoratively to distinguish new religions from older ones, each of which already claims to be the best or only way. The label "new religious movement" seems more neutral and is widely used, particularly in academic circles, to avoid such negative connotations. However, the word "new" is itself imprecise, for many of these groups have a rather lengthy history and have survived long after the death of the original founder.

Much of the research into new religious movements has been undertaken by sociologists, for they are interested in the processes by which new religions arise,

Students in Moscow learn ancient levitation techniques from India.

attract members, deal with the death of their founders, and then organize themselves into continuing religious traditions that may gradually enter the social mainstream. Many twentieth-century sociological theories looked at the difference between "churches" and "sects." If seen as ends of a continuum, "churches" are more established religious traditions; sects or cults are newer and more marginal. In the typology suggested by Professors Rodney Stark and William S. Bainbridge, a church typically accepts and accommodates itself to the society in which it operates. A sect, by contrast, rejects its social environment as "worldly" and "unbelieving," i.e., opposed to its beliefs. Sects usually have previous ties to a religious organization but have broken off from it, often in the attempt to return to what they perceive as its pristine original form. Cults are independent religious traditions, but they may also be in conflict with the surrounding society.

According to Stark and Bainbridge's typology, cults can be further defined by the degree to which they influence their followers' relationship to society. What they call "audience cults" do not require conversion, and allow their followers great flexibility. They may sample many religious movements and attend workshops here and there, making their own choices about what to believe and do. New Age groups tend to fall in this category. California-based Dr. Deepak Chopra, for instance, has such a large following that over ten million copies of his books such as *The Seven Spiritual Laws of Success* have been sold in English and his workshops on subjects such as physical healing, emotional wellbeing, and spiritual growth are often sold out even though they may cost thousands of dollars. However, those who practice his teachings based on ancient Indian ayurvedic principles plus psychological "self-knowledge" do not become members of a distinct religious group.

"Client cults" offer some kind of service, usually some kind of therapy. Involvement with the organization may become deeper and more socially defining over time. Scientology, which is based on the writings of L. Ron Hubbard (1911–1986), is considered such a group. The initial agenda is therapeutic: "auditing" in order to clear the mind of the negative effects of past experiences and past lives with the help of a counseling instrument called an "E-meter." But once this process begins, clients learn of more complex levels of involvement, and other members may become their primary social group. Auditing often leads to membership in the Church of Scientology. This institution is based on Hubbard's idea that the mind is directed by a spiritual entity which he called the *thetan*. Hubbard taught that the *thetan* is trapped in the material world but that its freedom can be obtained through a gradual process of detachment. Step by step, following precise directions, the *thetan* can move up "The Bridge" to "total freedom." Higher levels of involvement in this process are said to confer secret wisdom, or *gnosis*, and the freed "Operating Thetan" begins to have out-of-body experiences. "Advanced Organizations" have been established to offer these higher levels of experience, culminating in the "Sea Org" which consists of members who have committed themselves to work for Scientology by signing the "billion-year contract." They move to one of the Sea Org centers throughout the world, where they undertake a disciplined program of work and study and attempt to abide by a strict code of conduct, "to help get ethics in on this planet and the universe, which is the basic purpose of the Sea Org."[2] Those reaching this Sea Org level—which has been compared to monastic orders in Christianity or Buddhism—are a small subset of the reportedly millions of clients who register for the auditing sessions with Scientology. The organization thus remains primarily what Stark and Bainbridge call a "client cult."

What Stark and Bainbridge call a "cult movement" is a full-fledged organization that requires conversion and does not allow dual allegiances to other organizations. Some offer a total way of life, with community-based lodging and work as well as group worship. Commitment to this way of life ranges from partial, with people still involved with family and friends outside the movement, to total, in which they are largely cut off from the wider social environment. Groups anticipating an imminent time of great changes in the world may take this path of separation.

When members of a new religious movement anticipate that the end times or new world order are coming soon, they tend to be regarded as eccentrics by the rest of their society. To maintain their faith, they may isolate themselves from mainstream society and try to prepare for the coming changes. Alternatively, those who anticipate the end of the present world may accept social scorn and try to share their prophecies with others in order to save them from the anticipated coming destruction or prepare them for the new world order.

The expectation of major world changes appears in many established religions, including Hinduism, Zoroastrianism, Judaism, Christianity, Islam, and some indigenous religions. Hindus, for instance, anticipate that the current depraved age of Kali Yuga will be followed by the return of Sat Yuga (when *dharma* will again prevail). This anticipation leads periodically to the formation of movements which preach that the time of great changes is imminent. In Christianity, the last book in the Bible, Revelation, predicts an **apocalypse**, or dramatic end of the present world. Revelation foretells a titanic war at Armageddon between the forces of Satan and the forces of God, with great destruction, followed by the **millennium**, a 1,000-year period of special holiness in which Christ rules the earth. Some nineteenth-century Christians developed the idea of the **rapture**, using Paul's letter to the Thessalonians (1 Thess. 4:17) to say that

Actor Tom Cruise speaks at the inauguration of a new Scientology church in Madrid.

Christians would be caught up in clouds to meet Jesus when he returned to earth. As indicated in Chapter 9, this idea has been revived in our times.

Charismatic leadership

Formation of new religious movements often begins in the same way as many established religions: A charismatic figure emerges who develops a dedicated following of people who regard him or her as their guru (such as Buddha), prophet (such as Muhammad), or messiah (such as Jesus). Huge movements have developed around such beings who are thought to be divinely inspired. From time to time, new figures arise and attract a lot of followers, such as the contemporary spiritual leaders Rev. Sun Myung Moon and Sathya Sai Baba. They have developed far-flung and diversified service and propagation organizations which may help their movements to survive their own eventual physical deaths.

Sociological research suggests that after a charismatic founder dies, those groups who are able to routinize that charisma into the authority of a religious institution survive, and may later produce other charismatic persons. When an institution has grown or allied with other similar institutions to encompass a large part of the civil community, it may begin behaving more like what Stark and Bainbridge call a "church" rather than a "sect." In general, churches take responsibility for the larger community and respond to its needs; sects take responsibility for themselves and for their own members. Rev. Moon's organization and Sathya Sai Baba's organization have both begun this process of helping the larger community during the lifetime of their founders.

UNIFICATION MOVEMENT

myreligionlab

The Lord of the Second Advent and the Ideal of True Parents
SUN MYUNG MOON

The Unification Movement has been founded by the charismatic leader Sun Myung Moon, who has proclaimed himself and his second wife, Hak Ja Han, to be jointly the Messiah. He was born in 1920 in what is now North Korea into a family of farmers. At that time, Christians met underground, hiding first from the Japanese occupation authorities and then from the communists. Many of the Christian churches had strong messianic expectations. Moon's parents converted to Christianity, and the young Moon became a Sunday School teacher. He says that in Easter 1935, while he was praying in the mountains, Jesus appeared to him in a vision. Jesus reportedly told him that it had not been God's desire that he be crucified, for his mission on earth was left unfinished. By Moon's account, Jesus asked him to complete the task of establishing God's kingdom on earth.

To this end, Moon developed the "Unification Principle," according to which God created the universe in order to manifest true love, and the human family is considered the primary institution for the growth of love. Based on spiritual and moral education in the family, people are to live for the sake of others in all situations. However, according to Moon's theology, humans do not live according to God's design; selfishness prevails in human relationships and in relationships between ethnic groups and nations. From the time of Adam and Eve, false love has been passed down from generation to generation, infecting the whole human race.

Moon began to teach publicly in North Korea, where communist leaders were seeking to quash religious activity. He was arrested and tortured, and his apparently lifeless body was thrown into a snowdrift. After his followers nursed him back to health, he continued preaching in public, was arrested again, and sentenced to hard labor in a concentration camp. Moon was liberated when American forces bombed the prison.

In the 1970s, the Unification Church staged a series of well-publicized rallies in the United States and saw a rapid growth in membership. Middle-class youths put aside their careers, gave up their worldly possessions, broke off from their girlfriends and boyfriends, and devoted themselves to the religious path. They saw their sacrificial and ascetic way of life as a rejection of the materialistic and hedonistic American lifestyle. However, alarmed parents accused the church of brainwashing their adult children. The church was viewed with suspicion by the established Christian churches and vilified by the political left because of its anti-communist activities. In 1982, Rev. Moon was subjected to criminal prosecution over a purported tax liability of $7,300, but the ruling was criticized by the National Council of Churches as a "miscarriage of justice" and a denial of religious liberty, and it was overturned by the Supreme Court.

Dodging controversy and mockery, the Unification Movement began engaging in large-scale international activities reportedly designed to transform the world. For instance, the Unification-sponsored Inter-Religious Federation for World Peace and the Religious Youth Service have created international inter-religious dialogues among scholars of religion and political leaders, and service projects in many countries. Such expensive projects are financially supported by members' door-to-door sales and their establishment of business companies such as industrial-scale fishing ventures. The Unification Church has become extremely financially successful and even wields some political power; for instance, it is the owner of a major Washington, D.C. newspaper, *The Washington Times*. It claims to be getting one million hits a week on its website.

A unique aspect of the movement's work is massive wedding ceremonies in which thousands of couples matched by the movement or already-wed couples wanting to dedicate themselves to "live for the sake of others" and "create an ideal family which contributes to world peace" are simultaneously "blessed" by Rev. and Mrs. Moon. With the seemingly charismatic Rev. Moon announcing himself as the "Second Adam," Unificationists view these mass weddings as a movement to create one human family, with couples of all races and nationalities being "engrafted" onto "God's lineage of true love." Rev. and Mrs. Moon also undertake global speaking tours, giving the same prepared speeches in many countries to announce that they are the True Parents of all humankind.

In addition to Rev. Moon's self-avowed transmissions of revelations from Jesus, it is also said that Mrs. Moon's deceased mother and Rev. and Mrs. Moon's son, who died in a car crash, are assisting Unificationists from the spirit world, through the help of a medium. Hundreds of thousands of members have participated in workshops designed to free them from evil spirits. The spirits are then said to be given training in the Unification Principle and duly "blessed." People cite miraculous physical healings and visions of spirits leaving their bodies. There are also liberation ceremonies for ancestors and even historical "infamous personages," such as Hitler, Lenin, and Stalin. A Unification spokesman reports that they have been "blessed as the representatives of all wicked people, thereby opening the gate for the 'liberation of Hell.'"[3]

Among his many projects to "build the kingdom of Heaven on earth," Rev. Moon has bought and renovated an inner-city university in Bridgeport, Connecticut. The University of Bridgeport now serves an ethnically diverse body of 5,300 students and specializes in career-oriented programs. Like the participants in other projects founded by Rev. Moon, these students are not typically Unification members. Moon's charismatic leadership is kept in the background. At conferences such as the Assembly of the World's Religions, the World Media Conference, and the International Conference on the Unity of Sciences, he or his wife may appear only once to present his philosophy, and many in attendance will not agree with it. Nevertheless, the Unification website claims that as a result of the Moons' activities and their blessings as the "True Parents:"

> *True love has now triumphed over evil. All the satanic barriers have been broken down. The Completed Testament Age has dawned. God's true love, which was lost at the fall of man, has made its triumphant reappearance in the world. This love is the power of new life for all individuals, marriages and families the world over.[4]*

SATHYA SAI BABA

Another charismatic leader with a huge following is Sathya Sai Baba of India. He travels very little and now moves around with the help of a wheelchair, but international crowds coming for his *darshan* are so large that spaces are allotted according to a lottery system. Perhaps a million people attended his eightieth birthday celebration, including top political leaders of India, despite some controversies surrounding him.

Born in 1926, Sathya Sai Baba claims to be the reincarnation of Shirdi Sai Baba, a saint who was greatly loved by people of all religions, and furthermore claims that he is an Avatar, an earthly manifestation of the Divine. According to biographical material written by devotees, his mother believes he was divinely conceived when a "big ball of blue light"[5] rolled toward her and seemed to enter her body. When the boy was fourteen, he was reportedly stung by a large scorpion, after which he went into silence broken occasionally by spiritual songs and discourses, weeping or laughing. Spiritual phenomena, his personal magnetism, and his claims of being Shirdi Sai Baba drew people to him. Eventually their numbers grew to the point that large buildings had to be built for their food and accommodation. Now his center in Puttaparthi has become a world pilgrimage center including a massive ashram, an educational system from primary schools to a free accredited university with three campuses, a museum of world religions, a planetarium, indoor and outdoor stadiums, free super-specialty hospitals, a railway station, and an airport. Sathya Sai Baba usually gives *darshan* daily to hordes of followers, moving among them to accept letters, materialize things such as rings, necklaces, watches, or sacred ash in his hand to give them, and choose some for private interviews in which he speaks as a clairvoyant about matters in their personal lives. His followers also claim that he manifests things in their homes far away, such as turmeric powder, holy water, Shiva lingams, fruits, and gems. Many other miracles are attributed to him, such as controlling the weather, changing the color of his clothing, disappearing physically, appearing in two places at the same time, bringing a dead man back to life, and healing people. Such apparent spiritual magic is not unique to him in India, but it adds to his charismatic appeal. He refuses to allow scientists to study his materializations of objects, so he is subject to accusations that he is simply a magician. He himself has said that the miracles are trivial compared to "my glory and majesty, as a mosquito is in size and strength to the elephant upon which it squats."[6] On another occasion he said, "I teach that no distinction should be made between the names Rama, Krishna, Ishwara, Sai—for they are all My names."[7]

Despite the attribution of Godhead to himself, Sathya Sai Baba does not claim to be starting a new religion, but rather preaches the simple universal message of truth, righteousness, nonviolence, love, and peace. His Sai Organization has study circles around the world and runs value-based free schools, medical institutions, digital radio networks, and large-scale projects to provide drinking water to drought-prone areas of India. Its centers also encourage their members to provide selfless service in their communities through projects such as food banks, feeding of the homeless, tree planting, park cleanups, medical camps, blood donation, and collecting old spectacles to be donated to the poor.

Offshoots of older religions

In previous chapters we have looked at contemporary versions of ancient religions, such as Hare Krishna in Hinduism and Soka Gakkai in Buddhism. Since newer offshoots of older religions are often sufficiently different from the parent religion to be considered new religious movements—whether they regard themselves as such or not—we will examine three contemporary examples below: the Mormon Church, Jehovah's Witnesses, and Radhasoami.

MORMON CHURCH

The chief feature of the Mormon Church, more formally known as the Church of Jesus Christ of Latter-Day Saints, that distinguishes it from the many variations of mainstream Christianity is that Mormons believe not only in the Bible but also in another scripture, *The Book of Mormon*. Mormons believe that in 1822, under angelic guidance, Joseph Smith found the book in New York State, engraved on golden plates. *The Book of Mormon* purports to be the account of several of the lost tribes of Israel, who crossed the ocean to become the ancestors of the American Indians, and the appearance of Jesus to them in the Americas after his death and resurrection. Mormon is one of the faithful who is believed to have survived tribal conflict and managed to write down the teachings about Jesus in the Americas for posterity. In 3 Nephi of *The Book of Mormon*, for instance, it is written that after "tempests, earthquakes, fires, whirlwinds, and physical upheavals attest the crucifixion of Christ," Jesus appeared to the Nephites as "a Man descending out of heaven; and he was clothed in a white robe; and he came down and stood in the midst of them." Jesus reportedly gave them teachings very similar to the Sermon on the Mount from the New Testament, and urged them to practice baptism by immersion and not to quarrel over doctrine.

myreligionlab

Mormon
Journey
by Sea
THE BOOK
OF MORMON

Convinced of the authenticity of *The Book of Mormon*, followers of Joseph Smith moved from one place to another to escape persecution and try to build a "New Jerusalem," "the land of Zion." With great effort, they built a great city in Illinois which they called Nauvoo, Hebrew for "beautiful place," and began to develop some political power, but then Joseph Smith was assassinated by angry area residents. In the struggle for succession, several separate groups of Latter-Day Saints developed, the largest of which was led by Brigham Young (1801–1877) to Salt Lake City, Utah, to build "Zion in the Wilderness" and restore what the Mormons consider true Christianity, as opposed to the **apostasy** (abandonment of principles) which they feel characterizes the Christian churches.

By now, the Mormon Church numbers thirteen million followers worldwide. Its members control great material wealth and also exercise considerable political influence in the United States, especially in Utah. The Mormon Church's success is perhaps due partly to the efforts of its 65,000 volunteer missionaries, and partly due to the appeal of its emphasis on clean living and strong family values in contrast to the prevailing Western culture. All men are ordained to the priesthood, and authority resides in fathers as the heads of the family households. Bishop Thomas Thorkelson from California explains:

> *The father at the head of his household holds the priesthood of God. That father can baptize his child when the child reaches the age of accountability. When the child gets sick, the father can heal it. When the children go off to school, the father gives them a blessing just like Abraham blessed his sons. He is the patriarch of his family and lays his hands upon their heads and gives them a blessing.*
>
> *The Church also teaches that a father should periodically interview each of his children. As holder of the priesthood, the father calls his children in and they kneel down in prayer, and he asks for discernment as he talks with his kids. He talks*

Mormons have become politically powerful and well established, and the Mormon Tabernacle Choir in Salt Lake City, Utah, is world-famous.

with them about everything in their lives. If they are old enough, they talk about dating, about their relationships with the opposite sex. They talk about honesty. Or what happens if there is a child in school who is not accepted by the other members of the class. We try to teach them that you need to go out and make a special inclusionary effort. We talk about what happens if somebody wants to copy your term paper, what happens if somebody wants to cheat on a test. How do you maintain what you know is right and honest, and still maintain your status as a welcome person within the community?[8]

Following the revelations given to Joseph Smith, Mormons typically eschew alcohol, tobacco, coffee, and tea, and eat meat only sparingly, thus focusing on a healthy diet of vegetables, fruits, and grains. They have developed a strong social welfare system to help families in need but also make them self-sufficient. Using volunteer labor alone, they have developed large-scale farms, ranches, peanut product factories, coal mines, and the like, using the symbol of the hive, in which honey bees cooperate in order to meet the needs of all the members. Children are trained in preaching from a young age, as part of the system of shared responsibility. Sexual conduct outside marriage is strongly discouraged, and only virgins can be missionaries.

Mormon theology is still evolving, due to its principle of continuing revelation by which all believers may receive revelations directly from God. The head of the church is specially empowered to receive divine guidance on contemporary issues that are not clearly addressed in the Bible and *The Book of Mormon*. Theological beliefs are also subject to change, the most controversial of which—from the point of view of other Christians—may be the nature of God. For some time, Mormons believed that the "Heavenly Father" was originally a man but had risen to exaltation, and that humans can likewise become like gods. This belief still exists, but the recent prophet, President Gordon Hinckley (1910–2008), did not stress the controversial first part of this doctrine, and restated the second half: "We believe in the progression of the human soul. We believe in the eternity and the infinity of the human soul, and its great possibilities."[9]

JEHOVAH'S WITNESSES

Whereas Mormons turn to *The Book of Mormon* and the Bible for guidance, Jehovah's Witnesses place their faith squarely and hopefully in the Bible alone. Their belief structure and their religious life refer constantly to biblical passages, and their missionaries traverse the globe, going door to door to invite people to study the Bible with them as the inspired and accurate Word of God. They feel that mainstream Christian churches began to deviate from the Bible in the second and third centuries by developing untrue doctrines: that God is a Trinity, that the soul is resurrected after death, and that the unrepentant wicked endure eternal torment rather than the utter annihilation that the Witnesses predict for them when God's kingdom appears. They foresee a new world in which people of all races (including many raised from the dead) will join hands in peace. They believe that this will happen only after the majority of humanity is destroyed for not obeying the Bible. In the understanding of Jehovah's Witnesses, God will not let anyone, including "false Christians," ruin

myreligienlab
Life in a Peaceful
New World
JEHOVAH'S WITNESSES

the earth. Those who are of the true religion will be saved from the general destruction, reunited with their dead loved ones in a paradise on earth (except for 144,000 who will live with God in heaven). According to the teachings, in the earthly paradise there will be no pain, no food shortages, no sickness, no death.

The founder of Jehovah's Witnesses, Charles Taze Russell (1852–1916), supported a prediction that 1873 or 1874 would be the date of this apocalypse. When that period passed uneventfully, the date for the "harvest of believers" was changed to 1878, and then 1914, 1925, and 1975. As the dates came and went without any apparent end of the world, Russell and his successors developed the idea that Christ had arrived, but was invisibly present. Only the faithful "Jehovah's Witnesses" would recognize his presence. Their mission is to warn the rest of the populace about what is in store. They thus go from house to house, encouraging people to follow their program of studying the Bible as an announcement of the millennium and to leave politics and "false religions." The latter include mainstream Christian churches, as above. They explain that prevailing problems such as crime, terrorism, social violence, pollution, deforestation, and global warming will soon come to an end because God has made biblical promises to save the planet, as no human institutions can:

> Soon our anxieties about the future will be over, for God will take charge of planet Earth by putting in place his own government, called God's Kingdom. Jesus Christ had that wonderful prospect in mind when he taught his followers to pray: "Let your kingdom come. Let your will take place, as in heaven, also upon earth." (Matthew 6: 9–10).
>
> God's Kingdom will neither cooperate with nor work through human political leaders. Rather, it will eliminate every vestige of human self-rule, as indicated in the following prophecy of Daniel about "the last days," the time in which we live. (2 Timothy 3:1) "In the days of those kings the God of heaven will set up a kingdom that will never be brought to ruin. ... It will crush and put an end to all these [man-made] kingdoms, and it itself will stand to times indefinite." (Daniel 2:44) Those words offer no comfort or hope to people who prefer rulership by man, but to all who desire God's sovereignty as expressed through his Kingdom, they glow with promise.[10]

During the 1930s and 1940s in the United States, many Jehovah's Witnesses were persecuted and arrested for their refusal to engage in military activities. Their trials became tests of the preservation of freedom of speech, press, assembly, and worship, and ultimately they won forty-three Supreme Court cases. They have been similarly successful in high courts of other countries. The movement continues to grow, with reportedly "some 6,000,000 persons today who are telling the good news of Jehovah's Kingdom by Christ Jesus in over 230 lands" and who "feel that they properly refer to themselves as Jehovah's Witnesses."[11] Despite their apocalyptic expectations, their website shows them as ordinary people concerned about the state of the world who go door-to-door to deliver their message:

> In most ways Jehovah's Witnesses are like everyone else. They have their problems—economic, physical, emotional. They make mistakes at times, for they

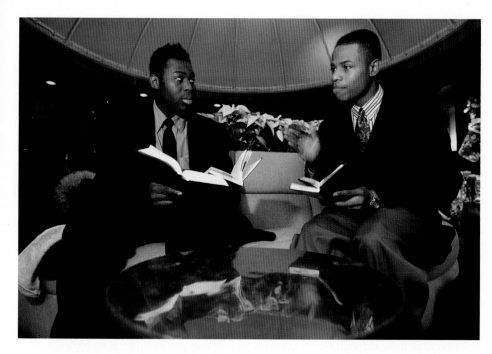

A Jehovah's Witness shares Bible study lessons.

are not perfect, inspired, or infallible. But they try to learn from their experiences and diligently study the Bible to make needed corrections. They have made their dedication to God to do his will, and they apply themselves to fulfill this dedication. In all their activities they seek guidance from God's Word and his holy spirit. ... They understand that many of the prophecies of the Bible have been fulfilled, others are in the course of fulfillment, and still others await fulfillment.[12]

RADHASOAMI

The Radhasoami movement is an outgrowth of Sikhism in India. Its leaders often have Sikh backgrounds, but while orthodox Sikhs believe in a succession of masters that stopped with the Tenth Guru and was transferred to the holy scripture, Radhasoamis believe in a continuing succession of living masters. The first of the Radhasoami gurus was Shiv Dayal Singh. In 1861, he offered to serve as a spiritual savior, carrying devotees into "Radhasoami," the ineffable Godhead. Some 10,000 took initiation under him. After his death in 1878, the movement eventually split into what are now over thirty branches, each with its own living master, although there is theoretically only one of these at a time on the earth. The Punjabi branches are known collectively as Sant Mat, or Path of the Masters.

The most popular of the branches is Radhasoami Satsang Beas, with its well-organized center in Punjab near the river Beas. A biographer of Baba Sawan Singh (1858–1948), the saint through whom many of the branches trace their lineage, describes the typical Radhasoami attitude that contemporary Sikhism suffers from lack of a living guru who would guide them in inner spiritual practice:

The basic spiritual core of Sant Mat and the Sikh teachings is practically the same. Soami Ji of Agra only simplified the earlier teaching and gave it out in clear and

An Interview with Wolfgang Hecker

In 1958, Maharishi Mahesh Yogi began teaching the practice of Transcendental Meditation (TM) based on ancient Vedic techniques. Maharishi's extensive travels and worldwide organization introduced the TM technique to millions of people. For most, TM is a practical part of the daily routine to enrich one's personal life. But for a select few, including Wolfgang Hecker of Germany, TM has become a way of life. Since 1999 he has been living in the Valley of the Saints in the Indian Himalayas as one of a hundred advanced practitioners chosen by Maharishi Mahesh Yogi to practice TM for the sake of bringing greater harmony to the world. Wolfgang has been meditating for so many years that he seems to be in a constant state of inner happiness, and even his skin appears to be translucent and radiant. Wolfgang recounts:

"I came to TM like almost everyone has—through the recommendation of a friend. I was very much attracted to Maharishi's technique because I saw on the face of my friend that inner peace and happiness that radiates from people who practice TM.

"Right in the very first instruction, I had exactly the experience I was always looking for. I was nineteen and interested in spiritual development. Immediately I had that experience of pure transcendental consciousness. The mind became more quiet, and more quiet, and more quiet, completely effortlessly, completely naturally, completely without any doing. The activity of the mind settled down. I was resting deeply within my own self, silent and yet fully awake at the same time, like the teacher had told me in the introductory lecture. I had that experience right away in the first meditation.

"After the personal instruction, you come again for an hour on three consecutive days. You discuss further experiences with the teacher so that you are completely self-sufficient and can meditate on your own. You start practicing twenty minutes in the morning and twenty in the evening, sitting comfortably with eyes closed.

"What I found very attractive was that you are not joining a club or an organization. It's not a religious practice, it's not a philosophy. There are Buddhists, Muslims, Christians, Hindus, people who don't believe in anything. All kinds of people practice Transcendental Meditation—housewives, doctors, anyone.

"Maharishi always encouraged scientific research on the TM technique, showing that its results could be proved scientifically and would be repeatable and reliable. In the early 1970s, a scientist named Dr. Robert Keith Wallace did the first research on brain wave coherence. Every state of consciousness—waking, sleeping, dreaming—has its own very specific brain waves and biochemistry. During TM, a fourth major state of consciousness occurs in which the brain's functioning is more orderly. Any parameter you can measure on the body at that time is pointing to greater orderliness in the physiology, and a deep layer of rest.

"There are advanced techniques, of which the most well known is Maharishi's yogic flying technique. This technique has its origin in the ancient Vedic tradition. It is a very powerful tool to enhance mind–body coordination, which brings benefits on all levels of life to the individual who is practicing it. But above that it was found by scientific research that if large groups practice yogic flying together, not only the individual consciousness of every practitioner is enlivened but also the coherence and orderliness in collective consciousness is increased. It was found that a larger number—6,000, 7,000, 10,000 people—practicing yogic flying together in one place would so dramatically increase the orderliness in the collective consciousness of everyone on the globe that positive trends would be increasing and negative trends would be decreasing.

"Yogic flying is one of many *siddhi* techniques that Maharishi has been teaching. You first practice TM in order to come to that peaceful, very, very silent, unbounded level of pure consciousness inside. And then you begin the technique of the yogic flying. It is like dropping a pebble into a silent lake. Ripples appear. So you can observe how from silent, abstract nothingness, a wave of creation arises. Here the laws of nature begin the process of creation. And as a meditator you can experience this within your own consciousness.

"In the case of the yogic flying *siddhi*, the body lifts up and the person makes a hop, so to say, in the air. His body moves up and there is a transformation from heavy to something light. But for the practitioner, all his attention is on the inner, rather than the outer. When the unbounded quietness wells up in waves of life and living, then the experience is one of bubbling up of bliss. So on the individual level, the yogic flying technique is the most powerful tool to transform the personality. Inner silent happiness nourishes one's daily life. And with mind and body coordination enhanced, scientific research has shown greater effectiveness and joy in life."

*lucid terms in the local language. ... In the course of time, however, the emphasis
of the [Sikh] teachings gradually shifted from spiritual practice under the guidance
of a living master to the practice of rituals and external observances. Many devout
Sikhs began to confine their religious activities to reading and reciting the holy
book, little realizing that it enjoins upon the readers the necessity of internal
practice of the sound current to attain ultimate salvation.[13]*

Radhasoami is primarily an esoteric path, without exoteric ceremonies.
Initiates are taught a secret yoga practice of concentrating on the third eye with
attention to the inner sound and inner light. "Radha" refers to the Prime Spirit
Current; "Soami" means the Prime Sound Current. The two are said to have min-
gled at the beginning of creation, and the primal sound continues to reverberate.
Radhasoamis are taught that there are three divisions of creation, with various
subdivisions. The lowest is the material-spiritual region, in which coarse matter
predominates over spirit. In the middle division, spirit predominates and matter
in a fine, pure form is mixed with it. The highest division is pure spirit, home of
the Supreme Creator, where sound and spirit currents intermingle. An instructional booklet explains that the prescribed method for the ascent:

*consists in raising the spirit from its present seat towards higher regions by means
of contact with the Sound Current and attraction of the spirit towards that Current
which is coming from the higher regions of creation. ... The result would be its
exaltation and elevation into the regions of higher bliss and joy, and eventual
entrance into the purely spiritual regions.[14]*

The faithful are told that the experience must be both initiated and guided by a
perfected being "who is possessed of all the powers of the purely spiritual regions."[15]

The Radhasoami movement now claims an estimated 1.7 million initiates.
Those in the Agra area of India have created whole spiritual suburbs where they
live and work as well as worship together. Outside of India, devotees gather in
satsangs (spiritual congregations), who are supposed to support each other in the
path. They are required to be vegetarians, to meditate every day, to forgo alcohol
and, if possible, tobacco, and to be employed.

Combinations of older religions

Mixtures of more than one religion have historically arisen in many places. As we
have seen, Buddhism, Confucianism, and Daoism have long intermingled in
China, to the extent that it is difficult to sort out the threads as distinct traditions.
When this process produces what seems to be a new religion of sorts as a combination of normally differing beliefs, it is referred to as **syncretism**.

CAODAISM

One of the most extreme contemporary examples of syncretism arose in
Vietnam early in the twentieth century. The new religious movement Caodaism
was formed in 1926 in Vietnam by several people who understood that God was
instructing them that religious leaders such as Moses, Yi king (in China),

Buddha, Laozi, Confucius, and Jesus had all been God-inspired to start religions in their home regions. However, these all became distorted by local customs, and through lack of communication between different regions the religions went their separate ways. According to the revelations, this multiplicity of religions kept people from living together harmoniously. Caodaists thus practice a syncretistic religion made from parts of many world religions, including Judaism, Christianity, Islam, Buddhism, Confucianism, and Daoism, plus the indigenous Vietnamese religion Geniism. For instance, Caodaists believe that before God there was the Dao. God was born in the Big Bang, and then created yin and yang, with the "Mother Buddha" presiding over yin aspects of the cosmos. Such a mixture of religious elements is supposed by Caodaists to be the basis for the "Third Alliance between God and Man," a self-description which is written in many places in Caodaist temples.

Caodaist beliefs have been developed through the process of spiritual mediumship, or "channeling." By various means that have precedents in both Eastern shamanistic practices and European spiritualist séances, spirits in Caodaism are thought to convey written messages between heaven and earth. Typically, the medium goes into trance and writes messages received from the spirits with a quill pen. Above a Caodai altar, a great eye with lines radiating from it represents this communication from Cao ("high") Dai ("palace"), where God reigns. Many of the spirits who are thought to carry these communications to earthly mediums are from French culture, such as Victor Hugo, Joan of Arc, and Louis Pasteur, reflecting the strong French influence in Vietnam since its colonization by France in the nineteenth century. Other spirits are Chinese gods, such as Li Po, who reportedly revealed the architecture of the Great Divine Temple in Tay Ninh, center of the faith. In the early years of the religion, séances were held throughout Vietnam, with miracles, healing of the sick, and direct orders to individuals by name to join the new religion. But because there was already a strong tradition of individual channeling of spirits, there was a perceived threat to the institutionalization of Caodaism. In 1936 a decision was taken that official Caodai séances could only be held in the Holy See at Tay Ninh. Having become thus centralized and institutionalized, Caodaism played a prominent role in Vietnamese society during the turbulent war years and became the third largest religion in Vietnam, after Buddhism and Roman Catholicism. Now its central management is under the control of a communist-appointed committee and official séances have stopped, though worship continues in the Holy See temples. Outside Vietnam, members of Caodaism are left with the dilemma of trying to understand what Tay Ninh would likely advise if it were officially guiding them through its link with Cao Dai.

AFRICAN-INSPIRED SYNCRETIC RELIGIONS

In contrast to the institutionalization of spiritualism in Caodaism, other syncretic mixtures that have emerged more organically include a variety of new religious movements in the Caribbean and Latin America. These have evolved from mixtures of Catholic traditions implanted there earlier, and African religions carried by slaves. They are characterized by a prevailing interest in contacting and cooperating with spirits. **Santeria** ("way of the saints," or Lukumi, as its practitioners increasingly prefer) blends some of the deities and beliefs of slaves from

In the syncretism of Santeria, the Yoruba river goddess Oshun is merged with the Christian Our Lady of Charity, patron saint of Cuba.

Dahomey, baKonga, and Yoruban cultures with images of Catholic saints. Since the slaves were prevented from openly practicing their ancestral faiths, they continued to do so in symbolic ways, such as hanging a white cloth from a doorway or tying bananas with red string, and also by worship of the African *orisa* in the form of Catholic saints. For instance, the female *orisa* Oshun is worshiped in Nigeria as the patron of love, marriage, and fertility, and is associated with river water. In Cuba and in areas of the United States with large Cuban populations, devotions to Oshun have merged into reverence of the Virgin Mary as Our Lady of Charity, the patron saint of Cuba. She is said to have appeared to three shipwrecked fishermen at sea.

Santeria specialists have techniques for "magical" intervention in people's lives to help solve problems that cannot be fixed by ordinary means. The *santeros*, for example, say they are able to clear away negative spiritual influences around people, help them get jobs, heal sickness, attract mates, block their enemies, and get ahead financially. They see the world as a mesh of interconnections among all beings, linked by the energy known as *ashe*. Human efforts are required to keep the *ashe* flowing properly through creation and to nourish the *orisa*. Then, by knowing how to feed and communicate with the *orisa* and understanding the principles of energy, practitioners are thought to be able to wield some control over the environment.

Where remnants of slave populations have coalesced, the renewed practice of African traditions has given the people a link with their cultural heritage, a sense of inner integrity, and a means of sheer survival. But these African traditions have been viewed with some suspicion by the dominant societies. For instance, traditional African methods of communicating with the spirits include divination and the consecrated slaughter of animals, in the context of a community meal. The latter practice was outlawed in Hialeah, Florida, as "animal sacrifice," but in a landmark judgment in 1993 the United States Supreme Court overruled the ban as an unconstitutional barrier to religious freedom. According to a majority of the Supreme Court justices: "Religious beliefs need not be acceptable, logical, consistent, or comprehensible to others in order to merit First Amendment protection."[16] Santeria has become so popular in Latin America and the United States that it has an estimated 100 million practitioners, and there are pilgrimages to Nigeria for people seeking to explore the roots of their religion. It is strengthening its ties to Africa as it gains legal and social acceptance and feels less need to mask its practices as Catholic variants.

Syncretism has also developed in Africa itself. For example, a number of "new" religions in West Africa combine ritual elements of indigenous and Christian traditions which had been brought by missionaries. The missionaries regarded worship of ancestors as religiously invalid, but communications with ancestors and spirits had been a major aspect of the indigenous religions. The syncretistic new religions take seriously problems with the spirit world, such as retaliations from spirits who have not been treated respectfully, and mix Christian prayers and incense with fetishes, talismans, divining, chanting, and drumming. This syncretistic mixture gives a sense of power against evil spirits and is also applied to contemporary, this-worldly problems. These groups are most popular in urban areas, where they offer a refuge from unpleasant aspects of city life. Those such as the Brotherhood of the Cross and Star are deeply committed to serving the people in areas where governments have failed them. They operate their own schools, food shops, industries, healthcare centers, and transportation services. Those who once felt like nobodies, alienated within modern impersonal culture, now feel recognized as important individuals within a loving group. The movements revive the traditional African community spirit as a stable support network within a changing society. They may also build a sense of African pride and spiritual destiny. Rev. William Kingsley Opoku of Ghana, International Coordinator of the African Council of Spiritual Churches and member of the Brotherhood of the Cross and Star, asserts:

Madame Blavatsky, mystic and founder of the Theosophical Society.

> *African Scriptures confirm that the world peace process will finally be founded in Africa, and the whole world will come and help build it, to signify the unity of mankind under the Government of God on earth.*[17]

THEOSOPHICAL SOCIETY

Another version of syncretism centers on the realization that all prophets have brought essentially the same messages to humanity. A prime example of this realization is the Theosophical Society, founded by the Russian aristocrat Madame Helen Blavatsky (1831–1891). "Theosophy" means "divine wisdom," as revealed to Madame Blavatsky by unseen "Ascended Masters." Madame Blavatsky was a fierce character with notable psychic powers. She traveled around the globe studying with masters of esoteric schools and said she had undergone initiations with Tibetan masters. She founded the Theosophical Society with the motto, "There is no religion higher than truth." It was an attempt, she said, "to reconcile all religions, sects and nations under a common system of ethics, based on eternal verities."[18]

The Theosophical Society introduced ancient Eastern ideas to Western seekers, especially Hindu beliefs such as *karma*, reincarnation, and subtle energies. Madame Blavatsky was particularly interested in the secret esoteric teachings of each religion, which collectively she called the "Wisdom Religion" or the "secret doctrine." Madame Blavatsky insisted that:

> *Theosophy is not a Religion. Theosophy is Religion itself. A Religion in the true and only correct sense, is a bond uniting men together—not a particular set of dogmas and beliefs. Now Religion, per se, in its widest meaning is that which binds not only all MEN, but also all BEINGS and all things in the entire Universe into one grand whole. ... Theosophy is RELIGION, and the Society its one Universal Church; the temple of Solomon's wisdom,—in building which "there was neither hammer, nor axe, nor any tool of iron heard in the house while it was building" (1 Kings, 6); for this "temple" is made by no human hand, nor built in any locality on earth—but, verily, is raised only in the inner sanctuary of man's heart wherein reigns alone the awakened soul.[19]*

The Theosophical Society now has members in seventy countries. The movement has splintered into several factions, which use the same name, and has also spawned other groups, such as the Agni Yoga Society founded by Nicholas Roerich (1874–1947), a Russian painter, philosopher, and humanitarian. When he traveled in the Himalayas with his wife, Helena, he painted the spiritual light

myreligionlab
The Wisdom-Religion
Esoteric in All Ages
HELENA BLAVATSKY

In Pearl of Searching, *the Russian painter Nicholas Roerich depicted a spiritual seeker and his guru in the Himalayas, a magnet for spiritual aspiration.*

A young dance troupe in Singapore points to the Baha'i vision of a united future for humanity.

he perceived in those mountains and placed in his paintings holy figures from many religious traditions. After his death, Helena encouraged students to revere unseen masters from India as well as Jesus. Now a steady stream of Russian pilgrims visit Roerich's mountain home in Kulu, India, seeking to establish the same connection with Indian spirituality that they see in his paintings.

BAHA'I

Universalist beliefs have also manifested in a "new" global religion, the Baha'i faith, which attempts to unite all of humanity in the belief that there is only one God, the foundation of all religions. The Baha'i faith was foreshadowed in Persia in 1844 when a young man called the Bab ("Gate") announced that a new messenger of God to all the peoples of the world would soon appear. Because he proclaimed this message in a Muslim state, where Muhammad was considered the Seal of the Prophets, he was arrested and executed in 1850. Some 22,000 of his followers were reportedly massacred as well. One of his imprisoned followers was Baha'u'llah (1817–1892), a member of an aristocratic Persian family. He was stripped of his worldly goods, tortured, banished to Baghdad, and finally imprisoned in Palestine by the Turks.

From prison, he revealed himself as the messenger proclaimed by the Bab. He wrote letters to the rulers of all nations, asserting that humanity was becoming unified and that a single global civilization was emerging.

Despite vigorous initial persecution, this new faith has by now spread to over five million followers in 233 countries and territories around the world, involving people from a wide variety of racial and ethnic groups. They have no priesthood but they do have their own sacred scriptures, revealed to Baha'u'llah. Baha'is compare this new messenger to previous great prophets, such as Abraham, Moses, Jesus, Muhammad, Krishna, and the Buddha. In fact, they see Baha'u'llah as the fulfillment of the prophecies of all religions. He did not declare himself to be the ultimate messenger, however. Rather, he prophesied that another would follow in a thousand years.

myreligionlab

A New Revelation from the Unifier
BAHA'U'LLAH

The heart of Baha'u'llah's message appears in the *Kitab-i-Iqan* ("The Book of Certitude"). God, Baha'u'llah says, is unknowable. Mere humans cannot understand God's infinite nature with their limited minds. However, God has become known through divine messengers, the founders of the great world religions. All are manifestations of God, pure channels for helping humanity to understand God's will. The spiritual education of humans has been a process of "progressive revelation," said Baha'u'llah. Humanity has been maturing, like a child growing in the ability to grasp complex ideas as it grows in years and passes through grade school and college. Each time a divine messenger appeared, the message was given at levels appropriate to humanity's degree of maturity. Baha'u'llah proclaimed his own message as the most advanced and the one appropriate for this time. It contains the same eternal truths as the earlier revelations, but with some

The Baha'i Model for Governance of the World

One of the most unusual features of the Baha'i faith is its own organization, which it sees as a good model for democratic governance of the whole world. Everywhere that people have converted to Baha'i faith, there is a highly organized framework designed not only to propagate the faith but also to democratize its leadership. Campaigning, electioneering, and nominations are prohibited, thus avoiding the empty promises to voters, corruption, and negative campaigning that tarnish elections in contemporary worldly democracies.

In the Baha'i "administrative order," each local group yearly elects nine or more people to a local Spiritual Assembly. Each local member is asked to pray and meditate and then write down the names of nine adults from the local Baha'i community who seem best qualified to lead the community. The necessary qualities are those of "unquestioned loyalty, of selfless devotion, of a well-trained mind, of recognized ability and mature experience."[20] By this simple and unusual process, Baha'is feel they choose leaders who are mature and humble rather than politically bold and egotistical. By the same process, the Local Spiritual Assemblies elect the National Spiritual Assemblies, and by the same process, the National Spiritual Assemblies choose the nine members of the Universal House of Justice,

seated in Haifa. Baha'is feel that this framework allows both grassroots access to decision-making and a superstructure for efficient international coordination of activities. However, women are not seated at the Universal House of Justice, and this omission is currently the subject of intense debate.

Within these elected groups—and also within business, school, and family settings—Baha'is attempt to reach decisions by a nonadversarial process of "consultation." The point of the process is to investigate truth in depth and to build consensus rather than struggle for power. Participants are enjoined to gather information from as many sources as possible and to be at once truthful and courteous to each other. Any idea once proposed is thereafter considered group property; it does not belong to one person or group, but rather is investigated impartially. As Svetlana Dorzhieva, formerly Executive Secretary of the National Spiritual Assembly of Baha'is of Russia, Georgia, and Armenia, explains: "What is wonderful is that when a person says his opinion, he just forgets that it belonged to him. It is offered and then it is discussed."[21] Attempts are made to reach unanimous consensus, but failing that, a majority vote may be taken. The success of this process is demonstrated in the fact that people from very diverse backgrounds manage to work and worship together.

---

new features, which humanity is now ready to grasp, such as the oneness of all peoples, prophets, and religions, and a program for universal governance for the sake of world peace and social justice. Contemporary Baha'is are active in trying to develop a just order in the world, creating projects such as schools promoting global awareness, the European Business Forum encouraging business ethics, environmental awareness campaigns, and rural development projects.

Baha'i Houses of Worship, which are open to all, have nine doors and a central dome symbolizing the diversity and oneness of humanity. Devotional services include readings from the scriptures of all religions, meditations, unaccompanied singing, and prayers by the Bab, Baha'u'llah, and his successor 'Abdu'l-Baha, his oldest son. 'Abdu'l-Baha describes the unified world that Baha'is envision:

> The world will become the mirror of the Heavenly Kingdom. ... All nations
> will become one, all religions will be unified ... the superstitions caused by races,
> countries, individuals, languages and politics will disappear; and all men will

*attain to life eternal under the shadow of the Lord of Hosts. ... The relations
between the countries, the mingling, union and friendship of the people ...
will reach to such a degree that the human race will be like one family. ...
The light of heavenly love will shine, and the darkness of enmity and
hatred will be dispelled from the world.*[22]

Islam opposes Baha'i as theological heresy, for Baha'i denies that Muhammad
is the final prophet. Baha'i also finds theological legitimacy in religions such as
Hinduism and Buddhism, which Islam does not consider acceptable God-
worshiping traditions of revealed scriptures. Baha'is in Iran have been subjected
to persecution since the inception of the religion, a pattern that increased after
the 1979 revolution and establishment of the Islamic Republic of Iran.

Baha'is' attempts to unite the earth in faith extend into the political sphere,
where they actively support the United Nations' efforts to unify the planet. Their
goal is a unified, peaceful global society built on these principles:

1 The end of prejudice in all forms.
2 Equality for women.
3 Acceptance of the relativity and unity of spiritual truth.
4 Just distribution of wealth.
5 Universal education.
6 The individual responsibility to seek truth.
7 Development of a world federation.
8 Harmony of science and true religion.[23]

Social trends

New religious movements can also be seen as arising from social trends, with or
without connections to previous religions or singular charismatic leadership.
Examples of such general movements that have arisen in the past hundred years
or so include movements furthering racial/ethnic identity, affection for nature,
deep ecology, the "New Age" movement, and self-improvement. Since they are
rooted in present concerns, these may or may not survive into the future. Some
examples are explored below.

ETHNIC IDENTITY: RASTAFARI

As descendents of African slaves in the Americas struggled to build better lives for
themselves, religious ideals developed that mirrored their hopes. In 1895,
Alexander Bedward of the Baptist Free Church in Jamaica prophesied a coming
holocaust in which all the white people would be killed, leaving the Blacks, "the
true people," to celebrate the new world. He sat in his special robes as the predicted date came and went; eventually he was placed in an asylum for the insane. A
more generalized hopeful vision was spread by Marcus Garvey (1887–1940), who
saw a fundamental change in society that would be led by Blacks. Garvey linked
these dreams to the return of Blacks to Africa, from which their ancestors had been
taken as slaves; there they would rebuild a great civilization. A prophecy attributed

Rastafari male musicians carry the message of reasserting Black spiritual and social rights.

to Garvey—"Look to Africa when a black king shall be crowned, for the day of deliverance is near"[24]—was thought to have been realized when Ras (Prince) Tafari of Ethiopia was crowned as Haile Selassie, Emperor of Ethiopia. An elaborate mystique was built up around Haile Selassie as the living God (though neither Selassie nor Garvey shared this view). Hopeful lore was based on interpretations of Selassie's statements and passages from the Old Testament and the New Testament Book of Revelation. Poor Jamaicans (who likened themselves to the Jews in captivity in Babylon) repeatedly prepared to be given free passage back to Africa.

Haile Selassie's reign (until his death in 1974) did nothing to liberate Jamaican Africans, but Blacks in Jamaica nevertheless developed a new religious movement around these ideals. They intend to revive the "Way of the Ancients," their concept of the lost civilization of precolonial Africa, and to free people of African extraction from subservience. "Babylon," the oppressor, is collectively the United States, Britain (the former colonial power in Jamaica), the state of Jamaica, and the Christian Church. In protest against Babylon, Rastafarians wear their hair in long uncombed curls, called "dreadlocks," a lion-like mane symbolizing the natural nonindustrial life. Some give use of marijuana (*ganja*) religious significance as a sacrament. A distinctive music, reggae, evolved as an expression of Black pride, social protest, and Rastafarian millenarian ideals with the legendary Bob Marley as its musical prophet. In many areas the movement has developed mostly through men; they consider women incapable of experiencing Rasta awareness except through their husbands. However, by the end of the twentieth century women had begun to play more significant roles in the movement.

The Rastafari movement spread beyond Jamaica to Blacks and a few whites elsewhere in the Caribbean, North America, Europe, southern Africa, Australia, and New Zealand. It is very localized and diverse. Some Rastas insist that the truths they espouse are not just for people of African descent.

Thus in some places it has been adopted by other ethnic groups such as Native Americans, Indonesians, Maoris, and Thais. And after the Soviet Union fell, during the 1990s a Rasta subculture developed among Slavic youths in some formerly communist states. They adopted reggae music and marijuana and some let their hair grow into dreadlocks, in protest against the values of "Babylon." On the other hand, some black members insist that Rastafari is only for Blacks. For instance, in their Rastafari website www.earthcuture.roots.com, Ras Charles and French Dread write:

> *Rastafari is a movement of black people who know Africa is the birthplace of mankind, all mankind. … We must re-culture ourselves so we can have a sense of pride, in the turning from occidental culture, and taking into ourselves the power of our African culture, which has been hidden from us for so long.*[25]

NATURE SPIRITUALITY

If religion is defined in the broadest sense as that which ties us back to the sacred, one of the strongest trends in our time is that of the religion of nature. Many who are experiencing a reconnection with the natural world do not think of this path as a religion, for it has no clear structure. It seems to be growing spontaneously, cropping up here and there in diverse forms.

myreligionlab
Witchcraft
DIANE MARIECHILD

Reinvention of old practices   Some who seek to practice a nature-oriented spirituality look to the past for models. This trend is sometimes called **Neo-Paganism**, with reference to pre-Christian spiritual ways that are thought to have been practiced in Europe. Some call their way "Witchcraft," despite the negative connotations associated with this label. As Starhawk, minister of the Covenant of the Goddess, explains:

> *Modern Witches are thought to be members of a kooky cult, … lacking the depth, the dignity and seriousness of purpose of a true religion. But Witchcraft is a religion, perhaps the oldest religion extant in the West … and it is very different from all the so-called great religions. The Old Religion, as we call it, is closer in spirit to Native American traditions or to the shamanism of the Arctic. It is not based on dogma or a set of beliefs, nor on scriptures or a sacred book revealed by a great man. Witchcraft takes its teachings from nature, and reads inspiration in the movements of the sun, moon, and stars, the flight of birds, the slow growth of trees, and the cycles of the seasons.*[26]

Some Neo-Pagans try to reproduce some of the sacred ways of earlier European peoples, such as the Celts in the British Isles or the ancient Scandinavians. Reconstructing these ways is difficult, for they were largely oral rather than written traditions. After religions such as Christianity were firmly established, the remaining practitioners of the old ways were often tortured and killed as witches and blamed for social ills such as the plague. They were said to be in league with the devil against God, but the pagan pantheons had no devil—he was introduced by the Jewish–Christian–Muslim traditions.

The way known as **Wicca** can be partly traced to the writings of Gerald Gardner in England in the 1940s. He claimed to have been initiated into a secret coven of witches who allowed him to write about some of their practices as well as their historical persecutions by Christians, and added other rituals and "magickal" practices from various sources to replace those which had been lost because of the isolation and secrecy of the few remaining covens.

Another version of the attempt to return to old models is **Goddess spirituality**. Archaeological evidence from many cultures around the world was reinterpreted during the twentieth century as suggesting that worship of a female high goddess was originally widespread. Although there were, and are now, cultures that did not ascribe gender or hierarchy or personality to the divine, some that did may have seen the highest deity as a female.

A reverent address to Ishtar, an important Mesopotamian goddess, dating from some time between the eighteenth and seventh centuries BCE, suggests some of the powers ascribed to her:

> *Unto Her who renders decision, Goddess of all things. Unto the Lady of Heaven and Earth who receives supplication; Unto Her who hears petition, who entertains prayer; Unto the compassionate Goddess who loves righteousness; Ishtar the Queen, who suppresses all that is confused. To the Queen of Heaven, the Goddess of the Universe, the One who walked in terrible Chaos and brought life by the Law of Love; And out of Chaos brought us harmony.[27]*

Temples and images that may have been devoted to worship of the goddess have been found in almost every Neolithic and early historic archaeological site in Europe and West Asia. She was often symbolically linked with water, serpents, birds, eggs, spirals, the moon, the womb, the vulva, the magnetic currents of the earth, psychic powers, and the eternal creation and renewal of life. In these agricultural cultures women frequently held strong social positions. Hereditary lineages were often traced through the mother, and women were honored as priestesses, healers, agricultural inventors, counselors, prophetesses, and sometimes warriors. Goddess spirituality has thus been adopted by some contemporary feminists as their preferred religious way.

Scholars are now trying to piece together not only the possible characteristics of goddess worship, but also the circumstances of its demise. In Europe and West Asia, worship of the goddess may have been suppressed throughout the third and second millennia BCE by invading Indo-European groups in which dominant males worshiped a supreme male deity, often described as a storm god residing on a mountain and bringing light (seen as the good) into the darkness (portrayed as bad and associated with the female).

In replacing the goddess, patriarchal groups may also have devalued the "feminine" aspect of religion—the receptive, intuitive, ecstatic mystical communion that was perhaps allowed freer expression in goddess worship. Women have been the major

The Goddess and Women's Spirituality
CHARLENE SPRETNAK

An early female figurine, representing the Great Mother or Goddess (Halaf style, c.4500 BCE, Paris, Louvre).

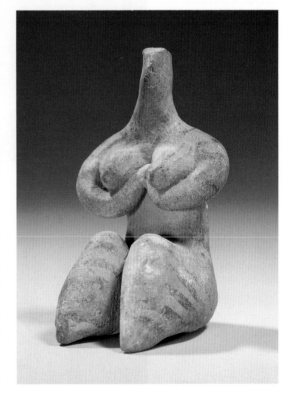

victims of this devaluation of the feminine, but there has also been distrust of mystics of both sexes.

To revive appreciation of the Goddess, including the goddess within themselves, as well as women's spirituality, contemporary women have pieced together and invented rituals for both individual and group use. Diane Rae Schulz writes in *Awakened Woman* e-magazine:

> *The practice of goddess spirituality can take many forms, from constructing a small altar or meditation space in one's home, to participating in ritual circles with other women, to large seasonal celebrations which include men and children. My first experience of the practice of goddess spirituality was an all women's Samhain (Halloween) spiral dance. The ritual involved meditation on the goddess Hecate, the dark aspect of the triple goddess, the goddess of death and rebirth, and it culminated in a whirling spiral dance—scores of women of all ages holding hands and singing, weaving in and out, re-enacting an ancient celebration of the power of women. I left the gathering feeling uplifted, energized, and reassured of women's unique spiritual unity.[28]*

Yet other people seeking to return to old models are members of new religions known collectively as **ethnic religions**. These have emerged since the fall of communism as revivals of pre-Christian ethnic traditions in countries such as Russia and in eastern Europe. In Estonia, pagan rituals are now celebrated in a rather happy, mocking fashion as a form of entertainment. In other places such as the

Russian Neo-Pagans create a ritual celebration of the summer solstice in a forest outside Moscow.

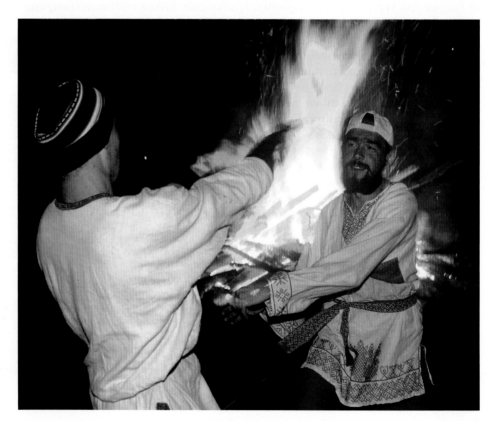

Udmurt Republic in Russia, faith in pre-Christian prayer and ceremony had been maintained at least up to communist times, only partially replaced by Christian worship. Special groves were reserved for communal prayers to the Progenitress in summer and late autumn. Now that freedom of religion is permitted, people are returning to the traditional agrarian rites for the earth's fertility and human links with the cosmic rhythms and energies. Some members of ethnic religions question why they should revere the myths of West Asian desert tribes, as in Judeo-Christian tradition, rather than the ethnic myths of their own ancestors and native lands. Though newly revived on the basis of folklore, mythology, and ethnic pride and given the label "ethnofuturism," the antecedents of these ways may be very ancient. Images of animal guardians have been found in peat bogs that date back as far as the eighth millennium BCE.

Teachers from earth-affirming religions that were never totally destroyed, such as certain Native American sacred ways, are highly valued as guides to worship for the natural world. From them, contemporary seekers have learned to use traditions, such as vision quests, sweat lodges, and medicine wheels. But the traditions are complex, requiring lifelong training, and are interwoven with ways of life that have passed or developed in different environments. Neo-Pagans from non-native backgrounds usually cannot experience them in their original fullness. What remains is the intent: to honor and cooperate with the natural forces, to celebrate the circle of life rather than destroy it.

In the absence of sure knowledge of ancient traditions, Neo-Pagans often develop new forms of group ritual. Usually they are held outside, with the trees and rocks and waters, the sun, moon, and stars as the altars of the sacred. Speakers may invoke the pantheistic Spirit within all life or the invisible spirits of the place. At ceremonies dedicated to a phase of the moon or the change of the seasons, worshipers may be reminded of how their lives are interwoven with, and affected by, the natural rhythms. Prayers and ritual may be offered for the healing of the earth, the creatures, or the people.

Certain spots have traditionally been known as places of high energy, as indicated in Chapter 2, and these are often used for ceremonies and less structured sacred experiences. Ancient ceremonial sites in the British Isles, such as Stonehenge and Glastonbury Tor, draw a new breed of tour groups wanting to experience the atmosphere of these places.

Neo-Pagan festivals are popular gatherings where participants shed their usual identities and perhaps their clothes, create temporary "kinship groups," and enjoy activities such as ritual fires, storytelling, dancing, drumming, and workshops on subjects ranging from astrology to old methods of herbal healing.

Deep ecology In addition to groups that are looking to replicate or reinvent past ways of earth-centered worship, many people in nontraditional societies are now seeking new ways of connecting themselves with the cosmos. What is called deep ecology is the experience of oneness with the natural world. By contrast, most Western religions have cast humans as controllers of the natural world, of a different order of being than bears and flowers, mountains and rivers. Australian deep ecologist John Seed refers to this attitude as **anthropocentrism**—"human chauvinism, the idea that humans are the crown of creation, the source of all value, the measure of all things."[29]

> *What is man without the beasts? If all the beasts were gone, men would die from a great loneliness of spirit. For whatever happens to the beasts soon happens to the man. ... The earth does not belong to man; man belongs to the earth. This we know. All things are connected like the blood which unites one family.*
>
> *Attributed to Chief Seattle[30]*

During the twentieth century, many people came to a new awareness of our planetary home when they first saw it photographed from space. Rather than a globe divided by natural political boundaries, it appeared as a beautiful being, its surface mostly covered by oceans, wreathed in clouds, floating in the darkness of space. Some scientists have taken up this metaphor of the earth as a being and are finding evidence of its scientific plausibility. Biogeochemist James Lovelock (b. 1919) proposed that the biosphere ("the entire range of living matter on Earth, from whales to viruses, and from oaks to algae") plus the earth's atmosphere, oceans, and soil can be viewed as "a single living entity, capable of manipulating the Earth's atmosphere to suit its overall needs and endowed with faculties and powers far beyond those of its constituent parts."[31] Lovelock named this complex, self-adjusting entity Gaia, after the Greek name for the Earth Goddess. In elaborations of his Gaia hypothesis, Lovelock emphasizes the "feminine" and divine characteristics of this being:

Any living organism a quarter as old as the Universe itself and still full of vigour is as near immortal as we ever need to know. She is of this Universe and, conceivably, a part of God. On Earth she is the source of life everlasting and is alive now; she gave birth to humankind and we are part of her.[32]

A corollary to the Gaia hypothesis is the concept that humans are becoming the global brain of the planet, its mode of conscious evolution. In the "body" of Gaia, the tropical rainforests function as the liver and/or lungs, the oceans as the circulatory system, and so on. As the evolving brain of the planet, we are becoming conscious of the dangers our activities pose to these other parts of "our body." Peter Russell, author of *The Global Brain*, warns that we have little time to become fully conscious of our potential destructiveness, our connectedness to everything else, and to take appropriate action to forestall environmental disaster:

As a species we are facing our final examination; ... it is in fact an intelligence test—a test of our true intelligence as a species. In essence we are being asked to let go of our self-centred thinking and egocentric behaviour. We are being asked to become psychologically mature, to free ourselves from the clutches of this limited identity, and express our creativity in ways which benefit us all.[33]

Those who perceive a oneness of all life may be inspired to take political action to protect other members of the earth's body. Many support "green" political agendas on behalf of the environment. In Australia, Britain, and the northwest coast of the United States, people have chained themselves to giant trees to try to keep loggers from cutting them down. Julia Butterfly Hill spent 736 days living high in a 1,000-year-old redwood tree to protect it from loggers. She braved winter storms, high winds, and harassment by helicopter, refusing to come down until an agreement was negotiated with the logging company to protect the tree and the surrounding virgin forest. She was sustained by spirituality. As she wrote:

> One day, through my prayers, an overwhelming amount of love started flowing into me, filling up the dark hole that threatened to consume me. I suddenly realized that what I was feeling was the love of the Earth, the love of Creation. Every day we, as a species, do so much to destroy Creation's ability to give us life. But that Creation continues to do everything in its power to give us life anyway. And that's true love.[34]

Similarly, in 1974, the women and children of Reni, a Himalayan village, wrapped themselves around trees to protect them from woodcutters seeking wood for the cities. They knew that the trees' roots were like hands that kept the hillside from washing away, that they shaded the plants they used for medicine and homes for the animals and birds. They said, "The trees are our brothers and sisters."[35] Although some view such actions as romantically naive and hopeless, the "Tree Hugging" movement grew to such proportions in northern India that the government banned commercial woodcutting in Uttar Pradesh.

NEW AGE SPIRITUALITY

A great variety of spiritual movements developed in the West in the 1970s and 1980s that drew on many characteristics of other "new" movements mentioned already—progressive millennialism, interest in the supernatural and "channeled" revelations from invisible beings, reverence for nature, and universalism. In addition, they are often characterized by a quest for self-improvement but in highly individualistic, anti-institutional formats. Collectively, these ways, rather than being called "religions," are therefore often called "New Age spiritual movements."

A special working group in the Vatican studying New Age groups concluded that they are among the "contemporary signs of the perennial human search for happiness, meaning, and salvation," which people from mainstream institutions may not have found in their own religion due to clergy's lack of attention to such central spiritual themes as "the importance of man's spiritual dimension and its integration with the whole of life."[36] As promoted in books and workshops, this amorphous but widespread movement anticipates that a network of personally transformed individuals will eventually lead to the transformation of the planet. Author Marianne Williamson voiced this hope in 1994:

> A mass movement is afoot in the world today, spiritual in nature and radical in its implications. After decades of declining influence on the affairs of the world, there is once again a widespread consideration of spiritual principles as an antidote to the pain of our times. Like flowers growing up through pieces of broken cement, signs of hope and faith appear everywhere. These signs reflect the light of a transcendent force at the center of things, present in our lives in a corrective and even miraculous manner, a light we can reach personally through internal work of a devotional nature. We are experiencing now an alteration of collective consciousness, centered not in government or science or religion per se. It is the rising up of our true divine nature, a reassertion of God in the consciousness of modern man.[37]

The roots of New Age spiritual movements are many, including Western esotericism, Spiritualism, Theosophy, astrology, and introduction of the Eastern religions to the West. Another antecedent is found in discoveries about spiritual healing, developed into a full-fledged religious movement by Mary Baker Eddy (1821–1910) as Christian Science. In her *Science and Health with Key to the Scriptures*, Eddy proposed that negative inner states such as hatred, fear, selfishness, and envy obscure one's relationship with God's love. When they are surrendered, healing occurs naturally as one's true spiritual being emerges. Only God is real; the physical body, with its ailments, is not. Christian Scientists usually refuse medical treatment, turning instead to prayerful affirmations.

A related trend is New Thought, which emphasizes the power of positive thinking. This diverse movement spread widely due to the efforts of Emma Curtis Hopkins (1849–1925). At first such groups were quite open to female leadership, but during the twentieth century some tended to revert to patriarchal male structures, with women only in supporting roles. Some are based on the teachings of a single charismatic leader, with organizations that support dissemination of their teachings without church buildings, a priesthood, or other features of organized religions.

One of the manifestations of New Thought that has proved relatively long-lived is the Unity School of Christianity, which dates back to 1886. Its inspirational publication, *The Daily Word*, is now available in twelve languages. Like many other new religious movements, the Unity School makes extensive use of the Internet for sharing its teachings and practices. On *The Daily Word*'s website, each day a different positive affirmation is posted for reflection, such as this one:

> *Life-giving energy flows throughout my body. I am renewed.*
> *Divine energy flows in and through God's creations, renewing, restoring,*
> *uplifting. I see this energy in the exuberance of a child, in the beauty of a flower*
> *blossom and in the vibrant display of autumn's colors. I feel it in the warmth*
> *of the sun's rays, the freshness of a gentle breeze.*
> *As I align my thoughts with life and wholeness, I feel divine energy in*
> *my own body as well. I am in the flow of life-giving energy, and it is in me. ...*
> *I am renewed in mind, body and spirit, Thank You, God.*[38]

New Age spirituality is often mystical, favoring direct communion with the unseen. The Findhorn community is a striking example. One of its leaders, Dorothy Maclean, studied with Sufi masters, learning how to receive "inner guidance," before joining with Eileen and Peter Caddy in developing Findhorn, a transformation of desolate dunes on the coast of Scotland into a lush farming community. Dorothy's role was to receive communications from the energies that she called the plant *devas*, after the Hindu term for the invisible "shining ones." Dorothy developed a cooperative relationship with the *devas*, asking for their "advice" on matters such as what nutrients the plants needed. The Findhorn community receives thousands of visitors every year, has its own eco-village, and hosts workshops on many topics designed to elevate human consciousness.

The main thrust of the 1970s and 1980s New Age movement was the belief that a new era was arising in which poverty, war, racism, and despair would give way to a new feeling of global human community, with peace, harmony, and happiness prevailing. Since this was not to be accomplished through any religious or political organization, the idea developed that groups of people could act as receivers for positive cosmic energies so that their effects would create a "planetary consciousness" that would spread to the rest of the world. This belief was strengthened by widespread distribution of a book, *The Hundredth Monkey*, which described what later turned out to be a false report that monkeys on a Japanese island were affected by behavioral changes of monkeys on another island. Many New Age groups thus gathered to receive the cosmic energies and try to create enough critical mass to change the world.

The longed-for era of peace and harmony did not emerge, and talk of a "New Age" gradually faded away. However, the many professionals who were making a living as workshop leaders, holistic health practitioners, publishers of New Age literature, and the like were still on the scene. Collectively they shifted to emphasizing transformation in individual consciousness, perhaps coupled with the longer-term goal of global transformation.

While part of the New Age movement lost its millennial nature and focused instead on personal growth and the search for mystical communion through techniques such as meditation, a different millennial thrust developed in some circles: the idea that gradually "higher consciousness" will spread among enough humans for others to be drawn into the same enlightened worldview and thus the whole world will "ascend." This idea was popularized by the bestselling 1993 novel by James Redfield, *The Celestine Prophecy*, which claimed to be true and presented "nine key insights into life itself—insights each human being is predicted to grasp sequentially, one insight then another, as we move toward a completely spiritual culture on earth." The Ninth Insight is this:

> As we humans continue to increase our vibration, an amazing thing will begin to happen. Whole groups of people, once they reach a certain level, will suddenly become invisible to those who are still vibrating at a lower level. … It will signal that we are crossing the barrier between this life and the other world from which we came and to which we go after death. This conscious crossing is the path shown by the Christ. … At some point everyone will vibrate highly enough so that we can walk into heaven, in our same form.[39]

Sequels to the novel followed, including *The Tenth Insight*, in which spiritually evolved people create a new global spiritual culture.

Sociologists note that many people who participate in nature rituals and New Age movements are nomads, dabbling here and there without any deep commitment to what Stark and Bainbridge called "audience cults." In countries allowing freedom of religious choice, they may wander through a growing supermarket of spiritual offerings, taking a bit here and there according to their needs of the moment. Sandra Duarte de Souza describes "spiritual nomadism" in contemporary Brazil, where most people remain nominally Christian but many are also attracted to nature-oriented New Age groups. As opposed to a "radical change of life, marking the biography of the converted forever and demanding his faithfulness, … the idea of 'religious transit' admits the 'walk through' several religions, does not demand intestinal changes in the way of life of the 'transilient,' and exempts or attenuates the commitment."[40] Of course, the same can be said of established religions—that many people belong to them without deeply transformational inner commitment.

myreligionlab

A Course in Miracles Summarized
HELEN SCHUCMAN

Opposition to new religious movements

Throughout history, new religious movements have met with opposition from previously organized religions, which perceive them as threats to their own strength or brand them as heresies.

Baha'is claim that after the 1979 establishment of the Islamic Republic of Iran persecution of Baha'is has become official government policy. According to the Baha'i website, since that time:

> *more than 200 Baha'is have been executed or killed, hundreds more have been imprisoned, and tens of thousands have been deprived of jobs, pensions, businesses, and educational opportunities. Formal Baha'i administration had to be suspended, and holy places, shrines, and cemeteries have been confiscated, vandalized, or destroyed.[41]*

In Russia, various foreign-based new religious movements are fighting for freedom of worship against a 1997 law, passed at the behest of the Russian Orthodox Church, which restricts the activities of groups that were newly introduced to Russia. Lawyers defending these groups have had some success in court cases with reference to Jehovah's Witnesses and organizations sponsored by the Unification Movement.

With or without prompting by established religions, nations may attempt to suppress new religious movements. China has taken strong measures to stamp out Falun Gong. As described in Chapter 6, it is one of many movements based on traditional Daoist Qigong energy practices, but with a living charismatic teacher, Li Hongzhi, who now lives in exile in New York City, from where he has spread Falun Gong to thirty countries. In 1999 the Chinese government characterized the movement as an "evil cult." When approximately 10,000 people staged a silent protest next to the compound of the Communist Party leadership in Beijing, the government responded by banning Falun Gong, alleging that it had "been engaged in illegal activities, advocating superstition and spreading fallacies, hoodwinking people, inciting and creating disturbances, and jeopardizing social stability."[42] Subsequent protestors were reportedly jailed and beaten, followed by wave upon wave of peaceful protests by members who met the same fate. Some are said to have died from torture while in police custody. Claims of human rights abuses of Falun Gong practitioners continue. But the movement still persists in China and other countries, and practitioners claim that Falun Gong has brought them physical healing, inner peace, and answers to the central questions of life.

In addition to negative reactions from governments and previously organized religions, new religious movements usually meet with opposition from family members of those who join. They may be worried about violence that has been associated with some new religious movements and widely reported in the media. A catastrophic example occurred in Waco, Texas, in 1993, when a community of Branch Dravidians was besieged by federal officials. As FBI agents moved into the compound to end the fifty-one-day siege, a fire broke out and approximately eighty of the Branch Dravidians died as the fire engulfed their compound. The Branch Dravidians had been anticipating the millennium and trying to obey what they understood as God's will, preparing for the end of the world as prophesied by their messiah, David Koresh. There is a widespread feeling that this tragedy might have been avoided if law enforcement agencies concerned about weapons allegedly stored in the compound had not been so provocative. Another spectacular violent incident occurred in 1995, when members of the Aum Shinrikyo movement were accused of launching a poison gas attack on the Tokyo subway. Media reports described the movement as a doomsday cult making chemical weapons under the leadership of Shoko Asahara.

Religion-related violence is not limited to new religious movements. As we will see in the last chapter, religious extremists who claim to be followers of major established religions are resorting to violence in many parts of the globe. Are the followers of new religious movements different? Whether old or new, if movements are sincerely expecting imminent world changes and have isolated themselves to prepare for the end, they distance themselves from other points of view. In isolation and group solidarity, seemingly irrational beliefs—such as the apocalyptic scenario of the biblical book of Revelation—may seem to make perfect sense.

In addition to isolation and group support in their beliefs, religious movements may turn violent in response to hostility from the surrounding culture. This response is called "deviance amplification" in the literature. Specialists in new religious movements, Massimo Introvigne and Jean-François Mayer, have observed that when some groups perceive threats from the outside they encourage their members to feel that they are not of this world. When under attack from the outside and also perhaps shaken by defections of disillusioned members, they may conclude that suicide is their only good option. People enter the group of

Falun Gong members doing their meditation practices.

their own free will, but when the trend toward suicide or violence becomes apparent they may find it difficult to leave if the leader is extremely charismatic or even coercive. Families of those who join unfamiliar religious movements may thus fear that they may be dangerous.

There is also concern that new religious movements may cause psychological damage, especially to vulnerable young people. In the United States, the "anti-cult" movement employed special agents who captured and "deprogrammed" followers of new religions, at the request of their parents. However, the claim that members of new religious movements had been "brainwashed" has been largely discredited. As Professor Catherine Wessinger notes, mainstream social and religious institutions all practice some kind of indoctrination in which people's thinking is molded. This process is also used by parents in socializing their children. According to the research on new religious movements, Wessinger writes:

> Usually the processes utilized by members of NRMs to attract and socialize converts are not different from those used in mainstream families and institutions. Belief in brainwashing offers a simplistic explanation for why people adopt unconventional beliefs. It obscures the fact that people adopt alternative beliefs because those beliefs make sense to them, and that people join groups because those groups offer them benefits. [The new religious movements that she examined] all regarded people in mainstream society as being brainwashed by television, the media, educational institutions, and by the values of materialistic society. They believed that their respective groups taught the truth as opposed to the delusions of the brainwashed people in external society. In most cases, the members willingly undertook the discipline and lifestyle of their unconventional religion, which they believed would lead to achieving salvation, their ultimate concern.[43]

In addition to the discrediting of the brainwashing theory of why people join new religious movements, the coercive deprogramming techniques of the anti-cult movement have been deemed illegal in themselves. The Cult Awareness Network went bankrupt in 1996 after one of its deprogramming victims won a multimillion dollar damage suit against it. Nevertheless, what are now called "countercult" activities continue in the hands of other organizations, such as the American Family Foundation. Countercult activities are also rampant on the Internet, which is now a hotbed of allegations against new religious movements. These can be posted by anyone, without any editorial control.

There are also governmental efforts to eliminate or control new religious movements in Europe, where governments are struggling with issues of religious freedom versus public safety. France is home to hundreds of new religious groups, including several that have committed mass suicide. There has been concern that some are using a religious front to carry on illegal businesses or extort money from gullible followers. Some are neo-fascist groups in the guise of medieval cults whose intentions seem to involve the propagation of white supremacy ideas and hatred of immigrants.

The French government has enacted secularizing legislation that inhibits the practice of many mainstream religions, in addition to countercult legislation and police scrutiny of groups such as Mormons, Jehovah's Witnesses, and Scientology, as well as evangelical and charismatic Christian groups. In Italy, by contrast, the Supreme Court in 1997 overruled a lower court judgment that had defined "religion" only as Judaism or Christianity; nonprofit recognition and tax exemption was extended to Scientology by the court ruling. Germany grants tax-exempt status only to a few long-established religions, excluding not only new religious movements but also Islam, Hinduism, and Buddhism.

Will new religious movements last?

All of the major religions we have examined were once new and were once resisted by more entrenched institutions. Will any of today's new religious movements last more than a few generations? Those who study the sociology of religion are researching the secular factors that seem to predispose a new religious movement to become widespread and longlasting. One of these is a balance between similarities to existing beliefs (making it attractive and nonthreatening to potential converts) and differences compelling enough for people to convert.

A second factor is organization, personal commitment, and bonds between members that will survive the death of the prophet and the original followers. This factor includes efforts to propagate the new religion, including hagiographies —idealized accounts of the life of the founder designed to interest new members. These may diverge from the known facts, a common occurrence within the process of popular myth-making.

A third factor is the social setting: Times of great social change, places that allow freedom of choice in matters of religion, and societies with fragmented relationships between people are most conducive to the recruitment of new members. Fourth is the status of prevailing religions; if they have become merely institutional with little spiritual life they are susceptible to being supplanted by more vibrant new faiths. Fifth is the younger generations: Children must be continually born or recruited into the faith, taught its values, and given responsible parts to play in keeping the faith alive.

The spiritual aspects of new religions are also of major importance but they cannot easily be quantified. Among these are the genuine spirituality of the founder or spreader of the message, and the ability of the new teachings and their presentation to capture people's hearts, change their lives, motivate them to act collectively, and give them the courage to face social opposition. Finally, there is the necessity of divine assistance, in the parlance of theistic religions, or alliance with absolute truth, from the point of view of nontheistic religions.

myreligionlab
After the
Founder's Death
J. GORDON MELTON

Suggested reading

Barker, Eileen, *New Religious Movements: A Practical Introduction*, London: Her Majesty's Stationery Office, 1989. A sociological study on the effects of new religious movements on people's lives.

Blavatsky, H. P., *The Key to Theosophy*, Los Angeles: The United Lodge of Theosophists, 1920. A wide-ranging survey of esoterica from many of the world's religions.

Bromley, David G. and Phillip E. Hammond, eds, *The Future of New Religious Movements*, Macon, Georgia: Mercer University Press, 1987. Interesting sociological analyses of the likelihood of long-run success of some contemporary movements.

Bryant, M. Darrol and Donald W. Dayton, *The Coming Kingdom, Essays in American Millennialism and Eschatology*, Barrytown, New York: International Religious Foundation,

1983. Studies of Christianity-based movements, such as Jehovah's Witnesses and Mormons, which foretell a dramatic coming of the Kingdom of God on earth.

Cleary, Thomas and Sartaz Aziz, *Twilight Goddess: Spiritual Feminism and Feminine Spirituality*, Boston: Shambhala, 2002. Explorations of feminine principles and Goddess worship in a variety of religions.

Daschke, Dereck and Michael Ashcraft, *New Religious Movements: A Documentary Reader*, New York: New York University Press, 2005. New religious movements speak for themselves in these excerpts from founders and followers.

Dawson, Lorne L., *Comprehending Cults: The Sociology of New Religious Movements*, Oxford: Oxford University Press, 1998. Sociological study of the emergence and members of new religious movements, and predictors of violent tendencies.

Dawson, Lorne L., *Cults and New Religious Movements: A Reader*, Oxford: Blackwell Publishing, 2003. Original source material from a variety of new religious movements.

Gaver, Jessyca Russell, *The Baha'i Faith: Dawn of a New Day*, New York: Hawthorn Books, Inc., 1967. The history and beliefs of Baha'is, in appreciative detail.

Hall, John R., Sylvaine Trinh, Philip Schuyler, eds, *Apocalypse Observed: Religious Movements, Social Order and Violence in North America, Europe, and Japan*, London: Routledge, 2000. Articles analyzing situations within which violent new religious movements have developed.

Melton, J. Gordon, *The Church of Scientology*, Salt Lake City, Utah: Signature Books, 2000. A scholar analyzes the development of Scientology as a movement to clear the mind, a church, and a social service organization, and describes controversies it has faced.

Melton, J. Gordon, and Christopher Partridge, *New Religions: A Guide*, Oxford: Oxford University Press, 2004. Over 200 groups and new religious movements are described according to their roots in older traditions or New Age alternatives.

Miller, Timothy, ed., *When Prophets Die: The Postcharismatic Fate of New Religious Movements*, Albany, New York: State University of New York Press, 1991. Contemporary case studies of how the followers of strong founders have or have not succeeded in keeping the faith alive.

Miller, Timothy, *America's Alternative Religions*, Albany: State University of New York Press, 1995. A lengthy survey of the major alternative traditions in America, with chapters written by scholars specializing in specific groups.

Plaskow, Judith, and Carol Christ, eds, *Weaving the Visions: New Patterns in Feminist Spirituality*, San Francisco: HarperCollins, 1989. Inclusive, goddess, feminist, and womanist perspectives from several religions.

Rinehart, Robin, *One Lifetime, Many Lives: The Experience of Modern Hindu Hagiography*, Atlanta, Georgia: Scholars Press/The American Academy of Religions, 1999. A profound study of devotees' approaches to chronicling the life and significance of their guru after his death, reinventing him over time.

Seed, John, Joanna Macy, Pat Fleming, Arne Naess, *Thinking Like a Mountain: Towards a Council of All Beings*, Philadelphia: New Society Publishers, 1988. Some of the leaders of the deep ecology movement offer a collection of thoughts and exercises leading one into the experience of kinship with all life.

Starhawk, *The Spiral Dance: A Rebirth of the Ancient Religion of the Great Goddess*, San Francisco and London: Harper and Row, 1979, 1999. A lyrical, experimental introduction to the interweaving of the God and Goddess principles.

Stark, Rodney and William Sims Bainbridge, *The Future of Religion: Secularization, Revival, and Cult Formation*, Berkeley, California: University of California Press, 1985. Includes a sociological classification of religous groups in relation to their broader environment.

Wessinger, Catherine, *How the Millennium Comes Violently: From Jonestown to Heaven's Gate*, New York: Seven Bridges Press, 2000. Develops the theory that violence is catalyzed by certain types of interactions.

Key terms

apocalypse The dramatic end of the present age.

apostasy The accusation of abandonment of religious principles.

cult Any religion that focuses on worship of a particular person or deity.

ethnic religions New religions that emerged since the fall of communism as revivals of pre-Christian ethnic traditions in eastern Europe and Russia.

Goddess spirituality Worship of a female high goddess in ancient times, now revived in many places.

millennium One thousand years, a term used in Christianity and certain newer religions for a hoped-for period of 1,000 years of holiness and happiness, with Christ ruling the earth, as prophesied in the Book of Revelation.

Neo-Paganism Nature-oriented spirituality referring to pre-Christian sacred ways.

orisa Yoruba term for a deity.

rapture Nineteenth-century belief amongst some Christians, using Paul's letter to the Thessalonians, that Christians would be caught up in clouds to meet Jesus when he returned to earth.

Santeria The combination of African and Christian practices that developed in Cuba.

sect A subgroup within a larger tradition.

syncretism A form of religion in which otherwise differing traditions are blended.

Wicca Neo-Pagan sect of a secret coven of witches traced to the writings of Gerald Gardner in England in the 1940s.

Review questions

1. Define and give an example of a new religion, a cult, a sect, an audience cult, a client cult, and a cult movement.
2. What are the common themes and the differences among nature spirituality, deep ecology, and New Age spirituality? Give examples of each.
3. Define "syncretism" and give at least two examples of syncretic religions.

Discussion questions

1. Describe and compare the arguments made by those who advocate tolerance for new religious movements and those who believe they should not be tolerated.
2. Do you think that any legal limits should be placed on new religions? If so, by what criteria? If not, why?
3. Can you envision qualities and beliefs that would constitute a positive new religion?

Additional Internet resources

Center for the Study of New Religions http://www.cesnur.org

Cults http://religioustolerance.org/cultmenu.htm

Hartford Institute http://www.hirr.hartsem.edu/denom/new_religious_movements.html

Online Texts about Cults and New Religions http://www.skepsis.nl/onlinetexts.html

myreligionlab

For further activities and resources, including access to MyReligionLibrary, please visit MyReligionLab at www.myreligionlab.com

KEY TOPICS

• GLOBALIZATION 500

• SECULARISM 501

• RELIGIOUS
  PLURALISM 502

• RELIGION IN
  POLITICS 507

• INTERFAITH
  MOVEMENT 510

• RELIGION AND
  SOCIAL ISSUES 517

• RELIGION AND
  MATERIALISM 522

• RELIGION AND
  THE FUTURE OF
  HUMANITY 523

CHAPTER 13

RELIGION IN THE TWENTY-FIRST CENTURY

In the twenty-first century, the global landscape is a patchwork of faiths. Religious expressions are heading in various directions at the same time, and political conflicts involving religions are assuming great importance on the world scene. Religious perspectives and influence are being sought in the effort to solve pressing global challenges. Therefore, as we conclude this survey of religions as living, changing movements, an overview of religion is necessary to gain a sense of how religion is affecting human life now and what impact it may have in the future.

Globalization

Human factors in the global landscape are not what they once were. In contrast to earlier centuries, in which regions were relatively isolated from each other, two major world wars and other violent conflicts, technological advances, and population shifts have brought us into closer contact. Our world has been "shrinking" through increasing urbanization (over half of all people now live in cities) and globalization. Primarily through markets and businesses, regional and national economies have become part of an interconnected global network. Cultural and social connectivity is also increasing, through technological innovations such as the Internet and air travel, political alliances such as the European Union, and the entertainment industry.

Global integration has thus far been largely a one-way process, with Western ways dominating and other cultures and societies tending to be submerged. The 2008 financial meltdown in American banks threatened economies and jobs around the globe. Over eighty percent of all websites are in English, particularly American English. Television programming tends to follow the models created in the United States of quick-bite newscasts and popular series such as *Who Wants to be a Millionaire?* And an estimated eighty-three percent of the film offerings in Latin America and fifty percent in Japan consist of Hollywood movies.[1]

Intermixing or overlaying of cultures is also occurring because of immigration. The United States was built on the basis of immigration from various countries and has historically been known as a "melting pot." Political violence and natural disasters continue to send people far from their homelands in search of refuge.

Oppressed in Tibet, Tibetan Buddhists have established a new homeland in India, and lamas are being requested to give *dharma* teachings in many countries. Violence in Iraq, Afghanistan, Sri Lanka, Sudan, and elsewhere is increasing the numbers of refugees seeking asylum in other countries, with the United States, Canada, France, Italy, and the United Kingdom being favored destinations. These countries and others such as Australia and Malaysia are also continuing to receive immigrants who leave their homes in hopes of economic gain.

Secularism

Until the Iranian revolution in 1979, which brought Islam to the fore as a potent social force, there was a common assumption by Western intellectuals that "Europe's past is the world's future." That is, just as many Europeans had lost interest in religion since the Enlightenment (see Chapter 1), the whole world would eventually secularize. This assumption that religion would become irrelevant in people's lives was shared by capitalism, communism, and liberalism.

Charles Taylor, Professor of Philosophy at McGill University, describes three forms of Western secularism. One refers to "public spaces":

These have been allegedly emptied of God, or of any reference to ultimate reality. Or taken from another side, as we function within various spheres of activity— economic, political, cultural, educational, professional, recreation—the norms and principles we follow, the deliberations we engage in, generally don't refer us to God or to any religious beliefs; the considerations we act on are internal to the "rationality" of each sphere—maximum gain within the economy, the greatest

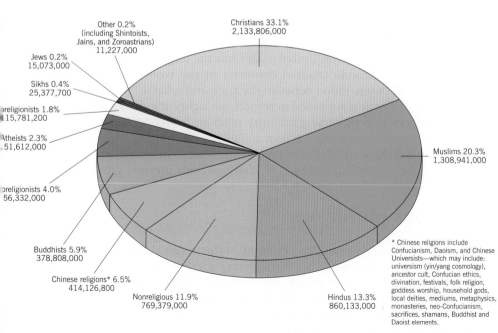

Other 0.2%
(including Shintoists,
Jains, and Zoroastrians)
11,227,000

Christians 33.1%
2,133,806,000

Jews 0.2%
15,073,000

Sikhs 0.4%
25,377,700

oreligionists 1.8%
15,781,200

Atheists 2.3%
51,612,000

oreligionists 4.0%
56,332,000

Muslims 20.3%
1,308,941,000

Buddhists 5.9%
378,808,000

Chinese religions* 6.5%
414,126,800

Nonreligious 11.9%
769,379,000

Hindus 13.3%
860,133,000

This chart shows current followers of the world's religions. Percentages of the world's population following each religion or none, and approximate numbers of followers are based on statistics in the Encyclopaedia Britannica 2006 Book of the Year, *London, EB, 2006, p. 282.*

* Chinese religions include Confucianism, Daoism, and Chinese Universists—which may include: universism (yin/yang cosmology), ancestor cult, Confucian ethics, divination, festivals, folk religion, goddess worship, household gods, local deities, mediums, metaphysics, monasteries, neo-Confucianism, sacrifices, shamans, Buddhist and Daoist elements.

benefit to the greatest number in the political area, and so on. This is in striking contrast to earlier periods, when Christian faith laid down authoritative prescriptions, often through the mouths of the clergy, which could not be easily ignored in any of these domains. …

Professor Taylor also describes another form of secularism—its individual dimensions (which he again sees mostly with reference to Western Christianity):

In this second meaning, secularity consists in the falling off of religious belief and practice, in people turning away from God, and no longer going to church. In this sense, the countries of western Europe have mainly become secular—even those who retain the vestigial public reference to God in public space.

Yet a third meaning of secularism is the social condition in which religious faith is only one of various possibilities. In Taylor's words:

Belief in God is no longer axiomatic. There are alternatives. And this will also likely mean that at least in certain milieus, it may be hard to sustain one's faith. There will be people who feel bound to give it up, even though they mourn its loss. This has been a recognizable experience in our societies, at least since the mid-nineteenth century. There will be many others to whom faith never even seems an eligible possibility.[2]

As religion has become an option which some have rejected, there has been a spate of books by Western authors overtly critical of religion, such as *The End of Faith* by Sam Harris (2005), *The God Delusion* by Richard Dawkins (2006), *Breaking the Spell* by Daniel Dennett (2007), *When Religion Becomes Evil* by Charles Kimball (2006), and *God is Not Great: How Religion Poisons Everything* by Christopher Hitchens (2008). Even half a century ago, such literature would have been unthinkable.

Yet a fourth meaning of secularism applies to countries such as the United States, India, and Turkey, where the modern constitutional separation of religion and state may be referred to as "secularism," even though individuals may have strong belief structures. The United States has the largest percentage of church-going people in the industrialized countries of the world, yet its constitution insists on a wall of separation between the state and religion. In a secular democracy, the government is supposed to respect the rights of individuals to their own religious beliefs, thus protecting minority religions from oppression.

In all four senses, secularism is now under siege or waning. Many religions are undergoing a resurgence, either in their home regions or elsewhere, and political secularism is being threatened by politicized religious pressure groups.

Religious pluralism

Within these social, political, and cultural contexts, the global picture of religion is changing. A major feature of contemporary religious geography is that no single religion dominates the world. Although authorities from many faiths have historically asserted that theirs is the best and only way, in actuality new religions and new versions of older religions continue to spring up and then divide, subdivide, and provoke reform movements. Christianity claims the most members of any global religion, but Christianity is not a monolithic faith. Thousands of forms of Christianity are now being professed.

With migration, missionary activities, and refugee movements, religions have shifted from their country of origin. It is no longer so easy to show a world map in which each country is assigned to a particular religion. In Russia there are not only Russian Orthodox Christians but also Muslims, Catholics, Protestants, Jews, Buddhists, Hindus, shamanists, and members of new religions. At the same time, there are now sizable Russian Orthodox congregations in the United States. Buddhism arose in India but now is most pervasive in East Asia and popular in France, England, and the United States. Islam arose in what is now Saudi Arabia, but there are more Muslims in Indonesia than in any other country. There are large Muslim populations in Central Asia, and growing Muslim populations in the United States, with over fifty mosques in the city of Chicago alone.

Professor Diana Eck, Chairman of the Pluralism Project at Harvard University, describes what she terms the new "geo-religious reality":

> Our religious traditions are not boxes of goods passed intact from generation to generation, but rather rivers of faith—alive, dynamic, ever-changing, diverging, converging, drying up here, and watering new lands there.
>
> We are all neighbors somewhere, minorities somewhere, majorities somewhere. This is our new geo-religious reality. There are mosques in the Bible Belt in Houston, just as there are Christian churches in Muslim Pakistan. There are Cambodian Buddhists in Boston, Hindus in Moscow, Sikhs in London.[3]

myreligionlab
The Next
Christendom
PHILIP JENKINS

HARDENING OF RELIGIOUS BOUNDARIES

As religions proliferate and interpenetrate geographically, one common response has been the attempt to deny the validity of other religions. In many countries there is tension between the religion that has been most closely linked with national history and identity and other religions that are practiced or have been introduced into the country. With the collapse of communism, Protestant congregations rushed to offer Bibles and religious tracts to citizens of formerly atheistic communist countries, with the idea that they were introducing Christianity there. But Orthodox Christianity, established more than a thousand years ago in Russia, had continued to exist there, even though the church structures were limited and controlled by the state. People from the more established religions seek to find a balance between freedom of religion for all and the threat they perceive to their traditional values, customs, and sense of national identity from religious minorities.

One issue that arises as religious boundaries come to the fore is that of legal jurisdiction. Can Muslim minorities in a pluralistic nation-state be governed by their own traditional Shari'ah laws, or must they accept the common law of the country? And vice versa: Must other religious minorities in a Muslim-ruled country be subject to the laws of Shari'ah? In some northern states of Nigeria, for instance, Muslims and Christians clashed over attempts to implement full Shari'ah jurisdiction, which could mean applying punishments such as stoning to death in cases of adultery, flogging for those convicted of sexual intercourse outside of marriage, and amputation of the hand of a person convicted of theft.

Religions are now practiced far from the countries where they originated. This Tibetan Buddhist nun is practicing on the Holy Island of Lindisfarne in the United Kingdom.

Another issue arises concerning which religions will receive state funding. Registration requirements are another means used to help control or at least track the introduction of religions into countries where they did not originate. Another is outright banning of new or minority religions. In 1997, the Russian parliament passed a law prohibiting religions that had not officially existed in Russia longer than fifteen years from distributing religious materials or newspapers or running schools. The law protects the traditional status of the Russian Orthodox Church and Islam, Buddhism, and Judaism with some concessions to Protestant and Roman Catholic Christianity.

Religious symbols have become the focus for the French government's attempts to keep religion within bounds. In 2004, a controversial law was passed forbidding wearing of religious symbols including Muslim veils, Sikh turbans, Jewish yarmulkes, and large Christian crosses in French public schools and colleges. The government has also tried to restrict the activities of new religious movements, as well as charismatic and evangelical Christian groups, even though its constitution states "France shall respect all beliefs."

In some previously communist countries, old animosities between people of different ethnic groups resurfaced with great violence once totalitarian regimes toppled. These intense ethnic and political struggles have often pitted people of different faiths against each other, as in former Yugoslavia. Where there had been a seemingly peaceful society, horrifying atrocities arose among largely Orthodox Christian Serbs, Roman Catholic Croats, and Muslims.

Boundaries between religions also hardened in recent times because of the clash between fundamentalism and modernism. Along with the salient features of modernity—complex technologies, globalization, urbanization, bureaucratization, and rationality—have come the values known as **"modernism."** They include individualism, a preference for change rather than continuity, quantity rather than quality, efficiency rather than traditional skills and aesthetics, and pragmatism and profiteering rather than eternal truths and values. Modernism is perceived by some fundamentalists as threatening the very existence of traditional religious values; contemporary secular culture seems crude, sacrilegious, and socially dangerous. In 2004, Jerry Falwell (1933–2007), who founded the "Moral Majority" in the 1970s in the United States, described what he saw as signs that America was "losing its soul":

> During the past 35 years or so, we have expelled prayer from our schools and legalized abortion on demand. Our divorce rate has soared to 50%. There are one million teen pregnancies each year. We have a drug epidemic. We are considering legalizing same-sex marriages and trying hard to normalize the gay and lesbian lifestyle. School violence has burst upon the scene. Our culture is collapsing. Hollywood, television, video games, internet pornography and other influences are destroying our children and our values. America is in serious jeopardy of self-destroying.[4]

Some fundamentalists have tried to withdraw socially from the secular culture even while surrounded by it. Others have actively tried to change the culture, using political power to shape social laws or lobbying for banning of textbooks that they feel do not include their religious point of view. As described by the Project on Religion and Human Rights:

> Fundamentalists' basic goal is to fight back—culturally, ideologically, and socially—against the assumptions and patterns of life that are taken for granted in contemporary secular society and culture, refusing to celebrate them or to embrace them fully. They keep their distance and refuse to endorse the legitimacy of any culture that opposes what they perceive as fundamental truths. Secular culture, in their eyes, is base, barbarous, crude, and essentially profane. It produces a society that respects no sacred order and ignores the possibility of redemption.[5]

Fundamentalism sometimes turns to political means to accomplish its objectives. At the same time, political leaders have found the religious loyalty and absolutism of some fundamentalists an expedient way to mobilize political loyalties. Thus, Hindu extremists in India have been encouraged to demolish Muslim mosques built on the foundation of older Hindu temples and to rebuild Hindu temples in their place. The United States, which had prided itself on being a melting pot for all cultures, with full freedom of religion and no right of government to promote any specific religion, has witnessed attempts by Christian fundamentalists—the "Religious Right"—to control education and politics, and a simultaneous rise in violence against ethnic and religious minorities. Buddhism, long associated with nonviolence, became involved in the violent suppression of the Hindu minority in Sri Lanka. Christians and Muslims are clashing in Indonesia, Nigeria, India, and elsewhere. Violence among different branches of the same religion also rages—Roman Catholic churches in Northern Ireland have been burned by Protestants, and Sunni and Shi'ite Muslims have taken up arms against each other. The Internet reveals the sentiments and activities of a troubling number of hate groups promoting intolerance, bigotry, hatred, and violence against specific others in the name of religion.

RELIGION AFTER 11 SEPTEMBER

The stunning attacks by terrorists on United States targets in 2001 brought instant polarization along religious and ethnic lines. Hundreds of hate crimes were committed in the United States against Muslims and foreign immigrants who were

myreligionlab
The Battle for God
KAREN ARMSTRONG

mistaken for Muslims. As some Americans responded in fear and rage, these groups were suddenly seen as "outsiders." With the subsequent bombing of Afghanistan and Iraq, the perpetrators of terrorism such as Osama bin Laden incited Muslims to see the world in terms of Muslims versus the infidels, and to join together to drive the United States out of its strategic positions in Muslim lands. Both sides claimed that God was on their side and their cause a holy one.

While the Christian Identity movement promoted ideas of Christian supremacy in the United States, leaders of Al Qaeda selectively cited passages from the Holy Qur'an to give the appearance of spiritual legitimacy to their militant teachings. After 11 September, Osama bin Laden proclaimed:

> *These events have divided the world into two camps, the camp of the faithful*
> *and the camp of infidels. ... Every Muslim must rise to defend his religion. ...*
> *God is the greatest and glory be to Islam.*[6]

Once groups have taken such oppositional standpoints, violence seems inevitable. In search of sensational news that sells, the media often fan local issues into widespread conflicts. Dr. Rosalind Hackett, Professor of Religious Studies at the University of Tennessee, describes the media coverage of interreligious tensions in Nigeria:

> *There is plenty of evidence of how local conflicts get transformed into national issues*
> *by virtue of media coverage, especially if that coverage is particularly biased and*
> *provocative, which it often can be. It is important to note that the coverage may*
> *be determined by media ownership—i.e. Muslim or Christian. These incidents*
> *of ethnic and religious violence also get reported more internationally because*
> *Nigeria is seen by many as a barometer of what is going on in the rest of*
> *Africa, and because it represents an interesting case of a country which has*
> *moved from being renowned for its religious tolerance up to about 30 years*
> *ago to one known the world over for its interreligious tensions and conflict.*[7]

In some areas, inter-religious animosities have been stirred up to the point that people are even ready to sacrifice their lives as suicide bombers, kill innocent people in terrorist attacks, conduct assassinations, or drop bombs on populated areas, for the sake of what they consider to be a holy cause. Study of suicide bombers in organizations such as Al Qaeda and Hamas in Palestine shows that the suicide attackers tend to be well educated and to come from relatively well-off families. Theirs is not the easily exploited despair of poverty and ignorance; it is the conviction of ideology. Pilots dropping bombs and soldiers treating prisoners brutally may similarly be motivated by the conviction that they are doing the right thing and attacking evil by "countering terrorism." And some who kill innocent people may not be motivated by any kind of principles. Instead, they may be emotionally angry and callous, or simply hired killers working for money without any scruples. As public support for such violence is waning, wages offered for suicide attackers are reportedly declining.

Given the plurality of religions in the world and the extremism that some of their adherents are espousing, is a global "clash of civilizations" inevitable in the future? As noted in Chapter 1, some observers are now saying that the real problem is not conflict among religions but rather a "clash of ignorance."[8] Rigid exclusivist positions do not represent the heart of religious teachings. Whether state-sponsored or incited by militant extremists, violence finds no support in any religion. Thus there has been a strong outcry against fundamentalist violence by the mainstream religions from which militants have drawn their faith. Muslims are trying to point out that jihad must not be confused with terrorism, for jihad (spiritual struggle, particularly against one's own inner flaws) is the holy duty of every Muslim, whereas terrorist killing of innocent people is forbidden by the Holy Qur'an. Likewise, many Christian organizations have come out strongly against violence of any sort, including state terrorism. Roman Catholic theologian Vimal Tirimanna explains:

> Ordinary human experience shows that terrorism can never be a moral good, because of the horrendous evils it causes to human lives and to property. Let us not forget here that terrorism also damages the very existence of the terrorist himself/herself as a human being with others; it is demeaning of his/her own basic human dignity. Terrorism is an evil also because it is always a deliberately planned act to hurt, to damage, to injure other human lives, and also to devastate God's creation. Moreover it is intimidation which seeks to eliminate the basic human freedom of the would-be victims and which tends to impose the will of the terrorists forcefully on those who are at the receiving end. Terrorism, no matter whatever form it takes, no matter who are its perpetrators, and no matter what "noble" goals it seeks to promote, can never be justified by a conscientious person.[9]

Religion in politics

The future of religion is sure to include its engagement with politics. In many countries, religious groups have become associated with political parties or political interest groups—such as the linkage of Hindu religious fundamentalists with exclusivist nationalist political movements in India, and the linkage between neo-conservative politicians in the United States and evangelical Christian beliefs. Such politicians then frequently legitimate their agendas by giving them a religious color or by claiming they are defending religion. When religious groups are mobilized for political purposes, people oriented toward power rather than toward spirituality thus tend to be propelled into leadership roles, while still justifying their actions in religious terms. The political agenda can even become a global one, as in the case of Al Qaeda. Bruce Lincoln, Professor of the History of Religion, observes:

> The Al Qaeda network ... understands and constructs itself as simultaneously the militant vanguard and the most faithful fragment of an international religious community. The goal it articulates is the restoration of Islam in a maximalist form and its consequent triumph over its internal and foreign enemies. Those enemies include, first, the Western powers, who are not only non-Muslims, but non-, even anti-religious ("infidels"); second, postcolonial state elites, whose Islamic commitments have been egregiously compromised ("hypocrites"); third, that part of the Enlightenment project committed to religious minimalism and ascendancy of the secular state.[10]

After 11 September, President Bush proclaimed a global politico-religious agenda: to attack any nation suspected of harboring terrorists and thus presumably bring peace, with God's blessings resting securely upon America:

In the face of today's new threat, the only way to pursue peace is to pursue those who threaten it. We did not ask for this mission, but we will fulfill it. The name of today's military operation is Enduring Freedom. We defend not only our precious freedoms, but also the freedom of people everywhere to live and raise their children free from fear. … The battle is now joined in many fronts. We will not waver; we will not tire; we will not falter; and we will not fail. Peace and freedom will prevail. May God continue to bless America.[11]

Some international observers feel that this triumphalist policy has increased rather than decreased terrorism and violent deaths, and many religious leaders have questioned its ethics, as well as its political usefulness.

This confrontational approach was reversed early in the Barack Obama presidency. In an historic speech to the "Muslim world" given in Cairo University in June 2009 (see Box), President Obama spoke sympathetically about resolving political tensions between Islam and the West, as well as political tensions in areas such as West Asia between people of different religious traditions. Barack Obama and his wife Michelle are a striking example of contemporary pluralism, for even though they are Protestant Christians their family backgrounds include Christian, Muslim, and Jewish ancestors, and their extended families live in such diverse cultures that they collectively speak English, Indonesian, French, Cantonese, German, Hebrew, Swahili, Luo, and Igbo. Obama's "politics of hope," which earned him the Nobel Peace Prize, could be a harbinger of a sea change in political relationships among people of different faiths.

Religious fervor is a potent force that has often been tied to political movements.

Excerpts from Obama's Historic Cairo Speech

We meet at a time of great tension between the United States and Muslims around the world, tension rooted in historical forces that go beyond any current policy debate. ... Tension has been fed by colonialism that denied rights and opportunities to many Muslims and a Cold War in which Muslim majority countries were too often treated as proxies without regard to their own aspirations. Moreover, the sweeping change brought by modernity and globalization led many Muslims to view the West as hostile to the traditions of Islam.

Violent extremists have exploited these tensions in a small but potent minority of Muslims. The attacks of September 11, 2001, and the continued efforts of these extremists to engage in violence against civilians has led some in my country to view Islam as inevitably hostile not only to American and western countries but also to human rights.

All this has bred more fear and more mistrust. ... And this cycle of suspicion and discord must end. I've come here to Cairo to seek a new beginning between the United States and Muslims around the world, one based on mutual interest and mutual respect, and one based upon the truth that America and Islam are not exclusive and need not be in competition. Instead, they overlap and share common principles, principles of justice and progress, tolerance and the dignity of all human beings. ...

Just as Muslims do not fit a crude stereotype, America is not the crude stereotype of a self-interested empire. The United States has been one of the greatest sources of progress that the world has ever known. We were born out of revolution against an empire.

We were founded upon the ideal that all are created equal. ...We are shaped by every culture. Drawn from every end of the Earth, and dedicated to a simple concept, *E pluribus unum*: Out of many, one. ...

When violent extremists operate in one stretch of mountains, people are endangered across an ocean. When innocents in Bosnia and Darfur are slaughtered, that is a stain on our collective conscience.

That is what it means to share this world in the twenty-first century. That is the responsibility we have to one another as human beings. This is a difficult responsibility to embrace, for human history has often been a record of nations and tribes, and, yes, religions subjugating one another in pursuit of their own interests.

Yet in this new age, such attitudes are self-defeating.

Given our interdependence, any world order that elevates one nation or group of people over another will inevitably fall. ...

The same story can be told by people from South Africa to South Asia, to Eastern Europe to Indonesia. It's a story with a simple truth: Violence is a dead end. It is a sign neither of courage nor power to shoot rockets at sleeping children or to blow up old women on a bus. That's not how moral authority is claimed, that's how it is surrendered. ...

All of us have a responsibility to work for the day when the mothers of Israelis and Palestinians can see their children grow up without fear, when the holy land of three great faiths is the place of peace that God intended it to be, when Jerusalem is a secure and lasting home for Jews and Christians and Muslims and a place for all of the children of Abraham to mingle peacefully together as in the story of Isra, when Moses, Jesus, and Mohammed—peace be upon them—joined in prayer. ...

Freedom of religion is central to the ability of peoples to live together. We must always examine the ways in which people protect it. ...

It's easier to start wars than to end them. It's easier to blame others than to look inward. It's easier to see what is different about someone than to find the things we share. But we should choose the right path, not just the easy path. There is one rule that lies at the heart of every religion, that we do unto others as we would have them do unto us.

This truth transcends nations and peoples, a belief that isn't new, that isn't black or white or brown, that isn't Christian or Muslim or Jew. It's a belief that pulsed in the cradle of civilization and that still beats in the hearts of billions around the world. ...

We have the power to make the world we seek, but only if we have the courage to make a new beginning, keeping in mind what has been written. The Holy Qur'an tells us, "Mankind, we have created you male and female. And we have made you into nations and tribes so that you may know one another."

The Talmud tells us, "The whole of the Torah is for the purpose of promoting peace."

The Holy Bible tells us, "Blessed are the peacemakers, for they shall be called sons of God."

The people of the world can live together in peace. We know that is God's vision. Now that must be our work here on Earth.[12]

While separation of religion and state is one of the defining principles of modern democracy and also of some totalitarian states, certain religious beliefs and symbols are so deeply ingrained in people's minds as part of their culture that they may still influence policies and worldviews. In Israel, for instance, even totally secular Jews beset by violence on their borders and terrorism within may subconsciously harbor the ancient Jewish dream of a world at peace—and thus rule out any consideration of ending the Zionist political experiment. As Charles Liebman, Professor in Religion and Politics at Bar-Ilan University, writes:

> *Surely the dream of the Jewish prophets, the notion of "the wolf shall dwell with the lamb and the lion shall lie down with the kid, and nation shall not lift up sword against nation, neither shall they know war anymore" is for many, whether they call themselves religious or secular, an important vision of the future and, therefore, a source of how we behave in the present.*[13]

For other religious cultures such as Islam and Sikhism, the combination of religion and polity is perceived as a positive goal—the possibility of the mundane world reordered according to spiritual ideals. Even Buddhism has become engaged in politics, and to some Buddhists' thinking, a proactive approach to political change is desirable.

Interfaith movement

What can religions do to end the increasing political deadlock and hatreds between followers of various religions? There is already an existing countercurrent growing in the world. At the same time that boundaries between religions are hardening in many areas, there has been an acceleration of **interfaith dialogue**—the willingness of people of all religions to meet, explore their differences, and appreciate and find enrichment in each other's ways to the divine. This approach has been historically difficult, for many religions have made exclusive claims to being the best or only way. Professor Ewert Cousins, editor of an extensive series of books on the spiritual aspects of major religions, comments: "I think all the religions are overwhelmed by the particular revelation they have been given and are thus blinded to other traditions' riches."[14]

Religions are quite different in their external practices and culturally influenced behaviors. There are doctrinal differences on basic issues, such as the cause of and remedy for evil and suffering in the world, or the question of whether the divine is singular, plural, or nontheistic. And some religions make apparent claims to superiority which are difficult to reconcile with other religions' claims. The Qur'an, for instance, while acknowledging the validity of earlier prophets as messengers of God, refers to the Prophet Muhammad as the "Seal of the Prophets" (Sura 33:40). This description has been interpreted to mean that prophecy was completed with the Prophet Muhammad. If he is believed to be the last prophet, no spiritual figures after he passed away in c.632—including the Sikh Gurus and Baha'u'llah of the Baha'is—could be considered prophets, though they might be seen as teachers. Similarly, Christians read in John 14:6 that Jesus said, "I am the way, the truth, and the life; no one comes to the Father but by me." But some Christian scholars now feel that it is inappropriate to take this line out of its context (in which Jesus's disciples were asking how to find their way to him after they died) and to interpret it to mean that the ways of Hindus, Buddhists, and other faiths are invalid. Relationships with other faiths was not the question being answered.

Many people of broad vision have noted that many of the same principles reappear in all traditions. All religions teach the importance of setting one's own selfish interests aside, loving others, harkening to the divine, and exercising control over the mind. What is called the "Golden Rule," expressed by Confucius as "Do not do unto others what you do not want others to do unto you," and by the Prophet Muhammad as "None of you truly have faith if you do not desire for your brother that which you desire for yourself," is found in every religion.

The absolute authority of scriptures is being questioned by contemporary scholars who are interpreting them in their historical and cultural context and thus casting some doubt upon their exclusive claims to truth. Some liberal scholars are also proposing that there is an underlying experiential unity among religions. Wilfred Cantwell Smith, for instance, concluded that the revelations of all religions have come from the same divine source. Christian theologian John Hick suggests that religions are culturally different responses to one and the same reality. The Muslim scholar Frithjof Schuon feels that there is a common mystical base underlying all religions, but that only the enlightened will experience and understand it, whereas others will see the superficial differences.

> *If the religions are true it is because each time it is God who has spoken,*
> *and if they are different it is because God has spoken in different "languages"*
> *in conformity with the diversity of the receptacles. Finally, if they are absolute*
> *and exclusive, it is because in each of them God has said "I."*
>
> *Frithjof Schuon*[15]

RESPONSES TO OTHER FAITHS

With these contrasting views, there are several different ways in which people of different religions may relate to each other. Diana Eck, Professor of Comparative Religion and Indian Studies at Harvard Divinity School, observes that there are three responses to contact between religions. One is **exclusivism**: "Ours is the only true way." Eck and others have noted that deep personal commitment to one's faith is a foundation of religious life and also the first essential step in interfaith dialogue.

Eck sees the second response to interfaith contact as **inclusivism**. This may take the form of trying to create a single world religion, such as Baha'i. Or it may appear as the belief that our religion is spacious enough to encompass all the others, that it supersedes all previous religions, as Islam said it was the culmination of all monotheistic traditions. In this approach, the inclusivists do not see other ways as a threat. Some Sikhs, for instance, understand their religion as actively promoting interfaith appreciation and thus propose that their holy scripture, the Guru Granth Sahib, could serve as a roadmap to harmony among people of all religions, without denying the right of each religion to exist as a respected tradition.

myreligionlab

Can We Share in Others' Spiritual Traditions?
MARCUS BRAYBROOKE

The third way Eck discerns is **pluralism**: to hold one's own faith and at the same time ask people of other faiths about their path, about how they want to be understood. Uniformity and agreement are not the goals—the goal is to collaborate, to combine our differing strengths for the common good. From this point of view, for effective pluralistic dialogue, people must have an openness to the possibility of discovering sacred truth in other religions. Raimundo Panikkar, a Catholic-Hindu-Buddhist doctor of science, philosophy, and theology, has written extensively on this subject. He speaks of "concordant discord":

We realize that, by my pushing in one direction and your pushing in the opposite, world order is maintained and given the impulse of its proper dynamism. ... Consensus ultimately means to walk in the same direction, not to have just one rational view. ... To reach agreement suggests to be agreeable, to be pleasant, to find pleasure in being together. Concord is to put our hearts together.[16]

Professor Arvind Sharma of McGill University, who grew up in India as a Hindu, goes beyond Eck's categories to describe a fourth possibility, which he calls **universalism**. From his personal experience, he states that by studying different religions a person may learn about the diversity within one's own religion and then the diversity of the world's religions, and yet still somehow develop an inner connection with all religions:

In the end one might emerge with the tacit knowledge of being the legatee of not just one's tradition, however tolerant, or the various religious traditions of humanity, however diverse, but of the entire religious heritage of humanity, in the singular. The experience could be compared to that of geographical discovery, when what one thought was one's separate country turns out to be part of a continent, and then what one thought were different continents turn out to be part of a single globe. ... It involves the concrete realization of a religious tradition of humanity.[17]

This feeling of universalism is sometimes referred to as religious tolerance, in the sense of respect and even appreciation for all religions. However, the same term can also have negative connotations, as explained by Wendy Brown, Professor of Political Science at the University of California, Berkeley:

Despite its pacific demeanor, tolerance is an internally unharmonious term, blending together goodness, capaciousness, and conciliation with discomfort, judgment, and aversion. Like patience, tolerance is necessitated by something one would prefer did not exist. ... In this activity of management, tolerance does not offer resolution or transcendence, but only a strategy for coping. ... As compensation, tolerance anoints the bearer with virtue, with standing for a principled act of permitting one's principles to be affronted; it provides a gracious way of allowing one's tastes to be violated.[18]

Brown proposes that the kind of "religious tolerance" she is referring to becomes possible when religion is already relegated to the background in a society as having no claim on public life, or else as a solution to insolvable conflicts among dueling absolutist approaches to religious belief. It may also stem from the superior and condescending attitude of a religion in power toward religious minorities whom it is in a position to regulate. It typically does not spring from conviction that religions have equal truth claims, or even that religions are dealing with truths.

> *"Spirituality is not merely tolerance. … It is the absolute recognition of the other's faith in God as one's own."*
>
> *Sri Chinmoy*

INTERFAITH INITIATIVES

People of all faiths have been discovering each other for some time now. A major global assembly was held in Chicago in 1893: The Parliament of the World's Religions. The figure who most captured world attention was Swami Vivekananda (1863–1902), a disciple of Sri Ramakrishna. He brought appreciation of Eastern religions to the West, and made these concluding remarks:

> *If the Parliament of Religions has shown anything to the world it is this: It has proved to the world that holiness, purity, and charity are not the exclusive possessions of any church in the world, and that every system has produced men and women of the most exalted character. In the face of this evidence, if anybody dreams of the exclusive survival of his own religion and the destruction of others, I pity him from the bottom of my heart.*[19]

After that initiative, ecumenical conferences involved pairs of related religions that were trying to agree to disagree, such as Judaism and Christianity. Now a large number of interfaith organizations and meetings draw people from all religions in a spirit of mutual appreciation. In 1986, Pope John Paul II invited 160 representatives of all religions to Assisi in honor of the humble St. Francis, to pray together for world peace.

Two years later, the Assisi idea was extended to include governmental leaders, scientists, artists, business leaders, and media specialists as well as spiritual leaders.

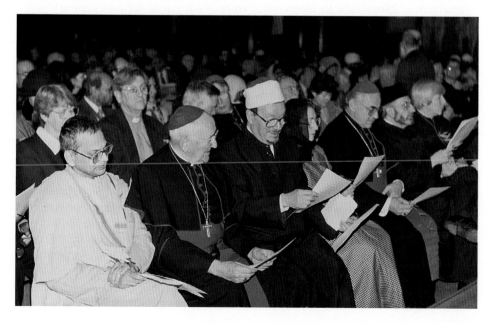

Leaders of many religions gather in Westminster Cathedral, London, in 1996 on the tenth anniversary of the Assisi interfaith gathering.

Some 200 of them from around the globe met in Oxford, England, in 1988 at the Global Forum of Spiritual and Parliamentary Leaders on Human Survival. They held their plenary sessions beneath an enormous banner with the image of the earth as seen from space. Statements of concern for the environment brought participants to the conclusion that the ecological dangers now threatening the entire human race may be the key that draws us together. But it was spiritual camaraderie rather than shared fear that brought the participants together. Dr. Wangari Maathai, leader of the Green Belt movement in Kenya, observed:

> *All religions meditate on the Source. And yet, strangely, religion is one of our greatest divides. If the Source be the same, as indeed it must be, all of us and all religions meditate on the same Source.*[20]

In 1990, a great assembly of spiritual leaders of all faiths, with scientists and parliamentarians, took place in what, until a few years before, would have been the most unlikely place in the world for such a gathering—Moscow, capital of the previously officially atheistic Soviet Union. The final speaker was Mikhail Gorbachev, who called for a merging of scientific and spiritual values in the effort to save the planet.

Throughout 1993, special interfaith meetings were held around the world to celebrate the 100th anniversary of the Parliament of the World's Religions. The largest 1993 centenary celebration was again held in Chicago. It gathered hundreds of well-known teachers from all faiths and thousands of participants to consider the critical issues facing humanity. It included an attempt to define and then use as a global standard for behavior the central ethical principles common to all religions. The provisional conference document signed by many of the leaders, "The Declaration Toward a Global Ethic," included agreement on the Golden Rule:

> *There is a principle which is found and has persisted in many religious and ethical traditions of humankind for thousands of years: What you do not wish done to yourself, do not do to others. Or in positive terms: What you wish done to yourself, do to others! This should be the irrevocable, unconditional norm for all areas of life, for families and communities, for races, nations, and religions.*[21]

The global gathering model has been replicated in various locations, drawing participants from around the world to deliberate how religions can collectively help to solve the world's problems. Many people have also had the vision that the United Nations could be home to representatives or leaders from all faiths, jointly advising the organization on international policy from a religious perspective.

Questions arise in such an effort, in addition to the necessity for substantial funding. Which religions should be represented? As we have seen, most major religions have many offshoots and branches that do not fully recognize each other's authority. And which, if any, of the myriad new religious movements should be included? Should indigenous religions be included? If so, could one representative speak for all the varied traditions? Would such an organization reflect the bureaucratic patriarchal structures of existing religions, or would it include women, the poor, and enlightened people rather than managers? If the members of the body were not elected by their respective organizations, but were rather simply interested individuals, what authority would they have?

The Internet conveys the efforts of many organizations to provide accurate information about a variety of religions to help overcome ignorance and intolerance. The Ontario Consultants on Religious Practice, for instance, sponsor www.religioustolerance.org, a rich offering of articles and resources on a long list of religions plus essays on interfaith themes. Some nongovernmental organizations are also attempting to develop curricula for teaching children about the world's religions in classrooms.

Classroom materials for values education have also been prepared for universal use by such august institutions as the Oxford University Press. Its Indian series "Living in Harmony: A Course on Peace and Value Education" uses stories and activities drawn from all religions to inculcate virtues such as honesty, nonviolence, religious tolerance, and respect for the environment. The editors explain:

The destiny of a nation depends on the character of its people. Character is not merely the awareness of some values, but also the commitment to uphold them in practice. To our sages and seers, education was incomplete without nobility of character. ... The dream of a peaceful society cannot be realized without achieving a profound transformation in the character of its people and in their attitudes and relationships with one another. ...

Education should be a tool for empowerment, not just employment. It must impart not merely knowledge but wisdom, not merely skills but character. It must help every child to develop an inner core of peace, a profound respect for Nature, and a belief in truth and justice.[22]

Sikhs, Hindus, Muslims, and Christians enjoy a children's interfaith education class together in Gobind Sadan, New Delhi.

Local and national inter-religious groups and projects are quite active in Britain, with its increasingly multi-cultural population. The Leicester Council of Faiths, for instance, includes representatives from Christianity, Hinduism, Islam, Sikhism, Judaism, Jainism, Buddhism, and the Baha'i faith. Their efforts include developing a multifaith Welcome Centre, ensuring that there is balanced representation of all faiths at civic events, providing multifaith counseling and a multifaith chaplaincy service in some healthcare institutions, informing the various faiths about political matters that affect them, and working with the National Health Service on care that is sensitive to people's specific faiths.

In some places, interfaith efforts are being applied directly to difficult real-life situations, such as the conflicts between Protestants and Catholics in Northern Ireland. In Israel, the Interfaith Encounter Association brings Muslims, Christians, and Jews together for intimate sharing of cultural and spiritual experiences from each other's traditions. For example, twenty Christian, Muslim, and Jewish women went to the home of one of the Muslim women for a traditional Ramadan fast-breaking dinner. Her family welcomed them, gave them a tour of their garden, and helped them pick figs before sunset. The meal thoughtfully included many kosher delicacies for the Jewish guests, with the hostess explaining the meaning and customs of Ramadan. Such person-to-person contacts seem very effective in developing warm friendships among people of different faiths. There are even groups bringing together the families and friends of those from all sides who have been killed in conflicts.

myreligionlab

God Will Break
All the Barriers!
BABA VIRSA SINGH

Baba Virsa Singh prays to the Light some perceive as shining through all the prophets and pervading all Creation.

In India, where communal violence between people of varying religions is daily news, the Sikh-based interfaith work of Gobind Sadan is bringing together volunteers of all religions in practical farm work on behalf of the poor, and in celebrations of the holy days of all religions. Baba Virsa Singh, the spiritual inspiration of Gobind Sadan, always quoted from the words of all the prophets, explaining:

All the Prophets have come from the same Light; they all give the same basic messages. None have come to change the older revealed scriptures; they have come to remind people of the earlier Prophets' messages which the people have forgotten. We have made separate religions as walled forts, each claiming one of the Prophets as its own. But the Light of God cannot be confined within any manmade structures. It radiates throughout all of Creation. How can we possess it?[23]

Although Baba Virsa Singh passed on in 2007, his teachings and his practical approach to interfaith harmony are being carried on by his followers. One new initiative is interfaith education for children. Poor children from the community and surrounding area gather weekly to learn the interfaith philosophy of Baba Virsa Singh and to act out stories from the lives of all prophets. In the context of that living interfaith community, Sikh, Hindu, and Muslim children eagerly play the roles of figures from traditions other than their own and regard them all as messengers from the same divine source.

Where people have seen their relatives tortured and killed by fanatics of another faith, reconciliation is very difficult but necessary if the cycle of violence and counterviolent reactions is to be halted. Andreas D'Souza and Diane D'Souza, who are working to heal hatreds among Muslim victims of violence in India, point out that we tend mentally to divide society into opposing camps:

> In our world today, particularly in Western countries, we are tending to demonize the other. It is "us," the sane and balanced, against "them," the demented, violent, and inhuman. We must resist this attempt to polarize "the good" and "the bad," for it leads to complacency at best, and to the rationalization of violence, death, and destruction at worst.[24]

However, embedded within religions themselves is the basis for harmony, for all teach messages of love and self-control rather than murderous passions.

Religion and social issues

Within every religion, there are contemporary attempts to bring religious perspectives to bear on the critical issues facing humanity. Today we are facing new issues that were not directly addressed by older teachings, such as the ethics of genetic engineering. Some are old issues which persist into the present, such as the ethics of abortion and sexual activity outside of marriage. And some issues have reached critical proportions in our times, such as terrorism, HIV/AIDS, global recession, the gap between rich and poor, climate change, and the deterioration of the natural environment. Many religious groups are re-examining their scriptures for teachings that would support careful environmental stewardship, in the face of dire warnings about global warming and other looming disasters. At the 1994 Cairo Conference on Population and Development, Christian and Muslim delegations took strong stands on behalf of just economic development, and education and healthcare for women, rather than forced population control or abortion as means of stabilizing population. Buddhists are spearheading efforts to ban landmines. Hindus and Muslims are trying to stop the spread of immoral, violent, and cynical mass media communications, to help protect the minds of the young. Racism and violence are challenging people of all faiths to deepen their spiritual understanding and to ponder appropriate responses to these scourges. Poverty, injustice, and human rights abuses in societies are being addressed by many religious groups. The Catholic liberation theologian Gustavo Gutierrez asserted in 1994:

> In the last analysis, poverty means an unjust and early death. Now everything is subordinated to market economies, without taking into consideration the social consequences for the weakest. People say, for example, that in business there are no friends. Solidarity is out of fashion. We need to build a culture of love, through respect of the human being, of the whole of creation. We must practice a justice inspired by love. Justice is the basis of true peace. We must, sisters and brothers, avoid being sorry for or comforting the poor. We must wish to be friends of the poor in the world.[25]

In contrast to this ethic, in today's world there is an increasing gap between rich and poor, and poor people are homeless and dying from malnutrition and starvation in the same countries where many wealthy people are benefiting from their cheap labor and politicians are benefiting from their votes. India, home to the world's largest tribal populations, is also the world's largest democracy, a richly agricultural country with plentiful grain surpluses that are exported or left to rot because of inadequate storage facilities. Urban areas are becoming very smart throughout the country, and many large homes and high-rise apartments are being built with teak and marble decor. However, despite promises of politicians to the tribal peoples languishing out of sight in rural areas, over eighty percent of them remain below the poverty line, sick, malnourished, ill-educated, lacking

RELIGION IN PUBLIC LIFE

Jimmy Carter

When Jimmy Carter left the White House after being the President of the United States from 1977 to 1981, he did not retire from public service. He went on to become involved in Habitat for Humanity, which helps to build houses for the poor, and to found the Carter Center, which works on many fronts to help governments solve conflict through peace talks rather than violence. The Carter Center also promotes development, health, and human rights in many countries. Jimmy Carter explains the philosophy that underlies all these efforts:

Bringing deaths and injuries, massive destruction of property, and the interruption of normal law and order, war is the greatest violation of basic human rights that one people can inflict upon another. Starvation, exposure, and disease caused by war often produce more casualties than the fighting itself. War touches not only soldiers in battle and leaders in government but ordinary citizens—men, women, and children—as well.

Because of numerous bloody struggles [in our times, many of them in poor countries], millions of people have lost their homes, livelihoods, and opportunities for medical care and education. Children in particular suffer—many do not know when to expect their next meal, whether they will ever attend school again, or where their parents might be.

It is one thing to say that we each have the right not to be killed. It is another to say that we each have the right to live comfortably, with adequate food, health care, shelter, education, and opportunities for employment. It is even more powerful to say that we each have the right to worship as we choose, to say what we choose, and to be governed by leaders we choose. And perhaps the most powerful statement of all is to say that we each hold these rights equally— that no one person is more entitled to any of these rights than the next, regardless of his or her sex, race, or station in life.[26]

Ex-President Carter is a highly respected and effective statesman whose personal intervention and reconciliation efforts during his presidency brought the Camp David peace accords between the leaders of Egypt and Israel. He has not always been successful in accomplishing his high ideals. But Jimmy Carter is a deeply religious person, a committed Christian who brings a strong grounding in faith to the inevitable trials and setbacks in life. He asserts:

Faith is the gift of God, and it is more precious than gold; to face life, we should put on the shield of faith, the breastplate of faith and love. … Without a central core of beliefs or standards by which to live, we may never experience the challenge and excitement of seeking a greater life. We will have ceased to grow, like Jesus, "strong in spirit, filled with wisdom; and the grace of God upon him" (Luke 2:4).[27]

basic services, and hungry. Although the central government has legislated many programs designed to alleviate poverty, aid has not reached the people who need it, because of mismanagement, corruption, and a lack of direct participation by tribal people in implementation of poverty alleviation programs. Uneducated and facing extreme poverty, they are easy prey to unscrupulous moneylenders who charge such high interest that poor farmers fall more deeply into debt each year, especially when crops fail. As a result, thousands have committed suicide because they see no other way out. Some faith-based NGOs such as the Swadhyaya Movement (see Chapter 3) and Gobind Sadan (see Chapter 11) are trying to help people on a local scale, but there is as yet no concerted, sincere, large-scale effort by religiously conscientious people to change this bleak picture of structural

In the midst of difficulties, Jimmy Carter is comforted by a personal sense of the presence of God. He reflects:

In addition to the intellectual realization of a supreme being, we have a purely subjective need to meet a personal yearning. We have an innate desire to relate to the all-knowing, the all-powerful, and the ever-present—to some entity that transcends ourselves. I am grateful and happy when I feel the presence of God within me, as a tangible influence on my thoughts and on the ultimate standards of my life. It is reassuring to me to know that God will always be with me and cares for me. I think of the words of Isaiah: "When you pass through the waters, I will be with you; and through the rivers, they shall not overwhelm you; when you walk through fire you shall not be burned, and the flame shall not consume you; For I am the Lord your God. … You are precious in my sight, and honoured, and I love you" (Isaiah 42:2–4).[28]

Jimmy Carter is now one of the leaders engaged in a deep struggle to restore fundamental American values in government. He explains:

In recent years, I have become increasingly concerned by a host of radical government policies that now threaten many basic principles espoused by all previous administrations, Democratic and Republican. These include the rudimentary American commitment to peace, economic and social justice, civil liberties, our environment and human rights. Also endangered are our historic commitments to providing citizens with truthful information, treating dissenting voices and beliefs with respect, state and local autonomy, and fiscal responsibility. At the same time, our political leaders have declared independence from the restraints of international organization and have disavowed long-standing global agreements—including agreements on nuclear arms, control of biological weapons and the international system of justice. Instead of our tradition of espousing peace as a national priority unless our security is directly threatened, we have proclaimed a policy of "preemptive war," an unabridged right to attack other nations unilaterally to change an unsavory regime or for other purposes. …

I am extremely concerned by a fundamentalist shift in many houses of worship and in government, as church and state have become increasingly intertwined in ways previously thought unimaginable. As the world's only superpower, America should be seen as the unswerving champion of peace, freedom and human rights. … We should be in the forefront of providing human assistance to people in need. It is time for the deep and disturbing political divisions within our country to be substantially healed, with Americans united in a common commitment to revive and nourish the historical political and moral values that we have espoused during the last 230 years.[29]

injustice, even though India is home to many of the world's religions. To varying extents, the same widening gap between rich and poor in India is evident in other countries as well. Until individualism gives way to genuine concern for the community, this pattern may persist and worsen in the years to come.

The HIV/AIDS pandemic, which some feel is already the greatest social crisis in the world, with tens of millions already dead, infected, or orphaned in Africa alone, may continue to grow in the future. It has been a particularly difficult subject for religions to come to grips with, since it involves intimate behaviors that they do not usually discuss. Though late in starting, the response of religions is now growing rapidly, with dialogues, debates, and actions being undertaken from local to international levels by religious institutions. In Uganda, one of the worst-hit countries in Africa, the disease was identified in 1982. People thought that those who contracted the disease must be victims of witchcraft, revenge from angry ancestors, or the wrath of God. Once the connections of the disease with sexual promiscuity, homosexual contact, and drug use were made, the issue was shrouded in stigma and denial. But by 1992, the government recognized that its future development could be seriously imperiled by the disease, so it organized the Uganda AIDS Commission. Catholic, Protestant, and Muslim leaders have been active members and chairs of the commission, and have helped it to be candid about the problem and also sensitive to the people's religious beliefs and practices. They developed a basic program called "ABC": abstinence, being faithful, and condoms. Since limiting the number of sexual partners is considered the most important way of stopping spread of the epidemic, Ugandans have encouraged "zero grazing" for monogamous, mostly Christian couples, and "paddock grazing" for polygamous relationships among Muslims. But even this simple program, which has apparently shown considerable success, runs into many subtle barriers related to people's religious cultures, such as traditional acceptance of wife-sharing, spontaneous sexuality during celebrations, and allowance for men to "inherit" their relatives' widows.

Reproductive restrictions are proposed by many religious groups, for the sake of safeguarding the family and the preciousness of human life. Homosexual preferences are controversial when the actors are in roles of spiritual leadership. As we have seen in Chapter 9, the issue of homosexuality in the clergy may split the Anglican Church between conservatives and liberals. Sexual intercourse outside of marriage is discouraged by many religions. Even within marriage, contraception may be subject to religious guidelines. The Roman Catholic Church tries to prohibit contraception by any means other than abstinence during the most fertile days of the woman's monthly cycle, and also forbids abortion and sterilization. In 1965, in an historic document called *Gaudium et Spes* ("Joy and Hope"), the Second Vatican Council recommended that individual freedom should be consciously subsumed to concern for the common good and commitment to God:

> *The intimate partnership of life and the love which constitutes the married state*
> *has been established by the creator and endowed by him with its own proper laws.*
> *… Married couples should see it as their mission to transmit human life and to*
> *educate their children. … This involves fulfilling their role responsibly as human*
> *beings and Christians, judging matters correctly in a spirit of obedient respect for*
> *God, reflecting and working together; it also involves taking into consideration their*

*own well-being and the well-being of their children already born or yet to come,
being able to read the signs of the times and assess their own situation on the
material and spiritual level, and, finally, an estimation of the good of the family,
of society, and of the church. ... Married people ... must be ruled by conscience—
and conscience ought to be in accord with the law of God in the teaching authority
of the Church, which is the authentic interpreter of divine law. ... special mention
should be made of those who after prudent reflection and joint decision
courageously undertake the rearing of a large family.[30]*

Such recommendations do not have the force of law except in theocracies.
Many couples make their own sexual choices, including the moral decision not
to have large families, to help curb population growth and to use their time and
resources to rear a few children as best they can.

Legalized abortion has been a hot issue for decades, with strident conflicts continuing between "pro-life" and "pro-choice" factions, both of whom cite ethical principles to support their causes. *In vitro* fertilization has also been controversial ever
since its inception. It is seen by infertile couples as a last hope in their efforts to bear
children, but some people have religious objections to the procedure. A Sunni
Muslim *fatwa* issued in Egypt in 1980 is still considered valid in many Muslim circles: IVF is permitted if the husband's sperm is used and if the partners are currently
married to each other. Because many fertilized eggs die during IVF attempts without becoming viable embryos, the spiritual question arises of whether and when
the embryo should be considered a human being, with human rights. According to
legal decisions from Al-Azhar University in Cairo, the earliest time at which the
embryo has differentiated organs and a soul is forty-two days after fertilization, so
research involving surplus embryos is allowed up to fourteen days after fertilization.

The newest reproductive choice issue involves reproductive cloning research,
which could potentially be used to create a duplicate of an existing human being.
Experiments with animals have sometimes resulted in live births, but many of
these cloned animals have later developed major defects, some of which did not
manifest until the animal was mature. Many ethical and social questions have
been raised: Should a clone be considered the offspring or the twin of its progen-
itor? Who is socially responsible for the clone? What happens to deformed
humans who result from cloning research? Does a clone have a soul? Are human
beings wise and restrained enough to use such technology carefully?

Concern over other social problems has in recent years been eclipsed by concern over terrorism. The terrorist attacks in the United States in 2001 and in other
countries have brought a sea change in ways of thinking. The future may hold a
more serious inquiry into the motives and concerns of people who are willing to
risk their lives and kill others. In addition, as pointed out by Dr. N.
Radhakrishnan, Chairman of the Indian Council of Gandhian Studies, peacemaking has always been a dangerous business:

*To stand up and challenge any established belief or order requires extraordinary
courage and conviction. The price paid by those who mustered strength to do so or
swim against the current has been enormous. ... Ironically, notwithstanding threat
of death, persecutions, imprisonment, crucifixion or torture, their tribes have only
been steadily increasing.[31]*

myreligionlab
Is Religion Killing Us?
JACK NELSON-
PALLMEYER

Religion and materialism

All religions teach that one should not hurt others, should not lie, should not steal, should not usurp others' rights, should not be greedy, but rather should be unselfish, considerate, and helpful to others, and humble before the Unseen. These universal spiritual principles were swamped by the expansion of capitalism in the twentieth century, as the profit motive triumphed as the most important value in economies around the world.

William J. Byron, who teaches courses in corporate responsibility at Loyola College, observes that integrity has fallen by the wayside in the "new corporate culture." Instead, "secrecy, easy money, and the violation of trust define a framework for the test of character in the world of business."[32] Spiritual principles were notoriously absent in the sub-prime lending by American banks that led to a severe global recession starting in 2008. Economist Thomas Friedman described the situation as "a near-total breakdown of responsibility at every link in our financial chain."[33]

Material greed characterizes the lives of many individuals as well as organizations. As Vaclav Havel, former president of the Czech Republic, wrote to his wife Olga when he was imprisoned for his courageous human rights work:

> The person who has completely lost all sense of the meaning of life is merely vegetating and doesn't mind it; he lives like a parasite and doesn't mind it; he is entirely absorbed in the problem of his own metabolism and essentially nothing beyond that interests him: other people, society, the world, Being—for him they are all simply things to be either consumed or avoided or turned into a comfortable place to make his bed. Everything meaningful in life, though it may assume the most dramatic form of questioning and doubting, is distinguished by a certain transcendence of individual human existence. Only by looking outward … does one really become a person, a creator of the "order of the spirit," a being capable of a miracle: The re-creation of the world.[34]

One of the religious commentaries on the consequences of unprincipled, never-satisfied greed has come from the Vatican, where in the midst of global recession Pope Benedict XVI called upon governments, corporations, political leaders, and individuals to look at their economic responsibilities from a spiritual perspective of love and truth. He proclaimed, "Only with love illumined by reason and by faith is it possible to achieve goals of development endowed with humane and humanizing values."[35]

myreligionlab
Sacred Whispers
in the World
LEE W. BAILEY

Some individuals and corporations have now stepped back to consider how to reconcile spiritual motives with earning a living. Books on voluntary simplicity have proliferated on the bestseller lists. Typically, they encourage the relatively wealthy to cut back on their breakneck work pace for the sake of their own spiritual peace, and to cut back on unnecessary individual expenditures for the sake of sharing with others. Many people are also taking a second look at the effect of economic systems. Liberal capitalism, for example, is being reinterpreted not as a means of allowing industrious people to climb out of poverty, but as a potentially amoral system. In free market capitalism, as Pope Paul VI commented: "The right to the means of production is absolute. It has no limits. It has no social obligation."[36]

A new social consciousness that reflects religious values is beginning to enter some workplaces. Professor Syed Anwar Kabir, a faithful Muslim on the faculty of the Management Development Institute in New Delhi, India, teaches his managerial students to do mind-stilling meditation daily in order to listen to their own conscience and make ethical choices from a base of inner tranquility. He observes:

> *Businessmen themselves say that the uninhibited, reckless way in which you accumulate wealth will not give you a good name. For a company to survive in a highly competitive world in the long term means creating an image in the mind of the public, creating good will, creating its own impact and niche in the market. ... If you treat human beings not as means but also as ends, naturally it is reflected in your products and services and creates an impact in the world of consumers so that they also come to respect the company's principles and strategies.*[37]

However, in the twenty-first century, power-mongering, self-interest, and corruption are at the forefront of economic and political activities; honesty, altruism, service, harmony, justice, and the public good are not the primary motivating forces in most government actions.

Religion and the future of humanity

The new century has begun with flagrant materialistic greed, crime, amorality, ethnic hatreds, violence, and family crises, together with ignorant demonizing, power-mongering, and moneymaking in religions themselves. But being sick, perhaps the world is ready to be cured. There is indeed a global increase in interest in religion, particularly in new forms of traditional religions as well as new religious movements.

The negative signs of our times are interpreted by some as the darkness before the dawn, chaos from which will emerge a new and greater order. As Yasuhiro Nakasone, former prime minister of Japan, has optimistically stated: "Perhaps we are undergoing a trial—a test that will facilitate the rebirth of the human race."[38]

Baba Virsa Singh confidently asserted that sweeping change in the hearts and actions of humanity is not difficult at all for the One who has created the entire cosmos. He reminded people of the value of practicing the eternal spiritual teachings and advised them to ignore religious leaders who do not practice what they preach and who have led people away from the truth because they themselves are not connected to it. He said that truth and love are ultimately very powerful:

> *Anticipate that day when God transforms the world, and the Truth, which is now hidden, comes out and starts working among the people again. That day is upon us.*[39]

Drawing inspiration from the past in order to greet the future, contemporary Russians gather in a Moscow park to celebrate the spring equinox according to ancient Slavic rites.

The world stage is ready for a true moral and spiritual revolution, in which people of every faith truly begin to practice in their own lives what their prophets have taught. The words of the late French sage Teilhard de Chardin are often quoted in these apocalyptic days:

Some day, after mastering the winds, the waves, the tides, and gravity, we shall harness for God the energies of love. And then, for the second time in the history of the world, man will have discovered fire.

Suggested reading

Barney, Gerald O. and others, *Threshold 2000: Critical Issues and Spiritual Values for a Global Age*, Ada, Michigan: CoNexus Press, 2000. Projections of environmental and social crises in the twenty-first century, with multifaith spiritual perspectives that may offer solutions.

Braybrooke, Marcus, *Faith and Interfaith in a Global Age*, Grand Rapids, Michigan: CoNexus Press and Oxford: Braybrooke Press, 1998. One of the world's central interfaith coordinators surveys the interfaith movement.

Brown, Wendy, *Regulating Aversion: Tolerance in the Age of Identity and Empire*, Princeton, New Jersey: Princeton University Press, 2006. Deep exploration of tolerance as an exercise in power, a means of managing what we actually dislike.

Byron, William J., *The Power of Principles: Ethics for the New Corporate Culture*, Maryknoll, New York: Orbis Books, 2007. A critical survey of cynical, self-serving motives that have taken the place of old ethical principles in business.

Cenkner, William, *Evil and the Response of World Religion*, St. Paul, Minnesota: Paragon House, 1997. Leading scholars from many religions explore the diversity of religious beliefs about a major spiritual issue: Why is there evil and suffering in the world?

Fisher, Mary Pat and Lee W. Bailey, *An Anthology of Living Religions*, second edition, Upper Saddle River, New Jersey: Prentice Hall, 2008. Readings from the various religions, following the outline of this book, to deepen understanding of the material herein.

Forward, Martin, *Ultimate Visions: Reflections on the Religions we Choose*, Oxford: Oneworld Publications, 1995. Interesting personal essays by scholars and leaders of many religions, reflecting upon why they like their religion and how it can contribute to a future of harmony among all religions.

Kelsay, John and B. Twiss Sumner, eds, *Religion and Human Rights*, New York: The Project on Religion and Human Rights, 1994. A sensitive introduction to conflicts caused by religious "fundamentalism," with positive suggestions as to the potential of religions for insuring human rights.

Khan, Hazrat Inayat, *The Unity of Religious Ideals*, New Lebanon, New York: Sufi Order Publications, 1927, 1979. A master of Sufi mysticism explores the underlying themes in the religious quest that are common to all religions.

Knitter, Paul F., *The Myth of Religious Superiority*, Maryknoll, New York: Orbis Books, 2004. Exclusivism, inclusivism, and pluralism as perceived from Hindu, Sikh, Buddhist, and Western perspectives.

Marshall, Katherine and Lucy Keough, *Mind, Heart and Soul in the Fight Against Poverty*, Washington: The World Bank, 2004. Encouraging report from the world's largest development bank as it attempts to work with religions to alleviate poverty, unemployment, debt, and HIV/AIDS.

Smith-Christopher, Daniel L., *Subverting Hatred: The Challenge of Nonviolence in Religious Traditions*, Maryknoll, New York: Orbis Books and Boston Research Center for the 21st Century, 2007. Articles delineating teachings of nonviolence from each of the major world religions.

Swidler, Leonard, ed., *Toward a Universal Theology of Religion*, Maryknoll, New York: Orbis Books, 1988. Leaders in interfaith dialogue grapple with the issues of transcending differences.

Taylor, Charles, *A Secular Age*, Cambridge, Massachusetts: Belknap Press of Harvard University Press, 2007. The history of secularization of Western culture from strong belief to disintegration and meaninglessness.

Tobias, Michael, Jane Morrison, and Bettina Gray, eds, *A Parliament of Souls: In Search of Global Spirituality*, Ada, Michigan: CoNexus Press, 1994. Interviews with twenty-eight spiritual leaders from the 1993 Parliament of the World's Religions, plus supplementary material.

World Scripture: A Comparative Anthology of Sacred Texts, New York: Paragon House/ International Religious Foundation, 1991. A thematic compendium of appealing excerpts from the scriptures and oral traditions of many religions.

Key terms

exclusivism The idea that one's own religion is the only valid way.

inclusivism The idea that all religions can be accommodated within one religion.

interfaith dialogue Appreciative communication between people of different religions.

modernism Values that developed in the twentieth century including individualism, preference for change rather than continuity, quantity rather than quality, efficiency, pragmatism, and profiteering, all seen by some as threatening the existence of traditional religious values.

pluralism An appreciation of the diversity of religions.

Review questions

1. Define "globalization" and "secularism", and explain how each has affected religion in the contemporary world.
2. Describe the major themes of the interfaith movement.
3. Describe how religious leaders have responded to the issue of materialism in the contemporary world.

Discussion questions

1. Discuss the advantages and disadvantages of religions' involvement in politics and social issues such as sexuality and reproduction.
2. Compare examples of exclusivism, inclusivism, pluralism, and universalism. What do you consider the advantages and disadvantages of each position?
3. Do you agree or disagree with the statement at the end of this chapter that "The world stage is ready for a true moral and spiritual revolution, in which people of every faith truly begin to practice in their own lives what their prophets have taught."

Additional Internet resources

Council for a Parliament for the World's Religions http://www.parliamentofreligions.org/

Gobind Sadan http://www.gobindsadan.org

Internet Sacred Text Archive http://www.sacred-texts.com

The Pluralism Project at Harvard University http://www.pluralism.org

Religion and Ethics http://www.bbc.co.uk/religion

Religiously Motivated Violence http://www.religioustolerance.org/relviol.htm

myreligionlab

For further activities and resources, including access to MyReligionLibrary, please visit MyReligionLab at www.myreligionlab.com

NOTES

CHAPTER 1

RELIGIOUS RESPONSES

1   Karl Marx, from "Contribution to the Critique of Hegel's Philosophy of Right," 1884, *Karl Marx, Early Writings*, translated and edited by T. B. Bottomore, London: C. A. Watts and Co., 1963, pp. 43–44; Capital, vol. 1, 1867, translated by Samuel Moore and Edward Aveling, F. Engels, ed., London: Lawrence & Wishart, 1961, p. 79; "The Communism of the Paper 'Rheinischer Beobachter'," *On Religion*, London: Lawrence & Wishart, undated, pp. 83–84.

2   Karl Marx, "Religion as the Opium of the People," in Karl Marx and Friedrich Engels, *On Religions*, Moscow: Foreign Language Publishing House, 1955, p. 42.

3   Tenzin Gyatso, "The Monk in the Lab," *New York Times*, 26 April 2003, p. A29.

4   Mata Amritanandamayi, *Awaken Children!*, vol. IV, Amritapuri, Kerala, India: Mata Amritanandamayi Mission Trust, 1992, pp. 103–104.

5   Buddha, *The Dhammapada*, translated by P. Lal, 162/92 Lake Gardens, Calcutta, 700045 India. (Originally published by Farrar, Straus & Giroux, 1967, p. 97.) Reprinted by permission of P. Lal.

6   Mahatma Gandhi, quoted in Eknath Easwaran, *Gandhi the Man*, Petaluma, California: Nilgiri Press, 1978, p. 121.

7   *The Bhagavad-Gita*, portions of Chapter 2, translated by Eknath Easwaran, quoted in ibid., pp. 121–122.

8   Excerpted from Agnes Collard, in "The Face of God," *Life*, December 1990, p. 49.

9   *Brihadaranyaka Upanishad*, Fourth Adhyaya, Fourth Brahmana, 20, 13, translated by F. Max Müller, *Sacred Books of the East*, vol. 15, Oxford: Oxford University Press, 1884, pp. 178–179.

10 Jiddu Krishnamurti, *The Awakening of Intelligence*, New York: Harper & Row, 1973, p. 90.

11 Radhakrishnan, *The Hindu View of Life*, New Delhi: HarperCollins Publishers India, 1927, 1993, pp 17–18.

12 Martin Luther, as quoted in Gordon Rupp, "Luther and the Reformation," in Joel Hurstfield, ed., *The Reformation Crisis*, New York: Harper & Row, 1966, p. 23.

13 William James, *The Varieties of Religious Experience*, New York: New American Library, 1958, p. 298.

14 AE (George William Russell), *The Candle of Vision*, Wheaton, Illinois: The Theosophical Publishing House, 1974, pp. 8–9.

15 From *The Kabir Book* by Robert Bly, copyright 1971, 1977 by Robert Bly, copyright 1977 by Seventies Press. Reprinted by permission of Beacon Press.

16 John White, "An Interview with Nona Coxhead: The Science of Mysticism—Transcendental Bliss in Everyday Life," *Science of Mind*, September 1986, pp. 14, 70.

17 Abu Yazid, as quoted in R. C. Zaehner, *Hindu and Muslim Mysticism*, London: University of London, Athlone Press, 1960, p. 105.

18 Sallie McFague, *Models of God: Theology for an Ecological, Nuclear Age*, Philadelphia: Fortress Press, 1987, p. 133.

19 Dr. I. H. Azad Faruqi, Letter to Dr. Nishat Quaiser, 19 September 2005.

20 Maimonides, "Guide for the Perplexed," 1, 59, as quoted in Louis Jacobs, *Jewish Ethics, Philosophy, and Mysticism*, New York: Behrman House, 1969, p. 80.

21 Guru Gobind Singh, *Jaap Sahib*, English translation by Surendra Nath, New Delhi: Gobind Sadan, 1992, verses 7, 29–31.

22 Bede Griffiths, *Return to the Center*, Springfield, Illinois: Templegate, 1977, p. 71.

23 Antony Fernando, "Outlining the Characteristics of the Ideal Individual," paper for the Inter-Religious Federation for World Peace Conference, Seoul, Korea, 20–27 August 1995, p. 9.

24 Akka Mahadevi, in A. K. Ramanujan, *Speaking of Shiva*, London: Penguin, 1973: vol. 17, p.116, quoted in Vijaya Ramaswamy, *Walking Naked: Women, Society, Spirituality in South India*, Shimla, India: Indian Institute of Advanced Study, 1997, p. 33.

25 Pir Vilayat Inayat Khan, "The Significance of Religion to Human Issues in the Light of the Universal Norms of Mystical Experience," *The World Religions Speak on the Relevance of Religion in the Modern World*, Finley P. Ounne, Jr., ed., The Hague: Junk, 1970, p. 145.

26 Lame Deer, "How the Sioux Came to Be," in Richard Erdoes and Alfonso Ortiz, *American Indian Myths and Legends*, New York: Pantheon Books, 1984, pp. 93–95.

27 Joseph Campbell, *The Hero with a Thousand Faces*, second edition, Princeton, New Jersey: Princeton University Press, 1972, p. 29.

28 Dr. Syed Z. Abedin, "Let There be Light," *Saudi Gazette*, Jeddah, June 1992, reprinted in *Council for a Parliament of the World's Religions Newsletter*, vol. 4, no. 2, August 1992, p. 2.

29 Quoted in John Gliedman, "Mind and Matter," *Science Digest*, March 1983, p. 72.

30 Murray Gell-Mann, in Kitty Ferguson, Stephen Hawking, *Quest for a Theory of Everything*, London: Bantam Press, 1992, p. 30.

31 Ilya Prigogine, abstract for "The Quest for Certainty," Conference on a New Space for Culture and Society, New Ideas in Science and Art, 19–23 November 1996.

32 James Lovelock, in Bel Mooney, *Devout Sceptics: Conversations on Faith and Doubt*, London: Hodder and Stoughton, 2003, pp. 83–84.

33 Albert Einstein, *The World As I See It*, New York: Wisdom Library, 1979; *Ideas and Opinions*, translated by Sonja Bargmann, New York: Crown Publishers, 1954.

34 Paul Davies, excerpted from Bel Mooney, *Devout Sceptics*, 2003. London: Hodder and Stoughton, pp. 48–56.

35 Ellen Bernstein, "Creation Theology: Theology for the rest of us," in Rabbi Elyse Goldstein, ed., *New Jewish Feminism: Probing the Past, Forging the Future*, 2009, Woodstock, Vermont: Jewish Lights Publishing, pp. 42–43.

36 Stephen Hawking, *A Brief History of Time: From the Big Bang to Black Holes*, London: Bantam Press, 1988.

37 Jacqueline Kramer, "Mothering as Practice," in *Sakyadhita*, vol. 8.1, no. 1, Spring 2009, p. 5.

38 His Highness the Aga Khan, address to the School of International and Public Affairs, Columbia University, 15 May 2006.

CHAPTER 2

INDIGENOUS SACRED WAYS

1 Vine Deloria, Jr., *God is Red*, New York: Grosset & Dunlap, 1973, p. 267.

2 Lorraine Mafi Williams, personal communication, 16 September 1988.

3 Gerhardus Cornelius Oosthuizen, "The Place of Traditional Religion in Contemporary South Africa," in Jacob K. Olupona, *African Traditional Religions in Contemporary Society*, New York: Paragon House, 1991, p. 36.

4 Quoted by Bob Masla, "The Healing Art of the Huichol Indians," Many Hands: Resources for Personal and Social Transformation," Fall 1988, p. 30.

5 George Tinker, *Missionary Conquest: The Gospel and Native American Genocide*, Minneapolis: Fortress Press, 1993, p. 122.

6 Wilmer Stampede Mesteth (Oglala Lakota), Darrell Standing Elk (Sicangu Lakota), and Phyllis Swift Hawk (Kul Wicasa Lakota), "Declaration of War Against Exploiters of Lakota Spirituality," undated handbill reproduced on http://puffin.creighton.edu/lakota/war.html, 19 April 2001.

7 John (Fire) Lame Deer and Richard Erdoes, *Lame Deer: Seeker of Visions*, New York: Pocket Books, 1972, p. 100.

8 Knud Rasmussen, *Across Arctic America*, New York: G. P. Putnam's Sons, 1927, p. 386.

9 Interview with Rev. William Kingsley Opoku, August 1992.

10 Clyde Ford, *The Hero with an African Face: Mythical Wisdom of Traditional Africa*, New York: Bantam Books, 2000, p. 146.

11 Adapted from a Yoruba story told by Deidre L. Badejo. Deidre L. Badejo, "Osun Seegesi: The Deified Power of African Women and the Social Ideal," paper presented at the Inter-Religious Federation for World Peace Conference, Seoul, Korea, 20–27 August 1995.

12 Josiah U. Young III, "Out of Africa: African Traditional Religion and African Theology," in *World Religions and Human Liberation*, Dan Cohn-Sherbok, ed., Maryknoll, New York: Orbis Books, 1992, p. 93.

13 Jo Agguisho/Oren R. Lyons, spokesman for the Traditional Elders Circle, Wolf Clan, Onondaga Nation, Haudenosaunee, Six Nations Iroquois Confederacy, from the speech to the Fourth World Wilderness Conference, 11 September 1987, p. 2.

14 Quoted in Keith Basso, *Wisdom Sits in Places: Landscape and Language among the Western Apache*, Albuquerque: University of New Mexico Press, 1996, p. 127.

15 Te Urutahi, Waikerepuru of Aoeteroa, New Zealand, remarks at the Global Peace Initiative of Women Religious and Spiritual Leaders, Geneva, 7 October 2002.

16 Bill Neidjie, *Speaking for the Earth: Nature's Law and the Aboriginal Way*, Washington: Center for Respect of Life and Environment, 1991, pp. 40–41. Reprinted from *Kakadu Man* by Big Bill Neidjie, Stephen Davis, and Allan Fox, Northryde, New South Wales, Australia: Angus and Robertson.

17 Jaime de Angulo, "Indians in Overalls," *Hudson Review*, II, 1950, p. 372.

18 Kahu Kawai'i, interviewed by Mark Bochrach in *The Source*, as quoted in *Hinduism Today*, December 1988, p. 18.

19 Quoted in Matthew Fox, "Native teachings: Spirituality with power," *Creation*, January/February 1987, vol. 2, no. 6.

20 John (Fire) Lame Deer and Richard Erdoes, *Lame Deer*, op. cit., p. 116.

21 Tlakaelel, talk at Interface, Watertown, Massachusetts, 15 April 1988.

22 As quoted in Georges Niangoran-Bouah, "The Talking Drum: A Traditional African Instrument of Liturgy and of Meditation with the Sacred," in Jacob K. Olupona, ed., *African Traditional Religions in Contemporary Society*, New York: Paragon House, 1991, pp. 86–87.

23 Leonard Crow Dog and Richard Erdoes, *The Eye of the Heart*, unpublished manuscript, quoted by Joan Halifax, *Shamanic Voices: A Survey of Visionary Narratives*, New York: E. P. Dutton, 1979, p. 77.

24 Quoted in John Neihardt, *Black Elk Speaks*, 1932, Lincoln, Nebraska: University of Nebraska Press, 1961, pp. 208–209.

25 Mado (Patrice) Somé, interviewed 14 September 1989.

26 Igjugarjuk, in Knud Rasmussen, *Intellectual Culture of the Hudson Bay Eskimos*, report of the Fifth Thule Expedition, 1921–1924, translated by W. E. Calvert, vol. 7, Copenhagen: Gyldendal, 1930, p. 52.

27 Tsering, in Ian Baker, "Shaman's Quest," *Hinduism Today*, November 1997, p. 23.

28 From an interview conducted for this book by Tatiana Kuznetsova.

29 Ruth M. Underhill, *Papago Woman*, New York: Holt, Rinehart and Winston, 1979, p. 9.

30 In Mark St. Pierre and Tilda Long Soldier, *Walking in the Sacred Manner*, New York: Simon and Schuster, 1995, pp. 69–70.

31 Quoted by Black Elk in Joseph Epes Brown, *The Sacred Pipe*, Norman, Oklahoma: University of Oklahoma Press, 2002, p. 71.

32 Leonard Crow Dog and Richard Erdoes, in Joan Halifax, *Shamanic Voices*, op. cit., p. 77.

33 Interview with Wande Abimbola, 6 August 1992.

34 In Jean-Guy Goulet, *Ways of Knowing: Experience, Knowledge, and Power among the Dene Tha*, Lincon, University of Nebraska Press, 1998, p. 73.

35 Tlakaelel, op. cit.

36 In James Treat, ed., *Native and Christian: Indigenous Voices on Religious Identity in the United States and Canada*, New York: Routledge, 1996, p. 52.

37 "Aborigine aiming to be first native woman MP," *Asian Age*, 30 September 1998, p. 5.

38 In Lee Romney and James F. Smith, "Crowds hail Zapatistas' Arrival in Mexico City," *Los Angeles Times*, 13 March 2001.

39 Interviews conducted December 2006 by Savinder Kaur Gill, who gratefully acknowledges the assistance of team members and data providers of the Heritage Garden Project, Kampung Simpai, Pahang, Malaysia.

40 Jameson Kurasha, "Plato and the Tortoise: A Case for the death of ideas in favor of peace and life?," paper presented at Assembly of the World's Religions, Seoul, Korea, August 1992, pp. 4–5.

41 Jace Weaver, in Jace Weaver, ed., *Native American Religious Identity: Unforgotten Gods*, Maryknoll, New York: Orbis Books, 1998.

42   Winona LaDuke, *Last Standing Woman*, Stillwater, Minnesota: Voyageur Press, 1997, p. 17.

43   Winona LaDuke, as quoted by Jamie Marks, "A campaignless campaign," *Becker County Record*, 8 September 1996, p. 1A.

44   Winona LaDuke, as quoted by Willmar Thorkelson, "Indians ask for help in regaining land," *Post-Bulletin*, Rochester, Minnesota.

45   Winona LaDuke, *Last Standing Woman*, op. cit., p. 299.

46   "The Hopi Message to the United Nations General Assembly," submitted by Thomas Banyacya, Kykyotsmovi, Arizona, 10 December 1992, reprinted on http://www. 0alphacdc.com/banyacya/un92.html

47   Rigoberta Menchú, quoted in Art Davidson, *Endangered Peoples*, San Francisco: Sierra Club Books, 1994, p. ix.

CHAPTER 3

HINDUISM

1   Sukta-yajur-veda XXVI, 3, as explained by Sai Baba in *Vision of the Divine* by Eruch B. Fanibunda, Bombay: E. B. Fanibunda, 1976.

2   *The Upanishads*, translated by Swami Prabhavananda and Frederick Manchester, The Vedanta Society of Southern California, New York: Mentor Books, 1957.

3   *Chandogya Upanishad*, ibid., p. 46.

4   *Brihadaranyaka Upanishad*, ibid.

5   *The Patanjala Yogasutra with Vyasa Commentary*, translated from Sanskrit into English by Bengali Baba, second edition, Poona, India: N. R. Bargawa, 1949, pp. 96–97.

6   Swami Sivananda, *Dhyana Yoga*, fourth edition, Shivanandanagar, India: The Divine Life Society, 1981, p. 67.

7   Ramana Maharshi, *The Spiritual Teaching of Ramana Maharshi*, Boston: Shambhala, 1972, pp. 4, 6.

8   Bhakta Nam Dev, as included in Sri Guru Granth Sahib, p. 693, adapted from the translation by Manmohan Singh, Amritsar, India: Shiromani Gurdwara Parbandhak Committee, 1989.

9   Mirabai, *Mira Bai and Her Padas*, English translation by Krishna P. Bahadur, Delhi: Munshiram Manoharlal Publishers Pvt. Ltd., 1998, no. 46, pp. 76–77.

10   Ramakrishna, quoted in Carl Jung's introduction to *The Spiritual Teaching of Ramana Maharshi*, op. cit., p. viii.

11   Sri Swami Sivananda, http://www.dishq.org/download/godmother.htm, accessed 10/13/2007.

12   *The Thousand Names of the Divine Mother: Sri Lalita Sahasranama*, with commentary by T. V. Narayana Menon, English translation by Dr. M. N. Namboodiri, Amritapuri, Kerala, India: Mata Amritanandamayi Math, 1996, verses 1–2, 8, 158–161, 220–224, pp. 5–6, 11, 82–3, 106–107.

13   Swami Sivasiva Palani, personal communication, 26 October 1989.

14   Appar, as quoted in R. de Smet and J. Neuner, eds, *Religious Hinduism*, fourth edition, Bangalore, India: St. Paul's Society, 1996, p. 321.

15   T. M. P. Mahadevan, *Outlines of Hinduism*, second edition, Bombay: Chetana Ltd., 1960, p. 24.

16   A condensation by Heinrich Zimmer of the *Vishnu Purana*, Book IV, Chapter 24, translated by H. H. Wilson, London, 1840, in *Zimmer's Myths and Symbols in Indian Art and Civilization*, New York: Pantheon Books, 1946, p. 15.

17   Uttara Kandam, *Ramayana*, third edition, as told by Swami Chidbhavananda, Tiriuuparaitturai, India: Tapovanam Printing School, 1978, pp. 198–199.

18   Chapter III:30, p. 57. All quotes from the *Bhagavad-Gita* are from *Bhagavad-Gita as It Is*, translated by A. C. Bhaktivedanta Swami Prabhupada, New York: Copyright 1972, The Bhaktivedanta Book Trust. Reproduced with permission of The Bhaktivedanta Book Trust International.

19   Ibid., III:30, p. 57.

20   Ibid., IV:3, p. 64.

21   Ibid., IV:7–8, pp. 68–69.

22   Ibid., VII:7–8, 12, pp. 126, 128.

23   Ibid., IX:26, p. 157.

24   Srimad-Bhagavatam, second canto, "The Cosmic Manifestation," part one, chapter 6:3 and 1:39, translated by A. C. Bhaktivedanta Swami Prabhupada, New York: Bhaktivedanta Book Trust, 1972, pp. 59 and 275–276.

25   Swami Vivekananda, *The Complete Works of Swami Vivekananda*, vol. III, Mayavati, India: Advaita Ashrama, 1948, p. 259.

26   Swami Sivasiva Palani, op. cit.

27   *Thus Spake Sri Ramakrishna*, fifth edition, Madras: Sri Ramakrishna Math, 1980, p. 54.

28   Swami Prajnananda, introduction to *Light on the Path*, Swami Muktananda, South Fallsburg, New York: SYDA Foundation, 1981, p. x.

29   William F. Fisher, "Sacred Rivers, Sacred Dams: Competing Visions of Social Justice and Sustainable Development along the Narmada," in Christopher Key Chapple, and Mary Evelyn Tucker, eds, *Hinduism and Ecology*, Boston: Harvard University Press, 2000, p. 413.

30   Ibid., p. 410.

31   Somjit Dasgupta, interviewed 26 February 2006.

32   Aditi Sengupta De, "The 'holy' mess," c/o editor@ip.eth.net, 31 July 2000.

33   "Kumbha Mela," *Hinduism Today*, September 1998, p. 32.

34   Robert N. Minor, "Sarvepalli Radhakrishnan and 'Hinduism': Defined and Defended," in Robert D. Baird, ed., *Religion in Modern India*, New Delhi: Manohar Publications, 1981, p. 306.

35   Condensed Gospel of Sri Ramakrishna, Mylapore, Madras: Sri Ramakrishna Math, 1911, p. 252.

36   Ramakrishna, as quoted in Swami Vivekananda, *Ramakrishna and His Message*, Howra, India: Swami Abhayananda, Sri Ramakrishna Math, 1971, p. 25.

37   Swami Vivekananda, *Inspired Talks* (recorded by a disciple during the seven weeks at Thousand Island Park), third edition, Chennai: Sri Ramakrishna Math, 1921, p. 53.

38   Lectures delivered by Shastriji Pandurang Vaijnath Athavale at the Second World Religious Congress held at Shimizu City, Japan in October 1954.

39   Shri Pandurang Vaijnath Athavale Shastri, *Nivedanam*, third edition, Bombay, 1973, p. 6.

40   Shri Pandurang Vaijnath Athavale Shastri, discourse on 10 January 1988, Bombay, on the occasion of Diamond Jubilee Celebration of Shrimad Bhagvad Geeta Pathshala by Sagar-Putras of the Fishing Community, p. 5.

41   "Aims and Ideals of Self-Realization Fellowship," http://yogananda-srf.org/aboutsrf/aims_ideals.html, accessed 3/9/2009.

42   All quotations are from an interview with Dr. Karan Singh, 17 November 1998.

43   Abbreviation of Indian Supreme Court definition of Hinduism, as itemized in "The DNA of Dharma," *Hinduism Today*, December 1996, p. 33.

44 Excerpted from Mahatma Gandhi, "Hinduism of Today," *Young India*, 8 April 1926, in Mahatma Gandhi, *What is Hinduism?*, New Delhi: National Book Trust, 1994, pp. 24–25.

CHAPTER 4
JAINISM

1 *Awashyakchurni*, pp. 304–305, among many fasts listed in Muni Nathmal, *Shraman Mahavir: His Life and Teachings*, New Delhi: Today and Tomorrow's Printers and Publishers, 1980, p. 57.

2 Akaranga Sutra, translated by Padmanabh S. Jaini in *The Jaina Path of Purification*, Berkeley: University of California Press, 1979, p. 26.

3 Padma Agrawal, "Jainism: Mahavira as Man–God," *Dialogue and Alliance*, p. 13.

4 Acharya Kund Kund, *Barasa Anuvekkha (Twelve Contemplations)*, M. K. Dhara Raja, ed., New Delhi: Kund Kund Bharati, 1990, p. 32.

5 Ibid., p. 11.

6 Akaranga Sutra, Fourth Lecture, First Lesson, in *Sacred Books of the East*, F. Max Müller, ed., vol. XXII, Jaina Sutras part I, Oxford: Clarendon Press, 1884, p. 36.

7 R. P. Jain, personal communication.

8 Acharya Tulsi, as quoted in *Anuvibha Reporter*, vol. 3, no. 1, October–December 1997, p. 54.

9 Acharya Tulsi, "World Peace through Self-Restraint," in *Anuvibha Reporter*, Vol. 1, nos. 4, 5, July–December 2003, inside front cover.

10 Avasyaka Sutra, as quoted in Padmanabh S. Jaini, *Collected Papers on Jaina Studies*, Delhi: Motilal Banarsidass Publishers, 2000, p. 223.

11 Amitagati's Dvatrimsika, 1, as quoted in Padmanabh S. Jaini, ibid., p. 224.

12 Samani Sanmati Pragya, interviewed 11 December 1993, Rishikesh, India.

13 Address to the North American Assisi Interfaith Meeting in Wichita, Kansas, 31 October 1988.

14 Gurudev Shree Chitrabhanu, *Twelve Facets of Reality: The Jain Path to Freedom*, New York: Dodd Mead and Company, 1980, p. 93.

15 Lala Sulekh Chand, in "A Rare Renunciation," *The Hindustan Times*, New Delhi, 17 February 1992, p. 5.

16 Muni Amit Sagar, in "A Rare Renunciation," ibid.

17 Acharya Mahaprajna, "Without Controlling Desires, No Reform is Possible," from *The Daily Rising Kashmir*, posted on http://www.herenow4u.net, accessed 4/4/2009.

18 Acharya Tulsi, in S. L. Ghandi, "Acharya Tulsi's Legacy," *Anuvibha Reporter*, vol. 3, no. 1, October–December 1997, p. 2.

19 Jagdish Prasad Jain "Sadhak," "Forgiveness: Its Nature and Significance," *Hindustan Times*, 8 September 2006.

20 Acharya Shri Sushil Kumar, personal communication, 30 October 1989.

21 Acharya Mahapragya, as quoted in Prof. R. P. Bhatnagar, "Acharya Mahapragya: A Living Legend," in *Anuvibha Reporter*, January–March 1995, p. 8.

CHAPTER 5
BUDDHISM

1 Majjhima-Nikaya 1.80.

2 Muhaparinibbana Sutta, Digha Nikaya, 2.99f, 155–156, quoted in *Sources of Indian Tradition*, William Theodore de Bary, ed., New York: Columbia University Press, 1958, pp. 110–111.

3 "A message from Buddhists to the Parliament of the World's Religions," Chicago, September 1993, as quoted in *World Faiths Encounter* no. 7, February 1994, p. 53.

4 Majjhima-Nikaya, "The Lesser Matunkyaputta Sermon," Sutta 63, translated by P. Lal in the introduction to *The Dhammapada*, 162/92 Lake Gardens, Calcutta, 700045 India. (Originally published by Farrar, Straus & Giroux, 1967, p. 19.) Reprinted by permission of P. Lal.

5 Walpola Sri Rahula, *What the Buddha Taught*, revised edition, New York: Grove Press, 1974, p. 17.

6 Ajahn Sumedho, "Now is the Knowing," undated booklet, pp. 21–22.

7 Ajahn Chah, "Our Real Home," Samuel Bercholz and Sherab Chodzin Kohn, *The Buddha and His Teachings*, Boston: Shambhala, 2003, p. 93.

8 Ajahn Sumedho, cited in Satnacitto Bhikku, ed., *Buddhanature*, World Wide Fund for Nature, London, 1989.

9 Maha Ghosananda, *Step by Step*, Berkeley, California: Parallax Press, 1992, p. 42.

10 Sigalovada Sutta, Dighanikaya III, pp. 180–193, quoted in H. Saddhatissa, *The Buddha's Way*, New York: George Braziller, 1971, p. 101.

11 *The Dhammapada*, translated by P. Lal, op. cit., p. 152.

12 Ibid., p. 49.

13 Ajahn Chah in *A Still Forest Pool*, Jack Kornfield and Paul Breiter, eds, Wheaton, Illinois: Theosophical Publishing House, 1985.

14 Lankavatara Sutra, as quoted in Christopher Key Chapple, "Animals and Environment in the Buddhist Birth Stories," in Mary Evelyn Tucker and Duncan Ryuken Williams, eds, *Buddhism and Ecology*, Cambridge: Harvard University Press, 1997, p. 143.

15 *The Mahavagga* 1.

16 *Suttanipatta* 1093–4.

17 Majjhima-Nikaya 1:161–4.

18 *The Dhammapada*, translated by P. Lal, op. cit., pp. 71–72.

19 Samyutta Nikaya, quoted in the introduction to *The Dhammapada*, translated by P. Lal, op. cit., p. 17.

20 Chatsumarn Kabilsingh, *Thai Women in Buddhism*, Berkeley, California: Parallax Press, 1991, p. 25.

21 Joko Beck, as quoted in Lenore Friedman, *Meetings with Remarkable Women*, Boston: Shambhala, 1987, p. 119.

22 Mahaparinibbana Sutta ii.142.

23 Interview with Ashin Nyana Dipa, 10 May 2009.

24 His Holiness the Fourteenth Dalai Lama, speaking on 15 February 1992, in New Delhi, India, Ninth Dharma Celebration of Tushita Meditation Centre.

25 As quoted in Lenore Friedman, *Meetings with Remarkable Women*, op. cit., p. 75.

26 Dainin Katagiri, "Emptiness," in Samuel Bercholz and Sherab Chodzin Kohn, *The Buddha and His Teachings*, Boston: Shambhala Publications, 1993, p. 245.

27 David W. Chappell, personal communication, 26 July 1995.

28 As quoted by Joseph A. Adler, *Chinese Religions*, London and New York: Routledge, 2002, p. 86.

29 Platform Scripture of the Sixth Patriarch, Hui-neng, quoted in *World of the Buddha*, Lucien Stryk, ed., New York: Doubleday Anchor Books, 1969, p. 340.

30 From "Hsin hsin ming" by Sengtsan, third Zen patriarch, translated by Richard B. Clarke.

31 Poems by Chinese Zen master Kuon, translated into English by Urs. App, 1996, www.iijnet.or.jp.

32 Roshi Philip Kapleau, *The Three Pillars of Zen*, New York: Anchor Books, 1980, p. 70.

33 Bunan, quoted in Stryk, *World of the Buddha*, op. cit., p. 343.

34 The Most Venerable Nichidatsu Fujii, quoted in a booklet commemorating the dedication for the Peace Pagoda in Leverett, Massachusetts, 5 October 1985.

35 The Most Venerable Nichidatsu Fujii, ibid.

36 "Rissho Kosei-kai, Practical Buddhism and Interreligious Cooperation," brochure from Rissho Kosei-kai, Tokyo.

37 Lama Drom Tonpa, as quoted in "Gems of Wisdom from the Seventh Dalai Lama," *Snow Lion Newsletter*, vol. 14, no. 4, Fall 1999, p. 14.

38 Ibid., p. 14.

39 "Stories and Songs from the Oral Tradition of Jetsun Milarepa," translated by Lama Kunga Rimpoche and Brian Cutillo in *Drinking the Mountain Stream*, New York: Lotsawa, 1978, pp. 56–57.

40 His Holiness the Fourteenth Dalai Lama, *My Land and My People*, New York: McGraw-Hill, 1962; Indian edition, New Delhi: Srishti Publishers, 1997, p. 50.

41 His Holiness the Fourteenth Dalai Lama, evening address after receiving the Nobel Peace Prize, 1989, in Sidney Piburn, ed., *The Dalai Lama: A Policy of Kindness*, second edition, Ithaca, New York: Snow Lion Publications, 1993, p. 114.

42 Cuc Nguyen, personal communication, 6 July 2003.

43 Angarika Dharmapala, as quoted in Rick Fields, *How the Swans Came to the Lake: A Narrative History of Buddhism in America*, Boston: Shambhala, 1986, p. 122.

44 Thich Nhat Hanh, *Being Peace*, Indian edition, Delhi: Full Circle, 1997, pp. 53–54.

45 Richard B. Clarke, personal communication, 2 October 1981.

46 Alan Wallace in Brian Hodel, "Tibetan Buddhism in the West: Is it working? An interview with Alan Wallace," *Snow Lion Newsletter*, vol. 15, no. 4, Fall 2000, p. 17.

47 Stephen Batchelor, *Buddhism without Beliefs: A Contemporary Guide to Awakening*, New York: Riverhead Books, 1997.

48 Walpola Rahula, "The Social Teachings of the Buddha," in *The Path of Compassion*, Fred Eppsteiner, ed., Berkeley, California: Parallax Press, 1988, pp. 103–104.

49 Metta Sutta, as translated by Maha Ghosananda, in "Invocation: A Cambodian Prayer," *The Path of Compassion*, ibid., p. xix.

50 Maha Ghosananda as quoted by Alan Channer, "Twilight of the Khmer Rouge?," http://www.forachange.co.uk/index.php?stoid=32.

51 Maha Ghosananda, *Step by Step*, quoted in "Letter from Cambodia," Coalition for Peace and Reconciliation, January 2001.

52 Daw Aung San Suu Kyi, "Freedom from Fear," http://www.dassk.org/contents.php?id=416, accessed 3/5/2006.

53 Sulak Sivaraksa, "Buddhism in a World of Change," in *The Path of Compassion*, op. cit., p. 16.

CHAPTER 6
DAOISM AND CONFUCIANISM

1 Tu Wei-ming, "The Continuity of Being: Chinese Visions of Nature," in Mary Evelyn Tucker and John Berthrong, *Confucianism and Ecology*, Cambridge, Massachusetts: Harvard University Press, 1998, pp. 106–108.

2 *The I Ching*, translated by Richard Wilhelm (German)/Cary F. Baynes (English), Princeton, New Jersey: Princeton University Press, 1967, pp. 620–621.

3 Excerpt from verse 1 in *Tao-te Ching*, translated by Stephen Mitchell. Translation copyright 1988 by Stephen Mitchell. Reprinted by permission of Harper & Row, Publishers, Inc.

4 *Dao de jing*, Chapter 1, English translation by D. C. Lau, New York/London: Penguin Classics, 1963, p. 57.

5 Lao-tzu, *Tao-te Ching*, translated by D. C. Lau, London: Penguin Books, 1963, verse 25, p. 82.

6 Lao-tzu, ibid., p. 82.

7 Chuang-tzu, *Basic Writings*, translated by Burton Watson, New York: Columbia University Press, 1964, p. 40.

8 *Dao de jing*, op. cit., chapter 71, p. 133.

9 Chuang-tzu, *Basic Writings*, translated by Burton Watson, op. cit., p. 36.

10 Guanzi, "Inward Training," as quoted in Harold D. Roth, "The Inner Cultivation Tradition of Early Daoism," in Donald S. Lopez, Jr., ed., *Religions of China in Practice*, Princeton, New Jersey: Princeton University Press, 1996, pp. 133–134.

11 *Dao de jing*, op. cit., chapter 12, p. 68.

12 *Dao de jing*, op. cit., chapter 67, p. 129; chapter 46, p. 107.

13 *Dao de jing*, op. cit. chapter 77, p. 139.

14 Liu Zhongyu, translated by Lu Pengzhi, "Daoist Folk Customs: Burning Incense and Worshiping Spirits," http://www.eng.taoism.org.hk/religious-activities&rituals/daoist-folk-customs, accessed 3/22/2007.

15 *The Secret of the Golden Flower*, translated by Richard Wilhelm/Cary Baynes, New York: Harcourt Brace Jovanovich, 1962, p. 21.

16 Excerpted from Huai-Chin Han, translated by Wen Kuan Chu, *Tao and Longevity: Mind–Body Transformation*, York Beach, Maine: Samuel Weiser, 1984, pp. 4–5.

17 Sun Bu-er, in *Immortal Sisters: Secrets of Taoist Women*, translated by Thomas Cleary, Boston: Shambhala Publications, 1989, p. 50.

18 "Taoist Association of China," http://www.eng.Taoism.org.hk/daoist-world-today/contemporary-daoist-organizations, accessed 3/22/2007.

19 Huang Zhi An, interviewed 14 August, 2008.

20 Zhou Zhongzhi, "The Significance of Taoist Ethical Thought in the Building of a Harmonious Society," paper for "Continuity+ Change: Perspectives on Science and Religion," Metanexus Institute, Philadelphia, Pennsylvania, 3–7 June 2006, p. 3.

21 Quoted in *T'ai-chi*, Cheng Man-ch'ing and Robert W. Smith, Rutland, Vermont: Charles E. Tuttle, 1967, p. 106.

22 Ibid., p. 109.

23 "Brooms, Gourds, and the Old Ways, An Interview with Daoist Master An," *Heaven Earth: The Chinese Art of Living*, vol. 1, no. 1, May 1991, p. 2.

24 Yu Yingshi, "A Difference in Starting Points," *Heaven Earth*, ibid., p. 1.

25 The Analects, VII:1, in *Sources of Chinese Tradition*, vol. 1, William Theodore de Bary, Wing-tsit Chan, and Burton Watson, eds, New York: Columbia University Press, 2000, p. 23.

26 Ibid. XIII:6, p. 32, and Analects II: 1, as translated by Ch'u Chai and Winberg Chai in *Confucianism*, Woodbury, New York: Barron's Educational Series, 1973, p. 52.

27 Confucius, *The Analects*, translated by D. C. Lau, London: Penguin Books, 1979, VIII:19, p. 94.

28 *The Texts of Confucianism, Sacred Books of the East*, Max Müller, ed., Oxford: Oxford University Press, 1891, vol. 27, pp. 450–451.

29 The Analects, XI:11, in Ch'u Chai and Winberg Chai, *The Sacred Books of Confucius and Other Confucian Classics*, New Hyde Park, New York: University Books, 1965, p. 46.

30 Ibid., X:25.

31 Ibid., X:103.

32 Mencius, in de Bary, *Sources of Chinese Tradition*, op. cit., p. 91.

33 Ibid., p. 89.

34 From the Hsun Tzu, Chapter 17, in de Bary, ibid., p. 101.

35 Frederick Streng, *Understanding Religious Life*, third edition, Belmont, California: Wadsworth, 1985, p. 2.

36 Joseph A. Adler, "Confucianism as Religion/Religious Tradition/Neither: Still Hazy After All These Years," paper presented at American Academy of Religion Annual meeting, 18 November 2006, p. 5.

37 Chang Tsai's Western Inscription, in de Bary et al., *Sources of Chinese Tradition*, op. cit.

38 Mao Zedong, "Overthrowing the Clan Authority of the Ancestral Temples and Clan Elders, the Religious Authority of Town and Village Gods, and the Masculine Authority of Husbands," 1927, as quoted in Deborah Sommer, ed., *Chinese Religion: An Anthology of Sources*, New York and Oxford: Oxford University Press, 1995, p. 305.

39 *Quotations from Chairman Mao Tse-tung*, second edition, Peking: Foreign Language Press, 1967, pp. 172–173.

40 *China Daily*, 30 January 1989, p. 1.

41 Xinzhong Yao, "Confucianism and the Twenty-first Century: Confucian Moral, Educational and Spiritual Heritages Revisited," First International Conference on Traditional Culture and Moral Education, Beijing, August 1998, p. 4.

42 Alan Qiu, quoted in Jim Yardley and David Barboza, "Quake Stirs Unexpected Reaction in China," *The New York Times*, supplement to The Asian Age, 17 May 2008, p. 3.

43 Tu Wei-ming, "Confucianism," in Arvind Sharma, ed., *Our Religions*, New York: HarperCollins Publishers, 1993, pp. 221–222.

44 Korean Overseas Information Service, *Religions in Korea*, Seoul, 1986, pp. 55–57.

45 Mary Evelyn Tucker, in Tu Weiming and Mary Evelyn Tucker, *Confucian Spirituality*, New York: Crossroad Publishing Company, 2003, p. 1.

CHAPTER 7

SHINTO

1 Motohisa Yamakage, *The Essence of Shinto: Japan's Spiritual Heart*, Tokyo/New York/London: Kodansha International, English translation 2006, p. 12.

2 Yukitaka Yamamoto, *Way of the Kami*, Stockton, California: Tsubaki America Publications, 1987, p. 75.

3 Adapted from the *Nihon Shoki (Chronicles of Japan)*, I:3, in Stuart D. B. Picken, *Shinto: Japan's Spiritual Roots*, Tokyo: Kodansha International, 1980, p. 10.

4 Sakamiki Shunzo, "Shinto: Japanese Ethnocentrism," in Charles A. Moore, ed., *The Japanese Mind*, Hawai'i: University of Hawai'i Press, p. 25.

5 Yamamoto, *Way of the Kami*, op. cit., pp. 73–75.

6 *Nihongi, Chronicles of Japan from the Earliest Times to* AD 697, translated by W. G. Aston, Rutland, Vermont: Charles Tuttle, 1985, 1:176.

7 Kishimoto Hideo, "Some Japanese Cultural Traits and Religions," in Charles A. Moore, ed., *The Japanese Mind*, op. cit., pp. 113–114.

8 Ise-Teijo, Gunshin-Mondo, Onchisosho, vol. x., quoted in *Genchi Kato*, p. 185.

9 Unidentified quotation, Stuart D. B. Picken, ed., *A Handbook of Shinto*, Stockton, California: The Tsubaki Grand Shrine of America, 1987, p. 14.

10 Ibid.

11 Yamamoto, *Way of the Kami*, op. cit., p. 97.

12 Hitoshi Iwasaki, "Wisdom from the night sky," *Tsubaki Newsletter*, 1 June 1988, p. 2.

13 Motoori Norinaga (1730–1801), Naobi no Mitma, quoted in *Tsubaki Newsletter*, 1 November 1988, p. 3.

14 Tensho Kotaijingu oracle, English translation by Norman Havens based on Japanese translation by Kamata Jun'ichi, as reproduced in Brian Bocking, "Changing images of Shinto: Sanja takusen or the three oracles," in John Breen and Mark Teeuwen, eds, *Shinto in History: Ways of the Kami*, Honolulu: University of Hawai'i Press, 2000, p. 169.

15 In W. G. Aston, *Nihongi*, Rutland, Vermont and Tokyo: Tuttle, 1972, p. 77.

16 *Tenri kyoso den* ("Life of the Founder of the Tenri-kyo Sect") compiled by the Tenri-kyo doshi-kai, Tenri, 1913, quoted in Ichiro Hori, *Folk Religion in Japan*, Chicago: University of Chicago Press, 1968, p. 237.

17 Ofudesaki, as quoted in *Aizen Newsletter of the Universal Love and Brotherhood Association*, no. 17, September–October 1997, p. 2.

18 http://www.tsubakishrine.com/misogishuho, accessed 5/2/2009.

19 Jinja-Honcho (The Association of Shinto Shrines), "The Shinto View of Nature and a Proposal Regarding Environmental Problems," Tokyo, 1997.

ZOROASTRIANISM

1 *The Hymns of Zarathushtra*, translated by Jacques Duchesne-Guillemin/Mrs. M. Henning, London: John Murray Publishers, 1952, p. 7.

2 Yasna 33:14, *Songs of Zarathushtra*, the Gathas translated by Dastur Framroze Ardeshir Bode and Piloo Nanavutty, London: George Allen and Unwin, 1952, p. 66.

3 Yasna 34:5,4, ibid., p. 67.

4 T. R. Sethna, *Book of Instructions on Zoroastrian Religion*, Karachi, Pakistan: Informal Religious Meetings Trust Fund, 1980, p. 87.

CHAPTER 8

JUDAISM

1 Genesis 1:1. *Tanakh—The Holy Scriptures: The New JPS Translation According to the Traditional Hebrew Text*, Philadelphia: The Jewish Publication Society, 1985. This translation is used throughout this chapter.

2 Genesis 1:28.

3 Genesis 6:17.

4 Genesis 9:17.

5 Genesis 22:12.

6   Personal communication, 24 March 1989.
7   Deuteronomy 7:7.
8   Exodus 3:5.
9   Exodus 3:10.
10   Exodus 3:12, 14–15.
11   Irving Greenberg, "History, Holocaust, and Covenant," in Alan L. Berger, *Judaism in the Modern World*, New York and London: New York University Press, 1994, p. 129.
12   Exodus 34:13.
13   I Kings 9:3.
14   Daniel 7:13–14.
15   From the Talmud and Midrash, quoted in *The Judaic Tradition*, Nahum N. Glatzer, ed., Boston: Beacon Press, 1969, p. 197.
16   Jacob Neusner, *Recovering Judaism*, Minneapolis: Fortress Press, 2001, p. 25.
17   Jerusalem Talmud, Demai 22a, in C. G. Montefiore and H. Lowe, eds, *A Rabbinic Anthology*, New York: Schocken Books, 1974.
18   *Kaddish Shalem*, English translation by Rabbi Sidney Greenberg in *Likrat Shabbat: Worship, Study, and Song for Sabbath and Festival Services and for the Home*, Bridgeport, Connecticut: Media Judaica/The Prayer Book Press, 1981, p. 251.
19   Maimonides, *The Guide of the Perplexed*.
20   Quoted in S. A. Horodezky, *Leaders of Hasidism*, London: Ha-Sefer Agency for Literature, 1928, p. 11.
21   Moses Sofer, ethical testament cited in W. Gunther Plaut, *The Growth of Reform Judaism: A Sourcebook of its European Origins*, New York: World Union for Progressive Judaism, 1965, pp. 256ff.
22   Elie Wiesel, *Night*, New York: Bantam Books, 1960, 1982, p. 64.
23   Aviezer Ravitzky, *Messianism, Zionism, and Jewish Religious Radicalism*, Chicago: The University of Chicago Press, 1993, p. 1.
24   Paul Johnson, *A History of the Jews*, New York: Harper and Row, 1987, p. 430.
25   Ravitzky, *Messianism*, op. cit.
26   Maimonides' "First Principles of Faith," as quoted in Louis Jacobs, *Principles of Jewish Faith*, Northvale, New Jersey: Jason Aronson, 1988, p. 33.
27   Ibn Gabirol, Keter Malkhut, quoted in Abraham J. Heschel, "One God," in *Between God and Man: An Interpretation of Judaism, from the Writings of Abraham J. Heschel*, Fritz A. Rothschild, ed., New York: Free Press, 1959, p. 106.
28   Abraham Joshua Heschel, *Man is not Alone*, New York: Farrar, Straus & Giroux, 1951, 1976, p. 112.
29   Abraham J. Heschel, "One God," op. cit., p. 104.
30   Martin Buber, in *The Way of Response: Martin Buber— Selections from His Writings*, Nahum N. Glatzer, ed., New York: Schocken Books, 1968, p. 53.
31   Isaiah 65:25, JPS Tanakh.
32   Eli Epstein, interviewed 2 March, 2009.
33   Ismar Schorsch, "Learning to Live with Less: A Jewish Perspective," in Steven C. Rockefeller and John E. Elder, *Spirit and Nature: Why the Environment is a Religious Issue*, Boston: Beacon Press, 1992, p. 35.
34   *Likrat Shabbat*, translated from the Hebrew by Rabbi Sidney Greenberg, Bridgeport, Connecticut: Media Judaica/ The Prayer Book Press, 1981, p. 61.

35   Job 1:20–21.
36   The Jewish Prayer Book, as quoted by Jocelyn Hellig, "A South African Jewish Perspective," in Martin Forward, ed., *Ultimate Visions*, Oxford: Oneworld Publications, 1995, p. 136.
37   Leviticus 11:45.
38   Talmud Berakhoth 11a, in *Ha-Suddur Ha-Shalem*, translated by Philip Birnbaum, New York: Hebrew Publishing Company, 1977, p. 14.
39   Rabbi Nina Beth Cardin, *The Tapestry of Jewish Time*, Springfield, New Jersey: Behrman House, 2000, p. 36.
40   Excerpted from Ruth Gan Kagan, "The Sabbath: Judaism's Discipline for Inner Peace," paper presented at the Assembly of the World's Religions, Seoul, Korea, 24–31 August 1992, pp. 3, 7.
41   Sanhedrin 22a, quoted in *The Second Jewish Catalog*, Sharon Strassfeld and Michael Strassfeld, eds, Philadelphia: The Jewish Publication Society, 1976.
42   Rabbi Yochanan ben Nuri, Rosh Hashanah prayer quoted by Arthur Waskow, *Seasons of Our Joy*, New York: Bantam Books, 1982, p. 11.
43   Isaiah 55:6–7.
44   As quoted by Susahhan Heschel, "The Origin of the Orange on the Seder Plate," April 2001, http://www.miriamscup.com, accessed 7/3/2009.
45   Ibid.
46   Prayer quoted by Arthur Waskow, *Seasons of Our Joy*, op. cit., p. 175.
47   Rabbi David Saperstein, "Partners in Tikkun Olam," from *Jewish Spiritual Journeys, 20 Essays written to Honor the Occasion of the 70th Birthday of Eugene Borowitz*, Laurence Hoffman and Arnold Jacob, eds, West Orange, New Jersey: Behrman House, 1997, p. xxx.
48   Rabbi David Saperstein, press conference at the Dirksen Senate Office Building, http://www.interfaithalliance. org/ site/pp.asp?c=8dKOOW<CE&b=120706, accessed 4/14/2007.
49   Rabbi David Saperstein, "Religious Underpinnings of Social Justice," remarks on being given the Chernin Award by the Jewish Council for Public Affairs, 2003.
50   Rabbi Maria Feldman, "Why Advocacy is Central to Reform Judaism," Religious Action Center of Reform Judaism, http://rac.org/_kd_items/actions.cfm, accessed 4/14/2007.
51   Mordecai M. Kaplan, "The Way I Have Come," in *Mordecai M. Kaplan: An Evaluation*, I. Eisenstein and E. Kohn, eds, New York: Jewish Reconstructionist Foundation, 1952, p. 293.
52   Rabbi Karyn D. Kedar, "Metaphors of God," in Rabbi Elyse Goldstein, ed., *New Jewish Feminism: Probing the Past, Forging the Future*, Woodstock, Vermont: Jewish Lights Publishing, 2009, pp. 40–41.
53   Melanie Dinwiddie, Egalitarian Kebutah, http://ketubah works.com/images/ketubah_text_roses_egal.
54   Jewish Orthodox Feminist Alliance, http://www.jofa.org/ about.php/who, accessed 4/18/2007.
55   Rabbi Tirzah Firestone, "Transforming Our Stories through Midrash," in Rabbi Elyse Goldstein, op. cit., p. 115.
56   Ibid., p. 117.
57   "Declaration of the ELCA to the Jewish Community," as quoted in Joel Beversluis, *A Sourcebook for Earth's Community of Religions*, revised edition, Grand Rapids, Michigan: CoNexus Press-Sourcebook Project, 1995, p. 170.

CHAPTER 9
CHRISTIANITY

1 Publishing Department of Moscow Patriarchate, The Russian Orthodox Church, Moscow, 1980, p. 239 in English translation by Doris Bradbury, Moscow: Progress Publishers, 1982.

2 "Origen on First Principles," in Hugh T. Kerr, ed., *Readings in Christian Thought*, Nashville, Tennessee: Abingdon Press, 1966, p. 46.

3 *The Gospel According to Thomas*, Coptic text established and translated by Guilloaumont et al., Leiden: E. J. Brill; New York: Harper & Row, 1959, verse 77.

4 Luke 2:47, 49. Most biblical quotations in this chapter are from the *Revised Standard Version of the Bible*, copyright 1946, 1952, 1971 by The Division of Christian Education of the National Council of the Churches of Christ in the USA. Used by permission.

5 Mark 1:10–11.

6 Dietrich Bonhoeffer, *The Cost of Discipleship*, New York: Simon & Schuster, 1959, 1995, p. 90.

7 Matthew 6:25–27.

8 Matthew 7:7.

9 Luke 9:17.

10 John 6:48.

11 William, quoted in *The Gospel in Art by the Peasants of Solentiname*, Philip and Sally Scharper, eds, Maryknoll, New York: Orbis Books, 1984, p. 42.

12 Rosemary Radford Ruether, *Women and Redemption: A Theological History*, Minneapolis: Fortress Press, 1998, p. 18.

13 Matthew 5:21–22.

14 Matthew 5:44–45.

15 Mark 10:27.

16 Luke 10:25–37, *The New English Bible*.

17 Matthew 22:39.

18 Matthew 25:37–40.

19 Matthew 5:3.

20 Mark 1:15.

21 Luke 4:43.

22 Matthew 6:10.

23 Matthew 24:29–31.

24 Matthew 15:10, *The New English Bible*.

25 Matthew 23:27–28, *The New English Bible*.

26 Isaiah 56:7.

27 Jeremiah 7:11.

28 Mark 11:15–18, *The New English Bible*.

29 Mark 8:29–30.

30 John 11:27.

31 Matthew 17:2–5.

32 John 7:16, 8:12, 23, 58.

33 Matthew 26:28.

34 Mark 11:10.

35 Mark 14:36.

36 Joachim Jeremias, *New Testament Theology: The Proclamation of Jesus*, translated by John Bowden, New York: Charles Scribner's Sons, 1971, p. 40.

37 Mark 14:41.

38 Matthew 26:64.

39 Matthew 27:11.

40 John 18:35–38.

41 Matthew 27:46.

42 Matthew 28:18–20.

43 Elisabeth Schüssler Fiorenza, *In Memory of Her*, New York: Crossroad, 1983, 1994, p. xliv.

44 Acts 4:10–12.

45 Acts 1:10–11.

46 Christos Yannaras, *Elements of Faith: An Introduction to Orthodox Theology*, English translation by Keith Schram, Edinburgh: T & T Clark, 1991, pp. 65–66.

47 Acts 2:36.

48 Acts 26:18.

49 Philippians 3:8–10.

50 Acts 17:28.

51 *The Gospel According to Thomas*, op. cit., 82.

52 *Confessions of St. Augustine,* translated by Edward Bouverie Pusey, Chicago: Encyclopedia Britannica, vol. 18 of *Great Books of the Western World*, 1952, p. 64.

53 Rowan Williams, *Resurrection*, New York: The Pilgrim Press, 1984, p. 46 with quotations from John 14:19.

54 Archimandrite Chrysostomos, *The Ancient Fathers of the Desert*, Brookline, Massachusetts: Hellenic College Press, 1980, p. 78.

55 Ibid., p. 80.

56 From *A Hopkins Reader*, John Pick, ed., New York: Oxford University Press, 1953, quoted in D. M. Dooling, ed., *A Way of Working*, New York: Anchor Press/Doubleday, 1979, p. 6.

57 "St. Francis, Testament," April 1226, p. 3, quoted in Jean Leclerc, Francois Vandenbroucke, and Louis Bouyer, eds, *The Spirituality of the Middle Ages*, vol. 2 of *A History of Christian Spirituality*, New York: Seabury Press, 1982, p. 289.

58 *The Cloud of Unknowing and The Book of Privy Counseling*, Garden City, New York: Image Books, 1973 edition, p. 56.

59 Martin Luther, "A Treatise on Christian Liberty," quoted in John Dillenberger and Claude Welch, *Protestant Christianity*, New York: Charles Scribner's Sons, 1954, p. 36.

60 Ulrich Zwingli, "On True and False Religion," quoted in Harry Emerson Fosdick, ed., *Great Voices of the Reformation*, New York: Random House, 1952, p. 169.

61 John Calvin, "Instruction in Faith," quoted in Fosdick, op. cit., p. 216.

62 John Wesley, "The Repentance of Believers," sermon preached in Londonderry, 24 April 1767, on http://www. godrules.net/library/wsermons/wsermons14, accessed 7/17/2009.

63 St. Teresa of Avila, *The Interior Castle*, translated by E. Allison Peers from the critical edition of P. Silverior de Santa Teresa, Garden City, New York: Image Books, 1961, p. 214.

64 John Wesley, as quoted in Dillenberger and Welch, *Protestant Christianity*, op. cit., p. 134.

65 Sarah Grimke, "Letters on the Equality of the Sexes and the Condition of Women" (1836–1837), in *Feminism: The Essential Historical Writings*, M. Schneir, ed., New York: Vintage, 1972, p. 38.

66 *The Documents of Vatican II*, Walter M. Abbott, ed., New York: Guild Press, 1966, p. 665.

67 Fotini Pipili, in Iina Kyriakidou, "Greek women poised to take on all-male monastic community," *Asian Age*, 14 October 1997, p. 7.

68 Father Feodor, interviewed 29 October 1994.

69 St. Gregory Palamas, "Homily on the Presentation of the Holy Virgin in the Temple," in Sophocles, *22 Homilies of St. Gr. Palamas*, Athens, 1861, pp. 175–177, quoted in Vladimir Lossky, *The Mystical Theology of the Eastern Church*, New York: St. Vladimir's Seminary Press, 1976, p. 224.

70 Jim Forest, *Pilgrim to the Russian Church*, New York: Crossroad Publishing Company, 1988, p. 50.

71 John 14:2–10, *The New English Bible*.

72 Paul Knitter, in John Hick and Paul F. Knitter, eds, *The Myth of Christian Uniqueness: Toward a Pluralistic Theology of Religions*, Maryknoll, New York: Orbis Books, 1987, pp. 192–193.

73 Matthew 20:28.

74 John 3:16–17, *The New English Bible*.

75 Archbishop Desmond Tutu, "The Face of God," *Life*, December 1990, pp. 49–50.

76 Rev. Larry Howard, interfaith service, Syracuse, New York, 25 October 1992.

77 Thomas Keating, *The Mystery of Christ: The Liturgy as Spiritual Experience*, Amity, New York: Amity House, 1987, p. 5.

78 Thomas a Kempis, *The Imitation of Christ*, p. 139.

79 F. Ioann Kronshtadtsky, as quoted in F. Veniamin Fedchenkov, *Heaven on Earth*, Moscow: Palmnik, 1994, p. 70.

80 Julia Gatta, personal communication, 22 July 1987.

81 "Brief Order for Confession and Forgiveness," Lutheran Book of Worship, prepared by the churches participating in the Inter-Lutheran Commission on Worship, Minneapolis, Minnesota: Augsburg Publishing House, 1978, p. 56.

82 World Council of Churches, Baptism, Eucharist and Ministry, Faith and Order Paper No. 111, Geneva, 1982, p. 2.

83 Father Appolinari, interviewed 28 October 1994.

84 John 1:9.

85 Jim Forest, *Pilgrim to the Russian Church*, op. cit., p. 72.

86 Thomas Merton, *Contemplative Prayer*, Garden City, New York: Image Books, 1969, p. 67.

87 Bishop Paulos Mar Gregorios, World Congress of Spiritual Concord, Rishikesh, India, 11 December 1993.

88 Interview with Professor Kathleen Dugan, 4 February 1993.

89 *The Way of a Pilgrim and The Pilgrim Continues His Way*, translated by Helen Bacovcin, New York/London: Doubleday, 1978, 1992, p. 160.

90 Luke 1:38.

91 Quoted in Jim Forest, *Pilgrim to the Russian Church*, op. cit., p. 63.

92 His All Holiness Ecumenical Patriarch Bartholomew, *Encountering the Mystery*, New York: Doubleday, 2008, p. 67.

93 Associated Press, Vatican City: "Only Catholicism 'proper': Vatican," *The Globe and Mail*, 6 September 2000, A14; Philip Pullella (Reuters), "Vatican says no religion equals Roman Catholicism," *Asian Age*, 6 September 2000, p. 5.

94 Pope Benedict XVI, *Jesus of Nazareth*, as quoted in Father Raymond J. De Souza, "Benedict Asks: 'What did Jesus actually bring to the world?'", http://ncregister.com/site/article/3427, accessed 9/2/2007.

95 Joe Mannath SDB, "Sexuality, Celibacy and the Religious Quest," *Vidyajyoti Journal of Theological Reflection*, vol. 67, no. 1, January 2003, p. 54.

96 Sean McDonagh, *The Greening of the Church*, Maryknoll, New York: Orbis Books, p. 65.

97 Jonathan Edwards, "Sinners in the Hands of an Angry God," Enfield, Connecticut, July 8, 1741, http://www.ccel.org/ccel/edwards/sermons.sinners.html, accessed 7/20/2009.

98 I Corinthians 12:6–11.

99 Vazhayil Babu, interviewed 11 December 2008.

100 Roman I. Bilas, interviewed 25 October 1994.

101 In Allan Anderson, *An Introduction to Pentecostalism*, Cambridge: Cambridge University Press, 2004, p. 138.

102 Harvey Cox, *Fire from Heaven: The Rise of Pentecostal Spirituality and the Reshaping of Religion in the Twenty-first Century*, Reading, Massachusetts: Addison-Wesley, 1995.

103 Lamin Sanneh, *Whose Religion is Christianity? The Gospel beyond the West*, Grand Rapids, Michigan: William B. Eerdmans Publishing Company, 2003, pp. 22, 23.

104 Members of African Independent Churches Report on their Pilot Study of the History and Theology of their Churches, "Speaking for Ourselves," Braamfontein, South Africa: Institute for Contextural Theology, 1985, pp. 23–24.

105 Martin Luther King, Jr., "An Experiment in Love," in *A Testament of Hope: The Essential Writings of Martin Luther King, Jr.*, James Melvin Washington, ed., San Francisco: Harper & Row, 1986, p. 16.

106 Acts 4:32–35.

107 Desmond Tutu, quoted in Charles Vila-Vicencio, "Tough and Compassionate: Desmond Mpilo Tutu," in Leonard Hulley, Louise Kretzschmar, and Luke Lungile Pato, eds, *Archbishop Tutu: Prophetic Witness in South Africa*, Cape Town: Human and Rousseau, 1996, pp. 41–42.

108 Ibid., p. 37.

109 Ibid., p. 38.

110 Francis Cull, "Desmond Tutu: Man of Prayer," in Hulley et al., *Archbishop Tutu*, op. cit., pp. 31–32.

111 Desmond Tutu, in Vila-Vicencio, "Tough and Compassionate," op. cit., pp. 44–45.

112 Gustavo Gutierrez, quoted in Phillip Berryman, *Liberation Theology*, New York: Pantheon Books, 1987, p. 33.

113 Bakole Wa Ilunga, *Paths of Liberation: A Third World Spirituality*, Maryknoll, New York: Orbis Books, 1984, p. 92.

114 Dwight N. Hopkins, ed., *Black Faith and Public Talk*, Maryknoll, New York: Orbis Books, 1999, pp. 1–2.

115 Florence Muindi, quoted in Donald E. Miller and Tetsunao Yamamori, *Global Pentecostalism: The New Face of Christian Social Engagement*, Berkeley: University of California Press, 2007, pp. 40–41.

116 I Corinthians 11:7–12.

117 Rosemary Radford Ruether, *Women and Redemption*, op. cit., pp. 32–33.

118 Ivone Gebara and Maria Clara Bingemer, *Mary, Mother of God, Mother of the Poor*, Maryknoll, New York: Orbis Books, 1989, as excerpted in Ursula King, ed., *Feminist Theology from the Third World*, Maryknoll, New York: Orbis Books, 1994, pp. 277, 280–281.

119 Sallie McFague, *Models of God: Theology for an Ecological, Nuclear Age*, Philadelphia: Fortress Press, 1987, pp. 101, 106.

120 Thomas Berry, remarks at "Seeking the True Meaning of Peace" conference in San Jose, Costa Rica, 27 June 1989.

121 Thomas Berry, in Michael Valpy, "'Geologian' saw beyond a human-centric view," *The Globe and Mail*, 18 June 2009, http://v1.theglobeandmail.com/servlet/story/LAC.20090618.OBBERRY18ART2053, accessed 7/23/2009.

122 In Laurie Goodstein, "Evangelical Leaders Join Global Warming Initiative," *The New York Times*, 8 February 2006.

123 Father Denis G. Pereira, "A New Model for India's Pastoral Clergy," *Vidyajyoti Journal*, vol. 67, no. 1, January 2003, p. 67.

124 "Decade to Overcome Violence," World Council of Churches website, www.wcc-coe.org, October 1, 2001.

125 His All Holiness Ecumenical Patriarch Bartholomew, *Encountering the Mystery*, op. cit., p. 146.

CHAPTER 10

ISLAM

1 *The Holy Qur'an*, XCVI:1–5, English translation by Abdullah Yusuf Ali, Durban, R.S.A.: Islamic Propagation Center International, 1946. This translation is used throughout this chapter, by permission. Note that despite the layout of this translation, the Qur'an is not a work of poetry.

2 Abu Abdallah Muhammad Bukhari, Kitab jami as-sahih, translated by M. M. Khan as Sahih al-Bukhari, Lahore: Ashraf, 1978–80, quoted in Annemarie Schimmel, *And Muhammad is His Messenger*, Chapel Hill, North Carolina: University of North Carolina Press, 1985, p. 11.

3 *Sura* 8:18.

4 Maulana M. Ubaidul Akbar, *The Orations of Muhammad*, Lahore: M. Ashraf, 1954, p. 78.

5 *Sura* 41:6.

6 *Sura* 28:56.

7 Hadith quoted by Annemarie Schimmel, *And Muhammad is His Messenger*, op. cit., 1985, pp. 48, 55.

8 *The Holy Qur'an*, III:104.

9 Quoted by Mahmoud Ayoub, *The Qur'an and its Interpreters*, Albany: State University of New York Press, 1984, vol. 1, p. 14.

10 Footnote 5778, *Sura* 74:1, p. 1640.

11 *Sura* 42:15.

12 Islamic Society of North America, "Islam at a Glance," Plainfield, Indiana: Islamic Teaching Center.

13 Abu Hashim Madani, quoted in Samuel L. Lewis, *In the Garden*, New York: Harmony Books/Lama Foundation, 1975, p. 136.

14 Frithjof Schuon, *Understanding Islam*, translated by D. M. Matheson, London: George Allen & Unwin, 1963, p. 59.

15 *Sura* 2:136.

16 *Sura* 32:16–17.

17 *Sura* 3:63.

18 *Sura* 41:37.

19 Quoted by Abdur-Rahman Ibrahim Doi, *"Sunnism," Islamic Spirituality: Foundations*, Seyyed Hossein Nasr, ed., New York: Crossroad, 1987, p. 158.

20 *Sura* 17:13–14.

21 *Sura* 70:16–18.

22 *Sura* 2:256.

23 Hadith quoted by Syed Ali Ashraf, "The Inner Meaning of the Islamic Rites: Prayer, Pilgrimage, Fasting, Jihad," in *Islamic Spirituality: Foundations*, op. cit., p. 114.

24 Hammudah Abdalati, *Islam in Focus*, Indianapolis, Indiana: American Trust Publications, 1975, p. 88.

25 Syed Mousmen Hussain, interviewed 18 October 2006.

26 Ibrahim Keskin Hafiz, interviewed 9 April 2008.

27 Quoted by Muhammad Rida al-Muzaffar, *The Faith of Shi'a Islam*, London: The Muhammadi Trust, 1982, p. 35.

28 Hadith #535 cited in Badi'uz-Zaman Furuzanfar, Ahadith-i Mathnawi, Tehran, 1334 sh./1955, in Persian, quoted in Annemarie Schimmel, *Mystical Dimensions of Islam*, Chapel Hill: University of North Carolina Press, 1975, p. 118.

29 Rabi'a al-'Adawiyya al-Qaysiyya, quoted in Abu Talib, Qut al-Qulub, II, Cairo, A. H. 1310, p. 57, as quoted in Margaret Smith, *Rabi'a the Mystic and her Fellow-Saints in Islam*, Cambridge: Cambridge University Press, 1928, 1984, p. 102.

30 Jalal al-Din Rumi, opening lines of the *Mathnawi*, translated by Edmund Helminski, *The Ruins of the Heart: Selected Lyric Poetry of Jelaluddin Rumi*, Putney, Vermont: Threshold Books, 1981, p. 20.

31 Jalal al-Din Rumi, *Mathnawi-i ma'nawi*, translated and edited by Reynold A. Nicholson, London: 1925–1940, vol. 4, line 2102.

32 Hadith of the Prophet, #352 in Badi'uz-Zaman Furuzanfar, Ahadith-i Mathnawi, in Schimmel, *Mystical Dimensions of Islam*, op. cit.

33 Quoted in Javad Nurbakhsh, *Sufism: Meaning, Knowledge, and Unity*, New York: Khaniqahi-Nimatullahi Publications, 1981, pp. 19, 21.

34 Al-Ghazali, in *The Faith and Practice of Al-Ghazali*, translated by William Montgomery Watt, Oxford: Oneworld Publications, 1953, 1994, pp. 77, 130.

35 Idries Shah, *The Sufis*, London: Jonathan Cape, 1964, p. 76.

36 Jalal al-Din Rumi, *Mathnawi, VI, 3220–3246*, translated by Coleman Barks, *Rumi: We Are Three*, Athens, Georgia: Maypop Books, 1987, pp. 54–55.

37 As quoted in M. Fethullah Gulen, *The Messenger of God: Muhammad*, English translation by Ali Unal, Somerset, New Jersey: The Light, 2006, p. 191.

38 Treaty cited in Philip K. Hitti, *Islam and the West*, Princeton, New Jersey: D. Van Nostrand, 1962, p. 112.

39 Uzbek Khan, 1313 charter granted to Metropolitan Peter, as quoted in *Al Risala*, June 1994, p. 12.

40 Dalil-ul-Arifin, p. 37, as quoted in W. D. Begg, *The Holy Biography of Hazrat Khwaja Muinuddin Chishti*, Botswana, Africa: G. N. Khan, 1979, p. 41.

41 Indonesian president Suharto, quoted in *Hinduism Today*, July 1989, p. 20.

42 Annemarie Schimmel, speaking on "Islam's Hidden Beauty," tape from New Dimensions Foundation, San Francisco, 1989, side 1.

43 Jalal al-Din Rumi, *Mathnawi, IV*, in *Rumi: We Are Three*, op. cit., p. 52.

44 Muhammad Mashuq ibn Ally, "Theology of Islamic Liberation," in Dan Cohn-Sherbok, ed., *World Religions and Human Liberation*, Maryknoll, New York: Orbis Books, 1992, p. 47.

45 Amina Wadud, *Qur'an and Woman*, New York: Oxford University Press, 1999, pp. ix–x, xiii, xx; Amina Wadud, "Alternative Qur'anic Interpretation and the Status of Muslim Women," in Gisela Webb, ed., *Windows of Faith: Muslim Women Scholar-Activists in North America*, Syracuse: Syracuse University Press, 2000, p. 11.

46 Seyyed Hossein Nasr, "The Pertinence of Islam to the Modern World," *The World Religions Speak on the Relevance of Religion in the Modern World*, Finley P. Dunne Jr., ed., The Hague: Junk, 1970, p. 133.

47 Shirin Ebadi, http://nobelprize.org/nobel_prizes/peace/laureates/2003/ebadi-lecture-e.html, accessed 8/17/2009.

48 "Islamic TV channel to counter the West," *Asian Age*, 20 October 1998, p. 1.

49 Ardeshir Cowasjee, "As Pak mocks education," Dawn, in *Asian Age*, 8 January 2004, p. 16.

50 Noordin Kassam, talk at Gobind Sadan Institute for Advanced Studies in Comparative Religion, New Delhi, 4 March 2006.

51 Hadith of the Prophet, as quoted in *Fakhr al-Din Al-Razi, Tafsir al-Fakhr al-Razi*, 21 vols, Mecca: al-Kaktabah al-Tijariyyah, 1990, vol. 7, p. 232.

52 *Sura* 22:39–40.

53 *Sura* 2:190.

54 *Sura* 2:217, 192.

55 Quoted in Karen Armstrong, *The Battle for God:*

Fundamentalism in Judaism, Christianity and Islam, London: HarperCollins, 2000, p. 240.

56 Azizah Y. al-Hibri, "The Taliban and Islamic Teaching," in *Sightings*, an e-mail journal published by the Martin Marty Center at the University of Chicago Divinity School, 14 March 2001.

57 Osama bin Laden, videotaped address, 7 October 2001, in Bruce Lincoln, *Holy Terrors: Thinking about Religion after September 11*, Chicago: University of Chicago Press, 2003, pp. 102–3.

58 Tony Blair, then prime minister, quoted in Alan Cowell, "Britain Proposes Allowing Schools to Forbid Full-Face Muslim Veils," *New York Times*, 21 March 2007, p. 21.

59 John L. Esposito, *The Islamic Threat: Myth or Reality?*, New York: Oxford University Press, 1993, pp. ix–x.

60 Asaf Hussain, "Fundamentalism—An Islamic Perspective," *International Interfaith Center News*, December 2000, p. 7.

61 Mahmoon-al-Rasheed, "Islam, Nonviolence, and Social Transformation," Glenn D. Paige, Chaiwat Satha-Anand, and Sarah Gilliatt, eds, Honolulu: University of Hawai'i, Center for Global Nonviolence Planning Project, 1993, p. 70.

62 Dr. A. K. Abu'l Majd, quoted in the video "Islam," Smithsonian World series, Smithsonian Institution and WETA, Washington, D.C., originally broadcast 22 July 1987, transcript pp. 6, 17.

CHAPTER 11

SIKHISM

1 *Songs of Kabir*, translated by Rabindranath Tagore, New York: Samuel Weiser, 1977, p. 45.

2 Puratan, quoted in Khushwant Singh, *Hymns of Guru Nanak*, New Delhi: Orient Longmans Ltd., 1969, p. 10.

3 Guru Nanak, Guru Granth Sahib, translated by Dr. Gopal Singh, New Delhi: World Book Centre, 1997, p.150.

4 Guru Nanak, as quoted in W. Owen Cole and Piara Singh Sambhi, *The Sikhs: Their Religious Beliefs and Practices*, London: Routledge and Kegan Paul, 1978, p. 39.

5 Sri Rag, p. 59, quoted in Trilochan Singh, Jodh Singh, Kapur Singh, Bawa Harkishen Singh, and Kushwant Singh, translators, *The Sacred Writings of the Sikhs*, reproduced by kind permission of Unwin Hyman Ltd., 1973, p. 72.

6 Bhagat Ravi Das, Rag Sorath, Guru Granth Sahib, p. 657.

7 Guru Granth Sahib, p. 724.

8 Guru Har Rai, as quoted in Dr. Gopal Singh, *A History of the Sikh People*, New Delhi: World Sikh University Press, 1979, p. 257.

9 Guru Gobind Singh, *Bachittar Natak*, autobiography.

10 Guru Granth Sahib, p. 1022.

11 Nikky-Guninder Kaur Singh, *The Birth of the Khalsa: A Feminist Re-Memory of Sikh Identity*, Albany: State University of New York Press, 2005, p. 126.

12 From Dr. S. Radhakrishnan, letter in the Baisakhi edition of *The Spokesman*, 1956, reprinted as introduction to Giani Ishar Singh Nara, *Safarnama and Zafarnama*, New Delhi: Nara Publications, 1985, pp. iv–v.

13 Mul Mantra, quoted in Singh, *Hymns of Guru Nanak*, op. cit., p. 25.

14 *Jaap Sahib*, verses 84, 159, English translation by Harjett Singh Gill, New Delhi: Gobind Sadan Institute for Advanced Studies in Comparative Religion, 2007.

15 *Adi Granth* 684, quoted in Cole and Sambhi, *The Sikhs*, op. cit., p. 74.

16 Inderpreet Kaur, interviewed 20 March 2007.

17 Guru Nanak, Guru Granth Sahib, p. 141.

18 Ibid.

19 Guru Nanak, Guru Granth Sahib, p. 473.

20 *Anand Sahib*, verse 14.

21 Excerpt from Guru Gobind Singh, *Rahitnamas*, as translated by Gurden Singh.

22 Ibid.

23 Jap Ji verses 9–10.

24 Baba Virsa Singh, quoted by Juliet Hollister in *News from Gobind Sadan*, August 1997, p. 1.

25 Baba Virsa Singh, "Challenge to Religious Leaders," *Gobind Sadan Times*, August 2000, p. 1.

26 Baba Virsa Singh, in *News from Gobind Sadan*, April 1997, p. 3.

27 Excerpts from daily Ardas of Sikhs, in English translation.

28 Baba Virsa Singh, in *News from Gobind Sadan*, May 1994, p. 4.

29 Guru Gobind Singh, *Dasam Granth*.

CHAPTER 12

NEW RELIGIOUS MOVEMENTS

1 Friday M. Mbon, "The Social Impact of Nigeria's New Religious Movements," in James A. Beckford, ed., *New Religious Movements and Rapid Social Change*, Paris and London: Unesco/Sage Publications, 1986, p. 177.

2 "Code of a Sea Org Member," J. Gordon Melton, "A Contemporary Ordered Religious Community: The Sea Organization," paper presented at the 2001 CESNUR conference in London, http://www.cesnur.org/2001/london2001/melton.hem, accessed 9/26/2009.

3 Andrew Wilson, "Visions of the Spirit World: Sang Hun Lee's 'Life in the Spirit World and on Earth' Compared with Other Spiritualist Accounts," *Journal of Unification Studies* 2, 1998, p. 123.

4 http://www.unification.org/rev_mrs_moon.html?148/30, accessed 10/3/2009.

5 http://media.radiosai.org/Journals/Vol_04/01DEC06/03-coverstory.htm

6 http://www.sathyasai.org/discour/1974/d740609.htm

7 Sathya Sai Baba, 17 May 1968, "Sathya Sai Speaks, vol. VIII, Chapter 19. On the occasion of the World Conference of Sri Sathya Sai Seva Organization, http://www.srisathyasai.org.in/Pages/SriSathyaSaiBaba/BabaHimself.htm, accessed 9/30/2009.

8 Thomas Thorkelson, interviewed 21 February 2004.

9 Gordon B. Hinkley, PBS interview broadcast, 18 July 1997.

10 "A Secure Future under God's Rule," http://www.watchtower.org/e/200805/article_03.htm, accessed 10/2/2009.

11 "Jehovah's Witnesses: Who are They?", http://www.watchtower.org/e/jt/article_01.htm.

12 www.watchtower.org.

13 Julian P. Johnson, *With a Great Master In India*, Beas, Punjab: Radha Soami Satsang Beas, 1934–2002, pp. 88–89.

14 *A Brief Description of Radhasoami Faith and a Short Note on the Holy Samadh*, fourth edition, Agra, India: S. D. Maheshwari, 1984, p. 10.

15 Ibid., p. 11.

16 Justice Anthony M. Kennedy, United States Supreme Court majority opinion summation in the Church of the Lucumi vs. The City of Hialeah, 11 June 1993.

17 Rev. William Kingsley Opoku, personal communication, 6 February 1993.

18 H. P. Blavatsky, *The Key to Theosophy*, Los Angeles: The United Lodge of Theosophists, 1920, p. 3.

19 H. P. Blavatsky, "Is Theosophy a Religion," *Lucifer*, November 1888.

20 "The Baha'is: A Profile of the Baha'i Faith and its Worldwide Community," Leicestershire, UK: Baha'i Publishing Trust, p. 42.

21 Svetlana Dorzhieva, interviewed 26 October 1994.

22 "Abdu'l-Baha," as quoted in "One World, One Faith," *National Spiritual Assemblies of the Baha'is of India*, New Delhi: Baha'i Publishing Trust, 1979, p. 3.

23 Adapted from "The Baha'i Faith," New York: Baha'i International Community (unpaginated).

24 Quoted in Ernest Cashmore, *Rastaman*, London: Unwin Paperbacks, 1983, p. 22.

25 "An Introduction to Rastafari," Ras Charles and French Dread, http://www.earthcultureroots.com/rastafarism.html, accessed 10/6/2009.

26 Starhawk, *The Spiral Dance: A Rebirth of the Ancient Religion of the Great Goddess*, San Francisco: Harper & Row, 1979, pp. 2–3.

27 Quoted in Merlin Stone, *When God was a Woman*, San Diego, California: Harcourt Brace Jovanovich, 1976, p. x.

28 Diane Rae Schulz, "Discovering Goddess Spirituality," *Awakened Woman* e-magazine, http://www.awakened woman.com/goddess_spirituality.htm, accessed 5/9/2007.

29 John Seed, "Anthropocentrism," *Awakening in the Nuclear Age*, Issue #14 (Summer/Fall 1986), p. 11.

30 Chief Seattle, "Chief Seattle's Message," quoted in *Thinking Like a Mountain: Toward a Council of All Beings*, John Seed, Joanna Macy, Pat Fleming, and Arne Naess, eds, Santa Cruz, California: New Society Publishers, 1988, p. 71.

31 J. E. Lovelock, *Gaia: A new look at life on Earth*, Oxford: Oxford University Press, pp. 9, 11.

32 James Lovelock, *The Ages of Gaia*, New York: Bantam Books, 1990, p. 206.

33 Peter Russell, "Endangered Earth: Psychological roots of the environmental crisis," *Link Up*, Issue #38 (Spring 1989), pp. 7–8.

34 Julia Butterfly Hill, circleoflifefoundation.org./review4. html.

35 David Albert, "A Children's Story: Gaura Devi Saves the Trees," *Awakening in the Nuclear Age*, op. cit., p. 15.

36 "Jesus Christ: The Bearer of the Water of Life: A Christian Reflection on the 'New Age,' Pontifical Council for Culture, Pontifical Council for Interreligious Dialogue, http://www.cesnur.org/2003/vat_na_en.htm, accessed 10/7/2009.

37 Marianne Williamson, *Illuminata*, New York: Riverhead Books, 1994, p. xvii.

38 Daily Word, http://www.dailyword.com, accessed 10/8/2009.

39 James Redfield, *The Celestine Prophecy*, London/New York: Bantam Books, 1994, cover and pp. 276–77.

40 Sandra Duarte de Souza, "Religious Transit and Ecological Spirituality in Brazil," paper presented at "The Spiritual Supermarket: Religious Pluralism in the 21st Century," 19–22 April 2001, London School of Economics, sponsored by the Center for Studies on New Religions, Italy, p. 4.

41 "Persecution," http://www.bahai.org/dir/worldwide/ persecution, accessed 10/5/2009.

42 Xinhua, "China Bans Falun Gong," *People's Daily*, 22 July 1999.

43 Catherine Wessinger, *How the Millennium Comes Violently*, New York: Seven Bridges Press, 2000, p. 6.

CHAPTER 13
RELIGION IN THE TWENTY-FIRST CENTURY

1 Jayati Ghosh, "U.S. dominates culture trade," *Asian Age*, 24 June 2008, p. 7.

2 Charles Taylor, *A Secular Age*, Cambridge, Massachusetts, and London: Belknap Press of Harvard University Press, 2007, pp. 2–3.

3 Diana Eck, "A New Geo-Religious Reality," paper presented at the World Conference on Religion and Peace Sixth World Assembly, Riva del Garda, Italy, November 1994, p. 1.

4 Jerry Falwell, http://www.falwell.com/?a=meet_falwell, accessed 7/9/2004.

5 Charles Strozier et al., "Religious Militancy or 'Fundamentalism,'" *Religion and Human Rights*, New York: The Project on Religion and Human Rights, 1994, p. 19.

6 Osama bin Laden, videotaped address, 7 October 2001, reprinted in Bruce Lincoln, *Holy Terrors: Thinking about Religion after September 11*, Chicago: University of Chicago Press, 2003, p. 103.

7 Rosalind Hackett interviewed, "The Shari'a Debate: Religion and Politics in Nigeria," Religioscope, 26 April 2002, http://www.religioscope.com/info/articles/ 012_nigeria.htm, accessed 2/2/2009.

8 His Highness the Aga Khan, address to the School of International and Public Affairs, Columbia University, 15 May 2006.

9 Vimal Tirimanna, "Can the War against Terrorism be Won?", *Vidyajyoti Journal of Theological Reflection*, July 2004, vol. 68, no. 7, pp. 529–530.

10 Bruce Lincoln, *Holy Terrors*, op. cit., p. 75.

11 George W. Bush, address to the nation, 7 October 2001, reprinted in Bruce Lincoln, ibid., pp. 100–101.

12 Excerpted from The White House transcript of President Barack Obama's speech at Cairo University, 4 June 2009, http://www.msnbc.msn.com/id/31102929/ns/politics-white_house, accessed 10/19/2009.

13 Charles S. Liebman, *Religion, Democracy, and Israeli Society*, Amsterdam: Harwood Academic Publishers, 1997, pp. 7–8.

14 Ewert Cousins, speech at North American Interfaith Conference, Buffalo, New York, May 1991.

15 Frithjof Schuon, *Understanding Islam*, London: George Allen & Unwin Ltd., translated from French, 1963, p. 41.

16 Raimundo Panikkar, "The Invisible Harmony: A Universal Theory of Religion or a Cosmic Confidence in Reality?", *Toward a Universal Theology of Religion*, Leonard Swidler, ed., Maryknoll, New York: Orbis Books, 1987, p. 147.

17 Arvind Sharma, *One Religion Too Many*, Albany, New York: State University of New York Press, 2010.

18 Wendy Brown, *Regulating Aversion: Tolerance in the Age of Identity and Empire*, Princeton, New Jersey: Princeton University Press, 2006, p. 25.

19 Swami Vivekananda, speech for the Parliament of the World's Religions, Chicago, 1893.

20 Wangari Maathai, speaking at the Oxford Global Survival Conference, quoted in *The Temple of Understanding Newsletter*, Fall 1988, p. 2.

21 "Towards a Global Ethic," Assembly of Religious and Spiritual Leaders, at the Parliament of World Religions, Chicago, 1993.

22 Valson Thampu, Malini Seshadri, and Prema Raghunath, *Living in Harmony: A Course on Peace and Value Education*, Book 6, New Delhi: Oxford University Press, 2006, p. iv.

23   Baba Virsa Singh, in Mary Pat Fisher, ed., *Loving God: The Practical Teachings of Baba Virsa Singh*, second edition, New Delhi: Gobind Sadan Institute for Advanced Studies in Comparative Religion, 1995, pp. 7–8.

24   Andreas D'Souza and Diane D'Souza, "Reconciliation: A New Paradigm for Missions," Hyderabad, India: Henry Martyn Institute of Islamic Studies, p. 5.

25   Gustavo Gutiérrez, address to the World Conference on Religion and Peace, Riva del Garda, Italy, November 1994.

26   Jimmy Carter, *Talking Peace*, New York: Penguin Books, 1995, pp. xi–xii, 21.

27   Jimmy Carter, *Living Faith*, New York: Random House, 1998, pp. 5, 13.

28   Ibid., p. 32.

29   Jimmy Carter, "This Isn't the Real America," *Los Angeles Times*, 14 November 2005.

30   *Gaudium et Spes*, "Holiness of the Marriage and the Family," 48, and "The fruitfulness of Marriage," 50, The Second Vatican Council, http://www.osjspm.org/majordoc_gaudium_et_spes_part_2.aspx, accessed 10/21/2009.

31   Dr. N. Radhakrishnan, "Glenn D. Paige and a Nonkilling World," New Delhi: Indian Council of Gandhian Studies, 2007, p. 1.

32   William J. Byron, *The Power of Principles: Ethics for the New Corporate Culture*, Maryknoll, New York: Orbis Books, 2006, p. 51.

33   Thomas L. Friedman, "How greedy cynics brought down Citi," *New York Times*, in *Asian Age*, 27 November, 2008, p. 6.

34   Vaclav Havel, *Letters to Olga*, translated by Paul Wilson, London and Boston: Faber & Faber, 1988 edition of 1983 original, pp. 236–237.

35   Pope Benedict XVI, General Audience, 8 July, 2009 and encyclical *Caritas in Veritate*, 29 June 2009.

36   Pope Paul VI, *Populorum Progressio Encyclical*, 1967.

37   Professor Syed Anwar Kabir, interviewed 12 April 1995.

38   Yasuhiro Nakasone, speech at the Sixth World Conference on Religion and Peace, Riva del Garda, Italy, 4 November 1994, p. 3.

39   Baba Virsa Singh, *Loving God*, op. cit., p. 60.

GLOSSARY

In the glossary, most words are accompanied by a guide to pronunciation. This guide gives an accepted pronunciation as simply as possible. Syllables are separated by a space and those that are stressed are underlined. Letters are pronounced in the usual manner for English unless they are clarified in the following list.

	as in	
a		flat
aa		father
aw		saw
ay		pay
ai		there
ee		see
e		let
i		pity
ī 1		high
o		not
ŏŏ		book
oo		food
oy		boy
ō		no
ow		now
u		but
ă, ĕ, ŏ, ŭ		about (unaccented vowels represented by "ə" in some phonetic alphabets)
er, ur, ir		fern, fur, fir
ch		church
j		jet
ng		sing
sh		shine
wh		where
y		yes
kh		guttural aspiration (ch in Welsh and German)

A

absolutist Someone who holds a rigid, literal, exclusive belief in the doctrines of their religion.

Advaita Vedanta (ad v ī ee ta ve dan ta) Nondualistic Hindu philosophy, in which the goal is the realization that the self is Brahman.

Adi Granth (Guru Granth Sahib) Sacred scriptures of the Sikhs.

Advent The month of spiritual preparation leading up to Christmas.

African Instituted Churches Christian churches primarily founded or shaped in Africa.

Agni (aag nee) The god of fire in Hinduism.

agnosticism (ag nos ti siz ĕm) The belief that if there is anything beyond this life, it is impossible for humans to know it.

ahimsa (ă him să) Nonviolence, a central Jain principle.

Allah (aa lă) The one God, in Islam.

allegories Narratives that use concrete symbols to convey abstract ideas.

Ameshta Spenta In Zoroastrianism, six divine powers (the Good Mind, Righteousness, Absolute Power, Devotion, Perfection, and Immortality), personified and worshiped as deities with shining eyes and beautiful forms after Zarathustra's death.

Amida (ă mee dă) (Sanskrit: **Amitabha**) The Buddha of Infinite Light, the personification of compassion whom the Pure Land Buddhists revere as the intermediary between humanity and Supreme Reality; esoterically, the Higher Self.

amrit (am ret) The water, sweetened with sugar, used in Sikh baptismal ceremonies.

anatman (Pali: **anatta**) The principle that there is no eternal self.

anekantwad (ă nay kant wăd) The Jain principle of relativity or open-mindedness.

angel In the Zoroastrian, Jewish, Christian, and Islamic traditions, an invisible servant of God.

Anglicanism The Church of England, founded by Henry VIII when he split from Rome and formalized by Elizabeth I in 1559.

anitya (Pali: **anicca**) Impermanence.

Annunciation (ă nun see ay shun) In Christianity, the appearance of an angel to the Virgin Mary to tell her that she would bear Jesus, conceived by the Holy Spirit.

anthropocentrism (an thro po sen triz ĕm) The assumption that the whole universe revolves around the human species.

anti-Semitism Prejudice against Jews.

aparigraha (ă paa ree gră hă) The Jain principle of nonacquisitiveness.

apocalypse (ă <u>paw</u> kă lips) In Judaism and Christianity, the dramatic end of the present age.

apostasy Accusation of abandonment of religious principles.

apostle Missionary follower of Christ who spread his word.

arhant (<u>aar</u> hănt) (Pali: *arhat* or *arahat*) A "Worthy One" who has followed the Buddha's Eightfold Path to liberation, broken the fetters that bind us to the suffering of the Wheel of Birth and Death, and arrived at nirvana; the Theravadan ideal.

Ark of the Covenant In Judaism, the shrine containing God's commandments to Moses.

Aryan Invasion Theory Speculation originally advanced by Western scholars that the Vedas were written by people invading India rather than by people already there.

Aryans (<u>ayr</u> ee ăns) The Indo-European pastoral invaders of many European and Middle Eastern agricultural cultures during the second millennium BCE.

asana (<u>aa</u> să nă) A yogic posture.

Ascension The ascent of Jesus to heaven forty days after his Resurrection.

Ashkenazim An ethnic grouping of the Jews that migrated first to Italy, then spread throughout central and eastern Europe and thence on to the Americas.

ashram (<u>ash</u> ram) In Indian tradition, a usually ascetic spiritual community of those who have gathered around a guru.

Assumption Feast celebrating the bodily ascent of Mary to heaven.

atheism (<u>ay</u> thee is em) Belief that there is no deity.

atman (<u>aat</u> man) In Hinduism, the soul.

avatar In Hinduism, the earthly incarnation of a deity.

Avesta Holy text of Zoroastrian teaching and liturgy, only fragments of which have survived.

awakening Awareness of invisible Reality.

Axial Age Period dating approximately sixth century BCE during which a large number of great religious leaders and thinkers appeared in many parts of the ancient world, including the authors of the Upanishads, the Buddha, Mahavir, Confucius, Laozi, Socrates, and Zarathushtra.

B

baptism A Christian sacrament by which God cleanses all sin and makes one a sharer in the divine life, and a member of Christ's body, the Church.

Baptists Protestant denomination in which baptism takes place in adulthood.

barakah (bă <u>raa</u> ka) In Islamic mysticism, the spiritual wisdom and blessing transmitted from master to pupil.

Bar Mitzvah (baar <u>mitz</u> vă) The coming-of-age ceremony for a Jewish boy.

Bat Mitzvah (bat <u>mitz</u> vă) The coming-of-age ceremony for a Jewish girl in some modern congregations.

Beatitudes (bee <u>at</u> ĕ toods) Short statements by Jesus about those who are most blessed.

Bhagavad-Gita (<u>ba</u> gă văd <u>gee</u> tă) A portion of the Hindu epic *Mahabharata* in which Lord Krishna specifies ways of spiritual progress.

bhakta (<u>bak</u> taa) Devotee of a deity, in Hinduism.

bhakti (<u>bak</u> tee) In Hinduism, intense devotion to a personal aspect of the deity.

bhakti yoga In Hinduism, the path of devotion.

bhikshu (bi kshoo) (Pali: *bhikkhu*; feminine: *bhikshuni* or *bhikkhuni*). A Buddhist monk or nun who renounces worldliness for the sake of following the path of liberation and whose simple physical needs are met by lay supporters.

bodhisattva (<u>boo</u> dee sat vă) In Mahayana Buddhism, one who has attained enlightenment but renounces nirvana for the sake of helping all sentient beings in their journey to liberation from suffering.

Brahman (<u>braa</u> măn) The impersonal Ultimate Principle in Hinduism.

Brahmanas (braa mă năs) The portion of the Hindu Vedas concerning rituals.

brahmin (<u>braa</u> min) **(brahman)** A priest or member of the priestly caste in Hinduism.

Buddha-nature A fully awakened consciousness.

C

caliph (<u>kay</u> lif) In Sunni Islam, the successor to the Prophet.

Calvinism Protestant denomination founded by John Calvin in the sixteenth century and believing in predestination.

canon Authoritative collection of writings, works, etc., applying to a particular religion or author.

caste (kast) Social class distinction on the basis of heredity or occupation.

catholic Universal, all-inclusive. Christian churches referring to themselves as Catholic claim to be the representatives of the ancient undivided Christian church.

chakra (<u>chuk</u> ră) An energy center in the subtle body, recognized in *kundalini* yoga.

charisma (kă <u>riz</u> mă) A rare personal magnetism, often ascribed to a founder of a religion.

Christmas Feast on 25 December celebrating the birth of Jesus Christ.

Christology The attempt to define the nature of Jesus and his relationship to God.

Common Era Years after the traditional date used for the birth of Jesus, previously referred to in exclusively Christian terms as AD and now abbreviated to CE as opposed to BCE ("before Common Era").

communion see Eucharist.

comparative religion Scholarly discipline attempting to understand and compare religious patterns from around the world.

confirmation A Christian sacrament by which awareness of the Holy Spirit is enhanced.

Congregationalism Protestant denomination based on Calvinism, emphasizing the independence of each local congregation.

Conservative Judaism Branch that seeks to maintain traditional laws and practices while employing modern methods of scholarship.

cosmogony (kos <u>mog</u> ŏn ee) A model of the evolution of the universe.

Creationism Belief that all life forms were intentionally created by a Divine Being.

creed A formal statement of the beliefs of a particular religion.

crucifixion In Roman times, the execution of a criminal by fixing him to a cross; with reference to Jesus, his death on the cross, symbolic of his self-sacrifice for the good of all humanity.

crusades Military expeditions undertaken by the Christians of Europe in the eleventh to thirteenth centuries to recover the Holy Land from the Muslims; any war carried on under papal sanction.

cult Any religion that focuses on worship of a particular person or deity.

D

Dao (dow) (also **Tao**) The way or path, in Far Eastern traditions. The term is also used as a name for the Nameless.

darshan (daar shan) Visual contact with the divine through encounters with Hindu images or gurus.

Darwinism Belief that life evolved by biological processes such as natural selection.

davening (daa věn ing) In Hasidic Judaism, prayer.

deity yoga (dee i tee yō gǎ) In Tibetan Buddhism, the practice of meditative concentration on a specific deity.

denomination (di nom ě nay shun) One of the Protestant branches of Christianity.

dervish (der vish) A Sufi ascetic, in the Muslim tradition.

deva (day vǎ) In Hinduism, a deity.

Dhammapada (dam ǎ pǎ dǎ) A collection of short sayings attributed to the Buddha.

dharma (daar mǎ) (Pali: *dhamma*) In Hinduism, moral order, righteousness, religion. In Buddhism, the doctrine or law, as revealed by the Buddha; also the correct conduct for each person according to his or her level of awareness.

dhimmi (dě hem ee) A person of a non-Muslim religion whose right to practice that religion is protected within an Islamic society.

diaspora (d ī ass po ra) Collectively, the practitioners of a faith living beyond their traditional homeland. When spelled with a capital "D", the dispersal of the Jews after the Babylonian exile.

Digambara (di gǔm bǎ rǎ) A highly ascetic order of Jain monks who wear no clothes.

dogma (dog mǎ) A system of beliefs declared to be true by a religion.

Dreaming (Dream Time) The timeless time of Creation, according to Australian Aboriginal belief.

dualistic Believing in the separation of reality into two categories, particularly the concept that spirit and matter are in separate realms.

dukkha (doǒ kǎ) According to the Buddha, a central fact of human life, variously translated as discomfort, suffering, frustration, or lack of harmony with the environment.

Durga (doǒr ga) The Great Goddess as destroyer of evil, and sometimes as *sakti* of Siva.

E

Easter Movable feast in spring celebrating the Resurrection of Jesus Christ.

ecumenism (ek yoo mě niz ěm) Rapprochement between branches of Christianity or among all faiths.

enlightenment Wisdom that is thought to come from direct experience of Ultimate Reality.

epic A long historic narrative.

Epiphany (ee pi fǎni) "Manifestation"; in Christianity the recognition of Jesus's spiritual kingship by the three Magi.

eschatology (es kǎ tol ǒ ji) Beliefs about the end of the world and of humanity.

Essenes (es eenz) Monastic Jews who were living communally, apart from the world, about the time of Jesus.

ethnic religions New religions which emerged since the fall of communism as revivals of pre-Christian ethnic traditions in eastern Europe and Russia.

Eucharist (yoo kǎ rist) The Christian sacrament by which believers are renewed in the mystical body of Christ by partaking of bread and wine, understood as his body and blood.

evangelicalism Diverse Christian movement calling for a return to biblical faith, personal conversion experience, and spreading of the gospel.

evangelism (i van jě liz ěm) Ardent preaching of the Christian gospel.

exclusivism The idea that one's own religion is the only valid way.

excommunication Exclusion from participation in the Christian sacraments (applied particularly to Roman Catholicism), which is a bar to gaining access to heaven.

exegesis (ex a gee sis) Critical examination of a religious text.

F

Falun Gong/Falun Dafa A form of Qigong mixing Buddhism with Daoist energy practices, and emphasizing ethics—the development of truthfulness, benevolence, and forbearance.

Fatiha (fat haa) The first sura of the Qur'an.

fatwa In Islam, a legal opinion issued by an authority according to a particular school of law.

feng shui (fěng shwee) The Daoist practice of determining the most harmonious position for a building according to the natural flows of energy.

Five K's In Sikhism, the symbols worn by Khalsa members.

fundamentalism (fun dǎ men tǎl iz ěm) Insistence on what people perceive as the historical form of their religion, in contrast to more contemporary influences. This ideal sometimes takes extreme, rigidly exclusive, or violent forms.

G

Gamara In Judaism, commentaries on the Talmud, additional to the Mishnah.

Gathas In Zoroastrianism, metric verses or hymns which were the words of the prophet Zarathushtra.

Gayatrimantra (gī a tree man trǎ) The daily Vedic prayer of upper-caste Hindus.

Gentile (<u>jen</u> tīl) Any person who is not of Jewish faith or origin.

Geonim In Judaism, the administrators of the two great rabbinic academies in medieval Babylon.

ghetto An urban area occupied by those rejected by a society, such as quarters for Jews in some European cities.

gnosis (nō sis) Intuitive knowledge of spiritual realities.

Gnosticism (<u>nos</u> ti siz ĕm) Mystical perception of spiritual knowledge.

Goddess spirituality Worship of a high goddess in ancient times, now revived in many places.

gospel In Christianity, the "good news" that God has raised Jesus from the dead and in so doing has begun the transformation of the world.

gurdwara (gŏŏr <u>dwa</u> rä) A Sikh temple.

guru (g<u>ŏŏ</u> roo) In Hinduism, an enlightened spiritual teacher.

Guru Granth Sahib (goo roo granth <u>sa</u> heeb) The sacred scripture compiled by the Sikh Gurus.

H

Hadith (<u>haad</u> ith) In Islam, a traditional report about a reputed saying or action of the Prophet Muhammad.

haggadah (hă <u>gaa</u> dä) The nonlegal part of the Talmud and Midrash.

hajj (haaj) The holy pilgrimage to Mecca, for Muslims.

halakhah (haa laa <u>khaa</u>) Jewish legal decision and the parts of the Talmud dealing with laws.

Haredi (Ultra-Orthodox) Favoring detachment from non-Jewish culture, to focus on the Torah.

Hasidism (<u>has</u> īd iz ĕm) Ecstatic Jewish piety, dating from eighteenth-century Poland.

hatha **yoga** (<u>ha</u> thă <u>yo</u> gă) Body postures, diet, and breathing exercises to help build a suitable physical vehicle for spiritual development.

havan In Hinduism, a sacred fireplace around which ritual fire ceremonies are conducted.

heretic (<u>hair</u> i tik) A member of an established religion whose views are unacceptable to the orthodoxy.

hermeneutics The field of theological study that attempts to interpret scripture.

heyoka (hay <u>yō</u> kă) "Contrary" wisdom or a person who embodies it, in some Native American spiritual traditions.

hijab (<u>hay</u> jab) The veiling of women for the sake of modesty in Islam.

hijrah (<u>hij</u> ră) Muhammad's migration from Mecca to Medina.

Hinayana (<u>hee</u> nă <u>ya</u> nă) In Mahayana Buddhist terminology, the label "lesser vehicle," given to the orthodox southern tradition now represented by Theravada; in Tibetan terminology, one of the three vehicles for salvation taught by the Buddha.

Holocaust (<u>haw</u> lō cawst) The genocidal killing of six million Jews by the Nazis during World War II.

I

icon (ī kon) A sacred image, a term used especially for the paintings of Jesus, Mary, and the saints of the Eastern Orthodox Christian Church.

iconoclast One who attacks cherished beliefs or destroys sacred images.

ijtihad (ij ti <u>haad</u>) In Islam, reasoned interpretation of sacred law by a qualified scholar.

Imam (i <u>maam</u>) In Shi'ism, the title for the person carrying the initiatic tradition of the Prophetic Light.

imam (i <u>maam</u>) A leader of Muslim prayer.

immanent Present in Creation.

incarnation Physical embodiment of the divine.

inclusivism The idea that all religions can be accommodated within one religion.

indigenous (in <u>dij</u> ĕ nĕs) Native to an area.

Indra (<u>in</u> dră) The old Vedic thunder god in the Hindu tradition.

indulgence In Roman Catholic Christianity, granting of a remission of sins.

infidel (<u>in</u> fid ĕl) The Muslim and Christian term for "nonbeliever," which each tradition often applies to the other.

Inquisition (in kwi <u>zi</u> shun) The use of force and terror to eliminate heresies and nonbelievers in the Christian church, starting in the thirteenth century.

intelligent design The concept that scientific discoveries and recognition of complex life processes prove the existence of a single being, an Intelligent Designer.

interfaith dialogue Appreciative communication between people of different religions.

Islam In its original meaning, complete, trusting surrender to God.

Islamist A person seeking to establish Islamic states in which the rule of God is supreme.

J

Janam-sakhis Traditional Sikh biographies, especially stories of the life of Guru Nanak.

Jap Ji (<u>jap</u> jee) The first morning prayer of Sikhs, written by Guru Nanak.

Jehovah's Witnesses Movement holding that many modern Christian doctrines are false, and advocating what is regarded as early Christianity.

jihad (<u>ji</u> had) The Muslim's struggle against the inner forces that prevent God-realization and the outer barriers to establishment of the divine order.

Jina (<u>jī</u> nă) In Jainism, one who has realized the highest, omniscient aspect of his or her being and is therefore perfect.

jinn (jin) In Islam, an invisible being of fire.

jiva (<u>jee</u> vă) The soul in Jainism.

jnana yoga (ya na <u>yō</u> gă) The use of intellectual effort as a yogic technique.

Jujiao see Rujiao.

justified In Christianity, having been absolved of sin in the eyes of God.

K

Kabbalah (kă <u>baa</u> lă) The Jewish mystical tradition.

Kali (<u>kaa</u> lee) Destroying and transforming Mother of the World, in Hinduism.

Kali Yuga (<u>kaa</u> lee <u>yoo</u> gă) In Hindu world cycles, an age of chaos and selfishness, including the one in which we are now living.

kami (<u>kaa</u> mee) The Shinto word for that invisible sacred quality that evokes wonder and awe in us, and also for the invisible spirits throughout nature that are born of this essence.

kannagara (kă nă gă ră) Harmony with the way of the *kami* in Shinto.

karma (<u>kaar</u> mā) (Pali: *kamma*) In Hinduism and Buddhism, our actions and their effects on this life and lives to come. In Jainism, subtle particles that accumulate on the soul as a result of one's thoughts and actions.

karma yoga (<u>kaar</u> mă <u>yō</u> gă) The path of unselfish service in Hinduism.

kenotic (ki <u>not</u> ik) In Russian Orthodox Christianity, belief in the monastic pattern of ascetic poverty combined with service in the world.

kensho (ken shō) Sudden enlightenment, in Zen Buddhism.

kevala (<u>kay</u> vă lă) The supremely perfected state in Jainism.

Khalsa (<u>kal</u> să) The body of the pure, as inspired by the Sikh Guru Gobind Singh.

kirtan (<u>keer</u> tan) Devotional singing of hymns from the Guru Granth Sahib in Sikhism.

koan (<u>kō</u> aan) In Zen Buddhism, a paradoxical puzzle to be solved without ordinary thinking.

kosher (<u>kō</u> sher) Ritually acceptable, applied to foods in Jewish Orthodoxy.

kshatriya (<u>ksha</u> tree ă) A member of the warrior or ruling caste in traditional Hinduism, Jainism, and Buddhism.

kufr (<u>koo</u> fer) In Islam, the sin of atheism, of ingratitude to God.

kundalini (koon dă <u>lee</u> nee) In Hindu yogic thought, the life force that can be awakened from the base of the spine and raised to illuminate the spiritual center at the top of the head.

L

Lakshmi In Hinduism, the consort of Vishnu.

lama (<u>laa</u> mă) A Tibetan Buddhist monk, particularly one of the highest in the hierarchy.

langar (<u>lan</u> găr) In Sikh tradition, a free communal meal without caste distinctions

Lent The forty days of spiritual preparation leading up to Easter.

li (lee) Ceremonies, rituals, and rules of proper conduct, in the Confucian tradition.

liberal Flexible in approach to religious tradition; inclined to see tradition as metaphorical rather than literal truth.

Liberal Judaism see Reform Judaism.

liberation theology Christianity expressed as solidarity with the poor.

lifeway An entire approach to living in which sacred and secular are not separate.

lingam (<u>ling</u> ăm) A cylindrical stone or other similarly shaped natural or sculpted form, representing for Shaivite Hindus the unmanifest aspect of Shiva.

literati The philosophical form of Daoism, followed by intellectuals and artists.

liturgy (<u>lit</u> ĕr jee) In Christianity and Judaism, the rites of public worship.

Lubavich Hasidim Highly structured Orthodox Jewish movement that uses modern technology for propagation but has traditional lifestyles.

Lutheranism Modern denomination of the breakaway Protestant church founded by Martin Luther in 1517.

M

Mahabharata (mă haa <u>baa</u> ră tă) A long Hindu epic that includes the *Bhagavad-Gita*.

Mahayana (maa hă <u>ya</u> nă) The "greater vehicle" in Buddhism, the more liberal and mystical Northern School, which stressed the virtue of altruistic compassion rather than intellectual efforts at individual salvation.

mandala (man <u>daa</u> lă) A symmetrical image, with shapes emerging from a center, used as a meditational focus.

mantra (<u>man</u> tră) A sound or phrase chanted to evoke the sound vibration of one aspect of creation or to praise a deity.

mass The Roman Catholic term for the Christian eucharist.

materialism The tendency to consider material possessions and comforts more important than spiritual matters, or the philosophical position that nothing exists except matter and that there are no supernatural dimensions to life.

maya (<u>mī</u> yă) In Indian thought, the attractive but illusory physical world.

medicine Spiritual power, in some indigenous traditions.

medicine person An indigenous healer.

Messiah The "anointed," the expected king and deliverer of the Jews; a term later applied by Christians to Jesus.

metaphysics Philosophy based on theories of subtle realities that transcend the physical world.

metta (<u>met</u> ă) In Buddhist terminology, loving kindness.

Midrash (<u>mid</u> rash) The literature of delving into the Jewish Torah.

mikva (<u>mik</u> vă) A deep bath for ritual cleansing in Judaism.

millennium One thousand years, a term used in Christianity and certain newer religions for a hoped-for period of a thousand years of holiness and happiness, with Christ ruling the earth, as prophesied in the Book of Revelation.

minyan (<u>min</u> yăn) The quorum of ten adult males required for Jewish communal worship.

Mishnah In Judaism, the systematic summation of the legal teachings of the oral tradition of the Torah.

misogi (mee <u>sō</u> gee) The Shinto waterfall purification ritual.

mitzvah (<u>mitz</u> vă) (plural: *mitzvot*) In Judaism, a divine commandment or sacred deed in fulfillment of a commandment.

Modern Orthodoxy Branch of Orthodox Judaism, dedicated to the significance of Israel and Jewish law, which values secular knowledge and integration with non-Jews.

modernism Twentieth-century values including individualism, preference for change rather than continuity, quantity rather than quality, efficiency, pragmatism, and profiteering, all seen by some as threatening the existence of traditional religious values.

moksha (<u>mōk</u> shǎ) In Hinduism, liberation of the soul from illusion and suffering.

monistic (<u>mon</u> iz tik) Believing in the concept of life as a unified whole, without a separate "spiritual" realm.

monotheistic (mon ō <u>thee</u> iz tik) Believing in a single God.

muezzin (moo <u>ez</u> in) In Islam, one who calls the people to prayer from a high place.

mujahid (<u>moo</u> jǎ hid) In Islam, a selfless fighter in the path of Allah.

muni (<u>moo</u> nee) A Jain monk.

murshid (<u>moor</u> shid) A spiritual teacher, in esoteric Islam.

mystic One who values inner spiritual experience in preference to external authorities and scriptures.

mysticism The intuitive perception of spiritual truths beyond the limits of reason.

myth A symbolic story expressing ideas about reality or spiritual history.

N

naga (<u>naa</u> gǎ) A snake, worshiped in Hinduism.

Nam (naam) The Holy Name of God reverberating throughout all of Creation, as repeated by Sikhs.

Neo-Confucianism Confucianism stressing the importance of meditation and dedication to becoming a "noble person" established during the Chinese Han and Sung dynasties.

Neo-Paganism Nature-oriented spirituality referring to pre-Christian sacred ways.

Nicene Creed Basic profession of faith for many Christian denominations in East and West, including all Orthodox churches, framed in a council held in Constantinople in 381 CE, and proposed as a basis for unifying all Christians.

nirvana (ner <u>va</u> na) (Pali: **nibbana**) In Buddhism, the ultimate egoless state of bliss.

nontheistic Perceiving spiritual reality without a personal deity or deities.

O

occult Involving the mysterious, unseen, supernatural.

oharai Shinto purification ceremony.

OM (ōm) In Hinduism, the primordial sound.

original sin The Christian belief that all human beings are bound together in prideful egocentricity. In the Bible, this is described mythically as an act of disobedience on the part of Adam and Eve.

orisa The Yoruba term for a deity, often used in speaking of West African religions in general.

orthodox Adhering to the established tradition of a religion.

Orthodox Judaism Observing the traditional rabbinical *halakhah*; the strictest form of Judaism.

P

Pali (<u>paa</u> lee) The Indian dialect first used for writing down the teachings of the Buddha, which were initially held in memory, and still used today in the **Pali Canon** of scriptures recognized by the Theravadins.

Pahlavi Texts written or translated in Middle Persian from about the ninth century CE with detailed instructions about the rituals and customs of the Zoroastrians in Iran.

Panth In Sikhism, the religious community.

parable (<u>par</u> ǎ bǔl) An allegorical story.

Paraclete (<u>par</u> ǎ kleet) The entity that Jesus said would come after his death to help the people.

Parsis Persian Zoroastrians who avoided conversion to Islam by migrating to western India.

Parvati (<u>paar</u> vǎ tee) Siva's spouse, sweet daughter of the Himalayas.

passion narratives Descriptions in the gospels of Christ's suffering, betrayal, trial, and death.

patriarchal Group, society, or religion led by men in a fatherly role.

penance An act of self-punishment to atone for wrongdoings.

Pentateuch (<u>pen</u> tǎ took) The five books of Moses at the beginning of the Hebrew Bible.

Pentecost (<u>pen</u> tě kost) The occasion when the Holy Spirit descended upon the disciples of Jesus after his death.

Pentecostalism Charismatic Protestant denomination experiencing the manifestation of divinely inspired powers by signs such as "speaking in tongues."

Pharisees (<u>fair</u> ě seez) In Roman-ruled Judaea, liberals who tried to practice Torah in their lives.

phenomenology An approach to the study of religions that involves appreciative investigation of religious phenomena to comprehend their meaning for their practitioners.

pluralism An appreciation of the diversity of religions.

pogrom An attack against Jews.

polytheistic (pol ě thee iz ěm) Believing in many deities.

pope The Bishop of Rome and head of the Roman Catholic Church.

Prakriti (<u>praak</u> ri tee) In Samkhya Hindu philosophy, the cosmic substance.

prana (<u>praa</u> nǎ) In Indian thought, the invisible life force.

pranayama (<u>praa</u> nǎ ya mǎ) Yogic breathing exercises.

prasad (prǎ <u>saad</u>) In Indian traditions, blessed food.

presbyter A governor of the Christian Reformed Church that sprung from Calvinism.

Presbyterianism Protestant denomination based on Calvinism, governed by presbyters or officials of the church.

profane Worldly, secular, as opposed to sacred.

puja (<u>poo</u> jǎ) Hindu ritual worship.

Puranas (pǒo <u>raa</u> nǎs) Hindu scriptures written to popularize the abstract truths of the Vedas through stories about historical and legendary figures.

Pure Land A Buddhist sect in China and Japan that centers on faith in Amida Buddha, who promised to welcome believers to the paradise of the Pure Land, a metaphor for enlightenment.

Purgatory (<u>pur</u> gǎ tor ee) In some branches of Christianity, an intermediate after-death state in which souls are purified from sin.

Purusha (poo <u>roo</u> shǎ) The Cosmic Spirit, soul of the universe in Hinduism; in Samkhya philosophy, the eternal Self.

Q

qi (*ki*) (also *ch'i*) (chee) The vital energy in the universe and in our bodies, according to Far Eastern esoteric traditions.

Qigong (also **ch'i-kung**) (chee kung) A Daoist system of harnessing inner energies for spiritual realization.

Quakers Protestant denomination with no liturgy, but the expectation that God will speak through members of the congregation.

R

rabbi (<u>rab</u> ī) Historically, a Jewish teacher; at present, the ordained spiritual leader of a Jewish congregation.

raja yoga Mental concentration yoga (ancient technique for spiritual realization).

Ramayana (raa <u>maa</u> yǎ nǎ) The Hindu epic about Prince Rama, defender of good.

rapture Nineteenth-century belief amongst some Christians, using Paul's letter to the Thessalonians (I Thess. 4:17) to say that Christians would be caught up in clouds to meet Jesus when he returned to earth.

realization Personal awareness of the existence of Unseen Reality.

Reconstructionism Movement holding that Judaism is an evolving religious civilization.

redaction Editing, organizing

Reform Judaism Movement that began in the nineteenth century as a way of modernizing the religion and making it more accessible and open-ended.

reincarnation The transmigration of the soul into a new body after death of the old body.

relic In some forms of Christianity, part of the body or clothing of a saint.

religion A particular response to dimensions of life considered sacred, as shaped by institutionalized traditions.

Religious Zionism Holds as central the resettlement of the Jews in Israel.

ren (also *jen*) (yen) Humanity, benevolence—the central Confucian virtue.

Resurrection The rising of Jesus in his earthly body on the first Easter Day, three days after his crucifixion and death.

Rig Veda (rig <u>vay</u> dǎ) Possibly the world's oldest scripture, the foundation of Hinduism.

rishi (<u>rish</u> ee) A Hindu sage.

ritual A repeated, patterned religious act.

Rujiao (ree tzǔ yow) The Chinese term for the teachings based on Confucius.

S

Sabbath (<u>sab</u> ǎth) The day of the week set aside for rest and worship in Judaism and Christianity.

sacrament Outward and visible sign of inward and spiritual grace in Christianity. Almost all churches recognize baptism and the eucharist as sacraments; some churches recognize five others as well.

sacred The realm of the extraordinary, beyond everyday perceptions, the supernatural, holy.

sacred thread In Hinduism, a cord worn over one shoulder by men who have been initiated into adult upper-caste society.

Sadducees (<u>saj</u> ŭ seez) In Roman-ruled Judaea, wealthy and priestly Jews.

sadhana (<u>saad</u> hǎ nǎ) In Hinduism, especially yoga, a spiritual practice.

sadhu (<u>sad</u> oo) An ascetic holy man, in Hinduism.

samadhi (sa <u>maa</u> dee) In yogic practice, the blissful state of superconscious union with the Absolute.

Samkhya (<u>saam</u> khyǎ) One of the major Hindu philosophical systems, in which human suffering is characterized as stemming from the confusion of Prakriti with Purusha.

samsara (sǎm <u>saa</u> rǎ) The continual round of birth, death, and rebirth in Hinduism, Jainism, and Buddhism.

Sanatana Dharma (sǎ <u>na</u> tǎ nǎ <u>daar</u> mǎ) The "eternal religion" of Hinduism.

sangat A Sikh congregation, in which all are ideally considered equal.

Sangha (<u>sung</u> ǎ) In Theravada Buddhism, the monastic community; in Mahayana, the spiritual community of followers of the *dharma*.

sannyasin (sun <u>yaa</u> sin) In Hinduism and Buddhism, a renunciate spiritual seeker.

Sanskrit (<u>san</u> skrit) The literary language of classic Hindu scriptures.

sant A Sikh holy person.

Santeria The combination of African and Christian practices which developed in Cuba.

satori (sǎ <u>taw</u> ree) Enlightenment, realization of ultimate truth, in Zen Buddhism.

scientific materialism School of thought which developed during the nineteenth and twentieth centuries claiming that the supernatural is imaginary; only the material world exists, and from this point of view religions have been invented by humans.

sect A subgroup within a larger tradition.

secularism Government policy of not favoring any one religion.

Seder Ceremonial Jewish meal in remembrance of the Passover.

see An area under the authority of a Christian bishop or archbishop.

Semite (<u>sem</u> ite) A Jew, Arab, or other, of eastern Mediterranean origin.

Sephardim An ethnic grouping of the Jews that migrated first to Spain and then to North Africa, the Americas, and back to West Asia.

Seventh Day Adventists Protestant denomination or sectarian movement believing in infallibility of the Bible, honoring Saturday as the Sabbath, and anticipating the "end times."

shabd (shaabd) The Sikh term for a Name of God that is recited or a hymn from the Guru Granth Sahib, considered the Word of God.

Shahadah (shǎ <u>haa</u> dǎ) The central Muslim expression of faith: "There is no god but God," and Muhammad is the messenger of God.

Shakta (<u>sak</u> ta) A Hindu worshiper of the female aspect of deity.

shakti (<u>sak</u> tee) The creative, active female aspect of deity in Hinduism.

shaktipat (<u>shaak</u> tǎ pǎt) In the Siddha tradition of Hinduism, the powerful, elevating glance or touch of the guru.

Shaivite (sīv īt) A Hindu worshiper of the divine as Shiva.

shaman (shaa măn) A "medicine person," a man or woman who has undergone spiritual ordeals and can communicate with the spirit world to help the people in indigenous traditions.

Shangdi (also **Shang Ti**) In ancient China, a deity (or perhaps deities) with overarching powers.

Shari'ah (shă ree ă) The divine law, in Islam.

shaykh (shaik) A spiritual master, in the esoteric Muslim tradition.

Shekhinah (she kī nă) God's presence in the world, in Judaism.

Shi'a (adj. **Shi'ite**) (shee īt) The minority branch of Islam, which feels that Muhammad's legitimate successors were 'Ali and a series of Imams; a follower of this branch.

shirk (shirk) The sin of believing in any divinity except the one God, in Islam.

Shiva (also **Siva**) (shee vă) In Hinduism, the Supreme as lord of yogis, absolute consciousness, creator, preserver, and destroyer of the world; or the destroying aspect of the Supreme.

shudra (shoo dră) A member of the manual laborer caste in traditional Hinduism.

Sikh (seek) "Student," especially one who practices the teachings of the ten Sikh Gurus.

soma (sō ma) An intoxicating drink used by early Hindu worshipers.

spirituality Any personal response to dimensions of life that are considered sacred.

stupa (stoo pă) A rounded monument containing Buddhist relics or commemorative materials.

Sufism (soo fis ĕm) The mystical path in Islam.

Sunnah (soo nă) The behavior of the Prophet Muhammad, used as a model in Islamic law.

Sunni (soo nee) A follower of the majority branch of Islam, which feels that successors to Muhammad are to be chosen by the Muslim community.

sunyata (soon yă tă) Voidness, the transcendental ultimate reality in Buddhism.

sura (sŏō ră) A chapter of the Qur'an.

sutra (sŏō tră) (Pali: *suta*) Literally, a thread on which are strung jewels—the discourses of the teacher; in yoga, *sutras* are terse sayings.

Svetambara (swe taam bă ră) Jain order of monks who are less ascetic than the Digambara.

symbol Visible representation of an invisible reality or concept.

synagogue (sin ă gog) A meeting place for Jewish study and worship.

syncretism (sing kri tis ĕm) A form of religion in which otherwise differing traditions are blended.

synod In Christianity, a council of church officials called to reach agreement on doctrines and administration.

synoptic (sin op tik) Referring to three similar books of the Christian Bible: Matthew, Mark, and Luke.

T

Taiji quan (also **T'ai-chi chu'an**) (tī chee hwaan) An ancient Chinese system of physical exercises, which uses slow movements to help one become part of the universal flow of energy.

talit (ta lit) A shawl traditionally worn by Jewish men during prayers.

Talmud (tal mŏod) Jewish law and lore, as finally compiled in the sixth century CE.

Tanakh (ta nakh) The Jewish scriptures.

Tantras (tan trăs) The ancient Indian texts based on esoteric worship of the divine as feminine.

Tantrayana (tăn tră ya nă) see Vajrayana.

tariqa (ta ree ka) In Islam, an esoteric Sufi order.

t'fillin (tĕ fil in) A small leather box with verses about God's covenant with the Jewish people, bound to the forehead and arm.

thangka (tang ka) In Tibetan Buddhism, an elaborate image of a spiritual figure used as a focus for meditation.

theistic (thee is tik) Believing in a God or gods.

Theravada (ter ă vă dă) The remaining orthodox school of Buddhism, which adheres closely to the earliest scriptures and emphasizes individual efforts to liberate the mind from suffering.

Tipitaka (ti pi ta ka) (Sanskrit: **Tripitaka**) The foundational "Three Baskets" of the Buddha's teachings.

Tirthankaras (tir tăn kăr ăs) The great enlightened teachers in Jainism, of whom Mahavira was the last in the present cosmic cycle.

Torah (tō raa) The Pentateuch; also, the whole body of Jewish teaching and law.

transcendent Existing outside the material universe.

Transfiguration The phenomenon that took place when Christ, praying on the mountain, was irradiated with light and God spoke from the heavens.

transpersonal Referring to an eternal, infinite reality, in contrast to the finite material world.

transubstantiation (tran sŭb stan shee ay shun) In some branches of Christianity, the idea that wine and bread are mystically transformed into the blood and body of Christ during the eucharist sacrament.

Trinity The Christian doctrine that in the One God are three divine persons: the Father, the Son, and the Holy Spirit.

Triple Gem ("Three Refuges") The three jewels of Buddhism: Buddha, *dharma*, Sangha.

tsumi (tzoo mee) Impurity or misfortune, a quality that Shinto purification practices are designed to remove.

tzaddik (tzaa dik) An enlightened Jewish mystic.

U

Udasi (oo daa see) An ascetic Sikh order.

ulama (oo lă maa) The influential leaders in traditional Muslim society, including spiritual leaders, imams, teachers, state scribes, market inspectors, and judges.

ummah (o maa) The Muslim community.

Unitarianism Protestant denomination holding that God is One rather than Three persons.

universalism Acceptance that truth may be found in all religions.

untouchable The lowest caste in Brahmanic Hindu society.

Upanishads (oo <u>pan</u> i shăds) The philosophical part of the Vedas in Hinduism, intended only for serious seekers.

V

Vaishnavite (<u>vīsh</u> nă vīt) (or **Vaishnava**) A Hindu devotee of Vishnu, particularly in his incarnation as Krishna.

vaishya (<u>vīsh</u> yă) A member of the merchant and farmer caste in traditional Hinduism.

Vajrayana (văj ră <u>yaa</u> nă) (or **Tantrayana**) The ultimate vehicle used in Mahayana, mainly Tibetan, Buddhism, consisting of esoteric tantric practices and concentration on deities.

Vedas Ancient scriptures revered by Hindus.

vipassana (vi <u>pas</u> ă nă) In Buddhism, meditation based on watching one's own thoughts, emotions, and actions.

Vishnu (<u>vish</u> noo) In Hinduism, the preserving aspect of the Supreme or the Supreme Itself, incarnating again and again to save the world.

vision quest In indigenous traditions, a solitary ordeal undertaken to seek spiritual guidance about one's mission in life.

Vodou (<u>voo</u> doo) Latin American and Caribbean ways of working with the spirit world, a blend of West African and Catholic Christian teachings.

W

Wahhabism Islamic philosophy founded by Muhammad ibn 'abd al-Wahhab in the eighteenth century, discarding all practices not specifically approved by the Qur'an and Sunnah.

Wicca Neo-Pagan sect of secret coven of witches traced to the writings of Gerald Gardner in England in the 1940s.

wu wei (woo way) In Daoism, "not doing," in the sense of taking no action contrary to the natural flow.

Y

yang In Chinese philosophy, the bright, assertive, "male" energy in the universe.

yantra (<u>yan</u> tră) In Hinduism, a linear cosmic symbol used as an aid to spiritual concentration.

yi (yee) Righteous conduct (as opposed to conduct motivated by desire for personal profit), a Confucian virtue stressed by Mencius.

yin (yin) In Chinese philosophy, the dark, receptive, "female" energy in the universe.

Yoga (<u>yō</u> gă) A systematic approach to spiritual realization, one of the major Hindu philosophical systems.

yoga (<u>yō</u> gă) Ancient techniques for spiritual realization, found in several Eastern religions.

yoni (<u>yō</u> nee) Abstract Hindu representation of the female vulva, cosmic matrix of life.

yuga (<u>yoo</u> gă) One of four recurring world cycles in Hinduism.

Z

zakat (zak at) Spiritual tithing in Islam.

zazen (zaa <u>zen</u>) Zen Buddhist sitting meditation.

Zealots Jewish resistance fighters who fought the Romans and were defeated in the siege of Jerusalem.

Zen (zen) (Chinese: **Ch'an**) A Chinese and Japanese Buddhist school emphasizing that all things have Buddha-nature, which can only be grasped when one escapes from the intellectual mind.

zendo (<u>zen</u> dō) A Zen meditation hall.

Zion The original site of the Jerusalem temples, now often used to refer to Jerusalem itself as the heavenly city, the goal of Judaism.

INDEX

Page numbers in *italics* refer to topics mentioned in illustration captions. When that subject appears in the text on the same page, italics have not been used.

A

Aaron 247, 248
"Abba" 302, 313
Abbasid dynasty 260, 405, 413, 415
'Abdu'l-Baha 483–84
Abedin, Dr. Syed Z. 19
Abimbola, Wande 51, 61
aborigines *see* Australian aborigines
abortion 362, 505, 517, 521
Abraham, Hebrew patriarch 241, *243*, 244–45, 293, 321, 381, 388, 400, 413
absolutists 18, 19
Abu Bakr, caliph 385, 387, 404
Abu Bin Le 64
Abu Yazid 9
Acoma Pueblo, New Mexico 37
Acts of the Apostles 317, 318, 355, 370
acupuncture 201
Adam 242–43, 277, 348, 394, 400
Adi Granth *see* Guru Granth Sahib
Adler, Joseph 207
Advaita Vedanta 81, 116
Advent 353
Afghanistan 404, *422*, 431–32, 448
Africa: AIDS 520; Christianity 39, 338, 368, 369 *see also* African Instituted Churches; indigenous cultures 33–34, 38, 39, 40, 41, 42–44, 50–52, 53, *54*, 66; Islam 387, 411, 412, 415, 417–18, 420, 421, 423; new religious movements 465, 478–80
African Americans 372; and Islam 420–21; Kawnzaa 60–61
African Instituted Churches 369, 370
afterlife, belief in 237, 394–96
Aga Khan Development Network 427
Aga Khan IV 29, 406, 427
Agni 78, 92, 98
Agni Yoga Society 481
agnosticism 13
Agrawal, Padma 123–24
Ahavat Olam (Jewish prayer) 277

ahimsa (nonviolence) 125–26, 128–29
Ahmadiyyah Movement 420
Ahura Mazda 235, 236, 237, 238
Ahuras (lords) 235
AIDS 517, 520
Aikido 227, 232
Ainu people 39, 50
Akal Takht ("Eternal Throne") 460
Akan people 51
Akaranga Sutra 125
Akbar, Mogul emperor 417, 445, *459*
Akhand Path 455, 457
Akiva, Rabbi 256, 257
Akka Mahadevi 15
Al-Azhar university, Cairo 406, 413, 521
Alexander the Great 236, 252
Alexandria, Patriarchate of 343
Alhambra, Granada *414*
Ali, Abdullah Yusif 390
'Ali, cousin of Muhammad 385, 387, 404, 406, 408
Ali, Noble Drew 420
Allah 391, 392, 408
allegories 16–17
Ally, Muhammad Mashuq ibn 422–23
Amar Das, Guru 444
Amarnath cave, Kashmir 106
Amaterasu 218, 219, 221, 222, 228, 229
Ambedkar, Dr. B.R. 180
American Family Foundation 496
Ameshta Spenta 237
ammas 325
amrit (holy water) 442, 446, 452, 458, 460
Amritanandamayi, Mata 5, 115
Amritsar: Golden Temple 444, 445, 452, 457, 459, 460
An, Master 203
Ananda, the Venerable 140, 150
anatman (no self) 142, 153
ancestors: Africa 40; in China 185–86, 206; and indigenous peoples 40, 41–42, 184
anekantwad (nonabsolutism) 125, 128
Angad, Guru 444
angels: Christianity 360; Islam 394, *395*
Anglicanism 336–37, 362
Angra Mainyu 237

anicca (impermanence) 142, 153
Anishinaabe people 68
Annunciation 357
Anthony of Padua, St. 360
anthropocentrism 489
Antioch, Patriarchate of 343
Antiochus IV Epiphanes, king of Syria 252, 254, 283
anti-Semitism 260–62, 264, 266, 293
Anubrat Movement 133
Apache people 45
aparigraha (nonattachment) 125, 127–28
apartheid 371
Apocalypse 467
apocalyptic literature 254, 299
apocalyptic movements 467–68, 495
the Apocrypha 150, 262, 299
apostasy 472
Appear, Shaivite saint 90
Appolinari, Father, Russian Orthodox priest 352
Aquinas, St. Thomas 331, 347
Arafat, field of 400
Aramaean people 246
Aranyakas 78
Archambault, Marie Therese 63
archetypes 15–16
arhant (worthy one) 147–48
Arius and Arianism 324
Ariyaratne, Dr. A.T. 180
Arjun Dev, Guru 445, 453, 455
Arjuna 94, *95*
the Ark of the Covenant 248, 249, 250
artha (worldly success) 100
Arunachala mountain 107
Arya Samaj 110, 112
Aryans 74
al-As, Amir ibn 412
Asahara, Shoko 495
asanas (yoga postures) 82
Ascension: Jesus 354, 355; Muhammad 386
asceticism 110, 114, 321, 325, 407; Hinduism 88, 100, 109–10; Jainism 121, 122, 123, 128–29, 133
Asherah, Canaanite goddess 246
Ashin Nyana Dipa 154
Ashkenazi Jews 261–62, 272, 286–87
Ashoka, King 148, 171
ashrams (retreat communities) 102
'Ashura 406
Assisi interfaith initiative 513–14

Assumption of Mary 355
Assyrian empire 250
astrology 104, 115, 492
Asvaghosa 136
Athavale, Pandurang Shastri 113
atheism 11–12
Atisha 167
atman (self or soul) 79, 81
audience cults 466, 493
Augustine of Hippo 323, 330, 355
Aum Shinrikyo 495
Aung San Suu Kyi, Daw 179
Aurangzeb, Mogul emperor 417, 446, 452
Australian aborigines: acculturation 63; cosmology 38; customs and beliefs 34–35, 45, 46–47, 48, 52
Avalokiteshvara 158, 168
avatars 92, 470
Avesta 236
Avignon papacy 330, 332, 334
awakening 8
Ayers Rock (Uluru), Australia *35*
Azusa Street Revival 366

B

Baal Shem Tov 263–64
the Bab 482, 483
Babur, Mogul emperor 117, 441
Babylonia 250, 251, 257, 258, 259, 277
Badejo, Deirdre 43
Baghdad 259, 413, 415
Baha'i 482–84, 494, 510, 511
Baha'i Temple, New Delhi *14*
Baha'u'llah 482–83
Bahubali 124, 132
Bainbridge, William S. 466, 467, 468, 493
Baisakhi festival 458
Bakole Wa Ilunga 372
Balfour Declaration (1917) 270
Bali, Hinduism in 77, 111
Banyacya, Thomas, Hopi elder 69, 70
baptism 350, 352
Baptists 337
Bar Mitzvah 281–82
Baraitha 298
barakah (blessing) 408
Bartholomew, Patriarch 360, 376
Bat Mitzvah 282
Batchelor, Stephen 175
the Beatitudes 309
Bebbington, David 363
Beck, Joko 153

Bedward, Alexander 484
beguines 331
Benedict, St., rule of 325, 330
Benedict XVI, Pope 361, 372,
    522 *see also* Ratzinger, Cardinal
    Joseph
Benedictine orders 325
Ber, Dov 264
Bernadette, St. 358
Bernstein, Ellen 26
Berry, Father Thomas 375
Beth Cardin, Rabbi Nina 280
Bhadrabahu, Jain saint 122
Bhagat Ravi Das 444
Bhagavad-Gita 5, 94, 96, 113, 449
Bhagavata Purana 96
Bhago, Mai 452
Bhai Kanahia 452
bhakta (devotee) 84, 440
bhakti (devotion) 84–85, 86,
    112, 113
bhakti yoga 82, 84–85
Bharat 124
Bharatiya Janata Party (BJP)
    117
bhavanas (loving relationships)
    111
Bhikkhu, Buddhadasa 177
bhikshunis (Buddhist nuns) 139,
    151–52
bhikshus (Buddhist monks) 139,
    151
Bhutan 166, 170
the Bible 299–301, 467–68, 473;
    historical–critical study 19–20,
    300, 341; New Testament 300–
    301, 303, 312, 317, 318, 322,
    341; Old Testament 299, 302
Bilal 385
Bilas, Roman 367
bin Laden, Osama 431, 432–33,
    506
Bingemer, Maria Clara 374
birth control 362, 424, 520–21
BJP (Bharatiya Janata Party)
    117
Black Elk, Sioux visionary 53
Black Muslims 379
Blake, William: *The Act of
    Creation 10*
Blavatsky, Madame Helen
    480–81
Bodhidharma 161
bodhisattvas 156–58, 159, 165,
    168
Bohm, David 23, 24
Bolshevik Revolution (1917)
    266, 344
bomohs (shamans) 64–65
Bön 166–67
Bonhoeffer, Dietrich 304–5
Book of Changes see I Ching
Borobudur, Java *154*
Bourne, H.: engraving
    of Miriam *248*
Bowker, John 4
Brahma 88, 90, 91, 96, 110

Brahmadatta, King 146
Brahman 79, 81, 85
Brahmanas 78
brahmins 85, 97, 98, 100, 101,
    103
Brahmo Samaj 112
brainwashing 469, 496
Branch Dravidians 494–95
Brazil 231, 265, 364, 369, 493
Brotherhood of the Cross and
    Star 480
Brown, Wendy 512
Buber, Martin 275
the Buddha 5, 121, 135–36,
    138–41, 142, 143, 146, 147,
    151, 154, 158 *see also*
    Amitabha (Amida) Buddha
Buddhacarita (Acts of the
    Buddha) 136
Buddha-nature 163
Buddhism: branches 148–49,
    160; Chan 161, 197; in China
    149, 152, 158, 160–61, 184,
    199, 203, 211; and
    Confucianism 214; and Daoism
    197, 199, 202; the Dharma
    138–39, 140, 141–48, 150–51,
    153–54, 155, 156, 161, 170,
    510; festivals *155*, 170–71; and
    Hinduism 80, 91, 111, 144;
    and indigenous peoples 34, 35,
    39, 55, 66; in Japan 149, 152,
    158, 160, 161, 164–66, 217,
    227–28; Jodo Shinshu 164,
    171; Mahayana 149, 156–60,
    166, 167, 170; Nichiren
    164–66; and politics 510; Pure
    Land 164; and Shinto 227–28,
    231; and social issues 177–80,
    517; spread of 135, 148, *149*,
    157, 160, 166, 465; in Sri
    Lanka *140*, 149, 155, 170, 171,
    178, 180; Theravada 149–56,
    157, 159, 170, 178; in Tibet
    149, 158–59, 166–68, 170,
    171, 501; timeline 137;
    Vajrayana 166–68, 170; in the
    West 135, 164, 166, 170,
    171–77; Zen 160–64, 171–74,
    219; and Zoroastrianism 235
Buddhism for Development 178
Buddhist Churches of America
    171
Bunduk, Nym: *Snakes and Emus
    46*
burqa 422, 431, 432
Buryat people 24, 34, 41, 47, 55,
    60
Bush, George W. 507–8
Byron, William J. 522
Byzantine Empire 326, 328, 411,
    412, 413

C
Caddy, Eileen and Peter 492
Caiaphas, Joseph 314
Cairo: Al-Azhar university 406,
    413

Cairo Conference on Population
    and Development (1994) 517
Cairo Speech (Obama, 2009)
    508, 509
Caitanya, Shri 91, 114, 440
caliphs 387, 404, 407, 413
calligraphy 163, *389*, 412
Calvin, John and Calvinism 336,
    364
Cambodia 149, 178, *179*
Campbell, Joseph 18
Canaanites 244, 245–46, 249
Caodaism 477–78
Caravaggio: *The Conversion of St.
    Paul 319*
Carmelite Order 340, *359*
Carter, Jimmy 518–19
Carthusian Order 330
caste system 99–100, 117, 452
catacomb churches 345
Cathars 330
Catherine of Siena, St. *332,*
    334
Celestial Masters (Daoist
    priesthood) 197
The Celestine Prophecy (Redfield,
    James) 493
celibacy 328, 336, 361–62
Chagall, Marc *247*
Chah, Ajahn 142–43, 144
chakras *81*, 82
Chalcedon, Council of (451)
    324–25, 329
challah (braided bread) 281
Chan Buddhism 161, 197
Chand, Baba Siri 449
Chand, Lala Sulekh 129
Chandogya Upanishad 79
"Changing Woman" 40
Chappell, David 160
charisma 28, 468–71
"Charismatic Renewal" 368
charismatics 365–68, 375–76
Chartres Cathedral, France 48
Cheng Yen *178*
Chiapas people 63
Chin, Ann-ping 212
China: ancient traditions
    184–87, 189; Buddhism 149,
    152, 158, 160–61, 184, 199,
    203, 211; Christianity 199,
    211; Cultural Revolution 199,
    209; Islam 199, 211, 417; map
    185; new religious movements
    494; scholars 199, *205*, 209,
    210, 212; Tibet, invasion of
    (1950–1959) 168; timeline 188
    see also Confucianism; Daoism;
    Falun Gong
Chinese New Year celebrations
    198, *201*
Chinmoy, Sri 513
Chishti, Khwaja Muinuddin 417
Chitrabhanu, Shree 128, 132
Cho, David Yonggi 367
Chona, Papago medicine woman
    57
Chopra, Dr. Deepak 466

Christian Science movement 492
Christianity 259, 298, 467–68;
    central beliefs 347–49;
    charismatics 365–68;
    contemporary issues 360–70,
    368–70, 372–76; creation-
    centered 375; early church
    318–26; and the ecumenical
    movement 375–76; and the
    Enlightenment 340–41; and
    feminism 373–75; and
    Hinduism 111, 117–18; and
    indigenous peoples 34, 39, 63,
    66; and Islam *361*, 390–91,
    412–13, 415, 417–18 *see also*
    Crusades; and Judaism 255,
    259, 260–61, 298–99, 302,
    306, 309, 310, 312, 319–20;
    liberation theology 370–73;
    liturgical year 352–55; major
    divisions 335; Mary, devotion
    to 302, 357–59, 374; sacred
    practices 349–60; saints and
    angels 331–32, 334, 340,
    359–60; services and
    sacraments 349–52, 364;
    timeline 311; world
    distribution *326*; and
    Zoroastrianism 235, 236, 302
    see also Bible; Eastern
    Orthodox Church; Jesus;
    Protestant Christianity; Roman
    Catholic Church
Christmas 353–54
Christology 324
Church of England *see*
    Anglicanism
Church of the Holy Sepulcher,
    Jerusalem 415
circumcision 244, 259, 279,
    320–21
Cistercian Order 330
Clare, St. 332
Clarke, Charmaine 63
Clarke, Richard 174
client cults 466–67
cloning research 521
The Cloud of Unknowing (anon.)
    332
Cluny, France 330
Collard, Agnes 5–6
collective unconscious 15, 114
Columban Fathers (SSC) 362
Common Era (CE) 301
communion *see* Eucharist
comparative religion *see*
    comparative religion
Complete Perfection Daoism
    194, 197, 200
confirmation 350, 352
Confucian Classics 204, 207,
    208, 214
Confucian Temple, Qufu, China
    213
Confucianism 184, 187, 203;
    and Buddhism 214; under
    communism 199, 209–11, 213;
    contemporary 211–13; and
    Daoism 184, 187, 189, 203–4;

in East Asia 213–14; followers 206–7; in Japan 214, 217, 228; map *185*; and Shinto 214, 227, 228; as the state cult 207–8; timeline 188; virtues 205–6, 209 *see also* Confucius; Neo-Confucianism

Confucius 203, 204

Congregationalism 337, 340–41

Conquistadors 339

Conservative Judaism 287, 290, 292

Constantine I 321, 324, 326

Constantinople 326, 416 *see also* Istanbul

Constantinople, Patriarchate of 343

conversos (converted Jews) 261

Coptic Christians 360

Coptic Cross *360*

Cortés, Hernán 38

"Counter-Reformation" *see* Roman Catholic Reformation

Cousins, Ewert 510

Coxhead, Nona 9

Cranach, Lucas, the Elder: *Martin Luther 334*

creation accounts: African 42; Genesis 242–43, 251, 275, 277; Native American 17; Polynesian 17

creation-centered Christianity 375

Creationism 24

creeds, Christian 324

the cross as Christian symbol 323, *360*

Crow Dog, Leonard, Lakota holy man 52, 57, 60

Cruise, Tom *467*

Crusades 261, 328–29, 415

Cult Awareness Network 496

cults 465–67, 493, 494–96

Cultural Revolution, China 199, 209

Cyrus, king of Persia 236, 251

D

Da Liu, Master 191

Dada *see* Athavale, Pandurang Shastri

Dagara people 42, 53

Dahomey people 39

Daido Loori Roshi, John 172, 173

Dalai Lama, 7th 167

Dalai Lama, 14th 4, 157, 158, 168, 169, 171, *356*

Damascus 412–13

dances: dervishes, Sufi *8*, 407, 410; sacred 52, 57, *61*; sun dance 58–59

Dao (Tao) as the way 187, 190, 191

Dao de jing (Tao te Ching) 20, 190–91

Daoism 184, 187, 189–90; and Buddhism 197, 199, 202; and

Confucianism 184, 187, 189, 203–4; contemporary 199–202; longevity/immortality 195–96; map *185*; organized groups 194; popular religion 194–95; sects 196–97, 199, 200; teachings 190–94; timeline 188

Daoist Association of China 197, 200

darshan (visual contact with the divine) 97, 470

Darwin, Charles 21

Darwinism 21, 364

Dasgupta, Somjit 105

davening (intensity of praying) 281

David, king of Israel 249–50, 273

Davies, Paul 25, 26

Dawkins, Richard 12–13, 502

Dayal Singh, Shiv 475

Dead Sea Scrolls 252

death ceremonies: Daoist 199; Hinduism 88, 98; Zoroastrian 238

deep ecology 489–91

Deguchi, Madame Nao 229–30

deity yoga 167

Deloria, Vine, Jr. 33

Dene Tha people 36, 61

Dennett, Daniel 502

Dep, Sanisah 64, 65

Dera Sach Khand 460

deras (communities) 460

dervishes, Sufi *8*, 407, 410

desert fathers 325

designs, auspicious 103–4

devas 78, 492

"deviance amplification" 495–96

The Dhammapada 144

Dharamsala, India *148*, 159, 168

dharma: in Hinduism 73, 87, 91, 92, 93, 100, 103; in Jainism 130

Dharma (Buddhist teachings) 138–39, 140, 141–48, 150–51, 153–54, 155, 156, 161, 170, 501

Dharmapala, Angarika 171

dhimmis (protected people) 413, 416–17

diaspora, Jewish 259, 278

Diego, Juan 358

Digambaras 122, 123, 127

disciples of Jesus 300, 304, 306

Divali festival: Hinduism 108, 109, 130; Jainism 130, 132

divination: Africa 53, *54*, 479–80; China 186–87; oracle bones 186–87; *Yijing (I Ching)* 187, 189, 204

dogma 6, 339

Dome of the Rock, Jerusalem 413, *419*

Dominican Order 331

Dong Zhongshu (Tung Chung-shu) 207

Dorzhieva, Svetlana 483

dragons *186*

Dravidian people 74

Dream Time/Dreaming 46–47, 52

drumming 480, 489

D'Souza, Andreas and Diane 517

dualism 9, 80–81, 237, 301, 320

Duarte de Souza, Sandra 493

Dugan, Kathleen 356–57

dukkha (suffering) 142, 143, 153

Durga *86*, 87, 106, 109, 444

Durga Puja festival 109

Durkheim, Emile 4

Dussehra festival *92*, 109

E

earthworks *44*

Easter 354

Eastern Orthodox Church 299, 327–29, 335, 338, 339, 341, 342–46; and the ecumenical movement 376; Greek Orthodox Church 343–44; green issues 360; Mary, devotion to 358; sacraments 350, 351, 354; saints and angels 359–60; spirituality 345–47 *see also* Russian Orthodox Church

Ebadi, Shirin 425, 430

Eck, Diana 503, 511–12

ecumenical movement 375–76

Eddy, Mary Baker 492

Edwards, Jonathan 364

Efe pygmies *40*, *60*

Egypt 271; Coptic Christians 360; Islam 404, 406, 413, 415, 420, 429; Israelites 246–47, 284

Eightfold Path 139, 143–44, 160

Einstein, Albert 23

El, Canaanite god 246

Eliade, Mircea 10

Elijah, Hebrew prophet 250, 313

Elizabeth I, queen of England 336–37

England: Buddhism *504*; Christianity 327, 332; and Islam 434–35; Jews 261; medieval mysticism 332; new religious movements 486–87; Pentecostalism *367*; Protestant Reformation 336–37; sacred sites 489; Sikhism 459, 462

enlightenment 8, 161, 163–64

the Enlightenment 3, 21, 290, 501; and Christianity 340–41; and Judaism 264–65, 271, 290

Enoch, Book of 262

Epiphany 353

Episcopal Church 337

Epstein, Eli 276

Erdoes, Richard 17

escapism 28

Esposito, John 435

Essenes 252, 255, 259, 299

Esther 284

Ethiopian Orthodox Church 329

ethnic religions 488–89

ethnofuturism 489

the Eucharist 328, 336, 339, 341, 350–51

euthanasia 180

evangelical churches 337–38, 363–64, 375–76

Evangelical Lutheran Church 293

Eve 242–43, 277, 348, 400

evolution, theory of 21, 364

exclusivism 11, 290, 462, 506–7, 511

excommunication 327

exegesis 258, 278

Ezekiel, Hebrew prophet 16, 253, 262

Ezra the Scribe 242, 251

F

faith 5, 249

Falun Gong (Falun Dafa) 202, 494, *495*

Falwell, Jerry 505

Farid, Shaikh 440

Farrakhan, Louis 421

Faruqi, Dr. I. H. Azad 12

fasting 423; Christianity 352; Hinduism 97, 103, 109; Islam 399–400

Fatah 433

Fatiha 390

Fatima, daughter of Muhammad 387, 406, 415

Fatimid caliphate 413, 415

fatwa (legal opinion) 406, 521

Feldman, Rabbi Maria 290

feminist movement 27, 112; and Christian theology 373–75; Islam and feminism *396*, 431; Jewish feminism 285, 286, 291–93

feng shui 194

Fenix, Sister Jocelyn *372*

Feodor, Bishop 345

Fernando, Antony 14–15

Festival of Floating Bowls, Thailand 171

Festival of the Tooth, Sri Lanka 171

Feuerbach, Ludwig 3

Findhorn community 492

Finney, Charles Grandison 363

Fiorenza, Elisabeth Schüssler 316–17

fire ceremonies: Hindu *78*, 103; Zoroastrian *235*, 236, 238

Firestone, Rabbi Tirzah 292, 293

Five Beloved Ones *(Panj Piaras)* 446, 458

"Five K's" 447–48, 458

Five Pillars 396–400, 402–4

Ford, Clyde 42

Forest, Jim 354

Four Noble Truths 139, 142–43, 160

Fox, George 337

France: Buddhism 174;

Christianity 330, 337, 358; contemporary issues 504; Islam 412, 421, 434; Jews 264; new religious movements 496
Francis of Assisi, St. 331–32
Franciscan Order 331, 356
Frashokereti 237
"Free Churches" 337
French Revolution (1789-1799) 264
Freud, Sigmund 4–5
Friedman, Thomas 522
Fromm, Erich 5
Fujii, Nichidatsu 165
functional perspectives 4–6
fundamentalism 18–19, 504–7; Buddhist 178; Christian 19, 363, 364, 365, 369, 505, 506; Hindu 117, 505; Islamic 18–19, 401, 432, 435, 505–6, 507; Sikh 19, 462

G
Gabriel, archangel 384, 394
Gaia hypothesis 24, 490
gambling and game playing 38, 67, 69
Gandhi, Indira 459
Gandhi, Mahatma 5, 99, 111, 118, 125, 131, 165, 417
Ganesh 90, 106, 109
Ganesh Chaturti festival 109
Ganges River 88, *104*, 110
Gardner, Gerald 486–87
Garvey, Marcus 484–85
Gathas (Zarathushtra) 235–36, 237, 238
Gatta, Mother Julia 351
Gaudium et Spes 520–21
Gautama, Siddhartha *see* Buddha
Gayatrimantra 77, 100
Ge Hong 193
Gebara, Ivone 374
Geertz, Clifford 29
Gell-Mann, Murray 23
Gemara 257
genetics *21*
Gentiles 250, 259, 271, 302, 320–21
Germann, Father 359
Germany 331; Jews 261, 265, 289, 290 *see also* Holocaust; new religious movements 497; Protestant Reformation 334–36, 337
al-Ghazali, Abu Hamid 396, 408–9
ghettos, Jewish 261, 264, 267
Ghosananda, Maha 143, 178, *179*
Giacometti, Alberto: *Walking Man 6*
Giotto: *The Nativity 302; The Raising of Lazarus 305*
Global Forum of Spiritual and Parliamentary Leaders on Human Survival, Oxford (1988) 514

globalization 500–501
glossolalia 366
gnosis 8, 322, 466
Gnostic Gospels 322
Gnosticism 322
Gobind Sadan *2*, 456, *515*, 516–17, 519
Gobind Singh, Guru 13, 440, 446–47, 448, 449, 450, 452–53, 454, 455, 457, 458, 460, 462
goddess worship 86–88, 90, 111–12, 115, 357, 487–88
Golden Mother of the Celestial Pool 199
"Golden Rule" 511
Golden Temple, Amritsar 444, 445, 452, 457, 459, 460
Good Samaritan 308
gopis 96
Gorbachev, Mikhail 345, 514
gospels, Christian 299, 300–301, 309–10, 314 *see also* John; Luke; Mark; Matthew
"The Great Ape" Jakata Tale 146
Great Britain *see* England
Great Goddess *487*
Great Schism 330
Great Spirit 17, 40, 47, 48, 52, 58, *60*
Greek Orthodox Church 343–44
Greenberg, Rabbi Irving 249
Gregorian Order 330
Gregorios, Paulos Mar 356
Gregory I, Pope 327
Gregory VII, Pope 327
Gregory XI, Pope 334
Griffiths, Bede 13–14
Grimke, Sarah 340–41
Guadalupe, Virgin of 358
Guanyin (Kannon) 158
Guevara, Esperanza: *John the Baptist 303*
guilt 5, 28
gurdwaras 454, 457, 459–60, 461, 462
Guru Granth Sahib (Adi Granth) 444, 445, 447, 448, 449, 450, 451, 453, 455, 457, 458, 460, *461*, 511
Guru ka Bagh 448
gurus: Hindu 97, 102, 112; Sikh 441–49, 450, 451, 460
Gutierrez, Gustavo 372, 517

H
Habitat for Humanity 518
Hachiman 220
Hackett, Rosalind 506
Hadith 383, 395, 404, 405, 424
Hafiz, Hajji Ibrahim Keskin 403
Hagar 244, 293, 381, 400
haggadah (nonlegal teachings) 256, 285, 286
Hagia Sophia, Istanbul 328, 416
hajj (pilgrimage to Mecca) 400, 402–4, 418
al-Hakim, caliph 415

halakhah (proper conduct) 256, 265, 287, 290
al-Hallaj, Mansur 408
Hamas 433, 506
Han dynasty, China 189, 196, 199, 207, 208
Hanh, Thich Nhat 174, 177
Hanukkah, Jewish festival 283
Hanuman 92, *93*, 94
Har Krishan, Guru 446
Har Rai, Guru 446
Hare Krishna movement 91, *114*, 115, 471
Haredi (Ultra-Orthodox) Judaism 287, 288
Hargobind, Guru 445–46
Harris, Sam 502
Hasan 406
Hasidism 263–64, 281, 287
Hasmonean kings 252–53
havan 98, 103
Havel, Vaclav 522
Hawai'i 47
Hawking, Stephen 26
Hayut-Man, Yitzhak (with Omer): *The Throne of Shekhinah 258*
healing 49; Christian 358–59; Christian Science 492; Daoist 195–96, 201; in Santeria 479; shamanistic 56, *62*
health and religion 4, 520
Heart Sutra 159, 228
"Hebrew" 246
Hecker, Wolfgang 476
Heian period, Japan 227
hell 237, 395–96
Hellenism 252
Henriques, Francisco: *The Last Supper 314*
Henry VIII, king of England 336
Hensel, W.: painting of Miriam *248*
hermeneutics 299
Hermetic tradition 409
Herod Antipas, ruler of Galilee 310
Herzl, Theodor 270
Heschel, Abraham Joshua 274
Heschel, Susannah 285
heyoka (sacred fool) 52
al-Hibri, Azizah Y. 431
Hick, John 511
Hideo, Kishimoto 223
Highest Purity Daoism 197
hijab (the veil) 423, 504
hijrah (migration) 386
Hildegard of Bingen 331
Hill, Julia Butterfly 490–91
Hillel the Elder 256, 259
Hinckley, Gordon 473
Hinduism 8, 9, 13, 73, 467; beliefs 78–80; and Buddhism 80, 91, 111, 144; and Christianity 111, 117–18; contemporary 99, 104, 106, 111–18; deities 78, 85–91; epics 91–95; festivals *92*,

97–98, 107–11, 130; gurus 97, 102, 112; and Islam 111, 117, 416–17, 440; origins 74–80; philosophical systems 80–85; Puranas 91, 96–97; reverence of trees and rivers 88, 106, 109–10; rituals 97–99, 100, 101; sacred thread ceremony 100, 101; and Sikhism 440, 441, 442, 446, 450, 453, 456, 459, 461, 462; and social issues 517; timeline 76; way of life *96*, 97–111
Hirohito, Emperor 229
historical–critical study of the scriptures 19–20, 300, 341
Hitchens, Christopher 502
Hitler, Adolf 266, 267
HIV/AIDS 517, 520
Holi festival 107, 108
Holiness movement 365–66
the Holocaust 239, 266–68, *269*, 277, 278
Holocaust Memorial Day 286
Holy Trinity 323
The Holy Trinity, Lavra, Russia *342*
homosexuality 285, 362, 505, 520
Hong Kong 197, 199, 200, *201*, 213
Hong Kong Taoist Association 200
Hopi people 38, 48, 57, 67, 69–70
Hopkins, Dwight 372
Hopkins, Emma Curtis 492
Hopkins, Gerard Manley 331
Hoshea, king of Israel 250
Howard, Larry 348–49
Huai-Chin Han 196
Huang, Al *202*
Hubbard, L. Ron 466
Hubble Space Telescope *22*
Huichol people 36, 56, *60*
The Hundredth Monkey 493
Husayn 404, 406
Hussain, Asaf 435
Hussain, Dr. Syed M. 401
Hussein, Saddam 430, 431
Huxley, T.H. 13

I
I Ching (Yijing) 187, 189, 204
Ibn Gabirol 273
ibn Ziyad, Tariq 412
icons 346, 359–60
Ifa 42, 61
Igjugarjuk, Inuit Shaman 54
ijtihad (reasoned interpretation) 424
Imams (leaders, guides) 406
The Imitation of Christ 349, 355
immanence 10
in vitro fertilization 521
Inari 220
incarnation doctrine 11

inclusivism 511
India 73; Christianity 111, 112, 117–18, 322, 365; indigenous cultures 38, 47, 67; Islam 111, 416–17; map 75; social issues 518–20; Zoroastrianism 236, 238 see also Hinduism
indigenous peoples/cultures 33–34; Africa 33–34, 38, 39, 40, 41, 42–44, 50–52, 53, 54, 66; and ancestors 40, 41–42, 184; and Buddhism 34, 35, 39, 55, 66; and Christianity 34, 39, 63, 66; circle of right relationships 39–40; contemporary issues 33–34, 37, 38, 55, 62–63, 66–70; cultural diversity 38–39; distribution of 34; and the environment 36, 43–48, 67; group observances 56–61; India 38, 47, 67; individual observances 61–62; and Islam 39, 66; lifeways 36, 38; oral traditions 34, 50–52; sacred ways 34–37, 40–41, 67; spiritual specialists 42, 50–56, 61; and women 40–41, 43, 49–50, 52
Indonesia 404, 411, 417
Indra 78
indulgences 334
Indus Valley civilization 74–75, 104
infanticide, female 453
inipi (sweat lodge) 60
the Inquisition 261, 330, 415
Insight Meditation Society 171
Interfaith Encounter Association 516
interfaith movement 510–17
International Association of Buddhist Women see Sakyadhita (Daughters of the Buddha)
International Council of Thirteen Indigenous Grandmothers 69
International Network of Engaged Buddhists 180
International Society for Krishna Consciousness (ISKCON) 91, 114–15
Internet resources: and Christianity 361; and contemporary religion 500, 505, 515; indigenous cultures 37; Judaism 276, 285; new religious movements 465, 487, 492, 496; Sikhism 462
Introvigne, Massimo 495
Inuit people 41, 54
Iran 235, 236, 238, 404, 423, 425, 429–30, 484, 494
Iranian Empire 235, 236
Iraq 235, 271, 369, 404, 407, 412, 413, 415, 430–31, 434
Ireland 337

Isaac, Hebrew patriarch 244, 245, 381
Isaiah, Hebrew prophet 251, 254, 262, 275
Ise Shrine, Japan 220, 221
Ishmael (Isma'il) 244, 381, 400
Ishtar, Great Mother Goddess 284, 487
ISKCON (International Society for Krishna Consciousness) 91, 114–15
Islam 381, 385, 388, 467; and Baha'i 482, 484, 494, 510; central teachings 391–96; and Christianity 361, 390–91, 412–13, 415, 417–18 see also Crusades; culture 260, 413–15; feminism 396, 431; Five Pillars 396–400, 402–4; and Hinduism 111, 117, 416–17, 440; history 381, 383–88; and indigenous peoples 39, 66; jihad 428–30, 432–34, 507; and Judaism 260, 271, 286, 390–91, 413, 415, 433; Muslim resurgence 421–36; and politics 508, 509, 510; and Sikhism 442–43, 445, 452, 456, 462, 510; and social issues 517; spread of 387, 411–18; timeline 382; West, relationship with 418–21, 429, 432–33, 434–35, 503, 508, 509; and Zoroastrianism 235, 236, 409 see also Muhammad; Qur'an; Shi'ite Muslims; Sufism; Sunni Muslims
Islamists 422, 429, 431, 433, 435
Isma'il see Ishmael
Israel 239, 246, 254, 259, 271, 419–20, 510, 516; contemporary 269, 270–73; map 243; tribes 244, 246, 250 see also Zionism
Israel (Jacob), Hebrew patriarch 243, 244, 246
Istanbul 416
Italy 174, 496–97; Buddhism 501; Christianity 330, 331, 334, 337; Jews 261, 286; new religious movements 496–97; Roman Catholicism 337
Iwasaki, Hitoshi 225, 227, 232
Izanagi 222

J
Jaap Sahib 13, 450, 455
Jacob (Israel), Hebrew patriarch 243, 244, 246
Jade Emperor 194, 198
Jagganath (Hindu festival) 97–98
Jain, Jagdish Prasad 132
Jain, M.P. 131
Jain, R.P. 126
Jainism 80, 91, 111, 121; asceticism 121, 122, 123, 128–29, 133; cosmology 122;

ethical pillars 123–28; festivals 130, 132; history 121–23; purification 127; spiritual practices 128–30, 132; as a world religion 132–33
Jakun people 64, 65
James, William 7
janam-sakhis (traditional biographies) 441, 442–43
Janmashtami festival 109
Jap Ji 450, 455
Japan: Ainu people 39, 50; Aum Shinrikyo 495; Buddhism 149, 152, 158, 160, 161, 164–66, 217, 227–28 see also Zen Buddhism; Christianity 217; Confucianism 214, 217, 228; map 221; new religious movements 465, 495; tea ceremonies 163, 219 see also Shinto
Jataka Tales 146, 147
Jehangir, Mogul emperor 445
Jehovah's Witnesses 338, 473–75, 494, 496
Jeremias, Joachim 314
Jerusalem 250, 251, 252, 255, 271, 413, 415; Church of the Holy Sepulcher 415; Dome of the Rock 413, 419; Patriarchate of 343; Temples 241, 250, 251, 252, 254, 255, 283, 286; Western Wall 254, 255
Jesuits (Society of Jesus) 339
Jesus 255, 259; authorities, challenges to 310, 312–13; baptism 303; birth and preparation 298, 301–3; in contemporary Christianity 345–47, 353, 370; crucifixion 313–16; in Islam 390–91; life and teachings 301–6, 308–10, 312–18; as the Messiah 255, 260, 300, 301, 303, 309–10, 312, 319–20, 353; ministry 303, 304–6, 308–10; proof of existence 298–99; Resurrection and Ascension 316–18, 355; resurrection and ascension 354; and women 26, 306, 308, 316–17
Jewish Orthodox Feminist Alliance 292
Jews 239; anti-Semitism 260–62, 266, 293; Ashkenazi Jews 261–62, 272, 286–87; Hasidic Jews 263–64; history 239, 241–73; and Roman Catholic Church 261; Sephardic Jews 266, 287 see also Holocaust; Judaism
jihad ("holy war") 428–30, 432–34, 507
Jina 123
jing (energy) 195
Jinmu 217–18, 222
jinn (immaterial beings of fire) 394

Jinnah, Mohammed Ali 417
jiva (soul) 123
jivatma (self) 131
jnana yoga 81, 84
Joanna 306, 316
Job 277–78
Jodo Shinshu Buddhism 164, 171
Joel 318
John, Gospel of 300–301, 304, 310
John of the Cross, St. 340
John Paul II, Pope 360, 513
John the Baptist 303, 310, 313, 353
John XXIII, Pope 341
Jordan 271, 420
Joseph, St. 302
Joseph of Arimathea 316
Josephus 252, 298
Judah 250–51
Judah the Prince 257
Judaism 239, 467; anti-Semitism 264; and Christianity 255, 259, 260–61, 298–99, 302, 306, 309, 310, 312, 319–20; contemporary 286–94; and the Enlightenment 264–65, 271, 290; feminism 285, 286, 291–93; Hasidism 263–64, 281, 287; Hellenism and 252; holy days 282–86; and Islam 260, 271, 286, 390–91, 413, 415, 433; Kabbalah 262–63; major branches 261–62, 263–64, 265, 272, 286–91; in the Middle Ages 259–62; Orthodox 265, 271, 277, 279, 287–88, 291, 292, 293; and politics 510; rabbinic tradition 244, 255–59, 299; sacred practices 278–82; spiritual tenets 273–78; timeline 240; and Zoroastrianism 235, 236, 252, 259 see also Jews; Torah; Zionism
Judas Iscariot 313, 314
Julian of Norwich 332
Junayd 408
Jung, Carl 15–16

K
Ka'bah 381, 383, 385, 387, 402, 403
Kabbalah 262–63
Kabilsingh, Dr. Chatsumarn 151
Kabir 8, 440–41, 449
Kabir, Syed Anwar 523
Kaddish 259
Kagan, Ruth Gan 280
kahuna (shaman–priests) 47
Kali 87, 111
Kali Yuga 91, 96, 442, 446, 467
kama (love) 100
Kamakura period, Japan 227
kami (spirits) 219–20, 221, 222–23, 224, 225, 226, 227–28

Kanchi (of Choctaw tribe) 34
kannagara (Natural Religion) 219–20, 225
Kannon (Guanyin) 158
Kapila 80
Kaplan, Rabbi Mordecai 290–91
Kapleau, Philip 163
Karenga, Maulana Ron 60
karma 481; Buddhism 80, 144–45; Hinduism 80; Jainism 123–25; Sikhism 450, 453, 454
karma yoga 82, 84
Kassam, Noordin 427
Katagiri, Dainin 159
Kaur 447
Kaur, Amardeep *447*
Kaur, Gur Ramandeep *447*
Kaur, Inderpreet 451
Kaur, Malika Preet *447*
Kawai'i, Kahu 47
Keating, Father Thomas 349
Kedar, Rabbi Karyn D. 291–92
kenoticism 333
kensho 8, 163
kevala (state of perfection) 125
Khadijah, wife of Muhammad 383–84, 385, 386
Khalistan 459
Khalsa ("Pure Ones") 447, 454, 458, *461*
Khan, Pir Vilayat Inayat 15
Khan, Uzbek 415–16
khanda (sword) 458, 461
al-Khayr, Abu Sa'id Abu 408
Khomeini, Ayatollah 429–30
Khrushchev, Nikita 344
kibbutzim *270*, 286
Kimball, Charles 502
King, Martin Luther, Jr. 370
kirpan (small sword) 461, 462
kirtan (devotional singing) 455, *458*
Kitab-i-Iqan (The Book of Certitude) 482
kitchen god 194
Knitter, Paul 347–48
koan (Zen puzzle) 163
Kogi people 67
Kojiki 217
Kong, Master *see* Confucius
kontombili (spirit beings) 42
Kook, Rabbi Abraham Isaac 288
Korea 149, 152, 160, 184, 213, *214*, 367, *368*, 369, 469
Koresh, David 494
kosher food 279
Koyukon people 47
Kramer, Jacqueline 27–28
Krishna *84*, 85, 90–91, 92, 94–95, 96, 108, 109, 110, 115
Krishnamurti, Jiddu 4
Kronshtadtsky, Ioann 349–50
kshatriyas 99
Kufa, Iraq 412
kufr (ungratefulness, unbelief) 393
Kumar, Acharya Sushil 127–28, 133

Kumbha Mela (Hindu festival) 110–11
Kund, Acharya Shri Kund 124–25
kundalini (energy center) 88
kundalini yoga *81*
Kung storyteller, Botswana *51*
Kurasha, Jameson 66
Kushner, Rabbi Lawrence 245
kusti (sacred cord) 238
Kwanzaa celebration (first fruits celebration) 60–61

L

Ladakh 170
Laden, Osama bin *see* bin Laden, Osama
LaDuke, Winona 68
Lakota Sioux people 17, 39–40, 48, 52, 57, 58–59
Lakshman 92, *93*, 94
Lakshmi 87, 90, 104, 109
Lalibela, Ethiopia *329*
lamas 167, 171
Lame Deer, Lakota holy man 17, 39–40, 48
langar (community meal) 444, 449, 454–55, 456, 460
Lantern Festival, China 198
Laos 149
Laozi (Lao-tzu) 190, 191, 193–94, 196, 199
Lapp people 56
Last Supper 306, 313, 351
Latin America 367, 368, 369, 372, 374
Lazarus *305*, 312
Lazarus, Emma 266
Lebanon 271
Leicester Council of Faiths 516
Lenin, V. I. 344
Lent 354
Leo I, Pope 327
levitation *466*
li (ceremonial rites) 185–86, 204, 206, 228
Li Hongzhi 202, 494
liberals, religious 19
liberation theology 370–73
Liebman, Charles 510
lifeways 36, 38
Lincoln, Bruce 507
lingams 89, 97, 106, 110
Lingayats 89–90
"The Little Flower" (St. Thérèse of Lisieux) *340*, *359*
Liu Zhongyu 194
Lohari festival 107
Lotus Sutra 156–57, 164–66
Lourdes, France 358
Lovelock, James 490
Loyola, Ignatius 339; *Spiritual Exercises* 339
the Lubavich Hasidim 288–89
Luke, Gospel of 300, 302, 306, 318
Lukumi *see* Santeria
Luria, Isaac 262–63

Luther, Martin 7, 293, 334–36, 337, 338, 339
Lutheranism 337
Lyons, Oren 44

M

Maathai, Dr. Wangari 514
Maccabean rebellion 252, 283, 298–99
McDonagh, Sean 362
McFague, Sallie 11, 374–75
Maclean, Dorothy 492
McLeod, Hew 462
McPherson, Aimée Semple 366
Madani, Abu Hashim 392
madrasas 426
Magha Puja Day (Sangha Day) 170–71
the Magi 236, 302, 353
Mahabharata 91, 93–95, 100, 105
Mahadevan, T.M.P. 91
Mahadevi (Akka) 15
Mahakala 90
Mahaparinibbana Sutta 153
Mahaprajapati 139
Mahaprajna, Acharya 129–30, 133
Maharishi Mahesh Yogi 114, 476
Maharshi, Ramana 84, 107
Mahashivaratri 109–10
Mahavira (Mahavir) 121–22, 130, 132
Mahayana Buddhism 149, 156–60, 166, 167, 170
Maimonides 13, 260, 274
Maitreya, Radhikamohan 105
Maitreya Buddha *159*
Majd, Dr. Ahmad Kamal Abu'l 436
Malaysia 64, 66–67, 200, 459
Malcolm X 420
Mali Empire 418
mana (sacred power) 48
mandalas 168
Mandate of Heaven 187, 199, 219
Mannath, Father Joe 361–62
mantras 82–83, 97, 101, 114, 168, 170
Manu, Code of 99–100
Mao Zedong 209–10
Maori people 36, 45, 48–49
Mara 139
Marcos, Chiapas leader 63
Mark, Gospel of 300, 314, 317
Marley, Bob 485
Martha 306, 312–13
Marx, Karl 3
Mary, the Virgin: devotion to 302, 357–59, 374; and Oshun 479
Mary Magdalene 306, 316
Mary of Bethany 306
Masorti (Conservative) Judaism 287, 290
mass *see* Eucharist

materialism 2, 3, 17, 67, 175, 369, 421, 522–23
Matthew, Gospel of 300, 302, 310, 312, 314, 316
maya (illusory world) 81
Maya, mother of the Buddha 136
Mayer, Jean-François 495
Mecca 381, *385*, 386–87, 400, *402*, 403, 416, 418
medicine people 53 *see also* shamans/shamanism
Medina 386–87, *400*, 407, 428
meditation: Buddhism 152–53, 161, 163, 167–68, 171; Christian contemplative prayer 355–57; Daoist 195; Hindu *82*, 83, 102, 105; positive effects 4; techniques 8; Transcendental 114, 476
mediums 52, 186
Medjugorje, Herzegovina 358–59
Meiji, Emperor 218
Meiji Restoration, Japan 218, 227, 228–29
Menchú, Rigoberta 70
Mendelssohn, Moses 265
Mengzi (Mencius) 206–7
men's movement 37
menstruation 49–50, 57, 279
Merneptah Stele 249
Meron, Michal: *The Ten Commandments* 249
Merton, Thomas 355, *356*
Mesoamerica 34, 36
Mesopotamia 242, *243*, 244, 259, 284, 321, 487
the Messiah 253, 254–55, 259, 262, 263, 269; Jesus as 255, 260, 300, 301, 303, 309–10, 312, 319–20, 353
metaphysics 24, 208
Methodism 337, 340, 348, 369
Mevlevi Dervish Order 410
Mexico 36, 38, 56, 59, 61–62, 63
Mian Mir, Islamic saint 445, 452
Micah 250, 254
Midrash 256, 257, 258, 285, 290, 293
mikva (ritual bath) 279
Milarepa 168
millennial movements 467, 474, 493
Ming dynasty, China 208
Minkowski, Maurycy: *After the Pogrom* 267
Minqin Wang 186
Mirabai, Rajput princess 84–85
Miraj *386*
Miriam 247, *248*, 285
Mishnah 257, 298
misogi (purification ritual) 226, *230*, 231
missionaries 338, 340, 369, 370, 480, 503

Mithraism 237
Modern Orthodoxy (Judaism) 287–88
modernism 504–5
Mogul Empire 117, *416*, 417, 441, 445, 446, 448, 449
moksha (liberation) 80, 100
monasticism: Buddhist 139, 150–52, 154, 168, 170, 171, 172–73; Christian 325, 327, 330–31, 332, 333, 340, 343, 344; Daoist 200; Hindu 114–15; Jain 122–23, 126, 128–29; kenoticism 333
Mongolia 149, 166, 170; Mongols 333, 415–16, 419, 441
monistic religions 11, 81
monotheism 10, 235, 237, 245–46
Moon, Sun Myung 468–70
Mordecai 284
Mormon Church 471–73, 496
Moses 239, 242, 247–48, *249*, 313, 388
Mother Goddess 86, 357, *487*
Mount Athos 343, *346*
Mount Fuji 218
Mount Hira *384*
Mount Huashan *189*
Mount Kailas 44, 48
Mu'awiyya, caliph 404
mudras (sacred gestures) 88
muezzin 385
Muhammad, Elijah 420, 421
Muhammad, the Prophet *16*, 26–27, 255, 271, 381, 383–88, 389, 399, 404, 406, 407, 412, 413, 482, 510, 511
Muhammad, Warith Deen 420
Muindi, Florence 372–73
mujahid (fighter in the Path of God) 428
Muktananda, Swami 102
Mul Mantra 450
Mundaka Upanishad 9
murshid (teacher) 408
music and religion 83, 104, 105, 204, 341, 362, 485
Muslims *see* Islam; Shi'ite Muslims; Sunni Muslims
Myanmar (Burma) 149, 155, 156, 179
mysticism 7, 8, 9, 13, 23, 56, 262, 331–32, 334, 339–40, 407
myths 2, 17–18

N

Nachman, Reb 264
Nag Hammadi manuscripts 301, *321*, 322
Naga Panchami 109
Naganuma, Myoko 165
Nagarjuna 159
nagas (snake spirits) 42, 109
Nakasone, Yashuhiro 523
Nakayama, Miki 229

Nam (name of God) 450, 453, 454, 455
Namdev, Bhagat 84, 440
Nanak, Guru 440, 441–43, 444, 450, 452, 453, 455, 462
Nanaki, Bibi 452
narieka (doorway of the heart) 56
Narmada River 104
Nasr, Seyyed Hossein 424
Nasrudin, Mulla 409–10
Nathan 262
Nathaniel, Archimandrite 346
Nation of Islam 420–21
Native Americans: and Christianity 63; contemporary issues 38, 63, 67, 68, 69; creation accounts 17; *Descendants of the Eagle* story 17; earthworks *44*; and New Age movements 37, 489; reservations 67, 68; shamans 53, 54; spiritual practices 39–41, 45, 49–50, 57–60; sun dance 58–59
nature spirituality 486–91
Navajo people 39, *41*, 53, 67
Nazis 266, 267
Nebuchadnezzar, king of Babylonia 250
negative aspects of religion 28–29
Nehru, Jawaharlal 104, 116
Neidjie, Bill 45
Neo-Confucianism 208, 228
Neo-Paganism 37, 486–89
"Neo-Pentecostal" churches
Nepal 42, 45, 54, 149, 166, 170
Neusner, Jacob 257
New Age spirituality 37, 466, 484, 491–93
"New Atheism" 12
New Israelite Temple Association 265
New Mexico *49*
new religious movements 465–97
New Testament 300–301, 303, 312, 317, 318, 322, 341
New Thought 492
Newton, Isaac 21
Nguyen, Cue 170
Nicene Creed 324, 327–28
Nichiren Buddhism 164–66
Nigeria 423, 505, 506
Nihongi 217, 219
Nipponzan Myohoji 165
nirvana *140*, 141, 143, 147–48, 159
Niwano, Rev. Nikkyo 165
Nizamuddin Aulia *409*
Noah 244
Noahide Code 277
Noble Eightfold Path 139, 143–44, 160
Non-Chalcedonian Churches 329

nontheistic religions 11, 141, 153
Northern Ireland 505, 516
Numinous Treasure Daoism 197

O

Obama, Barack 508, 509
Obatala 42, 50
Ogoni people 66
oharai (purification ritual) 227
Old Testament 299, 302
Olodumare 43
Olokun 42, 50
OM symbol 83
Omer, Hannah (with Hayut-Man): *The Throne of Shekhinah* 258
Ontario Consultants on Religious Practice 515
Oomoto movement (Shinto) 229–30
Oosthuizen, Gerhardus Cornelius 35
OPEC (Organization of Petroleum Exporting Countries) 421
Opoku, Rev. William Kingsley 42, 480
oracle bones 186–87
Oracles of the Three Shrines 229
oral traditions 34, 50–52
Orang Asli people 64–65, 66–67
Oriental Orthodox Churches 329
Origen 299
original sin 337, 339, 358
orisa (spirit beings) 42, 50, 61, 479
Orthodox Judaism 265, 271, 272, 277, 279, 287–88, 291, 292, 293
orthodoxy 18
Oshun 479
Osun 34, 42, 43
Otto, Rudolf 9
Ottoman Empire 416, 420, 422
Oxford University Press 515
Oya 42

P

Padmasambhava 166
Pahlavi shahs (Iran) 429
Pahlavi texts 236
Pakistan 236, 404, 417, 427, 431–32, 459, *459*
Palani, Swami Sivasiva 88, 98
Palestine 252, 255, 270, 271–72, 328, 419–20, 433, 506
the Pali Canon 150, 151, 156, 159
Pali dialect 139, 149
Palmer, Samuel: *The Waterfalls, Pistyll Mawddach, Wales 9*
Palmerston, Lord 419
Palmo, Tenzin 174
Panikkar, Raimundo 512
Panj Piaras (Five Beloved Ones) 446, 458
Pann, Abel: *The Wandering of Adam and Eve 242*

Panth (community) 444, 460–61
papacy 326, 327, 329–30, 332, 334, 341, 360; Avignon papacy 330, 332, 334
parables of Jesus 308, 309
Paraclete 391
Parham, Charles 365–66
Parliament of the World's Religions, Chicago (1993) 141, 513, 514
Parsis 236, 238
Parvati 88–89, 108, 109
Paryushan Mahaparva festival 132
Passover 247, 273, 284–86, 313, 354
Patanjali 82
patriarchal religions 26, 27
Patterson, Dudley 45
Paul, St. (Saul) 259, 300, 318, 319, *320*, 321, 322, 325, 365, 373
Paul VI, Pope 522
Peace Pagodas 165
penance 349, 350
Peng Ying Zian Guang (Fung Ying Seen Koon) Daoism 200
Pentateuch 241–42, 251, 281
Pentecost 318, 354–55
Pentecostalism 335, 363, 365, 366–67, 369, 370, 372–73
Pereira, Denis G. 376
Perfection of Wisdom scriptures 159–60
Persian Empire 252, 259, 387, 411–12, 414
Pesach (Passover) 247, 273, 284–86, 313, 354
Peter, St. 304, 317, 318–19
Pharisees 252, 255, 259, 299, 310, 312, 319
Philistines 255
Philokalia 345, 346
philosophy and religion 2, 80–85
piercing rituals, Native American 59
pilgrimage: Buddhism 141, *154*, 155; Chinese religions *189*; Daoism 199; *hajj* 400, 402–4, 418; Hinduism 89, 104, 106–7, 110–11; indigenous groups 60; Islam 381, 394, 400, 402–4; Jainism 132; Shinto *218*, 224; Sufi *409*
Pinga 54
Pinyin transliteration system 184
Pit River Indians 46
Plato 20
Plum Village community, France 174
pluralism 502–7, 506, 512
pogroms 266, *267*
Poland, Jews in 261–62, 263, 264, 267
politics and religion 28–29, 369, 427–35, 507–10
polytheism 10–11, 13, 236
Pompey 253

Pongsak, Ajahn 178
Pontius Pilate 315
popes *see* papacy
Prabhupada, A.C. Bhaktivedanta Swami 114–15
Pragya, Samani Sanmati 127
Prakriti 80–81
prana (life energy) 82
pranayama (breath control) 101
prasad (sanctified food) 97
prayer: Christianity 355–57; Hinduism 77, 97, 99, 103; Islam *385*, 397–99; Judaism 259, 262, 274, 277, 279–78, 281; Sikhism 455, 457, 458
prayer wheels/flags *166*, 168
Presbyterianism 337, 369
Prigogine, Ilya 23
the profane 10
Project on Religion and Human Rights 505
Protestant Christianity: contemporary issues 362; denominations 336–39; and the ecumenical movement 376; fundamentalism 363; missionaries 338, 340, 503; sacraments 351, 352, 364 *see also* evangelical churches; Protestant Reformation
Protestant Reformation 334–39
the Pseudepigrapha 262
puberty 100, 101
puja (ritual worship) 97, 98–99
pujaris (priests) 97
the Punjab 457, 458, 459, 475
punye (good deeds) 131
Pure Land Buddhism 164
Purgatory 334
purification rituals: Jain 127; Shinto *218*, 222, 225–27, *230*; Zoroastrian 238
Purim, Jewish festival 284
Purusha 80–81

Q
"Q" 300
Al Qaeda 432–33, 506, 507
qi (ch'i) (energy) 187, 194, 195, 200, 201
Qigong (Ch'i-kung) 202, 494
Qin (Ch'in) dynasty, China 199, 204
Qing dynasty, China 208
Qiu, Alan 211
Quakers 337, *338*, 348
quantum mechanics 22–23
Queen Mother of the West 196
"Queen of Peace" (Medjugorje) 358–59
Qumran settlement 252, 262
the Qur'an 20, 381, 383, 384, 388–91, 393, 394–95, 396–97, 404, 405–6, 407, 409, 412, 420, 423–24, 428–29, 432, 433–34, 507, 510
Qurayshites 383, 385, 386, 412
Qutb, Sayyib 429

R
rabbis 255, *256*, 258, 299
Rabi'a 407
racism and religion 371, 372
Radha *84*, 96, 108
Radhakrishnan, Dr. N. 521
Radhakrishnan, Dr. S. 7, 449
Radhasoami movement 475, 477
Rahul, son of the Buddha 138
Rahula, Walpola 142, 177
raja yoga 81, 82
Ram Das, Guru 444
Rama 90, 92–93, 94, 109
Ramadan 384, 399–400, 401, 423
Ramakrishna 85, 102, 111–12, 513
Ramakrishna Movement 112
Ramananda 440
Ramayana 90, 91, 92–93, 105, 113
Ranjit Singh, Maharaja 448
the rapture 364, 467–68
al-Rasheed, Mahmoon 435–36
Rashtriya Svayamsevak Sangh (RSS) 117
Rastafari movement 484–86
Ratzinger, Cardinal Joseph 360 *see also* Benedict XVI
Ravana 92, *93*, 94
Ravitzky, Aviezer 269, 272
Reconstructionism (Judaism) 287, 290–91, 292
Redfield, James 493
Reform Judaism 265, 271, 272, 287, 289–90, 292
reincarnation 79–80, 118, 138–39, 450, 481
relics: Buddhist 141, 153, 155, 171; Christian 327, 334, 336, 339, 359, 360
Religious Zionism 272, 288
Rembrandt van Rijn: portrait of Jesus 299; *The Three Crosses 315*
ren (jen) 205
Responsa literature 259–60
Revolutionary Association of the Women of Afghanistan 431
Rig Veda 74, 78
Rinzai Zen 163
Rishabh, First Tirthankara 124
Rishikesh, India *95*
rishis (Hindu sages) 77, 78–79
Rissho Kosei-kai 165–66
Rites, Book of 206, 207
rituals 2, 14–15, 56–62; Hinduism 97–99, 100, 101; Jain 127; Native American 59; Shinto *218*, 222, 225–27, *230*; Zoroastrian 238
Roerich, Nicholas 481–82; *Pearl of Searching 481*
Roman Catholic Church: contemporary issues 360–62, 368, 520–21; and the ecumenical movement 376; liberation theology 370–73; Mary, devotion to 358–59,

374; medieval 331–32, 334; monasticism 332; sacraments 339, 350, 351, 352; saints and angels 359 *see also* papacy
Roman Catholic Reformation 339–40
Roman Empire 241, 253, 255, 259, 298, 299, 309, 310, 318, 321, 326–27
Romania *347*
Rosh Hashanah, Jewish festival 282–83
Rothschild family 264, 270
RSS (Rashtriya Svayamsevak Sangh) 117
Ruether, Rosemary Radford 306, 373
Rumen, Catherine *374*
Rumi, Jalal al-Din 407, 410, 418
Russell, Charles Taze 474
Russell, George William (AE) 7
Russell, Peter 490
Russia 170; Buddhism 465, 504; ethnic religions 488–89; Hinduism 465; Islam 415–16, 417, 504; Jews 263, 264, 266, 267, 293, 503, 504; Mongol invasions 333; new religious movements 465, 483, 486, 488–89, 494, 504; religious pluralism 503, 504; Spring Equinox festival *523 see also* Buryat people
Russian Orthodox Church 333, 342, 343, 344–45, 354, 357, 358, 494, 503, 504

S
Sabbath 256, 273, 280–81
Sacha Sauda community 460
sacraments, Christian 350–52
sacred reality, understandings of 1, 10–14
sacred sites *35*, 48–49, 60, 67, 68, 489
sacred thread ceremony (Hinduism) 100, 101
Saddleback Church, California 362, *363*
Sadducees 252, 299, 310
sadhanas (yogic practices) 82, 105
sadhus (Hindu ascetics) *88*, 110
Sagar, Muni Amit 129
Sai Baba, Sathya 470–71
Sai Baba, Shirdi 470
Sai Organization 471
saints: Christian 331–32, 334, 340, 359–60; Hindu 445; Islamic 394, 445, 452; Sikh 440–41, 460
Sakyadhita (Daughters of the Buddha) *174*, 175, 177
salaat (prayer) 397, 398
Salah-al-Din (Saladin) 415
Salvation Army 375

samadhi (spiritual absorption) 82, 83, 85
Samantabhadra 130
samatha (calm) 152
samsara (cycle of birth, life, and death) 80, 102, 123, *125*, 127, 130, 144–47, 149
Samuel, Hebrew prophet 249
sangat (congregation) 448, 454
the Sangha 139, 150, 151, 154, 170, 262
Sangha Day (Magha Puja Day) 170–71
sannyasins (Hindu renunciates) 100, 102, 138
Sanskrit 74, 83, 93
Sant Mat 475
Santeria 39, 478–79
sants (holy people) 440–41, 460
Saperstein, Rabbi David 288–89
Sarah *243*, 244, 293, 381
Saraswati 87
Sarnath *138*, 139, 170
Sarvodaya Shramadana Sangamaya movement 180
Sat Yuga 467
Satan 277, 278, 303, 394
satori 163–64
Saudi Arabia 399, 400, 403, 404, 423, 427, 432
Saul, king of Israel 249–50
Saunders, Eliza 63
Savarkar, V. D. 117
Sawan Singh, Baba 475
Sayadaw, Mahasi 152
Schechter, Solomon 168, 290
Schimmel, Annemarie 418
Schorsch, Ismar 277
Schulz, Diane Rae 488
Schumacher, E. F. 178
Schuon, Frithjof 392, 511
science and religion 4, 20–26, 340, 364
scientific materialism 3, 21
Scientology 466–67, 496, 497
Scopes, John Thomas 364
Seattle, Chief 490
Second Vatican Council (1962) 341–42, 370, 376, 520
the Secret of the Golden Flower 195
"Sect Shinto" 229–30
sects 465
secularism 501–2
Seder meal 284, 285, 313, 354
Seed, John 489
Selassie, Emperor Haile 485
Self-Realization Fellowship 114
Semites 246
Sengen shrines 220
Sengtsan 161
Sephardic Jews 266, 287
Sergius, St. 333, *342*
Sermon on the Mount 308
Sethna, Tehmurasp Rustamji 237
Seva Panthis 452
Seventh Day Adventists 337–38
Seymour, William Joseph 366

Shah, Hajji Waris Ali *408*
Shah, Idries 409–10
Shah Jahan, Mogul emperor *416*, 449
Shahadah 391, 396–97
Shaivites 88–90
Shaktas 86–88, 106
shakti (female aspect of deity) 86, 88
shaktipat (power of a glance, word, touch, or thought) 102
Shakyamuni Buddha 158 *see also* Buddha
shamans/shamanism 37, 42, 53–55, 61, 64–65, 199
Shang dynasty, China 186–87
Shangdi (Shang Ti) 187
Shango 42
Shankara (Sankara) 81
Shari'ah 405, 406, 419, 422, 423–24, 431, 503
Sharma, Arvind 512
Shavuot, Jewish festival 286, 354–55
shaykh (spiritual master) 408
the Shekhinah 258, 281, 293
shen (spirit) 195
Sheng 190
Shichi-go-san (Seven-Five-Three) Festival *224*
Shi'ite Muslims 387, 396, 404, 406, 414, 429–30, 431, 435
Shinran 164
Shinto 184, 217; and Buddhism 227–28, 231; ceremonies 219, 223–24, 232; and Confucianism 214, 227, 228; contemporary 230–33; festivals 217, *224*–25; *kami* 219–20, 221, 222–23, 224, 225, 226, 227–28; nature, kinship with 217, 218–19, 220, 225, 232–33; purification rituals *218*, 222, 225–27, *230*; roots of 217; "Sect Shinto" 229–30; shrines 217, 218, 220–23, 224, 227, 231, 232; "State Shinto" 228–29; and the West 227, *230*, 231
shirk (Islamic sin) 393
Shiva 75, 86, 88–90, 96, 101, 104, 108, 109, 110, 116
shrines: Buddhist 39, 153, 155; Daoist 199; Hindu 86, 99, 104, *106*; indigenous peoples 38, *49*; Shinto 217, 218, 220–23, 224–25
Shuddhodana, King, father of the Buddha 139
shudras 85, 99, 100
Shunzo, Sakamiki 219
Sikh Empire 448
Sikhs/Sikhism 440; Baisakhi festival 458; central beliefs 450–53; and Christianity 456; contemporary 457, 459–62, 475; "Five K's" 447–48, 458; Guru Nanak 440; gurus

441–49, 450, 451, 460; and Hinduism 440, 441, 442, 446, 450, 453, 456, 459, 461, 462; interfaith movement 511, 516–17; Islam 442–43, 445, 452, 456, 462, 510; and Islam 442–43, 445, 452, 456, 462, 510; and politics 510; sacred practices 453–55, 457; *sant* tradition 440–41, 460; timeline 443; and Zoroastrianism 235
Sikkim 166, 170
Simhat Torah, Jewish festival 283, *284*
Singapore 200, 211, 213, 459
Singh 447
Singh, Dr. Karan 116
Singh, Manmohan 457
Singh, Nikky-Guninder Kaur 447–48
Sioux people 59 *see also* Lakota Sioux people
Sita 92, 93, 94
Sivananda, Swami 83, 87
Sivaraksa, Sulak 180
"Six Day War" (1967) 271
Smart, Ninian 1–2
Smith, Joseph 471, 472, 473
Smith, Wilfred Cantwell 511
social issues and religion 2, 112, 177–80, 370, 372–73, 484–93, 502, 517–23
Soen Nakagawa-roshi 158
Sofer, Moses 265
Soka Gakkai International 165, 471
Solomon, king of Israel 250
Soma 78
Somé, Mado 53
Song dynasty, China 208
Songstan, king of Tibet 166–67
South Africa 371
South America 338, 364, 369
Spain: Inquisition 261, 330, 415; Islam 260, 412, 413, *414*, 415, 418, 434; Jews 260, 261; mysticism 339–40; Protestant Reformation 337
Spenta Mainyu 237
Spinoza, Baruch 265
spirit animals 54, 56
Spiritualism 478, 492
Sri Lanka: Buddhism *140*, 149, 155, 170, 171, 178, 180; Christianity 322
Stanton, Rabbi Alysa *292*
Starhawk 486
Stark, Rodney 466, 467, 468, 493
"State Shinto" 228–29
Stations of the Cross 356
Steindl-Rast, Brother David 5
Stepanova, Nadezhda Ananyevna 55
storytellers 50–52
Streng, Frederick 5
stupas 141, 154, 170
Sudan 433

Sufism *8*, 407–10, 411, 417, 440
Sugihara, Chiune 268
Suhrawardi, Shihabuddin 409
suicide bombers 506
Sukkot, Jewish festival 283
Sumedho, Ajahn 143, 174
Sun Bu-er 196
sun dance, Native American 58–59
Sunday, Elisabeth 47
Sunnah 383, 404, 405, 432
Sunni Muslims 404–6, 407, 417, 431, 435
sunyata (emptiness) 159–60
"superstring theory" 23
Susanna 306
Susanoo 222
sutras (sayings) 125, 129, 150, 154, 159, 166, 228 *see also* *Lotus Sutra*
Suzuki, D. T.: *Zen Buddhism* 177
Svetambaras 122–23
Swadhyaya Movement 113, 519
Swan, Madonna 57
sweat lodges, Native American 60
symbols 14–17; Christian 323, *360*, 504; Daoism *186*, *190*; Hinduism 83; indigenous cultures 39, *40*, 50–51; Islamic 407, 421, 504; Jainism *125*; Sikh 447, 461–62, 504
synagogues 255, 281, 292
syncretic religions 477–84
synod, Eastern Orthodox Church 345
synoptic gospels 300–301
Syria 252, 271, 404, 411, 412–13
Szold, Henrietta *270*

T

Taiji quan (T'ai chi ch'uan) 201, *202*
Taiwan 152, 170, *178*, 197, 199, 200, 211, 213
Taj Mahal, Agra *416*
the Taliban 431–32
talit (prayer shawl) 280
the Talmud 241, *256*, 257, 259, 262, 273, 277, 287; Babylonian Talmud 258, 259, 277; Jerusalem Talmud 257–58
Tamerlane 441
Tamil Nadu 90
the Tanakh 239, 241, 246, 255, 257, 258
Tang dynasty, China 199
Tantras 88
Tantrayana Buddhism *see* Vajrayana Buddhism
Taoism *see* Daoism
Tara 167
tariqas (esoteric orders) 408
Taylor, Charles 501–2
tea ceremonies, Japan *163*, 219
Teg Bahadur, Guru 446

Teilhard de Chardin, Pierre 375, 524
Temple of Heaven Complex, Beijing *209*
the Ten Commandments 248, *249*, 277, 286
"Ten Lost Tribes of Israel" 250
Tenjin shrines 220
Tenrikyo movement (Shinto) 229
Teresa of Avila, St. 340
terrorism 29, 271, 376, 401, 425, 427, 430, 431, 432–34, 505–6, 517, 521
t'fillin (phylacteries) 279–80
Thailand 149, 154–55, 171, 177, 178
thangkas 168
theistic religions 10
Theodosius, St. 333
Theosophical Society 480–82, 492
Theravada Buddhism 149–56, *157*, 159, 170, 178
Thérèse of Lisieux, St. *340*, *359*
Thomas, Gospel of 301, 322
Thorkelson, Bishop Thomas 472–73
Three Marks of Existence 139
Tian (Heaven) 187
Tian ho (Tien-hou) 194
Tiananmen Square 210–11
Tiantai Zhiyi 157
Tibet: Buddhism 149, 158–59, 166–68, 170, 171, 501; Chinese invasion (1950–1959) 168; indigenous religions 44, 48
Tinker, George 37
the Tipitaka 150
Tirimanna, Vimal 507
Tirthankaras 122–23, 124, 130, 132
Tisha Be-av, Jewish festival 286
Tlakaelel 48, 61–62
Toltecs 48
Tokugawa period, Japan 218
Tonpa, Lama Drom 167
the Torah (tenets of faith) 239, *241*, 248, 249, 251, 252, 255, 256–57, 257–58, 262, 265, 273–78, 281, 282, 285, 286, 287, 291
Tosefta 298
transcendence 10
Transcendental Meditation (TM) movement 114, 476
Transfiguration of Christ 312–13, 355
transubstantiation 339
Tree Hugging movements 491
Treister, Kenneth: Holocaust sculpture *268*
Trent, Council of (1545–1563) 339
the Triple Gem 150–52, 170
Trotsky, Leon 266
"True Pure Land" Buddhism 164

Tsalagi people (Cherokee) 39
Tsering, Nepali shaman 54
Tsomo, Karma Lekshe 176
Tsubaki Grand Shrine, Japan 227
Tsubaki Shrine, United States 227, *230*, 231
tsumi (impurity) 225
Tu B'shvat, Jewish festival 283–84
Tucker, Mary Evelyn 214
Tudi gong (T'u-ti Kung) 199
Tulsi, Acharya 126, 130, 133
Tunisia 415
Turkey 235, 262, 404, 410, 416, 422, 433
Tutu, Desmond 348, 371
tzaddik (enlightened saint and teacher) 264
Tzevi, Shabbatai 262
Tzu Chi Foundation *178*

U

the Udasis 449
Ueshiba, Mirihei 227
Uganda AIDS Commission 520
ulama (scholars) 405–6, 415, 429
Ultra-Orthodox Judaism 287, 288
Uluru (Ayers Rock), Australia *35*
'Umar ibn al-Khattab, caliph 394, 404, 412
Umayyad dynasty 404, 405, 407, 412, 413
ummah (Muslim community) 405, 411, 413
Underhill, Ruth 57
Unification Movement 468–70, 494
Unitarianism 337
United States: and Afghanistan 431, 433; anti-cult movement 496; Buddhism 164, 166, 171–74, 501, 503; Daoism 201; evangelicalism 337–38, 364, 365–66, 375, 507; and Iraq 369, 430–31, 433; Islam 420–21; Judaism 265–66, 272, 285, 290, 291; new religious movements 469–70, 471–73, 479–80, 494–95, 496; Orthodox Church 343–44, 503; Pentecostalism 365–66, 369; Shinto 227, *230*, 231; Sikhism 459, 462; war on terrorism 381, 430–31, 433, 507–8; Zoroastrianism 238
Unity School of Christianity 492
universalism and universalist religions 11, 482, 491, 512
untouchables 99, 117

Upanishads 78–79, 81, 85, 91, 96, 116
Urban VI, Pope 330
Uthman, caliph 404
Uttaradhyayana Sutra 129
Uvavnuk, Inuit shaman 54

V

Vaduma people 66
Vaishnavites 90–91, 108
vaishyas 99
Vajrayana Buddhism 166–68, 170
Valmiki 92–93
Vandiver, David 307
Vatican II (1962) 341–42, 370, 376, 520
the Vedas 74, 75, 77–80, 91, 96, 99, 116, 118
Vedic age 74, 77–78, 80, 86, 103
Vedic religion *78*, 86, 98, 99, 101
Vesak festival 170
VHP (Vishva Hindu Parishad) 117
Vietnam 149, 160, 177, 477–78
Vimalakirtinirdesha Sutra 166
vipassana (insight) 152, 171
Virgin Mary *see* Mary
Virsa Singh, Baba 456, 462, 516, 523
Vishnu 88, 90, 92, 96, 101, 110
Vishtapa, King 236
Vishva Hindu Parishad (VHP) 117
vision quests 58, 61–62
Vivekananda, Swami 96, 112, 513
Vladimir I, king of Russia 344
Vodou 39
vodu (spirit beings) 39, 42
Vohu Manah 235
Vyasa 77, 81, 96

W

Wach, Joachim 10
Waco, Texas 494–95
Wadud, Amina *396*, 424
al-Wahhab, Muhammad ibn 'Abd 432
Wahhabism 432
Wakan Tanka ("Great Spirit") 59
al-Walid, Khalid ibn 411, 413
Walid II, caliph 413
Wallace, Alan 175
Warren, Rick 362, *363*
Wat Indra Viharn, Bangkok *155*
Watts, Alan: *The Way of Zen* 177
Weaver, Jace 67
Weber, Max 28
Wei, Lady 197
Weiss, Ellen 288

Welwood, John 28
Wesley, John 337, 340, 363
Wessinger, Catherine 496
Wheel of Birth and Death, Buddhist 144–47
White Buffalo Calf Woman 60
White Cloud Monastery, Beijing 197, 200
White Earth Land Recovery Project 68
Whitefield, George 363
Wicca 486–87
Wiesel, Elie 268
Williams, Lorraine Mafi 34–35
Williams, Rowan 323
Williamson, Marianne 491
witchcraft 486
women and religion 26–28, 487–88; Baha'i 483; beguines 331; Buddhism 27–28, 139, 151–52, 174, 175–77, 179; Christianity 27, 325, 331, 340–41, 362, 373–75; Confucianism 208, 210; Daoism 196, 197; Hinduism 86, 88, 89, 91, 100, 103, 104, 107, 112, 139, *166*; in indigenous cultures 40–41, 43, 49–50, 52; Islam 18–19, *396*, 397, 405, 421, *422*, 423–24, 425, 426, 431, 433; Jainism 122–23; and Jesus 26, 306, 308, 316–17; Judaism 256, 257, 279, 280, 290, 291–93, 306; as priests 362, *374*; Rastafari movement 485; Sikhism 447, 452–53, 457 *see also* feminist movement; menstruation
World Council of Churches 352, 356, 376
world religions, percentage of followers *501*
World Tree *16*, 51
wu wei (actionless action) 192–93

X

Xunzi (Hsun Tzu) 206, 207

Y

Yahweh 242 *see also* YHWH
yakeduras (shamans) 155
Yamakage, Motohisa 218
Yamamoto, Princess 221
Yamamoto, Yukitaka 218, 220, 226
yang *186*, 187
Yannaras, Christos 318
yantras (symbols) 83, 86, 88
Yao (sage king) 205

Yao Xinzhong, Professor 211
Yashodara, wife of the Buddha 136, 139
Yasukuni Shrine, Tokyo 231
Yazid, caliph 404
Yellow Emperor 190
Yeshe Tsogyal 167
YHWH (YHVH) 247, 248, 249, 283
yi (righteous conduct) 207
Yiddish 261
Yijing (I Ching) 187, 189, 204
yin *186*, 187
yoga 81–85, 167
Yogananda, Paramahansa *102*, 112, 114
Yoido Full Gospel Church, Korea 367, *368*
Yom Kippur, Jewish holy day 282, 283
yoni 89
Yoruba people 34, 39, 42, 50–51, 52, 66
Young, Brigham 472
Young, Josiah, III 43
Yu Yingshi, Professor 203–4
Yup'ik people 47
Yurok people 49

Z

zakat (charity) 399
Zarathushtra 235–36, 237
Zayd 385, 412
zazen 161, 163, 171, 172
Zealots 255, 299, 310
Zen Buddhism 160–64, 171–74, 219
Zen Mountain Monastery, New York 172–73
Zen Oxherding Pictures 162
Zhang Daoling (Chang Tao-ling) 197
Zhang Zai 208
Zhao Ziyang (Chao Tzu-yang) 210
Zhou (Chou) dynasty, China 187
Zhou Zhongzhi 200–201
Zhu Xi (Chu Hsi) 208
The Zhuangzi 190
Zhuangzi (Chuang tzu) 191, 192, 196
Zionism 269–71, 272, 286, 287, 419, 510; Religious Zionism 272, 288
Zohar ("Way of Splendor") 262
Zoroastrianism 235, 467; contemporary 238; spread 236; teachings 236–38; Zarathushtra's mission 235–36
Zum-Zum 400, *402*
Zwingli, Ulrich 336, 339

CREDITS

The author and publishers wish to acknowledge, with thanks, the following photographic sources.

Frontispiece: © P Deliss /Godong/Corbis.

CHAPTER 1 2 Alexandra Engel; 6 Hirschhorn Museum and Sculpture Garden, Smithsonian Institution, Washington, D.C. (Gift of Joseph H. Hirschhorn) photo Lee Stalsworth/© succession Giacometti 2010; 8 © Sarah Errington/Hutchison Picture Library; 9 © Tate, London 2010, photo John Webb; 10 LKP Archives; 11 © Brian Vikander/Corbis; Leon Neal/AFP/Getty Images; 14 © Courtesy of the architect Fariborz Sahba/photo Chars Nolley; 15 Alexandra Engel; 16 Iranian hanging for prayer niche, Mihrab design with Tree of Life, 19th century, wool embroidered in silk, 75 x 50 ins. The Metropolitan Museum of Art, Rogers Fund, 1910 (10.33.1). Image copyright The Metropolitan Museum of Art/Art Resource/Scala, Florence; 21 © kjpargeter/ClipArtOf.com; 23 © Space Telescope Science Institute/Corbis; 26 www.worldreligions.co.uk.

CHAPTER 2 35 Tim Graham/Getty Images; 37 Photo from Lucy M. Lewis, American Indian Potter by Susan Peterson; 40 Pygmy Fund Photo: Jean-Pierre Hallet; 41 Courtesy Smithsonian Institution, National Anthropological Archive, Washington, D.C.; 43 Ohio Historical Society; 44 Musée des Arts d'Afrique et d'Océanie, Paris/Bridgeman Art Library; 47 © Elisabeth Sunday; 48 Mary Pat Fisher; 51 Mat Farbman © Life Magazine/Getty Images; 53 Photo by Marisol Villanueva; 54 Hutchison Picture Library; 56 © Olivier Martel/Corbis; 58 © Bert Gunn; 61 Hutchison Picture Library/Juliet Highet; 62 Photo Dana Salvo; 65 © Mary Pat Fisher; 69 Photo by Marisol Villanueva/Grandmotherscouncil.org.

CHAPTER 3 77 © Paul A. Souders/Corbis; 78 © Mary Pat Fisher; 79 Alexandra Engel; 82 Circa Religion Photo Library/William Holtby; 82 © Mary Pat Fisher; 84 V&A Images; 86 V&A Images; 87 Hutchison Picture Library/Christine Pemberton; 88 © Chris Hellier/Corbis; 89 (top) © Walter Allgoewer /age fotostock/Imagestate; 90 Metropolitan Museum of Art, Rogers Fund, Harris Brisbane Dick Fund, 1964 (64.251), age © 2010 The Metropolitan Museum of Art/Art Resource/Scala; 90 © Mary Pat Fisher; 92 © Lindsay Hebberd/Corbis; 93 V&A Images; 95 Mary Pat Fisher; 96 Circa Photo Library/Bipin J. Mistry; 98 Hutchison Picture Library/Nancy Durrell McKenna; 101 © Mary Pat Fisher; 102 Photo of Paramahansa Yogananda, copyright © 1953 renewed 1981 Self-Realization Fellowship, copyright © 1984 Self-Realization Fellowship. All rights reserved. Reprinted with permission; 103 Gurmeet Thukral; 104 © Harish Tyagi/epa/Corbis; 105 © Mary Pat Fisher; 106 Hutchison Picture Library/Dave Brinicombe; 107 Mary Pat Fisher; 108 © Amit Bhargava/Corbis; 109 (above) © Mary Pat Fisher; 109 (below) Gurmeet Thukral; 110 © Gideon Mendel/Corbis; 112 Topfoto; 114 © Matt Morreale, Yoga Maya Films; 115 Sandhya S., Kannada Matruvani, Mata Amritanandamayi Mutt.

CHAPTER 4 122 © Mary Pat Fisher; 123 Mario Tama/Getty Images; 128 V&A Images; 130 © Mary Pat Fisher.

CHAPTER 5 136 Hutchison Picture Library/Ivan Strasbourg; 138 Circa Religion Photo Library/William Holtby; 140 Hutchison Picture Library/ Robin Constable; 145 V&A Images; 148 Alexandra Engel; 150 © Caroline Penn/Corbis; 152 Hutchison Picture Library/Juliet Highet; 155 (top) © Hutchison Picture Library/Robin Constable; 158 World Religions PL/ Claire Stout; 159 Chinese, Northern Wei Dynasty, Maitreya Altarpiece, dated 524, gilt bronze, ht. 30¼ ins. The Metropolitan Museum of Art, Rogers Fund, 1938 (38.158.1a-n) © 2010 The Metropolitan Museum of Art/Art Resource/Scala; 163 Hutchison Picture Library/Bernard Regent; 164 Christie's Images/Corbis; 166 Patrick Field, Eye Ubiquitous/Corbis; 167 V&A Images; 168 © Ryan Pyle/Corbis; 167 © Louise Gubb/Corbis Saba; 172–173 Zen Mountain Monastery, Mount Trumper; 174 Sonam Wangmo; 176 Karma Lekshe Tsomo; 178 Buddhist Tzu Chi Foundation.

CHAPTER 6 186 (below) © Asian Art & Archaeology, Inc./Corbis; 189 © Keren Su/Corbis; 190 The Mansell Collection; 193 © Asian Art & Archaeology, Inc./Corbis; 198 ChinaFotoPress/Getty Images; 201 © Kevin Fleming/Corbis; 202 Photo Si Chi Ko, courtesy of C. Al Huang, Celestial Arts Publications, Berkeley, California; 205 AKG-Images; 209 © Dallas and John Heaton/Free Agents Limited/Corbis; 210 © Mary Pat Fisher; 214 © Setboun/Corbis.

CHAPTER 7 AND ZOROASTRIANISM 218 www.worldreligions.co.uk; 223 John Lander/OnAsia.com; 224 Hutchison Picture Library/Jon Burbank; 226 Ernest Haas/Getty Images; 230 Tsubaki Grand Shrine of America; 235 ©Hutchison Picture Library/Tim Page.

CHAPTER 8 242 HUC Skirball Cultural Center, Museum Collection, gift of Mrs Simon Kuhn, HUCSM 66.538b, Photo John Reed Forsman; 247 Cathedral of St. Etienne, Metz, France/Giraudon/Lauros. © Vitrail de Marc Chagall réalisé en collaboration avec Charles Marq/ADAGP 2010; 248 Getty Images; 249 Courtesy of The Studio, Old Jaffa, Israel, Michal Meron; 253 Richard T. Nowitz/Corbis; 254 Erchov Alexei Konstantinovich/Shutterstock; 252 Corbis/Bettmann; 258 By the Academy of Jerusalem team: artist Hannah-Aliza Omer and cyber architect Dr. Yitzhak Hayut-Man, concept. Image courtesy of the Academy of Jerusalem and High-Or Ltd. The series is shown at www.thehope.org/artgal.htm; 267 Photo The Jewish Museum/Art Resource/Scala, Florence; 268 © Patrick Ward/Corbis; 272 © Gyori Antoine/Corbis; 275 Zionist Archives, New York; 276 © Mary Pat Fisher; 281 © Dave Bartruff/Corbis; 282 Marco Di Lauro/Getty Images; 283 The Israel Museum, Jerusalem, Photo © The Israel Museum, David Harris; 284 © Eyal Ofer/Corbis; 286 David Sapperstein; 292 AP Photo/Al Behrma; 294 © Laura Turbow.

CHAPTER 9 299 Mr. and Mrs. Isaac D. Fletcher Collection, Bequest of Isaac D. Fletcher, 1917 (17.120.222), © 2010. Image copyright The Metropolitan Museum of Art/Art Resource/Scala, Florence; 302 © Photo Scala, Florence; 303 © Ernesto Cardenal, courtesy of Peter Hammer; 305 © 1990 Photo Scala, Florence; 314 National Museum of Ancient Art, Lisbon, Portugal/Bridgeman Art Library; 315 © The Trustees of the British Museum; 319 © Vincenzo Pirozzi, Rome fotopirozzi@inwind.it; 321 Institute for Antiquity and Christianity, Claremont, California; 323 © Archivio Iconografico, S.A./Corbis; 328 © The British Library; 329 © Bob Krist/Corbis; 331 Photo Mary Larosa; 332 © 1990 Photo Scala, Florence; 334 Fotomas Index; 337 National Portrait Gallery, London/Bridgeman Art Library/Getty Images; 338 Courtesy of the Library Committee of the Religious Society of Friends in Britain; 340 Solent News/Rex Features; 342 Dima Kartuchnikov; 344 © Hutchison Picture Library/ Vadim Krokhin; 347 Colorific!/P. Turnley/Black Star; 350 www.worldreligions.co.uk; 353 Chris Fairclough Colour Library; 356 Photograph of Thomas Merton and the Dalai Lama. Used with permission of the Merton Legacy Trust and the Thomas Merton Centre at Bellarmine University; 357 Hutchison Picture Library/Liba Taylor; 359 AP Photos/Lee Celano; 363 Monica Almeida/The New York Times/Redux/Eyevine; 366 Flower Pentacostal Heritage Centre; 367 David Gallant/Corbis; 368 © Pascal Deloche/Godong/Corbis; 371 Corbis/Bettmann; 372 Courtesy of Maryknoll Sisters; 374 www.worldreligions.co.uk.

CHAPTER 10 383 Susan Griggs Agency/Robert Azzi; 384 N.A.A.S./Peter Sanders; 385 Hutchison Picture Library; 388 Getty Images; 387 V&A Images; 395 The Bodleian Library, Oxford; 396 Nafise Motlaq/OnAsia.com; 397 www.world religions.co.uk; 403 Big Stock Photo; 408 © Mary Pat Fisher; 409 © Imagestate Media Partners Limited, Impact Photos/Alamy; 410 ©Hutchison Picture Library/ Christopher Tordai; 414 The Art Archive/Dagli Orti; 416 © Hutchison Picture Library/Nigel Smith; 419 C. Steele-Perkins/Magnum Photos; 422 www.world religions.co.uk; 425 © Montserrat T. Diez/epa/Corbis; 426 © Mary Pat Fisher; 430 Atta Kenare/AFP/Getty Images; 434 © Dallas Morning News/Corbis Sygma.

CHAPTER 11 441 From Biography of Guru Nanak by Kartar Singh, Hemkunt Press, New Delhi 110028; 449 © Mary Pat Fisher; 454 © Mary Pat Fisher; 455 Painting by Mehar Singh, courtesy of Gobind Sadan, New Delhi; 456 Mehar Singh/Gobind Sadan; 458 © Mary Pat Fisher; 460 © Ekaterina Sabitova; 461 Alexandra Engel.

CHAPTER 12 466 © Georges de Keerle/Corbis Sygma; 467 AP Photo/Paul White; 472 © Paul Schermeister/Corbis; 475 Robert Maass/Corbis; 479 Hutchison Picture Library/ M. MacIntyre; 480 Mary Evans Picture Library; 481 Nicholas Roerich Museum, New York; 482 © Baha'i International Community. www.media.bahai.org; 485 Hutchison Picture Library; 479 Bridgeman Art Library; 488 © Viktor Korotayev/Reuters/Corbis; 495 AFP/Stephen Shaver.

CHAPTER 13 504 Hutchinson Library/Nigel Howard; 508 © Keith Bedford/Reuters/Corbis; 513 Courtesy of Brother Daniel Faivre; 515 © Mary Pat Fisher; 516 © Mary Pat Fisher; 518 © Jonathen Weizmann/Reuters/Corbis; 523 Valeriy Lipenkov.